JNU

The Making of a University

Educated at St Xavier's College, Ranchi, and at Centre for Historial Studies, Jawaharlal Nehru University (JNU), Rakesh Batabyal has been a fellow of the Indian Institute of Advanced Study, Shimla (1996–1999), National Institute of Panjab Studies (2004), and was the inaugural chair of Contemporary Indian History at Tokyo University (2010). As deputy director of the Academic Staff College of Jawaharlal Nehru University, he has contributed in making the college one of the most dynamic academic centres in the country. Batabyal teaches history of media at the Centre for Media Studies in JNU.

Rakesh Batabyal's *Communalism in Bengal: From Famine to Noakhali (1943–47)*, (Sage Publications, 2005), and *The Penguin Book of Modern Indian Speeches*, (Penguin Books, 2007), are widely received works in modern Indian history. Batabyal brings his training in philosophy to examine issues of contemporary history.

JNU

The Making of a University

RAKESH BATABYAL

HarperCollins *Publishers* India

First published in India in 2014 by
HarperCollins *Publishers* India

HarperCollins *Publishers* India, Cyber City, Building 10-A, Gurugram,
Haryana – 122002, India

P-ISBN: 978-93-5177-007-7
E-ISBN: 978-93-5177-008-4

2 4 6 8 10 9 7 5 3 1

Typeset in 10.5/13.5 Electra LT Std
By Saanvi Graphics Noida

Printed and bound at
Repro India Ltd.

*

HarperCollins *Publishers*, Macken House, 39/40 Mayor Street Upper,
Dublin 1, D01 C9W8, Ireland

For Prof. Bipan Chandra

1928–2014

Contents

1

A University is Conceived

> A great university reflects the character of the whole nation. A great university will need great sacrifice on the part of the community and all concerned.[1]

On a cold winter afternoon in 1964, the air was electric with anticipation in the Rajya Sabha, the Upper House of parliament, as M.C. Chagla, the minister of education at the time, presented the Jawaharlal Nehru University Bill. Chagla, the first Indian chief justice of the Bombay High Court, was one of the most respected members of the Indian judiciary. A veteran at law-making, he had just completed the proceedings on a bill to amend the Banaras Hindu University Act of 1915 amidst a furore in parliament. The JNU Bill was unique and complex. It evoked a wide spectrum of emotions and opinions; some called the bill a worthless piece of legislation, while others considered it the beginning of a personality-cult trend. For Chagla, the JNU Bill, which was poised to herald a new chapter in the history of education in India, also signified a landmark metamorphosis in India's political and social history.

Chagla proposed to set up a university in Delhi, which would not only reduce concerns about the massive increase of students enrolling at the University of Delhi, but would also be of international standard, to live up to the high reputation of Jawaharlal Nehru. The university was designed to bring the frontiers of science and technology within easy reach of the Indian students, and simultaneously integrate humanistic learning into the curriculum. The JNU idea had a deep personal resonance for Chagla as he always had the utmost regard, respect and admiration for the first prime minister of India, Jawaharlal Nehru.

In 1965, following heated debates in the Rajya Sabha and the Lok Sabha, the bill was sent to a select committee of parliament for further discussion. The bill successfully became an Act in December 1966. At this time, however, Chagla, who had been its chief proponent, was no longer the education minister. However, he moved the bill in the Lok Sabha as the Union foreign minister.

By the time the vice chancellor of the university had been appointed, Chagla's political profile had undergone several changes. He had not only resigned from his post as the education minister, but had also fallen out of favour with the Congress party, and was no longer a member of the cabinet. Chagla was an almost forgotten entity by the time JNU was launched. And by 1989, nobody remembered Chagla although he was the brain behind the founding of the university. He had been completely erased from public memory not only in Indian politics but also in the annals of JNU. Considering the passion with which he had defended its creation during a period of major upheaval and turmoil in Indian politics—JNU may not have seen the light of day if it were not for Chagla's unstinting efforts—this book, in its exploration of the establishment of the modern, post-Independence Indian institution, the Jawaharlal Nehru University, will discuss the visionary contributions of people like Chagla.

After Nehru What?

When Jawaharlal Nehru decided to appoint M.C. Chagla to the post of minister of education in his cabinet, it was in the teeth of strong opposition from other politicians, their contention being that Chagla had not risen through the ranks. This continued to remain an issue even later in the history of Indian democracy where politicians as a class found it difficult to accommodate a layman in their midst.[2] In addition to India's defeat in the Chinese war, Jawaharlal Nehru was dealing with a generally difficult political climate. The pro-Hindi debate versus the anti-Hindi agitation in Tamil Nadu had taken an ominous turn. The anti-Congress rhetoric of the socialists as well as the anti-communist aggression from the Swatantra Party and several members of the Congress party created friction in the polity. The socialists, with their anti-elitism slogans, were the most significant participants in the anti-

English campaign along with the Jana Sangh. The vehemently debated 'official national language' dilemma finally ended with the moving of a resolution in 1959 by Home Minister Govind Ballabh Pant. Nehru had temporarily assuaged the feelings of the non-Hindi-speaking states, but a permanent solution was yet to be found. The national language controversy seemed to have been suspended in a limbo for five years.

It was a devastating loss for the entire generation when Jawaharlal Nehru passed away on 27 May 1964. Not only was he a political giant in the history of the world, but was also an acclaimed intellectual, a great and compassionate human being. By the 1960s, Indian polity seemed to have reached an impasse with a disheartening prognosis of India's imminent break-up. Concurrently, the second wave of the cold war had most of the world in its grip. However, these stand-offs were rendered relatively insignificant in the face of India's staggering bereavement. Nehru had supporters and opponents but no obvious successors, which raised the question: after Nehru, who?

Lal Bahadur Shastri, a member of Nehru's cabinet, was elected by the Congress to succeed Nehru as prime minister. Under his able leadership, the new ministry effectively debunked the gloomy hypothesis of India's balkanization. Shastri used his experience and expertise to form a new cabinet: he retained Chagla in the education ministry. Chagla was commendable in his efforts to sustain the memory of Nehru. He compiled Nehru's principles into a pledge, and, as the Union education minister, he issued a circular making the pledge a mandatory reading in every school assembly. This was resented by Ram Manohar Lohia, the socialist leader in parliament. Although Lohia's complaint about Chagla was addressed to Shastri, the prime minister forwarded it to Chagla himself—demonstrating an effective management approach to deal with conflict within the organization.

The intellectual vacuum left by Nehru's death however was large. His successors needed time to get to grips with the various issues and their ramifications, and to understand the diplomacy and tact with which each problem needed to be handled. The communists, who had been criticizing Nehru for his alleged pro-bourgeois, middle-road economic policy, had in fact lost their benefactor in a radically changed national and global situation. The 1960s was not an easy period for the Left, particularly in the post-China-war situation. In 1964, they would split almost vertically and a couple of years later another section, with more radical ideologies, would splinter the communist movement even further.

The socialist parties, not to be left behind, were having a field day indulging in their favourite pastime—in-fighting. The Praja Socialist Party (PSP) and the Samyukta Socialist Party (SSP) had decided to go their separate ways. The communal forces were recovering lost ground with the Jana Sangh active and recouping. The Swatantra Party, supposedly against socialist visions, could have, in theory, evolved into a serious adversary of the ruling party. However, the bulk of its leadership consisted of the erstwhile kings and maharajas and that did not augur well for the party's expansion in a democratic set-up.

It was in this political and intellectual climate that the education minister introduced the bill to establish the new university. The socialists, as we shall see, turned out to be the most trenchant critics of the bill, while the communists were compiling an ideological critique of the nature of the university itself. The main burden of the socialist critique was about the name of the university. There was an inherent logic in their stance as they were, at the time, also involved in a bitter struggle with the vested groups in the case of the Banaras Hindu University (BHU)—the socialists supported the education minister's contention that BHU should be re-named (as originally intended) 'Kashi Vishwavidyalaya', and eliminate 'Hindu' from its name. However, their case against the naming of the new university after Jawaharlal Nehru emanated from their party's pathological dislike of Nehru combined with a fear of establishing new authoritarian university edifices.

Powerless Education Ministry, but Striding Ahead

The ministry of education in India in the 1960s did not have a strong profile but the first minister of education, Abul Kalam Azad, with his passion for learning, had imbued the department with a certain degree of distinction. As education was a state subject, most of the educational institutions came under the jurisdiction of the state governments, and the Central government merely held advisory powers over these. Only the Central universities like the University of Delhi, the Visva-Bharati University, the Banaras Hindu University, the Aligarh Muslim

University and a few others were directly under the control of the ministry. The Indian Institutes of Technology (IITs) and the Indian Institutes of Management (IIMs) were in the process of being set up.

Chagla was appalled to discover that the standard of school education across the country lacked consistency and their teachers were paid badly and differentially. Salaries in schools and colleges were abysmally low—lower than, as Chagla declared, 'what we pay our *chaprasis*'. It was not surprising that there was widespread discontent among India's teaching faculty.[3] In a conversation with the prime minister, Chagla mentioned that if the government could afford to appoint a Pay Commission to increase the salaries of the civil servants with dearness allowance, they should be able to do the same for the teachers who were also engaged in work of 'much importance if not of greater importance than the work done by civil servants'.[4] Chagla also discovered that in 1963-64, Tamil Nadu was, in fact, the only state where the three Ps, namely, Provident fund, Pension and Promotion of teachers in schools and colleges, had been streamlined. In other places the salary system was in utter chaos.

With the minister at its helm, the Education Commission was making good progress in identifying areas for improvement and implementing effective changes on a practical level in the academic institutions across India. The University of Delhi was staggering under the exponential increase in the influx of students every year and was close to saturation point with its academic responsibilities. Chagla strongly believed it would be useful to have a second university in Delhi, with new colleges, faculty and infrastructure, which could help absorb the overflow from the old university. At one of the brainstorming sessions in the Education Commission, the launch of a brand new innovative university was discussed, and Chagla, who was already contemplating the idea of another Central university located in Delhi, was convinced that it was a very good notion, though starting a new university in a relatively poor country was not going to be easy.

From a political standpoint, the leaders from Delhi were naturally seeking to get their constituency included in the proposed university. The increase in the number of students also helped them to buttress their demand. Shanta Vasisht, for example, wanted the university to be located somewhere in the eastern part of Delhi (which was her constituency). In the debate on the first University Grants Commission (UGC) report in 1958, communist leader Bhupesh Gupta had argued that the snags besetting Indian education basically boiled down to numbers—the universities around the country were struggling to cope with the sudden increase in the numbers of students.[5] In the case of JNU however, the larger body of legislators countered the issue of numbers and supported a special university. Chagla systematically presented a sound counter-argument supported by facts and figures for JNU.

It was around this time that the ministry and the University Grants Commission had formulated a rule, which disallowed the naming of educational institutions after personalities. As Nehru was held in high esteem and deep affection, Chagla and several other members of the House felt this new convention for naming universities should not be applicable in this case. They had a fight on their hands about naming the new enterprise 'the Jawaharlal Nehru University'.[6] Most of the earlier universities in India had come into being following demands based on regional, political and linguistic groups:

- The demand for a university separate from the Madras University was raised for the Telugu-speaking people.
- It was during this time there was an organized effort to establish a university for cultivation of Marathi language and culture in Poona.
- The Karnataka University came into being on the basis of linguistic claims.

Several earlier requests for establishment of regional universities were recorded but they did not have enough backing. The Jawaharlal Nehru University had no such regional, linguistic or political agenda.

The proposed curriculum and ethos of the new university were discussed at length in the Rajya Sabha. Chagla wished to establish a high-quality university that would give India an edge in science and technology. During the debate in parliament, Chagla said: 'Unless we attach the greatest importance to science our country will not progress. We are very backward in science.'[7] Furthermore, he wanted the new university to have world-class departments in technology and agricultural science.

Chagla had been the Indian ambassador to the United States and later high commissioner to the United Kingdom and so he must have had the opportunity to study the education systems in the Western world closely. The United States and the Soviet Union had progressed with giant leaps in scientific development following the world wars. The Soviet Union's launch of the Sputnik had spurred America into hugely increasing its investments in the development of science and technology. Not to be outdone, India geared itself to face the new challenges of the twentieth century, and channelled manpower and resources into setting up steel plants and further its advancement in agricultural technology. By 1964, China had exploded its atom bomb, and the hydrogen bomb was in the pipeline. India, seeking an edge, was moving into the fields of nuclear technology. The father of the Indian nuclear programme, Homi Bhabha, had maintained India's non-aggressive stance with the new nuclear technology.[8] The situation was rapidly changing around India, putting tremendous stress on the policymakers.[9]

The nation's politics underpinned the parliamentary discussions about the actual location of Chagla's university project. Chagla's primary concern was India's deficit in science and technology that could only be met by upgrading the standards in education and providing access to modern university facilities to the growing student population in India. As it was the nation's onus to create an environment to facilitate scientific training and technological advancement, it was important that education was factored into the policymaking processes of the government. Nehru himself had felt that India needed a strong national infrastructure to move into the modern world's arena of scientific and technological advancement.

The communists, in their evaluation of Jawaharlal Nehru, had commended his progressive-mindedness: Nehru's greatest contribution to the Indian society was his 'modernity'.[10] They, however, criticized his 'socialism' which, according to them, did not have scientific logic—as opposed to the socialists' opinion that it would only take a few able men to make a change in society, the communists believed that it was the power of the working class that was the key to bringing about revolutionary change in this world.[11] This then was the context in which the ministry of education was making the blueprint for the JNU.

Introducing the JNU Bill

Chagla presented the JNU Bill in the the Rajya Sabha and initiated the discussion on it. A utopian university of unsurpassed excellence was beginning to take shape in the minds of the cabinet members, until Bhupesh Gupta, the down-to-earth communist leader, joined the debate and introduced a sense of realism and practicality to the discussions: '… let us not have Cambridges and Oxfords and Princetons and Harvards here;' but rather, 'let us create universities and colleges that our people need, that our development needs, for the re-making of our material and cultural being'.[12]

To Bhupesh Gupta, the proposal needed to be viewed from the perspective of the prevailing economic conditions in India. 'The first thing', according to him, was to ensure the doors of the universities are thrown wide open to 'the sons of the working people, the workers, the peasants and the middle classes'.[13] One needed, he pointed out, 'not only provision for money for this but also a different outlook'.[14] This 'different' outlook would have to include the primary role of the state undertaking to provide grants, scholarships and other subsidies for such education. Making a very significant point, Gupta said that the investment made in 'imparting higher scientific and technical education to the poorer sections of the community will have been repaid in course of time in creative and even constructive labour which would go to the benefit of the entire society'.[15] These government benefits would be applicable to students from both the lower- and middle-income groups. For this, he asserted, higher education had to be made affordable.[16] He therefore urged the members, in his inimitable manner, to take Nehru's socialist ideas and socialistic perspective seriously and let the emphasis of this debate about the university shift 'from the upper classes to the classes that are economically at the bottom layers of the society'.[17]

The proposed name of the university polarized the parliamentary proceedings. Gupta did not object to the name, and instead chose to focus on Nehru's socialistic views and how they could be incorporated into the new university's educational programmes, which, in his opinion, would be the greatest tribute to Nehru.[18] Socialism would not only need to be included in the university curriculum, it would form the bedrock of the university's ethos—serving the poor and the needy rather than the rich. He raised a very serious issue: given the income disparities in the country when young boys and girls from the poorer classes lacked the opportunity or wherewithal to enter the portals of our universities, the question naturally arose whether this university was going to be open for them.[19] The question was important and he felt that, in the interests of the country, it deserved an answer.[20]

The Government of India would need to take India's socio-economic profile and its own cultural needs into account, and plan for the new university appropriately. It was the poorer sections of the community which needed university education; a high-flying expensive institution would make no sense at all in a poor country. Gupta's argument was level-headed and had no taint of anti-universalism, although his communist ideology coloured his rhetoric.

How one reconciled universalistic notions with the patriotic, class-based position was the million-dollar question. Over the last two hundred years, Indian nationalists and intelligentsia have attempted to harmonize the two, and tried to maintain a universalistic shape, justice being its core value, despite struggling with a significant handicap of economic class inequalities. Patriotism has, more often than not, conformed to this standard set by the universalistic outlook and has effectively prevented any one class from overtly dominating the nationalist programme. In many communist societies, over the last century, patriotism has been seen as a unique virtue, and, when invoked, it helps overcome the class differences that incite revolutions. In the Indian context, patriotism has been integrated into the very rubric of nationalism.[21]

Gupta's argument for a new and advanced university which would be accessible to all economic classes was not intended as a case for patriotism. However, it had a definite tang of anti-colonialism: Oxford and Cambridge had become symbols of colonial intellectual hegemony and there was a need to break this control. His speech was reminiscent of a similar intervention by Dange during the debate on the foundation of the Poona University in 1947, which could be summarized as the first communist statement on educational institutions in India.

The Socialist Blockade

While the communists tried to see the new university in the context of scientific socialism, the socialists were disgruntled for different reasons. A completely unexpected obstacle was raised by the socialist leader, Asoka Mehta, who had in a sense reneged on his party when he joined the Planning Commission as its deputy chairman. The fifteenth informal consultative committee meeting of MPs on education was held on 3 December 1964. The plan to establish a second university in New Delhi was on the agenda, with the proposal to introduce a bill in parliament for this project, involving an outlay of approximately Rs 10 crore over a specified period. On 2 December 1964, while the bill was being debated in the Rajya Sabha, the minister received a letter from Asoka Mehta, expressing his consternation with regard to the new project. The main points of his argument were:

(a) that the proposal had at no stage been brought to the notice of the Planning Commission for consideration or consultation, and no provision had been made for it in the plan's outlay on education.
(b) that the education ministry had agreed with the Planning Commission that 'as far as possible new universities should not be established by states in the next plan period'.[22]

Mehta was political and polite as he attempted to forestall the minister from going ahead. He indicated that many states were in a mood to establish new universities but the Planning Commission was not supporting such moves on account of shortage of finances. He, therefore, argued that if the Centre went ahead and set up one university in the capital, which already had one, it would be difficult for the Planning Commission to retain the position that it had taken.[23] Purportedly, V.K.R.V. Rao, whose advice he had sought, had said, 'establishment of a second university in Delhi cannot automatically be considered a high priority'.[24] Mehta did not want the matter to be discussed in the advisory committee.

Chagla, just as polite and frank in his written response to Mehta, expressed his surprise at the timing and substance of the letter. He pointed out that this university had been under discussion since 1959 and the proposal was not a spur-of-the-moment occurrence. 'A working group was set up in the ministry of education to study the problem of expansion of facilities for school and college education in Delhi during the next two decades and recommended that a new university should be established in Delhi if the efficiency of the present university is not [to be] impaired.'[25] In not so many words, he communicated his concern that the Planning Commission was either not keeping abreast with important discussions (such as the JNU Bill) in the House, or was merely creating a hold-up for reasons unknown. He wrote:

> In 1960, the UGC also supported this proposal as it took the view that the Delhi University had become unwieldy and cumbersome and it would be desirable to set up another university to enable the present university of Delhi to arrest dilution of academic standards. This proposal was strongly supported by University of Delhi in 1961 both on administrative and academic grounds. In view of the urgency of the proposal to set up a second university in Delhi, expressed both by UGC and Delhi University, the project was included in the parliamentary report of the working group on the fourth five-year plan of general education on which all concerned authorities were represented. According to parliamentary report, it was decided to include the proposals regarding a second university in Delhi in the scheme for establishment of new university during the fourth plan formulated by the UGC. The parliamentary report of the working group was considered at a meeting in the Planning Commission on 23 June 1964, under the chairmanship of Dr Rao. It is, therefore, not correct to say that the purpose with regard to the new university had at no stage been brought up to the Planning Commission for consideration or consultation. The proposal for the new university was put up to the cabinet and approved by the cabinet on the 7 August 1964. Before putting the proposal to the cabinet, all the appropriate ministries including the ministry of finance and the UGC were consulted. Long before August 1964, I had been stating both before parliament and outside, the need for a second university, and sufficient publicity has been given to the proposal. After the cabinet approved of the proposal, the site for the university has been selected and earmarked and an expert committee has considered the necessary details and a bill has been actually drafted which is now being considered by the University Grants Commission. My surprise is therefore, due to

> the fact that the Planning Commission should, at this very late date, think it fit to raise objection to the establishment of this university. On 24 August 1964, an informal meeting was held in Planning Commission in the deputy chairman's room attended by, among others, the ministers of home affairs and finance. The meeting suggested that as an item of avoidable expenditure new universities in Delhi and Bangalore should be postponed. This proposal was put before me, but I took the view that so long as the cabinet decision stood, it must be implemented.
>
> I fully realize the financial position of most of the states and I agree with you that the view taken by me and also the UGC and publicly expressed by me on many occasions is that we should go slow about the establishment of new universities and consolidate the universities which already exist. Also that the state should not legislate about establishment of new universities without the approval both of the ministry and the UGC. I might point out that neither Calcutta nor Bombay have asked for a second university, and when they do so, their proposal will be carefully considered. If I might respect the proposal for establishment of a second university in New Delhi that was put up before the cabinet after very careful consideration—after all the educational authorities, who were concerned with the proposals, had strongly urged upon the ministry to set up the new university—I might add that my intention is that the new university should not be a duplication of the old but should really be a model university incorporating in it many new ideas in higher education which have been accepted and adopted in many parts of the world. I might further add that a little before the late prime minister died, I discussed the matter with him and he gave his strong support to this idea. I am also surprised at the suggestion that the expert committee, to which you have referred, should have held public hearing or invited written evidence. As you know, neither the committee nor the UGC functions in that way.[26]

While Chagla agreed that 'it is for the Planning Commission to advice cabinet about the resources available and how they should be allocated', the final say on the policy lay with the cabinet. And they, 'after careful consideration of the whole matter, had laid down the policy that a second university should be established'. Therefore, he was emphatic that it did not seem to be right 'that a member of planning commission should publicly give expression of opinion which opposed the declared policy of the government'.[27] He therefore very politely regretted that he could not 'accede' to the request of postponing the 'discussion at the informal consultative committee meeting which is to be held tomorrow'.[28]

It was apparent the nationalists were all for the setting up of the new university, while the socialists, some members of the Communist Party, and N.G. Ranga and Dahyabhai Patel of the Swatantra Party were opposed to the purpose, location, ideology and intended name of the new university. Asoka Mehta persisted with his opposition and, when the bill was under way, responded to Chagla on 3 January 1965, citing the opinion of V.K.R.V. Rao. (It is to be noted that, Dr Rao, when he gave his evidence in the joint committee some time later, did not say a word opposing the new university.) Mehta now brought up the issue of 'a uniform policy' regarding setting up of new universities.[29] 'If the new universities were to come up,' he was now arrogating the role of both the ministry and the UGC, 'it is essential that criteria for setting them up should be clearly predetermined and uniformly applied.'[30] These criteria would have enabled them to allocate limited funds, for outlays on the establishment of new universities.[31]

The Lok Sabha Debates the JNU Bill

On 20 September 1965, the deputy education minister, Shri Bhakt Darshan, moved the bill in the Lok Sabha and began by listing the names of the twenty members of the joint committee of the parliament.[32] Although Chagla's outline of the proposed university at the Rajya Sabha was definitive and unique, it had morphed into a vague, amorphous idea when it was eventually presented by Bhakt Darshan as a bill in the Lok Sabha. Two points, however, were very clear:

(a) The new university was to help manage the overflow from Delhi University. Delhi's population had doubled in two years following the arrival of partition refugees, resulting in a phenomenal rise in the number of students seeking admission in colleges.[33] Subsequently the number of colleges too had gone up from seven during 1947-48 to thirty-five in 1964-65, while that of the enrolled students went up from 4,583 to 30,640 in the same period.[34] It was estimated that by 1980 there would be approximately sixty colleges with an enrolment of 60,000 students, as 2,000 students on an average sought admission every year. Chagla had argued that the Delhi University had become an unwieldy and cumbersome institution and its academic and research standards were being diluted due to this heavy pressure of numbers.[35] It was due to this that the UGC had apparently recommended setting up of another university in Delhi, so that the academic standards of the present university did not suffer further.[36]

(b) It was to be named after Pandit Jawaharlal Nehru.

The broad outline of the proposed university as approved by the cabinet was as follows:

1. The new university will be a teaching university, with the same affiliations as the Delhi University.
2. The new university will be a multi-faculty institution with emphasis on the subjects of medicine, agriculture, engineering, technology and other professional studies.
3. The new university will be federal and affiliating in character with an enabling clause in its constitution to make it possible for existing autonomous institutions of higher learning in New Delhi to join whenever they chose to do so. The physical line of demarcation between the two universities would be the Ajmeri Gate—all the institutions on the north of the Ajmeri Gate plus some institutions like Azad Medical College, a little south of this line, would be under the jurisdiction of Delhi University, while the new university would cover the rest of the Union territory of Delhi.
4. The new university would be located in south Delhi near Munirka village, i.e., Ramakrishanpuram, where a site measuring 600 acres had already been earmarked.[37]

The minister, presenting the new university's unique features, said that due to the unprecedented changes in science and technology, universities across the world had been radically reorganized and reoriented. The new institution, he indicated, would not only help relieve the present Delhi University of some of its burden but also integrate the latest ideas and experiments in the field of higher education in its academic and administrative structures. It was also envisioned to embody a unique synthesis of humanities, science and technology. In promoting the spirit of university, the new university was to be a fitting memorial to one of the greatest Indian leaders.[38]

These were the broad outlines which needed to be delineated. While it would have on its administrative side, 'a department of collegiate education to look after and supervise the work of the affiliated colleges', it would have the authority to associate existing autonomous institutes, governed by their own Acts and 'deemed universities' within the jurisdiction of the new university, as its constituent units.[39] The old idea of affiliation was to be, therefore, retained but with a new system of federating affiliations. Chagla was aware of the complexity of the proposed affiliations and in fact said that he would have liked the new university to have started on a clean slate so that it could develop on entirely new lines from the very beginning.[40]

There was a sense that the federating self-governing institutions within the university were going to give the university its unprecedented uniqueness. To quote him: 'The idea is that the existing autonomous educational institutions such as the following may be persuaded to join the university within a federal framework, which will ensure their maximum autonomy and at the same time bring them within the fold of the new university for the purpose of mutual consultation and conferment of diplomas and degrees: IIT Delhi, AIIMS, IARI, ISIS, IIPA, Jamia Milia. Jamia Milia is a "deemed university" and we propose to bring it also under the umbrella of this new university.'[41] The possibility of affiliating educational institutions outside Delhi was also raised. Chagla's expertise in matters of law is apparent in the way he systematically worked at setting up a process to expand the jurisdiction of the Central university—which could, in due course, be the standard against the overarching chaos prevalent in educational affairs. JNU would spearhead this movement in India and work on the same lines as the large educational institutes in the USA.

The Jawaharlal Nehru University would reflect the vision of Indian leadership and the typical enlightened liberal understanding of postgraduate study and research of Chagla's era. The minister was of the opinion that the university would produce great scientists and engineers, and also those well versed in humanities.[42] To facilitate this, 'while science and technology will constitute the core of the new university at the post-graduate level' there will be facilities for 'specialization in social sciences and languages not only of India, but also of different countries of the world, so that this university caters to the harmonious development of both sciences and humanities' on an international level.[43]

There had been a concern amongst the educational policymakers in India that too many people study social sciences and humanities with no value addition to the knowledge, and Chagla's plan for the JNU curriculum paid attention to the needs of the nation in a global setting: 'It is however proposed that the studies in social sciences in the new university will be geared to the needs, requirements and aspirations of the country. They shall be relevant to the realities of our developing nations.'[44] The university would, 'set up special institutes to achieve excellence in selected spheres of social sciences, i.e., it is contemplated that institutes such as the following may be established:

1. IIMC [Indian Institute of Mass Communication]
2. Institute of Russian Studies
3. Institute of Indian Languages
4. Institute of Asian Languages
5. Institute of African Languages
6. Institute of International Law and Diplomacy
7. Institute of International Affairs.'[45]

Chagla deliberately kept the bill brief and flexible.

Several members of parliament had been active politically before Independence and the idea of popular control—the most decisive political idea of the national movement for freedom—had been their credo too. The debate in parliament began with an attack on the bill itself. It was referred to as a bad 'piece of legislation as it kept a lot of things unarticulated'. Almost as a tradition, most of the bills for universities or institutions were discussed threadbare in the legislative assemblies and parliament. The colonial officials had kept the universities under their control and one of the foremost struggles of the nationalist leaders and intelligentsia had been to incorporate democratic debate of the curriculum and administration of the universities. After a long-drawn-out battle, the debate on higher education had managed to wrest a space in the legislative agendas and it was imperative that this continued to remain open. Hence, the legislators were not quite happy when the JNU Bill was presented to them as a fait accompli. On the other hand, the new democracy was now trying to trust Indians to make their own institutions with minimum control by watchdogs. Thus, while the state was willing to come forward to repose some trust in them, the popular representatives were finding it difficult to harmonize this new turn by the state.

The most powerful voice against the bill's brevity was that of the oldest member in the House, M.S. Aney, who disapproved of the lack of adequate detail in the JNU Bill especially in a 'democracy like ours'.[46] To him the bill was extraordinary in that it was for the first time that a bill was brought before the House for constituting a university wherein all the details about the nature and compositions of all of its important bodies, were to be prescribed not by the parliament but by 'some other body'.[47] He, it was clear, did not like the idea because university bills so far discussed in the parliament had been mainly concerned with the 'mechanism that should exist in the universities'.[48] This gave an idea of the House's expectations of the composition of the court, the board, the syndicate, the executive council and so on, and from this they could 'understand what the elements composing those bodies would be and who would be entrusted to perform the tasks entrusted to them'. However, he felt the bill gave the parliament no clue whatsoever about the nature of the bodies, people and their capacity to execute the responsibility entrusted to them. To him, the new format of the JNU Bill was tantamount to a blank cheque being forwarded without any democratic debate and consensus.[49] The Rajya Sabha's approach to the JNU Bill seemed to him to be autocratic and undemocratic, and he therefore did not feel like congratulating the government.[50]

The bill had empowered the executive council of the new university to make its own statutes. Sinhasan Singh, the member from Gorakhpur, objected to this as he thought that making statutes was the job of the parliament.[51] He thought that the right of the parliament was being 'snatched'.[52] To Jwala Prasad Jyotishi, the terseness of the bill showed absence of any overarching philosophy, and he was unable to see the soul of Pandit Nehru in the bill. 'Universities', he argued, 'are not built with only cement and bricks', but required an atmosphere blending science and spiritualism.[53]

The next element of the discussion pertained to an undercurrent of political misalignment rather than the merit of the bill and its impact as a poor precedent on democratic processes for future generations. The legislators were reluctant to set a prototype for developing personality cults and were therefore unwilling to name the new university after Pandit Nehru. A vibrant democracy was demonstrated in this legislative debate against establishing institutions without due parliamentary process and oversight, and the political leaders were fulfilling their responsibilities by voicing their misgivings. There were criticisms as to why there were so many institutions in Nehru's name. Prabhat Kar of Hooghly complained that there already were so many institutions named after Nehru, many of them in hibernation, and therefore questioned the need for one more institution to be named after him, and that too, ostensibly, to relieve Delhi University. He wondered whether this was not the handiwork of the lobby of bureaucrats and academicians as the institution would provide a large number of well-paid jobs. He was not far off the mark when he complained that while one could hardly get a good lecturer, there were too many academicians who were anxious to become 'vice chancellor, registrar, or God knows what else'.[54] He was against adding to the number of such institutions.

The opposition to the proposed university's name became louder with many outspoken members arguing against it. They cited the recent University Grants Commission guideline against universities being named after personalities. L.M. Singhvi, an erudite lawyer and an independent member, noted the 'dichotomous situation' because while Ravi Shankar Shukla University was denied this privilege by the

University Grants Commission, a university named after Nehru was being passed by the parliament.[55] M.S. Aney was also worried about its future implications when he said that there was nothing fundamentally wrong with the idea to start JNU, but then it would start an intransigent trend, as there would be 'a plethora of universities in India named after the distinguished men in this country'.[56] He was apprehensive of this danger.[57]

Kishen Pattanayak, a firebrand socialist from Orissa, was one of the most vociferous against naming the university after a personality. He argued against setting any such precedence, which, once set, would allow people with a lot of money to start naming universities after all sorts of personalities.[58] He felt that the atmosphere in the Lok Sabha was politically charged and the loss of perspective would soon permeate the overall political and intellectual world. It was sad indeed that these discussions were about Nehru, the founder of the modern nation—with its industrial, democratic, secular and international framework.

The third element of debate was regarding the enabling features of the bill in its technicality. The absolute autonomy of the new university through the bill was criticized. D.C. Sharma flagged the contemporary institutional profile in Delhi, the uncontrolled and almost anarchic institution-building process in Delhi, where many enterprising persons had started institutions indiscriminately. He elaborated that it was through their contacts with intellectuals as well as people in authority that they managed to get their institutions recognized as deemed universities.[59] While the growth of institutions with some degree of independence was not a bad idea, he argued that 'institutions should not grow in their own way, in an isolated manner, without coordination and control from some central institution'.[60] Therefore, while he appreciated that the new university was bringing some institutions together 'under the shelter of some responsible bodies' and thereby performing a great service, he was very keen that the controlling body of the university, which was going to bring all these institutions under its direction must 'consist of men very versatile and very learned' and in possession of 'comprehensive experience and world-wide knowledge of the system of education existing at present'.[61]

L.M. Singhvi, who had a keen interest in education and was politically opposed to the Congress, first saw the JNU Bill as a 'worthless piece of legislation' and observed that the idea of incorporation, while an 'attractive idea', was fraught with disastrous consequences for existing institutions.[62] As many of these educational institutions were independent or voluntary organizations, he did not think it was at all necessary for the new university to spread its umbrella over these institutions also. His cautionary note was that the autonomy of these institutions needed protection.[63]

In the 1960s, India as a nation had not yet been completely centralized into several departments, and the education department was one of these. The states and cities were dynamic and the history of urban India in the 1950s and '60s shows that, notwithstanding the poverty and squalor, the cities were more or less on par with each other. The urban boom of isolated cosmopolitan cities in the post-1980s was yet to happen. Therefore, the location for JNU need not have been Delhi at all as there were several equally urban localities at this point in time which could have easily sustained a brand new university. Kishen Pattanayak, of the Socialist Party, criticized the basis for the establishment of a new university in Delhi, which was the increase in Delhi's population, by pointing out that there was a steadily increasing population in other parts of the country as well. He also advised the minister against retaining the position of a pro-vice-chancellor in the new university. Some members wanted the university to be located somewhere other than in Delhi. Congress member from Gurdaspur, Dewan Chand Sharma, saw Delhi as a wasteland 'where mostly hollow men' and climbers of all types—social climbers, political climbers, etc.—lived, and therefore was not the place where the university should be established. Moreover, Pandit Nehru, he said, held the Ganga very dear, and in his last will and testament had paid a very glowing tribute to it. The university, therefore, should be established somewhere along the banks of the Ganga so that the cultural flow of the Ganga could mingle with the cultural unity which Pandit Nehru preached.[64]

There was also a strong voice in favour of starting rural universities instead of a university for the urban population. Chandrabhan Singh and Diwan Chand Sharma suggested that the minister establish the new university anywhere but in Delhi, and that it should be a rural university.[65] This idea was endorsed by Yashpal Singh from Kairana.[66] Onkar Lal Berwa, who felt the university could come up with just 70 lakh rupees as outlay, proposed Rajasthan as the venue, and that it should be in the name of Rajendra Prasad. There were enthusiastic supporters for such a line of argument, and members like Shri Balmiki, Saraju Pandey and Shiv Narain also added their voices to prioritize a 'university for the poor'.

There were two significant threads in this debate which underlined a worrying development for the country. On the one side was the pro- and the anti-Hindi agitation, and the second was the communal polarization that the country would see around the issue of Aligarh Muslim University versus the Banaras Hindu University.

R.K. Khadilkar who was involved with educational institutions suggested that the new university ought to reflect the innate pan-Indianness and cosmopolitan nature of India unlike the Banaras Hindu University, which was essentially 'Hindu', and the Aligarh Muslim University, which was essentially 'Muslim'.[67] In addition, he recommended that the university include an 'Institute of Indian languages'.[68] He strongly disapproved of the correspondence courses which were to be included in the curriculum of JNU according to the bill, and of the post of a pro-vice-chancellor.[69] He was categorical that this should be 'a post-graduate university', and one that would commemorate Panditji and his ideals.[70]

Notwithstanding the attack and critique of the bill, there was a subtle subtext in the entire debate that the members of the House wanted something big, novel and unique with which Jawaharlal Nehru's name could be associated. It had to be more than merely a second university for Delhi or merely 'an academic explosion to meet the population explosion of Delhi'. As another parliamentarian pointed out, Jawaharlal Nehru was important to the entire country, not just Delhi.[71] He was suspicious that the whole exercise smacked of the hijacking of Jawaharlal Nehru's name for a very limited and narrow purpose, i.e., to relieve the University of Delhi of its overload. It was not the correct way to honour the late prime minister. This university, which appeared to be shaping up like any other residential university run by the Central government, could not 'arrogate to itself the name of Pandit Jawaharlal Nehru' if it was not going to make any contribution to 'those fields which Pandit Jawaharlal Nehru held very dear to his heart like the fields of internationalism, peace, cultural unity of India, scientific approach to life, etc'.[72]

The minister was even requested to withdraw the bill or rename it the Delhi University Bill. Basically, the sentiment in the House was, 'we should have the Jawaharlal Nehru University in some other way, in some other place, in some other form and in some other environment'.[71] However, despite all the criticisms and suggestions, the motion was finally adopted on 21 September 1965, and the JNU Bill was sent to the joint committee of parliament for giving its final shape in the light of the discussions it had provoked.

2

Legislating the University: The Jawaharlal Nehru University Act

> I do hold very strongly that we should say goodbye to this lack of trust in our teachers. There is too much of distrust between one group of people and another ... The teachers of the universities are not angels; they are not super human beings ... they are Indians like all of us. If we are not going to trust them, whom are we going to trust?[1]

The year 1965 was a bad one. The monsoons had failed and there was famine in many parts of the country. The subsequent failure of monsoon in the following year precipitated a severe food scarcity in India, with a decline of 17 per cent in overall agricultural production and 20 per cent in foodgrain production. To make matters worse, inflation had reached an all-time high of 12 per cent making life in India extremely difficult. India's reserve of foodgrain had been depleted to a mere two months' worth of stock. The Indian government had no option but to seek foreign aid to overcome the crisis.

Pakistan capitalized on this vulnerability to make a second foray in its war with India. The United Nations intervened and brought about a ceasefire. However, Pakistan persisted and, beginning with a clash to occupy the marshy land in the Rann of Kutch, the Pakistani army was preparing an onslaught in the northern and western sectors of India with rabid anti-India propaganda in April 1965, forcing the Indian government to rearrest Sheikh Abdullah in May 1965.[2] Using this as an excuse, the UN and the British government suspended their aid to India. By the end of August, a full-scale war was in the offing with the three-pronged Pak attack under its 'Operation Grand Slam'.[3] It was in such a situation that the defence minister had a premonition that this was the 'beginning of trouble in this part of the world' as encirclement of India by hostile countries was now complete.[4] India seemed to have been strategically surrounded. This had a considerable impact on the defence budget and therefore debilitated India's development programmes.

Foreign aid to India nearly ground to a halt.

During Nehru's term as prime minister of India, the resolution of the pro-Hindi versus anti-Hindi national language debate had merely been postponed with Nehru's proposed three-language formula. However, with the new political developments in 1965, this controversy again moved to the forefront. The attempt to alter the ethos of the existing two Central universities, Aligarh and Banaras, had culminated in another form of communal upheaval.[5] It was during this time that the preparations for the final legislation for the new university began in earnest. The timing seemed singularly inauspicious.

Meeting of the Giants

The motion to move the JNU Bill for discussion in the joint committee coincided with the day the Indian army was mobilized into war, 31 August 1965.

The joint committee had in its ranks some of the most erudite members of parliament. Its chairman was Gopal Swarup Pathak, an eminent jurist, later the vice-president of India. There were prominent members of the Socialist Party such as Hem Barua and Mukut Bihari Lal; the latter, a student of Harold Laski at the London School of Economics and professor of political science in BHU, was the seniormost leader of the Socialist Party in Uttar Pradesh. P.K. Kumaran and H.N. Mukerjee were noteworthy Communist Party voices. The committee also included the educationist and Anglo-Indian leader, Frank Anthony, peasant leader N.G. Ranga, and both the education ministers, Chagla and Bhakt Darshan. In the debates in the Rajya Sabha, one saw the prominent role played by Prof. Tara Chand, a legendary teacher who started his career in Kayastha Mahavidyalaya in the first decades of the twentieth century and emerged as one of the most important historians of the time establishing what came to be known as the Allahabad School of Indian Historiography. P.N.

Sapru, another member, one of the most eminent public figures of the twentieth-century India, had also played quite a crucial role in India's political history. It was clear that the most eminent educationists had been invited to participate in the consultations on JNU.

On 20 September 1965, the bill was discussed in the Lok Sabha, and agreed upon on the following day, which also coincidentally was the day the war with Pakistan ended. The country was in an understandably jubilant mood at this time. The ethos, structures and functioning of the Aligarh and Banaras universities were rediscussed with new, positive and creative frames of mind. The joint committee had only just re-examined the Banaras University amendment bill.

The JNU Bill received three memoranda. The first came from V.S. Jha, member of the Education Commission, the second, from K.P. Govil, registrar, BITS Pilani, and the third from R.P. Budhiraja, a resident of Delhi. The committee invited the opinions of eight eminent scholars—V.K.R.V. Rao, Triguna Sen, D.S. Kothari, A.C. Joshi, N.H. Bhagwati, V.S. Jha, K.G. Saiyidain and Sri Ranjan.

V.K.R.V. Rao, one of independent India's most prominent economists, had been the vice chancellor of the of the Delhi University and the founder of institutions like the Delhi School of Economics, the Institute of Economic Growth and the Institute of Social and Economic Change in Bangalore. A short time later, he became the education minister and inaugurated the Jawaharlal Nehru University in 1969.[6]

Triguna Sen had made pioneering contributions to engineering education. He, however, reserved his fondness for the Jadavpur University, which he had served almost from its inception in 1955. First as the rector and later as the vice chancellor of Jadavpur University, he unrelentingly worked for the growth of the university and his contributions remain unparalleled in making the university a premier institute of learning in India. He came to Banaras Hindu University in 1966 to calm the prevailing ferment and then succeeded Chagla as education minister soon after the JNU Act was passed.

Prof. D.S. Kothari, the eminent physicist, was at this time heading the University Grants Commission and also heading the Education Commission that Chagla had put into motion to survey the education system of the country. He gave JNU his endorsement in light of the global changes during this time.

A.C. Joshi was vice chancellor of Banaras Hindu University while V.S. Jha held the position of secretary to the Government of Central Provinces, Education Department, Nagpur. Jha worked in collaboration with the Secondary Education Commission, which the Government of India had constituted in 1952 under the chairmanship of Lakshmanaswami Mudaliar, the vice chancellor of Madras University. Jha went on to become the vice chancellor of Banaras Hindu University and was a member of the Education Commission headed by D.S. Kothari.

N.H. Bhagwati, a retired judge of the Supreme Court, was vice chancellor of BHU when violence had erupted in 1964-65. He, however, did not emerge unscathed from the unfortunate episode and the education minister was far from pleased with the way the incident had been handled in BHU.

K.G. Saiyidain was a distinguished educationist who had returned from Germany and worked closely with Zakir Hussain. He was respected for his views on a wide range of educational philosophies.

Sri Ranjan, the vice chancellor of Agra University (he was earlier the vice chancellor of Allahabad University), had done significant work on the separation of organic acid through paper chromatography, a pioneering frontier field in the early 1950s. The technique was later used in many areas of scientific investigations into plant physiology.[7]

For three consecutive days starting on 17 October 1965, the joint committee discussed the JNU Bill with the above illuminati. Therefore, JNU had the best intellectual minds of India to process the bill. Although the debates were contentious, there was common ground in a much wider sense, which formed the basic outlines of the new university.

Making It a Unique Institution

As the intention to make the institution unique was the overwhelming sentiment right from the introduction of the JNU Bill in the Rajya Sabha in 1964, discussion pivoted around the theme of uniqueness rather than on other details. The joint committee enthusiastically responded to this sentiment. The first person who gave evidence in the joint committee was V.K.R.V. Rao. Although years later a student leader of JNU wrote that Rao as an education minister wanted to make JNU an elitist university,[8] this was not borne out by facts. Rao's intentions were far superior and sublime than attributed to him by this student leader.[9]

G.S. Pathak set the tenor of the committee's proceedings when he posed his first question to Rao: What in Rao's opinion was going to be the 'uniqueness of the proposed university'? Rao, speaking from his rich experience, explained that 'uniqueness' had a twofold meaning here. As a university, it should be different from all other universities in this country and therefore be unique in itself.[10] Furthermore, as a university bearing Jawaharlal Nehru's name, it should embody three basic principles: national integration, establishment of a decent society, and a universalistic philosophy. The desire for national integration in 1965 must have been the principal driving force for these academicians. Fierce communal and linguistic disturbances had created very violent situations in many parts of the country. The pro- and anti-Hindi agitations had threatened to balkanize the country by mid-1965. One of the instruments to foster national integration that Rao proposed was to have a department of Indian languages and a truly national student body. In his opinion, the 'national representation' in Delhi University consisted of Bengalis and the south Indians of Delhi, which gave the university a superficial semblance of a national university although it was not.[11] He suggested there be a quota system allocated to students from each state.[12]

When JNU's uniqueness was being discussed, Rao emphatically recommended a *federating* and *postgraduate university* rather than a new university serving merely as an extension to the old Delhi University colleges; according to him, most of these lacked standards and would merely be deadweight on the new institution.

From Rao to Sri Ranjan, who was the last of the eight to give evidence, the general opinion was radically opposite to the original proposition of the bill which had aimed at affiliating the existing colleges of Delhi University en masse to the new institution. Rao made no bones about being 'not happy about affiliation' of the seventeen colleges of the Delhi University to the new university.[13] They were of uneven standards and some of them were a disgrace to the Delhi University itself. Rao, who had been involved with the administration of the Delhi University at some very crucial times, had a lot of insight into the issues at stake regarding affiliation. He was frank to admit that many of these colleges were forced on to the Delhi University by political powers, and it would be unfair to now force them on to the new university: 'For heaven's sake do not start the Jawaharlal Nehru University,' he pleaded. 'Name it after anybody, other than Nehru if the new university is going to affiliate with these colleges and turn into a third rate university.'[14]

H.N. Mukerjee and his communist colleagues must have been delighted with this new form of opposition to the JNU Bill, although the communists had an entirely different axe to grind in their objection to the new university. The vehemence of Rao's stand against affiliating these colleges could have utterly ruined any chances of establishing an entirely independent new university.

It would be useful to summarize the discussion by paraphrasing the exchange at Rajya Sabha on the day:

Hiren Mukerjee (representative of the communist ideology): Instead of a federal postgraduate university, if JNU turns out to be what many people fear, a replica of the routine Indian universities, would you recommend we either drop the idea altogether or omit the name of Jawaharlal Nehru from it?[15]

V.K.R.V. Rao: I am against a run-of-the-mill university to be named after Pandit Jawaharlal Nehru.[16]

However, he had a solution to the problem of relieving the Delhi University's burden and suggested a combined university comprising both residential and day scholars, catering solely to postgraduates.[17]

The evidence of the consulting team, like Rao, Kothari and Sen, further strengthened the dominant sentiment of bestowing Nehru's name on a completely new concept of a university with no affiliations from the old-fashioned institutions that were in existence at the time.

Rao was aware that it was advanced studies and research—not undergraduate studies—which gave a degree of consequence to a university and he wanted this to be the 'hallmark of this university'.[18] However, he acknowledged that a university also needed life and laughter as opposed to the scholarly sobriety of a purely postgraduate university and he wanted a small part, *only a small part*, of the university to be dedicated to undergraduate studies, just so the university would have versatility and vitality.[19]

Triguna Sen, the next consultant on the panel to give evidence, focused on the two divergent themes that were now on the table: (a) affiliating existing Delhi University colleges and (b) a new university dedicated to Nehru's philosophy. It would not be easy to inject new ideologies into the affiliated colleges as they were already fully formed, functional and cast in stone.[20] 'It will be difficult,' he was quite sure, 'to my mind to inculcate that spirit with which we are starting this university under the name of Jawaharlal Nehru in those institutions.'[21]

Sen took a firm stand that one could either have a unique university that embodied Nehru's ideologies or opt to have an affiliating institution which was merely an extension of Delhi University—not both. He thus effectively summarized the gist of the debate in parliament.

According to the original idea, as the education minister indicated, the new university would be the first of its kind to include advanced levels of research and tie in with existing institutions like the All India Institute of Medical Sciences (AIIMS), Indian Agricultural Research Institute (IARI) and the Indian Institutes of Technology. This idea was wholeheartedly supported by Jha, Kothari and Rao. However, the bill did not include any specific proviso as to how and when these technical institutions would become part of the new university. Rao and Kothari, who were very knowledgeable about academic administration, asserted that these institutions needed to be brought into the ambit of the bill at the outset before proceeding to actually passing the Act.[22] Rao, with his considerable experience of university administration, recommended to Chagla that the matter be earmarked for discussion by the joint select committee without further ado.[23]

Known internationally for his research on statistical thermodynamics and theory of white dwarf stars, Daulat Singh Kothari, from Udaipur, personified the public face and social commitment of Indian scientists. This achievement was further elevated by his association with Meghnad Saha. Kothari had been a student of Saha at Allahabad University and had studied applied physics. He did his early schooling at Indore and proceeded to Allahabad for his master's degree in science. He was a professor at the Delhi University between 1934 and 1961 when he was appointed chairman of the University Grants Commission. He did remarkably well on the UGC panel and remained its chairman until 1973. In his evidence, Kothari came straight to the point, and pointed out the impracticality of the education ministry's attempt to pass a bill without first finalizing affiliation of the federating institutions which were to be included in the new university. He asked the minister to first incorporate the institutions (which should be specifically named) in the bill itself and then pass the Act. Urging the minister to bring agricultural courses into the new university, Kothari strongly believed that the new university should contribute to raising the standards of agricultural education.[24]

Chagla's reluctance to make radical changes to the existing colleges and institutions demonstrated the typical dilemma of the Indian institution-building efforts, which strive to make new and improved academic institutions afresh but are disinclined to allow the old ones to die a natural death or be completely amalgamated into the new varsities. According to Chagla the autonomy of the target institutes was just as important as the new JNU. Kothari's response was succinct when he suggested that the whole idea of the new university be shelved until the ministry could be less indecisive: 'If the Government of India is not able to carry out what it itself feels is a unanimous academic opinion in the country, then let us not proceed with this. What is the use of establishing a university now and then wait for decades for things to happen?'[25] Despite Kothari's arguments, Chagla refused to be persuaded to encroach on the autonomy of the technology institutions and insisted on legislative restraint on the issue of institutional autonomy.[26] Kothari cited the recommendation about the AIIMS which would have provided the rationale for a merger. He cited the recommendation of the health ministry's committee under Lakshmanaswami Mudaliar, which had a British member, Prof. Rosenhein, that AIIMS should function as a subsidiary of a university.

Chagla, who was steeped in the idea of parliamentary sovereignty, was also conscious of its limits in a society which had just began establishing academic institutions and could not see how these illustrious institutions could be made subsidiaries of a brand new university 'without their consent'.[27] Notwithstanding the logic of Chagla's argument, Kothari was firm in his view that the step needed to be taken right away because it would be much more difficult at a future date.[28]

To summarize: Kothari and Rao's determination to bring the institutions engaged in high technology within the ambit of the JNU Act, so that the new university could commence as a postgraduate institution, inspired the members of the committee. Jayaben Shah, a member of the joint committee, endorsed their opinion and assured them that the government ministries could convincingly negotiate with the institutes and bring them under the confederation of JNU. Although Chagla continued to be ambivalent, another member of the joint committee, Amarnath Vidyalankar, was convinced that the government could achieve anything it set its mind to do; therefore amending the bill to include the affiliation of the science and technology institutions to the JNU would not be impossible. Kothari felt this would be the right way to do things, because Chagla's plan of action to pass the bill without further ado would be tantamount to putting the cart before the horse, and the new university would not have the benefit of having affiliations of the high-technology institutions.[29] Kothari pressed home his advantage by using Chagla's own view about including the agricultural institute within the new university. The surest way to improve the agricultural education in the country, Kothari argued, was to bring the agriculture research institute, IARI, doing postgraduate research work, under the fold of the university as a matter of priority.[30]

Chagla was unwilling to be high-handed with the institutes and dictate terms to them, hence his equivocation. Kothari suggested he be guided by expert academicians who could look at the situation objectively.[31] He reiterated that it was a pointless exercise to waste time deliberating on setting up an exemplar university and then waiting decades for it to actually materialize.[32]

The report of the joint committee had clarified some important features of the new university: (a) it would not include the Delhi University colleges and (b) it would in all likelihood be a postgraduate university.

Let Us Make It 'National'!

It was a first for India to have conceived of an institution with such a comprehensive national character. It was meant to provide unlimited access for people from all the regions and states of the country although

Mr M. Ruthnaswamy, a committee member, referred to the scope as the 'imperial range' with a negative nuance.[33] According to him, the concept had no precedent in the development any modern university.

The plan was for JNU to chart a new course for national integration. V.S. Jha and Triguna Sen felt that a good faculty with prominent and eminent professors would attract good students from all over the country. Kothari maintained that the focus should be on countrywide accessibility to a new postgraduate university, and not concentrated solely on the overburdened status of the existing Delhi University. V.K.R.V. Rao suggested that ideally every state ought to be represented in JNU with a quota system of students from each state. This would imbue a sense of national solidarity and integration into the new generation. Bhagwat Narayan Bhargava, a member of the Rajya Sabha, echoed Rao's sentiments on incorporating state-wise quotas for students and also endorsed Rao's plan to set up hostels named after different states and randomly populating them with students from different states—this would hopefully help foster national integration in future generations passing through the portals of JNU.[34] Kothari was confident that in the years to come Delhi would have many more universities and therefore JNU should focus on creating and cementing its character rather than solving Delhi University's problems.[35] Rao felt that the core value of the new university was going to be national, therefore the principles and sentiments of national solidarity and national integration should be inculcated here.[36] Kothari saw it differently and wanted the national character of the university to be facilitated by keeping a 'much greater proportion of postgraduate students than is the case of other universities'.[37]

The focal issues at this point were: (a) federating national-level science, technology and language institutions within the university and (b) national integration of students, faculty and the administrative board of JNU.

The location of the proposed university was another point discussed in the Lok Sabha. Raghunath Singh from Varanasi, Siddheshwar Prasad from Nalanda in Bihar, K. Hanumanthaiya from Bangalore and Prakash Vir Shastri from Bijnor, UP, had moved a resolution in the advisory council of the education ministry that the university should be set up somewhere in south India, perhaps in Andhra, Karnataka or in Kerala.

Krishnapal Singh of Jalesar put in a request for JNU to be situated in the interior or the rural heartland region, the state was not an issue.[38,39] Prakash Vir Shastri petitioned that Hindi be the medium of instruction in the new institutions. This demand, however, was countered by S. Kandappan, who associated this request with Hindi fanaticism.[40]

This aspect of the discussions in the Lok Sabha would coerce the government to consider establishing a new Central university in Hyderabad in the early 1970s.

H.N. Mukerjee and N.G. Ranga seemed to disapprove of Nehru and were against associating his name with the new university. However it was the Jana Sangh leader D. Thengari who wanted the name to be 'Rashtriya Visvavidyalaya'.[41]

The regional parochialism of the illuminati of Calcutta automatically resisted any development emanating from Delhi. This attitude would soon turn into almost a weapon in the hands of the political formations in the 1980s. Jyoti Basu and the CPI(M) claimed that Bengal was given a stepmotherly treatment by the Central government. While this stance gave the CPI(M) the macho image of a formidable opposition championing regional development, the attitude was taken to a ridiculous height in the 1980s by some intellectuals with their demand that the Third World revert to its primitive and traditional modes because the new-age metropolitan trends were not applicable to developing and underdeveloped countries.[42]

Are We Setting Up a Church?

From the outset the name of the new university was a bone of contention among the members of the Rajya Sabha. The socialists were not in favour of Jawaharlal Nehru's ideologies and were averse to using his name for the new university. The Jana Sangh echoed this sentiment; however, given their lower political stature, their objections did not carry much weight. According to these factions, although Nehru played an important role in the history of India, there were others who were just as worthy to be commemorated with a university.

The dispute over the name of the university was put on the back burner and the consultant academics who were called upon to give evidence focused on other aspects of the university, namely, integration, affiliation and curriculum. The committee inserted the following new schedule:

> To be worthy of its name, the university shall endeavour to promote the study of the principles and fulfil the ideals that Jawaharlal Nehru stood and worked for during his lifetime, namely, national integration, social justice, secularism, democratic way of life, international understanding and scientific approach to the problems of the country.[43]

Prof. Mukut Bihari Lal and Hem Barua disapproved of this schedule on the grounds that it was not right to represent the ideologies of a nation as 'principles and ideals of a great man'.[44] 'National ideals,' according to them, 'are to be studied and cultivated in life not because they are propounded and upheld by a great man but because they promote national good and the healthy growth of personality'.[45] They strongly opposed the idea of making Nehru an object of adulation and vesting him with qualities that personified the patriotic spirit. 'The university is converted into a church and the character and appeal of national ideals are considerably overcast with personality cult.'[46] Nehru had rebelled against Gandhi at one point in time; he was not the dyed-in-the-wool patriot that deserved hero worship or commemoration by naming a university after him; Nehru himself would not have appreciated being turned into a cult figure. It was not fair to Pandit Nehru or the youth of the nation to have an icon forced upon them as the patriotic prophet of India.[47] They objected to the schedule that attempted to combine the Act, the ordinances, and the national and social objectives of JNU. While social objectives of a university, they argued, are usually defined in the main body of the university Act, the ways to promote them are spelled out in ordinances. The two are hardly ever clumped together in a schedule in the manner proposed in the first schedule. They asked that the first schedule be dropped, and that the social objectives of the university be defined in the main body of the bill as national objectives.

The joint committee returned the bill after amending several clauses in light of the evidence given by the educationists. The bill was then moved to the Rajya Sabha on 1 December 1965. The minister acknowledged the revisions and changes, the foremost being the decision not to affiliate the seventeen to eighteen existing colleges of the Delhi University and start a university de novo.[48]

Although three-and-a-half hours were allotted to the discussion of the bill, it took three whole days to discuss the entire bill, and as many as 174 amendments were suggested, many of which were accepted including the amendment of some extremely important clauses and the first schedule itself. Prof. Mukut Bihari Lal, member of the joint committee, was the most impassioned critic of the bill. The mainstay of his argument was against naming the university after Jawaharlal Nehru as he was opposed to triggering personality cults. He had vociferously supported changing the name of the Banaras Hindu University and had proposed renaming it 'Kashi Vishwavidyalaya'. The socialists had also taken a stand against using Nehru's name for the university and the substance of the first schedule. This was beautifully elucidated by Professor Tara Chand when he discussed the bill on 2 December 1965. He spoke of the permanence of universities, which did not leave room to be defined by a mere personality cult, and hence rejected the schedule as well. Following this, he moved an amendment changing the wording of the schedule. Shakuntala Paranjpye seconded his motion.[49]

Chagla was adamant in his insistence on using Jawaharlal Nehru's name for the new university even while agreeing that it may not be proper to name universities after individuals. But he urged that an exception be made to this principle when men of outstanding stature were involved.[50] Mukut Bihari Lal, however, was intractable. In hindsight, perhaps one should have taken a policy decision on not naming universities after individuals. This became an almost facetious trend, particularly in the 1980s, when dozens of universities mushroomed with names of local and regional political and religious leaders. Now, with the ludicrous proliferation of names, one does not know how many Ambedkar Universities exist in the country and it is well-nigh impossible to identify the locations of these institutions.[51,] P.N. Sapru who also repudiated the first schedule and the many restrictions imposed on the autonomy of the proposed university, interrupted Mukut Bihari Lal.[52] Sapru believed that there were certain exceptional men, which included Nehru, 'who leave a permanent impression'.[53] Prof. Tara Chand agreed with this point of view, as did most of the members except the socialists—and they were not very happy with the first schedule either, or the proposed amendments to the bill.

From Congressman M. Satyanarayana's perspective, the objectives of the bill were the guidelines which would shape the university, which by all rights belonged to the future generations. The interpretations of many of the ideals and principles of today would undergo changes in future and it would be worthwhile to keep the ideals for which Nehru stood as the context and reference for posterity. The content of the first schedule had summarized the directive principles of the Indian Constitution and it was never said that they were Pandit Nehru's self-conceived concepts. Nor were they meant to be enforced in the university programme. Nehru, as a great Indian leader, merely symbolized these ideals and, we, as Indians, would also defend and stand for the objectives outlined in the schedule. The schedule was now amended as below:

> The university shall endeavour to promote the study of the principles for which Jawaharlal Nehru worked during his lifetime, namely, national integration, social justice, secularism, democratic way of life, international understanding and scientific approach to the problems of society.[54]

Chagla agreed with the amendment and concurred that a university exists to study and not to propagate. JNU would prove its worth by its own merit and be worthy of the great leader's name. He gracefully accepted Dr Tara Chand's modification of the schedule.[55]

The House still had misgivings about the words 'social justice' and 'secularism', which had been included in the revised schedule. P.N. Sapru deemed the term 'social justice' indistinct because it seemed to imply that socialism was to be a part of the JNU's curriculum. Another member of parliament took exception to the term 'secularism' that had slipped into the schedule.

Let Us Trust the Teachers

The debate on the bill in the Lok Sabha and the Rajya Sabha was focused on the name of the university and its possible national and international ethos. The emphasis shifted to the composition of the university faculty when the joint committee invited the evidence of the eight leading educationists. This panel made it clear that it was vital the new university had brilliant teachers at the heart of this enterprise.

V.S. Jha and Triguna Sen had disagreed with V.K.R.V. Rao who wanted a state-wise quota system to bring students to JNU. Jha and Sen were of the opinion that a good faculty consisting of eminent professors would attract good students from across the whole country. Jha, with his background of academic administration, had intervened to say that unless the proposed university had worthy teachers it had no great future. The policymakers would need to entrust the vice chancellor to appoint people according to his requirements without having to contend with the decrees of committees acting in a mechanical manner. 'If I am the vice chancellor,' Jha argued, 'then I would wish you to trust me to find the best man and leave me alone to do this task.'[56] He was more than willing to give the vice chancellor all freedom to choose his faculty as he 'may try all the methods possible to find the best man'. Jha drew a moral universe which was prophetic: 'All your selection committee only ensures a technical satisfaction that justice is done but the universities want something more than justice.'[57]

Bakar Ali Mirza pointed out to Jha that this blind trust in the post of vice chancellor could create problems in the long run. Jha partially agreed with this, however he insisted the vice chancellor be given a reasonable amount of control over the appointment of faculty and not be put under restraint. Reiterating his request for trust being reposed in the vice chancellor, Jha argued that instead of leaving the appointments to some ambiguous committees, it would be far more reasonable to trust a responsible vice chancellor.[58]

The members of the Rajya Sabha, across party lines, opposed Clause 8 which stipulated that a Visitor to the university would have the right to review the working of the university—the faculty, their modus operandi, the facilities, etc. Clause 8 became Clause 7 in the joint committee's report which said that the 'Visitor shall [also] have the right to cause an inspection be made, by such person and persons as he may direct, of the university.'[59] The scope of the inspection was quite wide: buildings, laboratories, equipment, institutions maintained by the university, the examination and teaching methodologies, any other work conducted or done by the university and other matters pertaining to the institution.[60]

Subclause 2 of Clause 7 clearly stated the visitor's authority to review the progress of the university. This seemed to be setting the stage for complications in the future as it said,

> Visitor may, from time to time, appoint one or more persons to review the work and progress of the university and submit a report thereon; and upon receipt of that report, the Visitor may take such action and issue such directions as he considers necessary in respect of any of the matters dealt with in the report, and the university shall be bound to comply with such directions.[61]

Subclause 3:

> Visitor may address the vice chancellor with reference to the result of such inspection and inquiry and issue such direction as he considers necessary in respect of any of the matters covered by the inspection or inquiry and the university shall be bound to comply with such directions.[62]

When the bill was presented in parliament, veterans like Mukut Bihari Lal and others immediately recognized the very binding provisos inserted within Clause 7 by the ministry officials. Mukut Bihari Lal was quick to point out that this clause had been taken from the Banaras Hindu University Act. Mohan Dharia, a member of the joint committee, explained the circumstances under which this section of the clause had been included. Visitorial inquiry and review was a feature that had been introduced into the university Acts following the controversy about the Andhra University's supervisory Act. This issue had culminated with the Inter-University Board threatening to derecognize the university if it went ahead with the Act. Furthermore, in the recent past when the Banaras and Aligarh Universities had similar issues, the ministry used visitorial inquiry to move beyond the groups and sections operating within the university to resolve the problems.

Now M.B. Lal, Sharda Bhargava and Tara Chand proposed amendments to this clause. As they had worked in various capacities in universities, they knew the problems which could ensue such supervisory inquiry and were the first amongst the panel to suggest deletion of this provision of visitorial review. In subclause 3, Mukut Bihari Lal wanted the university representative from the executive council to have the right to be present and be heard in an inquiry and Chagla agreed to the amendment. Visitor, it was now agreed, shall obtain the view of the executive council and only then cause an inspection or inquiry to be made. He, it was also agreed, would also address the vice chancellor with reference to the result of such inspection and inquiry. The clause was diluted by these amendments to give enough safeguards to the vice chancellor and the executive council.[63]

However, Prof. Tara Chand insisted the review clause be removed altogether with two arguments, which in hindsight sound quite valid. He reasoned that the university was not a technological institute and nor was it a laboratory, but rather consisted of numerous institutes and departments. Therefore, it was more or less impossible for one, two or three persons to inspect and report on the working of the university.[64] He also criticized it on moral grounds. Tara Chand felt it would be beneath the dignity of any university to accept inspection by rank outsiders.[65] Presenting a hypothetical scenario in which such an inspection was done, he was firm in saying that if he was teaching as a historian he would not allow anybody to come into his department to inspect his work.[66] He would rather leave the university than be subjected to such humiliation.[67]

As Mukut Bihari Lal pointed out, subclause 2 of Clause 7 was taken from the Banaras Hindu University Act which mentioned the visitorial inquiry. He wanted this to be amended as it severely countermanded the autonomy of the university.[68] His amendment was ranked number 185. Although P.N. Sapru, member of the university court, with experience of the pitfalls of visitorial inquiry, disagreed with Lal's opposition to the naming of the university, in this matter he supported Lal's objection to subclause 2 and condemned it as detrimental to the autonomy of the university.

In the strongest defence of academic autonomy, Ms Sharda Bhargava said that such a provision did not feature in the Delhi University Act. The amendment number 185, which was proposed by Mukut Bihari Lal and supported by Prof. Tara Chand and several other members, was accepted by Chagla, and adopted on 6 December 1965.

Most obvious, through this entire debate, was the underlying urge to create a completely autonomous institution, and this could be done by making the teachers the custodians of the university. This idea of trust underpinned the discussion on the provision of a second term for the vice chancellor. The opposition to extending the term turned ugly and personal when some rather unpleasant examples were cited. Tara Chand was clearly outraged with the accusations levelled at senior academicians: 'Teachers of the universities are not angels,' he retorted, 'they are not super human beings, they are Indians like all of us. If we are not going to trust them, who are we going to trust?'[69]

He underlined the irony in the fact that while one expected the teachers to develop the highest qualities of morality and intellect among young men, one did not trust them enough to do this with full responsibility.[70] He definitely did not like the tenor in which members tacitly assumed that the vice chancellors materialistically sought second terms and termed it unfortunate. He was perturbed at the way people depicted a vice chancellor as such a despicable human being that he or she would be unwilling to relinquish his or her salary or power for the greater good.[71]

To Tara Chand, the teaching faculty represented the soul of the university. 'The character and the functioning of the university depend,' he said, 'upon the trust that one places in the teaching staff of the university. They depend upon the arrangements that one makes for dealing with the students of the university.' Tara Chand, a legendary teacher, knew from experience that the students who would come to the university would not be children and would soon settle down in life in a couple of years or so, and hence it was important to take an interest in them 'not as boys and girls but as men and women'.[72] He therefore asked the people to develop such bodies in the new university where young adults could articulate their own concerns.[73]

Interaction with implicit faith between teachers and students would make for a higher quality of education. This automatically negated correspondence courses, which were generally considered inferior in quality and D. Thengari and Vimal Kumar Choradia suggested that long-distance education should be dropped altogether from the JNU curriculum.[74] Chagla agreed and assured the House that the university would not provide correspondence courses in light of these arguments and would take every precaution to see that quality was maintained.[75]

New Administrative Set-up

The panel of academic consultants was unanimous in their opinion that the ministry appoint an academician to the post of vice chancellor rather than retired judges or bureaucrats. The Lok Sabha agreed with this call and Chagla looked forward to appointing a person with a purely academic background to the post of the vice chancellor of JNU.

The innovation in this university bill was the brand new post of a 'rector'. There was a near unanimity about having the post of pro-vice-chancellor or registrar; however this plan was jettisoned as in universities like the Aligarh Muslim University and the Banaras Hindu University these posts had only become sources of problem and were constant irritants. The JNU Act attempted to resolve the matter by being innovative and provided for the post of the rector—perhaps more than one. In the joint committee, Triguna Sen, who had had to face the Banaras situation as a vice chancellor and had been reprimanded by his succeeding vice chancellor, A.C. Joshi, began his evidence by stating that the registrar should not administer the university in the absence of the rector and vice chancellor. Professor A.R. Wadia, a senior academician, was sceptical about this new rectorship, which meant different things in different universities.[76] Mukut Bihari Lal supported the creation of the rector's post.[77] P.N. Sapru enthusiastically endorsed Lal's view, and indicated there should be more than just one rector for JNU.[78] Chagla addressed Prof. Wadia's opposition and said, 'it is merely an enabling provision. As far as possible we will not have more than one rector, but supposing we need another, the parliament Act will need to be changed with due process.'[79]

Although the JNU Act was approaching fruition, Professor Mukut Bihari Lal, a socialist, who staunchly opposed naming the university after Nehru, was still not reconciled to the bill even at this stage. He saw in the bill the forebodings of an undemocratic and scholastically oriented institution. In his words:

> … it is my painful duty to inform you that I do not feel satisfied with this Bill and it is not possible for me, even at this stage, to extend my support to this Bill. I do feel that the university that will be constituted under this legislative measure, which, instead of promoting a scientific outlook and a scientific approach to problems will only promote scholasticism. I beg to submit that in my opinion, instead of promoting the democratic way of life, the university, constituted under this Bill, will promote autocracy and despotism in the University. I feel that this legislative measure is of an absolutely reactionary character, unworthy of the name with which this University is proposed to be associated.[80]

History, as Hayden White has argued, could be written in other tropes like irony.[81] Mukut Bihari Lal's resistance to the JNU Bill would have been the best basis for an irony-based historical plot. In many aspects, Lal symbolized one political segment's pathological opposition to the new university. The political and intellectual socialists, followers of Mukut Bihari Lal, remained some of the strongest critics of JNU, and, ironically, the students' union was spearheaded by socialist-minded students when, in 1983, violence broke out in JNU that would change the character of the university for all time to come. Curiously enough, it would not be the university statutes, but the various segments of students and teachers who would evince autocratic and non-democratic tendencies.

On the floor of the Lok Sabha, exactly twenty-three months after it was introduced in the Rajya Sabha, the Jawaharlal Nehru University Bill underwent the final phase of its career within the parliament. On 16 November 1966, at 2.44 p.m., M.C. Chagla, then the minister for external affairs, moved the bill, 'to establish and incorporate a university in Delhi' and, by 5.30 p.m., the bill was passed.[82] Shri Hanumanthaiyah, the eminent leader from south India, was the first to speak on the occasion. Although he had been critical of the bill, he was impressed with the way Chagla had carried the JNU Act through, and nearly put in a request for Chagla to be reinstated to the ministry of education from his current position in the ministry of external affairs. He believed that education was Chagla's forte rather than foreign affairs.[83]

It was backhanded compliment indeed for Pandit Jawharlal Nehru's achievements. The people's representatives of the world's largest democracy were able to speak freely, energetically and with great vehemence against the idea of naming an institution after the very the person who was in many ways instrumental in shaping this democratic order which allowed them their freedom of speech. What greater tribute could have been paid to the man by his countrymen?

A new university was no longer a distant possibility; its conceptual and legal foundation had been laid. It now required some strong hands and wise men to pull it all together and build a nice university.

3

The Nationalist Roots of a Modern University

> The university shall endeavour to promote the study of the principles for which Jawaharlal Nehru worked during his lifetime namely, national integration, social justice, secularism, democratic way of life, international understanding and scientific approach to the problems of society;[1] [and shall]
>
> foster the composite culture of India and establish such departments or institutions as may be required for the study and development of the languages, arts and culture of India.[2]

The first schedule of the JNU Bill which encapsulated the intellectual and philosophical premises of the university was almost the last item on the agenda during the discussions on the bill in the Rajya Sabha. The vision statement was construed as an attempt to impose Nehru's personal credo on to the new university and this generated a long and heated debate. The brainstorming sessions in the House indicated that there existed a far wider horizon of ideas beyond Nehru's personality. Many of these more progressive notions could just as well be embedded in the bedrock of the new university. Although the specific ethics contained in the schedule were not targeted, the underlying politically based motifs were apparent in the subtext of these criticisms.

The Modern Threshold

Attributes which define modern sensibilities in India have long been discoursed, primarily by a segment of academics, as being imported from post-enlightenment Europe in the nineteenth century.[3] Concepts such as nation, secularism, development, etc., were criticized as 'imported' metaphors. These imported metaphors are expounded in the theories explaining communal violence resulting in the disarticulation of society and partition.[4] The intensity of these critiques of nation and nation state correspond with two connected phenomena: intrusion of transnational corporations with a force hitherto unknown in human history (aided by the nation states of the United States, and other developed countries), and the impetus for an academic agenda of what has been termed 'global history'. One such effort, the Global Economic History Network, defines its motto as striving to push globalization in the national system of education with a missionary zeal.[5] There is therefore a close intellectual and academic collaboration between anti-modern academic discourse and extreme forms of attack led by transnational corporations on the national economies—nation states are perceived as impediments in the way the corporate and the American-state-supported groups seek to operate.[6] To enable this form of globalization, nation states in the Third World have to be conceptually destroyed.

Equality, an idea of justice and a critique of religion-based polity have been the ideological template for modern sensibilities. The intelligentsia saw in the inequitable, hierarchical and unjust social system the reflection of a system out of sync with the social and economic revolutions taking place thousands of miles away in Europe and particularly in Britain. These sensibilities led many of them to turn against the practices in their own society and try to envision a new society and polity for their country. The changes brought about by the French Revolution and the succeeding revolutions in Europe and elsewhere in the early decades of the nineteenth century were also not overlooked by the Indian intelligentsia.[7] The modern institutional arrangements with a new scientific education and democratic polity formed the basis of their vision. It is no wonder that it was the modern ideas of development, progress and the linked philosophical ideas of equality, justice and democracy that constituted the core of the new normative horizon in India as well.[8] A spectrum of social and political voices articulated this world view. This ranged from those coming from both the upper echelons and the so-called lower castes.

There have been recent efforts at dividing the intelligentsia and the leadership along caste lines in a heuristic, essentialist and intellectually pragmatic mode. The intelligentsia, mainly those from the upper castes who were trying to articulate ideas and organize changes to the society, was seen as demanding only reforms as opposed to those who came from the lower castes who were seen as attempting a complete rupture, i.e., revolution.[9] Interestingly, this divide demonstrates more of the present-day political divide than the divide that constituted the world of leadership in the nineteenth century. It was modernity that was on the horizon. This modernity sustained, first, the idea of equality; second, justice and the attendant rule of law which were to anchor the idea of equality; and it is here that the idea of an incipient democracy was to motivate the leadership and the intelligentsia.

The third and a very crucial idea, the nature of the modern state, had also come to define the template of the new social arrangement. The state and its location were pivotal in the intelligentsia's engagement. There were, however, shades of grey in construing the role of the state. From the days of Rammohun Roy to those of Gokhale, many Indian thinkers considered the state a collaborator in their efforts at social reform while there were others who were opposed to state intervention in Indian social issues altogether. This was the convergence point that later brought people like Gopal Krishna Gokhale and Lokmanya Tilak to attempt to unify public opinion ranged at opposite ends.[10] Having a colonial state which was also seen as biased and actively promoting a particular religion would not have been acceptable to a large section of the society and that complicated the case. However, it was in the realm of economics and state policies that the discourse would be most entrenched and in fact would soon define the core of Indian nationalism itself.[11]

When nationalism began emerging on the Indian horizon, it was seen in the context of a nation state. The notion of nation state in India was more or less on par with the nation state in the West. However, state making, which many associate with nation building in the US, was not quite as strong a component in the Indian nationalist context.[12] This is because the Indians were indigenous to India and had the inherent confidence of a people who had never been transplanted from their home state in the past. India, unlike the US where foreigners settled, or many other societies, where a centralized state may be weak historically, was home to monolithic state structures, the elements of which even the British used in order to entrench themselves in India. There was, however, one major difference. The mobilizing factor for nationalism in India was British colonialism and colonial domination. Therefore, Indian nationalism conjured up equality, justice and the end of discrimination between peoples and races, rather than language or culture as the template for a nation.[13] And it is here that the character of the discourse on states would substantially differ from similar discourses in Europe or in the United States.[14] The state here was to be attendant of the normative horizon which was in place and was to take forward the ideas defined by modern sensibilities. The idea and the design of an institution was part and parcel of these sensibilities.

Colonial rule projected itself as a successor state and quite often tried to, symbolically and in many other ways, create a public persona of it. There were however unmistakable signs, as was evident in the revolt of 1857, that it was always viewed as a foreign power. The basic premise of democracy was accepted and the related institutions were demanded and contested on those grounds. It was therefore an interesting contest where a subjugated people demanded the same rights and institutions which the advanced philosophers of the ruling country had been advocating. The intelligentsia increasingly gravitated to a democratic order—contours of that order crystallized with time. Some trends in recent intellectual discourse characterize all these under what is labelled as 'statist discourse' of the nationalists, imported, as is argued, from the West using the vehicle of post-Enlightenment knowledge and language.[15] What is obviously absent in this new discourse is the idea of democracy and equality which had become quite inalienable in the whole nation-making processes as well as in the discourse of nationalism in India since the nineteenth century.[16]

Biography of a Liberal

M. C. Chagla was born on 30 September 1900 in Bombay in a middle-class business family.[17] He went to the Jesuit-run St. Xavier's High School and College. He later went to Lincoln's Inn in Britain to study law. Upon his return to India he joined the bar of Bombay High Court as an assistant to the leading lawyers of the day including Muhammad Ali Jinnah. His rise in the court was steady: moving up to become the first Indian chief justice of the court after Independence. Nehru enlisted him for diplomatic work and sent him as a member of the first delegation of independent India to the United Nations and then in 1958 as Indian ambassador to the United States. Later he was the Indian high commissioner to England.

Since his early days, Chagla was enamoured by the politics and philosophy of Jawaharlal Nehru; they corresponded often and had open and frank exchanges of ideas. The admiration was mutual and Nehru appreciated Chagla's commitment to nationalism and justice. In April 1936, Nehru sought Chagla's opinion to set up an 'Indian Civil Liberties Union'.[18] Chagla's idea of justice was imbued with a sense of equality which explains his strong nationalist views. In one instance when he expressed his views regarding the role of the executive and the judiciary, Nehru advised him to exercise restraint as he was holding a public office.[19] Chagla agreed to be more circumspect.

In 1956, when there was an allegation in the parliament levelled against the finance minister by Nehru's own son-in-law, Nehru appointed Chagla to inquire into the Mundhra case. Chagla, known for his probity, indicted the minister for many lapses of omission and commission, which led to the resignation of the minister, T.T. Krishnamachari. It was Nehru's implicit trust in Chagla that made him appoint the latter as the ambassador to the United States and high commissioner to the United Kingdom, both very significant assignments considering the importance that both the countries carried in the post-Independence scheme of things in India. Nehru invited Chagla to join his cabinet as soon as he returned from London in 1963. He was given the education portfolio, which he held until 1966 when he was given the important portfolio of foreign affairs.[20]

Chagla was a liberal. The books that he read, the ideas that moved him and the education path that he travelled helped locate him in the nineteenth-century English liberal mould.[21] However, as a conscientious colonial subject he was also trying to evolve his location in the wider world—away from the British political and literary output. Individual liberty was the cornerstone of such an intellectual and political vision. Chagla, in his inaugural Spring Lecture series at Poona, on 1 May 1950, defined the contours of the democratic polity as being defined by liberty and law. He said that there 'must be faith in the uniqueness of personality and there must be a constant readiness to permit everyone to experiment with his own life and to work his own way to salvation'.[22] However, this liberty was to be guarded by the rule of law.[23] Chagla was one of the strongest defenders of individual and civil liberty. The conviction was so strong as to make him lead the whole civil liberty movement when Indira Gandhi, the daughter of his guide and philosopher, Nehru, imposed curbs on civil liberties during the Emergency.[24]

Chagla reflected the best of this modern tradition of defence of civil liberties when civil liberties were demanded not only for one's own group—a tendency that was evinced among most of the radical and left groups later. Chagla gave it a lot of thought and wrote on this topic. Nehru had approached him in 1936 to start a civil liberty union and Chagla inaugurated the Indian Civil Liberties Union along with Nehru.[25] Later, in the 1960s, Chagla again defended civil liberties of communists without sacrificing his personal stand as a nationalist.

Chagla and Nehru's Indian nationalist tradition—which militated against curbing civil liberty and tried to strengthen democracy—was not appreciated by the Hindu communal groups. From 1948 onwards, there were several instances when even the Communist Party also attacked Nehru and other nationalist leaders on the issue of civil liberties. When the Chinese war dealt a massive blow to India, the Communist Party of India thoughtlessly denounced the Indian nationalist leaders and blamed them for the Chinese intransigence.

However, it was the Hindu communal hardliners within the state who used the Chinese war as a pretext to attack the Communist Party and its activists. In universities like Delhi and Rajasthan communist intellectuals were actually physically assaulted. Thus, by the time Chagla, a jurist, became a minister in the Central cabinet, there was a pronounced anti-communist ambience in the ministries. On 30 August 1966, the prime minister's secretary, S. Banerjee, asked Chagla for his views on the Progressive Writers' Association (PWA) as the latter wanted the prime minister to inaugurate their sixth conference. The Intelligence Bureau had indicated that the PWA was a communist front and though a number of non-communist writers were its members, it was led by the members of the Communist Party of India.[26] The bureau opined against the prime minister attending the conference.[27] The prime minister, however, sought Chagla's advice on this.[28]

The latter's response was typical of the attitude of the nationalist leadership towards the communists. He held, he said, 'rather strong views about our attitude to what are described by the Intelligence Bureau as communist front organizations'. His experience, he said, was that 'the Intelligence Bureau dubs every leftist organization as communist-oriented'. He wondered why one should look upon communism in India as a contaminating disease. Chagla felt that when the USSR was considered a political ally in the international field, and India collaborated with the USSR in education (one of the best institutes of technology had been set up in Bombay with Russian professors), it was unreasonable to be prejudiced against the communists in any way.[29] As for the PWA, Chagla felt 'a writer should have perfect freedom to give expression to his ideas, to put into words his yearnings and his desire for a regimented society and the greatest evil in literature is conformity with the views held by those in authority'.[30] He therefore opined that they should 'give every encouragement to writers to write freely, express any views, adopt any ideology provided it is not subversive or against the security of our own country'.[31]

Referring to the PWA's invitation to the minister and the prime minister he said:

> With regard to this particular organization, the progressive writers organization, when Sajjad Jahir [Zahir] came to see me, I made it a point to see the list of those who were supporting the convening of the sixth conference and I found that the majority of them were not communists; they might hold advanced views, they may even be very much to the left, but they are very far from being members of the communist party. In my opinion, therefore this conference should get from us whatever support it can.
>
> They asked me to inaugurate it, but unfortunately the date does not suit me as I will not be in Delhi. If I could possibly participate in it without inaugurating it, I will certainly do so. My advice to the Prime Minister is that she should encourage these writers, most of whom are very talented and well known in our country.[32]

The prime minister was persuaded by Chagla's note and decided to 'go to the conference or find an opportunity of meeting the writers'.[33] It was wise advice and good championing of the values of right to freedom of speech in our political culture.

Later, as foreign minister, he helped communist leader Basavapunnaiah get his passport. In response to a report that suggested the UP government wanted to check appointment of 'subversive elements into the academic institution' by changing the recruitment procedures, he wrote:

> I think it is absolutely essential that we should maintain academic freedom and we do not want any witch-hunt in universities and institutions of higher education. Balliol has just elected an ex-communist as its master and Harvard and Yale refused to compel its professors to take the oath of loyalty in order to obtain federal aid. The word 'communist' is too lightly used and everyone who has radical views can easily be dubbed as a communist or a foreign agent. Our ordinary law is strong enough to look after those who are engaged in actual subversive activities.[34]

Upon receiving a representation from V.P. Gupta, welfare officer in the Indian Council for Cultural Relations (ICCR), an alleged communist, Chagla wrote to the home minister, Gulzarilal Nanda. His letter gives us an understanding of Chagla's humane, logical and rational nature. He saw a more 'fundamental question' than mere suspension of an officer who was involved not only in 'connection with the ICCR but our other organization also'.[35] The question was whether, 'we were going to exclude from services all people who are communist although they may not be guilty of any subversive activities; even though they may not actually participate in the work of the party and may be completely loyal to the country'.[36] Chagla pointed to the anomaly by reminding the home minister that the Communist Party in India was not banned and that India had the friendliest of relations with the USSR and other communist countries. He therefore wondered as to the grounds on which one could take action against the communists when a large number of Russians professors, 'avowedly communists', and IIT Bombay were collaborating together.[37] Chagla made a technical reasoning of equality in this regard:

> I can quite understand the government service rule that no employee of government should take active part in politics or in the affairs of any party and this should apply to every party whether it is Congress, the Muslim League, Jana Sangh or the Communist Party. But presumably a government servant can be a four-anna member of the Congress without inviting displeasure of the government. Why cannot he be a member of another political party which is not banned under the law? I know that we are opposed to the communist ideology as such, as much as we are opposed to the ideology of the Jana Sangh or the Muslim League, but in a free society citizens must be allowed to hold their own views unless those views are translated into action which conflict with the safety of the state.[38]

Chagla, therefore, was a quintessential liberal for whom the value of civil liberty was neither pragmatic nor political, but was self-evident and inherent. Chagla was also a staunch defender of private property; he considered it an intellectual, liberal and ideological position, and opposed the amendment to Article 31 of the Constitution. He was not one of those liberals who considered liberalism a convenient, non-left or anti-communist political ideology.

Secularism: the Core of Nationalism

What distinguished Chagla from many other Indian liberals was his robust upholding of secularism.[39] For Chagla, religion was a personal matter and secularism was not mere articulation of liberal principles of separation of church and the state. He saw the politics of Muslim and Hindu communalism as antagonistic not only to the principle of separation of religion and politics as per the liberal rubrics, but also as something that posed an impediment to social progress in India. Chagla very accurately recognized the intricate interconnection between Indian politics and the evolution of Indian nationalism.

Chagla took a keen interest in the politics of the country since his early years. Upon his return from London he worked with Jinnah. Chagla broke this association when Jinnah began talking about the two-nation theory, and he wrote publicly criticizing the idea. When the Congress ministries resigned in protest against not being consulted before dragging India into the Second World War, the Muslim League commemorated it as their day of 'deliverance' (from Hindu domination). Chagla admonished this:

> When I read of deliverance I thought that the British government had repented for its sins and misdeeds and overnight conferred freedom on India, and Mr Jinnah—the erstwhile champion of India's freedom—wanted us all to join in the song of victory. What Mr Jinnah wants us to celebrate, however, is the end of a government however wicked and iniquitous according to him, but elected by popular choice and commanding the confidence of the legislature, and the assumption of power by the governor as the representative of British imperialism which we have all sworn—including Mr Jinnah—to put an end to.[40]

Chagla would do his utmost to ensure that Jinnah did not assume the leadership of the faithful for a political cause. His stand was loud and clear: he was not one of Jinnah's followers and if his appeal had been made to them, he would have protested against this insult to the tenets of Islam.[41] Chagla criticized Jinnah's exhortation to the Muslims and condemned it as misuse of personal religion for political purpose. He cited the historical precedents and ramifications of using people's religious faith as a political agenda to disrupt an entire nation. A year later, in its annual session at Lahore in March 1940, the Muslim League declared that the two religious communities were now two separate nations and that the issue between the Hindus and Muslims was an international issue and needed an altogether different solution: creation of an independent Pakistan. Chagla came out strongly against this:

> It is indeed difficult to understand how and why India, which was one country, and the people of India who constituted one nation till recently, should have undergone a sudden transformation in

> Mr Jinnah's mind and have become a sub-continent on the one hand and two nations on the other. Even the misdeeds of the Congress are not sufficient to explain this cataclysmic change. The Muslim League was perhaps not conscious of the fact that it was going diametrically against the current of history and political progress. All over the world the present tendency for peoples is to coalesce and realize the harm that has been done by ideas of exclusive and aggressive nationalism. The League and Mr Jinnah are trying to divide communities that have already come together and have been sharing common citizenship for hundreds of years past.[42]

Gandhi was assassinated on 30 January 1948. Chagla, speaking at All India Radio's Bombay station, blamed communalism as the chief culprit. He was unequivocal in his view that it was 'not enough to call meetings, pass resolutions, and pay homage to him'.[43] It was more important to recognize the ideology behind the whole organized movement that killed Gandhi and decide which kind of ideology should prevail in the country.[44] He was absolutely clear that the need to build a strong secular state and fight against communal and sectarian ideologies were of paramount significance to develop a common bond of citizenship.[45]

The idea of evolution of a people inspired Chagla to give a compelling address on the Kashmir issue. His idea of this evolving history of India was part culture and part politics. His perception of Indian culture was clear cut and he believed that the Indian evolution had bequeathed an interesting and composite cultural mosaic which shaped India. In addition, modern political history unified India. It was from this vantage point that one understands his opposition to any idea which impeded this process of evolution. Here he found the idea of communalism was most inimical to not only the natural historical progression but was also contrary to the liberal design that he had of the society and its basic norms.

It was this concept that made him take a very strong stand on the Muslim communal idea which came in the shape of Jinnah's call for Muslim nationalism. However, after Independence it was Hindu communalism that he also had to contend with and his opposition to it was just as strong. As education minister, in 1964, when he was informed that a vice chancellor of a university in Madhya Pradesh had spoken at an RSS meeting, he immediately wrote to the home minister, Mr Gulzarilal Nanda: 'Vice chancellor of Ravi Shankar University gave a speech recently from the official platform of RSS praising the Sangh and holding it up to the people as an institution which had shown patriotism and helped the national cause.'[46] Gulzarilal Nanda too disapproved of this incident and responded: 'I do not like a vice chancellor and a university professor praising the RSS and advocating its cause. But what we can do in the matter will require careful examination. I am having this done and I shall write to you again.'[47] However, Chagla wrote to D.P. Mishra, the chief minister of Madhya Pradesh who was also very close to the academic community, and reported this unprofessional behaviour to him and requested him to take action. Dr Mishra in his reply said that he disliked the communal character of the RSS. He agreed with Chagla that it was highly improper for the vice chancellor and a professor to articulate their communal position in public meetings. Expressing his own sense of anguish that as the chief minister of Madhya Pradesh he had to witness the powerfully entrenched RSS particularly in the Madhya Bharat region recently included in the state,[48] Mishra went on to assure Chagla that the university faculty as well as the vice chancellor in question were strong nationalists and that he would talk to them regarding the event and in case they had articulated such ideas, he would try and tell them to desist from doing so in future.[49] Quite a strong statement from the chief minister of a state![50]

However, Chagla was not lulled by a mere promise of action, and sent a circular to the vice chancellors of the Central universities on 30 November 1965:

> My attention was drawn to the case of a vice chancellor of a state university who gave a speech from the official platform of RSS. The Home Minister and I considered this matter and we have come to the following conclusion:
>
> That it would be desirable if a convention could be established that a vice chancellor or a university teacher's right to freedom of speech should stop short of public support to political activity,

> open or disguised, which is inconsistent with the basic ideas of our constitution. It is certainly harmful if a vice chancellor or a university teacher support anti-democratic, anti-secular or pro-communal activities.[51]

A recent description of Chagla as a Muslim whose opposition to communalism was nothing but overzealous 'bending-over-backwards to prove his Indianness' is not only misplaced but it also ignores the intellectual trajectories of modern India. Kuldip Nayar was thus not very charitable to Chagla when he says that although Shastri initially considered Chagla as foreign minister, he later dropped the idea on the grounds that Chagla, being a Muslim, would bend over backwards to prove his opposition to Pakistan, an Islamic country.[52] Chagla's stand on the 1967 war in West Asia was completely in line with his Nehruvian idea of a foreign policy based on Indian support to aspirations and independence to all secular Arab nationalisms. The Western media projected his speech and stand as Muslim. Later on Chagla was quite scathing in his criticism of the government's attempt at gate-crashing the meeting of the Organization of Islamic Countries. Although a Congress member in the Rajya Sabha, he spoke against the government's decision as unfortunate and on communal lines.

Chagla was was thus not just a 'refined Muslim gentleman' as has been described by an educationist[53] recently. He was a doughty fighter for civil liberties and came out in opposition to curbs on citizen's rights during the Emergency.

Grounding Liberalism

Chagla had an abiding commitment in the individual's ability to raise one's own consciousness and he believed that the state could be a truly welfare and consciousness-raising instrument.[54] In all these, education according to him played a key role and it is very significant that when he became the education minister his ideas on education were in consonance with not only the liberal template but also with the values of the nationalist intelligentsia that he had stood for. He had a vision for education that was very closely tied with the idea of modernity and its core quest of democratic expansion and the deepening of justice.

Chagla reflected the best of the modern ideas on justice and equity in which state had a pivotal role.

Chagla's experience in handling the educational issues were not comprehensive but not very limited either. He had been the vice chancellor of Bombay University for a short while, therefore his scholarly mind, judicial approach and liberal humanist outlook made him an eminently suitable education minister. However, the domain of the ministry was limited. The Union government did not have jurisdiction over much of the primary and secondary education and in higher education there were only a couple of Central universities which were under the Centre's control. Therefore, while people were happy that an upright and judicious man had come to occupy the chair, they were also sceptical, as they knew that no education minister could succeed without the active support of the states, which were responsible for implementation of educational policies. The newspapers hoped that Mr Chagla and his deputy would be able to inspire the state governments into perceptible action.[55] The *Amrita Bazar Patrika* thought that 'the inclusion of a man of his stature in the cabinet would ensure intelligent handling of the problems of education at all stages'.[56] One does not know, however, how Chagla saw his own role, as V.K.R.V. Rao, who became a minister later in 1969, thought that his own role was to 'merely sermonise' and nothing else, as most of the powers were vested in the states.[57] Chagla, however, showed optimism about his potential as an education minister.

Chagla had an all-round idea of education and believed that education had to be seen from a national perspective and schools were equally important.[58] He was also acutely aware of the importance of facilities for children in schools and appreciated the Madras Parks, Play Fields and Open Spaces (Preservation and Regulation) Act 1959, and suggested the states to initiate legislations in this regard in view of disappearance of playing grounds in the cities.

The educational system with its vagaries was floundering to provide able manpower (both at the technical and non-technical levels) which was essential for the success of the Second Five-year Plan.[59] The state governments were proving unequal to the task of maintaining standards of education. There were disparities within and among states about age and streams. It needed streamlining. Chagla was considering the provision of evening and postal education. He began making concerted efforts to raise teachers' remuneration across the country.[60]

Textbooks and teaching methods of crucial subjects like history were haphazard.[61] He was attentive to the concern of historians who had been agitating over the fact that in most states history textbooks were shoddy, based on colonial understanding and stereotypes, and extremely communal. He therefore acceded to the request of setting up a writing board and also commissioned the NCERT to produce good textbooks in history. However it was Subhadra Joshi, a leading Congress member of parliament, who took the lead in this agitation for secular history. She also saw to it that the minister included non-communal historians in the board and therefore sent alternative proposals which incidentally were included in the board which later selected authors to write the NCERT textbooks. The names suggested by her included Bisheshwar Prasad, B.P. Saxena, Nurul Hasan, S.N. Sen, R.P. Tripathi, K.K. Dutta, K.P.S. Menon, Mohammad Habib and N.K. Sinha.[62]

Chagla was also very keen that the national ethos must be preserved in the textbooks that were to be prepared. However, his ideas in this field were best reflected in his stand that India needed its own textbooks. When the issue of collaboration with multinational publishing houses writing Indian textbooks was brought to him he wrote to the minister of industry, T.N. Singh, that the textbooks that students study 'are a matter of national concern' and what they should be studying should not be decided by any 'foreign agency'.[63] Though a matter of industrial collaboration, and an education minister did not have much say in it, he articulated his firm opinion that in matters of publishing textbooks for Indian students, it was necessary for Indian firms to have a majority share in the equity capital and not 40 per cent as suggested. 'This is more a matter of ministry of industry than for our ministry', he agreed.[64] His efforts to promote NCERT textbooks in all subjects therefore was not merely to push an ideology but an effort to create autonomous intellectual development of students and a sense of 'national unity' in their formative stage.[65]

Although constitutionally Chagla preferred limited control by the Central government in matters of education, it was evident from the debate on the first report of the University Grants Commission in 1958 that he wanted the Centre to assume a more hands-on approach to resolving the problems. When L.M. Singhvi presented his bill on education, Chagla, while agreeing that education was pivotal to Indian development, argued that 'we cannot go very far as a nation unless the educational standards of our people are raised'. Chagla was directly involved in the implementation of some of his basic ideas and set up model institutions and charted their course. The push to make structural changes to an existing system was a move by the Indian government which has been unprecedented and unequalled. The report of the Education Commission 1964–66 (known as Kothari Commission after its chairman Dr D.S.Kothari), therefore, was of singular significance as it provided the justifying arguments behind these changes.

Many so-called 'modern' Indian universities ran along colonial and very archaic feudal lines, and, somewhere along the way, vested interests of caste or community were beginning to take priority over developing the structures along modern democratic lines. It was apparent that Chagla primarily wanted to fulfil the modern promise to Indian universities, and the Aligarh and Banaras University bills, which he presented in parliament, proved his intention and intellectual predilections.

Aligarh Muslim University Agitation

Chagla, who had been keenly watching the academic life of Aligarh, was eager to promote the department of medieval history at AMU as a world-class department. As soon as he became the education minister, he took the opportunity to champion the cause of Aligarh Muslim University. He was determined that Aligarh Muslim University be developed into a first-class university with a larger canvas, playing a leading role in the new atmosphere of knowledge. Chagla persuaded Nawab Ali Yavar Jung Bahadur, a Hyderabad educationist and a radical and staunch nationalist, to come from Paris to Aligarh and assume charge of the university. Wishing him Chagla said:

> As you are assuming the office of the VC of the AMU on the 1st of March [1965], I feel I should write to you and send my best wishes for a very successful tenure of office. I know how difficult it was for me to persuade you to give up your diplomatic

> career and accept this post, but when I told you that it was a very challenging assignment and in my opinion, one of the most important in the educational world of India today, you agreed to accept the challenge. I have no doubt that with your past experience you will make one of the most successful VCs that AMU ever had. You have been a teacher, a minister in government, VC of Osmania and have rendered valuable services to the country's diplomatic posts. Today you will be called upon to make the AMU a modern, outward-looking institution of higher education which will be national in outlook and proudly taking part and playing its role in the educational development of our country. You can count on the full support of the government in your efforts to make your university one of the best and most national in our country.[66]

Jung too felt optimistic about undertaking this challenge, assured in the knowledge that he had the minister's personal confidence and support. Jung was soon to find out the ways of the university. He tried to rationalize the reservation for local students in professional courses so that the ambience of isolation was reduced and at the same time increasing a sense of competition. This became the issue on which there was a massive mobilization against him and he was grievously attacked in the meeting of the university court itself. He was nearly killed in the event and was brought to Delhi for treatment.

Chagla was incensed with this treatment of the vice chancellor. In a confidential letter to the home minister, Gulzarilal Nanda, on 3 May 1965, Chagla disclosed the real nature of the attack on the vice chancellor. He wrote that the student disturbance was undoubtedly aimed personally at Jung and it was organized by the communal and reactionary elements that comprised some students and members of the staff.[67] The reason for the assault was clear to Chagla: 'the national and liberal outlook of the vice chancellor'.[68]

The attack, in fact, jeopardized his plans to bring a new bill to change the character of the university. Chagla, therefore, promulgated the AMU ordinance to suspend the senate and court and gave their powers to the vice chancellor and the executive committee. This provoked many detractors, including those who had a vested interest in the university, to charge him of suppressing minority rights provided in Article 30 of the Constitution. Chagla was however very clear: Article 30 applied only to institutions established and administered by a community and as the AMU was established by legislature it did not qualify to be to treated as a minority institution requiring safeguards under the article.[69] 'We have always looked upon the Aligarh University as a national institution', he argued, 'where special attention should be given to all aspects of Muslim culture in the context of our secular society.'[70] He also brought the issue of parliamentary sovereignty and the idea of secular constitution to the foreground in his argument when he said that the government could not possibly assure a majority for any single community in the management of institutions created by legislature: 'Our right to promulgate the ordinance and pass the bill was being challenged and what was suggested was that there must be a statutory guarantee that there will be Muslim majority in the senate. On behalf of the government I could not possibly accede to this suggestion.'[71]

A strong mobilization apparently to save the university began to take shape. Many individuals like Syed Mahmud, an ex-Congressman, came out of hibernation, and mobilized Muslim public opinion. It also aroused the communal elements already powerful within the university. Syed Mahmud spearheaded the agitation by Aligarh University's old boys and accused Chagla of inciting passions and predicted that his actions would have repercussions in Pakistan. Chagla wrote to Asad Madani who too was spearheading the movement:

> When I described the incident in the Muslim University as communal, I made it quite clear that I did not use the expression to mean that there was any attempt to stir up feelings against the Hindu students or against the Hindu community as such. I was only emphasizing the fact that there is a reactionary element in the Aligarh University, which was opposed to the appointment of the new vice chancellor who has a national and modern outlook. I am convinced that such a communal element exists in Aligarh and it is in the interest of the Aligarh University that such an element should be deprived of every influence which it possesses in the administration of the university. The ordinance that has been promulgated has largely been done with this purpose.

In the same letter, he elaborated the Indian notion of secularism that was not against the cultural mosaic:

> Although I am a confirmed and convinced secularist, I am equally convinced in my mind that the secularism of India depends upon full encouragement being given to different cultures, which have contributed to making Indian civilization the glorious thing it is and, in this, the Muslim civilization has played a very big part. Therefore, it is both false and libellous to suggest that I am in any way opposed to the development and maintenance of Muslim culture. I want the Muslim culture to flourish in Aligarh University not in isolation but in the context of Indian nationalism. Aligarh University has to show to India and the world what role Muslim culture has played in Indian history and how important it is that culture is safeguarded. I therefore, think that your association, instead of suspecting my bona fides and expressing doubt, ought strongly to stand by me in the action that I am taking and give your full support both to the education minister and to the new vice chancellor.[72]

It was the time when Hindu communal mobilization had been drummed up on the issue of the Banaras Hindu University, and when there was a pro-Hindi agitation orchestrated by the socialists in Uttar Pradesh, that the Jana Sangh and the Muslim communal elements joined forces in a vicious campaign on a large scale. Chagla stood firm and there was subtle support from many leading Muslims. K.A. Hamied, the founder of pharmaceutical multinational CIPLA, wrote to him on 14 July 1965 and invited Chagla to a dinner that he was organizing where he had invited Muslim intellectuals, editors, etc., to meet and dispel the misconceptions about the whole episode.[73]

The attack against Chagla also revealed some of the most intriguing and exasperating aspects of Indian politics. Many Muslim politicians, who were supposedly nationalists, were in fact galvanizing opinion against him.[74] These campaigns would change Indian politics, primarily communal politics, in northern India.[75] But Chagla, an ardent Nehruvian, faced the entire agitation with determination and grace and refused to compromise his ideas of secular institution.

Language: The Anguish of a Nationalist

There had been intense moments in the politics of India where the question of language tried to occupy centre stage. It was evident that however strong linguistic allegiances were, India as a nation commanded a much larger commitment. The emotionally charged agitation for linguistically defined states in the 1950s nearly ripped the national fabric. Far more serious was the trouble that began in the 1960s when the southern part, especially Tamil Nadu, seemed to be breaking away from the country. Chagla's assumption of the ministership as well as his stand on the language issue provides us with a valuable insight into the mind of a nationalist.

This was an issue which had divided the country in the 1960s, and when Chagla was appointed as minister of education, there were voices that accused him of being a defender of English. Significantly, he was given a deputy minister, Bhakt Darshan, who was a prominent Hindi enthusiast. However, Chagla was soon moved to the ministry of external affairs as he was one of the few with the widest foreign exposure and, after Nehru, one of the few who could actually articulate much of the Nehruvian foreign policy vision at international fora. One of the toughest times he faced within a month of this appointment as foreign minister was the second Arab–Israeli war where Indian sympathy with the Arab forces precariously balanced the Indian position against Western blackmail. Although Chagla articulated this well, his stance was wrongly perceived as entirely pro-Muslim.

Soon however, the controversy about introduction of vernacular languages in higher education made Chagla resign from the post of external affair minister as he felt very strongly about it. It was a rarity that a person resigns on an issue that did not concern him as a minister. The first state which adopted the vernacular language in this manner was Gujarat (it would be quite significant to examine the long-term effects of the adoption of vernacular as the medium of higher education in Gujarat). The language policy of Uttar Pradesh, Madhya Pradesh, Rajasthan and Maharashtra, however, it seems, had a crippling effect on their universities. It not only failed to produce any worthwhile tradition beyond regional or local parochial assertions but also slowly surrendered certain positive and universalistic scholarly traditions that they had developed over the last century. In his resignation letter to the prime minister that he released to the press on 31 August 1967, he said: 'maintenance of unity of India' was the basic tenet of his political philosophy and that he regretted that in his opinion 'the educational policy of the government is likely to threaten, if not undermine, that unity'.[76] Chagla was almost prophetic. The educational system was rapidly crumbling amidst these developments and in the Vice Chancellors' Conference in September serious doubts were raised about the way things were moving.[77]

A product of the national movement, during which he had seen Hindi's unifying role, Chagla was convinced that Hindi must ultimately replace English and play the unifying role that English plays today. He, however, strongly believed that the changeover from English to regional languages must be gradual so as not to impair educational standards. He also advised that English should be continued, as this was an international and scientific link language and we must plan and usher the changeover from English to Hindi very carefully and gradually.[78]

He was referring to a full range of issues that the country would have to face in case a sudden change were to take place. For him the time limit of five years for undergraduate studies and ten years for all stages, proposed by all universities to change over to the vernacular, 'was hopelessly unpractical and unrealistic'.[79] Emphasizing the fact that recognized Indian languages are different and in unequal stages of their development, and, therefore, needing considerable attention and care to develop themselves, he rejected the idea that a crash programme of translation would overcome the problem of an absence of necessary literature and teaching aids in many such languages. 'It is not through translation', he argued, but through 'original work that a language is developed. And original works cannot be produced overnight.' He also mentioned how the Education Commission had also pointed out the need for 'careful preparation for this purpose and the fact that both the manner and the time of translating would have to be left for a decision by the university system'.[80]

The idea of excellence was an integral part of the idea of a future social order during the last two hundred years and all institutions were created out of a respect for this notion of excellence. Chagla believed that the telos of every university was 'work for excellence' and should not be reduced to being a mere 'factory for the production of graduates'. He wondered what would happen to this idea of excellence if teachers were asked to lecture in a language in which they were not proficient and would have to arm themselves with 'shoddy books hastily produced to order'. He also pointed to a very significant issue, the issue of linguistic minorities: 'What will happen to students whose mother tongue is different from the regional language?' In fact, he foresaw that the minorities in this case would be 'practically shut out from universities of a state which would be teaching in the regional language'.[81] The universities would be hit by another turn of events as a consequence of the policy of recruitment at a national level: 'What will happen to the teachers who are not conversant with the regional language? Most universities recruit professors on an all-India basis and make use of the best talent available. Are these professors to be turned out? And do we, after five years, make our universities purely regional with students only from the state and cease to employ teachers outside its boundaries?'[82] This actually began happening in 1967 when the English-speaking faculty of Rajasthan University began to look for opportunities outside the state.

Chagla was concerned about the teaching of the sciences, and felt that the impact would be more acute and widespread in this area as it was an international domain and the students and researchers would be hit by the paucity of standard material as it would be well-nigh impossible to translate and publish good material. Building a pool of scientists and scientific research was a long and laborious process, 'and therefore, a sudden change over from English to the regional languages must result in precipitous lowering of standards'. Parochializing a university would therefore lead to restricting the boundaries of sharing research and dialogue among the scientific community.[83]

Whether or not he had exaggerated his fears, he saw clear signs that the consequences of the policy were going to be far-reaching. It was not a simple Anglophile's nightmare of a world without English but a concerned citizen's anguish over the populist pressure over governance where the result was perceived to be undesirable. 'I strongly feel,' he ended his note to the prime minister with whom he was not going to work any longer, 'that the steps that we are taking are irreversible.'[84] He was emphatic that, unlike other policy measures of the government where mistakes could be corrected, mistakes in education would have a permanent impact. 'It affects millions of our people and a whole generation may suffer,' he said, 'because we were more concerned with our present difficulties and pressures and did not look sufficiently ahead into the future.'[85]

A careful reading of Chagla's writings on many important issues gives us some idea of his political, social and cultural views. He was a liberal humanist with a keen eye on public affairs right from the very beginning. However, in the ideological context of India, that liberalism as a personal and political philosophy was much more nuanced than the purely classical definition of liberalism: (a) liberalism had no place for the colonialist when, as a matter of fact, in many ways, colonialism was defended by the liberals and (b) the quintessential liberals were completely out of place with the gradual enlargement of the base of Indian national movement and were increasingly sidelined except for a very limited role that eminent Indian liberals such as Tej Bahadur Sapru, Bhulabhai Desai, M.R. Jayakar performed in facilitating dialogues on constitutional issues. Many liberals resurrected themselves in the freedom movement by donning a completely different garb as Jinnah had done by metamorphosing his ideological stance on to the Muslim communal side while people like Jayakar appealed to the Hindu communal side. It is here that the idea of nationalism in India is very significant in moderating the tenor of liberalism. There have been attempts to try and define a liberal space for the Indian intellectual and political life. The location of nationalism and secularism has become a target for criticism in these liberal writings.[86] In an extreme form of such liberal articulation, a kind of North American communitarianism gets mimicked for India.[87]

Liberals like Chagla held secularism as the unifying factor in a country of pluralities. And JNU was the vision of such liberals who anchored their liberal attitudes principally in the ethos of nationalism, anti-colonialism and secularism which they believed would be coterminous with an autonomous national educational culture in sync with the historical evolution of the society.

4

Radical Decade: The 1960s

The 1960s were easily the point of entry into a new phase for institutions in the contemporary world. There were unmistakable signs that the older institutional frameworks in many fields of human existence were either questioned or were beginning to show cracks. The hippie movement and the radical and violent campuses in the United States, for example, demonstrated the gap between the generational aspirations and the core values of traditional institutions. The music group, the Beatles, which emerged from the not too radical Britain, was a major symbol of the attack on the established socio-cultural order. In terms of discourse, institutions themselves became sites of contention. Intellectuals contested not only the existing institutional designs but also the legitimacy behind such designs. The students' sit-ins in the United States, strikes in Paris and student rallies at Hyde Park, London, all in 1968, were open demonstrations of a larger fatigue, if one may call it that, with the lack of dynamism of the institutions, academic and non-academic, to catch up with the political and social changes.[1]

Education Explosion and Change

The changes were most visible in the sphere of educational institutions. The student profile across the world underwent tremendous changes during the 1960s. The transformation had its root in the structural modifications that began to take place in Europe after the Second World War. Secondary education in many parts of Europe was still considered a privilege. In many countries compulsory primary education, which was introduced only at the tail end of the nineteenth century, was not properly implemented, and in pre-communist eastern Europe as well as the peasant heartland of Spain, Italy, Ireland, etc., children dropped out of school quite early. However, there were changes in the 1950s, and one saw Britain, Italy and France changing the structure by raising the school-leaving age—to fifteen (in England in 1947, and sixteen in 1972) and to fourteen in Italy in 1962. The numbers were now telling a different story. The number of full-time students in Italy doubled between 1959 and 1969. In France the 'bacheliers' (high school graduates) increased fivefold. Europe seemed to be full of young people; in France, for example, there were 8 million people between sixteen and twenty-four, constituting 16.1 per cent of the total population.[2] The old European gap between the majority who had not been to institutions beyond primary school and those who had been to secondary school and beyond was narrowing.

When it came to the new entrants moving up, there was an issue. The universities were mostly integrated with the existing architecture of the cities and hence it was difficult for them to sustain the new wave unless the cities enlarged their own absorption capacity. They all needed the help of the state now, and different countries used different approaches to secure this. The British universities and some of the Scandinavian countries built new universities in the provincial cities and country towns, e.g., Lancaster in England and Aarhus in Denmark.

Traditionally, in Europe, there was not much of an issue of moving from secondary to higher levels if one passed the prescribed national level tests. In addition, state after state removed whatever impediments there were for the potential student. There was something like an explosion now. A typical Italian university, for example, the University of Bari, which traditionally had 5,000 students, now had to take in 30,000 students; Naples, 50,000; and University of Rome, 60,000. In West Germany where there were 108,000 students in 1950, the number by the end of 1960 rose to 400,000.[3]

The explosion in student population had a negative impact on the quality of instruction. To quote Tony Judt, one of the finest historians of the period, 'all over Europe there were vastly more students than ever before—and the quality of their academic experience was deteriorating fast. Everything was crowded—the libraries, the dormitories, the lecture halls, the refectories—and were in distinctly poor condition (even, indeed especially, if it was new).'[4] The falling academic standards were very graphically described by Raymond Aron, the sociologist, who bore the brunt of the anger of the radical intellectuals and the student leaders of 1968. In describing the university that he returned to teach in, long after 1955, he said: 'In 1955 it was already true that most students had to fend for themselves in a world that was different from that of the lycée [secondary school]. Each year as the number of students ... increased, and without a precise goal or any particular vocation, the old pattern became more and more anachronistic.'[5] To him Sorbonne almost seemed like a relic of the nineteenth century.[6] By 1968, he saw another transformation. To quote him:

> Between 1955 and 1968, from a sheltered position, I witnessed the transformation of the old Sorbonne. University theses were abolished; theses for the troisième cycle were introduced. I had a single assistant in 1955, ten years later there were ten looking after the students. The increase in both teachers and students could be seen from year to year. The Descartes amphitheatre was full when I gave my lectures; I was addressing hundreds of listeners who I did not know. I decided to leave Sorbonne in 1967 and to become the director of studies at the École Pratique des Hautes Etudes, because I had the feeling that the building was cracking, that we were paralysed, sterilized by a system at the end of its tether.[7]

There was, however, a silver lining. This explosion in numbers had been taking place without any serious crisis in the economies,[8] which were on the whole looking up and, with an additional effort, the situation could be given a new direction. In the Third World on the other hand, the recently independent countries began to build institutions in the 1950s and '60s although they were cash-starved and lacked the support of the Marshall Plan or the economic umbrella of the United States which covered Japan.[9] The Third World also had to bear the brunt of the cold war where any help was linked to political subscription to one side or other.

Many countries including India, Indonesia, Nigeria, Kenya and China had to start building from scratch as the erstwhile colonial powers had not only left nothing much for institution building but had also placed a huge burden of a ruptured and disarticulated socio-economic fabric. While for many African and Asian countries it was the beginning of their stories, for India, it was a new phase. After the euphoria of Independence more or less settled, new tensions began to test the endurance of the still surviving structures. The floundering universities had begun sending out their distress signals and the leadership had an inkling that the Centre had to step in with some kind of new institutional design.

In the Vortex of the Cold War

The 1960s formed the midpoint between two periods of crises in contemporary Indian history. Extreme poverty, food shortages and critical all-time lows in the socio-economic indicators were the hallmarks of the 1950s. The 1960s saw the economy in a strange flux where, in spite of the fact that many new industries and projects like Bharat Electronics Limited (1954), Heavy Engineering Corporation (1958), Bhilai Steel Plant (1955), Durgapur Steel Plant (1960), Rourkela Steel Plant (1955), Sindri Fertilizer Factory (1952), etc., had been functioning during the first two plans, their contribution to real life had not been felt beyond their local environs.[10] As most of these large industries were basically infrastructural in nature, they had long gestation periods before they could generate profits. On the other hand, agriculture, notwithstanding major efforts in the 1950s to improve the condition by bringing the Zamindari Abolition Act, the Land Ceiling Act and steps in improving rural conditions through the community development projects, did not achieve any technological breakthrough and was still in the primitive stages of operation. Dependence exclusively on the monsoons was starkly revealed when two successive years of drought in 1965 and 1966 brought the country to the brink of a food famine.[11] The situation was complex as the economy could not rely solely on internal production and had to turn to international trade and aid to tide over the crisis.

The world situation had completely changed after the Second World War with the Soviet Union and the United States of America emerging as the two central forces of the new world. In addition to helping rebuild the destroyed Western economies, America had also become the centre of military might. On the other hand, the Soviet Union had emerged as the other major power that now occupied almost half the world stage either alone or in ideological collaboration with the other socialist country, China. The Soviet-led forces in eastern and central Europe and in Asia, just after the war, had made America take a stand to counter any further communist expansion.[12] The Warsaw Pact countries in Europe, China and other communist forces in East Asia and Africa consolidated into the communist bloc, which was confronted by the Western capitalist bloc led by the United States, Britain and France.[13]

The independent foreign policy that India adopted in world affairs was viewed with suspicion by both the communist and the capitalist blocs. The experience of the Indian representatives, J.L. Mehta and Vijayalakshmi Pandit, in the United States and the Soviet Union had been singularly exasperating. Vijayalakshmi Pandit was not even given an audience by Stalin.[14] Gradually, however, the situation with respect to bilateral relations improved, although the non-aligned status of India was neither understood nor liked. The death of Stalin in 1954 and the split between the Soviet Union and Chinese Communist Party made a slight improvement to India's relations with the Soviet Union, and Khrushchev's visit to India helped bring a better understanding between India and the USSR.

The international fallout of the Sino-Soviet split in 1956, combined with the domestic economic stress, put complex pressures on the Indian policymakers, which was compounded by the Chinese aggression in 1962 and the subsequent war with Pakistan in 1965. A large section of population suffered acute privation and the polity was also under duress. It was in this situation of stress that the leadership was pressurized by the United States to apply its policy prescriptions, namely, liberalization of trade, devaluation of currency and acceptance of its wide-ranging advice on agricultural policy and practices.[15] The new Indian leadership under Lal Bahadur Shastri had been working with the United States of America and had close policy and administration links. However, with the situation developing in many parts in the world where American forces worked against the local national interest, the Indian leadership and intelligentsia were keeping a wary eye on the developments.[16] They had witnessed Sukarno's government in Indonesia toppled with active American help, and the massacre of a couple of million people carried out under the pretext of clearing Indonesia of communists. Soon after, the American leadership under Johnson would commit itself to the Vietnam War against the nationalist and communist forces, which would be ranged against a regime supported and fostered by Washington. While the Vietnam situation was yet to unfold into a total war, Indira Gandhi visited the United States and agreed to devalue the Indian currency, which turned out to be a nightmare both politically and financially for India.[17] Similarly, India was ready to have a large collaboration with the USA in the agricultural arena.[18] However, as trade liberalization involved changes in the Indian economic policy at a fundamental level, the country needed time to make adjustments. It was in this economic situation that the cold war entered a new phase with the escalation of hostilities in Vietnam. Policymakers in the United States were progressively turning Vietnam into an issue of ego and legitimacy for the US army as well as the state. The situation in Vietnam generated waves of protest from not only across the world but also from the appalled American public and its university students, and it soon acquired a national dimension by the fall of 1968.[19] And it is at this juncture that a new university was being set up in India.

The Crisis of Institutional Design

Institution designing for higher education in post-Independence India relied on manpower-planning models, which were used for economic forecasting—primarily labour demands in various sectors.[20] In a developing country with a relatively weak technological and scientific institutional base, the focus was to develop manpower for industrial projects that the economy was fostering and hence had an inward-looking orientation. This was the time when science and technology were consolidating their institutional bases, most often outside the university structures. Although the Council for Scientific and Industrial Research (CSIR) was in trouble at the time, it was on its way to simultaneously consolidate and start new institutions. There appeared to be serious gaps in the government's design of the institutional map. This was also the time when India felt the abrasiveness of hard-nosed strategic thinking in American institution planning.

The post-war United States had by now become proactive in

establishing its dominance in the South-East Asian region,[21] a region vested with both national and international interest for its oil resources, etc. Any forward drive by Soviet Union was also to be thwarted so as to check the proliferation of communism. The instruments of an anti-communist strategic policy were put in place in the early 1950s, which could be instantly activated through direct and indirect intervention anywhere in the world. Many foundations like the Rockefeller Foundation, Carnegie Endowment for Peace, etc., not only became involved in this anti-communist project, but were also brought into the ambit of the academia. Thus the cold war front presented a formidable alliance of foundations, academia and the state department. This combination struck a death blow to the already gasping liberal universities in the United States. McCarthy had already dealt a crippling blow to the left and oppositional trend in the academia and big money aligned with the state and the businesses to produce a new star system which would stifle all dissident voices. The recent literature on this topic has started a lively debate on the way the professoriate became the willing executioners of the global operations of the policies of the anti-communist phalanges which were quite often very oppressive.[22]

The intellectual product of this alliance was the development of a model of American intervention in the Third World and more so in the areas where there were real or perceived threats from/of communist expansion. The intellectual architecture for such intervention saw its genesis in the Harvard Department of Social Relations where sociologist Talcott Parsons's System Theory formed the template for understanding the political system in these societies and to devise policy prescriptions for the state department.[23] Once the templates were decided, the idea took root that to stop communism from expanding, these societies required de-modernization, and here the intellectual project was joined by financial assistance from Rockefeller's International Development in 1950. Harvard, Michigan, Illinois, Princeton, MIT and Stanford were harnessed in different capacities to work for the cold war project of the American state in the fields of social science, science, communication studies and policy formulation. MIT had the reputation of being the most ardent agent of support, having buttressed the US state during the Second World War, and now, with the cold war, its backing was almost guaranteed.[24] Its Center for International Relations pitched in, with W.W. Rostow and Max F. Millikan now designing the economic policies of the American state. The center also rose up to become the major institution taking up American interests in the Third World.[25] W.W. Rostow came out with the celebrated anti-communist manifesto which delineated the stages of economic growth where the grand theory was that the communists were to be attacked at the stage of take-off in those societies that were planning economic development.[26]

The defence establishment was closely cooperating with the whole behavioural enterprise. Hans Speier, former director of Project Troy and chair of the advisory of committee to the CIS communications programme, was the head of the Rand Research Council that was run by the US air force. He was a key supporter of the positive role the military played in post-colonial societies. His position echoed the position of many behaviouralist academics like Lucien Pye, Samuel Huntington, and others, who viewed the military as an ally of the American state against the expansion of communism in these societies. The common feature of the developing area programme, comparative politics programme and behavioural science programme, all taken together with strong financial support from Ford and Rockefeller, was the attack on the state if it was not held by the military. By the beginning of the 1960s, the Indian political scene was rife with accusations of how the money from PL-480 was used for political subversion.[27] By 1967, the Asia Foundation, which sponsored institutions, was found to be colluding with the American state department.[28]

The strategic idea was to capture the imagination of the elite in the Third World societies. The closely knit and calibrated move by the foundations, American business interests and the state won over the Indonesian army and, through coups, killings and capture, completely changed the destiny of Indonesia.[29] Now they began their work on the Indian Army with their area studies man, Stephen Cohen, who, following the patterns advocated in other 'Third World countries', tried to recommend changes in army recruitment and training so that the army could become an integral part of the behaviouralist, conservative political-science-and-anthropology-dominated agenda called 'Nation Building'.[30] This included making army recruitment more comprehensive, less cohesive and involved in more substantive civil works.[31] Working towards the same goal was also the concerted efforts to influence and penetrate another pillar of perceived stability of the Indian system, namely, the bureaucracy. This was done through the slogans of modernization and training. The Indian Institute of Public Administration (IIPA) was soon to undergo a complete change with the Ford Foundation effecting a leadership change by apparently foisting its own nominee as the director.

US representatives had worked in close proximity with the bureaucrats in the 1950s and had known the importance of this segment.[32] In the early 1960s, the American agencies began to approach the government offering to help with training and modernization of the Indian bureaucracy.[33] Thus, the Ford Foundation and its coordinators became active within the Indian Institute of Public Administration, the institute in charge of training mid-career bureaucrats. Very soon there was an intense outcry in parliament by the members who wished to know how the Ford Foundation had placed its own choice as the director of the IIPA.[34] Public administration, an otherwise underdeveloped discipline, could have been developed by the Indian bureaucracy and intelligentsia and raised to great heights as it was the only country in human history that was developing as an unalloyed democracy and its bureaucracy was given the role to implement wide-ranging policies that covered almost all the facets of human affairs. The Indian economists simultaneously gained experience and contributed to developing a completely new discipline of development economics. The Indian bureaucracy could have contributed to the development of public administration in similar ways and evolved the IIPA as one of the most innovative centres in the world. Instead, since the 1960s, it became a disciplined satellite controlled by centres of developed countries making it one of the least stimulating institutions in the country.[35]

India had moved close to the United States particularly after India's debacle in the war against China and more so after Lal Bahadur Shastri became the premier. By 1966, India was persuaded by the US lobbies to sign what was known as the Indo-US education treaty. Indira Gandhi who was visiting the United States was actually unaware of the massive opposition to it in India, and allowed it to be announced by President Johnson.[36] The opposition was against the access that the pact would have given to the American educational institutions and agencies while operating in India. The argument by the opposition parties to the treaty, particularly by leaders like Bhupesh Gupta and H.N. Mukerjee of the Communist Party India (CPI), was sound as they pointed out that it would have killed the Indian academia as, compared to the academia in the United States, India had a minuscule institutional and human resource presence and any treaty providing free access would kill the Indian potential. Judging from the context of the 1960s, this argument could not be faulted.

Discourse on the Decline

Two components constituted the discourse on institutions and institutional design. The government was spurred to appoint an Education Commission to report on the present and future of the Indian higher education system. There were, however, many things which were quite obvious to the public eye. It was public knowledge that the universities were witnessing declining standards. Although the European universities too were complaining of falling standards, the Indian problem was compounded by two additional factors, namely, increasing corruption and the existence of social classes that actually benefited from the discourse of decline.

A new element had entered the university life since the 1950s. Corruption in the selection of teachers had always been the bane of universities like Calcutta and other old universities, and this remained the biggest issue in the Indian university systems. However, many well-established universities now complained of the corruption in many other areas including administration. A letter from a teacher in the Agra College to the UGC chairman, C.D. Deshmukh, encapsulated how colleges were beset with problems and corruption.[37] By the 1960s, the colleges and universities were emerging as the major centres of corrupt practices, particularly casteism and clientelism.

This was also the time when there were tectonic shifts in Indian politics particularly after Nehru's death. The elections of 1966-67 returned a mixed verdict. Parties opposing the Congress came to power in many states. There was no ideological and programmatic compatibility in these combined oppositions to the Congress party. These amorphous combinations would very soon try to develop the student body as their potential constituencies. The opposition,

Dravida Munnetra Kazagham (DMK) in Tamil Nadu, the Communist Party of India (Marxist) (CPI[M]) in Bengal and various socialist parties in Bihar and Uttar Pradesh, began to attract the youth power of the university students.[38] This would make a significant impact in the domain of higher education. Many universities felt the strain of state policies, protest movements, and student violence.[39] This created a new discussion on how Indian universities were declining because they were now supposed to be infested with youth interested only in politics. It was part of such a discourse, which, from 1958 onwards, began curtailing students' participation in politics. On the other hand, it strengthened the corrupt practices of the administration, and organizations like the RSS (Rashtriya Swayamsevak Sangh) gained entry through the back door.

The talk of decline of the universities was but a reflection of the new class structure emerging in India which would try and establish its hegemony in post-Nehru Delhi. In the newly emerging democratic structure, power emanated from proximity to the ruling political class combined with the capitalist class, which was assisting in stabilizing the state. In Delhi, the capital, it was the bureaucracy and the erstwhile landed and business aristocracy which dotted the landscape of power along with personalities from politics, media and the cultural fields. New spaces were emerging which would provide hegemonic opportunities.

The constitution of these emerging self-composed enclaves was very significant. It was from there that both the discourses about the decline of the university and brain drain would emanate. Indian universities were declining, it would be argued, and therefore the progenies of India's new elite, who would have gone through the routine public school, would inevitably need berths at Oxbridge. By sheer virtue of their social background and constructed academic reasons (decline of the Indian university), the wards needed to be invited back; hence the brain drain. Since it was almost a given that the Indian universities were declining, they were cut off from having links with national or international bodies.

This helped the bureaucrats insulate the international bodies from the country's academic bodies and thereby monopolized the roles and positions in them for themselves and their family members. Thus, by the end of the 1960s the universities in India had virtually no connection with the international or even national organs where their students and teachers could get any formal, informal or practical training and international exposure. Thus, while any American or Canadian university could send its students to the UN bodies for work or training, no Indian university could do that. The bureaucracy, and what I call the 'socintelligentsia' (the socialite intelligentsia), and the classic Indian family network hijacked all these opportunities and virtually throttled the Indian universities in this way. This new class of Indians were extremely negative to the Indian university-bred academics unless they looked and sounded like one of them or were one of them; hence the discourse of continuing decline of the Indian university was most appropriate for such self-legitimation.

This discourse emanating from this conglomerate in the capital also coincided with the new political changes in the provinces, which in turn, provided currency to the discourse of the decline. There were new shifts in social bases of the political formations in most of the states:

- In Tamil Nadu, for example, the non-Brahmin parties, particularly the Dravida Munnetra Kazhagam would oust the Congress from its dominant position.
- In Bihar and Uttar Pradesh the rich, landowning agricultural classes would come to occupy central positions and constitute a bloc against the Congress.
- There were also indications of new emerging segments of hitherto completely absent tribal voices in south Bihar and Rajasthan.

While electorally, the coming of these forces into the political arena would change the landscape of politics, their arrival would also herald the changing face of many institutions—the Indian university being one of them. Wherever the classes had significant power, they could change the colour of the institutions, but where, for example in south Bihar, the powerful politics of the northern side would not allow any space to the tribal leaders of the south, the tribals languished when the spaces specifically earmarked for them, i.e., the constitutional provision of 7.5 per cent reservation, were denied and grabbed by the upper castes of north Bihar.[40] But from a distance, the period's crises would still be seen in terms of decline. It is here that I make a slight distinction between the discourse of decline and the decline itself.

Decline of the Universities: Bihar

The real issue of decline of the Indian universities can be located in the taking over of their administrations for non-academic purposes. And the purpose in most cases was primarily to provide jobs and access for people of one's own ilk. Thus, increase in population and limited institutional availability of spaces meant that caste, community and kin networks would soon be reworked in the universities as well. Increase in the number of universities in too short a period aggravated rather than solved this problem.

Let us start with Bihar. Patna University, started on 1 October 1917, was, at first, a purely affiliating and examining university with some teaching departments coming gradually into existence. The demand for a completely residential and teaching university was met when in 1951, the state legislature passed the twin Acts of Patna and Bihar Universities—Patna was made teaching and residential while Bihar, teaching and affiliating, with headquarters in Patna. In 1960, four teaching-cum-affiliating universities were set up in four divisional headquarters: Ranchi, Patna, Muzaffarpur and Bhagalpur. This Act changed the residential character of Patna University. The situation soon changed when political pressure made the government reverse its decision. Patna regained its residential character and Magadh University catered to the affiliating needs of the Patna division.

With so many universities established in just a couple of years, the standards began to fall and, on 21 February 1964, a panic-stricken government appointed a commission under K.S.V. Raman, ICS, to inquire into the working of the Bihar University. Its report presented in 1965 was alarming. It said: '... rot in Bihar University had run deep. Lawlessness and indiscipline were widely prevailing and in almost every event caste had been the dominant issue and no holds had been barred in this inter-caste in-fighting.'[41] Soon, another effort was made to understand the whole phenomenon when a university inquiry commission was appointed in February 1966, which more or less said the same things about the rot. S.P. Sinha and K. Ahmad, professor and educational administrator respectively, explored the archaeology of the decline and suggested that 'the university education in this state was in a very perilous condition and its future depended on the courage and fearlessness with which we could face this perilous situation'.[42] There were 'so much confusion, mismanagement and indiscipline that no self-respecting person is prepared to undertake the onerous responsibilities of a vice chancellor'. In their candid report they wrote:

> The difficulties that they have to face in their dealings with the teachers and the students, the fast deteriorating academic condition, the impossibility of carrying on the work of administration even with a modicum of efficiency, the ruined finances, all these have been brought to the notice of the chancellor and the government. But the matter is not receiving the urgent attention that it deserves. Some of the vice chancellors have tendered their resignation. At one time, the post of the vice chancellor was considered to be one of honour and dignity, but now it has fallen so low that the post now goes begging, as good and capable men refuse to accept the position.[43]

The report was also candid about the senate of the university and opined that the wrangling and the bitterness in the senate was a direct reflection of the general malady that had afflicted the political body. Academic rectitude, they argued, was not what moved the senate members but narrow political or caste considerations.[44] Bihar University too was in a bad condition where, in all the highest academic bodies, there could, 'never be any frank and unbiased discussion of educational problems. These groups which are based on caste alignments have completely vitiated the academic atmosphere.'[45]

The unstable national politics increased the intrusion of corruption and caste patronage in the university politics and did not allow anybody to intervene and arrest its decline. Another commissioner, K. Abraham, was appointed in November 1969 after a serious caste riot between Rajput and Yadav groups took place on 29 June 1969 in Gaya College where pistols and daggers were brandished—one person was killed and seven injured, including two professors. Virulent casteism and groupism was found to be at the root of all the trouble in Magadh University.[46] The caste battles inside the institutional premises reached a climax when a Rajput versus Bhumihar riot took its toll in Rajendra College, Chapra, and its principal, Bhola Prasad Singh, was murdered on 9

May 1971.[47] Similarly, Ranchi University became the site for a clash between tribal and non-tribal students, and in June 1968, there were violent clashes near Ranchi city.

Chagla, the education minister, had got wind of the acrimonious atmosphere in the Bihar universities. He told Kothari that the only way out that the governor, the chancellor of Bihar universities, could take was to invite scholars from outside to apply for the post of the new vice chancellor, someone who would not be part of the caste politics which had overshadowed everything else in the state.[48]

Unfair discrimination on the basis of caste and kinship, in Bihar for example, was not limited to the issue of mere appointment of faculty or admission of students; caste prejudices had spread like cancer into the most vital area of academic life, evaluation. A report by a journalist, Janardan Thakur, on the conditions prevailing in Ranchi University was representative of what was happening in other universities and colleges in the state. The fact that the write-up was published by the *University News*, a monthly magazine of the association of the Indian universities, a semi-official body, demonstrated that this state of affairs had been accepted even at the level of the education administration in the country. Arguing that the qualities of sycophancy, slyness, dishonesty, mediocrity were needed for success in the local universities, the author of the article was brutally frank when he said that one required to be either closely connected to some minister, a mighty politician, a powerful officer, a university overlord or to have parents with a lot of money to top the university exams.

He put Ranchi University in the spotlight of his disdain when he advised the prospective examinees in the postgraduate department to first grab a seat in the private lodge of their professors. 'Never mind if it's a crowded dark hovel, or if the room opens on a suppurating drain, or if the "chowki" (bed) creaks and wobbles every time you move.'[49] Continuing, he sarcastically advised students to, 'continue buying the milk that your professor's cow produced without a murmur about the degree of its dilution or its high price, because unadulterated milk is not available anywhere anyway' and consider this an investment. What he detailed was a completely slavish life that a student needed to lead in order to get a good position in the university. Education was to be given the lowest priority and, he concluded, was 'the least part' of the result.[50]

In Uttar Pradesh, the Mudaliar and Gajendragadkar Committees had already revealed that there were caste and communal approaches in recruitment of teachers in BHU. Aligarh Muslim University was plagued by kinship and client relations occupying the largest spaces in recruitments.[51] The Chatterjee Committee that inquired into the AMU affairs had given a detailed criticism of the appointment pattern where people of the same family and clan were given most of the teaching jobs. In the case of Aligarh, Bashir Hussain Zaidi, the vice chancellor, attributed the limited social base of intellectual recruitment to the fact that a large number of Muslim families had decided to migrate to Pakistan leaving behind a sudden hiatus in Aligarh.[52]

The BHU Conundrum

The Banaras Hindu University had been in the throes of crises since the late 1950s and the Mudaliar Committee had examined its earlier problems.[53] However, in the 1960s, the university would face two major phases of the crisis that would destroy the university forever. The first emerged when the Ministry of Education tried modernizing the university administration and change its name in 1964-65. The entrenched interests, which included all the top functionaries of the university, instigated a communal mobilization against the bill which vitiated the atmosphere of not only the city but of the entire country, forcing the ministry to abandon the project. However, the forces unleashed this time made the university a place where communalists and criminals had wanton freedom from the authorities. This resulted in the second major crisis in 1967–69 resulting in the appointment of the Gajendragadkar Committee which exposed many unpalatable truths about the university.

In the 1960s, there were portents of difficult times to come. The BHU amendment ordinance was promulgated on 14 June 1958, replaced by the amending Act No. 34 of 1958, passed on 20 September 1958. A bill proposing a comprehensive amendment to the BHU Act 1915 was introduced in the Lok Sabha on 5 May 1961. This bill could not be passed before the dissolution of the Lok Sabha in March 1962. Later, this amending bill was introduced in the Rajya Sabha on 5 May 1964, and it was referred to the joint committee of the parliament on 25 November 1964. The joint committee had thirteen sittings in all between December 1964 and August 1965. The bill sought to abolish two key posts in the university set-up. These two posts had, in the past, led to factional quarrels between the university authorities. After the passage of the bill by the parliament the tenure of one of the leading functionaries would have come to an end, and his main rival in the university's politics, who had until then enjoyed the support of a majority of the members of the existing executive committee, would also have been worse off. All these affected vested interests were anxious to get the bill shelved.[54]

Vested elements of the BHU administration instigated the students with the help of the RSS to agitate against the bill. They paraded through the city in a demonstration for the 'protection of Hinduism' as the bill in parliament was going to delete the word 'Hindu' from the university's name.[55] The real intention was to delay the passage of the bill. The most worrying feature of this agitation was the active involvement of the office of the vice chancellor and other functionaries in instigating the students and the other subversives. For example, a cyclostyled handbill bearing the vice chancellor's signature permitted the use of microphones in meetings, and asked students 'to chalk out the programme of the students' [association] vis-à-vis the change in the name of the university'.[56]

The city was initially lukewarm to this agitation which was effectively taken over by the RSS cadres who began the agitation along extremely communal lines with slogans like 'Hinduism in danger' or that deletion of the word 'Hindu' was the beginning of the end. All these finally led to a massive city-wide mobilization which even mobbed one of the most known public faces of the Congress, Kamalapati Tripathi. The socialists were in a tricky position, and Prof. Mukut Bihari Lal, who had been a key figure in the discussion of the BHU Bill in the parliament and one of the most respected professors of political science, and also the seniormost leader of the Socialist Party, was garlanded with shoes by a group of students obviously belonging to RSS. This incident also precipitated the agitation which was coloured with communal propaganda, and the fact that Chagla was a Muslim seemed to provide an additional ingredient to this line of attack.

The agitation simmered down as soon the Central leadership decided to shelve the bill to stop the rioting, which was exactly what the rabble-rousers wanted. But the RSS wanted to continue the agitation for its own mobilization purposes. Although the RSS tried to outsmart the students' association, it soon realized that its cover could be blown and its insidious presence behind the agitation would be exposed; therefore their activities also stopped for a while. It is at this point that the non-communal, secular and other segments of population began counter moves by sending letters of complaint to the prime minister, ministers, etc., requesting them to investigate the role of the university authorities in the entire episode. This investigation led to the discovery that the BHU's original name was 'Kashi Viswavidyalaya' and that in the original piece of legislation it was the pro-British elements which inserted the 'Hindu' into the English translation of the Kashi Viswavidyalaya in order to counter Aligarh Muslim University's name. The disclosure helped people desist from participating in any further demonstrations.

However the damage was done, and although the communists, socialists and others in the parliament asked the government to go ahead with the legislation, a slightly shaky government did not want to take a political risk, and shelved the bill. The decision was marked by strong dissent. Communist leader Renuka Ray, Vaishampayan and S.K. Pottekkatt, and others like R.P.N. Singh and Savitri Nigam protested strongly. Mukut Bihari Lal who had played a lead role throughout the proceedings also came out strongly saying that, 'since its inception the BHU is also known as the Kashi Viswavidyalaya. The emblem of the university bears both the names, and now, when we are discarding English in favour of Indian languages, it is but proper that the university be also known in law as the Kashi Viswavidyalaya.' However, the strong agitation and the communal overtones given to all these protests finally forced a weak and unstable leadership to withdraw and seek a compromise. A diluted Act was passed in the Lok Sabha but the issues of Banaras remained unresolved and the university was again plunged into turmoil within a couple of years.[57]

AMU Slide

Aligarh had been in the throes of one controversy or another.[58] Being the intellectual citadel of the Muslim League during the 1940s, barring a few scholars like Mohammad Habib, a large number of students and teachers had been converted to the idea of Pakistan and the two-nation theory which the founder of the university had advocated in a completely different context in his opposition to the anti-colonial character of the Congress. It took quite a consolidated effort of the national leadership to bring some semblance of stability and assurance in the university. However, in the absence of any sustained anti-communal drive, the level of communalization that remained, continued to be an intellectual and political force.

Badruddin Tyabji was appointed vice chancellor and he seemed to have a clear picture of the internal dynamics of the university.[59] He was very keen to improve the prospect of the students and, as he said years later, he thought that if the students of the university's own school and college get assured admission in the professional courses, there were definite advantages for the students and the university. He therefore raised the internal reservations to 75 per cent, which meant that only 25 per cent of the students from outside could now join the university at the higher levels. Tyabji was on the right track and had effectively brought the situation in the university under control.[60]

The next vice chancellor, Ali Yavar Jung, was recommended by Tyabji to the prime minister and the education minister. Chagla had wanted Tyabji to continue but he wanted to return to his foreign service. Ali Yavar Jung (Mirza Ali Yar Khan) was born in Hyderabad (the Deccan) on 16 February 1905, educated at Madrasa-i-Aliya and Nizam College during 1918 and 1922. He then went to Queen's College, Oxford, for his BA in modern history, following which he spent a year in France where he worked with Sylvan Levy and Alfred Martineau studying the French in India. Between 1927 and 1935, he was reader and professor of history at Osmania University. After that he joined the Nizam's services. From 1946 onwards, he was in the Indian delegation to the United Nations. He became the vice chancellor of Osmania University for a year and then again in 1948–52. Yavar Jung was also doing serious work with the UNESCO and this was probably the best time that India had with its engagement with the UNESCO.

When he was approached to become the vice chancellor of AMU, Jung wrote to the education minister that he would like to bring S.R. Dongerkerry from Bombay as the registrar who, Chagla agreed with Yavar Jung, was one of the best registrars they had ever seen. Yavar Jung eventually joined the university and began his work. One of his major decisions was to bring freshness and competitiveness in the university by reducing the reservations that Tyabji had introduced, and this led to a violent clash. On the day of the court meeting, about one thousand students collected and an effigy of the vice chancellor was paraded. Oddly enough, the effigy was not made of dry grass as is usually done in such cases, but stuffed with soda water bottles, hockey sticks and brickbats. This shows that a lot of planning preceded the riot. And the students were incited to attack selected members of the court—the nationalist and progressive teachers were targeted for attack and dragged out of the hall.[61] An eyewitness narrated the incident with sadness when he said that the 'students became unruly, entered the hall and started beating several members of the court'. 'They also', he said, 'manhandled Nawab Ali Yavar Jung and it took him several months to recover from these injuries.'[62]

From all accounts, the hooliganism was engineered by three groups working in close collaboration: Jamat-e-Islami, the Majlis-e-Ittehadul-Muslimeen and the Rastriya Swayamsevak Sangh (RSS). These groups and their patrons were opposed to making the Aligarh University a really secular and progressive seat of learning. Polarization between these groups and the secular, progressive nationalist and communist opinion at Aligarh had already become quite clear before Badruddin Tyabji became vice chancellor. He used his administrative skill to maintain a balance between the communal groups and the nationalist elements and worked out policies which would satisfy both. When Ali Yavar Jung was made the vice chancellor, attempts were made to block the appointment by putting forward the claims of pro-vice-chancellor, Yusuf Hussain Khan, who had support from the Majlis-e-Ittehadul-Muslimeen and the Jamat-e-Islami.

Such dastardly violence infuriated Chagla. He immediately suspended the university statutes and bodies, and the university instituted cases against many of those who were supposed to have been involved in the whole episode. With the violence, the local factionalism within the university was brought to light. Senior professors now came out into the open to criticize the violence and, in this, Prof. Nurul Hasan, also an active member of the Communist Party of India, took the lead. Nurul Hasan and those who supported him wanted strict action taken by the state government and wanted no leniency shown towards anybody responsible for the violence.

Chagla's suspension of the statutes and promulgation of the ordinance brought many factions on to the field. The AMU old boys' association suddenly became very active with Dr Syed Mahmud, an old Congress leader from Bihar, jumping on to the bandwagon and demanding that Chagla must resign. The Hindu communalists were also ready to give it an anti-national colour with the 1965 war in the background.[63] Syed Mahmud accused Chagla of attacking the Muslim community. In his response to Syed Mahmud, Chagla squarely put the responsibility for the sorry state of affairs in the university on the strong communal and reactionary elements which had to be rooted out if Aligarh University was to play a proper role in India.[64] That role, according to him, was 'to develop the best elements of Muslim culture, not in isolation but in the context of Indian life, and to make a definite contribution to that composite culture which we should all cherish and of which we should all be proud'. There was tremendous pressure on Chagla, but to his credit, he remained determined and was in constant touch with the governor, the chief minister and the prime minister. His argument was that AMU, as a national heritage, should develop along modern lines to become one of the world centres of advanced studies on Muslim culture.

AMU: The Communal Onslaught

Chagla referred to the AMU campus's hostility to the vice chancellor as a communal opposition, and he was right although he was not aware that the attacks on the university had been a recurring phenomenon since the 1950s and that the Jana Sangh and RSS had joined the fray with their onslaughts since the early 1960s. Aligarh University, which had been the intellectual centre for the Pakistan movement, was limping back to normalcy after Partition under the soothing hands of its vice chancellor, Dr Zakir Hussain. However, since the 1950s, it was beset with problems like mass migration to Pakistan creating a dearth of good faculty, and the institution of 'Visitorial enquiry' created impediments to the academic progress of universities from which it took time to recover. By the mid-1950s, just as the AMU began to academically regain its moorings, the RSS and the Jana Sangh decided to make Aligarh the Muslim and Urdu metaphors for the enemy of the nation. Their chief target was the un-nationalized Muslims and the 'communists' in Aligarh. The communists in Aligarh were a new breed, and their presence was providing the university with a connection to the larger life of the nation; its historians, Mohammad Habib for example, were the most respected in the country. Obviously, from the Hindu communalists' perception, this was not to be encouraged at any cost.

The police firing in Aligarh in 1961 during the students' disturbance, in which students lost their lives, led to inquiries which brought to light the role of Jana Sangh leaders—local, provincial and national—in the well-orchestrated attack against the university. It was soon to be proved that the Aligarh issue was part of a 'separatist act'. Atal Bihari Vajpayee claimed that 'as long as the university was not emancipated from the clutches of the communalist-cum-communist incubus, the danger of recrudescence of communal trouble in western Uttar Pradesh would always persist'.[65] Jana Sangh held its national general council in Varanasi in the same year where it declared that the AMU should be Indianized.[66] Soon Vajpayee and Balraj Madhok moved a resolution in the parliament declaring that it was time to 'nationalize and Indianize'.[67] Both terms were interchangeably used by Madhok and Vajpayee. The term *Bharatiyakaran* was used for Indianization.

Jana Sangh leaders clamoured for an inquiry into 'the communal and anti-national character of the university', because, as Madhok declared, 'the two-nation theory was born and cherished in the Aligarh University. They say they have a separate culture. When you have a separate culture, separate language, separate history, then you are a separate nation. It is this talk of separate nation, separate culture and separate history which goes against Indian nationalism.'[68] The Jana Sangh leaders declared that the Aligarh University by and large 'continues to be the centre of the mentality' which resulted in the partition of this country.[69] Madhok declared that they would continue to raise their voice against the university so long as they thought this university was the plague spot of India.[70]

Madhok explained the party's stand in his article in the RSS mouthpiece, the *Organizer*:

> Nationalism as conceived and preached by the Congress and its allies had given a new lease of life to Muslim separatism and has become the biggest ally of communism. It has still failed to draw inspiration and sustenance from the ancient roots of Indian national life that has stood the test of time. It is neither national nor secular. It is based on compromises with separatism and communalism which it seeks to employ for the political gain of the Congress. But in doing so it is cutting at the roots of Indian nationalism. It is un-Indian, un-Hindu and un-Bharatiya.[71]

Jana Sangh, despite its bold proclamations, was intellectually and politically a marginal force. But there was an extra amount of sensitiveness within the university, which felt under siege in the current crisis. It was therefore an opportunity for Muslim communal elements and other vested interests to take a lead in exploiting the situation in AMU.

The spread of the AMU agitation and its transformation into a wider Muslim communal agitation had strong Hindu communal support, which had interests in retaining the character of the university because it helped them target the Muslim separatist trends in an atmosphere of fear and suspicion; also, the local colleges wanted to be part of the university through affiliation. It is in this situation that the Indo-Pakistan conflict escalated and ended up in a full-scale war in 1965. Now the second part of the nationalization thesis unfolded itself, when there was talk of the pro-Pakistan elements within India, and therefore the need to Indianize was very important. The Delhi meeting of the central committee of the Jana Sangh resolved that, 'there should be no political bargaining with Indian Muslims. They must be guaranteed all constitutional rights due to them in this secular state. But all separatist tendencies and attitudes betraying a pro-Pakistan bias must be curbed and the outlook of Indian Muslims must be nationalized.'[72]

The communal attack on it by the Hindu communalists strengthened the Muslim communal groups' claims as the defenders of the university. Both these forces attacked the intellectuals and those who wanted the university to find its way to fulfil its intellectual promise and align with the larger intellectual and historical forces operating in the outside world. The more the Muslim communalists reigned inside, the easier the Hindu communalists found it to show the university up as a metaphor for the essential Muslim separatist psyche and to describe it as un-Indian, needing to be Indianized—but how this was to be done was never spelt out.[73] It was at this juncture that Chagla tried to intervene in the matters of the university as an educator. But the agitation that ensued increasingly sucked Banaras University into its ambit, deepened the communal polarization of the groups, and doomed Chagla's entire effort.

Assassination of an Institution

The Aligarh experience for Chagla was a bitter one though his efforts to intervene in the university were for reasons academic, not political. But a delicate and more personal matter awaited Chagla in Osmania, whose vice chancellor, a contemporary of Chagla in England, faced removal by the Congress ministry in Andhra Pradesh.

On 25 November 1965, the Andhra Pradesh legislature passed identical amendments to the Acts governing the state's three universities. As a result, one of the three, Osmania, feared for its independence. Under the new legislation, the governor, the chancellor of Osmania, Andhra and Sri Venkateswara universities, acting on the advice of the Andhra Pradesh government, would directly appoint the vice chancellor of each university, rather than choose from a panel submitted by the university. The Government of Andhra Pradesh would also have the authority to give mandatory instructions to the universities regarding major educational policies. This piece of legislation changed the history of Indian higher education for the worse. The law minister of the state cabinet who would have had a hand in preparing the bill was none other than the future education minister of India, P.V. Narasimha Rao, who would draft the new education policy of 1986—another irony.

There were charges against the vice chancellor of Andhra University, and the state government had no weapon at its disposal to sack him. It wanted to change the law. But that would have hit D.S. Reddy, who was a very good administrator, steering Osmania University to new heights. The university was not only expanding under his leadership but was also producing quality teaching and research. The vice chancellor sent a confidential letter to D.S. Kothari on 14 August 1965 about the draft bill in Andhra Pradesh. The bill was about to change the character of the three universities in Andhra. The move had created unrest in Osmania where the students and teachers struck work and protested against the government's plan. The teachers' association filed a case in the high court of Andhra Pradesh against the Act, when it was promulgated. The episode suggested to a contemporary political commentator that 'patterns of university autonomy based on British models are being challenged by radical changes in the environment, composition and purposes of universities'.[74]

Chagla wrote to Chief Minister K. Brahmananda Reddy on 13 October 1965 arguing that although university education was a state subject and that the state had complete right and freedom to pass any law it wanted, it would have been better had it been done in coordination with the University Grants Commission which was helping the state universities in their development. Any change in existing legislation, he cautioned, might adversely affect the autonomy of the universities in the state for which the UGC had also been working.[75]

He requested the chief minister to wait for the new bills which were already in the parliament, namely, BHU Bill and JNU Bill. Chagla felt that these new Acts could give the chief minister an idea of the way the Central government was thinking on the issue. The UGC had also issued the report of the committee on a model Act for universities. The Education Commission was due to submit its report by the end of March in the following year.[76] He cautioned the chief minister that it would be 'unfortunate if', he concluded, 'the opposition to the bill assumes an agitational form'.[77]

Chagla also got in touch with the UGC chairman, D.S. Kothari, and emphasized that 'in dealing with broad principles of university structure, organization and policy, it is most important to maintain some coordination on an all-India level'.[78] UGC was yet to assume the character that it would do later in the 1980s and '90s, and therefore the talk by the education minister in evolving machinery for 'development and coordination of higher education on a national basis in the country' reflected his thinking about the national educational space.

The Andhra government's insistence in passing the bill was obstructing Chalga's vision and therefore one can, in hindsight, sympathize with him. It was no longer the case of a friend named Dr Reddy, the vice chancellor, but rather a contest between the local politics and the desire to create a national space for higher education to expand.[79] He persevered with the case until the end, and even when the bill was passed he wrote to K. Brahmananda Reddy on 27 November 1965:

> My dear Chief Minister ... I do not suppose it is much good my saying anything about the contents of your letter as I see from the newspapers that the bill has already been passed by the Andhra assembly. I sent on your letter to Dr Kothari, Chairman, UGC, and in his view there are features in the bill which are not in the best interests of the state universities and their progress. I do not know whether it will still be possible for you to withhold the assent of the governor to the bill and, in the meanwhile, appoint a small committee consisting of representatives of your government, of UGC and of the education ministry here to go fully into the whole question and make a recommendation to your government with regard to what amendments should be made in the bill affecting the three state universities.[80]

He also referred to the fact that although education was a state subject, the Centre was vested with the responsibility of 'coordination and determination of standards in institutions of higher education'. Since this required an all-India coordination, the state government should not bring legislation without prior consultation with the Union government. Chagla was obviously upset and was at his wits' end. Writing to Kothari on 21 December 1965, he expressed his apprehension that, 'if this is the position, I do not think any state will consult the UGC before starting a university'.[81] He knew that the only control the Centre had was 'financial control'.[82] He seemed prepared to shed his constitutional liberalism when he suggested refusing funds to recalcitrant universities. 'Although I appreciate the argument that once a university is established it should not be starved of the necessary finances, the only preventative we have against the state running amuck and setting up new universities, is the refusal to finance them from the Centre. I hope you look into this aspect of the matter.'[83]

Chagla, leaving no stone unturned, spoke to the new prime minister, Indira Gandhi, who responded by suggesting that since the matter had already become controversial, it would be better if the prime minister was not brought into the issue. She, however, assured all her support to him in finding a solution of his liking. In an astute political manner she asked him to write to the CM endorsing a copy to the governor. Alternatively, he could, she advised, write to the governor himself, mentioning that the prime minister attached great importance to the choosing of a 'right type of VC to succeed Dr D.S. Reddy'.[84] Chagla agreed with the suggestion except that he did not use the expression, 'a right type of vice chancellor to succeed Dr D.S. Reddy', as this might make people exclude Dr Reddy and he was very keen that the latter rather than someone else was appointed.[85]

Chagla subsequently wrote to the governor, Pattom A. Thanu Pillai, on 13 April 1966. He requested him to exercise his individual judgement in giving assent to the bill which had now been passed by the assembly. He indicated the assurance of the law minister that the governor could exercise his individual judgement and would not be compelled to act on the advice of the ministry.[86] Giving specific details about the bill, he subtly outlined the instructions. 'The impending Act', he wrote, 'provided that the term of office of the vice chancellor came to an end within ninety days of the passing of the bill.' He indicated to the governor that it was for him, the chancellor, to appoint the vice chancellor and therefore he expected that the former would appoint the best person for the post. Giving broad hints about what he wanted, he now drew the governor's attention to Osmania and said that it was one of the best universities built up by the fine work of its present vice chancellor, D.S. Reddy, and that he and the prime minister, wished that the governor would try and appoint Dr Reddy.[87]

However the situation slipped out of the Centre's control as the politics of the state were moving very fast. The Osmania teachers who initially lost in the high court went on to win their case in the Supreme

Court, which passed strictures against the state government for passing such an Act. Although the judgment allowed D.S. Reddy to continue till the end of in his term, losing the government's support at a time when the political landscape was rapidly changing left him ineffective. With his retirement, the university gradually moved into the orbit of political control. This in turn pushed the university increasingly into the provincial political abyss full of castist, regional and parochial issues. What happened to Osmania has now become a part of history. It was the assassination of an institution.

The Language Bomb for Rajasthan

The crisis that manifested in the institutional domain was exacerbated by the political tumult that was caused by the language agitation during the 1960s, reaching its climax in 1967. The Hindi agitation in the northern states affected the academic lives of the universities more than any other segment.

Take the case of the University of Rajasthan. It was a premier university and, under the vice chancellorship of Mohan Singh Mehta and later M.V. Mathur, efforts were made to bring scholars from across the world and, by 1964-65, the university could boast of some of the best faculties and departments in the country—sociology, history, political science, economics, philosophy, English, mathematics and chemistry to name a few. M.V. Mathur, the vice chancellor, was one of the most respected educationists in the country. It was very difficult to find such a constellation of good scholars teaching in one good university in a backward country. For the backward economies in the world, the paucity of good teaching faculty has been the most serious problem.[88] In that sense, Rajasthan University was definitely very fortunate and was reckoned among the top three universities in the country.

The anti-English agitation, which the socialists and the Jana Sangh had been leading since the early 1960s, was beginning to take an ominous turn. The political class which had seen power in linguistic politics was not ready to give time for the university to transition from English to Hindi as medium of instruction. The local publishing mafia was also ready to finance any move to impose Hindi as they had glimpsed a gold mine from the impending change. The university and colleges became the prime targets of the gold rush by all these vested interests. By the beginning of 1967, the vice chancellor had declared that English would be an optional subject in the second and third year of the three-year degree course; however, in the pre-university years and in the first year of the degree course, it would be a compulsory subject for all the students. It was thought that English was required for professional courses, postgraduate studies and for the all-India services, and therefore should be retained.[89]

In the first week of September 1967, the Academic Council and syndicate of the University of Rajasthan met. Vice chancellor M.V. Mathur was satisfied that the views of the student bodies were also considered. However, this move did not mollify the Hindi fanatics and, on 5 September 1967, there was an anti-English agitation.[90] The police had to open fire on the agitating mob and thirty-two people were arrested. There were news reports about meetings in different parts of the state. The meeting in Bikaner criticized the anti-Hindi policy of the government.[91] The director of college education, R.S. Kapur, and the minister for home affairs, Damodar Lal Vyas, were severely censured by the local Hindi media.[92] In all, the government was under siege. The college teachers, with grievances against the college directorate, and several members of the Rajasthan University syndicate joined forces with the anti-English agitation.

The movement, however, was creating a dangerous stir in the heart of the pro-Hindi agitation land, Uttar Pradesh. Interestingly, in all the major Hindi speaking states, Bihar, Uttar Pradesh and Madhya Pradesh, the Samyukta Vidhayak Dal (SVD) ministries had Jana Sangh and the Samyukta Socialist Party in power and both had strong pro-Hindi positions. The Jana Sangh and its ideological mentor, the RSS, created what came to be known as 'the Hindi Sena'; the youth were exhorted to enrol as Hindi 'sainiks' (soldiers) to counter the new bill which the Centre had brought in to resolve the official language controversy. The Samyukta Socialist Party had shed its strong anti-English position and now was advocating the right of every language to be used for official purposes not only within a particular state but also at the Centre; English was incompatible with democracy. So for the link language it was prepared to wait until all the states came to an agreement. The Jana Sangh on the other hand felt that the use of all the national languages for interstate and state–Union communications would only cause confusion and delays, and insisted on the replacement of English with Hindi because, to them, national unity was synonymous with Hindi as the official language, and were therefore reluctant to accept the SSP's position.

In Delhi, it was the Hindi Sena and the Jana Sangh which joined forces under the leadership of the mayor of Delhi, Hans Raj Gupta. Delhi also saw the coming together of the RSS Seva Sanchalaks of Jammu and Kashmir, Punjab, Haryana, Rajasthan, Himachal Pradesh and Delhi. In the university campus, vice chancellor Prof B.N. Ganguli was not spared, the Delhi University students' union was, as it were, on fire.[93] The Hindi sainiks in Uttar Pradesh and the Samajwadi Yuvak Sabha were up in arms, and the new anti-English tirade had begun to accommodate the historical Hindi–Urdu chasm into its movement. The major call to protest was given by Madhu Limaye, the quintessential stormy petrel of Indian politics, who in the conference of the Samajwadi Yuvak Sabha asked them to launch a vehement protest from the three universities in Uttar Pradesh: Lucknow, Allahabad and Banaras. Atal Bihari Vajpayee exhorted the Hindi sainiks to lead the way. On 2 December 1967 the deputy chief minister, Ram Prakash Gupta, and his family defied police orders prohibiting any gathering of people. This made it difficult for the chief minister to maintain his neutrality. People were left to their own devices and the state was not guaranteeing the safety of anyone in this battle.

Bihar was displaying its special brand of anti-English-ism. It was the coal tar movement where the leading Hindi enthusiasts along with some lumpen elements in Patna decided to blacken the English signboards and legends with coal tar. The chief of the Bihar Hindi Academy, Ramdayal Pandey, and its finance secretary, Shankar Dayal Singh, the former Speaker of the legislative assembly, Lakshmi Narayan Sudhanshu, along with Dhanik Lal Mandal and Bhola Prasad Singh coal-tarred signboards and nameplates. On 5 December 1967, about a thousand students with tin cans of coal tar and brushes in their hands stood on both sides of Ashok Rajpath, the busiest thoroughfare in Patna, and smeared all the signboards written in English. Shopkeepers shut their shops. Coal tar was thrown on drivers and occupants of cars.

However, there was no popular support for such actions and, despite the Hindi Sahitya Sammelan calling for a bandh on 8 December 1967, the response was poor except for some straggling groups of students smearing nameplates.[94] Most shopping centres wore a bizarre look with black smudges on shop fronts, and paper or cloth veils covering English letters on the signboards. The cars moving on the roads carried handwritten Hindi legends pasted over English numbers.[95]

While all this could be considered an expression of the newly arrived sections to the field of education, political formations like the socialists and the Jana Sangh, the RSS besides facilitated these late entrants with a campaign marked with a distinct negativism.

The Emerging Mind Space

While the crisis was engulfing the universities, an important development was simultaneously taking place unbeknownst to the polity. It was the coming of age of an indigenous intellectual tradition, which also used the same space that freedom and democracy had provided. Since the early 1960s, historical scholarship had matured to such an extent that there was an outright rejection of many ideas that the colonial historians had injected into the understanding of Indian history and society.[96] The writings of Mohammad Habib, R.N. Dandekar, P.V. Sukhtankar, D.D. Kosambi, K.M. Ashraf and R.S. Sharma earlier, and later of Nurul Hasan, Satish Chandra and many others, thoroughly rejected many historical myths propagated by the colonial history writings and by implication demonstrated that the ideas the RSS was propagating stemmed from illiteracy.[97]

The Indian History Congress, founded in 1935, had emerged as the largest professional congregation of historians in India, and was the platform for the most advanced ideas in any particular discipline in the country. With its serious engagement with everyone interested in teaching, researching and writing Indian history, it contributed to the democratization of the discipline. By the time the Aligarh University historian, Prof. Nurul Hasan, became the education minister in the 1970s, Indian historians had already changed the contours of historical discourse. And the education minister himself was the product of these renovated ideas.

Many restrictions on the academia and intellectual world began to be relaxed around this time, quite often with the prime minister's personal intervention. Many communists got jobs and positions in universities, which in the 1960s was well-nigh impossible. Indian leadership was contesting the dominance of the developed world and the intellectuals were coming up with a sophisticated critique of colonialism at this point of time.[98] It is through this critique of colonialism that scholars demonstrated how Hindu communalists, as well as their Muslim and Sikh counterparts, were in fact following the trajectory laid down by the colonial political studies and historiography.[99] By 1969, this intellectual section became the major bulwark against communal ideas, and more so in the case of the Hindu communal idea of Indianization, which it attacked as un-historical and even undemocratic as it was meant to attack the Muslims. They argued that the idea of India had historical underpinnings, and it was trained historians as well as the democratic policy of the modern state that should be the crucial elements in determining Indianness, not communal groups like the RSS or Jana Sangh. On the contrary, they argued that these groups had a very un-Indian philosophy.

This is the time that the work of R.N. Dandekar had come to fruition and Sanskrit scholarship was at its pinnacle. Before this, the final volume of the momentous *History of Dharmashastras* had been published in 1962, and its author P.V. Kane (1880–1972), was felicitated in 1963 with India's highest civilian honour, Bharat Ratna. Dandekar, one of the finest scholars of Sanskrit and Indology, had also published his very fine, nuanced work *Some Aspects of the History of Hinduism* in 1967, and would soon publish a tract on Hindu cosmology.[100] This was the time when the Bhandarkar Oriental Research Institute reached its height of glory. The institute was named after Ramakrishna Gopal Bhandarkar, one of the first four graduates of Bombay University, who became one of the tallest Sanskrit scholars, (he was also the pioneer of social reform movement in India) and set up the Prarthana Samaj along with Atmaram Pandurang Tarkhadkar, Justice M.G. Ranade, Justice N.G. Chandavarkar and Waman Abaji Modak. The institute not only did a pioneering job in collecting Sanskrit manuscripts, but also became the premier institution of research on Indian history primarily through Sanskrit sources.[101] While the Sanskrit scholarship and the great Indological tradition at Poona peaked, an increasingly different historical scholarship was ensuring that Indian history was no longer a part of the indological studies enunciated by colonial scholars and their colonial subjects.

A similar trend was also seen in the field of philosophy. The philosophical thinking was now on its way to ground itself in epistemology, asking serious questions using the contemporary philosophical template. Daya Krishna, for example, challenged the conventional argument that 'Indian thought was a means to spiritual salvation'.[102] Independently, K.C. Bhattacharya in Calcutta was raising certain fundamental issues in philosophy which the Kantian philosophers in Europe would raise a couple of decades later. Philosophers were trying to retrieve philosophical discourse from a lot of very hackneyed religious, cultural and Sanskrit mumbo-jumbo. Major contributions in this field were made by philosophers like A.P. Rao, Kalidas Bhattacharya, Sibajiban Bhattacharya, Daya Krishna, Jitendra Nath Mohanty, Bimal Krishna Matilal, Rajendra Prasad, Pranab Kumar Sen, and many others.[103]

Daya Krishna attacked the religious and hackneyed interpretations which tagged Indian philosophy along six schools of philosophy, four orthodox and two heterodox. He also critiqued the idea of treating Indian philosophy as merely the extension of Indian religious life. Several other philosophers vindicated Daya Krishna's argument by writing some of the finest papers in philosophy which had none of the cultural claptrap. The Pratap Centre of Philosophy at Amalner, a fascinating effort by individuals and groups, publishes one of the best journals, the *Indian Journal of Philosophy*, which celebrated its silver jubilee in 1967. Thus, philosophy was coming into its own and was now interpreting tradition not merely by referring to the tradition of philosophy but also by placing it on an analytical footing or along the lines of a phenomenological understanding as was beginning to be done in Europe.

In this sense, Indian philosophers were quite up to date with the times because phenomenological understanding of philosophy had reached France only in the 1940s and had been put into wider philosophical use only in the 1950s and 1960s by philosophers like Marleau Ponty, and Sartre. J.N. Mohanty had worked in the 1950s itself on Edmund Husserl who was the fountainhead of phenomenological thought and one who decided to place philosophy on a more stable platform, i.e., mathematics, following his teacher Brentano.[104] It was Husserl's disciple, Heidegger, who developed the existentialist thinking out of Husserl's efforts. Heidegger argued that all questions of truth were already captured in the post-Socratic paradigm of European knowledge and, in order to break out of it and even ask a question afresh, one had to transcend this paradigm. Philosophy was a tool to liberate the *Being* from its mundane existence. In the hands of French philosophers, Sartre and Marleau Ponty, existentialist thinking came to many contemporary thinkers including many in India. Mohanty himself attempted to connect this with Indian thought in his paper, 'Phenomenology and Existentialism: Encounter with Indian Thought'.[105] Similarly, Rama Kant Sinari was engaged in critically examining Indian thought in his book *Structures of Indian Thought* in the same phenomenological way as Brentano or Husserl or Heidegger would have done.[106]

While philosophers were intimately engaged with the questioning processes in the sciences, the early part of the twentieth century saw the coming of a strong science–philosophy interface with the writings of Karl Hempel, W.V.O. Quine and Karl Popper, leading up to Thomas Kuhn's now famous foray into the historicity of science, which proved that the early inquiry into science was not just an extension to its philosophical pursuits but rather the quest for a scientific tradition in its own right. It was in this light that Brajendra Nath Seal had written about the positivism of the ancient Hindus; and the sociologist, Binoy Kumar Sarkar, tried to resurrect positivist trends in Indian society so that scientific traditions could be emphasized. There was a very strong current in the early 1960s to separate the search for tradition within, and work towards linking Indian thought with, global epistemologies. The philosophers were key in this endeavour. Those who worked on logic were seen to be delving deeper into the logical structures of science like R.K. Shukla who was probing the connection of modern logic to science.[107] P.K. Sengupta, a leading philosopher, wrote a book by the name *The Logical Structure of Science*.[108]

It was in this milieu that Debi Prasad Chattopadhyaya emerged with a fascinating historical evaluation of Indian philosophical thinking, and questioned the mainstream view that Indian philosophy's sole concern was the concept of Brahman, an effort Daya Krishna too was making but from a different vantage point. From the scattered references in the ancient philosophical literature which were completely hostile to the ancient materialistic schools, Debi Prasad Chattopadhyaya reconstructed the philosophy of Lokayata, which consistently denied the existence of Brahman and viewed *pratyaksa* (perception) as the sole means of knowledge. He demolished the so-called 'interpretation of synthesis' which sought to combine the diverse philosophical traditions of India to form a ladder that led to the philosophy of Advaita Vedanta.[109] Very soon his *Indian Philosophy: A Popular Outline* tried to establish the real, and not what was popularly dished out, context of philosophical discourse.[110] He argued that philosophical development moved in a dialectical manner paving the way for contradictions to mature into real solutions. The capstone of his work was his masterly *Indian Atheism* which tried to account for atheism in India, which, he found, constituted a mainstream and not a peripheral space in Indian religious consciousness.[111] In fact, Chattopadhyaya was doing to philosophy what Kuhn had done to scientific world—putting it on the historical radar.

It was at this time that the debate had just begun to examine the lineage of philosophical traditions having the medieval as well as Islamic roots. In this sense, it was not from any philosophical or analytical terms but from a historical context that the quest began. At a fundamental level, scholars like S. Alam Khundmiri of Osmania University, were bringing deep scholarly reflections to bear on the way philosophical thinking among the leading Islamic scholars entered the public sphere over the last couple of centuries.[112] However, to counter the trends and shades that the Muslim communalism had forced, many serious scholars located philosophy much more within history than before. While the analytical trend of Indian philosophy was moving away from the historical, the trend in Islamic philosophical discourse was entering the domain of history and more particularly the ideas and correct assessment of people like Shah Waliullah and Shaikh Sirhindi. With a brilliant piece of historical analysis, Irfan Habib of Aligarh highlighted the way the mediocre principles of these personalities were projected to be part of the separatist agenda.[113].

Thus, while Debi Prasad Chattopadhyaya was trying to bring ancient Indian philosophy into the contemporary historical gaze,

Irfan Habib, Athar Ali and other contemporaries were trying the same with medieval Islamic thought in India.[114] Political science was a poor cousin of history and Moin Shakir, a political scientist of Marathwada University, emerged as the leading scholar on the political thinking of Indian Muslim leadership and showed the trajectories of communal and secular thinking. He made an invaluable contribution by examining the political ideas of leading intellectuals from Khilafat to Partition, the most significant phase in the political life of Indian Islam when the idea of community as defined by religion seemed supreme.[115]

However, away from the rarefied world of academic philosophy, it was the literary and cultural sensitivities, which marked the new world of intellect. The increasing desire for sophistication in what was called 'socialist realism' which had been the hallmark of progressive literary and cultural productions since the early 1940s had been giving way to various experimentations in the 1960s and by the end of the decade one saw a completely new genre of socialist ethos painting on a new canvas. The major contribution came from the new cinema from the West, particularly Italy and France. The realism (realismo) or thereafter new realism (novorealismo) of film-makers like Antonioni, Vittorio De Sica, Fellini and Renoir had quite an impact on India which would be hard to imagine today, inundated as we are with the Bombay and Hollywood cinema. Vittorio De Sica's 1946 production *Sciuscià* and his 1948 release *Bicycle Thief* are, even today, the most popular among the film literati. Renoir, influenced by the neo-realism of Antonioni, had visited India to shoot his film *River* and left with an already married lady. He influenced Satyajit Ray who was on the verge of making the first of his Apu trilogy. By the end of the 1960s, the creative life of people like Ritwik Ghatak, who was simultaneously experimenting beyond the frame of realism and neo-realism and making strong political statements, was coming to an end. This inspired others to join in to translate political and literary lives into films. *Meghe Dhaka Tara* (1960), *Komal Gandhar* (1961), *Titas Ekti Nadir Nam* (1971), etc., influenced not only a group of students like Mani Kaul and Kumar Sahani to make films but also to accept politics as something more complex than mere utterances of socialist shibboleths as depicted in Guru Dutt's movies in the late 1950s; and, in the 1960s, Dutt's film, *Saheb, Bibi aur Ghulam*, made the idea of romance more complex and nuanced.

A similar movement could be seen in literary creations. The socialist realism of Vinda Karandikar's collection *Swedganga* in 1949, which pioneered the tradition of reality, reached maturity in Narayan Gangaram Surve's *Maze Vidyapeeth* published in 1966, which talked about the whole life as a canvas of tough experience: talking about real life without referring to socialism as such. The creative field of the 1960s saw a range of writings which simultaneously gave expression and attacked the earlier hope and utopia of post-Independence prosperity and cleaner societal development, creating a more radical and cynical attitude. Marxist writers and poets across the country were bringing sensitivities of realism into literature and invoking a closer connect with the people. Kannada literature, for example, was defining new sensitivities by radicalizing its anti-caste ideology. Literary giants like Shivaram Karanth, turned the spotlight on to the huge changes happening in society. Girish Karnad's *Tughlaq* in 1964 brought to the fore the violence of ideological clashes taking place within the society. Likewise, Bhyrappa engendered a radical shift in Kannada literary sensitivity with his *Dharmashree*, *Vamshavruksha* and *Grihabhanga*.

In Marathi, the large number of journals generally referred to as 'Little Magazines', expanded the sensitivities in a similar manner, especially with the idea of a 'Dalit' (person of oppressed lower caste) and the need for expanding the democratic horizon. In Hindi, creativity was bursting forth with the writings of new poets and writers like Raghuvir Sahay, Sarveshwar Dayal Saxena, Muktibodh and Dhumil. They defied the period by questioning clichés. For instance, *Apka Banti* by Mannu Bhandari broke the innocence of the Hindi literary universe from a new standpoint: women depicted with a natural freedom to engage in relationships with more than one socially sanctioned male.[116] The Malayalam cultural scene was dynamic with new creativity taking the ongoing social and political renaissance to new heights. Takazhi Sivasankara Pillai's *Chemmeen* and its cinematic depiction shook the social conscience of the time. The Sahitya Pravarthaka Sahakarana Sangham and the Kerala Grandhasala Sangham movements reached their peak and raised popular consciousness on tricky social topics.

These tectonic shifts in the intellectual life of the country was happening on the fringes of university life. Most of the writers and creative artists were either teachers in small colleges or they were outside the university system. In reality the cultural and intellectual revolution that the left movement had brought in the 1940s and 1950s—the Indian People's Theatre Association (IPTA), Indian Progressive Writers Association (IPWA), etc.—had taken place outside the universities. This was highly significant as the universities which were expanding at the cost of the local colleges were devoid of the new creative energies, and very soon a large intellectual life outside of the academic milieu came into existence. The national movement during this phase saw creative people leaving, or not even joining, the university world as they did not want to be excluded from the excitement of the literary and creative movements. Intellectual life outside the university was more creative and dynamic. It was only in the mid-1960s that one saw the beginning of the inclusion of the university into the creative spaces that had been enlarged to encompass new voices even if they were disparaging.

While language remains one of the issues around which the politics of education was structured, the students' agitations that spanned most places in the country began to talk about autonomy and their need to speak out. In a series of interviews across the country, the youth talked about their need to talk and of having some space for themselves.[117] The socialists, the RSS and Jana Sangh leaders were talking about giving students more autonomy by invoking the issue of language.[118] The students were, in fact, looking for new democratic spaces which neither the existing university system nor the political parties were able to provide. Their joining the language agitation was only an indication of their desire for those spaces—the language agitation had never originated from any university campus, they were announced from the political pulpits and conferences of socialist parties and the RSS.

Designing a University for the New Times

Universities were beginning to occupy the central public space. The nationalist movement since the 1920s had in fact bypassed the university. The students either left the universities to join the movement or carried on some kind of political role outside the university. Except for the scientists who retained a university affiliation, the university was not a major forum for politics. It was in the late 1950s and '60s that the universities morphed into sites of political articulation. The youth was no longer someone potentially looking for a placement in the job market; he was now both a student and a political propagandist.

The 1960s was the period of disillusionment. There was a mismatch between the academia and the expectations of the new world such as the promises of the republic. Modelled on the British academia and strict disciplinary codes, the professors seemed to have lost the script, and part of the crisis was the non-academic consideration in the selection and promotion of both teachers and students. This was resented by the disillusioned generation. The stagnation of the economy in the cities where the universities were located did not give much hope either. Within the academia, favouritism in the appointment of teachers had become a discouraging but established bias.[119]

The students, therefore, wanted to speak out, and language was of utmost importance. The new entrants from rural backgrounds, who had been educated in the vernacular medium, had difficulties with the English curriculum in the universities. Also, with the education system's lack of innovation and experimentation, it was easier to resort to cramming in English medium. All this created a vicious cycle.

The new ruling segment led by Nehru, although not apathetic, was not very enthusiastic about the Indian academia. The primary reason was the lack of exposure to the university system as such, and secondly, the national movement had no space for the literati in the academia as it had sufficient legitimacy; in any case, the universities were sequestered enclosures. Much of the Gandhian movement attempted to delegitimize the colonial intellectuals in the existing universities and worked towards creating and popularizing parallel institutions. Thus in post-Independence India, although the wheels were set in motion to establish social sciences and humanities in the universities, Nehru was more intent on creating new institutions of science and technology rather than planning ways and means by which the teaching of science and technology could be incorporated into the existing universities. During the first two post-Independence decades, the nationalists, despite their apprehensions, did not tamper with the existing structures of the universities or their autonomy.

The change in the leadership's attitude towards the university appeared in the 1960s. Indira Gandhi was the first to actively allow intellectuals from universities to join her as advisors or become part of her team. She was the first to seek as well as provide legitimacy to the Indian universities. Perhaps she felt reassured by the intellectual legitimacy provided by the academia. Also, the national movement which had supported the Nehruvian leadership now needed an injection of freshness to appeal to the newcomers to the political arena. The national polity needed to include people who were born after Independence and had only faint memories of the freedom movement. Mrs Gandhi was aware of one contingent who ascribed the failure and corruption of the Congress to her, and considered her the pretender and false prophet of the great national movement. The scorn for the khadi cap was a live metaphor of this trend. The delegitimization was also sharpened by the rhetoric of the new political formations of the socialist parties, communists and the Dravidian party in Tamil Nadu, which attacked the national alliances or components of the national movement in some form or other. While the socialists attacked the Congress's corruption, the communists felt the Congress was handicapped by its class composition and inability to bring social change. They saw the Congress government as merely the continuation of colonial rule in Indian garb. To the Dravidians, the Congress represented a Brahminical party. Therefore, the Congress needed the intellectual support of indigenous intelligentsia located in Indian Universities.

It was at this juncture that the politics of language returned to centre stage. The scope of the language agitation moved from denial of the central role of English, as in the intellectual discourse articulated by Lohia and the socialists, to the denial of any role for Hindi as it smacked of Brahminical and north Indian dominance over Dravidian society in Tamil Nadu. From this deadlock emerged a different kind of politics that influenced the universities.

The universities resented political interference and wanted autonomy. However, as many responsible people in hindsight saw, on many occasions state intervention was necessary. Political and social scientists have indicated that the crux of the problem lay in the fact that the changing political contours of the country and the structures that were developed before the extension of democracy were outdated and could not cope with the increase in numbers and the arrival of the new segments of population into the universities. A very penetrative analysis by Mahadevi Verma, one of the most distinguished Hindi poets of her time, in her convocation address to Vikram University makes this point. The new segments, both social and economic, had a segment steeped in traditionalist thinking on the one hand and an unyielding university segment on the other. As university jobs were not many, they began to reflect not only the economic frustration but also social and cultural angst.

The JNU Bill had inadvertently charted a completely new way for Indian universities. The Visva-Bharati University Act of 1951, was the first Act that had formalized an already existing institution in independent India by the parliament. The JNU Act created a brand new institution. The context of the political transitions and institutional crises had shaped the bill and therefore circumvented the issues which plagued the other universities. The posts of pro-chancellor and pro-vice-chancellor were, for example, discarded. At the core of the institutional design there was democracy where academia was an independent factor and not a mere appendage or instrument of state or bureaucracy or even the ruling classes. It was a new state of autonomy, which was to be manifested in the bill and in the Act.

5

Born amidst the Rocks

> Shri Amarnath Vidyalankar: What do you suggest we could do as legislators to avoid those defects and to prevent this university from falling into the same rut?
>
> V.S. Jha: Three things—give it adequate finance, entrust it to the right people and give it ample freedom.[1]

The university began to take shape amidst a declining credibility of universities as well as the emergence of new intellectual sensibilities. There was a gap of approximately three years before the university became operational. These three years contained some of the most defining moments in the contemporary history of India. There was a sea change in the world of politics—both global and national—and in the regional and cultural reflections of the new age.

Vice Chancellor of a New Kind

During the parliamentary debate on the JNU Bill, the education minister maintained that one of the unique features of the university would be that, unlike other universities, the vice chancellor would be selected first, who would then be involved in the gradual process of starting up the university.[2] It however meant, going by the precedence of university formation in India, inundating the new vice chancellor with a lot of spadework and other responsibilities, which were not predetermined. It has been noted that some of the members of the House were a touch envious of this prerogative and objected to the appointment of a vice chancellor preceding the launch of the actual university. M.S. Aney, a senior parliamentarian, felt that this was not a good step in a democracy.[3] Notwithstanding these protests, the post of vice chancellor, by virtue of the fact that he was to start the university and make its statutes, became a kind of lynchpin for the new institution. The question remained as to the kind of person that needed to be chosen and entrusted with such a radically new experiment.

The 1960s was a transitional phase in the role and position of the vice chancellor. Under the colonial regime, universities were under strict official control and even those personalities who had emerged as powerful vice chancellors actually had strong official support. Although scholar-administrators like Ashutosh Mookerje were very powerful and independent vice chancellors, British official control remained paramount. In the scenario after Independence, two kinds of vice chancellors emerged. In universities like Banaras, where leading public personalities became vice chancellors they were merely part-time and nominal holders of office while the actual day-to-day administration was done by the pro-vice-chancellor, and a team of people began to control the universities in which the family and friends of the founders played a part. Associates of Tagore in Visva-Bharati, for example, kept themselves active as informal and yet effective advisors to the vice chancellor, quite often to the chagrin of the latter. Interference was accepted as most of these people commanded a lot of respect. But this was not the case in many other places where the interference created nothing but problems for the vice chancellor and impeded his functioning.

Universities like Bombay, on the other hand, had vice chancellors who were for the most part, part-time. The registrar was the key functionary. S.R. Dongerkerry, registrar of Bombay University, for example, emerged as one of the most respected names in the annals of university administration in India owing to his efficiency and commitment.[4]

Calcutta University had eminent academics as vice chancellors but the institution's administration was carried out by the registrar, pro-vice-chancellor and controller of examinations, who were also academics. Madras witnessed a very long tenure for its vice chancellor, A. Lakshmanaswami Mudaliar, spanning over twenty-seven long years. While he helped smoothen its transition process from a colonial to a free Indian institution, he kept intact the colonial bureaucratic elements in the university. C.R. Reddy, educationist, one of the most outspoken intellectuals of pre-Independence India and one of the founders of the non-Brahmin Justice Party in the Madras Province, served as the vice chancellor for a long time as well (1926–1931 and 1936–1949), and shaped Andhra University. It was personalities such as these and an all-India frame of reference during the national movement that made Andhra University the home for scholars like V.K.R.V. Rao, Hiren Mukerjee, S. Radhakrishnan, Humayun Kabir, S. Gopal and many others who were on its faculty.

The late 1950s and the 1960s saw new trends. The structure of universities and the position of vice chancellors remained static despite new democratic changes taking place in the country. In fact, this was the time when visionary and energetic vice chancellors could take the lead to change the ethos of their universities to keep them in sync with the new times. This did not happen for two reasons. First, the universities were straitjacketed by the administration and the bureaucracy which were by themselves too rigid to allow the educational institutes any leeway to grow and evolve. Second, most of the vice chancellors were either retired judges or people who had 'no connection with the people in direct ways', as someone pointed out in his response to the select committee's question, and were too exhausted to do justice to the variegated role of vice chancellor. (The situation had completely changed by the year 2000 when judges were no longer in the running for this job, and the post was more or less monopolized by academia and bureaucracy and in some cases by former army generals or police officers.) The universities could have probably synergized the state drive to start new institutions considering all the institutional changes taking place elsewhere in the world. In the United States, for example, spurred by the intensity of the cold war and the launch of the Soviet spacecraft, Sputnik, the American federal government brought in massive institutional changes in the university system. It not only increased funding for scientific research but also provided a lot of incentives to state initiatives in other areas of research. In India, however, the subject of casteism seemed to be dominating the discourse in politics, which increasingly brought universities under political and bureaucratic control.

In the meeting of the select committee for the JNU Bill, M.F. Mohsin had asked Dr Triguna Sen what kind of personality profile would be the best fit for the role of vice chancellors. The latter had responded by listing the traits, which are *not* suitable in vice chancellors. 'The present system of appointing retired judges or retired ICS officers', he felt was proving 'counter-productive', as they did not have 'contact with people', and therefore should not be 'made vice chancellors'.[5] In his response to the question as to how to make a university unique, V.S. Jha emphasized the close link between the university and its vice chancellor, and said: '... the Act can state the uniqueness only in certain general terms. The real individuality, the real personality of the university is to be built by those who are in charge of the university.'[6] To Jha the whole university was 'a reflection of the personality of the vice chancellor'.[7] He felt that for the university to flourish, the vice chancellor would have to be given three things—adequate finances, the right people and ample freedom.[8]

In both the Rajya Sabha and the Lok Sabha there were discussions on the functionaries of the university when the clauses of the bill were debated on 6 December 1965. Following Jha's evidence, some people petitioned for a president instead of a vice chancellor and a chancellor. This was rejected out of hand by one of the most vocal members in the house, P.N. Sapru, who in his characteristic way said that though he liked the American language, he did not like the word president to be imported for the vice chancellor.

Sharda Bhargava who had had some experience with the institutions of Rajasthan was also a vocal member during the discussion on the bill and argued that there should be no chancellor and just one rector, and that the registrar should be the secretary of the university.[9] Most senior members and, interestingly, all those who were involved with the universities, namely, B.N. Prasad, P.N. Sapru and A.R. Wadia, were unanimous that there must be a chancellor.[10]

By the beginning of 1969, we hear of the government talking to four people which included a director of public instruction (DPI) (which could have been V.S. Jha). The only clue we have of the identities of these four people is an account that suggests that G. Parthasarathi's name was mentioned to the prime minister by Chagla. Chagla mentions that in a dinner hosted by a Union minister, he asked Indira Gandhi whether she had found 'someone for the post of vice chancellor of the Jawaharlal Nehru University,' for the founding of which he had worked so hard. She in turn asked him whether he had someone in mind. 'On the spur of the moment', Chagla reminisced, 'I said, "Why not Parthasarathi? He has just returned from the United Nations, and I think he will do very well."'[11] Chagla remembered that she 'immediately agreed but asked me whether Parthasarathi would accept the appointment if requested to do so'.[12] 'As it happened', Chagla wrote in his memoir:

> He was present at the dinner, and was at the moment standing in a corner talking to someone. I remarked to the prime minister that it was my habit to take decisions quickly where the instinct is sound; decisions taken quickly turn out to be good decisions. I left her, pulled away Parthasarathi from the person he was talking to, took him aside and asked him whether he would accept the vice chancellorship if it was offered. Without a moment's hesitation he said, 'yes'. I went back to Indira, and told her about Parthasarathi's reaction. And the appointment of the first vice chancellor of Jawaharlal Nehru University followed as a matter of course.[13]

It shows his high admiration for GP (G. Parthasarathi) but it appears that the sudden gush of appreciation or recommendation was not so sudden after all and that Chagla and GP had known each other for some time as GP had apparently worked with Chagla during the latter's tenure as foreign minister.

Gopalaswamy Parthasarathi, known among his acquaintances as GP, was the son of the N. Gopalaswamy Ayyangar, former prime minister of Kashmir, a constitutional lawyer and India's first representative in the United Nations. A versatile personality, Parthasarathi, worked as correspondent for the Press Trust of India in London, and was then called by Nehru to join the foreign ministry.[14] He thereafter worked as one of the most reliable mediators in the many assignments that India had been involved with, for example, the Indo-China discussions. Parthasarathi also became a trusted aide to and close friend of U. Thant, and was one of the most respected diplomats in the United Nations. As Chagla pointed out,

> He was an extremely able administrator, and in diplomacy he was as though to the manner born. He worked with me in New York when I went there as External Affairs Minister during one of the west Asia crises. He was on the best of terms with the whole diplomatic corps, and he was a friend and confidant of the Secretary General, U. Thant. Relations between U. Thant and Parthasarathi were most intimate and on many matters U. Thant consulted him and took his advice.[15]

Indira Gandhi would also find in him one of her most trusted aides. It was therefore not accidental that he did not escape the careful and appreciative eye of the minister who offered him the ambassadorship of the United States as a successor to B.K. Nehru. Parthasarathi's letter in response to Chagla's offer gives an idea of the high esteem in which Chagla held him.

> I am deeply appreciative of the generous way in which you have referred to my work in New York and if I may say so with respect, it is characteristic of you to provide such warm-hearted encouragements. You have asked me whether I would like to succeed B.K. Nehru in Washington. You have also been good enough to say that if I preferred to remain in my present post, you will not distrust me. I have given a great deal of thought to your kind enquiry ever since I received your letter three days ago. I find it difficult to express a personal preference. The only test is where I would be more useful to our government. Obviously, I cannot be objective in making such an assessment and will happily abide by your decision.
>
> I agree with you that the next three years or so will be crucial in the development of our relationship with the United States. We have a large stake in the healthy development of this relationship on a basis of equality and deeper understanding of each other's policies and needs. In view of the weighty considerations you have urged and the challenging nature of the assignment in the present context, I shall be glad to serve in Washington. You will no doubt let me know your final decision after discussing the matter with the prime minister.[16]

On the other hand, even Parthasarathi could not have been untouched by the suave, gentlemanly Chagla on one side and his robust nationalist defence of India's stand either on Kashmir or during the Arab-Israel war in West Asia in 1967. He conveyed the general mood at the United Nations when Chagla resigned from the cabinet. 'Your decision to resign from the government', Parthasarathi wrote to him, 'has been received with profound regret and disappointment in the United Nations. U. Thant spoke to me yesterday in the highest terms of respect about you. So did many colleagues. All of them recalled with admiration the great contribution you made during the recent west Asian crisis.' But what was important was his own personal feeling of sadness: 'May I say personally', Parthasarathi wrote to Chagla, 'your decision to leave the Ministry of External Affairs (MEA) is a sad blow. It was a pleasure to work for a chief who stood for high principles and in whose basic approach one was in entire accord. I shall treasure the memories of our close association ... '[17]

If Parathasarathi was Chagla's find for the post of vice chancellor, the latter was indeed lucky. To have someone to build an institution with a horizon broad enough to incorporate and assume the idea of the university, which Chagla and the members of the parliament had debated, was not going to be easy. There were other qualities that made Parthasarathi a remarkably successful vice chancellor. His strong Madras University connection where his wife was still teaching would help him to immediately get to the academic resources in Madras and the southern part of India. On the other hand his long years in diplomacy and stints across the world would help him avoid a parochialism, which was fast becoming the byword for academia across the country and particularly in the intellectual centres like Calcutta, where, apart from provincial parochialism, a political sectarianism was emerging; while Madras, another major centre for science, was witnessing a change of era with the vice chancellorship of A. Lakshmanaswami Mudaliar coming to an end after twenty-seven years of continued stewardship.[18] Furthermore, there were visible signs of change in the Madras University. The resignation of the leading physicist G.N. Ramachandran and his shift to the Indian Institute of Science, Bangalore, was an indicator of the centre of gravity of science teaching shifting away to other institutions. Parthasarathi, therefore, could embark on a truly national project.

Parthasarathi's Summer of 1969

Delhi's temperature had begun touching the unbearable forties when Parthasarathi assumed office on 28 April 1969. He was given an office in the Vigyan Bhawan annexe. Some of the senior members in Rajya Sabha, for example, Tara Chand, Pandit S.S. Tankha and P.N. Sapru, who were either teachers or deeply involved with education, had argued for two terms for the vice chancellor. However, after a long debate, the Act finally stipulated only a single term.[19]

Parthasarathi spent the first three months discussing matters with academics. Around July–August, the government gave him a team which in all probability would have been hand-picked by himself. He was keen, excited and awed about his new project:

> When Mrs Indira Gandhi asked me to take up the task of launching the university, serving as its first vice chancellor, my inner feelings were of two kinds. I was enthusiastic about the prospect of making a modest contribution to the building of an institution to be named after Jawaharlal Nehru. Coupled with that sense of excitement was a clear awareness of the magnitude of the responsibility that I was being called upon to undertake.[20]

Parthasarathi, like many of this generation, had an intuitive understanding of the unfolding world order. He also had the advantage of being a diplomat and hence aware of the quantum of work that had gone into putting the Nehruvian vision into operation. This must have given him a vantage point to understand the movement of ideas in the global scenario. Therefore, when it came to institution building he would have had a very lofty view. Intellectually, he wanted to set the institution at that level. On the other hand, his having been a journalist before moving into diplomacy, which involved living in and thinking of the perpetual changes, must have inhibited any detailed and deep study of any particular discipline. And it is here that his personality came to be of crucial importance in starting something from scratch.

Intellectual self-reliance defined the core issue of new institution building at a time when the West started attacking any such efforts in Africa and Asia. This self-reliance would be a positive force and an added advantage in any circumstance not merely from an antagonistic cold war perspective. As JNU was like a blank slate, a tabula rasa, intellectual self-reliance would be the key requirement for the new vice chancellor.[21]

Parthasarathi was new to university administration, and this worked in two ways. One, with diplomacy and judgement, he cross-checked his applicants and brought together the best academic talent from across the country. However, his not being from the academia diminished his self-reliance somewhat when he had to rely on others' opinions on academic issues.

Paying his tribute to Parthasarathi, Manmohan Singh, who later became the prime minister of India, saw Parthasarathi as a 'great reconciler'.[22] 'His emphasis was [on] a multidisciplinary approach for solving real life problems.'[23] Dr Singh added that Parthasarathi 'insisted that there were several layers of rationality and any single discipline which claimed that it had understood all that went into the pursuit of rationality, would be an imperfect view of the complex entities that one dealt with in human affairs'.[24]

One of Parthasarathi's greatest qualities was his enthusiasm, which did not abate throughout his career, which ignited a corresponding creative enthusiasm in people across the country. There was a multitude of people seeking employment in the new university. The times were tumultuous, particularly in Bengal where the Naxalite movement had brought many institutions to a standstill. But it was a sense of intellectual excitement that Parthasarathi evoked which made many, like the eminent mathematician, Prof. Yashpal, get engaged with the JNU project. Although they knew that they would not be joining the new university, as Yashpal reminisced, they were concerned.[25] G. Parthasarathi would also consult him for his views and opinions.[26]

Advisors and Executives

Provisions had been made for the academic advisory committee and executive council within the JNU Act and there were debates about who ought to be part of the academic advisory committee. Many senior intellectuals joined the new projects spearheaded by Parthasarathi, and a large segment of Indian intelligentsia was part of the academic advisory body and executive committee. This was significant both for him and the new university as no university had ever been given this much autonomy. There were important and interesting issues which had to be sorted out systematically, which was done with excited anticipation and Parthasarathi's characteristic enthusiasm.

The original plan, according to Chagla, was to appoint the vice chancellor as soon as the bill was passed and provide him with an academic advisory committee consisting of some of the best educationalists of India. They were, however, not to be from among the staff of the university.[27] At least four persons recommended deleting the clause 'not being members of the staff': Mukut Bihari Lal, Mulka Govinda Reddy, Shakuntala Paranjapye and D. Thengari. Lal's contention was that somebody suitable could be within the university. Thengari's argument was, 'barring the members of the staff from being on the AAC would imply the staff were in a lower status when compared to those appointed to this committee'. He certainly had a point there because this was reflected in the reluctance of the advisory board members to join the university's faculty but recommended their own kinsmen or students for these posts. M.S. Swaminathan or M.N. Srinivas or V. Ramalingaswami, for example, never considered joining the university but ensured that at least some of their relatives joined the new departments that they were setting up.

Chagla accepted the amendment which removed the restriction concerning the faculty and the motion to pass Clause 14 was duly adopted. It was propitious that the clause was eventually dropped a few years down the line at the request of Lal, Sapru and Tara Chand; otherwise S. Gopal, who went on to play a crucial role in the university, would not have been able to join the JNU's advisory panel.

For the advisory committee, Chagla garnered the best creative intellects in the contemporary Indian academic and institutional life—M.G.K. Menon, director of the Tata Institute of Fundamental Research, Bombay; V. Ramalingaswami, who then was the director of All India Institute of Medical Sciences; M. N. Srinivas, a sociologist of singular eminence; K.N. Raj, economist at the Delhi School of Economics;

S. Gopal, who was the foremost amongst the historians and had been the director of Historical Research Division of the Ministry of External Affairs and had also been teaching modern and contemporary history at Oxford; J.P. Naik, who had immense knowledge of the nuances of education system of India.[28] The term for the committee was fixed for a year.

The executive council, which had been constituted earlier, had an interesting mix of powerful people: B.D. Nag Chouduri, connected with the Planning Commission but primarily with the scientific establishment; M.V. Mathur, highly respected in the educational field, at the helm of the Rajasthan University and the director of Asian Institute of Educational Planning and Administration; Nurul Hasan, professor of history and the education minister. The other members were R. Ramanna, Department of Atomic Energy; S.M. Katre, director of the Deccan College of Post Graduate and Research Institute; P.N. Dhar, director of the Institute of Economic Growth; M.S. Swaminathan, director of Indian Agricultural Research Institute (IARI); and M. Chalapati Rao, editor of *National Herald*, New Delhi.[29]

The people on the academic advisory committee and executive council seemed too close to the establishment. But this could have been deliberate because the prime minister might have wanted to emphasize the role of intellectual giants behind the new university enterprise. There was a distinct lack of representation in these committees from the universities of Madras and Calcutta. Although some of these universities were in a state of decline they had quite a significant number of academicians who had international fame and exposure to working on frontier areas and who would have been able to make considerable contributions to JNU by providing new angles on planning the academic programmes in disciplines like mathematics or philosophy, which were in a slump during this period. Calcutta University was floundering and senior scholars from the advanced centre of Visva-Bharati were migrating to the West.[30] Had philosophy been incorporated at this point, JNU could have contributed to salvaging it from a phase of banality. Kalidas Bhattacharya, one of the foremost philosophical minds, who had recently been the vice chancellor of Visva-Bharati languished as this discipline withered and atrophied. Young scholars like A.P. Rao and many others were looking for opportunities to spread their wings, and JNU would have been tailor-made to provide sustenance to this fresh talent and also to philosophy as a subject.

Science and scientists in JNU soon began to make connections with the science bureaucracy in the capital and willingly became its torch-bearers instead of evolving a distinct institutional and experimental path of JNU. This was probably not the best move. Several state universities had become captives to local bureaucracy and petty politicians and there were no guarantees that the Central universities would not follow suit.

Creating Structures

Notwithstanding these criticisms, the committees proved to be very effective and made some of the best possible academic engagements to provide the new university with a durable and flexible structure. It is to their credit that that university withstood the test of time despite pressures and attacks on its very foundations by various stakeholders.

The committee planned the programme for the new university at the outset with certain basic points of departure:

(1) Distinguished Indian scholars living abroad were to be offered appointments in the university on attractive terms. This is an interesting concept which flowed against the current of the popular 'brain drain'. In the 1960s, offspring of bureaucrats and other wealthy Indians who found it difficult to compete with local students, went abroad for college education, and the 'brain drain' scare was raised to accommodate these students back in India alongside high achievers in various professions abroad who were seeking to return to their homeland. A foreign degree was considered a leveller, and programmes like these were initiated to bring them back. The new university got many good people from this pool and also a few whose academic credentials nobody could ascertain.

(2) The committee felt it was imperative that no distinction would be made between teaching and research. A team of six or eight persons would be assigned to work on new ideas evolved by educationists and then translate them into practical policies for

> the university. Another suggestion was to appoint more than one professor in each discipline to provide the much needed elasticity and incentive.

One more innovative idea was to start centres for Chinese and Pakistani studies.[31] Nurul Hasan, S. Gopal and G. Parthasarathi were dynamic personalities and could sway the committee discussions to seeing their points of view as was done, for example, in the setting up of a school of social sciences. The committee debated on the pros and cons of establishing 'centres' in schools rather than university 'departments'. This issue was discussed in parliament as well where some members like M.B. Lal had suggested that since the term 'school' conveyed different things to different people, it would be advisable to retain the traditional terms 'faculty' and 'department'. Sapru, however, could see the idea behind the term 'school' as proposed by Chagla, and endorsed it. [32] Chagla too clarified that the modern tendency was not to have one subject-based faculty but to have multidisciplinary schools of studies headed by a dean and that this was the endeavour here as well.[33] The old system of organization was increasingly felt to be very conservative and restrictive as it generally made the department watertight and discouraged interdisciplinary studies and research. All things considered, it was agreed that, to begin with, the university should establish centres in schools around clearly identified problems or areas of study.

The School of Social Sciences, it was tentatively agreed by the advisory committee, would consist of the centre for the study of social systems which would also study tribal societies and backward classes; the centre for the study of scientific and technological advances which would focus on developing societies with special reference to their economic and social implications, including problems connected with international transfers of technology; the centre for disarmament studies; the centre for regional planning; the centre for educational studies; the centre for historical studies; and the centre for linguistics.

The year 1969 was the time when radical social movement grew around nuclear weapons, and there was a need for immediate disarmament.[34] The anti-nuclear movement in 1969 began in France against the French government's decision to construct two nuclear reactors in Fessenheim.[35] In light of the intense international pressure against which the Indian nuclear programme was also working, there must have been a felt need for a proper study of disarmament. The experience of Parthasarathi at the UN and Gopal as an advisor at the external affairs ministry and Raja Ramanna at the Tata Institute of Fundamental Research (TIFR); must have contributed to this collective feeling: they all felt that there must be a department of disarmament studies. In fact, they thought that it should be taken up on a priority basis and such a centre could try and study 'nuclear disarmament; arms control; regional security; developments in military technology and their impact on the arms race; economic consequences of rising arms expenditure; etc'.[36]

At this juncture, Parthasarathi emphasized the importance of establishing a school of international relations and diplomacy. The members too agreed. Some however felt that they might be duplicating many facilities that already existed at the Indian School of International Studies (ISIS). The historian, S. Gopal, was the first to suggest that the JNU explored a working relationship with the ISIS.[37]

Some proposals, for example, for the centre for educational studies were included in this second meeting, but were considered 'not clearly visualized'. J.P. Naik, who brought the proposal, was requested 'to prepare a paper showing the type of research work that is already being done in education; the important gaps that have to be covered and the manner in which the centre for educational studies would develop'.[38] Concern regarding the non-availability of personnel of the right quality was again stressed. It was finally decided that there may be a working subgroup for this under the overarching umbrella of the School of Social Sciences.

As the area covered by the School of Social Sciences was very large, it was agreed that there should be separate subgroups for different centres and that their views and reports should be finally coordinated into one by the main working group consisting of S. Gopal, M.N. Srinivas, K.N. Raj and J.P. Naik. The group for the centre for regional planning had four very distinguished scholars including three of India's leading economists: M.S. Gore of Delhi School of Social Work fame, T.N. Srinivasan who had not left India yet, Mrinal Dutta Chaudhuri and K.N. Raj himself. One of the biggest centres planned was the centre for the study of the social systems with M.N. Srinivas himself being part of the subgroup along with Rajni Kothari, Rasheeduddin Khan and Ramakrishna Mukherjee as invited members.

It was at this meeting that the most visionary of centres was ideated and a sub-group was constituted with M.G.K. Menon, B.S. Minhas, Sukhamoy Chakravarty and Anand Sarup of the Planning Commission as its members. This was to be a centre for the study of the scientific and technological advances in developing societies.

There was to be a centre for linguistics for which S.M. Katre of the Deccan College was made the convenor. S. Gopal was very clear that for the study of history 'the need for the study of linguistics is indisputable', but it need not be linked with the department of history. He felt that there should be a separate centre of linguistics, and the history department would obviously work in close association with it.[39] Nobody mentioned archaeology. The reason may be that in the milieu of scientific temper, collective vision seemed to view archaeology with its tentative conjectures, colonial past and pseudo-scientific career not worthy of a serious and scientific university department. And there were already too many such centres in the country to waste resources upon.

In 1970, there were no university-level centres to study and research environmental sciences. M.G.K. Menon suggested that a school of environmental and theoretical sciences should be established with a 'character of its own with applied mathematicians, physicists, geophysicists, geochemists, meteorologists, hydrologists and oceanographers' working together. He, however, was also of the view that the university should not start individual departments like these as there were already specialized national institutions already in place working on specific issues. For example, ionospheric physics was being researched by National Physical Laboratory (Delhi), Physical Research Laboratory (Ahmedabad), Space Science & Technology Centre (SSTC, Thumba), several universities (Andhra, Calcutta, Delhi, etc.) and Astrophysical Observatory (Kodaikanal), while geology and geophysics were studied in classical form at several places with the oceanography department centred at Andhra University. Meteorology and hydrology did not have a major status. JNU, he suggested, could link certain core areas and devise programmes like 'meteorology, oceanography, hydrology and ecology (pollution of air and water)'.

For the innovative environmental and theoretical sciences, it was proposed that the studies should be based 'not only on the traditional patterns of large-scale observations and data-collection, but with model-building, computer-simulation, extensive use of applied mathematics and new experimental techniques'.[40] Menon's working paper also suggested, as a 'working proposition a group of about four scientists with a few years of post-doctoral experience in each of the fields taken up and an equal number of scientists at post-doctoral or pre-doctoral levels'.[41]

Scouting for the Pioneers

G. Parthasarathi lost no time in getting people to start the centres and schools and began communicating with several people. Statute 28, which provided a special mode of appointment, facilitated invitations to scholars to join the university. The joint committee and the educationists who gave their evidence before the committee mooted that many a time able, senior and productive people hesitate to attend interviews. Chagla had included a provision to invite people for the positions of professors, readers and lecturers—all these posts were to be covered by statute—although in the Rajya Sabha, M.B. Lal and P.N. Sapru were convinced that lecturers needed to compete for their position. However, P.N. Sapru also felt that the professors did not require to be interviewed.[42] Chagla agreed to this suggestion and retained the invitation provision for professors and readers. Furthermore, in the joint committee, the eminent educationalist, K.G. Saiyidain, recommended that the appointments to these posts should be for a five-year tenure, using the American contract system.

The appointment of the registrar has always been crucial, and the vice chancellor zeroed in on N.V. Murthy who had helped set up the Poona Film and Television Institute and requested him to join his team. Murthy's contribution in giving shape to Parthasarathi's ideas was second to none. In his capable hands JNU sailed through the turbulent early 1970s when, despite all opposition and disturbances, the different aspects of the work to set up the university moved at speed. It was also his personality that set the tradition of the low-profile and non-interfering registrar at the time when the registrars were becoming the biggest irritants in the universities.

In the very first executive council meeting, Parthasarathi constituted a committee comprising Nurul Hasan, P.N. Dhar and himself to draft the statutes. The original statutes of JNU demonstrated Parthasarathi and Dhar's editorial skills and the perfect prose made them technically foolproof without sounding like jargon or legalese.

After the vice chancellor, importance would be accorded to the person(s) starting the centres and erecting the edifice of the university. A consensus of sorts emerged during the discussion that (except for a few centres) there should be more than one professor in any given department so that there would be academic elasticity. This was a time when the number of professorships in the universities were few and far between. This brought in all sorts of politics into play in the departments, which stunted the growth and expansion of the discipline itself. JNU needed to be saved from these issues.

Moonis Raza, senior professor of humanities and principal, Regional Engineering College, Srinagar, Jammu and Kashmir, was one of the first to be appointed. He was appointed not to any specific department but as a special planning officer for two years.[43] Raza, with a geography background, was teaching in a nondescript engineering college in Kashmir and was in no way within Parthasarathi's orbit of academic excellence for effective administration. It was, therefore, very obvious that this must have been due to the Communist Party of India or an Aligarh connection, and both these pointed to Nurul Hasan. However, his coming to JNU proved beneficial because he was instrumental in giving the campus an indigenous aesthetic and its earthiness, both long-time virtues. Rooted as he was in eastern Uttar Pradesh and the robust communist movement, Moonis Raza brought this energy to complement Parthasarathi's own finer aesthetic touch. Raza radiated vitality, vigour, a native intelligence and nationalist confidence that provided the university and its student community a sense of assurance in their academic career.

The second set of appointments made by JNU was for the Centre for Russian Studies, which was known, prior to its merger with JNU, as the Institute of Russian Studies. Three of its alumni, Ramadhikari Kumar, S.K. Mathur and Kumari Preeti Kaul got the opportunity to join the university.[44] As the appointed people had been students of the centre in its earlier avatar, this was not a difficult exercise. It was, however, more complicated to get the right kind of people to initiate the programmes suggested by the advisory committee for the other new centres.

For the history department, the initial invitations went to S. Gopal, Romila Thapar and Satish Chandra. Gopal was one of the most respected historians on modern India teaching at Oxford, and his status was markedly different from the others as he was also a key mover of the entire academic exercise. Romila Thapar, trained in London under A.L. Basham, supervisor of many other Indian historians, had a completely new and open approach to ancient history that was not in line with the kind of work the departments of Indology and archaeology were doing. Both the disciplines were increasingly being rejected for their pseudo-scientific assertions and half-baked conjectures, and people like D.D. Kosambi were already expositing that they needed to be part of the larger narrative of history. She had already brought a new and fresh dimension to the study of ancient Indian history through her books on Ashoka and the Mauryan Empire (her doctoral thesis, 1958) and a general introduction to ancient India.[45] Her popularity at the Delhi University as part of the new group and a Delhi literati made the founders of JNU to invite her. Satish Chandra was the product of the Allahabad University history department, which had teachers like Tara Chand, R.P. Tripathi, Ishwari Prasad and many more stalwarts. He joined as a reader at Aligarh in the early 1950s and his thesis entitled 'Party and Politics of Medieval India' became one of the pioneering works on medieval India.[46] By 1970, he was among the tallest medieval historians of his generation and was teaching at the University of Rajasthan at Jaipur where he encouraged the 'use of regional language sources for historical understanding of the regions'. However, his induction might also be part of Nurul Hasan's plans to strengthen the history department.

Parthasarathi was keen to bring in the leading chemical scientist, Prof. C.N.R. Rao, who was a professor at IIT Kanpur at the age of twenty-eight and had emerged as the leading scholar in the field from Kanpur. Parthasarathi was also trying to wean away George Sudarshan from the Institute of Mathematics at Madras, to set up the school of computer sciences. A distinguished scientist, S.K. Malhotra, was also invited. Meanwhile Dr Govindjee, who, with his ground-breaking work in photosynthesis had recently joined the faculty at Illinois, was invited.[47] He asked for some commitments from the university which the executive council somehow did not agree to, and decided not to go ahead with his appointment.[48] The negotiation with C.N.R. Rao also did not go very far. Sudarshan soon left Madras for the University of Texas at Austin. His inability to rope in Sudarshan and Rao made Parthasarathi lose heart regarding the science centres, and he did not go far in doing much for the visionary centre, school of environmental science.

Rasheeduddin Khan of Osmania University had done work on politics in Iraq (1920–31) but had also been writing on Indian politics. He gained an all-India profile also on account of his political connections and was soon nominated to the Rajya Sabha. He was brought to the new School of Social Sciences to start what was designed as the Centre for Political Development (a nomenclature that would change later). JNU took a special commitment from him that his political work would not come in the way of discharging his duties as a professor in the university.[49]

It was difficult to find people for the Centre for Science Policy. Of the people who had been writing, B.V. Rangarao was not only a senior scientist with the government of India but also a member of the Communist Party of India and that may partly be the reason why he was spotted and appointed.

Some of the scientists that were invited to join as readers included P.C. Kesavan, A.K. Rajan, S. Ambirajan and Javed Ashraf. K.R. Narayanan, of the Indian Foreign Service was also invited to join as professor at the School of International Studies.[50] Although he could not join, he came back as vice chancellor of the university a decade later.

In many appointments, one could see connections with the Communist Party of India. Many of the serious academicians across the country, both in the sciences and social sciences, were members of the Communist Party of India. What went wrong was that many of the excellent ones were not appointed and mediocrity had begun to creep in.

After protracted negotiations, the second set of invited scholars were ready to join now: Prof. Yogendra Singh for sociology, Bhabani Sengupta in international politics, Randhir Singh for the Centre for Political Development and Dr Debabar Banerji for community health. Susnigdha Dey who taught Spanish in the Delhi University was invited to start a Spanish department in JNU. The wheels were set in motion and, following the initial set of invitations and appointments, the vice chancellor began to expand his horizon. Within a year, he invited Bipan Chandra, a historian from the Delhi University who was emerging as a leading voice of Marxist interpretation of history, and K.K. Subramanian, a science policy scholar.

Rajarshi Majumder, an expert in biochemistry who taught at the New York University Medical School's department of biochemistry and had been working on protein synthesis, one of the most significant emerging fields, received an invite to join JNU.[51] Soon, another young leading scientist, plant biologist, Sipra Guha-Mukherjee, teaching in the United States, was sent feelers and she agreed to come back along with her husband N.P. Mukherjee, a mathematician and an alumnus of University of Delhi. She had worked with B.M. Johri of Delhi University and her Ph.D was on 'Tissue Culture of Onion'. She was one of the originators of the technique for production of haploid pollen plants through anther culture using *Datura innoxia* as experimental material during 1964–66 while working at the laboratory of S.C. Maheswari (another of Johri's students and son of the legendary Panchanan Maheswari, founder of the botany department at the University of Delhi in 1949). Earlier, another promising student of Maheswari, Sudhir Sopory, also joined JNU; he had given the arid, rocky and almost waterless Aravali lands focus as a sub-field in science. Sipra Guha-Mukherjee and Sopory, therefore, connected the rich plant-breeding efforts by Indian botanists with the new university. G.S. Singhal, another life scientist, was also appointed.

Offers went to some very dynamic young scientists, namely, R.K.S. Chaganti, a Harvard Ph.D with Mangeldorf, the crop geneticist, Pradman K. Qasba, a young pharmaceutical graduate from Pilani,[52] and K.M. Jayaraman Menon, an emerging biochemistry scholar working in the Medical Research Council of Canada at the time.[53]

Some other appointments had taken place in key areas and in regular areas in the institutions that the university had inherited, namely, the Indian School of International Studies and the Institute of Russian Studies. Dhanpat Rai was brought as an officer on special duty to start the library.[54] Girija Kumar, who had earlier been working as assistant librarian, was confirmed, and he maintained the library of the School of International Studies.[55] Rahmatullah Khan was selected for international law; he and Mohammad Ayoob were appointed at higher levels as associate professors.[56] Although P.C. Verma was selected for Pakistani studies, he turned it down and the post then went to I.N. Mukherjee, an economist from Patna.

Significantly, geography saw a number of appointments which may be credited to Moonis Raza's initiative. In political geography, R.C. Sharma was appointed. C.R. Pathak, who had emerged as the most articulate scholar on regional geography, was also appointed to develop the centre while K.P. Dhurandhar was given charge of cartography, and Atiya Aziz who was with town and country planning also joined the JNU team. In history, leading medieval history scholar, J.S. Grewal, Suvira Jaiswal for history of religion and B.D. Chattopadhyaya for epigraphy, numismatics and ancient Indian history were appointed, and they were the best in their generation. Grewal, however, declined. These were some of the best appointments that ever happened in India's academic history.

It is an irony that some of the faculty who were appointed lent their names to the new university and yet their very eminence became an impediment to the building of strong academic centres. A prime example of this phenomenon was that of Sisir Gupta. He had been the finest scholar to develop the foreign policy studies and also South Asian studies. Not only was he an expert on the foreign policymaking processes but was also of an immense scholarly disposition. His work on Pakistan published in the early 1960s has not been surpassed even today.[57] However, when he took leave in 1972 to become India's ambassador to Vietnam, his absence meant that the development of the university's Pakistan and South Asia Studies departments was adversely affected. In the social sciences, Satish Chandra was soon invited to be the vice chairman of the University Grants Commission. His absence meant that the medieval component of the history department could not have the direction that Nurul Hasan and the other founders had hoped for.

Parthasarathi was not a man of academic science but he brought the best scientists to his selection committees. V. Ramalingaswami, one of the best-known figures in the field of medical sciences in India and abroad provided the vision plan for JNU. He also sat through many selection committee meetings. The uniqueness of Parthasarathi's attitude was to respect people's worth and this bred a sense of democracy which infused the entire institution. It became easy for people to forward names for different positions without being made to feel like they were asking for special favours. Unlike this day and age when the vice chancellors arrogate to themselves all possible 'knowledge', Parthasarathi did not need to voice his opinion on each and everything. Increasingly however, opinion, judgements and knowledge seem to be free-flowing and this has a devaluing impact on research.

Parthasarathi felt it was more important to assure himself of the quality of the potential faculty rather than focus his attentions on the selection committee. He diplomatically conducted his inquiries about the credentials of the applicants before proceeding to persuade him or her to join the university. There were demands from the historians for a centre for economics. When Parthsarathi realized that he was going to have the Centre for Political Studies, he did not lose time to act upon the suggestion that Krishna Bharadwaj was the best person to start a centre for economics as the Delhi School stalwarts were not very keen. He invited her to join the university even before the centre came into being. Parthasarathi was informed about the young and brilliant Amit Bhaduri whom the radical social scientists were very keen to have on board. While Parthasarathi ruminated about this young scholar, he met K.N. Raj at a dinner event where Raj mentioned in passing his plan to appoint Amit Bhaduri to the Centre for Development Studies (Trivandrum). This crystallized Parthasarathi's opinion and he promptly appointed this student and colleague of Joan Robinson.

Most of those who were interviewed by the selection committee as young candidates remember the genteel, protective and reassuring figure of Parthasarathi. This has, over the years, notwithstanding a couple of bad years, remained one of the best traditions in the institution.

One person who knew GP and JNU well, Dr Manmohan Singh, remembered how the former conducted his meetings which he thought was worthy of emulation.[58] According to Dr Singh, Parthasarathi ensured that the selection committees brought out the best in the candidates. In the process, he never forced his views on members, yet he knew how to guide the deliberations 'gently but purposefully'.[59] Giving an example of a friend of his, a famous biologist whom Parthasarathi wanted in JNU, Manmohan Singh remembered how the latter went out of his way to cajole and persuade him to come and join the university.[60]

In some areas, however, there was the perceptible role of the education minister, Nurul Hasan, a father figure among intellectuals, who was also close to P.N. Haksar, D.P. Dhar, P.N. Dhar and others, who were close to the prime minister's policymaking group. Several members of the Communist Party of India found their way into the university in this early phase due to this combined influence. Some of them could not justify their being in a new and ambitious university as they neither grew academically nor did they allow the department to grow lest there be any competition.

Most of the appointments, barring some exceptions however, were made via the pool of a newly emerged, indigenous intelligentsia and, by the mid-1960s and the 1970s, a majority of them belonged to the leftist persuasion. Even those who are now considered torch-bearers of liberal tradition were closely tied with the socialist tradition. Most of them articulated, albeit in a professional manner, the coming of age of social science and historical research in India.

Appointments, notwithstanding some later criticism, were some of the finest, and the history of the university would prove that they were able to set a worthy tradition of scholarship. There was also an interesting trail of failed applicants who went on to become arch-enemies of the faculty of JNU. This in turn created enormous problems for the JNU students who faced, to their dismay, an antagonistic selector or interview panel particularly in Delhi University. The rising tide of Marxist history and political science swept over Delhi University as well. The internecine war within the left was more to do with jobbery than with ideology.

Another issue which Parthasarathi had to contend with was incorporating certain institutions which were either in the original targets set for the new university or stipulated by the international agencies and the power brokers in academic policymaking. As this required the delicate touch of a diplomat, Parthasarathi did well and began by bringing the three directors of three key institutes based in Delhi—All India Institute of Medical Sciences, the Indian Institute of Technology and the Indian Agricultural Research Institute—to arrive at an understanding. His Tamil background appeared to be working in his favour. V. Ramalingaswami of AIIMS and M.S. Swaminathan of IARI were enlisted into key roles in the new university. Swaminathan and Ramalingaswami were not only part of the advisory group for the sciences, they belonged to the university's executive council as well. The nation-making agenda was also getting under way.

By the end of 1973-74, Parthasarathi might have been experiencing a burnout as he was simultaneously working hard for the university and working with the prime minister as her advisor. Perhaps, after the initial thrust, he looked forward to a successor who could build up the schools of environmental science and computer science. He had shown interest in B.D. Nag Chouduri, who he felt had the wherewithal and know-how to execute this role as he was a scientist and, as a member of the Planning Commission, had a fairly good understanding of the nuances. More importantly, he would be acceptable to the prime minister, who continued as chancellor and therefore kept a weather eye on the university.

Parthasarathi had successfully and strategically accommodated the Institute of Russian Studies into the new university. There was an effort by the Ministry of Education to start a Russian studies department and Chagla had tried to persuade the Indian mission in Moscow to start a dialogue on this line. One could see the pro-Soviet shift of forces which were not necessarily communist in their ideological orientation. However, when it became part of the JNU it was five years old, and had already developed a programme in teaching the language. It soon became the basis on which JNU could develop the teaching practices of language centres and provided the blueprint for language courses. It had a three-year course and the students were exposed to native speakers of the language. The Institute of Russian Studies which merged in JNU provided a group of trained teachers and a course outline which later helped set up the School of Languages at the new university.

In the meantime, applications for land and affiliations began to pour in. The first of these came from Vardhamana Trust to provide land in the campus. Then came the proposal to affiliate the National Defence Academy and granting defence officers JNU degrees.[61] The last proposal was to start a centre for north-east India.[62] Although the proposal to include the School of Planning and Architecture (SPA) was seriously considered, for technical reasons it could not fructify and JNU rejected the terms and conditions of the school's offer.[63]

Even before the setting up of the university, one of the issues that provoked long debates in parliament was the incorporation of different institutions such as the Indian Institute of Mass Communication, the Indian Institute of Public Administration (IIPA), the All India Institute of Medical Sciences (AIIMS). The two institutes that were discussed during the early stages were the Centre for the Study of Developing Societies (CSDS) and the Indian School of International Studies (ISIS).

The CSDS discussions were somehow diffused and melded with the deliberations for a centre for political development and proposed Rajni Kothari as member of the advisory body. A detailed terms of negotiations were framed for absorbing the CSDS, according to which the research staff and the administrative staff would have been absorbed in the University.[64] However, there might have been some reservations as many research staff in CSDS did not have requisite qualification to become senior faculty as per the generally accepted norms in the university system. So, probably, their interest must have waned [65] and there was no mention of the CSDS again.

JNU needed to have an international studies department as per Chagla's vision and, although Parthasarathi had also wanted this included in the JNU programme, he was not impressed with the academic and policy output of the existing School of International Studies and wanted one de novo. Although M.S. Rajan, one of the school's earliest members, compiled the documentation for the school's merger with JNU, and mentioned that this collaboration was inevitable, it was Parthasarathi and Gopal's presence which forced this decision on JNU. From the very beginning, Parthasarathi was interested in integrating a new centre for international politics, diplomacy and disarmament into JNU and Gopal was just as keen on a unit dedicated to the study of international history and relations. By 1969, Indian School of International Studies had become a burden on the government and the plan was to dovetail it into a new institutional framework.

The JNU had pivotal appointments at other levels as well. K.D. Dhasmana, M.L. Sobti, R. Natarajan and S.G. Puthli were absorbed at the administrative officers' level. A young professional, P.N. Sharma, who had been an understudy to Prof P.V. Kelkar, the director of IIT Kanpur, was brought in as the coordinator of JNU. Having seen one of the best institutions being built and having had the experience of other educational establishments during his travels, Sharma had an understanding of how to build an institution. The coordinator was JNU's contribution to the academic lexicon in an Indian university as the coordinator took care of academic recruitments and other serious matters and therefore served as the buffer between the vice chancellor and the faculty in academic matters. Although this coordinator became the cynosure of political demonstrations later in the history of JNU and was targeted by the left-wing students and faculty, he retained his heightened sense of professionalism at all times.

Parthasarathi also appointed the first six stenographers in JNU who later went on to become officers of the university by the 1980s. They were: N. Balasubramaniam, O.P. Khera, Ramesh Kumar, Jagdeesh Lal and V. Raghunathan, who were the lifeline of the new order and all of them proved equal to their task in their various capacities.

With the schools beginning to function, the dean was the chief point of reference. Some members of parliament, during their deliberations, had aired their apprehension that the dean would undermine democracy in the new university. However, this fear was unwarranted. In many universities across the world, deans were appointed despite contestation; these deans provided an independent and representative character to the institution vis-à-vis the vice chancellor and the administration. However, it also has the drawback of dividing the school almost vertically.

Chagla presented a fait accompli: the statute 7(1) ordained that 'every dean of a school of studies shall be appointed by the vice chancellor for a period of three years and he shall be eligible for reappointment'.[66] It was bitterly opposed by Mukut Bihari Lal who thought it sounded undemocratic.[67] And P.N. Sapru, who had been supportive of all the innovations and novel experiments proposed in the JNU Bill, was also not very happy with the idea.[68] Chagla's argument was that since it was not a rank outsider, or he (the minister of education), but the vice chancellor himself who would appoint the dean, there would be no sacrifice of autonomy. Chagla brought back the original idea of trust into the discourse and argued that one needed to trust a good vice chancellor to appoint 'a first class man to be the dean'. In this there was no violation of the autonomy of the university.[69]

Though this did not completely mollify Lal, Sapru and the others who had objected, it abated the debate for a while. Significantly, the first dean of the School of Social Sciences happened to be Satish Chandra proving Chagla right once again that a first-rate vice chancellor would appoint first-rate deans. The university soon adopted the rotation system for appointment of deans in line with Triguna Sen's suggestion to the joint committee.[70] Sen had also indicated that the registrar ought not to officiate as the vice chancellor, but that it should be the dean's duty; the seniormost dean would gradually absorb and obviate the registrar's role in the academic administration of the university.

The rectorship was a German academic tradition and generally not found in the Anglo-American university system. It was also a theological college tradition and prevalent in the Latin areas. Even the parliamentary discussion regarding this post was handled with kid gloves, as it was created for JNU in an effort to do away with the posts of pro-vice-chancellor and pro-chancellor both of which had proven to be disastrous failures in AMU and BHU. As for the objections raised in the House regarding the number of rectors for JNU, Chagla had explained that this provision in the JNU Bill was merely an enabling clause.[71]

The Land Has Been Settled

G. Parthasarathi retired on 27 April 1974 and was succeeded by B.D. Nag Chouduri who joined the university as the second vice chancellor on 30 April 1974. Parthasarathi was a perfectionist in every aspect, especially with the setting up of the JNU departments, and left no stone unturned to ensure he got none but the best people to man the posts. He was, however, working with a handicap—as he did not belong to the academia he had to rely heavily on others for suggestions and advice, and it was not merely a matter of cross-checking or ascertaining a few points.

In the disciplines of social sciences this wasn't very difficult, but in the science field where the top scientists and the best available talent in Madras, Bombay or Calcutta would refuse to leave their labs and be averse to moving base mid-career to join other institutions, it was going to be an uphill task. Parthasarathi could empathize with this reluctance to relocate and when he could not convince E.C.G. Sudarshan to start the system sciences at JNU, he did not pressurize him. Similarly in the life sciences, he allowed the expert group to advise him, which sometimes diminished the quality when some members of this 'expert group' took unfair advantage and appointed their kith and kin instead of the best.

Parthasarathi seemed to turn a blind eye to environmental science, and simply ignored it. He could see the importance of the community health and biomedical engineering projects and the need for scientists to sit with the community as part of their work. Probably this was why he wanted Nag Chouduri, with experience of the Planning Commission, science and technology establishments and also having political patronage, to be his successor. Also, Parthasarathi was probably instrumental in getting Haksar appointed chairman of the selection committee so that there would be no problem in ensuring a smooth transition.

B.D. Nag Chouduri joined the university at a time when the political climate of the country and the nature of student politics were moving into a new phase, and he faced the first blast of it soon after he joined the university. Just as Parthasarathi seemed to have designed, it fell on Nag Chouduri to take the initiative to start the science department. The life sciences had already begun functioning and Nag Chouduri began the process to start the theoretical and environmental science programmes. The hurdles were structural in nature in the sense that one was starting a programme that was essentially interdisciplinary, and it proved difficult to find people already entrenched in their work to shed their disciplinary orientation.

The University Grants Commission had restricted its input and was prepared to provide for only fifteen positions and the university was finding it hard to get capable people willing to transfer to JNU's environmental sciences.[72] It was in this melee that a physicist's personal inclination made Nag Chouduri's to design a physics department, and again environmental science was left in the cold. Nag Chouduri began work on the computer science department, which was already halfway ready, and this became operational in the mid-1970s. The university was more or less born on the rocks of the Aravalis.

By the end of 1970, one saw a large number of people in place. By 1972, the faculty strength had gone up to 182 from 135, and this meant more incumbents in the JNU quarters and hostels as many professors were given accommodations in the hostels. Moonis Raza, Satish Chandra, Yogendra Singh, Bipan Chandra and Sivatosh Mookerjee joined the university's living quarters. It would be another year when many more would join and the dreary desert of Aravali would play the role of muse. The young faculty would live in the blocks of the old campus. Many of the teachers and staff who had left their Delhi University jobs to join JNU, and there were quite a lot of them, remained quite keen to stay in touch with things there, and this desire made them develop a housing society in west Delhi near the Haryana border. The JNU bus would go to all conceivable libraries, including the Delhi University library, and therefore the connection was retained.

The initial working space for the new recruits was in the Vigyan Bhawan, which in a way incubated many ideas and blueprints. With the new programme in operation, the university began to shift to the National Academy of Administration (NAA) campus where community living and desire to establish something fresh enthused people. The living in this part of the Aravalis was extremely tough for almost everyone. However, the dream of a novel institution coming up was what made them put up with the rigorous conditions. With each new recruitment, newer people began to inhabit the campus and to evolve new ethos for community living.

6

Antedating the Dream: School of International Studies

G. Parthasarathi who had seen the art of diplomacy from close quarters was aware that diplomacy was quickly moving into a much more specialized and rigorous genre and was therefore keen to start a new centre, particularly a department of disarmament studies.[1] S. Gopal too was keen to have a department of international studies and more particularly a centre for disarmament studies. In his memo on the history department, Gopal stated that a disarmament studies department, which would 'have to draw upon the other departments of social studies and sciences' should be a priority.[2] 'Whether disarmament studies should be developed in a separate department of the Jawaharlal Nehru University or in association with the Indian School of International Studies is a matter which will require careful consideration.' 'I myself would favour', he opined, 'its study in a department of the university.'[3]

When the Academic Advisory Committee in their second meeting, held on 29 August 1969, considered a proposal regarding the establishment of a School of International Relations and Diplomacy, it was suggested that the university should establish a working relationship with the Indian School of International Studies.[4] This was to avoid unnecessary duplication and to save resources. Although Parthasarathi was not too happy, he went along with the idea so as to avoid a good deal of expenditure by not 'duplicating facilities which already exist' in the ISIS.

The Academic Advisory Committee also decided to constitute the working group for the centre of disarmament studies, which included Dr S. Gopal, Dr K. Krishna Rao and Dr Vikram Sarabhai. Later on, the administrator-turned-strategic-expert, Shri K. Subrahmanyam, was co-opted to this group. The working group met on Monday, 22 September 1969, but unfortunately, Vikram Sarabhai could attend neither this nor any subsequent meeting. The meeting took place at 4 p.m. with the vice chancellor too being present. It began by endorsing the idea that detailed studies of disarmament problems should be organized in the Jawaharlal Nehru University.[5] While various aspects of the subject were studied in various departments of government and by some non-official bodies, nowhere in India was disarmament studies, in its entirety, undertaken. However, disarmament studies would have to start from scratch and this raised some special problems.

The group felt that disarmament studies should be split into various heads: the history of disarmament negotiations since 1919 and independent India's role in them, especially since 1954; the various aspects of the problem of arms control and the efforts since 1870 to secure this. This would be studied under five categories:

1. conventional arms,
2. nuclear arms,
3. chemical and bacteriological weapons, and arms deployment in the oceans and in space,
4. weapons technology and its impact on disarmament and arms control; current negotiations on disarmament and the efforts to create security systems, with special reference to India and the stability of Asia; economic aspects of disarmament with special reference to India, and
5. the legal aspects of disarmament.

The group favoured setting up an interdisciplinary team for research and collection and analysis of relevant data at the centre for disarmament studies. During these discussions, Gopal thought it would be a good idea to include the Indian School of International Studies (ISIS), but Parthasarathi, although keen to have international studies, objected to this plan even though he was very much part of India's diplomatic and international political scenario and known to the school. Gopal, who, during his long stint as director of the historical division of the Ministry of External Affairs, had been invited to be a member of the academic advisory body of ISIS, and therefore had a bit of understanding of the strengths and weaknesses of the school, advised the new university to have a relationship with the school.

The Beginnings

The Indian Institute of International Affairs was brought into existence by the British Government in the 1930s. But it was a colonial enterprise; it was extremely non-representative and composed of members from the Indian ruling aristocracy. Upon closer examination, it is clear that the institute was merely a forum set up by the British and restricted to close associates: the local native rulers and loyalists, who affirmed the decisions of the colonial bureaucracy and the British Parliament. It was organized along the dominion lines and as was peculiar to all colonial institutions, 'it would give no opinion' and rather 'disseminate knowledge' which meant the policies taken at the highest realm of government (colonial policies).[6]

The idea of starting an independent organization in India for the objective study of international affairs was first broached in a circular issued on 24 August 1943 with the signatures of Hriday Nath Kunzru, president, Servants of India Society, and the Hon'ble P.N. Sapru, member, Council of State. They explained the idea thus:

> The war has stimulated active discussion, all over the world, of problems of post-war reconstruction based on national freedom and international collaboration. Such questions as:
>
> a. the application of the principles of the Atlantic Charter to all parts of the world;
> b. the future of dependencies and colonies with special reference to their political status and the economic and social interests of the indigenous populations;
> c. the establishment of an executive council on behalf of the United Nations for international purposes; and generally,
> d. the creation of machinery which would guarantee a lasting world peace, were receiving serious attention the world over.
>
> In view of the urgent need for a thorough study of the questions referred to above, and the importance of India being represented

> at any conference that may be held hereafter for their discussion by delegations capable of voicing the views and aspirations of the great majority of the people, the immediate establishment of an independent organization for the study of world affairs is necessary.[7]

The Indian Council of World Affairs might have been the Indian intelligentsia's response to the Indian Institute of International Affairs. The aims and organization of the council were nationalistic and, like the Indian National Congress, it wanted to disseminate knowledge of international affairs among the common people. In pursuance of this vision, Pandit Kunzru followed the model of the Servants of India Society and opened branches of the council all over the country. It seems there was not much of a revenue model for the institution and it depended on the support of the people, and later on the government. Many colleges and educational institutions were institutional members of the council and many researchers were sent invitations to attend the council lectures and seminars.

The circumstances under which the council was established are not very clear except that A. Appadorai and Kunzru played key roles. Appadorai, a historian who earned his doctoral degree with his thesis, 'Economic Conditions in South India, 1000–1500 AD, in the '1930s, had shifted to Delhi and gradually helped set up the council. The council was formally inaugurated in New Delhi on Sunday, 21 November 1943, with Tej Bahadur Sapru as president. The stated objective was to develop a policy of study and research by its own members, recognized research scholars and institutions in the country. While the officers and a majority of the members should be non-officials, to enable the council to build up a reputation as an authoritative body engaged in objective study free from official influences, the council would also have some officials among its members; indeed the knowledge and experience of many officials would be a great asset to the council.

The close association of the Saprus assured the institution its life and, in its initial years, even the property to start its operations from. Beginning with the modest address of Kasha House, in Connaught Place, the council was able to build an imposing edifice in the heart of Delhi. The building was constructed at a cost of Rs 8,39,128 approximately (of which until 1955 only Rs 7,14,795-4-5 could be collected) with money donated by a large number of people from across the country The new building was inaugurated by Nehru in 1955. Nehru had donated Rs 500 towards the construction. Its publication, *India Quarterly*, soon become an important organ of international affairs. The council also spread its dissemination activities through its branch organizations located in Ahmedabad, Allahabad, Amritsar, Bangalore, Bhavnagar, Bombay, Calcutta, Cuttack, Gwalior, Kanpur, Lucknow, Madras, Nagpur, Patna, Poona, Simla and Waltair.[9]

The idea of having a teaching-cum-research institute by the council finally gave shape to the Indian School of International Studies in the mid-1950s.

Emergence of a Discourse

On 3 October 1955, the vice-president of India formally inaugurated the Indian School of International Studies started by the Indian Council of World Affairs. Gradually, the ISIS had eleven departments and a big establishment. It had forty faculty members, thirty-seven research staff and forty-seven administrative and secretarial staff. The University of Delhi had decided to affiliate the school to the university, including preparing candidates for the Ph.D degree. A. Appadorai, who was the moving force of the council along with Kunzru, became the first director and professor of international relations. A number of distinguished people were part of its faculty. Sardar K.M. Panikkar, who had become a household name after becoming India's first ambassador to China in those turbulent times and who had also written a couple of books, was the professor of South Asian history and institutions. A distinguished Japanese scholar, K. Enoki, was its professor of East Asian studies. A. Aleem, a much respected scholar of Arabic in Aligarh Muslim University, was the professor of West Asian studies, while B.R. Chatterjee was professor of South-East Asian Studies. A student of D.G.E. Hall, the acknowledged master of South-East Asian history, Walter Sudan Desai, whose work on Burma had just been published, was brought in as a teacher of Burmese when Burma was still very crucial in the international scheme of things. P.K. Sircar taught geography and R. Gopalakrishnan was engaged to teach international law. A dynamic young man, Vidya Prakash Dutt, who had come back from Stanford University with a degree in international studies and a commitment to Marxism joined another Marxist scholar, K.P. Karunakaran, who was working on the political philosophy of Indian nationalism, as research associate at the Indian Council of World Affairs (ICWA), the parent body of the school.[10] A young scholar, M.S. Venkatramani, who had received his doctoral degree in the United States, joined as a lecturer on American studies while some more distinguished people were enrolled as part-time faculty.

The main focus of ISIS was India's foreign relations. Its strength, however, lay in the in-depth study of societies on which an educated opinion on policies could be based. This provided a larger template for the analysis of foreign policy. Soon, therefore, area studies began to occupy a crucial place in the school's academic programme, and its major areas of research and publication were the institutions of the United Nations and Commonwealth relations. The school was lucky to have among its early staff V.P. Dutt, who initiated the study on East Asia and more significantly Chinese studies, along with Vishal Singh, who was intellectually engaged with the South-East Asian scenario.[11] M.S. Agwani gave shape to a new understanding of western Asia from the perspective of Indian policies.[12] The school could not start an African studies section as African studies was already in the process of being established in Delhi University. But it gradually brought in people like Ram Rahul who came to specialize in central Asia as well.

The fifties was an expansive phase for Indian foreign policy, and its presence in major or even minor events of consequence in the world counted. Area Studies, therefore, began to define the school. Speaking to graduates on the fifth convocation of ISIS on 28 May 1970, Appadorai announced that the institute was all set to develop experts in international studies.[13]

While this was true of the overall mosaic of the institute, two major disciplines, history and political science, began to define the academic behaviour of most of the scholars here. Political science in India began as a discipline in a colonial setting but the way the political discourse evolved was quite interesting. The earliest major works were historically inspired and had a close link with the larger intellectual quest in vogue, particularly outside academia, for example, contesting colonial assertions. The first three doctoral theses in the discipline, submitted to Calcutta University, were significant in terms of their topicality, substance as well as in terms of the manner in which Indian intelligentsia responded to colonial claims. Upendranath Ghoshal studied ancient Indian political theories, while Sasankjiban Ray worked on the theory of sovereignty for his D.Litt. from Calcutta University in 1922, a decade after the university became a post-graduate teaching department. A year later, Narendranath Laha produced 'Ancient Indian Polity' for which he was awarded a doctoral degree in 1923.

In 1939, the year the Second World War broke out, some scholars met to form the Indian Political Science Association. The first few organizers were all historians like Tara Chand and Ishwari Prasad. This had a wider ramification as the discourse, which began on ancient Indian polity in the 1920s, was a response to colonial assertions that India did not have a central democratic polity.[14] However, with the deciphering of the Ashoka's pillar inscription in 1915 and identification of King Devanampriya with Ashoka, it changed the whole landscape of the ancient Indian polity. The confidence of the Indian intelligentsia was further boosted with the new discoveries of the Mohenjo-Daro and Harappa in the 1920s, which provided a new civilizational confidence to a people under servitude. Soon, the writings on the existence of the Ganarajya, republics in ancient time, helped the intelligentsia in countering arguments by the colonial administrators and the apologists of colonial power that because Indians lacked a democratic lineage their period under democratic tutelage would need to be extended. This was also the time when the national movement was entering a new phase and Mahatma Gandhi had already given the call for the non-cooperation movement.

The discipline of political science, or civics as it was called by the colonial academic bureaucracy, could not keep pace with the rapidly changing nationalist movement. The strictly monitored departments under the colonial regime would have had a role to play in this. The issues taken up for study were divorced from the political happenings of the time or were focused on very narrow administrative history.[15] The colonial university structure did not allow the constitutional development model to be upstaged by anything like the national movement or the study of ideologies like nationalism or Marxism or socialism. It was only in the 1950s that there were efforts in some places, particularly in the colleges and universities which were new and slightly less controlled than the ones like Calcutta, Bombay or Madras, to bring some discussion on socialism.

Writing in the late 1970s, a leading political scientist, V.M. Sirsikar, pointed out that 'the period 1947–60 was characterized by a general lack of interest in social science research in India'.[16] Compared to the eighty-three Ph.Ds awarded by all Indian universities combined during 1951–60, there were 285 Ph.Ds during 1961–70. This indicated a phenomenal growth in doctoral research as only twenty-one Ph.Ds were awarded in political science before 1951. During 1961–70, the ISIS came up and produced forty-nine theses, thirty-five of which were in political science, the largest in number. The second was Agra University with thirty-one, followed by Delhi with twenty, Lucknow with eighteen and Sagar with sixteen doctoral theses.

It was at this time that ISIS entered the scenario as a centre to study, research and advance ideas on foreign policy, area studies and international relations. Was it following an autonomous intellectual agenda? Most of its founding faculty were in fact self-taught in international relations, including area studies. Appadorai was a historian whose book, *Economic Conditions in Southern India* remains a classic.[17] M.S. Rajan, another initial member of the ISIS who came from outside academia developed himself first into an expert in commonwealth studies and thereafter an expert of non-alignment by sheer hard work anticipating the prescription of A.P. Rana that if 'formal training is not possible, it can be picked up from vast array of literature on the subject. This is not easy, but given enthusiasm, neither is it impossible.'[18] What helped them in this was also serious and continuous research work, which may not have been theoretically sophisticated and methodologically up to date, but indicated clear perceptions and focus at a time when leadership in these matters was also was quite educated and focused. Had India been a developed country or a first-world power, it might well have directed the discourse, notwithstanding the dissatisfaction of those who insisted that India's international relations lacked theory.[19]

Therefore, at a certain level, there seems to have been no major historical gap between the expansion of research in political science and the emergence of ISIS as a major centre for the study of political science. This had major implications. Apart from the empirical and liberal traditions that political science had imbibed, there was actually no ideological or serious methodological difference that would have separated international studies, area studies or political science. There was therefore not much difference if one shifted to international relations or foreign policy as one's area of research since it only implied expanding the horizon of the work, and could also, given space, articulate one's ideas like freedom or equality through analysing societies in the light of socialism, Marxism, nationalism and colonialism which were quite in vogue. Nationalism, for example, was the focus of the largest number of works at a time when political science itself was unable to evolve methods to analyse the movement. Similarly, a study of the Chinese revolution might have given many the space to articulate their perspectives on social revolution and, by critiquing the unsavoury side of communism, their faith in democratic transformation. The theoretical horizon was nationalism, colonialism and, significantly, communism. Some of the doctoral work by ISIS scholars, for example, 'Growth of Nationalism in India 1919–1928'; 'Political Philosophy of Indian National Movement'; 'Cambodian Independence Movement 1939–1955'; 'A Study of Indian National Army', etc., represent this mindset. Contrary to the latter-day argument of absence of theory in the work in area studies, the scholars at this time had shown that nationalism and anti-colonialism or Marxism were not so distant from abstract theoretical paradigms.

History, as a discourse, was almost a century and a half older than international studies. It had its own contours and evolved its own identity by challenging colonial discourse. It had a global perspective as it was in many ways reading the colonial history until it began to counter it. In the process, it had evolved certain presuppositions with serious ramifications: the Afghan war, the coming of the nation, the idea of British rule and the character of colonialism and the British Empire. It is here that history had a complete universe and therefore, for a historian, many aspects of international studies looked fragmented, and a bit sketchy. International studies in India adopted, quite often uncritically, anthropological categories from American discourse, for example, ethnicity. The first major work by an Indian scholar, which employed the category of ethnicity, was Urmila Phadnis in her book *Ethnicity and Nation Building in South Asia*.[20] Nationalism, colonialism, communism, etc., were categories and ideas that historians dealt with in international studies. However, with the ascent of the American influence in international studies, research and patronage witnessed efforts to exorcise the discipline of these concepts, words and ideas, to conform to the practices and ideas of American international and area studies.

Area Studies: The American Trajectory

The American political establishment after the Second World War encountered a vexing problem. The United States was the new power in the world and yet, many areas of the world, which were going to be affected by the new world power, were not known to the people and policymakers in the United States. The enterprise of knowledge production, therefore, was taken up in earnest by all stakeholders in the new power—the corporations, the political establishment and the universities. The National Defence Education Act (NDEA), Title VI, provided considerable finance, around $206 million between 1958 and 1973, to universities to 'start language institutions and centres to ensure' trained manpower of sufficient quality and quantity to meet the national defence needs of the country.[21] The foundations, closely associated with corporations, also contributed their resources.[22] The Rockefeller Foundation was the first and, between 1934 and 1942, it spent $1 million for language and area studies, which was increased manifold after the war to support military research.[23]

Carnegie Endowment also contributed around $2.5 million during 1947–51 as grants to universities and research councils.[24] The rationale for supporting the study of international relations was offered by its president John Gardner: '... the peace of the world now seemed to depend upon the development of a "sagacious and consistent foreign policy" by the United States, but, in order for American leaders to carry out such a policy, it would have to be grounded and supported in public opinion.'[25] This implied a mission for the Carnegie Corporation 'to educate 130,000,000 people', which made the educational system crucial. It required the training of a corps of university teachers, which, in turn, necessitated augmenting the stock of basic knowledge on these subjects and increasing the number of experts in them. The programme of the Carnegie Corporation in international affairs in the 1940s generously supported research in the study of international relations and helped develop many centres such as that for Japanese studies at the University of Michigan, South-East Asian Studies at Yale, Near Eastern Studies at Princeton and South Asian Studies at the University of Pennsylvania. The major undertaking of the programme, and the most generously supported, was the Russian Research Centre at Harvard (it received 23 per cent of the total grant).

Significantly enough, there was avoidance of social sciences and direct support to international studies or area studies. Foundations—Rockefeller, Carnegie and Ford predominantly—were there to solve practical problems. Foundations helped new departments and programmes which did not exist earlier. From 1950 to 1973, the Ford Foundation gave $278 million for area studies.[26] Ford Foundation, for example, invested $30.5 million during the period between 1959 and 1967 into the study of contemporary China.[27] Programmes in area studies succeeded in increasing the stock of scholarly knowledge about those parts of the world.

The 1960s exposed area studies as a major tool of intervention, and the political establishments, the state departments and Central Intelligence Agency (CIA) were accused in many cases, particularly in 1967-68, of using area studies knowledge and personnel to subvert academic and political discourse in Asia, Africa and Latin America. The exposés in the *Rampart* magazine and the *Newsweek* about how many universities in the United States closely linked themselves to the American state's cold war projects brought disrepute primarily to the area studies experts.[28] The matter came to such a head that the discipline itself came to be viewed with suspicion.

In India, for example, the political atmosphere was agog with news of penetration by the CIA into Indian educational institutions. The effort by the two governments to ink a US–India educational treaty was aborted at the last moment when the Indian political and intellectual establishments protested vehemently. The fact that the Indian School of International Studies had also taken funds for some of its projects from American foundations with dubious links made the ISIS vulnerable to such attacks at a time when it was trying to bring area studies into the orbit of the university structure. The ISIS somehow weathered the storm and, by 1970, managed to keep afloat as a stand-alone institution. Its merger with JNU provided it a new lease of life. In both its lives—pre-JNU and JNU—it was area studies which provided it with its lifeblood.

Institute or University: Contest for a Site for Area Studies

In India, Indian Council of World Affairs (ICWA) had emerged out of the nationalist inspiration to disseminate the nationalistic point of view as against the colonial 'Chatham House' views. By the 1950s and early 1960s it increased its spread to a larger world mostly with the support of the government except for some collaboration from the Carnegie Corporation when it wanted its help. This was the time of expansion in the realm of area studies as well. In 1954, the African studies department was started in Delhi University, and by 1964, India had Japanese and Chinese studies in Delhi, South-East Asia studies in Andhra University and South Asia studies in Rajasthan University. A move to locate area studies within the universities had begun. Noteworthy was the attitude towards the ISIS which was a stand-alone, degree-awarding centre but reliant on the government for finances. The Shiva Rao Committee which was appointed to recommend the possible course of action about area studies in Delhi University, and that of the ISIS, in fact, recommended that the African studies centre in ISIS was not necessary as the one which Delhi University already had was not doing well at all, indicating (albeit not explicitly) a gradual shift to the universities as the possible site for area studies.[29] The Shiva Rao Committee report and the response to it indicated an estranged relationship between the area studies centres and the universities. It suggested, much to the chagrin of ISIS authorities, that on many issues the ISIS should coordinate with the departments of the Delhi University.

While the school was hit where it hurt—its area studies programme—the worst was yet to come. Finances from the Government of India, scarce as they were, began to shrink further. The devaluation of the rupee and the famine had left a deep scar on the economy and it was at this juncture that a national seminar on organization of area studies was held in November–December 1967 at Delhi University. There was also a subcommittee appointed by the Academic Council of the University of Delhi. Both these bodies stressed that an area study programme should be deeply embedded in the various social science disciplines, its objective being to produce specialists of high quality in their respective disciplines. They also recommended 'provision of earmarked posts for the area in the concerned departments their work being coordinated through a centre devoted to the promotion of specialized studies in an area and not by creation of an additional or separate department of area study. The coordination work of this could be done by a committee of heads of the departments and should be associated.'[30]

Foreign policy

The Indian Council of World Affairs, with ISIS as the academic centre, tried to theorize India's foreign policy behaviour to help the bureaucracy and policymakers respond to certain basic contentions of international players. The fundamental premise of the foreign policy and international studies was 'power centric'. It was around the loci of power that reigning theories like realism, etc., came up in the area. It is here that the efforts of the council seemed to prepare an alternative to 'power-centric approaches to foreign policy'. In the deeply divided world of the cold war, Indian scholars, particularly the ISIS scholars who had developed links with American foundations and the universities, found to their chagrin that their perspective of the world, with no acceptance or avoidance of the mono-theoretical world of realism versus idealism which reigned in the world of international relations, invited sharp criticism. Their foreign policy regime of non-alignment was stigmatized as cloaking national interest, thereby negating any scope of going outside the power-centric approach that the scholars like Appadorai ventured to go.

Since June 1961, when the Central government accorded deemed university status to ISIS, the configuration within the school had begun to change. The Chinese war of 1962 also proved to be a watershed event for an institution that was specializing in international affairs and in a country where foreign policy until then was not left to what the American policy analysts (the policy elites) said. The Chinese war saw the deep cleavage between the left-leaning Nehruvian policy and a right wing that demanded a pro-American policy. There was also a major encouragement for international affairs, particularly in China studies. The socialists, the foremost critics of Nehruvian foreign policy, became very loud and the Jana Sangh and other pro-Americans also made their presence felt.[31] Therefore, from the mid-1960s, one saw a very interesting turn in the fortune of the school. V.P. Dutt, its scholar on China who had gone to work with Fairbank at Harvard and had in fact developed Chinese studies in the country, returned to set up the Chinese department in Delhi University. The other Marxist scholar, K.P. Karunakaran, had in the meantime emerged as the foremost scholar and the voice of an independent foreign policy for India.[32] He had already authored two volumes on India's foreign policy and had become a major contributor in the area. It was difficult for the government establishments, even in Nehru's liberal dispensation to let a communist occupy professorship of the most important think tank located in the capital. It had earlier not allowed K.M. Ashraf, the leading medievalist, to become a professor of history in Delhi University. Karunakaran was also denied the post of professorship. A confident Karunakaran resigned from the ISIS and went to Rajasthan University against the advice of many of his close friends. The ISIS recruited Bimla Prasad, an erudite scholar of liberal dispensation and with close relations with the socialist, Jayaprakash Narayan, as the professor at ISIS. Karunakaran went from institute to institute, with no stability of tenure and work, and India lost one of the most promising minds of international relations.

This was also the end of ISIS's association with Marxism. There were slight flirtations with socialism but no longer any strong ideological positions. Appadorai retired in December 1964 and became the member of the Union Public Service Commission (UPSC). Prof. Amiya K. Dasgupta, the seniormost professor was made the acting head for some time and then denied directorship, and M.S. Rajan, who was the administrative secretary, became its director. For many, it was a slight to them and particularly for Prof. Dasgupta.

Changing International Scenario

The international rivalry known as the cold war began to take an ominous turn with the Vietnam War turning ugly. Simultaneously, the communist movement was taking a new turn in China, and, estranged as it was from Russia now, it would take a more strident anti-American line and would also try to upstage the more balanced approach of Nehru at the non-alignment and other forums. The political voices at home were also sharper and divisions were along political lines. There were three critics of the Nehruvian foreign policy:

- The socialists were anti-Nehru on the Chinese question and, from the 1950s, they maintained a very strong opposition to Nehru's Tibet and China policy.
- The communists from the outset considered Nehru an American protégé although in the 1950s they had slightly slackened their accusations. However, soon, with the escalation of the situation in Vietnam, their anti-American position would again get articulated vociferously.
- The right wing and the Hindu communal groups had a pronounced American bias and they persistently accused Nehru of being pro-Russia and attacked his non-alignment as a hoax.

By the 1960s, this critique of foreign policy was nicely articulated by M.L. Sondhi in a pamphlet called, 'Want a national foreign policy'.[33] The Chinese aggression however changed the positions. The right and the socialists joined hands in attacking Nehru on China, while the communists were targeted by both. For Nehru, the imperative was not to let the attack turn into an all-out communist bashing which he always thought would be detrimental to democracy. The academic world was in crisis as the Marxist teachers were hounded out as were the communist cadres across the country.

By the mid-1960s, it was the anti-English agitation by the socialists in northern India that catapulted to the centre stage the already existing intellectual streams led by exceptionally brilliant leaders like Ram Manohar Lohia. It had in its armoury an intense dislike for the Congress and Nehru's foreign policy. Though socialist, it wanted India to take an anti-China position. In fact, the whole attack on Nehru's foreign policy was also an attack on the communists who were portrayed to be soft on the Chinese leadership. Ram Manohar Lohia's attacks were taken forward by the leaders like Surendranath Dwivedy, Kishen Pattanayak and others. It was at this time that the parliamentary attack began to focus on the ISIS. In 1965-66, the question was raised on not only the use of Hindi but also about the academic inefficiency of the institution. Researchers were personally attacked.[34]

The 1967–68 period was crucial: the foreign policy had taken an anti-American turn given the arm-twisting of India by the Americans for not endorsing the US attack on Vietnam. It came to a head when there were rumours of the CIA colluding with the Congress Syndicate and of the CIA being hand in glove with the socialists. Indira Gandhi swung to the left and within a year nationalized the banks and abolished the privy purses of Indian princes. All this meant that the old institutional foundation of the foreign policy regime was gone and a new era was to begin. In such a situation, ISIS was left high and dry with no affiliation, no finances of its own, and not much support with the new dispensation as most of the people it had lined up to champion its cause had been the old warhorses or those who no longer had any political base.

The debate on international affairs was, unlike as it happens today, not limited to some of the experts on international affairs. The political class was very much part of it and the debates between the socialists and the communists were quite often based on their analysis of foreign affairs. An increasing suspicion of the American intention, strengthened by the revelations that the CIA had a destabilizing role in many areas began to take root.[35] By 1967, when the Indian stand on West Asia and Vietnam was taken as a direct affront to the United States, it was clear that there would be pressure on India. It was at this juncture there were revelations that the ISIS had received Asia Foundation money. To top it all there were attacks by the socialists about the quality of research being done in the ISIS.

There were now arguments as to why the school did not have a Soviet studies centre. The director soon entered into a dialogue with the UGC requesting it to sanction posts in Soviet studies. But the credentials of the school were so dented that the UGC cold-shouldered these requests. This did not deter Appadorai, the director, from writing to the UGC chairman, Kothari, in March 1964 showing his 'keenness' to 'start the study of the Soviet History and Institutions'. He said that the institute had 'decided to start the study only after Indian scholars with an adequate knowledge of Russian had been trained in the subject, especially by study in the Soviet Union and acquiring first-hand knowledge of the country and its people'.[36]

The intent of the school was to promote its people who needed UGC-sanctioned posts and therefore the UGC was requested to sanction 'two posts of readers for the department of Soviet history and institutions', so that they could establish 'a full-fledged department of Soviet studies in our fourth plan period proposals'.[37] However, the UGC was unmoved. In its letter of 27 April 1966, the UGC said that while 'the commission agrees that the ISIS should continue to work on Soviet studies', it 'could not accept the proposal for the establishment of a department of Soviet studies'.[38]

A feeling of disillusionment became apparent in the institute. With no parallel employment or resources available, the pressure of an autonomous institute working wholly on government finances and relying on government support (which was unforthcoming), was now beginning to tell. Attacks from the socialists, exactly at this time, who, taking their cue from the supposed anti-Hindi stance of the school manifested by its apparent refusal to entertain Ved Prakash Vaidik's thesis written in Hindi, became lethal. One of the attacks was directed at the 'sub-standard research that the school produced'. On 31 March 1967, members of the Rajya Sabha charged the 'ISIS with receiving a lot of money from the CIA'.[39] Calling it 'totally untrue', an aggrieved Kunzru wrote to the minister of education, Triguna Sen, inviting him to the institute. Accepting that the institute received money from the Ford and Rockefeller Foundations in the past, he argued that the government of India had also accepted American financial help for those 'purposes which were acceptable to both of them', and Kunzru pointed out that the institute also received financial help from the Asia Foundation with the approval of the government. He insisted that they had received 'no assistance from the CIA either directly or indirectly'.[40]

Dark Clouds

In 1966, the estimates committee of the Lok Sabha came out with its report which added to the problems of the institute.[41] The report accused the school of accepting foreign funding—the bulk of this had come from Ford Foundation and the Rockefeller Foundation.[42] The committee commented adversely on the grants from Asia Foundation which included a grant of Rs 18,000 for a scholar's study trip to Sri Lanka.[43] Urmila Phadnis (nèe Bery), a student of political science, had worked in the Banaras Hindu University on the topic 'States' Integration into Indian State'. An extremely diligent researcher, she was appointed a reader in the South Asian studies department and began working on Sri Lanka. The school was having a funds crisis and Asia Foundation fellowships were available. Her Sri Lanka project had the ministry's approval.[44] However, this was the time when the fact that the Asia Foundation worked as cover for the CIA was discovered. It was denounced and attacked worldwide. The most aggressive in their attacks were the Communist Party of India and therefore many scholars personally became very anti-communist.

The parliamentary estimates committee also pointed out that the Indian Council of World Affairs dominated the Indian School of International Studies.[45] Soon there was a full-fledged discussion on the ISIS in the Rajya Sabha on 23 March 1968. The discussion pointed out anomalies in the school which included the fact that the director was the head of four departments. Hard on the heels of the estimates committee report came the report of the Chandra Reddy Committee. In January 1968, the Ministry of Education had appointed a committee under the chairmanship of Shri P. Chandra Reddy, the vice chancellor of Annamalai University. The other members of the committee were Prof. P.C. Chakravarty who was the head of department of Jadavpur University's international studies department, Prof. V.M. Dandekar, the director of the Gokhale Institute of Politics of Economics, and R.S. Chitkara, the deputy educational advisor in the Ministry of Education.[46] The committee was to recommend the amount of maintenance grant to be given to the institute.[47] The committee met four times in Delhi (27 January, 11 and 12 March, 3 and 4 June, and 3 October 1968), and also had meetings with the director and the heads of departments in the school.

The core issues that the committee tried to resolve were related to the institutional status of the ISIS as the advanced centre of international studies and its 'financial prudence'. The committee was sure that the ISIS was a special centre and as such its status needed to be expressly specified. However, the committee seemed inclined towards recommending that the ISIS should become a special centre like Delhi School of Economics, affiliated to Delhi University and yet retain its autonomy. The reason for this conclusion was the view that the best academic training in international and area studies can only be done by strengthening the core disciplinary training—a view which was at variance with that of the director of the institute itself, who defined international and area studies in deference to traditional disciplines.[48] According to the Reddy Committee, 'in order to achieve any real measure of depth and meaningfulness, studies in international relations and area studies must be academic-based, university-oriented and related to various academic disciplines and as such developed as a part of the university programme'.[49]

In a very poignant way the committee pointed out: '... the undertaking of area studies of the universities will, no doubt, lead to a progressive diminution of the school's uniqueness in the field of international studies; its responsibilities in the promotion of training and research in international studies will be more and more shared by the Indian universities. This loss of uniqueness however does not mean that the school can serve no useful purpose in future. Properly moulded it can, in our opinion, serve a very useful role by providing a model for university education in international studies and in assisting Indian universities to achieve excellence in the field.'[50]

On the administrative side, the committee felt that the institute should be re-affiliated to the Delhi University, but in the same breath, on academic consideration, thought that it should retain its present character but refrain from starting any new area studies, and consolidate. It may, if it felt the need, reorganize departments. The committee, however, found the institute quite profligate in its management of finances. It recommended slimming down the institute and consolidating its research and other affairs rather than spreading itself in an unwieldy manner. It found that the UGC had sanctioned the school sixteen research fellowships in the third five-year plan, most of them with the status and salary of lecturers in universities. The committee was appalled to find that these lecturer-type fellowships had been given in most cases to students of the school who could not even complete their doctoral dissertations in the course of their normal period of three to four years. The committee found this not only wrong in principle, but also that it introduced an invidious distinction between two sections of pre-doctoral students of the school—one section receiving normal scholarship or fellowship of the value of 250 or 300 rupees a month, the other receiving a lecturer's salary with allowances which may amount to about Rs 600. Significantly, the committee pointed out, these were offered, not as a reward for brilliant work, but for 'extraneous consideration'.[51] It asked the school to abolish them.

The other profligate ways of the school included a large number of research assistants attached to all heads of departments which the committee thought was 'not required'.[52] The school was found to be having a large number of secretarial staff which could not be justified, and it recommended retaining only forty-seven and reducing the staff in the long run. The committee also found the selection of the candidates not up to the mark.[53]

The report of the Chandra Reddy Committee completely demoralized the school. In August 1968, in another blow to the institute, the government placed a ban on placing more than a third of professors at a senior scale. Consequently, R.K. Khadilkar, A.D. Mani and Minoo Masani, members of the school's advisory board, the three most active people of the governing committee, were sent by the chairman to personally meet the prime minister, Indira Gandhi, and request her support and intervention.[54] They spoke to her about the controversies about the Indian School of International Studies.[55] Indira Gandhi asked them to send a note. In the note, they requested her to ask the education ministry not to freeze the budget at the 1967 level because this would prevent the growth of the institute. A.D. Mani met the prime minister again on 2 August 1968, and wrote to her on 3 August 1968 on the Ministry of Education's restriction and disapproval of placing more than one-third of its professors on the senior scale. He put the government order in perspective, and argued that this kind of order gives the government an undue say in determining the academic and the research work at an institute because following the trend, they would next want to decide which third would become professors and who would not. He did not see the ministry any more competent than the school to make such judgements. He also pointed to an eventuality where the professors of the school might look to the ministry for promotions bypassing the school authorities. Mani pointed out that these rulings would 'create unhealthy tendencies among the professors of the school and seriously affect discipline in the school and will also give a hand to the officials of the ministry in the internal academic affairs of the school. In effect, if not by intent, it would impinge on the academic autonomy of the school.'[56] He also spoke about the cut in the government's grant to the school for the current year of about Rs 3 lakh—the budget estimate of the school in respect of the year 1968-69 being Rs 15·14 lakh as against the ceiling placed by the Ministry of Education of Rs 12 lakh.[57] It was at this juncture of the life of the council and the school that JNU was coming up.

In 1969, when the governing committee met the education minister, it requested him to help the school tide over the financial crisis and provide it with autonomy. The minister assured the ISIS faculty that a final decision would be taken only after he had consulted every party in the case. It sounded ominous when he pointed out that the ministry was paying a maintenance grant to the school which was illegal. They were doing it because of a legal flaw in the UGC Act. According to the Act, only Central universities were entitled for the maintenance grant from UGC. He also told the ISIS representatives that the UGC Act was under review and a draft bill of amendments to the Act was pending before parliament. He was taking the opportunity provided by this hiatus to review the entire position with respect to institutions deemed to be of university status—whether such institutions should continue to exist as autonomous institutions or whether any changes were called for in their present position. He remarked that the constitutions of the deemed universities did not follow any particular model. He 'also felt that institutions deemed to be universities, could not, in fairness, enjoy greater autonomy than statutory universities. As an example of this he referred to the differing positions of a Visitor of the School and that of the Central universities.'[58]

Although he apologized for the government's error in accepting the recommendations of the Chandra Reddy Committee without giving a chance to the school to express its view, he made it equally clear that the government could not be bound by the views of the institution either.[59] He also asked the institute not to duplicate area studies like African studies and also to 'concentrate on the department of Asian Studies' rather than covering the entire world 'by developing European, the commonwealth, American, and studies on remote areas'.[60]

It was very clear that things were not going well for the school. The ministry was not ready to provide it finances and at the same time give policy exemptions. There were clear signs of a financial crunch[61] and there was no solution in sight with the parliament itself closely monitoring what it considered the ISIS's profligacy.[62] What was more damaging was the attack on what the leaders argued was the low and almost no standards that its scholarship displayed.[63]

The acute financial slump forced the council to clandestinely rent out its premises in 1969 to other organizations.[64] It was about this time that a new institution, Institute of Defence and Strategic Analysis (IDSA), came up in the rented premises. For this fledgling new institute, the scholars, the students and the sprawling library were a boon. The institute increasingly patterned itself after the school except that it was under the control of a strict bureaucratic regime that denied the academic institution any autonomy. The IDSA, under the directorship of Som Dutt and later K. Subrahmanyam, in due course emerged as a good policy institute but with a harsher and stricter regimented research climate, unlike the benevolent supervision of Kunzru, the dedicated servant of India Society.

ISIS joins JNU

It was serendipitous indeed that one of India's best diplomats was in charge of setting up of the Jawaharlal Nehru University while S. Gopal, the honorary advisor to the Ministry of External Affairs, was designing a centre to study diplomacy and disarmament. Gopal felt it was warranted that the university had a centre to study the disciplines as part of the contemporary history component. It was he who pointed out that the ISIS should be absorbed into the JNU to save unnecessary duplication and wastage.

The executive council of the new university at its meeting on 22 December 1969, approved 'in principle the proposal to take the Indian School of International Studies as a maintained institution of the university'.[65] It also 'authorized' the vice chancellor to conduct negotiation with the school 'in light of the discussions in the council'.[66]

The council felt that Indian School of International Studies 'could well form the nucleus of a school of international relations and diplomacy in the university'.[67]

Later the vice chancellor had a long talk with Pandit H.N. Kunzru, and on 30 December 1969 it was decided that:

- The society known as ISIS would stand dissolved and the assets and liabilities of the society would be vested in the JNU.
- The existing rights and service conditions of teachers, salaried officers and other employees of the school would be protected.
- The salaries would be according to the rules of the central university.
- There would be reorganization of the school.
- Location site of the ISIS would be reviewed as soon as the campus of the university developed.
- Existing arrangement of the library would be continued.
- Cooperation and suggestion with ICWA would be welcome.
- ... a board of management under the presidentship of Pandit Kunzru would deal with administrative problems involved in the taking over of the Indian School of International Studies by the university.[68]

The merger was complete with the signing of the agreement on 28 May 1970 and the university re-designated the ISIS as 'School of International Studies'. The notification issued showed JNU incorporating the school on and from 5 June 1970 with a resolution to change the statutes.[69] A reorganization followed which seemed to accept the recommendations given by the Chandra Reddy Committee. As a result of the reorganization, the new school had seven centres and seventeen divisions including two new centres, namely for diplomacy and disarmament studies. Parthasarathi, the mind behind the move, explained the nature and scope of the new centres in his inaugural address to the first summer school organized by the School of International Studies in March 1971. 'The main focus of the Centre for Diplomacy', he said, would be to study 'in depth the foreign policy of India'.[70] To him the 'foreign policy of a country was not a separate area of activity but part of its integrated national policy'.[71] In this, he hoped that the centre would make efforts to study political and economic trends and help redefine defence policy.[72] 'Disarmament studies', on the other hand, he thought would 'deal with problems of disarmament, including nuclear disarmament, arms control, problems of regional security, impact of technological developments on arms policy, economic consequences of disarmament'.[73] By 1971, JNU introduced an M.Phil. course, and by August 1973 an MA in international politics became one of the very first MA courses of the new university.[74] Parthasarathi took the initiative to ask for seventeen new faculty positions from UGC and followed it up.[75]

Many old-timers, including the directors of ISIS, did not like the reorganization but JNU was a godsend for the school in more ways than one. People who otherwise would not have made it to a university faculty now became full-fledged faculty of the new and prestigious university, and researchers who failed to make it into any good departments suddenly became scholars of a new Central university and in due course would become its faculty. The ISIS staff who had lived under tremendous stress after the Reddy Committee's recommendations to downsize the school, were now assured of university tenure and therefore the institute now reverted to profligacy in the new locale, without fears of financial cuts looming on their horizon any more. The ISIS would have petrified and splintered had it not come under the wings of the new university.

The Chronicle of a Death

When the ISIS become affiliated to the university, the Indian Council of World Affairs lost its flagship organization. 'Following the merge of the school with JNU early this year', the ICWA wrote to the Lt governor of Delhi seeking financial assistance as twenty-four out of thirty-four members of the university's library staff and nearly 20,000 volumes out of 55,000 belonging to the school were shifted by the university from Sapru House. Apart from the faculty that was key to the vibrant atmosphere of the ICWA, its research staff gradually diminished. Shivaji Ganguly got a research position in the USA and left.[76] Zafar Imam joined the Indian Council of Social Science Research.[77] Appadorai, the father figure, had been working on two research projects but left in June 1970.[78] The greatest loss, however, was the library, as JNU was to get the lion's share.[79] The bitter campaign to retain the library further weakened the position of the ICWA.

A bitter cold war to retain the library began to rage in the heat of a Delhi summer. It was finally agreed, after a negotiated settlement, that JNU would receive the books that belonged to the ISIS. Now the ICWA members decided to bring public pressure against the possible division of the library.[80] A delegation from the council which included Frank Thakurdas, Ram Ratan, D.R. Narang and Kunzru met the education minister, Nurul Hasan, on 16 May 1972. The council members were in a quandary when the minister asked for the reason for the delay in the delivery of the library. Nurul Hasan made it clear that 'the government had no obligation towards private institutions like the council but it was constitutionally responsible for looking after the interests of the JN University and other central universities'.[81] Hasan said, and quite correctly, that he needed to protect JNU's interest before assuring ICWA any assurance of assistance.

The Challenges of University Life

Though the ICWA was severed from its progeny, the ISIS, the researchers working there got a new lease of life in a different sort of institution, i.e., the university. The university provided them with a permanent station and freedom from financial constraints. For many, however, the university was a new domain with a lot of rules which seemed strange to them. The ISIS scholars were accustomed to gate-crashing international seminars but now the university made them participate only through the university, representing the university, which meant they had to take leave, etc., through due processes. And the university norms were more academic and perhaps this was why the first few applications for attending the conference by the SIS faculty, i.e., by Rajan and Vaidyanath were rejected by the executive council of the University. This new normative universe was in fact too much for them and this remained a long-term angst for the SIS faculty. New rules for visits of this nature were now in place.[82]

The new situation launched another series of problems. The scholars in the School of International Studies now felt the pressure to take cognizance of the social critique taking place in other departments like in the School of Social Sciences and also in the larger intellectual domain, the university. The new challenge was compounded when the university also acquired an oppositional or anti-establishment identity. The international relations scholars were not too happy with this new identity imposed on them by default as this damaged their professional life in India and abroad. As worse complexities in the Indian state were being exposed by the social scientists, there seemed to be fewer and fewer foreign policy formulations for which they could forward recipes. They found themselves unwittingly entrenched in power politics and a lobby-ridden existence, and they needed to vindicate their own position – all too problematic.

The second major issue which the new arrangement presented was the disciplinary problem. International relations was more or less a discipline guided and steered by the American state in its own national interests and had hundreds of books produced to make the discipline look more sophisticated in espousing critical realism. The most important approach of research has been to analyse how the Indian or for that matter the Third World elite arrived at making foreign policy decisions. The British as well as many European universities had a derisory attitude towards international or area studies and therefore the discipline, which was still trying to emerge, also faced the issue of academic dignity and, in a backward country, lacked the glamour that the international relations expert in an advanced country would attract. Any criticism of this would invite the opprobrium of being a cold war supporter or anti-American—which was neither a profitable nor a comfortable moniker for even non-political and academic reasons.

Soon however, the School of International Studies produced students who flooded the research institutes. The most notable scholars on India's international relations and foreign policy were from this school. The continuation of the colonial mindset, however, resulted in a constant struggle for the scholars, as foreign policy and international relations have close connections with the power elite who have close links with metropolitan centres of power and lobby and the latter try and position their own protégés in the departments of International Studies or Political Science and research institutions. The continued patronage of these elite provided a facelift for the school, unlike the locally produced scholars. In the area of international relations where many forces, both internal and external, are at work to influence research, the institutional setting of a university provides a cushion to a certain degree. Outside patronage however, had the effect of affecting the symmetry and academic well-being within the universities.

7

The Constitution of a Mainland

> As I drive around the campus now, I recall my first visit to the area on a scorching summer day. I stood with some colleagues on the highest point and surveyed the landscape—a scrubland with hardly a tree in sight. But it had a craggy charm of its own.[1]
>
> Entering the JNU gate for the very first time, however, did feel in a very strange way like I was coming home. ... Every time I was off campus outside in the city streets, I was tense, especially as it grew dark; but as the north gate loomed large and the noise from Ganga dhaba floated over, one felt safe and at home.[2]

During the debate on the JNU Bill in the Rajya Sabha, the Jana Sangh member, D. Thengari, had wanted a protective wall around Delhi University lest JNU encroached to affiliate its institutions.[3] The walls of brown rubble and stones, which eventually became the boundary walls of JNU, in fact were never uninviting. The once long trail of the walls by the early 1990s had either disappeared or shrunk as successive vice chancellors generously gifted lands to different institutions—both public and some privately inspired public institutions. This has led to the situation that entry into the university is now through many routes. Prof. Tara Chand, while debating on the nature of the university, indicated that there was a contradiction in that the university should live for hundreds of years but the general vision of the population constituting the university was not long term and, in this case, quite myopic. How true! The rubble walls, once many kilometres long, has shrunk to a bare minimum as many autonomous scientific institutions, reflecting the imperial annexation by science, increasingly usurped land from the university.

The Great Long Wall

When the first campus committee met, the walls were discussed, and the chairman of the campus committee, Padmaja Naidu, daughter of Sarojini Naidu, and erstwhile governor of Bengal, who had a keen eye for plants and landscaping, suggested that bougainvillea be planted along the compound wall wherever the rubble masonry was taken right up to the top. She recommended that the stones need not be cemented on the inside so that it would allow the creepers to hold on to the wall and go up to the top.[4] A scale drawing of the compound wall was made in consultation with Shri J.M. Benjamin, senior architect of Central Public Works Department (CPWD), and approved by the subcommittee for landscaping and horticulture headed by Padmaja Naidu. It was the consensus that the compound wall should be abutting the boundary of the JNU plot (which had a perimeter measuring nearly 28,000 feet) to avoid cattle and other domestic animals from straying into the compound and destroying the vegetation which was being planted by the directorate of horticulture. The compound wall was designed so that it would not block the view of the landscape—1'6" high random rubble wall with railing along the top for a height of 3'6" was considered the ideal proportion for the front where the buildings were to be constructed. As for the rest of the compound wall, the railing would be substituted by BRC fabric as in the offices of the defence headquarters.[5] The estimate for construction of the compound wall amounted to Rs 9,90,300 and was sanctioned by the Government of India.[6]

The main gate or the north gate—connecting the old and new campuses as well as the Munirka village, was planned along what came to be known as Baba Gang Nath Marg. The neighbouring Munirka village inhabited predominantly by Jat and Gujjar communities, had an ancient temple of Baba Gang Nath who belonged to the Nath Panth. The temple has grown big and is now quite visible at the junction where the road along the gate met the road which runs parallel to the western boundary of the university. The then puny little gate with the sleepy, khaki-clad security staff was always a welcoming sight. Most of the security staff were retired army jawans who were friendly and dignified and respected the dignity of students and staff. Immediately within the gates one would see people sitting on the pavements sipping tea and sometimes having 'samosas' from the lean-to shed that served as a little coffee shop, the Ganga Dhaba. The 'dhabas' went on to make some fascinating culinary innovations and inventions which, due to the lack of intellectual property rights regime, could unfortunately not be patented—bread pakodas, egg parathas, bread rolls. Soon, certain special brands evolved over time—Chacha's pakoda in the early 1970s, Madanji's tea, Francis's dosa and mango shake in the '80s, and Gopalan's fish curry meal in the '90s.

With bougainvillea bursting out of the rubble walls, the roads lined with amaltas looked glorious when they were in bloom. It is particularly magnificent at dawn during the summer months—which is otherwise pure hell with the heat of the rocky landscape spiralling the mercury to dizzying heights. The bus service was infrequent and one had to go to Outer Ring Road in Munirka to commute to other parts of the city, and resign oneself to the guaranteed disinclination of all the autorickshaw drivers to volunteer the services of their (faulty) meter-studded three-wheelers.

Although the JNU community was cast ashore like William Golding's children, unlike the island, goodness seemed to be trickling out. The city was ruthlessly arid, and full of the kind of crass Punjabi entrepreneurship which a Malayali, with a clannish compulsion for discourse on the latest debate emerging out of *Mathrubhumi*, or a Bengali, with his genteel elitism, found difficult to cope with. The campus was a haven for them. Moving to JNU for many meant coming to the mainland. Ensconced as they were in their class, region and ethnic shells, they suddenly found themselves at a place which held no meaning for all these virtual boundaries, and yet they could interact. For example, for a Punjabi youth from Chandigarh in 1971, names like Keya Deb or Avinash Wamanrao Rohankar or Syed Sahid Aakhtar Jaafri were completely alien, but the JNU ambience transcended the limited horizon of the particular and one became part of the larger universe.[7] It was a nation. It was the mainland.

Inhabiting the New Civil Space

The new university was very fortunate to find a very unusual host—National Academy of Administration, which was built in Delhi to relocate the academy training budding bureaucrats from Mussoorie. The academy was sited between the village of Ber Sarai and the cremation grounds of the Munirka village situated by a stream which flowed from Mehrauli, through Kishangarh, and across the land granted to JNU to develop the campus.

The story of the academy, like many other stories in independent India's administrative history, was a story of wastage of national resources by the bureaucracy without any responsibility or accountability. There were four six-storey blocks containing 400 suites with attached bathrooms. There was a separate six-storey block, consisting of sixteen flats on the ground and first floors for the VIPs, and thirty-two residential units for the female students.[8] The campus would have great facilities, i.e., a squash court, swimming pool, etc., to compensate perhaps for the lack of the wholesome Himalayan weather conditions. The academy for civil servants was transferred from the Metcalfe House in Delhi to Mussoorie in 1959. In the late 1960s, the training academy was to shift to Delhi, but it was delayed until 1969-70 and when the construction of the campus began it made the headlines: '5-Crore Luxury Campus for IAS Academy'.[9]

In the meantime, even as the academy was getting ready to welcome the future administrators of the republic, powerful vested interest groups came into their own. The academy never shifted as the vested interests, apparently represented by a very powerful minister in the Indira Gandhi cabinet, ensured that the bureaucrats changed their decision to shift the academy. Now the home ministry was very well entrenched with the bureaucrats who had no intention of bringing the training process under public scrutiny. Hence, the queen of the hills, Mussoorie, retained the civil servants under training and the Delhi sun never got to witness the glory of the administrators of the ranks (this included the two directors, two joint directors and two deputy directors) train themselves with some occasional and infrequent input from outside.

However, the abandoned project benefited JNU as the newly built campus became available to the new university at a throwaway rent to start its temporary operations. Different blocks became schools, i.e., the School of Languages, School of International Studies, and the School of Social Sciences, while the building located near Outer Ring Road, slightly away from the school buildings became the administrative building and the five-storey building closest to this with its big classrooms became the throbbing-with-life library. The block on the left in the extreme corner became the hostels including one for the girls with Suvira Jayaswal as its warden. The big lecture rooms were numbered L1 to L3. The common lecture room (L3) was a big assembly room; many important meetings and lectures by intellectuals both from within and outside the university were held in these sanctified halls.

The campus became the temporary residence of the fellows and students, and the class/lecture rooms became hallmarks of JNU teaching—the spacious rooms meant for the civil servants now could house individual teachers' rooms where classes and tutorial discussions could take place. The spacious dining halls and the club buildings provided a wonderful open space for students from various parts of the country to mingle, chat and interact. The post office, bank, coffee rooms and a supermarket also sprang up to cater to the needs of the JNU population. However, the swimming pool was perceived as a vulgar display considering the water shortage for millions and was forced to go dry.

The 'Sultanate' Skyline

The details of the composition of the executive and academic committees were not debated by the parliament perhaps because the members felt it was a slight to democracy. However, the members of parliament discussed the composition of the student body and the kind of campus the university should have. One member argued that though the university was going to be located in Delhi, all the sixteen states should be represented in the campus.[10] But how? V.K.R.V Rao had suggested the model of the Paris University, where residences known as Indian House, Moroccan House, etc., existed which was suggestive of the variety of the participants. He suggested that there could be sixteen small halls of residence named after each state but the residents in each house will not need to be essentially from the same state.[11]

Moonis Raza, became the first planning officer of JNU. A magnificent mind and the product of the communist movement of the early years, he was born in the eastern part of the erstwhile United Provinces, came to Aligarh where got inducted into the communist movement and worked for the party in Kanpur. He was sent by the party to Europe after he developed health problems, where he spent some time and finally returned to teach in Aligarh and then in the Regional College of Engineering in Kashmir. His forte was discourse transcending all disciplines; he could localize the discussion by either using Urdu shayari (poetry) or ideas recognizable to the enlightened aristocracy. Working with students and peer group geographers, he arrived at an idea of the possible design of space for the new university into which such a national idea could be translated. For someone who evolved intellectually through a rich indigenous knowledge base, academics was not something separate from society, and he felt that the future design of the university should reflect two core ideas:

a) the unity of knowledge which is the motto of our education and also the new university; and
b) the composite culture of India aligned with a world perspective.

With this perspective in mind, his proposal was to have the academic complex emerge as the nucleus of the campus. All its components should be in close proximity to each other. The library should, so to say, 'knit the entire complex, together' as it symbolized 'the unity of knowledge' and therefore 'should be the cynosure of the campus'.[12] As for the schools and centres, his suggestion was that they 'should not develop as independent units—empires in themselves, with frontier disputes and at best having ambassadorial relations with each other'. He seemed to have encapsulated the original idea of the university structure. The physical proximity of schools and centres to each other was intended to 'facilitate formal and informal contact between specialists in different disciplines and lead to the weakening of inter-discipline barriers'.[13]

The residential complex, similarly, accepting the parliamentary wisdom, was to reflect the unity in the diversity of India. Following the suggestion expressed in the joint committee, it was agreed that the residential units be dispersed all over the campus in 'sixteen nucleated blocks—each unit named after a state of the Indian Union'.[14] All the regions of India would be represented in each block. There was also the idea that 'each block should be planned in such a manner that it incorporates some characteristic architectural and landscape features of the state after which it is named'.[15] Raza emphasized that the university should reflect and add to the 'continuity of tradition in a modern milieu characterizing the personality of Nehru after whom the university is named.[16] He was thoroughly modern and was still rooted in and took sustenance from the past—not its fossils, but its elements throbbing in the present.

As Raza succinctly pointed out, the university campus was not coming up on virgin land. 'The skyline is studded, on the one hand, by the soaring minaret of the Qutab, and the rounded contours of the Palam Mosque, the Hauz-i-Khas and a number of other medieval structures and, on the other, by the multi-storied rectangular buildings of Indian Institute of Technology and National Academy of Administration.' The campus, therefore, he added 'should emerge as a unifying element in this diversity and should reflect the underlying unity of India's architectural tradition, which has and continues to defy time'.[17] The gradual evolution of the campus planning for the next twenty years kept up with this vision. However, contemporary times have shown that an aesthetic and grand vision has been substituted with prosaic monstrosities denoting a disconnect with both the past and the future.

The 1960s, as we have seen, was a time full of ideas notwithstanding abject poverty and acute problems. One of the ideas was the expansion of democratic voices through representation. Students were clashing with teachers and the heads of the universities across the world. The American universities saw the worst of their time with presidents quitting their jobs in quick succession. Many have argued in the parliament that one way to democratize the field of higher education was to break the distances created between the teacher and the taught which had turned into a yawning gulf in universities. The discussion on the JNU Bill had shown that the university was being visualized as breaking the tradition of segregating the teachers and students and bringing them together to create a democratic society. Hence, it was decided from the beginning to keep the residences of the students and teachers in close proximity.

There was also a concern about determining the optimum number of students that residential accommodation should aim for. It was believed that the 'organization of residential life of the students should not be looked upon as an instrument of furthering the objectives of the university'. What an ideal! It was also suggested that the units of students' residences should not exceed 200, and even that was thought to be on the higher side. The future development of the university on this front was quite tragic. The student unions in their myopic populism insisted from the beginning that it was against a higher student–teacher ratio and that the number of students had to be increased at any cost; therefore the demand for hostel space outpaced the construction of new hostels. The vice chancellor and the administration proved to be lackadaisical and demonstrated an utter lack of future planning on this front. To add to it, the University Grants Commission, with its own set of limitations arising from its 'clerical democratic' world view, competed with the populism-induced lack of innovation at the university. The results could be seen in the hostels that came up in the 1980s—a gigantic residential block reminiscent of communist era residential blocks in eastern Europe which provided residence but not the heightened sense of living. It is on this front that the JNU trampled upon the vision of its original planners the most. And, in hindsight, this lack of vision and student politics were equally responsible for increasingly turning an ecological dreamland into a massive urban slum.

Raza, being a geographer, was acutely conscious of the landscape. The vice chancellor too was an aesthete. Many senior teachers also, e.g., Sivatosh Mookerjee, contributed to the development of the idea of space within the university. The 'dry channels of monsoon "nalas" or the gullies and ravines sculpted by soil erosion, the disused quarries, the residual hills, the scattered boulders over gullied plains, the undulating dales and vales' were not daunting to Raza and his team as they believed that they were provided for by nature and the 'proper treatment of these elements of the landscape by the hand of man can lift a mere group of buildings to the stature of a place of higher learning'.[18] Therefore, the university was to be located as a natural campus with architectural remnants from the medieval. It is only in the twenty-first century when new money corrupted the whole system, and the natural forest and a great zone of biodiversity declared as reserved forest was given away to commercial malls that the contours of the skyline were drastically altered.[19] Now, while Qutab still hovers in the west, it is the shouting lights of the malls on the east that act as the constant reminder that one is inhabiting a space located between the medieval and the postmodern.

Bringing Red Brick to the Rocky Aravali

The campus committee was constituted and it decided to appoint an architect to design the new university. For a detailed blueprint they decided to have a national competition and nominated some of the best-known names in the field to assess the entries: J.R. Bhalla, president of the Indian Society of Architects; Robert Matthew, former president of the Royal Society of British Architects; H. Rahman, senior architect, Central Public Works Department (CPWD); P.K. Kelkar, director, IIT, Kanpur; and L.G. Selvam, construction advisor, Bureau of Public Enterprises, Ministry of Finance.

C.P. Kukreja Associates won the first prize for their design of the Jawaharlal Nehru University and the university decided to engage Kukreja to develop the master plan with appropriate conditions. The conditions drafted by the JNU lawyer was that Shri Kukreja:

a) be 'appointed as the architect in his individual capacity and not as a partner or agent of any firm or association of which he may be a member or partner', and
b) he shall satisfy the university that he has the resources to carry out the work efficiently and that he possesses or can develop a suitable organization for the efficient execution of the work.[20]

Kukreja was appointed in September 1970, and was given the job of generating a detailed sketch plan of one representative unit.[21] The university made the necessary legal provisions and the letter of appointment was approved by V.S. Desai of the Supreme Court.

The campus site was formally handed over by the Ministry of Youth Affairs on 20 October 1970. The priority was to quickly erect the residential complex and ensure that it was fully functional. This decision was probably prompted by the incomplete state of the National Academy of Administration campus, for which construction had begun several years ago and was still unfinished in the year 1970. Later, in February 1971, the assessors met and suggested that the complete designing work for Sector VI, which consisted of three units of hostels for 200 students each and seventy-five dwelling units for the staff, be entrusted to Kukreja as it would be 'faster, cheaper and retain a single flow'. The university was keen to have hostel accommodation for 600 students ready by July 1972.[22]

The National Academy of Administration complex, refurbished and operational now, came to be known as the old complex. One of the first residents of the university was Yogendra Singh who lived in the NAA before shifting to the newly constructed group of residences in JNU. The newly recruited teachers, particularly the bachelors, were lodged at the old campus. Many long-lasting bonds of friendship across disciplines were forged here. A set of three hostels—Kaveri, Godavari and Periyar—was built, which included a common room that is called the Nilgiri Dhaba today. Twenty-four residential units for the teachers came up opposite the Kaveri and Godavari hostels.

With the new architectural style, the buildings would soon be a noted landmark in the south Delhi landscape and would have its share of admirers and critics. *Hindustan Times* in its scathing critique called the new buildings 'faceless architecture'.[23] Referring to the hostels, the writer found the facades 'flimsy', deliberately constructed irregular, and give a feeling that they would come tumbling down with even a mildly lashing wind.[24] Rooms with massive glass panes in the front and back were thought to be hellish for the occupants during the summer.[25] The reviewer also found the absence of any landscaping an indication of the absence of any intention to 'maintain aesthetic identity and continuity with the surrounding'.[26] The JNU residents' critique of JNU's architecture was more muted but intellectually rooted. It argued that since geographers designed the campus and the buildings, no two rooms in any structure were of the same dimension or shape. The JNU architecture with its lack of many amenities for comfortable living, remained as a symbol to be hated while living within it.

Unlike the occasional visitor who liked JNU's wild expanse and red-brick buildings, the Sapru House scholars and the international studies researchers, who had lived in the comfort of the centrally located Lutyens's Delhi, initially found it difficult to get used to the barren expanses of the Aravali.[27] The DTC buses which faithfully provided public transport for both students and faculty were the common denominator for the JNU community where they would all meet up for the renewal of their commitment to a common quest to create a confident and independent intellectual space. The civility that has remained the hallmark of the JNU denizens, notwithstanding their bitter political differences, is not based on elitism, but perhaps attributable to common institutional incarceration.

On an approximate time scale, it took two-and-a-half years to begin the first course in JNU following the launch of the construction of the edifice. While the influx of students began, the political and intellectual atmosphere was rapidly changing. Some of the discussions were on international issues—the Vietnam War was in its final phase, the radical and communist phase in Latin-America was over and the Bangladesh war too was over. The campus students joined the university at a time when student movements around the world had either ended or were coming to an end. In India, the unity that the Bangladesh war had created among the nationalist left and other progressive forces, was however, intact.

The Tall Building

The library, as Moonis Raza and others planned, was designed to be the centrepiece of academic life, and remained the mainstay of the university. Its location and constitution in the life of the students has been extraordinary. The JNU library had integrated three libraries: the core, newly established JNU's central library, library of the Centre of Russian Studies, and the library of the School of International Studies which was earlier located in the Sapru House.

The ISIS library was the most advanced library in international and area studies, and was painstakingly put together over the years, since the inception of the school in 1955. It was originally established by the Indian Council of World Affairs and, when the ISIS came into its own in 1955, the latter telescoped into a section within the library. In the mid-1960s, when the parliamentary estimates committee remarked upon the ICWA's undue control over the ISIS, it became merely a matter of time before the ICWA's government-funded library caused a blip on the parliamentary radar. The Chandra Reddy Committee advised in its 1968 report that every attempt should be made to preserve the integrity of the ISIS library, as it was one of a kind. A functional division of the tomes could perhaps be considered. The issue became acute with the merger of the ISIS with JNU in 1970 when the division was imperative. A committee, which included M.C. Chagla and B.N. Ganguly, was set up to recommend the division of the library between JNU and the ICWA on a functional basis. The discussions about this division were prolonged as the ICWA realized that it had shrunk, and any division of its precious library would undermine it badly, but the merger of the ISIS with the JNU made this eventuality inevitable.

The ICWA had invested quite a lot of intellectual, organizational and financial resources in building up the school and its library. There was massive pressure from many members of the ICWA to somehow retain the library, but, as we have seen, the most important reason (perhaps the only reason), to include ISIS in JNU was its resources, symbolized by its library. A calling attention motion was raised in the Rajya Sabha about the situation in ISIS. Quite an intense, at times acrimonious, discussion followed the final division—and in the melee many books and resources were lost.[28] All said and done, the Sapru House library finally came to the new university and JNU assured the council that they would maintain it well. So a couple of ISIS staff remained to help set up the Sapru House library and stayed in the Gomati Guest House which was the hostel of the Sapru House scholars before the JNU affiliation. Incidentally, Gomati guest house became JNU's connect to the wider academic world as scholars from other universities across the country would stay there when they visited Delhi.

On 16 May 1972, the ICWA members met with the education minister, Nurul Hasan.[29] He seemed to be in no mood to please the council and categorically asked it to first fulfil its promises and only then would any other talk about the institute be entertained.[30] On 18 July 1972, the ICWA head, Pandit H. N. Kunzru, finally met Parthasarathi, the vice chancellor of JNU, to facilitate matters.[31] A negotiation committee was set up to discuss the issue.[32] The shifting of the ISIS library was taking place concurrently with regular meetings held until the middle of 1973.[33] The financial requirements of the library were discussed and somehow the matters began to settle down amicably with JNU pitching in to support the ICWA library with manpower.

In the meantime, the JNU constituted a very good advisory committee with three of the best librarians that India had produced in the last century: D.N. Marshall, B.S. Kesavan and A.K. Ohdedar. J.P. Naik was also included in this committee which would advise on the construction of the new library. At the same time, the new university opened with the library temporarily located in the NAA campus with Girija Kumar, who had joined ISIS as a professional assistant in November 1965, as the librarian of JNU. Although opinions vary about Girija Kumar being the best thing that happened to the library, he did seem to be a very wise choice, and people like Bipan Chandra and some others from Delhi University lobbied for him as they knew of his efficiency at ISIS. At the end of the day, it was Girija Kumar who masterminded the intellectual adventure of organizing a well-oiled library to cater to the university's research needs.

The library in the university increasingly became the epicentre of the university's academic and social life in more ways than one. It was built with fervour, zeal and assiduous labour of the pioneering staff. Compiling a book collection in a library is far more difficult than making a library building. There were ideas, suggestions and requests for books from many new teachers for their brand new courses at the time when the library building was still just a discussion. During this time, vice chancellor Parthasarathi was also doing his utmost and using his charm and charisma to acquire personal collections. He soon announced the gift of books by Kingsley Martin, a very well-known scholar and friend of India. The library bought the D.D. Kosambi collection of books for three thousand rupees.

In the early decades of the twentieth century, S.R. Ranganathan, overcome by a sense of patriotism and filled with an urge to prove himself and his mathematical mind, developed an elaborate classification system for libraries.[34] This brilliant system was handed down through generations by his devoted pupils and Girija Kumar used the very same system for cataloguing the collections in the JNU library. Ranganathan died the year the JNU library adopted his colon classification system. He had left Delhi when the Delhi Public Library accepted the Dewey Decimal System amidst a lot of controversy in 1955. It was therefore an interesting comeback of a system developed with nationalistic fervour in a national institution. There is nationalistic pride attached to the classification system which was extremely elaborate and on par with the classification in the Library of Congress. It required constant editing and updating as new disciplines and sub-themes emerged. In a developing country this could not be assured; therefore, by the 1990s, the system was faltering as new books and acquisitions were not being adequately classified under this system. By this time, with the proliferation of library systems, many professionals joined the university from institutions which had trained them in the simpler Dewey Decimal System. Thus by the advent of the twenty-first century the association with a proud system was severed and the Ranganathan system was discarded.

By the mid-1980s, the library was shifted to the new nine-storey building in the new campus and the life of the students became increasingly more organized. The School of International Studies and the Centre for Political Science were the last to shift to the new campus and, by the end of 1989, the new campus was fully functional with some of the employees' residential quarters still in the old campus.

The nine-storey library, the pinnacle of the academic complex, continues to be the centre of academic, political and social life of the university as Gopalan's large canteen hall was also moved to the new building, sometime during 1986-87. This was where the student leaders, cadres and non-cadre members of the communist parties and other student formations like the Free Thinkers or the non-representative and most often secretive extreme radicals would discuss politics, academics and other topics.

In its first few years, the library was manned by ex-ISIS staff, which, despite a few murmurs, was definitely advantageous to the new university. The ISIS library was geared primarily to cater to research scholars (unlike the general Indian university libraries) and was, therefore, a boon to JNU. Girija Kumar (the first librarian in JNU), an intellectual of calibre, who had travelled abroad in the early 1960s to seek research and library materials for his own research, was an asset to a research university. He was highly respected by his colleagues and generations of students. Although he was familiar with Delhi's wheeling-dealing world of publishers, he maintained an innate honesty. He was also a hard taskmaster, and his staff not only diligently followed Girija Kumar's example of physical work but were also intellectually motivated to bring out publications in support of the research university.

The canteens and eateries also evolved, each with their unique signature styles. The first tuck shop specialized in the north Indian dish, rajma chawal (kidney beans and rice). Soon, the India Coffee House joined up and their liveried waiters served good old coffee and vada (fried lentil doughnut) and cutlet in the big club building canteen at the old campus. Students and teachers alike began to patronize the canteens until the Students Federation of India members objected to the teachers partaking of the subsidy granted to the students. This created a divide and the offended faculty stopped using the common refectories. Somehow, in later years, the JNU community and the radical left's aversion to hygiene and aesthetics discouraged classy restaurants in the campus, and they soon made themselves scarce. However, labour-intensive enterprise has always been prized and therefore when Francis opened his single-window, one-man shop supplying dosa, idli, vada, uttappam and banana and mango shakes, he was an instant success. When Prof. Namwar Singh migrated to JNU from Jodhpur, he invited Madan Bhaiya, who brought the sophisticated cuisine of Rajasthani kachauri and served the School of Languages ever since.

Eventually it was the happy, old and absent-minded Gopalan, from Thrissur, who with great business acumen gradually consolidated the standing of the library canteen. He started serving south Indian meals for a minimal amount of Rs 3 and his Kerala-style fried fish and fish curry filled a vacuum in the culinary landscape in the campus and drew large numbers of people. He also subsidized many theses by freely providing chicken curry and rice to many struggling students in his library canteen. In the 1980s, the canteen emerged as the summit for social and intellectual discussion. It goes without saying that the canteen tables would be full before an election when the politicos would entice and dialogue with the non-politicos. It was also full when the civil service aspirants came in hordes the day after the Union Public Service Commission (UPSC) main exams.

This was the time to mingle with the mainstream and catch up with friends and classmates. Although JNU never developed either the tenure or contractual track amongst faculty, students had developed two predominant tracks: academic and civil service. Over a period of time, the university gradually developed a third track, the politico-academic track where the professional politician emerged as the winner in faculty recruitment. There was no discrimination between the students who took civil service examinations and those taking the academic track. The division into these two tracks was generally fluid as many who came to the university to do civil service inadvertently switched to the academic track and vice versa. There were supercilious offspring of the intellectuals and bureaucrats preparing for entrance exams for admission into Australian or American universities who made a high decibel critique of the people going into civil services and thereby wasting taxpayers' money. There were also the 'party' (political), particularly the extreme left which also looked upon the UPSC-wallahs with a self-righteous sneer. The library canteen not only provided cheap food but was also a meeting ground for the two streams of students. This may be a reason why the JNU academia and the civil servants share the academic common ground rather than the mere college bonding.

The Pilgrim Fathers

What kind of students were attracted to JNU?

- V.S. Jha had argued in the select committee that there was no need for a state-wise quota system for students as great teachers automatically attracted pupils. The fame of the Calcutta University and the Delhi University teachers who had been drafted into JNU attracted many young people who had just finished their bachelors or masters degrees, wanted to try something different enrolled into the new university.
- Many students and migrants who came to Delhi seeking jobs, or a purpose in life, or a sense of address would enrol in the School of International Studies which had now merged with the JNU. The school became quite popular as the first, second, or even third option for many students especially at the M.Phil. and Ph.D levels.
- The Centre for Russian Studies was a similar beacon, but slightly more purposive, and popularized by the CPI cadres through the Indo-Soviet Friendship Society in places like Andhra Pradesh, Tamil Nadu or Bihar's central belt (where caste [Bhumihar] and political party had become synonymous). After the initial burst of a radical peasant movement launched by Sahajanand Saraswati gradually settled down, the tenants

were now not only wealthier, but they had also gained a new socio-political status, i.e., Bhumihar-Brahmin, and acquired academic aspirations for their offspring which led them to JNU. This would explain the sudden influx of students from places like Begusarai or Nawada.

- The year 1974 was the beginning of student unrest in many states like Orissa and Bihar, and many middle-class students began migrating to BHU or Allahabad; with the advent of the JNU, they were provided with a brand new third option.
- Students from Calcutta arrived in droves as the Naxalite violence followed by the state action had made the lives of the institutions and their students miserable, and JNU came as a breath of fresh air. JNU gained immensely from the Naxalite violence, particularly from the Presidency College as very experienced and dedicated teachers like Tapas Majumdar in economics, Sivatosh Mookerjee in life sciences, and young scholars like Baudhayan Chattopadhyay, Sanjay Chandra and Saugata Mookerjee trod the path leading to JNU.

  The scions of the Bhadralok families of Bengal who knew the right department, the right people and the right kind of mix which would get them to the right kind of academic lineage or right kind of fellowship—which in turn translated into the right kind of Oxbridge, and later American institution—also made a beeline to JNU. Their choice of political formations was often reflected in their high level of professionalism, generally from the left side of the spectrum and preferably to the extreme, where responsibilities are few and visibility and opportunities to get into the global network of scholarship very high. This segment was at the vanguard of the abstract global and Indian revolution for the benefit of the poor from whom their own distance has always been almost legendary.
- Students specializing in political science, history, economics and international studies from the other Delhi colleges also gravitated to JNU.
- As JNU had no tradition of the sciences, it did not attract science students; however, the launch of the integrated School of Life Sciences brought in a crop of good science graduates.

- As the batches graduated, their friends and relatives followed their older siblings into the JNU campus. This increased familial bonding horizontally and there were many marriages where both the brides and the grooms were JNU students. Political ideology also helped cement these alliances (those in the same party tended to marry each other).

JNU introduced the fascinating phenomenon into the life of many. For the newcomers, the socialization and acculturation into JNU began with the visit to the tailors at Mohan Singh Place market in Connaught Place, who delivered within the hour a typical pair of blue jeans at Rs 45 (the price increased to rupees Rs 140 by 1989) and a couple of white or coloured kurtas from the famed Khadi Gramodyog Bhawan next door. Thus attired, the students presented the generic 1970s mien of the residents. The students from the various regions, the big cities, and those typified by old institutions like Fergusson College, Poona, St Xavier's College, Bombay and Calcutta, and Loyola College, Madras, Ravenshaw College in Cuttack, Cotton College, Gauhati, Patna College and Science College in Patna, St Xavier's College Ranchi, Allahabad University or St Edmund's or St Anthony's at Shillong, merged with those from Bhadrak College, Government College, Sira, in Karnataka, Degree College, Rajahmundry, the Farouk College, Calicut or Aloysius College, Mangalore, and were virtually indistinguishable. Large number of young, and sometimes not so young, people arrived from mofussil towns, villages and first or second-generation literate families, and provided the university with a mosaic of vitality and a genuine simplicity, which, notwithstanding their déclassé efforts, students from the entrenched academic middle classes, Delhi's bureaucratic classes, or the upcoming Punjabi population (famously termed 'papaji'), could not have given. This unpretentious and wholesome section was the one which learnt the language of intellectual commitment, followed them and asked questions. It is this section that helped the university zealously guard the autonomy of the intellectual. It was this section of the small-town non-radicals which also did not allow Delhi's social elite to capture the university.

By the early 1970s, universities and colleges all over the country had become extremely selective and were refusing admissions to students.

Language, caste, domicile and other categories began to dictate the criteria for admissions. Talk of the decline of standards in colleges that was very loud in the mid-1960s was no longer heard, but instead one saw that the colleges and universities were represented very negatively in various media. Education merely represented a degree certificate to gain employment. Apart from the Indian Institutes of Technology, JNU was the only institution which created an atmosphere of a horizontal-level meeting ground for young people without regard to divisions such as rural–urban, poor–rich, influential–obscure, high-status–not-so-high-status groups. It is here that the admission policy of the university became very significant.

The admission was entrusted to the teachers to fulfil Tara Chand's dictum in parliament that 'we should trust teachers'. The admission was at the school level and on the basis of interviews. Students were therefore given the opportunity to be interviewed by senior professors and be assessed for their research potential. In the foreign language diploma courses, entry was fairly easy. The admission process was given some structure over the years, and marks allocated for academic background, performance in interview, etc. However, the teachers began to be intimidated by the left-oriented students' body. And it is here the core of the left's politics in JNU began to take shape. By 1973-74, the left parties, particularly the CPI(M) began building its student movement through its student's wing, the Students Federation of India (SFI). JNU contained many left-wing sympathizers among teachers who embarked on a recruitment drive. It was soon understood that students from small towns from the back of beyond were easy constituencies. So the idea that people from backward regions should be given an opportunity began to be used as an admission criterion. The slogan that the left parties peddled was that JNU was an elitist university and had to be brought down to the level of the other universities. The higher teacher–student ratio which was seen as a desired goal of the university was shown to be an indicator of this supposed elitism.

Similarly, the criticism of the existence of two bathrooms in the teachers' houses as compared to the three for six students in the hostel was cited by the student leaders as an indication of class division. According to this line of argument, the teachers occupying a higher class position than the students was shown as detrimental to the interest of the students. The surest way to counter these, forwarded as political agenda, was to dominate the scene by having more students flooding the university and bringing down the student–teacher ratio. Informally there was a bias towards diversity and pro-backwardness within the new radical faculty, and the attempt was to formalize this into the admission policy itself. As several teachers were appointed through the party, it guaranteed that the students' demand would be met—as they were the demands of the party itself. The agitations therefore were merely an eyewash in a sense, as they were basically meant to pull into the orbit of a distant revolution the people who still had doubts about the connection between paying very low mess charges and the overthrow of the world capitalist system.

However, the all-India recruitment of both students and teachers contributed a lot to sustain certain traditions of scholarship which were coming under pressure due to the failure of institutions. It had taken almost an entire century to evolve the traditions of scholarship in many disciplines like sociology, political science, linguistics, history, etc., in places like Orissa, Rajasthan, Karnataka or Bihar, which were under threat of extinction due to rapid institutional decay. The increasing marginalization of free discourse and movement in academia would not replenish the traditions with new people from across regions and from outside the region. The migration of students from these places to JNU, therefore, not only assured the continuation of the tradition at a new place but also a replenishment. It is not surprising that intellectual leadership in many state universities in the 1980s and '90s was taken by those who went there from JNU.

The Clash of Civilizations

English was the lingua franca of the university. The university, on the other hand, was the product of the time of strong anti-English and pro-Hindi agitations in the north Indian belt. The JNU was located in the heart of the region where there probably was a strong pro-Hindi lobby. Apart from this, the home ministry's Hindi promotion cell which promoted the language through its army of Hindi officers, were sending out incomprehensible circulars, tempting many sensitive Hindi souls to consider committing hara-kiri. JNU somehow withstood the pressure.

English, in at least half a dozen different versions, was the lingua franca, and in this sense, the JNU community coped with English well before the theorists began their operation to present cartographies of English. For many, the abundance of the 'o' sound in English spoken by the Bengalis or Oriyas, the special sound of 's' and 'sh' and 'r' by the Biharis, or the ever ready 'sar' by the Tamil or Andhra English was an announcement of a new world. Many leading figures in politics and society in JNU used a completely democratic English.[35] Therefore, the society had been democratized before the quest for a democratic order could proceed.[36] It is completely false to suggest there was Hindi chauvinism.[37] Leaders of political formations like the Naxals valorize linguistics in order to bring culture into their fold. A fascinating déclassé effect took place in the campus when students from completely anglicized backgrounds began learning Bhojpuri and then landed up with a Ph.D topic in an American or British university on Bhojpuri radical thought. These students voluntarily crossed linguistic and class boundaries for a while with a view to academic exploration. The impact of the déclassé environment could also be seen in the large number of relationships between people of completely different social and economic backgrounds and in this aspect JNU became the biggest site for *pratiloma* marriages (marriage of an upper-caste girl and boy belonging to a caste lower in the hierarchy) in the first three years of the its existence.

The new social mosaic was built on an innovative culinary landscape. If JNU could attack the south Indians with something more pernicious than linguistic chauvinism, it was the amount of aloo (potato) in the staple diet of the north Indian. For a Malayali, a Bengali or a Konkani, the dry and arid scene with summer temperatures skyrocketing to beyond 40 degrees Celsius was most outlandish. In addition, the landscape of cuisine, cooked mostly by Garhwali and Kumaoni cooks with generous dollops of this remorseless tuber, was guilty of causing all sorts of gastronomic distress. While they created a cause célèbre for the north Indian cuisine, the bhindi (ladies' fingures), karela (bitter gourd), chicken and paneer (cottage cheese) were a daily reminder of being in a strange new land. The liberal dose of ghee (clarified butter) floating on the dal and chicken curry on a hot humid July afternoon contributed to the stomach rumbles.

The typical menu of the working-day mess was rice, dal (lentils) and subji (vegetables). On the food front (the only field the JNU community conceded), Delhi University was much better off than the JNU. However, JNU was in a league of its own with its creative ambience and camaraderie. Therefore, even if Samuel Huntington's civilizational clash theory may be seen as a falsehood due to its excessive dependence on religion, the clash between the regions here was palpable. The opening of jars of 'gunpowder' (roasted powdered lentils and spice) and fish pickle from Kerala or Tamil Nadu was changing the gastronomical horizon of the students from northern and eastern India about an entity called south India recognized so far by idli (rice and lentil steamed cakes), dosa (rice and lentil pancakes) and sambhar (lentil stew) and invoked by the bawdy linguistic caricature by Mehmood in Hindi films with a signature tune '*mutoo korika warihara*'. Complexities of the regional identities were better defined and the 'Madrasi' was now being deconstructed from its earlier status signifying anyone beyond the Vindhyas, a role Doordarshan would play for the larger country in the 1980s particularly through its programme of screening regional movies on Sundays at 2.30 p.m.

The 1960s was a world of permissiveness, sexual liberation and the great gender debate, particularly in the west. American Betty Freiden's *Feminine Mystique* was far more moderate than the British feminist Germain Greer's enraging *Female Eunuch*.[38] It went on to show how, in many important areas, the American was more moderate politically. Indian society was also witnessing currents of changing social norms as shown in man–woman relationships. One of the interesting reflections of this was the sudden phasing out in 1970 of the old heroes from the Bombay movies and the arrival of Rajesh Khanna symbolizing the arrival of the new mode of romantic expression. The portrayal of the man–woman relationships beyond fixed norms of society was also brought to the discourse now in many literary and cinematic reproductions which tried to expose the hypocritical attitude of the society.[39]

The country was experiencing the new sexual mores that had come to depict the new heroes and heroines in a different sexual context. While this was the era when Khushwant Singh was bringing the slightly exposed women into the pages of *Illustrated Weekly* and was creating a sensation, issues of sexuality were acquiring new dimensions in public places. The younger generations were replacing the middle-aged heroes and college romance was heralding the arrival of the matinee idol—matinee being the time when the girls and boys could come out and meet. It was a significant experience when JNU opened its door as a co-educational residential university. The residential character was also publicly displayed as the students and scholars thronged the capital's many public spaces. There was a major culture shock in the traditional northern Indian belt where the idea of co-education at the higher level was still strongly debated.[40] For the population outside the campus, JNU's postgraduate ladies began to be viewed as enigmas as well as 'available' ... while the genial and often simply clad JNU male students were considered emasculated leftist political leaders, which the media took a while to tag as 'intellectual'. The neo-economy in the 1990s and the coming of large number of women into the job market and the public spectacle of a large number of non-institutional and NGO workers with 'jhola' (sling bag) had increasingly marginalized the exotic value of the JNU male and female students. However, for insiders, the presence of ladies in their midst had a sobering impact on the men, the staff and the faculty.

There were ladies with definite political and social views, which they expressed, and the left movement (which included emancipation and gender equality) promoted women's articulation. These two aspects helped the larger democratic ethos to take shape in the life of the community. There was, however, another dimension to it. The leading student outfit, the SFI, always had many ladies in its fold. The presence of the ladies attracted a larger number of boys into the SFI camp. In many ways the parties would work like evangelists luring the young sheep to the Lord's services.

Put together in that desert clime, the teachers, relatively young and living close to the students' hostels, gradually developed social and personal relationships which lasted long years of political and career strain. The social life was marked by a real absence of parochialism which broke the shackles which Edward Shils noticed in Indian universities.[41] The number of inter-caste, inter-regional, and inter-religious marriages that began to take place in this campus cannot be compared to any other phase of Indian institutional lives at any point of time in Indian history. Another milestone was the progressive way of thinking.

The composite cultural mould and the constant interaction with other students and teachers enhanced the being, while the academic engagement made people acutely conscious of the issues in the real world. Notwithstanding the interlinkages between the island and the mainland, a portal had opened which took many by surprise. This was the opening up of the intellectual space for independent thinking—perhaps this was what G. Parthasarathi alluded to, albeit in a different context, as the space for autonomous intellectual.

The Admissions

The first admission took place in 1971 for the M.Phil. and Ph.D programme. In 1973, the MA admissions in many centres had begun. Although the economics centre in the JNU became operational from 1973, the admission of the first batch started later than in the other centres. Classes were held in the buildings leased from the National Academy of Administration. There were blocks containing big rooms with attached bathrooms. Block number one became the School of International Studies while block three housed the School of Social Sciences. Block one also became the residential complex for the married scholars and teachers, and included a mess hall. The State Bank of India established an office in the building adjacent to the pond, while a university printing press was planned in the space below the bank. The tall edifice between the club building and the lecture halls became the library. The library was open until 7 p.m. and gradually became the centre of all intellectual activity.

By the end of 1972, two sets of hostels came up in the northern part of the campus which one could access via pagdandi (a well-trodden narrow path—later a brick path came up), which emerged from the National Academy of Administration campus, now designated 'the old campus', and, after crossing a small half-built road it went through a patch of semi-arid vegetation and culminated at the hostel. The road connecting the old campus and the JNU main gate was constructed at lightning speed, within a day, when Prime Minister Moraji Desai, who became the chancellor in 1977, visited the campus for a court meeting. The DTC bus provided a regular ferry service between the old campus and new. Quite often the JNU's own red bus driven by one of the earliest revolutionaries appointed by JNU, comrade Tiwary, would also provide the ferry service, but its regular route was from JNU to Sapru House via all the major academic and cultural installations: Nehru Memorial Museum and Library, the National Museum, the National Archives of India, Max Müller Bhawan, Sahitya Academy, Indian Council for Historical Research and others. It was the lifeline not only of the local and residential scholars and students, but also of the visiting scholars putting up at the Gomati Guest House. The JNU scholars grew accustomed to visiting other centres of public discourse to attend forums and seminars, which had a negative effect, as JNU never considered developing a major convention centre of its own where debates from the outside world could be brought into the university.

The 1960s was a torturous decade for students across the world. In India, by the beginning of the new decade, the advanced centres of excellence were coming apart. Universities like Visva-Bharati, Osmania, Rajasthan, Banaras, Andhra, Kerala, Madras and Calcutta were pale shadows of their past. Many of them were unable to attract young minds to any exciting projects. The early spirit of student movements was waning. Some of these movements were entering their crucial phases in many places, mainly Bihar and Uttar Pradesh, where they would soon begin to consume institutions of higher learning. The Naxalite movement in West Bengal and parts of Bihar had triggered the trickle of students from Calcutta University towards the Delhi institutions. In 1971-72, these students came into the JNU campus and they had a decisive influence on the character of the university.

The first three batches of students came from a mixed bag of political affiliations: Marxists, non-communists, freethinkers. Over the years, JNU was home to students of many other political hues including the extreme right and the extreme left. Except for these two extremes, the rest had more or less reposed their faith in democratic structures. If academic work and activism were any indication, they reflected the overwhelming concerns, for example, extension of democracy and enlargement of the democratic space. Civil rights, especially those of the scheduled castes (SCs) and the scheduled tribes (STs), were of paramount concern. All tendencies which prevented democratic movements like communalism, fanaticism and sectarianism were critiqued and trends towards equality and justice upheld.

During the admission season, the faculty was very keen to have variety; many argued that to attract the widest variety of people there must be a different kind of admission system than the one merely based on marks, etc. There was broad consensus on this principle. However, on the question of whether admissions should be based on income and backwardness, there were disagreements, as many pointed out that income certificates can not only be faked but also procured easily as income yardsticks were variable. Gradually, the idea of deprivation points emerged where regions or districts were accorded points if they fell under the backward district denomination. This was a very significant innovation in the country's institutional policies and sustained JNU's admission policy for almost a decade until a new admission policy regime was established in 1984. While these deprivation points gave due weightage to people from disadvantaged regions and districts—and, coupled with the gender distinction, would in many ways reflect a true equalizing scale—it was also the beginning of the operation of the logic of backwardness which, in the later phase, would become a powerful vested interest in various kinds of politics. However, in its purest form the deprivation points and the interview-based admission was a balanced mix of social justice and trust in teachers to select the right kind of students. It also gave JNU its distinct student profile, which was truly national, varied and representative of disparate groups.

The admission by the faculty through interviews and based on deprivation points assured one that there was not only variety but also good students who liked to do research. The first five to six years in this sense were the best years for JNU. In fact, some of the ground-breaking research was done by the students of JNU. In course of time, students and teachers affiliated to the Students Federation of India demanded that the admissions be made on a more populist basis. A new category of urban–rural divide was brought in to argue what they alleged was a bias in admissions towards urban students. They, therefore, attacked any segment which tried to enlist students from good colleges. This was essentially shown as depriving the already deprived rural and backward-area students. In the end people insisted that teachers should not be allowed the privilege of selecting students. It was in this process that the SFI leaders leaked the admission list of the Centre of Historical Studies in which many from good colleges had scored high marks in their interviews.[42] It was a serious charge with serious connotations. It was known that in many regions college marks were inflated, while in universities like Delhi and Calcutta the evaluation of answer scripts were very strict, and marks were low generally.

The debate over the rural vs urban and elite vs non-elite soon became an electoral issue and political formations began to colour the space. While the newly recruited student members of the communist parties began to define community in terms of class, the solidity of the parties own ranks was very important and hence there were efforts to increase its numbers in the student body. However, it was not merely a matter of the admission policy. The importance, however, lay somewhere else. An entire generation of starry-eyed dreamers, careerists, idealists and political activists had landed in JNU with their dreams and capabilities. All of them, however, found themselves in a newly constructed intellectual world, a new discursive universe.

Making Life Political

The daily life in the university began to revolve around water politics, mainly in the campus mess, the library and the dhaba. A hydraulic society appeared to have come to roost, even though the JNU historians like Romila Thapar, Bipan Chandra and Satish Chandra had discredited this theory which was advanced by people like the Frankfurt school theorist Karl Wittfogel who had argued that the oriental despotism was based on the rulers' monopoly over water and resources vital for irrigation. The theory had argued that the oriental societies were ruled by those who controlled water and this control was at the root of the despotism of the oriental rulers. In the new democracy, however, water was supplied by the municipal corporation and tap water started around seven o'clock both in the morning and evening. The taps would run for two hours until nine o'clock. This was the time for daily ablutions. The bathroom practices also brought out the regional patterns in micro and macro ways. The south Indians were generally 'twice bathers' except some radicals who had no time for such deviation from their three-dimensional political engagement: discourse, debate and drinking. On the other hand, to match them were the others who were loth to take time off from their heavy engagements in discursive community. Conservation of water as a radical political statement, therefore, had its original contribution from JNU students.

The campus suffered from acute water scarcity in the mid-1980s when the campus was literally closed for want of water. Generally, the north Indians dirtied the bathrooms more than actually cleaning themselves compared to the south Indians. The strangest were the namazis (those who were going to read their namaz) from the northern belt, who would use the washbasins to wash their legs to the bewilderment of the hygiene-conscious. Protest was muted lest the secular ethos be hurt. Political sensitivity had a prized location and ranked above all sense of public hygiene. The men's bathrooms were dirtier than the women's and in both genders the contribution of north Indians to the per capita uncleanliness was far higher than that of the south Indians.

The hygiene politics were generally propounded by fascist powers that wished to cleanse the systems of irritants like the minority or the unclean.[43] The Indian communal parties had hygiene politics embedded somewhat in their philosophical core—they wanted the country to be cured of minorities, un-Hindu elements, etc. It was very significant that the politics of JNU developed along anti-hygienic lines with student formations more or less opposed to the communal parties and their hygiene politics. The same attack on hygiene was also translated into civic life and therefore the hostel, the mess and the shopping complex were some of the most unclean spaces in the university lives in the country.

However, these non-hygienic politics and civility also allowed JNU to be the most open campus anywhere in the world. There were dozens of students who were non-academic, scored low marks and did not even have the requisite honours degrees. JNU welcomed them and some of them are now teaching in world-class universities, making policies for universities as vice chancellors and building theories of international relations. Just as JNU would enthusiastically welcome a brilliant mathematician from Madras to study economics or history, it would allow a not-so-brilliant mind to think seriously about international theory. At JNU there was equal opportunity for a student from, say, Bhagalpur, to walk in for an interview as would his counterpart from a prestigious institution like Stephen's or Hindu College. Because of its larger number of departments and relaxed intake criteria, the School of International Studies was the easiest of places to gain entry. It became the hunting ground for the Delhi University's 'pass course' and 'sports quota' students who were never taken too seriously academically. They used JNU's 'open house attitude' to somehow gain good academic credentials—some even managing to peak in their chosen disciplines.

In addition, JNU was expansive with its hostel facilities, and one did not necessarily have to be a student to be entitled to be a resident—anyone who wished to contribute to the JNU culture were allowed in. Thus the musical genius of Sanne Naqvi from Lucknow with his deep voice and stock of Shakespearean dialogue lived in and entertained many in JNU for years without ever being a student. Many current IAS officers prepared for the civil service examination living in the hostels as what came to be known in JNU parlance a 'Permanent Illegal Guest' (PIG). Years before the idea that 'nations were imagined' could ignite minds, the JNU students generously extended some of their entitlements to foreigners—they ranged from simple tourists to scoundrels with foundation money. All made JNU their home. The JNU teachers used their influence to help many foreign academics with their legal issues and trouble with the authorities, e.g., photographing the borders at Barmer. Despite a vaguely anti-American air, JNU extended a certain openness both in the social sphere and the intellectual—the centres gave invitations to the largest number of American scholars during the Emergency when it was really difficult to invite scholars without inviting a needle of suspicion.

During admission time, JNU demonstrated its social self, outreaching, helping and quite often charitable towards hapless new candidates accompanied by their parents who would arrive from all over the country. They would be ably assisted by the JNU students, irrespective of caste, creed or connections. In a sense, this was JNU extending the frontiers of human well-being and the ideology of progress. The new students were soon to be socialized into the new milieu through 'pamphlets'. Pamphlet writing has been one of the greatest contributions of JNU's student community to the nation's intellect. Pamphlets would arrive at the mess table during breakfast, lunch and dinner time, for all to read. They would cover all issues, especially burning issues. Pamphlet-writing had taken on an art form—its writing and reading provided the students a new world: an insight into contemporary socio-economic and political issues. It also improved the pamphleteers' command over the language (English).

Pamphleteering required collective effort and included writing, cyclostyling and distribution just before meals and this helped community building in real time. While organizational viewpoints were being expressed, there were always spaces for individual viewpoints. In a society where fear of the mighty compelled subterfuge in anonymity, the intrepid JNU pamphlets were always signed even when the politics of caste and communalism began to appear in the body.

The feudal ethos would have found it difficult to see ladies debating just as furiously as the male speakers, however the tone had been set by the generally progressive teachers and some politically mature students in the first couple of batches. There were students who spent their time in debating and there were students who wanted to chart a different course. It all depended on the individual student. A left bias in urban youth found the rural youth conservative. However, the leftism of the urban youth was easily compromised while the rural youth of the early 1970s evolved their political ideas gradually and sustained it. The left-wing *Weltanschauung* combined with the progressive ideas of JNU transformed the landscape of minds in this section of population.

The leftism of this section of urban youth helped in shaping the discourse and took on the organized strength of the left parties which would otherwise have converted people into mere cadres and not independent minds. Spaces needed to be claimed by confidently articulating the demand and contesting opposing views, and this developed the confidence level of the students from their early days in the JNU. The new tradition of the post-dinner debate was a huge public spectacle which, although often fought along party lines, created less of a dogmatic communist than elsewhere among the intellectuals. For example, in the early 1970s a very well-read Trotskyite academic, Jairus Banaji, became a popular speaker and exposed the Stalinist authoritarianism that constricted communist movement in Europe.

This found the communist students of the campus looking for alibis and defences for Stalinism which they advocated.

In the 1960s, the student movement that developed in northern India, which demanded representation and democratization of the academic body, was underpinned by the new caste configuration, and this resulted in the rapid decline of many good colleges and institutions across northern India. Among the student leaders, it was the socialists who had a clear-cut dominance in the north Indian universities. Most of the political leaders who made their mark in the 1970s, '80s and '90s, had their origin in student movements. They were quite rooted in the realities of the caste-based north Indian society and were unable to transcend these narrow limits of observable realities. The student movements during the 1960s and '80s were circumscribed by narrowness: in the '60s, they led the anti-English and pro-Hindi agitation in most northern states, while in the '80s they turned into champions of caste-based politics.

In Delhi, the socialists targeted the Indian School of International Studies and the battle for the Hindi thesis of Ved Prakash Vaidik became part of the process. Very soon, significantly, many senior socialist leaders namely, Asoka Mehta, Nath Pai and R.K. Khadilkar, became the chief members of the school's governing bodies. Some of the teachers who later became CPI(M) members actually began their careers as socialists members here in the school. The issue of Hindi, which was controversial in 1966-67, was voiced by socialists like Kishen Pattanayak in parliament. Many students from Bihar and UP would come with some ideas of socialism from the tradition of Lohia and other socialist leaders in these places. Significantly, students from Bihar became very prominent in the ISIS—both before and after merging with the JNU. This had to do with multiple reasons which included a rapid decline of institutions in Bihar and easy entry to JNU. It was interesting that these socialistic inclinations of students also made them resistant to the communist parties's romantic pull.

The SFI Phenomenon

The socialist-minded students looked askance at the scattering of the socialist parties in 1980, and thus in 1983, there was a kind of demise of the student movement based on the ideas of Lohia, etc. In 1983, although they had strength in numbers and an idea to rally against authorities, the socialists were unable to fuse new strategies of mobilization, and this eventually marred their success. They became a victims of circumstance, and, despite the small, scattered pockets of socialists, they failed to become a part of the larger student movement in JNU.

There were some trends which were more urbane, oriented towards intellectually discussing Marx and related topics, international in outlook and with an interest in international thinking. For many students this was academically too sophisticated and was sectioned off as intellectual snobbery. Many of them suffered from deep cynicism and saw the faculty in poor light due to their superior reading and engagement with theory. While the leader of the group, Jairus Banaji, had the intellectual insight and exposure to lead his own personal intellectual life and commitment, for many others this cynicism increasingly bordered on arrogance and led to a peculiar intellectual hubris leading to haughty, fashionable, self-righteous superiority camouflaged in radical rhetoric about the disadvantaged poor, the marginalized and minorities.

In the communist current, it was the SFI that played a crucial role in institutionalizing and establishing the organized student movement in JNU. There were two trends in the communist movement across the country at this point of time: the new sectarians, CPI(M), and the existing movement that was intellectually accommodating i.e., the C.P.I. Most of the intellectually-inspiring teachers had come from the old party affiliation or were sympathetic to the old party while the new party was keen that the new space represented their hegemony. At the level of students, the numbers of cadres ensured party power. But at the faculty level, the new party had to win friends. It was the party's characteristic to demand complete loyalty. The party, therefore, adopted a strategy, which attacked the very foundation of JNU, and targeted the faculty who were abiding by the parliamentary mandate to mould the university according to the original plan, and were entrusted with powers and roles hitherto unheard of in the older Indian universities.

For many students the socialist world was chaotic and the Students Federation of India organized things neatly for them. Socialists were anti-officials, the SFI organized rallies against the officials; socialists were anti-government, and so was the SFI. There was anger against colonialism, and the SFI not only sympathized with it but also brought out a Mashal Julus (torchlight procession) against racial discrimination. In a nutshell, the SFI responded to the manifold student persona's angst in a time of scarcity and overall social anger. Thus, while the students in other places were placing themselves under the leadership of Jayaprakash Narayan, in JNU, a lot of them put their faith into the new formation called the Students Federation of India.

The CPI(M) was a new party with leaders of sectarian zeal after they broke with the parent party on sectarian agenda, and from 1964 onwards, the party had to build itself. With the new university opening, the party found a place to begin its student activities with a new spirit. Prakash Karat, who had, in the tradition of the communist leadership, returned from Britain and joined the CPI(M)[44] joined ISIS as a researcher while preparing to go abroad again for higher studies. He was involved in the 'consciousness-raising activities'. By virtue of ISIS getting merged with JNU in 1971, he got a readymade platform which the party was seeking. It was fortuitous that ISIS joined the new university exactly at the time Karat was enrolled in it as a research scholar.

The sectarian fervour of the new party, however, was matched by the equally strong liberal values that many of the students and teachers imbibed from their exposure abroad. This liberalism came to provide an abiding core value to the university. The debates and discussions were strong and so were the demonstrations, but the personal relationships and respect for dissenting voices was of the highest level. There was a decline in the core values of the JNU around the mid-1970s when the real India entered with its caste, language and political angularities. Until this time, JNU was insulated from these.

As had been the case with the CPI in the 1930s and the '40s, when the university youth were mobilized with fascinating efforts by P.C. Joshi and his comrades, CPI(M) considered JNU a good place to begin rallying the youth for the party. And they began this effort by targeting JNU's alleged elitist character and bringing it down to the level of the universities of Meerut and Gorakhpur. This plan struck a chord with many segments, especially with the students who camped at JNU for a couple of months or a year en route to Oxbridge. The attack on elitism came from a section which was itself trained in England and the attack was more tactical than with any real conviction. The first students' union president was trying to get a visa for the USA, the second president and builder of the union had gone all the way to England to get a certificate on Marxism like many of the earlier communist leaders. The only thoroughbred Marxists were Sitaram Yechury and others who had studied in JNU. The semi-rural students from the backwaters quite often caused pangs of conscience which was at the core of student politics in JNU, and from this emanated the demand of the left (of all shades) that excellence cannot be a criterion for institution building in such a poor country as it has no social relevance.

On the flip side of this attack on the elitist character of JNU, the students who had run away from run-down institutions found this criticism quite irritating, just as those from other elite institutions who were seeing in JNU the portents of a new space in the Third World that could critique the colonial and other forms of inequalities. The socialist-trained students from Benares, Bihar, Orissa and many other places who fought against English, were bemused by JNU's aura which seemed infused with a new spirit, and these students gradually moderated their opposition to English and began a new intellectual tour.

For the students from all over the country it was a difficult choice because what they saw in JNU was far superior to that in the institutions whose collapse they had witnessed in their own states. To add to it, the debates were new to them. The feudal, and quite often crude, values were what they were used to, and JNU presented a sanctuary. The realities in their own homes were changing fast. The student movement had new leaders, many had come to JNU in the heat of the 1974-75 movement and had grown up in JNU. Although the socialist slogans suited them, JNU was above that kind of language, and the disconnect was getting sharper as the academic tenor changed.

These new students were attacking the faculty not because they had any ideological disagreement but merely because they felt trapped between processes they were unable to handle. On the one side were the teachers, primarily in the social sciences, who were engaged in consciousness-raising discourses, mostly in English, and on the other side, there was the discomfort from the democratic setting of the university as they had just come from backgrounds steeped either in feudal ethos or in a deeply unequal urban spirit. It required time to negotiate with the new realities. The political outfits were providing easy-fix solutions—the student leaders were friends while the teachers (those who opposed the demands of the party leaders), were enemies not only of the students but also of democracy. By 1977–80, the regional and linguistic groups increased in concentration which meant that entry into the public space was no longer as an individual but negotiated through language, caste and region. This created tension, both individually and collectively. It also created strong anti-Marxist forces as these processes were defended in the name of Marxism.

As an organized force, like any other organized force, SFI wanted to create dominance in the social and intellectual life. The biggest hurdle was the intellectuals who were already established. From within the left, the CPI-affiliated teachers and students resisted such streamlining. However, the sharpest attacks were reserved for those who, although Marxists, were not ready to abide by the rules of the party and were ready to critique Marxist formulations intellectually. The Free Thinkers emerged at this juncture from the School of Social Sciences and were ready to take on the left's streamlining efforts in organization and social engineering at JNU. Although there were some socialist-minded students, the Free Thinkers articulated many problems better. They subscribed to the radical vision of the global youth but they refused the compulsory revolutionary telos, and this was what set them apart from other leftist groups. This was also the time when the CPI apparatchiki were using their connections to get jobs, go to Moscow and make careers. One of the early AISF leaders went to Moscow and from there to the US to become a radical historian. Similarly, many others made hay whilst the communist sun shone in eastern Europe.

Knowledge Production: The Collective Ways

A collective process of evolving a sense of belonging is what distinguishes an institution. JNU was a new community where people had come from different parts of the country. They followed their sectional knowledge, prejudices and interests. There were class, community and linguistic divisions which would have taken time to amalgamate seamlessly to form the JNU community. JNU scholars had rejected the colonial, and later on, Cambridge historians' thesis of Indian nationalism on the grounds of it being a reaction of the upper caste who refused to be collaborators of the colonial powers. But if JNU strove to reject the collaborative thesis of the colonial historians, its own collaborationist project of knowledge production had an interesting side. Ph.D writing came to Oxford in 1917, it came to JNU in 1971. The scorn which the British aristocracy reserved against the Ph.D degree was shared equally strongly by the Indian lower segments who saw the Ph.D as 'efforts at cutting grass' (a sheer waste of time).[45] On top of this the founding fathers, imagining that the new Third World intellectuals would take more time to conceptualize questions, had initially given a time period of five years for an M.Phil. and the whole of adulthood for a Ph.D. The founding students also thought somewhat along similar lines and decided to stay put even if they did not produce any Ph.Ds; they did something bigger: raised questions—sometimes about the university itself.

Many of these Ph.D students thought in terms of praxis and spent years organizing labour, peasants and even the government employees on field so that their practice could justify their theory. They could not, therefore, complete their theses in time. On the other hand, the parliament and its many intellectuals who had spent their earlier academic years under American munificence, were not ready to advance the same for the children of the lesser gods under the Indian sun. Some worked hard to support themselves and therefore also had to sublet the hostel room in their efforts of class upliftment of their families, in which case five years were a good period. Lastly, those who tried to develop a parallel discourse which also needed them to go to the origins of such a discourse, such as England or Africa or Germany, ended by settling down and marrying someone there to help him or her continue living in that discursive world for longer. There were also those for whom the sylvan surroundings of JNU and its tyrannical repetitiveness produced by the semester system actually saw the monsoons and winters passing by without any written output. Believing in the spoken word as their civilizational strength, they had been conducting their original discourse verbally. But the pragmatists in parliament and the parents who saw their wards being snatched by some Marxist bhoot (demon), were not ready to give any allowance for such a long time lapse, and they became the enemy. The first attack on this openness came with the reduction of time for all programmes.

But the life of the JNU community and its typical idiosyncrasies had gone on adding spice to the rich and varied life of the individual, despite the time spent on writing an M.Phil. or a Ph.D thesis and the efforts of the communist parties to make political morons out of unsuspecting spirits. Even the lighter moments at the dhabas added rich dimensions to their lives. Thus, JNU life in many cases prolonged the entry into those not-so-hallowed corridors of middle class urban existence.

The JNU community included the administrative staff, the assistants, the security staff, the library staff, the teachers (many teachers were also wardens, provosts and proctors, etc.) and students. The students' lives were not exclusive. The newspaperwallah was an important, perhaps even more important than the proctors, part of their lives. Similarly, the bearded gentleman called Dada (the Bengali honorific reference), the owner of Geeta Book Shop, was a well-respected man who trained many a student from the back of beyond in the art of reading whilst he shared 'the latest' with the more cultured. And soon, all were getting 'the latest'. The snobbery of dropping names of the latest books or French authors, prevalent in the main campuses and the highbrow league, was attacked by Dada who helped equalize the reading habits of all. An erstwhile member of the Communist Party of India, who was also very active in the Indo-Soviet Friendship Society, Dada came to the profession of a bookseller by choice and would scout for the latest, and his own understanding of the current debates in European Marxism was significant. He was an institution in his own right, many learnt the art of buying books from him, and people like him made the mind of the campus a place of equality, which attacked snobbery of all kinds at its root.

In the production of knowledge, the JNU staff also played a Herculean role by doubling as professional typists. Teachers and students both have preferred typists. The current generation of 10.30 a.m. to 4.30 p.m. university staff would be hard put to imagine the life of the staff of the earlier generation. It was rare that the students would get their theses typed in one continuous sitting. However, the serious scholarly type would try and finalize the project by May when his or her supervisor needed to leave for summer vacation. The civil service preliminary exams would take place around the first week of June which would have prevented the UPSC candidates' intellectual prowess to be scripted. So they would descend in droves to the typists after the preliminary exams (prelims in the local parlance) in the first week of June, with their written, half-written and even unwritten manuscript (which meant the flagged and marked portions from other books and documents). The typists were well trained as many professors writing their tomes on international disputes and other serious issues also required large volumes to be copied. Thus, from mid-June to the third week of July, until the theses were submitted, the campus would buzz with hyperactivity.

Typists knew English well and also the stylistics. They were good jugglers of work and would tamely type out the documents as long as the student perched by their side; however, out of sight also meant out of typewriter, so students left their seat beside the typist at their own peril. Everybody got their theses typed by JNU typists. This excluded some government officers' children whose father's typist, or mother's, would volunteer. But, very often, they all came back to the JNU typists as it was part of the common status marker and the JNU typists were also more familiar with the style sheet and knew where the footnotes appeared, and also the correct spelling of Clifford Geertz or Gerschenkron or Lu Xun.

However, the typists' knowledge of English and grammar could prove detrimental to those working in the field of linguistics. Thus, a student of linguistics who had worked on the common English errors and their analysis, found to her horror that not a single error which she had analysed was to be seen in the typed thesis. The typist had corrected all those errors taking pity on the candidate's poor English spelling! In the days of manual typewriting, one can only imagine how the hot and humid days of July must have turned into a nightmare for the linguistics student.

Thesis submission was also a test of human kindness. The consequentialists in moral philosophy argue that an act or a moral statement is as good or as bad as the consequences it brings. Notwithstanding the absence of a department for moral philosophy, students had the proverbial bias of Indian philosophy (the intuitive understanding of who was good or who was bad). It was the submission of the M.Phil. and Ph.D theses which was the litmus test of the consequentialist thesis. A supervisor was good if he or she helped in the final days in correcting or most often rewriting those pages. The office staff were good or bad depending on his or her dependability in rescuing the candidate who was submitting after the deadlines. It was at this critical time of the year that every thesis-submitting eye would seek out Mrs Kakkar at the School of Social Sciences for help, more than their supervisor or the chairperson. It was her diktat that would run. She exuded the milk of human kindness as she most often not only allowed late submission but allowed the students to take the thesis back for further typing. Her stern but smiling mien seemed to say 'in goodness we trust'.

Even though the campus was politically anti-communal, it participated in one particular communal endeavour in the spirit of communist sensibilities. This was in full display during the period of writing the thesis or dissertation. It showed the nation-building efforts at their peak as also the interdisciplinary character of the university. On many levels, the interdisciplinary efforts may be considered a failure as people who were appointed into departments other than their basic discipline were never accepted as such and remained uncomfortable throughout their term. It was in writing theses and dissertations, however, where the interdisciplinary nature of the campus came into play. One would be surprised to find that an environmental science Ph.D had better English than the average science scholar. The reason: an English or political science student writing on epistemological rupture probably wrote the final draft of the thesis.

Similarly, a sociology thesis might have gained a deep historical insight due to the fact that the friends who ended up writing the thesis were students of history who thought that they could display their sociologically inspired new thoughts. There were theses which were completely collective efforts and different chapters bore the stamp of ingenuity of different disciplinary practitioners. A biochemical science thesis, not claiming any interdisciplinary collaboration (as all environmentalists now announce from the rooftops), was virtually written by his friends from disciplines as diverse as German and economics, thereby giving the thesis deep interdisciplinary insights.

However the multidisciplinary nature generally ran riot during the entrance viva for the M.Phil. and Ph.D. The university's minds generally turned into 'Saraswati's playground' when hundreds of proposals on various topics for M.Phil. and Ph.D were discussed and written by students during the entrance viva in July; sometimes the student had never even heard of the country where he was going to work (e.g. Vanuatu or East Timor), at times the subject of his study would be that in which his knowledge was at best fragmentary. However, this was the only time when one witnessed the intellectual capital of the university in full bloom. Most M.Phil. aspirants' friends behaved like the typical RSS cadre who has knowledge of everything and, like a good communist, can blame even the summer sweat into a neat category of financial capitalism. The greatest recipient of such a vast intellectual repertoire was the School of International Studies and the School of Social Sciences, which mainly taught only M.Phil. and Ph.D. Friends and comrades or girlfriends or boyfriends helped arrive at the topic of research and many such researchers went on to occupy high academic and administrative positions later. Thus JNU's academia retained a symbiotic chord with the community in its knowledge production which may be the reason it refuted any ideas which suggested that education is a private good.

8

Life of the Mind

> Its major contribution is the promotion of Indian intellectualism. Until Independence our intellectual life was a province of the British intellectual life. And the trend continues in other institutes of higher learning. Western norms are still being applied to Indian conditions.[1]

The new university, anchored as it was on a commitment to pan-Indian nationalism, may be the first in the institutional history of modern India to repose trust in teachers to design and administer an institution. Between 1966, when the JNU Act was passed, and late 1969, when the university began to take actual shape, the grammar of Indian politics had already changed. The government which was to shoulder the responsibility of starting the university was going through a rough patch. Congress, the party in power, was split vertically. New groups of people were about to start a process of intellectual consolidation in a dreary desert site at the periphery of the capital.

The New Habitus

JNU provided the newly arrived intellectuals a space, both physical and virtual, which, fresh as it was, would help them experiment with, and develop, many of their ideas. Rasheeduddin Khan and K. Seshadri from Andhra, Tapas Majumdar and Boudhayan Chattopadhyay from Bengal, C.P. Bhambhri from Rajasthan, G.S. Bhalla from Punjab—they were all familiar with the changing socio-political dynamics of their respective states and, therefore, were able to guide any discourse pertaining to their region. The space also provided a politico-intellectual station to consolidate wider linkages. So much so that P.C. Joshi, the erstwhile general secretary of the Communist Party of India, was appointed to build an archive of the communist movement, the core of which was his own collection, vetted by senior scholars and then brought to JNU. This constituted what has since been known as the Archives on Contemporary History.

The arrival of students with links with progressive movements brought many writers, poets and cultural activists to the campus. Some, who decided to stay on at the JNU, became a permanent feature of the social life of the campus. Many such known, as well as unknown, figures helped create a large sophisticated universe. Although Sanne Naqvi, from Lucknow, with his Shakespearean English and chaste Hindustani, was never a JNU student, he was as much a part of the university community as the dishevelled Baba Nagarjuna, the famous Hindi poet, and a guest of poet Kedar Nath Singh. He could be spotted seated alone in one of the many roadside eateries within the campus.

Many with creative and radical ideas, for instance, Ritwik Ghatak with his unmatched cinematic insight and brilliance, would spend time at the Sapru House with the students, over packets of bidis and bottles of rum, discussing their own and others' films. Kumar Sahani, Mani Kaul, Raj Bahadur and, later, Prakash Jha in the mid-1980s, would screen and discuss their movies in one of the most reinvigorating atmospheres of the CRS (Centre for Russian Studies) auditorium—which was basically a 100-plus-seat small auditorium initially meant for the erstwhile institute of Russian studies to watch Russian movies and which later metamorphosed into the all-purpose auditorium for the School of Languages. However, as these were the days before television, multiplexes and the invasion of Hollywood, and significantly before the much discussed globalization, good international and national movies were well appreciated in JNU.

The presence of the broader left front brought certain ongoing intellectual engagements, and JNU not only provided the space to nurture those ideas but also sustained them. JNU, for example, would host A.R. Desai—born in Nadiad in 1915, educated at the Bombay University, and one of the most respected academic activists of the time, who believed that only a global revolution could change the capitalistic system—on his occasional visits to the new university. He was often seen in the company of Yogendra Singh.[2] Academic camaraderie made

JNU a very friendly space. It was also the first port of call for the two species of communist intellectuals, one from Calcutta and the other from Moscow.

With the arrival of the first batches of teachers and students, the mind of the new institution began to take shape. Two centres with discrete identities and academic trajectories were amalgamated into the new institution even before operations began. The School of International Studies was self-contained with a career of its own and high visibility among the city's policymaking literati due to the glamorous aura of international relations and policy debates in the high noon of the cold war. It was linked with the new requirements of the state, the external affairs ministry and the upper political–bureaucratic strata. It was, however, destabilizing for the faculty, staff and established researchers of the erstwhile Indian School of International Studies (ISIS), a research institution with an independent deemed university status, to adjust to the hurly-burly (and scrutiny) of the academic life of a university. Well-known scholars from various disciplines were inducted into the new university whilst ISIS was transplanted into its new environment. However, the excitement of being part of a large university and the financial stability with the termination of tenurial systems were reassuring for the school. The progressive attitude of the new teachers and students, primarily of the social sciences, also helped assuage whatever qualms remained.

The intellectual life began to pulsate with ongoing debates among the professionals. For new groups of students who had returned from the West with a completely new sensitivity and language of discourse, the atmosphere provided a space to articulate state-of-the-art concepts on Indian soil. Similarly, the arrival of students from the back of beyond added a whole new perspective. JNU became home to the largest number of students and scholars from the new states of Meghalaya, Manipur, Nagaland and Mizoram, as also from Assam—all in one place, for the first time, at a place outside Gauhati. The JNU community included the children of the landlords from Bihar, Andhra and other states who otherwise would not have selected Delhi University for university education. This was fairly significant in India's social history, because, to some degree, JNU deprived the old centres like Calcutta, Gauhati, Madras and Bombay of the privilege of being a meeting ground for the new generation of the literati.

In its newness, JNU had the added attraction of being bias-free and prejudice-free, while the local universities were collapsing under the weight of their inability to innovate and make an effective transition to a new institutional arrangement, which would accommodate the new social classes and yet provide excellence and institutional growth. The most tragic was the collapse of the disciplines of liberal arts and social sciences in these older universities, due mainly to overcrowding. The largest number of the newly empowered segments of population, most of them first-generation literate, made their way into the liberal arts stream. Their relative backwardness with regard to economic as well as socio-cultural capital barred their entry into the science, technological and professional arenas; hence the preference for liberal arts.

Sections of many of these groups began to capture the political and administrative structures of universities to facilitate their representation in the political space. The provincial politics at this time began to resonate with the idea of social justice and empowerment, which translated into the political expediency of requiring universities to expand and increase their capacities. This began to colour the discourse. Politics, invoking primordial loyalties like caste, language and religion, not only defined the regional socio-political discourse but also prevented any serious engagement with radical world politics invoking universal categories like class or revolution that was agitating the students the world over. JNU, unlike these provincial universities, attracted the student in tune with world politics rather than regional politics.

There were also students like Prakash Karat, Sunit Chopra, Rehana Butt and Jairus Banaji, who had returned from academic exposure in the West—particularly in England where they would have witnessed the student radicalism which had swept over the British universities in 1968. They had brought not only the British, European, Marxist and radical flavours, but also the overwhelming sense of democratic public conduct which overrode individual personalities. This was matched by the large number of Marxists and communists who landed in the university with their utopian vision of communist life, and strengthened the feeling of non-discriminate solidarity amongst students. This sensibility radiated to become part of the initial political life, and, notwithstanding their personal eccentricities, the students and teachers of the first generation made intellectual life in JNU a humanizing experience. This was the first campus which had Marxism meet with the best of social etiquette and the earthiness of Indian simplicity.[3]

The faculty was to frame syllabuses or courses, and, since the examination was also to be conducted by them, there was much excitement in the air. Courses such as capitalism and colonialism, the emergence of colonial economy and the Indian political economy, were heralding the dawn of a completely new intellectual horizon. The teachers who came from universities like Delhi or Calcutta were most excited as they could now frame their own courses easily, which, in those universities, was a hugely bureaucratic affair laced with the dictatorial and archaic attitude of the departmental heads. One consequence of this was the immediate decision to make headship rotational, initially for three years which was reduced to two years at the insistence of people from social sciences, although some in the SIS resisted because it meant loss of power associated with headship. Internal evaluation was completely new in the Indian university system. This also respected the spirit of the JNU Act which wanted to repose a lot of trust and responsibility in teachers.

In no time, the politically articulate sections began to pay attention to organizational matters. Deep cleavages existed among the newly arrived teachers particularly the social scientists as regards their understanding of the Indian society and the state. There was also the deep-seated sectarian divide between the Communist Party of India (CPI) and the Communist Party of India (Marxists) (CPI [M]), which was beginning to take an institutional form with the formation in 1971 of the Students Federation of India (SFI), the students' wing of the latter as against the All India Students Federation (AISF) of the former. While the larger academic and intellectual world was dominated by the CPI, the CPI (M) was emerging with a sectarian zeal and looking for converts so that they could catapult them to the high academic pedestal and steal intellectual dominance from the CPI. The ideological chasm between the two reflected their perception about the state, alliance with the Congress and the overall world situation: the former looked towards Soviet Union and the socialist countries as possible models of social development while the latter adopted the Stalinist model of the party, i.e., strong democratic centralism. The CPI(M) was also oriented more towards China which it considered more attuned to the communist revolution than the post-1956 Soviet Union which had denounced Stalin in the Twentieth Congress of the Communist Party.[4] The divide was to colour many intellectual debates in the campus. The Trotskyites argued against both these variants and would attack Stalin for his subversion of the global revolutionary telos of the communist movement.[5]

There was a students' association in SIS, which, notwithstanding efforts to keep its identity intact in a new federated arrangement, was absorbed within a new pan-JNU bonding. It was this organization which began to talk about the politics of the academia. To broadly describe its understanding of the situation, the politically articulate teachers were perceived as the spokespersons of the state and statist ideology and considered the adversaries of the students who tried to subvert the penetration of the state's ideological apparatus. This led to the attack against teachers who had taken on projects from state agencies like ministries, etc. The attack drew its logic from the instances of universities like Massachusetts Institute of Technology (MIT), Stanford, Illinois and Michigan in the United States which had turned themselves into satellite organizations of the American war-machine in the USA's war for world dominance in the 1950s and '60s. It is here that, for the first time, the global radical student politics made them take a stand against the research programmes of their own institutions. This, to them, indicated the respective teachers' subservience to the state's programme rather than engaging with the intellectual life of the people. There was surprisingly, however, one exception; they never attacked the teachers of the Centre for the Study of Regional Development which had received a number of projects from state agencies like ICSSR (Indian Council of Social Science Research).[6] In a developing country like India, research projects generally come from the state institutions and, in a new university starting afresh, this attack was quite destabilizing, especially in the departments for social sciences and humanities where there is more or less no funding from any source other than the state or the various communities.

One of the major planks of a political campus was hence defined. The criticism was further entrenched with the deeper invocation of the role of the intellectual, and it was for the first time in India that this question was posed in an educational environment. The role of the intellectual as part of the evolution of modern India has been viewed as that of social critics—Rammohun Roy in the 1820s, Jyotiba Phule and others in the 1870s, Gopal Krishna Gokhale, Dadabhai Naoroji, Rao Bahadur G.V. Joshi, Surendra Nath Banerjee and R.C. Dutt in the later part of nineteenth century and the early part of the twentieth century. The university youth of the later period of the 1960s and '70s was actually carrying two traditions—social critique as well as political agitation. The new university assimilated both of them and introduced a new dimension. There was an attempt to situate the intellectual on a universal plane by invoking intellectual tradition that transcended the parochial boundaries of issue-based students' or teachers' politics. Therefore, as an intellectual, it looked at itself with critical eyes in terms of its location in the regime of the day—the Indian state and global power relations. This debate came close on the heels of major changes in the orientation of the Indian state in the 1970s.[7]

Discovering the Colonial Contours

There had always been a demand from many quarters that universities be changed to suit the requirements of the new sections. Even though the intellectual climate had changed, on many levels, the orientation remained that of the old presidency universities, which in turn mimicked the metropolitan universities. In addition, there was the demand to decolonize the universities in the independent country. In the parliament too, the liberals were constantly harping on modelling the Indian academia on the metropolitan universities—they seemed to have an Oxford or Cambridge fixation. The communists and socialists attacked this fixation. The new climate favoured freshness and socialism provided a significant entry point.

Way back in 1964, Bhupesh Gupta exhorted in parliament that the new university must teach scientific socialism. Political theory included the history of the ideas of political sciences. Therefore, the responsibility to engage, both methodologically and analytically, with Marxism fell on the Centre for Political Development.

'Political Science' as a discipline stood at a crossroads by the mid-1960s. There was a feeling that the discipline was lackadaisical.[8] A senior political scientist from Banaras Hindu University, K.V. Rao, in his presidential address at the annual conference of the Indian Political Science Association in 1967, expressed this sentiment when he said that the most pathetic figure in the academic field today in India, next only to the philosopher and the historian, were the political scientists. Unhonoured, unwept and unsung, political scientists, he said, lived a life of excommunication, worse than the Dalits. He further added that the Indian political scientists were far behind in intellectual equipment to their American counterparts and that the greatest feat that the Indian political scientists could display was in writing cheap textbooks.[9]

The Indian Political Science Association, which was set up in 1939 with the initiative of Tara Chand and Gurmukh Nihal Singh, had become a sort of a meeting ground for a large number of political scientists. Rao, talking sarcastically about both his personal and professional frustration at its annual meeting in 1967, compared the political scientist with the Indian farmer and found the former more backward. The latter, he argued, 'considered himself to be the most ill-equipped, using the most antiquated tools and cultivating the most barren fields, until he met the Indian political scientist'.[10] Talking about the comparative advantage, or the lack of it, among the Indian scholars, he blamed the colonial mindset of the upper echelons of the political class in India for such a poor showing of the Indian political scientists. The expansion and the new institutional landscape were not helping matters as the new political leadership began to treat the academia as one more extension of their political space for patronage.

The relationship, therefore, began to be defined on hierarchical terms. The new entrants to the universities, both students and teachers, would help strengthen the core of this relationship, as they both needed patronage of the state and the administration to consolidate their own position. This came at a time when the university system was at its most expansive phase and, therefore, the new institutional designs, which ought to have strengthened the idea of excellence, lacked any such motivation, to the extent that even the older literati was encouraged to give up the idea of excellence. This was a period of rampant casteism, nepotism and academic corruption in universities in all of the states. This further made the political class, in general, and the leadership, in particular, look down upon researchers from Indian universities and hence, except in rare cases, was not ready to extend the respect due to an academic, which it was ready to give to even mediocre foreign scholars. Access to primary papers for the Indian researchers, was treated as an extension of the privilege usually reserved for foreign scholars. Historical materials in the National Archives, for example, were not open to Indian scholars while the same were given to Oxford or Cambridge scholars, thereby giving them an upper hand at exactly a time when the Indian historians were coming into their own in attacking the colonial claims.

Talking about how foreign researchers got access to almost all resources and persons, for example, the most confidential of government files or influential politicians, Rao gave his own example by revealing that he had sought interviews with many politicians, both big and small, but found that many either did not open their doors, and if they did open their doors, did not care to open their minds.[11] Dr S. Radhakrishnan, the philosopher president, though retired, had flatly refused to meet him. This experience, he suggested, made it clear that 'we have no access to any knowledge of the political process through the interview method or case studies. Our only source is the Americans—we have to quote them, to make a living.'[12]

This lack of access was acutely felt in political science as the discipline itself was trying to find its feet, both in terms of an identity and its methodological moorings, and needed academic cooperation from both the leadership and the administration—its object of study as well as its facilitator. However, the dice seemed to be loaded against them. On the one hand, the campaigners for expansion of the American behavioural science agenda of 'political development' were camping with money and clout from foundations, while the Indian political classes were openly sneering at home-grown intelligentsia. Even the most progressive and extremely pro-Nehruvian scholars felt strongly when an extremely pro-Israel political scientist, Michael Brecher, could enjoy easy access to Nehru and write his biography. It was not jealousy as one American area studies expert would years later express himself.[13] It was an anger against the political class's unequal treatment of its own intelligentsia. Writing in a similar vein, a close observer of the capital's intellectual life wrote:

> The academic world has only followed the pattern set by the political leaders of free India. The late prime minister rarely had time to sit across the table with Indian academics, much less did he utilize any opportunities to carry on a meaningful dialogue to bridge the gap between the politicians and the academics. He was very generous with his time to all and sundry foreign scholars. Michael Brecher, the biographer of Nehru, was provided easy access to the great man including opportunities to travel with him across the length and breadth of the country.[14]

This was the time when the dominance of Anglo-Saxon political thinking seemed to be waning with very few scholars entering the field and the heyday of Harold Laski, who inspired many Indians at the London School of Economics, had also come to an end by this time. Ivor Jennings (1903–65), with his long innings in Ceylon where he went to set up the University of Ceylon, of which he was also the vice chancellor (1942–55), was probably the last of the British academics in the subcontinent. His authority was widely accepted and his classic works *British Constitution* and *Cabinet Government* were there to inspire political scientists to assess the Indian parliamentary democracy modelled on the mother of parliaments, i.e., the British parliament.[15] W. Morris Jones, a votary of Indian independence, was also there to give solidity to the political science camps with his *Parliament of India* and *Government and Politics of India*.[16] His becoming the director and professor of commonwealth studies in London kept the Indian social scientists linked in many ways to the British and commonwealth scholars. The last of the major British political scientists who would look at the Indian constitution and its initial working with sympathetic eyes was Grenville Austin.[17]

One was, however, witnessing the ascendancy of the American political scientists since the 1950s. They had begun descending on the former colonies with anthropologists and area study researchers. South-East Asia and West Asia were fast becoming the flashpoints of an impending clash with communist expansion and also a fight for oil and other resources. The clout and operation of the American foundations to metamorphose the entire academic and intellectual life had demonstrated itself in, apart from many others, Indonesia, where the foundations, in close cooperation with American businesses and the state department, not only changed the intellectual profile of the country but the country itself.

The area studies, particularly Indian studies in the United States, had originated more or less on Indological foundations. The pioneer in the field, Norman Palmer, was a Sanskritist and held the chair for Sanskrit in Pennsylvania since the late 1940s. The indological chord was strengthened by the coming of Robert Redfield's students such as Milton Singer, McKim Marriot, and some others who thought of studying the connectivity within the civilizational expanse by locating the links through the Indian texts and their contexts. The late 1950s also saw Chicago anthropologist, Bernard Cohn, revitalizing the field by combining ethnography with politics and textual analysis. There were also movements in places like Michigan where South Asian studies could be seen to be increasingly emerging from their earlier Indological core and moving into village studies and the study of law. Significantly, Norman Palmer retired in 1968, and with this the umbilical cord between Indological studies and area studies seemed to be cut.

It is here that one gets an understanding of the history of the process of post-war academic intervention. In one of the most massive efforts which began in the Harvard University's department of social relations, sociologist Talcott Parson's 'system theory' was adopted as the template for understanding the political system in the former colonies and Third World societies where systems and components were to be studied to identify the elements that held the system together. In the overall project of preventing communism from spreading among these societies, this understanding of system was to be applied. Once intellectually diagnosed, the institutions were to be supported financially to align with the security and strategic needs of the state department.[18]

'Deathly Hallows'

The 1950s saw the rise of behaviouralism as both an intellectual movement and as a cold war effort to produce counter-communist academic agenda. Behaviouralism emerged with the close cooperation of political scientists and, in the USA, anthropologists located in a couple of the leading universities. The leading American foundations like Ford,

Rockefeller and Carnegie supported the state department of the United States as the latter engaged itself in its pursuit of global dominance. Edward Shils, the brilliant sociologist and thinker wrote one of the foundational texts of the group in which he defined modernism and how modernization was the goal of post-colonial independent countries.[19] The foreign policy of the United States, it was argued, must capitalize on the drive to modernise by the erstwhile colonized countries.[20] These intellectuals also developed a completely new discipline called 'Comparative Politics' with the patronage of the American state and the foundations. In promoting comparative politics, they aimed at understanding how the politics of the post-colonial world differed from that of the industrialized world'.[21] Every effort now was to study, research and work on how the differences provided clues to the effort at 'uniform modernization' and how communism could be contained or countered through modernizing efforts. It was suggested that 'social uniformities of political behaviour' would provide the basic unit of comparison.[22] With the comparative methodology widely entrenched, one saw there were efforts to harmonize the idea of political development and that of modernization. This was done by Myron Weiner at MIT.

Gabriel Almond also consolidated the political development programme to support a programme of interdisciplinary seminars and training institutes on political development. He received a grant of $273,000 from Ford in April 1960. This would help him open developing area programmes in Third World countries.[23] Almond now gave the leadership to Lucien Pye and under the latter's leadership from Princeton, a series on political development would show the way. While Princeton would lead the political development project, MIT was already deeply involved in actively developing and intervening in anti-communist economic policymaking for the government. MIT had the reputation of being the most ardent supporter of the US efforts during the world war, and now with the cold war its support was almost guaranteed.[24] Its center for international studies now pitched in with W.W. Rostow and Max Milikan in designing the economic policies for the countries beset with the issue of poverty and which could be susceptible to communism.

The center became the main champion of American interests in the Third World.[25] W.W. Rostow came out with the celebrated *Non-*

Communist Manifesto which delineated the stages of economic growth with the grand theory that the communists were to be attacked at the stage of take-off in those societies which were planning economic development.[26] The economists involved in Indian planning were actively encouraged by the MIT, and there was a lot of collaboration which was, in hindsight, oriented to enable the US to monitor the developments in India.[27]

The defence establishment was closely cooperating with the whole behavioural enterprise. Rand Corporation, the major think tank of the United States Air Force, organized a conference in Santa Monica in August 1969, where Edward Shils (1910–95) and Lucien Pye (1921–2008) presented the key papers. Along with their arguments pleading for intervention, Hans Speier, the chair of the Rand Research Council, former director of Project Troy and chair of the advisory committee to the CIS communications programme, pointed out that the military had played three salutary roles in post-colonial societies. His position echoed the position of many behaviouralists which saw the military as a revolutionary force that has contributed to the disintegration of the traditional political order and also as a stabilizing force to keep some countries from falling prey to communist rule. Therefore the military was also seen as a the modernizing force apart from being seen as a champion of middle-class aspirations or popular demands for social change; it was also viewed as having the ability to provide administrative and technological skills to the civilian sectors of countries in which such skills are scarce. In fact, Lucien Pye did his best to make the army in the Third World the biggest supporter of American projects when he argued that that the civil leaders in post-colonial countries were psycho-pathologically anti-Western and anti-American while the military was not. The military also provided people the security and national identity, which they craved. Thus, it is the military leadership that required to be befriended or installed in the post-colonial countries for strengthening the hands of the United States against any enemy take-over or any inimical regime.

Samuel Huntington, who also belonged to this group of political scientists and anthropologists, suggested that, along with all these formulations supporting the military regime, there was another dimension to the policy. He was, as Gilman points out, anti-people in that he believed and wrote that the people should not be trusted and supported the idea that the military be the 'stabilizing factor'. However, he emphasized that more than anything else 'slowing the growth rate in the post-independent country should have been the foreign policy objective of the United States'.[28] One may see that this became the important national template for some groups of scholars in the Third World, albeit supported by the US agency, to talk against development, science and technology at the very initial stage of their development.[29]

The emergence of this strong and extremely innovative cabal of political scientists and anthropologists contributed to the disarticulation of the American academia itself. There were major disarticulations earlier, namely, the Second World War which meant many academic departments, for example, MIT, Illinois and Columbia, veered towards sponsored work for anthropological, physiological and scientific warfare and thereby transformed the American academia into a large storehouse of state policy. The eastern Europeans and the Jewish migrants gradually made their peace with the new academia in the sciences, some by taking these works against Germany first and against communism later, with a zeal generally associated with new converts. Thus, by the end of the 1970s, the American academia at the top was a gargantuan conglomeration of conformism where, for many to conform to the state policy was such an intimate game of their life that many outsiders could not even realize the reality, impressed as they were with the overt trappings of efficiency and academic orderliness that they encountered.

In this project, the critics, as one recent author shows, were ousted from the system itself. The American star system was born and, despite the attack on the system by the forces of opposition in 1968, the hold of these groups remained just as powerful. In 1990, when the modernizing theory was no longer required and needed to be discarded in order to legitimize traditional forces in Asia and Africa, a powerful attack on modernization, modernity, etc., would be launched in the Third World as an anti-modernist phalange. Here the postmodernist discourse of the 1990s would be of great help to legitimize the new project. Now a new section of intellectual compradors was available which was more powerful than the earlier area studies specialists as they would sneak into the mainstream leveraging the deep antipathy of the local upper classes towards its university system by sponsoring institutions which were supra university but ready to be satellites of the academic programme of the United States and other developed countries.

One of the key points in the Developing Programme, Comparative Politics Programme and Behavioural Programme—all with strong financial support from the foundations—was the attack on the state in the former colonies, if they were not held by military.[30] The Indonesian case is a singularly significant example. Just after the Second World War was over and Japan was made a kind of informal American satellite, the strategic interest of the United States in the Pacific was to get control of Indonesia with its vast pool of resources, primarily material. And, lo and behold, the state department, the foundations and the university conglomerate descended upon Indonesia. The benign undersecretary of state in charge of the Pacific, Dean Rusk, announced that, 'communist aggression in Asia required not only that Americans be trained to combat it there but we must open our training facilities for increasing numbers of our friends from across the Pacific'. Soon the training programme for the budding Indonesian elite began in right earnest with potential economists trained in MIT and later on at Berkeley, and political scientists trained at Cornell. Huge resources came in and the villages were mapped with a large number of research assistants working for the American anthropologists and their Ithaca Programme. The leading American hand in Indonesia was Sumitro Djojohadikusumo, professor of economics and rector at the University of Indonesia, who also led the political party that tried to oust Sukarno from power and bring an end to his nationalistic or socialistic policies. After a failed rebellion, he was forced to leave the country and live in exile from 1950 to 1967.[31] He led the department from Singapore and other places but all efforts to remove him were foiled by fierce opposition of the Ford and the Rockefeller Foundations who, in fact, silenced even the American officials on this. The counter-threat was that in case the Indonesian government insisted on Sumitro's removal, the foundations would remove all the professors, etc.

The Americans now moved parallelly to establish contact with the military elite and began meeting and training them—as Stephen Cohen was suggesting for the Indian military later in 1971.[32] By the mid-1960s, the foundations had helped create a new elite in Indonesia, replacing almost completely the old nationalists who were trained in the Dutch or nationalist period. The new elite were trained in Berkeley, MIT, and Cornell and would very soon be engaged in a different kind of programme—modernizing Indonesia. The synchronized efforts of the foundations, industry, and even magazines like *Time* and *Life* were alarmingly fast.[33] New people were put in place where economic and business policies were to be made, and all had been trained at the Indonesia Centre at Berkeley or at MIT. Sumitro Djojohadikusumo returned home and became the minister for trade and commerce—the waiting period for the CIA and the foundations was over.

The other members of the new government came from a closely knit team of Berkeley graduates or those who closely worked with them. Nitisastro Widjojo who became chairman of the National Planning Board was a Berkeley graduate (Ph.D, Berkeley, 1961) while his deputy on the planning board, Emil Salim, was his junior at Berkeley (Ph.D, Berkeley, 1964). The minister for finance, Ali Wardhana, was also a Berkeley graduate (Ph.D, Berkeley, 1962), and the Secretary General of the Marketing and Trade Research was Gatot Sibroto who had graduated from Harvard in 1964 and was the chairman of the technical team of foreign investment. Mohammad Sadli had a masters degree from MIT in 1956, whereas Barli Halim, the Secretary General of industry, was again a full-blooded Berkeley man (Berkeley, 1959).[34] Interestingly, it was the time when the Harvard sociologist, Daniel Bell, was pronouncing ideology to be dead in a post-industrial society in his book *Post-Industrial Society*.[35] Indonesia was entering into that kind of society where the old ideologies had to be buried. In a contemporary publication, A. Brackman, as if making a case against the communists, suggests that the PKI (Communist Party of Indonesia) should not be outlawed but systematically curbed. This is exactly what happened a year later.[36] Who says ideology was dead? It was killed by other ideologies.[37]

The so-called 'modernizing regime' finished off almost everyone linked to the nationalist and communist movement, and was trying to create an independent political existence in Indonesia. The new leadership had been struggling to strengthen the unity of a predominantly agrarian and diverse country, achieved during the anti-colonial fight, and form a national state. While it was clear that the CIA was involved from as early as 1958 to bring some kind of regime change and that the 1965 coup bore its unmistakable fingerprints, the people who were also trying to argue for such an eventuality, though ex post facto, were the American academics, who themselves were engaged in weakening any idea of an Indonesian state, both historically and in contemporary times which could have transcended the religious or communitarian divisions, leading to the free country becoming a new, unified nation.

American anthropologists of all political hues in their own country descended and, even though coming from entirely different political perspectives (Clifford Geertz, who was a part of the state department's projects, categorized the traditional Balinese state as a 'theatre state', while Benedict Anderson, representing the other end and holding radical anti-state positions, dubbed it as an 'imagined community') attempted, with one voice, to posit the idea that the Indonesian coup was a reaction against communist attempts to take over. While the local intelligentsia were yet to take stock of the Dutch colonial experience, they now had to intellectually face the arrival of heavily financed American academia with the strong backing of the state department whose policy line was to install regimes which had no truck with communists. They sponsored intellectual projects on Indonesia; they did their utmost to delegitimize the Indonesian state. One result was the legitimacy that the military derived as a uniting and stabilizing power amidst a supposed lack of any such unifying power historically. The effort was to paint a country as a fragmented state, as a tool in the cold war effort to delegitimize and also de-historicize non-Western, and newly independent, states.[38]

Indian intellectuals were alive to what was happening in Indonesia and other parts of the world, and leading scholars had criticized the happenings in Indonesia. This was also the time when there was strong opposition to the use or misuse of the PL-480 money by the American embassy. It was a coincidence that the *New York Times* exposé came along at this time, i.e., 1967, thus leading to a serious discussion among the intelligentsia and the political community about the real nature of CIA interventions. A scholar at ISIS argued that all of these were, in fact, exaggerating the role of the CIA and that it might be the CIA itself leaking information about men and materials that had become its liabilities.[39] Leading journalist, C. N. Chittaranjan, would strongly refute such efforts at what he thought was normalization of the role and operation of the CIA.[40] In India, the behaviouralist centre known as the Centre for Study of Developing Studies (CSDS) was accused of being funded by the Asia Foundation, which, in 1966, proved to be a front for the CIA. I am not sure whether it got money from the same funding source as Gabriel Almond, namely, the Rockefeller Foundation.[41]

The founding father of CSDS, Rajni Kothari, however, operationalized the concept that Talcott Parsons had provided for the 'system'. For Rajni Kothari, the Indian political scenario provided the best example of that system, the Congress system. The death of Nehru brought intellectual euphoria to those who thought that, in light of the new system theory, the Congress system based as it was on Nehru's personality, would begin to crumble.[42] Kothari kept a close eye on the Congress system for a decade and followed his initial report with a decennial review.[43] The rapid right-wing sway in these couple of years was coupled with increasing centrifugal tendencies in the political parties and the opposition parties, which had begun to wrest some initiative from 1964 onwards. This sway had come to the fore by 1966, making the American scholars start talking about this being a 'dangerous decade'[44] and speculating on Nehru's successors.

It was abundantly clear to the Western scholars that the Indian state was not held together by the military, and its structure was more permanent, and hence they attacked what they considered its most enduring component which held the society together—the Congress system. A continued watch over the health of that system too became part of this behaviouralist regimen. State, expectedly in this design, was seen as an impediment to democracy and therefore the whole institutional design of such sponsored centres was to attack the Congress system. The political behaviour was to be seen from the electoral and psychological make-up of the populace, which reflected themselves either through voting patterns (election studies), violence, or their attitude to tradition and culture (political psychology).

Interestingly, the newly established ICSSR, where Rajni Kothari had an important presence, began to sponsor election studies which, thankfully, could not become a very big phenomenon; otherwise it would have killed whatever serious discussions that the discipline began to evolve among the political scientists. There were also the

Huntingtonian elements which were to criticize development with an overall strategy of slowing growth and significantly, coming at a time when the foreign policy agenda had also begun legitimizing tradition, it found in Ashis Nandy one of the most intellectually strong defenders of tradition in India.[45] Interestingly, Huntington was a serious votary of bombing Vietnam and was later found to have been sponsored by the CIA.

The insularity of the American intellectual life began to catch up with India in the 1980s. The critique of its own assumptions about the Third World was now converging with its critique of modernity and a radical multicultural revolt in the US campuses. Rabid anti-communism and cultural explanations had already made a heady intellectual concoction here. While the society was trying to arrive at a certain unity, intellectuals were directing their energy towards isolated multiculturalism to keep their own minuscule relevance in a gigantic capitalistic leviathan. An anti-communist section of Indian intellectuals that advocated anti-modernity, anti-communism and what was called anti-secular path, now began to see consonance with radical Third World intellectuals in the American campus. The anti-Sikh riots of 1984, and the anti-Muslim riots of the 1980s provided a social base for an intellectual formation. There was thus an interesting conjunction between the extremely sectarian discourses of caste and communalism with the new-found love for the multicultural and the tradition in some sections. A critical eye still saw the connections with these academic agendas and the financial contributions from the Foundations and its forward linkages with the agenda-setting centres at the Ivy League universities.

Way to Recover the Self

It was political science in India that was destined to have the first brush with the American foundations. The discipline as such did not have too many scholars—a handicap even in later years—and, on top of that, the leading lights, except for a couple, were already beginning to talk in the language that Shils, Lucien Pye or others had designed for them. Rasheeduddin Khan, who joined the Centre for Political Studies as the first professor, and thereby with the role of shaping the centre, came from Hyderabad. He was emerging as a name to reckon with in the new intellectual horizon of the time with a nomination to the Rajya Sabha by 1970.

An alumnus of the Indian School of International Studies, Rasheeduddin Khan, fondly called Rasheed by colleagues and students, had worked on West Asian politics (Iraq), and from the late 1960s he was writing on the idea of a national frame for secular and integrative society. His efforts at identifying the patterns of Muslim politics in Hyderabad during the mid-1960s, at the time of the emergence of the Ittehad-ul-Muslimeen as a powerful force was best brought out in 'The Muslim Leadership and Electoral Politics in Hyderabad: A Pattern of Minority Articulation'.[46] It was a novel piece in Indian scholarship interpreting an Indian issue in innovative ways. He argued, much against the later day 'valorizing of identity', an American political science concept that influenced political science thinking in India, that being Muslim was not an identity but a part of the country's cultural mosaic and therefore the metaphors and terms would have to be different from the way they were routinely imported into the discourse. His deep-seated secularism and high political and intellectual status among the capital's literati and political circles provided the Centre for Political Studies with an elan and confidence, the lack of which C.V. Rao had complained about. His presence also attracted the students of Andhra and this would prove to be a blessing in disguise for JNU as it would get many politically sensitive students from Osmania University and other colleges and universities in Andhra as also a professor in the shape of K. Seshadri, who was himself a part of the communist movement in Andhra.

The centre would soon appoint Sudipto Kaviraj, the son of a communist party intellectual from Calcutta, with close CPI connections, to its faculty. Another young sociologist, an exceptionally capable scholar, was Rajni Kanth, who had come from Delhi University. However, his tenure at JNU was cut short as he migrated to the United States, due to personal reasons, and was lost to Indian academia.[47] Randhir Singh, the most celebrated Marxist teacher at Delhi University, joined the Centre for Political Studies, only to return soon to his parent university. Randhir Singh had emerged as one of the most brilliant expositors of Marxist theory and attracted a large number of youth to his classes even if they were not political science enthusiasts. His presence, even for a short while, in the new centre saw the end of the Ford Foundation encroachment as his presence ensured that the centre's name changed from 'Centre for Political Development' to 'Centre for Political Studies'.

Randhir Singh had also presented a working paper for the advisory group, which was in sharp contrast to two others by Appadorai and Rajni Kothari. It provided a very fresh and intellectually stimulating footing where the original vision of teaching Marxism was to be fulfilled.

In 1973-74, C.P. Bhambhri, who in his earlier years wrote on the Indian administration and political system, and showed an understanding of Marxian analysis in his later works, now joined the centre. A regular commentator on national politics and with a keen eye on the political happenings, Bhambhri was one of the first to realize the importance of understanding the bureaucracy in a developing country. His doctoral work on parliamentary control over the public sector must have given him some inkling as to the changes in the bureaucracy and its character.[48] It was a pioneering work in the expanding realm of political science and providing an avenue to analyse and explain the operation of politics at different levels without depending upon the ruling class and the supercilious attitude of even Nehru—a fact which was constantly bemoaned by the academics. Soon political studies at JNU had Imtiaz Ahmed, Zoya Khaliq, Aswini K. Ray and Zafar Imam to make it quite a big centre.

These scholars were already engaged with issues of Indian politics before they joined the university. One of their basic concerns that was soon reflected in the political and academic engagements was the character of Indian state. Bhambhri made the study of the state a long-term commitment. He saw the Indian state in two perspectives: firstly as a general theoretical position along the Marxian lines as class rule; secondly, he would relate it to the Indian condition and would argue that, given the global power structure, the state in India functioned as the modernizing factor and was, in many ways, the agency to extend the bourgeois democracy.[49] The real fight here was among the classes to capture the state and the role of intellectuals was to not only understand and analyse the processes involved but to side with the socialistic forces to bring the power of the labour to the fore.[50] Since the early 1960s, his writings were contesting the views advocating the study of political behaviour from an electoral angle. In contrast, he would argue that there was a larger goal behind the elections—politicization of the classes and bringing them inside the democratic experience.[51] A direct confrontation of ideas emerged when Rajni Kothari conducted the first series of election studies on the 1962 elections and analysed the electoral behaviour of the various segments of population. Bhambhri, along with S.P. Verma, came up with a fascinating study suggesting that rural voters were evolving a sophisticated political understanding and also electoral techniques which were in consonance with the unfolding of the Indian democratic polity. This was directly confronting the Kothari hypothesis of analysing the fragmentary nature of the groups and their factional voting patterns along primordial loyalties.[52] Bhambhri's ideas were getting crystallized by the 1970s, and he was now talking about the class character of the Indian state.

Rasheed, on the other hand, looked at the state from two quarters: as a member of the Rajya Sabha and close to the prime minister and her policy advisors, and as a scholar looking at minority politics and the process of regional integration.[53] He saw the state as an evolving but enveloping entity and, therefore, was acutely aware of the Indian state having a completely different historical trajectory. He, therefore, was trying to develop a theory about this. Though a member of the CPI, he was not Marxist in the way many others were—rigorous and serious. His intellectual concerns were primarily the plural character of Indian society.[54] He was trying, therefore, to understand and formulate certain propositions about the state in India that could be repositioned theoretically and intellectually to hold these diversities together. What was significant was that he was trying to evolve an idea of an 'Integrative state'—not a very well-formed idea—along with an idea of Indian federalism.[55] Had he shown more rigour in pursuing this line, he might have developed a new paradigm to define the nationalist state. But, with his involvement in the Rajya Sabha at a time when Indira Gandhi engaged intellectuals quite seriously and intensely, he did not have the requisite time and energy to devote to his ideas and the JNU centre. However, his initial concerns provided the centre with a sense of direction and a measure of autonomy from an overarching and ever-watching ascendancy of the American political science paradigm.

The idea of federalism nurtured by Rasheed would find its careful evolution at the hands of his colleague, Balveer Arora, and the centre would emerge as a major centre to take up federalism as a basic issue for research.[56] Centre–state relations and the idea of federalism also became the core of the intellectual engagement with movements for separate statehood such as in Uttarakhand and Gorkhaland. Here, notwithstanding an analysis of the sociological, ecological and other dimensions of the movement, a resolution was sought under the rubric of a strong federal structure with a robust sense of regional redistribution of resources with a sense of justice.[57] One of the best examples was the work on the Jharkhand movement by Upjit Singh Rekhi entitled 'Jharkhand Movement and the Tribal Polity'.[58]

The new university was determined to break the boundaries of isolated departments and the new pedagogic aesthetic facilitated this. Social science was organized in such a way that in the first year a degree was given in social science—pragmatically it was later changed so that the orthodox job market would not reject JNU students. However, the research and dialogue in these years remained without any boundary and, therefore, faculty appointments were also made with this in mind. The question of state was also no longer confined to merely being a subject in a political science classroom. Larger issues and forces were involved. The political and academic positions were intrinsically connected and both positions were being questioned. In the process, many discursive templates also spilled over to other issues of academic interests. For the issues of Jharkhand, Assam or Bodo movements, scholars also debated the larger issues of transformations taking place in those societies and did not launch an overnight intellectual crusade.[59] For example, while Bhaskar Khaund was trying to unravel the socio-cultural dimension of the Assam movement, Humayun Bhokt was looking into the sociological dimension of the Bodo movement.[60]

One of the most dominant positions at this time was the communist formulation of the idea that the 'Independence was false'—*Azadi Jhuti Hai*. The political and bureaucratic power was, it said, merely transferred from white rulers to brown rulers, and the capitalistic metropolitan classes retained their hold through the collaborating (comprador) Indian bourgeoisie. Therefore, the Independence was a mere pretence. This was the famous Ranadive line named after its proponent, B.T. Ranadive, who was more militant and radical in the Communist Party of India and targeted P.C. Joshi's leadership within the party. The British Marxist theoretician, R.P. Dutt's thesis along this line propounded more thoroughly in his now famous book *India Today*, added to Ranadive's resolution.

All the communist parties believed in the line with varying degrees of conviction. Thus the character of the state was coloured by this thinking and followers of communist parties as well as students and teachers affiliated to either the CPI or the CPI(M) actually believed in this theoretical formulation. The formulation was also the parties' recipe for revolution—both political and social. The aim was to situate the socialist model onto the political realm by overcoming the present bourgeois model. The enthusiasm to do so was evident with one of the earliest works by a political scientist, Nalini Chopra, entitled 'Role of Communist Movement as an Alternative in India'. The formulation was significant in that if one accepted that India's was a false independence, then the role of intellectuals had to be redefined.

There was a second position by other Marxist intellectuals who began arguing that India had gained political independence in 1947 but the local contradictions had remained. This meant that while the contradiction with the colonial power was resolved by wresting independence, India's political independence was therefore real but the job of 'completing the social revolution was', as Bipan Chandra, a major proponent of this thesis would argue, 'waiting to be fulfilled'. The issue, therefore, was to work towards the socialist transformation, which was the role of the intellectual.

Then there was a view that could be associated with either of the two positions, but the political orientation would have aligned this with the latter rather than the former. It held that India was a neo-colonial country.

Discourses Identified

Significantly, JNU students and scholars found this universe a questioning universe. They could express and articulate the deepest of their political and social thoughts without any fear of being attacked as was happening in many parts of the country. Therefore, the electioneering and the presidential debate became a very significant phenomenon at JNU. While electioneering helped ideas to take concrete shape, their critiques sharpened the responses and fine-tuned the ideas further. The presidential debate was a kind of community articulation or a totemic representation with the president representing the community's agreed and consensus views. The available discourses were that of socialist, communist and other forms of Marxist or nationalist discourses, but the overarching need seemed to be for an alternative paradigm. The hundred, and later on couple of thousand, students were not enthusiastic about the communal discourse from the beginning. The reasons were many. First, an all-Indian gathering prevents a narrow and exclusivist world view. Second, in a truly international atmosphere where the most radical efforts of intellectuals were talked about, narrowness and issues of identity generally looked stupid. The third factor was the engagement of the most erudite and popular teachers and their themes.

The underlying sentiment was opposed to all oppressive structures and the solution was to engage intellectually with them. One of these major structures was social stratification signified at its highest level by colonial and unequal international structures. Therefore, one of the most significant and long-standing intellectual exercise had to do with the engagement with the idea and practices of colonialism. JNU came into being around the time the colonial powers were making inroads into Africa, setting off the second wave of colonialism. This was coterminous with the use of military coups and talk of ethnicity. Now, with the help of the military, and the academic agenda of ethnicity, a new and final phase of the cold war began in the African arena. The word 'ethnicity' was an invention to ride over the complications and political undertones of race and the first book on this was by the American diplomat and political scientist, Patrick Moynihan.[61]

'Ethnicity' was invented to counter or replace the word 'race' but it soon became a generic concept easier to describe all different populations. But once the concept became aligned to politics, it had devastating consequences. It also had great strategic value for states which could now encourage fragmentary politics based on whatever point constituted the basic or core identifier of ethnicity—language, religion, etc. Africa now became the new killing fields, marked and separated on the basis of ethnicity. The new military rulers in many places began to take control of the universities. The universities of Makerere, Dar es Salaam, Nairobi and, later on, Ibadan too began to feel the pinch and started to lose their sheen and scholars—the great African migration of academia was about to begin. It is at this juncture that Angola and Guinea Bissau arrived at their—seemingly glorious—independence. Strange are the ways of colonialism. The Guinea Bissau intellectual, Amílcar Cabral, whose fight against the Portuguese colonialism became a legend, became a great inspiration in the campus in Aravali to further decolonize the mind.

There were very serious and studied responses to all assertions, and all rhetorical claims were debated at JNU. This was not a politically correct campus (which it later would become) where dialogue could displace debate and argumentation presumably to retain an air of superiority over those who were, based on some new readings, merely rhetorical. It is this which allowed the intellectual life here to be rooted deeply rather than being swayed by the intellectual fashion of the day or mired into the culturalogical position of East vs West, which the African and many Asian intellectual circles would make the mistake of getting sucked into.[62] The intellectual example that JNU created was of immense help to the intellectual universe in India generally as most of the rhetorical and radical voices in many parts of Africa and Asia turned out to be sponsored.

One such interesting case was the journal *Transition*. It was a journal published from Kampala and had become the flagship journal of the intellectuals of the newly independent East Africa. Its tone and tenor was so radical that even the most radical scholars and political leaders found it hard to match. Culturologists like Ali Mazrui were its regular contributors. However, it was soon discovered that the CIA was partly funding the magazine. Its extremely brilliant editor, Rajat Niyogi, was soon to leave his home, i.e., Kampala, and the last one heard of him was his death in one of New York's poor quarters.[63] Notwithstanding the American help, none of the culturological critics in India could become heroes like they did in Africa. It is only in the mid-1990s that these explanations entered in the guise of Edward Said's East–West dichotomy.

Journals like *Quest* edited by the poet, Abu Syed Ayub, scandalized the intellectual community when it came to be seen as sponsored by dubious foreign agencies. Significantly, *Quest* also tried to initiate debate, generally critical, on 'secularism', 'modernity' and 'science'. Some very obscure American scholars made their presence felt for the first and last time in the journal intervening on the issues of secularism, defence of tradition and traditional science (at a time when advanced science and technology was not shared with India). This goes to show exactly where the influence of the US foreign policy consensus was operating. *Quest* was to wind up soon and its editor, Abu Syed Ayub, resigned to save face. It reappeared with a new name, *New Quest*, later in the 1980s and its flagship topics would be post-colonialism and post-modernity.

The new groups that arrived in JNU in the summer of 1971-72 had been debating on the issues of state, society, class and the socialist order. There was a new-found closeness among the new generation of political leaders and thinkers. The 1967 Arab–Israel war in the Middle East saw India taking a strong position supporting the Arab stance. When the American forces began pounding Vietnam villages and war escalated, India did not endorse the US stance, angering their establishment. The latter hardened its position on the food aid that was committed and was being exported to India under the PL-480 Agreement. President Johnson decided to teach India a lesson by what came to be known as the 'tethering policy'—food ships would be delivered on a day-to-day basis making Indians almost beg for food.

The food crisis brought by Johnson's policy in turn strengthened the left within the Congress and the communist intellectuals' argument against the United States' unfriendly and selfish motives. This forced a new-found determination in Indira Gandhi, and the new leadership decided to exert its independence to counter American bullying. This was when Indira Gandhi gave the go-ahead to its agricultural science and policy establishment to launch what came to be known as the Green Revolution. Indira Gandhi was in many ways seen as moving towards the Soviet Union as it was exactly at this time that she was inducting many socialists and old communists into the policymaking circles. People commented that the Congress left was becoming quite assertive, particularly after the split in the Congress where the old guard and organizational men were moved out and Indira Gandhi increasingly came to lead a plethora of young leaders. The socialist mood in the Congress under her leadership was very obvious.

The freedom and new-found self-esteem must have been enjoyable to students and teachers of JNU. Anti-colonialism, Marxism and nationalism were the three core philosophies that engaged the agile minds in the campus. A new space for a new body of intellectuals was formed, which could now engage in one of the dialectical processes of knowledge production—a first in any institution in modern India. Now whether India was described as free or as a neo-colony, colonialism needed to be probed and this debate infiltrated in the academic and intellectual discourses already taking place in the country for quite some time; it was just accidental that many of the participants were either from the left or not associated to any party.

If India was a neo-colonial country, then it validated the new works from some radical intellectuals who, using some abstract Marxian formulation, argued that the global capitalist order would not allow any development in the peripheral societies. First enunciated by a brilliant Argentinian economist, Raúl Prebisch (1901–86), the unequal exchange and dependency theory became the core of this formulation.[64] It had contended that in the present world system, the countries in the periphery produce primary goods. They have to export them to the countries in the centre, which produce secondary goods and export them back to the periphery. As technology improves, the theorist argued, the centre, due to its already saved resources, can retain 'higher wages and profits' both through 'developed unions' and 'commercial institutions' and is in a favourable position vis-à-vis the countries at the periphery where the companies and workers remain weaker. Prebisch pointed to the decline in the terms of trade between industrialized and non-industrialized countries, which meant more export was needed to get the same value from industrial imports.[65] Through this system, all of the benefits of technology and international trade would accrue to the centre. From this, the idea of the dependency theory began to take shape, which argued that it was nearly impossible for the peripheral countries to achieve independent development.

Andre Gunder Frank, popularized this theory worldwide. Frank, a German refugee in the United States, completed his doctoral thesis with Milton Friedman, whose monetarist theory he would critique later. In 1970, he went to the University of Santiago, Chile, and got involved with the communist leader Allende's new policies. His experience and wide-ranging travel led to his writing the now classic, *Capitalism and Underdevelopment in Latin America*, which contained the famous theorization of the 'development of underdevelopment'.[66]

The volatile situation in Africa and Asia in the early 1970s made the thesis more popular among intellectuals as this was linked with the political idea that a revolution at a global scale was the only way to get out of the dependency status. The radical condition in Europe, the Arab world, and in the whole of Asia and Africa, actually endorsed such a formulation and created a revolutionary zeal. They argued that in the way global capitalism is constituted, there was no way that the dependent economies could come out of their dependent status and the colonial system. The Indian nationalist intelligentsia had said the same thing almost a hundred years ago and argued that unless India breaks free from colonialism there would be no escape from its backwardness. Bipan Chandra used Andre Gunder Frank's analysis of colonialism or 'dependence' in the context of Latin America to make his case for the development of underdevelopment in the context of India.[67]

Thus, the critique that state was enmeshed in global engagement and colonialism became a core issue. This time, however, it fitted in well with the views of the radical intelligentsia and the old communist formulations. The moot question was the nature of the independence that India achieved in 1947 and the economic development taking place if one assumed that the context was neo-colonial development. Was there no escape from the world capitalist system premised on unequal exchange, as Samir Amin, Immanuel Wallerstein and Emmanuel Arghiri would suggest?[68] Wallerstein proposed in his world system analysis that an escape was possible only in case there was a world revolution. Until then it was a zero-sum game and the metropolitan centres would not allow the periphery to grow at its expense. It was a seductive argument as one student of the time remembers.

> We were all young at that time and passionate about everything. At one level it had do with Frantz Fanon's *Wretched of the Earth* and Paulo Freire's *Pedagogy of the Oppressed*. We wanted to change the world and lived in the world created by the writings of Gunder Frank and Samir Amin, Marcuse and Marx, Camus, Sartre, Ivan Illich and Maurice Godelier. Our vocabulary

was replete with words like emancipation and empowerment, imperialism and oppression, freedom and revolution.[69]

Transcending the Colonial

One of the strongest features of the new intellectual life that had developed in the 1960s and '70s in India was its deep-seated anti-colonial streak. More than any other discipline, history had to take on with a boldness not seen before, both professionally and intellectually, the full might of the colonial disarticulation of the history and economy of Indian society. Therefore, the discipline had within itself the basic presuppositions of colonialism and the arguments to counter those premises. The spectrum which constituted the historians' world, included historiographical assumptions, factual details and the political undertones of the trajectories which colonial historiography took. The Indian historians in the 1920s not only read the same sources but debated on the historiographical presuppositions on the issues of democracy, state, republican sensibilities, pluralism, etc. The first-generation debaters unconsciously subscribed to the tripartite division of Indian society—Hindu, Muslim and modern—as described by the East India Company's clerk, James Mill, in his *History of India*. Later historians, with more advanced historical consciousness, tried to correct this. Although the Marxist paradigm with innovative ideas was brought out by Marxist intellectuals, historians immediately took control of the debate and steered it along the trajectories of the discipline itself and liberated it from the guidelines of the party. It is here that the importance of scholars like D.D. Kosambi lies.

The new university centres in Africa, particularly that of Ibadan, Makerere, Nairobi and Dar es Salaam, tried to create centres for history which would disentangle themselves from what they perceived as the colonial creation of African history that would get reasserted by the colonial universities and their publications like *Journal of African History*. In Nigeria, from its first Ph.D, A.E. Afigbo in 1964, to the scholars until the mid-1970s, almost everyone saw the universities in Britain and the United States as bastions of imperialism. They, therefore, not only tried to develop a new methodology for African history but also rejected the *Journal of African History* and developed their own quite popular journal, namely, *Journal of the Historical Society of Nigeria*. Leading scholars of the Ibadan University like Saburi Biobaku, Kenneth Dike, J.F.A. Ajayi, Adiele Afigbo, E.A. Ayandele, O. Ikime and Tekena Tamuno wrote for the journal and participated in the meetings of the historical society of Nigeria.[70]

In Nairobi, B.A. Ogot emerged as the most powerful voice of this African historical renaissance. He and his colleagues such as Jan Vansina, J. Anene and C.A. Diop demonstrated that the history of Africa was full of dynamic movements and left very rich sediments. They contested the Eurocentric hegemony of African history and tried to research on colonization, the African self and issues like slavery, etc.[71] In Dar es Salaam too the department of history became the centre to contest colonial historiography and actively promoted an Africa-centred history writing. The new nations found this history as something to be happy about as it provided a sense of confidence to, as well as an assertion of, the new national and African personality.[72] In the third and the most dynamic of the East African universities, Makerere, also the new generation rejected colonial stereotypes and invoked an Afro-centric history.[73] This invocation to abandon the Eurocentric mode and methods to try and evolve new historical tools, methodologies and explanations, brought the historians together almost on a pan-continental scale.[74]

The period seemed to be reminiscent of the Indian historiographical era which questioned many of the colonial assumptions. Here one may do well to quote of the doyen of Indian historians, R.S. Sharma:

> Western indologists of the nineteenth and the early twentieth centuries popularized the stereotypes of oriental despotism and the hold of religion and spiritualism. These came under heavy attack, largely justified, from Indian scholars. After India attained Independence, the west developed a kind of neo-orientalism based on sociology. As a concession to the independent republican status of India, western historians and indologists modified the idea of perpetual despotism, but they placed undue emphasis on the role of religion, particularly rituals, and the divinity of kingship.[75]

However, mounting a critique of the earlier historians, Sharma, writing in 1959 like many of his contemporaries, was indicating the limitations of such histories written in response to Western historians, and he showed great maturity when he said:

> But this nationalist ideology has its limitations. First, while it did serve to rouse the educated middle class against alien rule, it hardly appealed to conscious intellectuals interested in the masses of peasants and workers who were being drawn into the national struggle from 1920 onward.[76]

He further pointed out that by 'a fulsome adoration of ancient Hindu institutions', the histories 'tended to antagonize the Muslims though this was not done deliberately'.[77] It also gave a 'false sense of past values' and also made them shy away from 'the religious aspect of ancient Indian polity, and, as if to cover a sense of guilt, took too much pain to prove the secular character of ancient Indian state, little realizing that even in the western world the first completely secular state did not come into existence until 1783 and that India was not the only country where religion influenced political ideas and actions'. In its craze for proving the superiority of our ancient institutions over those of the ancient West, it hardly tried to examine them in the light of evolution of primitive tribes as known from anthropology or in the light of early institutions of other Indo-European peoples.[78] Thus, Indian historians were not only conscious of the limitations of their contemporary approaches but the advance of democracy was also getting reflected in their writings.

In order to refute the notion that Africa does not have a history, the African historians showed the presence of history on a continental scale at a time when nations were also beginning to be formed and consolidated after the first wave of independence. Actually, the nationalist phase in Africa was a phase of bringing history to Africa and not to any particular nation. It was the opposite in India—where history and nation making were either simultaneous processes or history followed nation making. Now, in Africa this meant that the consolidation of the new nation was liable to break the consolidation of history. This turned out to be fortuitous for colonial history to make a comeback with vengeance.

In India, however, the mid-1960s was the most critical phase for national development and the intelligentsia was exercised about that. The role of colonization came up afresh through the issues of labour, foreign trade and, most importantly, industry. The issues of development, which brought the issues of planning and equitable distribution of wealth to the fore, led to a searching probe into the colonial disarticulation of national and global economies. This in turn resulted in a debate on two crucial issues, namely, the role of trade particularly export and the role of foreign capital. The tribe of economists lived and thrived on these debates and many a career was made. However, more crucial for intellectual purposes was the role of historians who came in at this juncture when the debate on developing India, i.e., with industry and agriculture or with trade and foreign capital, etc., was witnessing the sneaky entry of the old colonial assertion that it had developed India by introducing commercialization of agriculture, increasing the volume of trade, and developing administrative structures—which were precisely the inputs seen as instruments of exploitation by the colonial regime. This was the time when historians strove to create an autonomous space for themselves and the discipline by using the opportunity created by the efforts of the Indian state to create an independent economic development.

The best came in 1963 when Morris D. Morris, an emerging economic historian, wrote that colonialism had helped India develop and that no such thing as de-industrialization of Indian economy had taken place. This premise was thoroughly criticized by historians Bipan Chandra, Tapan Ray Chaudhuri and Toru Matsui. The debate was to appear in a special issue of *Indian Economic and Social History Review*, a journal which began to take shape with the effervescence of Indian scholarship.

However it was the journal *Enquiry*, although not highbrow, but run quite passionately by young Marxists, which brought out the best in scholars—both from home and abroad. In its pages, the paper, 'Potentialities of Capitalist Development' by Irfan Habib, was published which, as we see later, had a significant place in the debate on Indian capitalism and colonialism. The Marxist historians, in many ways, were creating a new universe. First, they linked their argument with the early nationalists and their defence of a modern state. Secondly, in their argument they also fused the early nationalist secularism and anti-colonial spirit into a concrete reality. This fusion explains why Marxism and some notions of communism are entrenched in the Indian psyche, and the collapse of the Soviet Union or the turning of China into a capitalist society does not diminish the Indian Marxist historians' explanatory potential or the respect they command.

This was also the time when India, a former colony, was the happy hunting ground for experimental ideas of those who would make policies for the 'new states'. There were invocations to join the 'modernist' bandwagon.[79] To cite Shils: 'modern states must be "dynamic", above all else. To be modern, an elite, as the elites of the new states see it, "must not fear change; on the contrary, it must strive to bring it about". It does not wish to remain as it is.'[80] The policy imperatives of these new players in the international arena required that they knew and had connections with the political elite and what they saw as the policy. It was a new society, a new state and therefore the elite needed to be known so that politics could be formulated by influencing them. American anthropology started becoming active in many societies simultaneously. Interesting projects to study the locals began to ensue from Cambridge and Oxford and, due to the way the projects were structured, this denied any larger entities other than factions or groups to be studied.[81]

On the other hand, debate on modernity and tradition in India was far older than the American area studies scholars could fathom and it was the touchstone of Indian nationalism. Using agencies such as the army to frogmarch a nation into modernity was so far from the consensus that it cut no ice with the Indian society, which had been exposed to these futile exercises. The modernity and contemporaneity with which these scholars worked and took up issues opened up an entirely new world to the historians. In light of the advances made by the previous generation of scholars, such as D.D. Kosambi, K.M. Ashraf, R.S. Sharma, Irfan Habib and Nurul Hasan, Marxian analysis for history did not require to be invented.

It is for such scholarship that JNU provided one of the largest space to enable its historians to fill the gaps in the narrative. Romila Thapar, whose book on the Mauryas had talked about the imperial dimension of the Mauryan state, had the ability to make the behaviouralists look foolish with their idea that the former colonies were systems without a state—the state can be absent both as a theory and as an agency in such a systemic understanding of politics.[82] It was an important project as the Marxist state formation theory involved certain structural assumptions which were difficult to follow for an ancient Indian historian.

The issue of the state which the political scientists were to discuss was no longer reserved for them; it was in this context that the historian pitched in with much more decisiveness. The debate on the character of Indian state in modern times pivoted on the core of colonial operation, i.e., land revenue.[83] The debate even during the British colonial taxation was about the right to property where the British had to concede the existence of the state. It planned itself as the successor state. The British state could not be as grand as the Mughal Empire; however, the main issue was whether the state-to-state structure was bestowed by the British, and this debate still goes on. Historians had been taking up the cudgels on behalf of the character and presence of the state in India with colonial administrators and historians. Some of the best efforts have come from U.N. Ghoshal for ancient India. He talked about Hindu polity while K.R. Kanungo talked about the medieval polity.[84] Similarly, Romila Thapar had recently written a long historical text on the Mauryas.[85] Sibesh Bhattacharya of Allahabad University was writing on the Mauryan state through a brilliant and critical exposition of *Arthasastra*, the prime text of the time.[86] Medieval state was brought to light through detailed works by Irfan Habib, Satish Chandra, Athar Ali and others of Aligarh University.[87] K.A. Nilakantha Shastri and T.V. Mahalingam of Madras University brought out the centrality of the Chola state while, in the east, Amalendu Guha excellently brought out the political architecture of the Ahom state in Assam.[88]

The intellectual project delegitimizing the state structures in the Third World so that either the military is installed as the stabilizing factor or the process of growth is shown to slow down had the foreign policy aims of contaning the expansion of communism.[89] This, along with certain peculiarities of American intellectual life which included the complete annihilation of Marxist scholarship during Joseph McCarthy's crusade, and deep provincialism of the American socio-political life, had allowed an inbuilt resistance against any universal intellectual premise.[90] This would soon make the project of exploring all avenues to designate the political structure obtained in India as a 'segmentary state' as against the general academic view of the existence of a large state structure, a very serious and celebrated intellectual project of some American scholars.[91]

The template of a larger and connected civilizational universe which underlined the works of anthropologists like Robert L. Park and his students in the 1940s was now completely abandoned for ideas of 'segments and factions'.[92] Park's work on the Yucatan villages then spread through his Chicago students to Asia which tried to explore the connectivity within the civilizations. This was one of the largest work on network relations even before network became a fashionable technical work in the twenty-first century.[93] The theoretical frame helped anthropologists like Milton Singer's exceptionally rigorous and path breaking research on urban centres like Madras, or on works about the evolution of many pilgrim centres evolving into a larger civilizational matrix.[94] Since the 1960s the academic establishment in the United States increasingly squeezed out ideas of connectivity. The idea of fragmentation began to gain orthodoxy. The factions within the society and the role of the elites in shaping the policy regimes seemed to be the focus of the day. Between civilization and fragments, the location of the modern nation state in India became an intellectual problem for the American scholarship in the 1960s. This was a problem whose burden would later shift to their Indian students in the 1980s.

By the time the ideas like 'the absence of state' or 'mock or theatrical state' or 'shared sovereignty' were shown as reasons why the state in these societies has been the biggest impediment to democracy, and why democracy needed to be expanded (even at the cost of the state, as put forward by the leading behavioural political thinker in India, Rajni Kothari), historians in India had already established that state and sovereignty in India had a robust and hoary past. They not only applied conceptual frames of materialist analysis, but scholars like Romila Thapar pioneered a non-Marxian understanding of the evolution of the state structure in her works which found its fruition in *From Lineage to State*, a theme which many of her students and colleagues in JNU began to take forward.[95] This became extremely crucial for the new nation-making processes at this juncture as they needed state structures and institutions not only for the welfare and developmental agenda of a post-independence country ravaged by colonial power, but also to give space and time to evolving structures which were being attacked by different ideological and secessionist movements.[96]

State, Class and Ideologies

The talk about the presence of the state structure was also linked to the debate over the contemporary character of the state and its lineages. The state was characterized by communist and left parties as the organ of the ruling coalition of the big bourgeoisie (in collaboration with foreign capital) and the big landlord. On the other hand, the post-Independence Indian state drew its legitimacy from the anti-colonial struggle that won India freedom. Could it therefore be surmised that if the anti-colonial movement brought the big bourgeoisie or landlord to power, ipso facto it was they who controlled and guided the anti-colonial movement too? The Marxist historians' characterization of national movement at the beginning of the 1970s was part of this teleological characterization of the national movement as a bourgeois movement which could bring only bourgeois political freedom but no social revolution.[97]

The communist parties, both the CPI and the CPI(M), inherited the explanation that imperialism was still holding the country in its clutches with the help of the collaborationist classes, i.e., capitalist or big bourgeoisie (comprador bourgeoisie) and the big landlord (the feudal landlords). The state was, therefore, seen as the ruling organ of the landlord and the big bourgeoisie. Notwithstanding some dilution during the next couple of decades, the theoretical and intellectual formulations of the parties and the intellectuals articulating their views held itself tight.[98]

In 1964, when the Communist Party of India split into two, namely, the Communist Party of India (CPI) and the Communist Party of India (Marxist), the new party, CPI(M), was in fact more uncompromising on this definition of the Indian state than the CPI. There was a second split when the more radical pro-China section formed itself into the Communist Party of India (Coordination), finally christened as CPI (Marxist-Leninist) which was further to the left and saw itself as the vanguard of an impending overthrow of the Indian state by the organized peasant forces. As a matter of fact, it waged a war against the

Indian state in the Naxalbari and other regions, believing that armed revolution was the only way to wage a war against this combination of classes that wielded state power.

The intellectual assemblage in JNU, particularly in the School of Social Sciences, had all these three ideologically rooted in their understanding of the Indian state. Since the debate had used an intrinsically Marxist methodology or analysis, where the modes of production and the resultant social formations were analysed and debated, the boundaries of engagement were coloured by the circuitous Marxist methodology and understanding. It was against such a backdrop that serious developments were happening in the political and social arenas. Between 1969 and 1972, the state was not only fighting communal and right-wing forces but Indira Gandhi, the prime minister, was using the state's powers to go directly to the people by nationalizing private banks; she abolished the privy purses and then nationalized coal mines (all owned by the Indian big bourgeoisie). This was indicative of the fact that the state was quite independent of the formulations put forward by the Marxist intellectuals and the communist parties. At this juncture, K.N. Raj, one of the most respected economists, and also quite radical, published his article on the class character of the Indian state where he argued for a different formulation. Polish economist, Michał Kalecki, had advocated in his classic paper 'Observations on Social and Economic Aspects of "Intermediate Regimes"' that in the context of a less developed economy an intermediate regime composed of 'lower middle-class and rich peasantry would be performing the role of the ruling classes (due to the absence of a fully-developed bourgeoisie)'.[99] The stability and viability of the political system in such a regime was to be maintained by different innovations, such as land reforms. There was a word of caution however: they merely maintained the class balance and not raised productivity of the land as such.

Kałecki altered the formulation of the communist parties in fundamental ways:

- One, it classed intermediate regimes as national economies with uniquely individual dynamics, which meant that the argument of a global capitalist order, on which the communist parties had been premising most of their formulations, stood weakened.

This was not acceptable to both the dependency theorists in Latin America and the communist parties in India. In Kałecki's formulation, the notion that the big landlords and the big bourgeoisie—the combination against which the communist parties argued—formed the Indian ruling classes, was altered.

- Second, it weakened the argument of the international comprador status of the big bourgeoisie.

K.N. Raj argued that the character of India's ruling establishment was different from what had emerged within the serious academic analysis, particularly among the leftists. Raj has been among India's most respected economists and had been in the forefront of the national planning and was someone who had been closely working on the changes that new technology and new infrastructural projects were bringing to the land and land relations. Coming from a person like Raj who could not have been brushed aside as an anti-Marxist, the intermediate regime characterization touched a raw nerve. The response came from no less a person than the seniormost leader of CPI(M), its general secretary E.M.S. Namboodiripad.[100] EMS (as he was popularly known) defended the communist understanding of the class character of Indian state as a combination of the big peasantry and the big bourgeoisie (which was also linked to the bourgeoisie outside India). He argued that Kałecki's formulation was based on the assumption of national economies (and not an integrated world economy) discussed in the communist conference in 1964, which was also not accepted by the communists. To him it also did not fit into the class description of Indian situation.[101]

Closely allied to the discussion of the Indian state was the serious discussion on the peasantry. For historians, it was very crucial not only to understand the way colonialism brought changes to the agrarian structure but also the way they transformed the related realms of lives. For the Marxist scholar and the communist parties it was important to know the clear divisions within the peasantry so that mobilization for revolution can be carried out, for example, in Telangana as a continuation of the separatist movement in Andhra Pradesh. The most significant idea was that there was feudalism in the villages and the relations between the rich peasantry—the small landholders and tenants—and the landless agriculturalist were that of non-wage or rather pre-capitalist forms of feudal relations. In many cases the upper caste, upper-class rich peasants, as they were categorized, were supposed to be suppressing all and that these rich peasants, or the zamindars, constituted a dominant presence. This dominance was maintained by having a major share in the new democratic polity.

Serious Marxists scholars like Sulekh Gupta and Daniel Thorner, however, could see that the Indian agrarian sector was showing divisions along class lines and, unlike feudal landlords and poor peasants, they had rich, poor and middle-class peasants dotting the rural scene.[102] Daniel Thorner highlighted the capitalist penetration into the village indicating that the communist party needed to stop thinking along outdated lines.[103] K.N. Raj's now famous work on the green revolution's impact on the rural scenario also indicated the increasing differentiation and inequality, but along class lines.[104]

Of the first major intellectual contests that JNU witnessed, the characterization of Indian peasantry, can be cited as being the most prominent. Scholars of different radical hues and many affiliated with the communist parties maintained that the Indian agrarian scenario was coloured by feudalism, semi-feudalism or pre-capitalist exploitation. While there were arguments with sophisticated mathematical analysis like that of Amit Bhaduri, the debate brought a very high level of political and polemical usage. The pages of the Indian journals, particularly *EPW*, along with pamphlets, tutorials and seminar papers, which finally led to dissertation and thesis, were all coloured by this fabulous debate. The debate also had sociological issues attached.

Following the classical Marxist model of the modes of production, Utsa Patnaik had argued that Ashok Rudra, another economist, was mistaken in thinking that the growing capitalist phenomenon was purely a capitalist development.[105] She argued that while there were capitalist elements in agriculture, as suggested by many, they did not amount to a capitalist mode of production coming to stay. The argument invited strong criticism from Marxist scholar, Paresh Chattopadhyay, who came in to defend Ashok Rudra.

Ashok Rudra (1930–92) was one of those economists who had obtained degrees in statistics and got a lead role in the planning set-up led by Mahalanobis. But he evolved into a leading public intellectual taking up issues on model building and planning, agricultural economics and the role of intellectual. His detailed fieldwork, particularly in Punjab in the 1950s and '60s, made him challenge any theoretically predetermined conclusions. While he criticized the neo-classical economists' propositions of allocative efficiency in Indian agriculture, he also picked up issues with Marxists economists. The debate centred around the nature of the classes that dotted the agrarian scenario and, following somewhat close to what Daniel Thorner had argued back in the early 1960s, he showed that there were two classes in rural India: big landowners and agricultural workers (though in some areas there may be a third class, that of 'subsistence farmers').

But Utsa Patnaik was categorical in her rebuttal. 'To substitute one's own empiricist concepts for Marxist concepts', she argued, 'and then to declare that there is no empirical proof of "Marxist" propositions, is really a bit too much for anyone to swallow.'[106] Utsa Patnaik found fault with his definition of class, which, according to her was 'empiricist' and did not emerge from the theory of class itself. Marx, to her, had already defined this very well. She argued that though she did not have 'an objection to anyone holding a non-Marxist theory of historical development or employing a non-Marxist concept of class', it became imperative, she thought, to point out the source of confusion misleading people, 'when the person concerned insists that he is talking about Marxist concepts'.[107]

Jairus Banaji entered the debate at this juncture by arguing that Paresh Chattopadhyay, who had come in defence of Ashok Rudra, was having a bookish idea of Marxism, not matched by the realities which are at the core of Marxism. His use of strong polemics charmed the radical hearts of the students of the campus when he wrote that Chattopadhyay's 'apparent preoccupation with clear definitions and his abundance of textual Marxism' basically 'conceal a real atrophy of theory'.[108] He described such practice by using historical analogy: 'His thought', as Trotsky said of the historian Pokrovsky, 'is gripped in the vice of rigid social categories which he puts in place of live historical forces.'[109]

Banaji of the Centre for Historical Studies was an activist with Trotskyite beliefs particularly of the need for world-wide revolution. Many young economists with strong communist support had been in the debate and thus Banaji's entry was seen by the researchers and students not only on intellectual terms but also in terms of equality of the intellectual life of faculty and students.

The debate was closely argued in the pages of *Economic and Political Weekly* and set the standard of debate on the contemporary agrarian relations within the Marxist scholarship. Banaji became a magnet for students who found it intoxicatingly fresh that he could single-handedly take on the dominant Marxist scholars of the CPI(M) and CPI. He soon had a strong following and had discussions in what come to be known as the Marx club. His presence in these initial years of JNU proved to be crucial for two reasons. First, his scholarship and involvement in the cause of labour were more than a match for most of the CPI(M) variety who pretended to be activists among scholars and scholars among activists. Second, it was the only time when a Trotskyite could find an open arena to critique and defeat the Stalinist arguments; being a minuscule minority, they were generally overwhelmed by the other organized communist parties. Thus, his presence gave the initial shock to the otherwise arrogant Marxist-party-affiliated scholars.

The debate on the mode of production and the agrarian economy was also in keeping with the larger debates that had been taking place in the international scene. This was also the climax of the Soviet–China split with the Chinese version totally discrediting the Soviet community of workers and encouraging anti-colonial mobilization in Africa and the Middle East. In trying to counter the Maoists political ideology, many scholars were involved in devising models of peasant resistance like James Scott or Eric Wolf on the one hand, and Eric Hobsbawm or Rodney Hilton on the other. However, in India, the peasant leaders were stepping forward with their own experience.

Two of the legendary peasant organizers, Ravi Narayan Reddy and P. Sundarayya, had their own testimonies about their understanding of the peasant movement in India.[110] Sunil Sen, another CPI veteran, had recently published his history of the peasant movement in India. The attention that the agrarian conditions received had two sources. Marxist scholars, since the 1940s, had tended to write and research on them, e.g., D.D. Kosambi, R.S. Sharma, Irfan Habib, Sulekh Gupta and Daniel Thorner; while other historians like Eric Stokes and Asiya Siddiqi brought 'the peasants' into the historiographical realm. Soon, JNU began to emerge as a sort of habitat for the *Homo Academicus*

Indicus Peasantus. The largest number of students who joined JNU had either come with some understanding of the peasant world or were very close to the movements taking place in historical or spatial terms. The debate over the differentiation of peasantry indicated that it was essential for the political party, CPI(M), to argue that, notwithstanding the differentiation on the field, original political categories still hold.

Those who were close, at least to the theatre of the national movement, e.g., Gujarat, wrote some of the best works on Gandhi. Shirin Mehta produced one of the best works on Gandhi and the Bardoli movement.[111] On the other hand, the intellectual debate also excited people who were interested in agrarian history to align the finding with new trends in academia, e.g., the long-term agrarian change in Punjab was debated by students like Mridula Mukherjee Neeladri Bhattacharya, Indu Agnihotri and Mukul Mangalik.[112] Some, like T.C.A. Raghavan, tried to go far deeper and see the changes in the Narmada Valley area while Alok Bandyopadhyay tried to even compare the changes in the two regions primarily in economic terms.[113]

The debate over agrarian relations was of tremendous help in the crystallization of many ideas. Three significant strands could be discerned:

- The agrarian transformations were deeper than what met the eye, and the mere concept change could not comprehensively convey all of that and therefore would not do;
- The plea for a colonial mode of production had now begun to take root and held a meaning for even those who belonged to the communist parties allergic to the category;
- Excellent studies mapping the change in the agrarian structure could be found in the works of sociologists like Pradip Bose, or the historians like Ram Subas or Ravindran Gopinath, in different locales like Bengal, Uttar Pradesh and Kerala.[114]

This linked into the earlier historical discourse about agrarian changes and therefore new studies came forth from historians. They studied not only contemporary times but delved deeper into the regions' histories. Many of these studies were directly inspired by the earlier works of mainly Marxist scholars. However, except for a couple of works like that of Rajan Gurukkal's 'The Agrarian System and Socio-Political Organization under the Early Pandyas, AD 600-1000,' very few actually adhered to the orthodox Marxist formulation.[115] Rattan Lal Hangloo tried to recover the agrarian system of Kashmir (1846–1900) with quite an eclectic approach.[116] The Deccan region also was a field of particular attention and inspired many new works.[117] One could also see a mature analysis in two different times and contexts in the works of K.N. Ganesh and Brahmanand who were engaged with the agrarian structure of the early medieval Venad and western India during 1880–1930.[118] The agrarian studies were part of a larger debate; hence even when they do not speak of the politics, they were deeply entrenched in the political debate.

Agrarian Relations and Change

It was significant that people were conscious of the need to try and catch the fleeting moments so that they could understand the changing dimensions. G.K. Karanth, a sociologist, tried to delve deeper into the changes and continuities in the agrarian relations in a Karnataka village, while political scientist, Jagpal Singh, using class as a frame of analysis, captured the rapidly changing dynamic of the villages in western U.P.[119] This upswing in agrarian studies came at a time when some of the evolved traditions of research on agrarian relations, for example in Sri Lanka, witnessed steep decline. Sri Lankan scholars in JNU now began to work on changing agrarian relations in the irrigated and non-irrigated land in Sri Lanka.[120]

There was also attempts to link the peasant movement to the larger political trends, and in the process, the examine the course of development of the Indian National Congress as a political party since the 1920s. Political scientists demonstrated an effort to capture ongoing political mobilization and agrarian movements. Chinnaya Suri on Andhra, K. Kumar on Thanjavur and M.H. Assadi on Karnataka, for example, provided rich narratives of the respective political struggles and typologies of politics and movements.[121]

The historians, on the other hand, probed deep political questions embedded in the agrarian movement. For example, Alok Sheel brought out the relationship between the Congress and the raiyats in three agrarian movements between 1928 and 1940, while Sri Kishan's dissertation explored the linkages between the Communist International, the CPI, and the agrarian question in India during the same period, i.e., 1920–45.[122] Similarly, a deeper analysis of the economy and class linkages in peasant movements was studied by Inukonda Thirumali, where the author characterized the movements as 'uprisings' and showed the class cleavages sharply operating in Telangana in his work entitled 'Lords and Peasants in Telangana, 1920-48: An enquiry into the people's uprising in Nalgonda and Warangal districts'.

There was also the time dimension. The 1970s were closer to the period of Naxalite and other uprisings, and, as participants in many movements, these historians had a keen understanding of the processes and hence were able to critique the movements in their work which at times made an attempt to dialogue, and simultaneously explore the nature of the economy, politics and society behind the movements.[123] The 1980s brought greater complexity into ideas in politics, which was now overpowering the earlier innocence and hence the various works began to show the efforts made to grapple with the complexities. For example, the unionization of the workers in both Kerala and Andhra created a new dimension for the political class.[124] Developmental administration was also observed to be eroding the mass base of many old political formations.[125]

The most difficult exercise was to track the transformation of the movement in peasant society resulting from the influence of the anti-colonial movement, which was the largest non-violent mass movement in human history. The historians began a deep study of the relationship between the Congress and communist parties and the peasant movement and some of the finest works started emanating from the university, e.g., Gyan Prakash Sharma's work on the Congress, peasant movement and agrarian legislation in Bihar in 1937–39, and Lata Singh's efforts to understand the Congress and the Bihar Kisan Sabha movement in 1934–39.[126] The congruence between the Congress and the communists was the manifestation of the efforts to link peasant mobilization and its successes and failures to the programmes of the political parties. It was very much a contemporary political battle that sharply brought out the finer nuances and the integrative processes of the mobilization. For example, the role of bureaucracy, development planning and integrating the tribal economies became some of the crucial aspects of understanding the politics of these parties. It also influenced the students in other centres as they had found a new paradigm on which they could work.

So, if the agrarian system was either merely evolving or transformed by colonialism (which actually was the case), how did the peasants respond to colonization? This is where the real contribution of the JNU scholars lay. The peasants and tribals responded to both the internal and external inequalities as they began to develop a better understanding of the situation. It is here that the difference between the romantic and fashionable interpretations versus the real understanding lay, and people generally understood that the peasants do not inherently have a developed political consciousness, on which to base their ideas.

The keen eye for differentiation could discern the presence of peasant radicalism. For example, in Andhra, the Telangana region had no change in the land system for twenty-one years or so, until the communist movement grew very strong and the regional disparities began to be seen. The Telangana leaders and the Andhra organizers were able to intellectually articulate their movement and, therefore, the younger generation, even if they were not leftists, were moved by the peasant movement, and in this area JNU became a major habitat of the scholar who could capture this spirit and motivate them to academically express the experience, thus taking it to a larger theoretical level. The presence of K. Seshadri, who was earlier a part of the communist movement in the state and had joined the political science department in JNU, was a blessing in disguise to many students who would first approach him. Having Rasheeduddin Khan on the rolls was a further attraction for the students from Andhra.

Three intellectual trends were visible:

- One was the immediate arrival of those who actually were the products of the movements; they were young and keen to see what had happened and how movements could be taken further. There was a sense of anticipation as well as angst. It was in the Centre for Political Studies that Shanta Sinha arrived to work on the Maoists in Andhra, and although her thesis displayed a camaraderie towards the Maoists, it also had a firm commitment to see them in the larger intellectual-political frame.[127] Similarly, there were efforts to look for lineages of peasant radicalism in the anti-Mulki agitation, Rampa rebellion and the results of the factional fights within the Congress party.[128] By the mid-1980s, when the political heat was slightly lower, there were attempts to study the diverse movements and their characteristics. 'Agrarian Movements in Andhra: 1921-1971' a panoramic study by Chinnaya Suri stands out in this context.[129] By the end of the decade, JNU scholars were exploring peasant radicalism in different districts like Adilabad, Karimnagar, East Godavari, Nalgonda and Warangal.[130] Some of them were high on the revolutionary mood of the time, which was creating slight problems in assessing the movement on its own terms.

❖ The second trend related to the processes of social and political change, which in the long run provided the template for secular and progressive movements in the Andhra regions. This trend was set by V. Ramakrishnacharyulu in his work on Veeresalingam and his reform efforts.[131] Later on, there were efforts to actually see the state's response to different social movements.[132] The work not only became one of the pioneering ones on social movement in India, it also provided an inkling of the imminent national and liberation movements in Andhra. The scholars kept a track of the land reform legislation and the efforts on development policies of the tribal region.[133] It is this mix of understanding long-term movements of politics and ideas that gave the scholars on Andhra a hold on the critique of policies, and some of the finest works on what is generally known as public administration came from this. For example, the linkage between unionization, bureaucracy, politics and rural development in Andhra Pradesh came from a scholar of political science.[134]

❖ A third trend seen since the 1980s was that of the increasing visibility of the Scheduled Caste component of the population in the politics of the state.[135] The general idea was to look for the politics of their participation in the political processes of democracy, e.g., in elections. However, the reservation policy and its impact was also woven into the narrative by scholars like Aluri

Sundar Kumar Das in his work on 'Scheduled Caste Political Elite in East Godavari District during 1951-1981'.[136]

Similarly, scholars from Nagaland were looking for a larger frame of reference than mere ethnicity and Christianity which became the hallmark of mission-oriented scholarship. One of the pioneering research was by Piketo Sema who presented a very dispassionate account of the Naga uprising during 1946–63.[137] By the late 1970s, the term 'identity' had invaded the academia and S.K. Chasie went deeper to reconstruct the Naga identity from 1878 to 1974, while Ahu Sakhrie tried to unravel the sociology of the Naga Movement.[138] The complexities that these studies exposed enlarged the dimension of studies on contemporary history.

The most difficult issue was taking a historiographically autonomous position and challenging the orthodoxies that were becoming quite prominent by the 1980s and, by the mid-1980s, the formulations were showing signs of rigidity. The relationship between colonialism, peasant movement and the larger political movement (of which the peasant movement became part) was more delicate to handle, and it required an extremely independent scholarship. The writing was on the wall in the heavy debates of the 1970s but they began to be stylized in supporting party formulations. There were exceptions: Majid Siddiqi, Mridula Mukherjee and others who were incidentally researching in the history department and primarily engaged with the issue of the relationship between the peasant mobilization and the mobilization of the national movement for freedom. Siddiqi's work was attacked in the CPI(M) journal showing the party's antagonism to the formulation that the two mobilizations had a symbiotic rather than an antagonistic relationship.[139] Bipan Chandra, who guided these works was an inspiration with his own writing on 'Peasant and National Integration'.

There were however new moves in the metropolitan centres where the peasant movements were stigmatized and delinked from the national movement so that no China-like situation emerged. Such works began to appear in 1982 from England where groups like the subaltern theorists would try to delegitimize the national movement by calling the peasant and tribal movements autonomous with a life world of their own. The writings, replete with rhetoric and logical faults, were soon mimicked by many centres. The first full-blown critique of it appeared from JNU's Mridula Mukherjee who exposed the whole project as being based on mistaken premises, wrong historiographical assumptions about both the peasants and their movement, and also a prejudiced reading of the Indian national movement.[140] That critique however, came a bit late as the group had already excited the imagination of a large number of impressionable students of other remunerates.

While the agrarian class structure became the crucial intellectual flashpoint, the role of the industrial and commercial classes (bourgeoisie) also came under intense scrutiny. The idea that the Indian big bourgeoisie, for instance the houses of Tatas and Birlas, were a comprador bourgeoisie was the received wisdom sanctioned by R.P. Dutt's book, and, later on, the political resolutions of the communist parties. The most retrogressive role played by the lower commercial section during the famine and post-Independence scarcity years led to the casting of the business classes as the people's enemy. The fact that some big business houses had close links with communal organizations further distanced the intellectuals from them.

In the early 1970s, Bipan Chandra had begun clarifying that the big bourgeoisie in India was not necessarily a comprador bourgeoisie, and it had its own class interests which many a time clashed with colonial interests and the interests of the colonial capitalist class. In his paper 'Jawaharlal Nehru and the Capitalist Class, 1936', which was attacked by communist intellectuals, Chandra agreed that there was a class difference between the villagers and their feudal landlords, but he argued that this big bourgeoisie was not necessarily a comprador collaborator like the colonial bourgeoisie who exploited society. On the contrary, they were probably aware that they stood to benefit more from a nationalist government than they could under a colonial government.[141] This concept was rejected by the other leftists. Rasheeduddin Khan's student, Kamal Mitra Chinoy, went on to produce a thesis on the line that the bourgeoisie was a comprador one.[142] To a sociology student, however, every institution was a product of colonial collaboration and there was no escape except by bringing about a world revolution. Last heard, this student was heralding a revolution through American agencies in the United States. Bipan Chandra's idea was historically researched by his student, Aditya Mukherjee, who showed how the

Indian capitalist class had its own interests that clashed with those of the colonial state or the metropolitan bourgeoisie.[143]

Making the Historical Horizon

What was the real nature of the Indian historical processes? Had it arrived into the capitalist phase as was predicted for all other societies, or did it have a different trajectory? These were very big questions which have engaged historians in the West vis-á-vis their own societies. Did it pass through certain stages like the ones suggested in the transition debate where capitalism in Europe is supposed to have arrived after the decline of feudalism? The European debate on the transition was one of the most scintillating debates in contemporary intellectual life. The dominance of the Indian historians in the debate had already linked the intellectual discourse to the great tradition of the historical debate taking place in the West.

The gap between Indology and Indian history was more or less bridged by the mid-1960s, which also indicated maturity of the intellectual life. One of the key players in this effort was Romila Thapar whose work and active interest in installing new historical analysis into the heart of historiography made a difference. By this time her book, *Asoka and the Decline of the Mauryas*, had already become a hit and her article on the barbarians further made her position unassailable in writing Indian history. She differentiated her work on Asoka with the work on Buddhism by the contemporary leading historians like G.C. Pande whose leaning towards Indology was very obvious.[144] By this time she had also published a book on ancient Indian history where there was, in general, a complete world view.[145] She, more than anybody else, symbolized the coming of ancient Indian history to a modern age. From the modernist sensibilities that she displayed in *Asoka and the Decline of the Mauryas*, it was taken for granted that she would enter the debate over the Indian state.[146] The state system that had existed during the sixth century BC had evolved from the lineages, she argued with an innovative use of the anthropological works on Africa and other sources, i.e., genealogy and epics such as the Ramayana representing growth of monarchy, etc. She entered the domain of the Indologists to conduct a real historical reconstruction. However, this was also the domain which would invite the attention and anger of those for whom the epics represented something more than mere historical reconstruction. She was the first to talk about communal interpretation in ancient Indian history way back in 1969, and those who subscribed to the communal view did not view her reconstruction very positively. Her students from the Centre for Historical Studies began to use the epics and other sources like the Puranas to reconstruct a very rich historical narrative of the pulsating life in the India of ancient times. While some of her students constructed the religious processes in eastern India, others examined the evolution of state structure. By the 1980s, one saw Romila Thapar's delineation of the state structure as an extremely important contribution from a completely different angle.

One of the most intricate issues in Indian history has been the transition to the newer times. The discourse on transition from the ancient period to the feudal period had been very significant from the time of its classical enunciator, R.S. Sharma, to its critique by B.D. Chattopadhyaya at a later date. R.S. Sharma, following the pointers in D.D. Kosambi's works, had argued in the late 1950s and early 1960s that the decline of the cities and consequent indication of decline of economy coincided with the establishment of feudalism in the society, particularly in northern India, where the new form of *samantashahi* (Indian version of feudal system) began to assume control of the political economy.[147] Later on, R.N. Nandi, with his comprehensive knowledge of history, discussed the collapse of the market economy of towns into a subsistence economy of agriculture which followed widespread decay and desertion of towns from the third century AD, which seemed to be the key factor in our understanding of the origins of feudalism.[148]

B.D. Chattopadhyaya an alumnus of Sanskrit College and Presidency College, Calcutta, began to gradually reflect a different understanding of the socio-economic processes when compared to Marxist scholars like R.S. Sharma and Nandi. Although Chattopadhyaya shared the same background as R.S. Sharma, with a rich knowledge of epigraphy, archeology and numismatics, he presented a fresh perspective for not only those interested in the debate over transition but also to those interested in the historical methodology and usage of various sources, by bringing an empirically rich exploration of the diffusion of urban centres in the early medieval times. He argued that the original hypothesis about the decline of the urban centres was error-prone. In his presidential address to the Burdwan session of the Indian History Congress entitled 'Political processes and structure of polity in early medieval India: Problems of perspective', he criticized the segmentary state theories of Burton Stein and Kenneth Hall by arguing that the state was never a static system.[149] While he was doing his best to refute a transition to a new stage, it was obvious that he was referring to a new political economy. The issue of moving from one type of economy to another, with a different set of indicators, remained unexplained. B.N.S. Yadava of Allahabad University, for example, had shown that the Kali age could be understood as an age of transition between the eighth and tenth centuries.

The second major contribution in the discipline of history in India came from the powerful centre of medieval history at Aligarh. Limping back from its honeymoon with the Pakistan movement, Aligarh got mired in communal controversy from the 1960s—most of it not of its own making. Weathering all these, the centre was painstakingly built with hard work by people like Nurul Hasan, Muhammad Habib, Athar Ali and Irfan Habib among others. Muhammad Habib, the historian who headed the department in the 1950s was its symbol to the outside world. His initial efforts with the secular and, increasingly, the Marxist lines were matched by the organizing efforts of Nurul Hasan. In the late 1950s and the 1960s, it was Nurul Hasan who contributed the most to build the Centre for Advanced Studies by developing a rich repository of manuscripts, which included work, produced by the research assistants, besides translated works, etc.

With Nurul Hasan being the education minister with a hand in JNU's working, JNU benefited by having Satish Chandra, his closest ally, intellectually, as the founder of the medieval history department in JNU. However, Satish Chandra very soon moved to the UGC where he stayed until the mid-1980s. Hence medieval history could not get the treatment required and its growth was halting and without focus. Satish Chandra's later interest in regional history took up much of his time.

Around this time, modern history, with economic history at its core, constituted the new field of study in the department of contemporary history and was chaired by Sarvepalli Gopal. Although Gopal's early works pertained to British policy, an increasing amount of radical intent became apparent in his teaching and works. The centre and Gopal had a mutual influence on each other. When Gopal was invited to write Nehru's biography, it was a crowning achievement for an Indian historian as, given the completely colonized minds of Indian upper classes, there was a good chance that this project would have gone to a third-rate European. As a matter of fact, the establishment was seeking a Briton to do the honours, but opted out when they learnt about the best historian who happened to be based in Delhi.

Writing Nehru's biography was like working in a minefield, especially in a campus resonating with the left-wing ideas and communism, as in many instances Nehru was described as a renegade both to the revolution and to democracy (e.g., on the issue of the summary dismissal of Namboodiripad's ministry in Kerala). Gopal was like a breath of fresh air in historical debates. Unattached to any of the communist parties (or any party at all), Gopal provided a comprehensive horizon to modern Indian history which was in dire need of social and political confidence to break free of the colonized mindset that plagued the other centres of Indian history.

Educated in England, Sarvepalli Gopal, like many of the earlier Oxford graduates, came to teach first in Andhra University at Waltair, which had been established by dint of sheer hard work and dedication by C.R. Reddy. It was when he eventually returned to teach at Oxford that Gopal received the invitation to join the Centre for Historical Studies, JNU. He was a cheerful, friendly person with a slight aloofness about him which evoked reverential awe. But he was a tremendous team player and lent vibrancy and energy to his department. He was well connected with the capital's literati, political elite and corridors of power, and was up to date with the current events. Unlike the other academics who dabbled in politics, Gopal held no political aspirations at all and his dedication to academics strengthened the centre that was in its initial phase.

This bonding provided confidence to the centre to withstand the criticisms from both the left and the right-wingers. The first strike against the centre came from the left and particularly the CPI(M), which viewed established scholars like Bipan Chandra, S. Gopal, and Romila Thapar as threats to its aim in establishing its dominance among the teachers. They were superior intellectuals, mascots of the new university, and sympathetic to the left cause and hence could not be branded as anti-left. As for their next line of attack, the centre, despite a modicum of political division within, stood firm against the CPI(M)'s intimidatory tactics on the issue of admission. The CPI(M) thereafter remained the arch critic of the centre. The attack on the centre was not merely because of technical matters but also because of the intellectual opposition that the party received from the centre to its attempts at gleichschaltung.

Communal opposition was there as well, particularly from the Hindu communal groups which from the beginning saw the centre as an anathema to their cause as the three authors who wrote about communal historiography were located there. As mentioned earlier, the Marxist historiography, beginning in the 1960s, was the first major breakthrough to take Indian scholarship as well as historical understanding out of the labyrinth into the new processual history, which maintained that history is about people and not kings and soldiers, and that what mattered most were the larger historical processes. In these processes, the most significant aspects were the study of how people lived their lives, the nature of society and the practices they followed to legitimize political authority. Here, colonialism was found to be a major exploitative system; at the same time, the exploitative social system of medieval and ancient India was also seriously scrutinized.

The notion of a pan-Indian Hindu community was recognized as a construction of the colonial historiographers as much as the notion of an all-India Muslim community. For example, the works of D.D. Kosambi, R.S. Sharma and many others brought out many facets of ancient India, repudiating the claim of a unified Hindu India. Irfan Habib, Nurul Hasan and others demonstrated how the medieval rule was as exploitative for the peasants, be they Muslim or Hindu, just as other systems were. Bipan Chandra recreated the milieu of the early Indian nationalists, who were the first to document and analyse British imperialism and its debilitating and impoverishing role. In the critique of the colonial system, he demonstrated that the early intelligentsia had set the basic principles that transformed into Indian nationalism on a later day.

These scholars along with many new generation, non-Marxist scholars were throwing open many important issues related to caste, community, politics and religion for historical analysis, which went against the grain of the communal groups who looked for legitimation and justification of their present-day claims in history. By 1977, however, the communal formations were sharing power with the Janata Party. There was a perceptible shift in the Indian state's policies relating to the offices that the Jana Sangh and RSS members held. The foreign ministry with Atal Bihari Vajpayee at its helm displayed a rapid change of policy towards Israel. Although India had always been sympathetic towards the Jewish predicament after Hitler's atrocities, it did not endorse the Israeli treatment of the Palestinian population. Interestingly enough, the Hindu communal groups had admired Hitler, but, paradoxically, they also looked towards Israel as a strong state, to be admired and befriended. The Jana Sangh injected a communal perception into India's foreign policy because the Hindu communalists viewed the Israel–Palestine conflict through the prism of its own anti-Muslim prejudice.[150] The other minister from this group, Lal Krishna Advani, was given the information and broadcasting portfolio, which meant the media was under his control. The Hindu communalists also got the prerogative to directly intervene in the education sector: it succeeded in getting certain textbooks removed from the school reading lists. This was part of the larger attack on the institutions of historical scholarship, which included making non-academic appointments in institutions, and awarding projects and fellowships, not necessarily of a high standard, that were meant to advance the communal historiography.

Since the early 1940s, there were demands that Indian schools use textbooks written by Indians. The colonial government had kept a strict control over the textbooks and, by the 1940s and '50s, a few British publishers monopolized the textbook publication business. The communist leader, S.A. Dange, had drawn attention to this fact way back in 1947 in the Bombay legislative assembly.[151] Mahatma Gandhi also gave importance to books written by those who taught students directly. By the 1960s, the Indian school and college system had all sorts of textbooks with varying standards. There were therefore two critical issues before a perceptive education minister. First, to introduce textbooks written by Indians which would provide a national perspective rather than the current textbooks. Second, to ensure the printing of books within India, and make them available to all sections of society. M.C. Chagla, the education minister, was very alert to these needs and he insisted that it was high time that books were both written and printed in India.[152] However, school education was in the domain of the states; therefore a national consensus was gradually evolved, where the model textbooks were discussed in detail and written with great care, so that the states, even if they did not adopt these, could model their textbooks on these. Organizations like Sampradayikata Virodhi Committee, under the dynamic Congress leader Subhadra Joshi, played a key role in the campaign for new textbooks, which were not communal.

On the basis of a note from the prime minister's office in 1977, the education minister, Pratap Chandra Chunder, himself a littérateur from Calcutta, took the decision to remove four of these model school textbooks, which were written by eminent historians, namely, the textbooks on Medieval India (Romila Thapar), Modern India (Bipan Chandra), Freedom Struggle (Bipan Chandra, Amales Tripathy and Barun De) and Ancient India (R.S. Sharma). However, as we have seen, several intellectuals had been at the forefront of the political battle for some time now and the communal design behind this move was immediately understood. Very soon, an all-India movement against the removal began, which was reflected in the media.

Beginning in the early 1960s with a critique of Nehruvian policies, the majority of these intellectuals had developed their own sophisticated analysis of colonialism and communalism in the new-found freedom of the collective space in the universities, rare among Third World countries. The leadership's independent stance against major powers during the nascent stage of the nation's Independence had also emboldened them and provided them with the self-assurance required for intellectual engagement. When Emergency was imposed in 1975, it was this trust in the leadership which was badly bruised. At this time, however, faith in the democratic vision of the leadership provided the intellectuals with the confidence to fight their own battles when the textbooks were removed. This act was perceived as not only an attack on their scholarship, but also the continuation of the communal attack in the garb of 'Indianization'. A stiff resistance ensued and a fringe segment of (communal) intellectuals now came out in the open to attack these historians as well as the intellectual tradition that they had developed.

They argued that the revoking of textbooks was not wrong as these intellectuals were patronized by the Congress regime, and it was only natural that the new regime should be patronizing a new set of intellectuals.[153] Some individuals and groups took advantage of the communal attack, and launched tirades against the historians concerned. The argument was that as the Marxists had used state patronage earlier, they had no right to counter the communalists who were now using the state to subvert the earlier regime (Congress). Such arguments were made to neutralize the communal aspect of the attack.[154] This idea falsified the rich intellectual tradition that had evolved quite independently of the state. While some scholars took this opportunity to attack Marxist historiography by avoiding the role of communalism, they ended up seeing this as merely reflecting a different cultural policy—another sanitized version of history.[155]

The Centre for Historical Studies (CHS), however, with the strong bond that it had developed, withstood the pressure and put up a stiff resistance to the large-scale attack and the teachers led from the front with Romila Thapar, Bipan Chandra and others defending the extant school of thought and countercharging the radical pretenders, while S. Gopal came up with a glorious condemnation of those who were attacking history in his article 'Fear of History'.[156]

While CHS was attacked for being anti-Hindu, historians were bringing out some of the best works on the Brahmanical religion: for example, Suvira Jayaswal's brilliant historical account of Vaishnavism in her *Origins and Development of Vaishnavism* and Champakalakshmi's *Vaishnava Iconography in the Tamil Country*. This was also the time when K.N. Panikkar, whose earlier works were on traditional British policy history, began to work on Indian social history and came up with an all-India account of the nineteenth-century social and religious reform movement which tried to provide a picture of the intellectual response of the British rule.

Reading the Running Water: Attempt to Understand the Culture

While the constitution of a historical construct was providing the community with a deep and diachronic perspective of issues, the community was extremely contemporary. How does one ground oneself in these fleeting times? Marxism could give only one handle. The freshness of the Aravali ridges provided the quest for autonomy. A Marxist political scientist, who has been trying to understand the contours of Indian society and its polity from a Marxist stance, gave the best expression of the mood of his generation when in a brilliantly sarcastic manner he pointed out the absurdity of the discussion in the area studies or international relations: 'What is the use of teaching balance of power to the students of powerless countries?'[157] Striking the same intellectual note, a student, who had studied sociology in this atmosphere, had written a thesis which tried to show the class composition of the Shiv Sena movement in Bombay and demonstrated how the 'sociology in Indian universities' was taught using completely alien methods and manners.[158] Though he talked from a radical Marxist perspective, the subtext expressed the dissatisfaction over the practice of the discipline and attempted to harmonize the issue at hand—the epistemological practices in Indian society.

It was a subtle invocation to the social scientists to carry out a historical examination, similar to the work that Kuhn had done in the case of scientists in 1962. One of the first efforts was made by C.N. Venugopal by comparing the sociological approach of G.S. Ghurye and Radhakamal Mukherjee. In the mid-1980s another sociologist from the Centre for the Study of Social Systems, Archana Singh, wrote her thesis on the sociology of D.N. Majumdar.[159] Later, there were efforts to embark on a non-colonial paradigm to understand tribes by scholars like Vikram Nanda.[160]

The sociologists in the school, particularly Yogendra Singh, who had trained with D.P. Mukherjee and Radhakamal Mukherjee in Lucknow in the 1950s, were exceptional in their ability to theorize on different scales, from micro to macro, and one could see in their writings an innate Indianizing and harmonizing effort. This was most evident in Yogendra Singh's critical writings on the state of knowledge on social stratification and modernization.[161] While his work and that of many of his students lacked flamboyance, they attempted to examine Indian reality with the unconfessed efforts at Indianizing, both in terms of theory and sociology. It could well be that working in a discipline, which by its origin and theoretical underpinning was most Western while the object of its study was very Indian, any effort to naturalize or Indianize the discipline required skill and patience. However, Indianizing efforts were fraught with the dangers of downhill slides into overly nativistic propositions. This had happened in many sociology centres in central and eastern Europe in the 1920s and continued into the mid-1930s. The famed sociology department of Bucharest University had turned right-wing and dallied with the Nazi parties during the 1930s.[162]

These efforts were very significant because sociology is a difficult discipline and society needs to be studied on its own terms. It was fairly strange that when the British and American scholars studied their own societies they were called sociologists; when they turned their focus on societies outside their spheres they became anthropologists. The hapless Indians had to play the role designed for them by their colonial academic masters. In the first sociology departments in Bombay and Calcutta, Indian students were trained in methodologies developed and perfected to study other societies. There was therefore the original fault line where we were studying our society with methods that were designed from an alien point of view. From M.N. Srinivas, who studied with G.S. Ghurye at Bombay and later reworked his same thesis with Ghurye's supervisor Radcliffe Brown at Oxford, to the most talked about sociologist in the 1960s, Louis Dumont, it was the functionalist model, later combined with structuralism making it a structural-functionalist model to study the society that was in vogue.[163]

Indian society needed to be known and studied and caste was the best handle to study it. Therefore, Indian sociologists made caste the reference point. It came to a point where caste and Indian society were indistinguishable in the sociologist menu, and when Louis Dumont wrote his *Homo Hierarchicus*, Indian ingenuity as projected by a French mind, it created a monstrous hierarchical system based on the notion of purity and pollution, and it loomed large over the intellectual horizon.[164]

The environment in JNU provided a very interesting workspace for sociologists. It was symbolically a late arrival. Although a couple of Delhi School of Sociology students had sneaked in (e.g., P.N. Mukherjee), the faculty were mostly trained in their early years in Lucknow (Yogendra Singh, R.K. Jain), or Poona (T.K. Oommen), or Jaipur (K.L. Sharma) and had therefore a completely different attitude to Indian society and the methodological tools to be applied while studying it. In Lucknow, Radhakamal Mukherjee had consciously argued for Indian categories for Indian society and exhorted students to make universal concepts which could incorporate not only sociological realities but also disciplines.[165] D.P. Mukherjee was more concerned, as an early Marxist thinker, about the dialectics of modernity and tradition. He was also very Indian in his sensibilities.[166] Another of the Lucknow school scholars, A.K. Saran, in fact rejected sociology itself and was of the opinion that the discipline had no wisdom at all.[167]

Now, the presence of this group of people, who were in no hurry to propagate a structural-functional model or to show its inadequacies to an American sociologist or a British anthropologist marshalling data from an Indian village, must have lent a freshness in comparison to the stuffiness of highbrow centres. The students got the space, time and the legendary Indian leisure to innovate. Sociology had always been a godfather-based discipline, where, right from the selection of topics to research to their appointment in a centre, a student had to depend on a godfather; the unshackled democratic atmosphere at JNU liberated the discipline from its colonial and domineering self-definition.

The other dimension was existential. Sociology being a discipline without many opportunities, civil services or teaching were the only two options. Delhi University's elitism refused employment to JNU students in their small number of otherwise available college departments, which gave the sociology students, many of whom came from different disciplines, an existential challenge. The centre very soon had students and teachers working on real-life issues with theoretical tools available through the latest thoughts and debates already taking place in JNU. The sociologist in JNU, therefore, survived Dumont's structuralist overdose and the pomposity of cognizing reality by distilling knowledge and reality from reading texts. The reality that was to be grappled with was a much more difficult commitment due to a large number of villages. The variety and background of the students made up for what the discipline lacked in terms of methods—the ability to connect.[168] One commitment was to decolonize the mind.

This invocation to decolonize the mind was not happening in a vacuum. Apart from thoroughly critiquing its own intellectual traditions, the intellectuals had begun to sense the international political mood. In the early part of the 1970s, there was a general movement of Third World solidarity which appealed to the sympathetic British Labour. The Soviet movements were also a moving force. This matched the genuine Indian intellectual and political traditions of Third World unity. The liberation movements in Africa and the radicalization of Latin America began to affect the larger intellectual current. There was a sort of symbiosis among the struggles in different parts of the world through the communist parties and the publication of literature. The African mood could be judged with the publication of the now famous classic by Walter Rodney, *How Europe Underdeveloped Africa*.[169]

Understanding the Globe

There was a discordant and uneasy relationship between the social sciences and foreign policy oriented scholars. A meeting ground was gradually emerging with the issues of secularism, and national sovereignty was beginning to be seen as the bedrock of India's foreign policy. The second issue was more contradictory and animated: the intellectual life of JNU.

The initial thrust for an intelligentsia, sensitive towards the nuclear programme of India came from the Chinese explosion but it was difficult both resource-wise and in terms of India's ability to mobilize a strategic support group. The political powers were very keen that India adopted a nuclear programme. As predicted a couple of months earlier by Leonard Beaton in his book *Spread of Nuclear Weapons*, China exploded the nuclear bomb in October 1964. Two kinds of reactions were voiced: first, reinforcement of the demand for India's nuclear weapon; and second, what K. Subrahmanyam referred to as an elite perception, 'acceptance of an air defence protection from the western powers vis-à-vis China'.[170]

The USA let down India and broke their promise to take action against the Pakistani use of US military equipment against India.

Against this backdrop, the demand for a nuclear programme became stronger.[171] This sensitive issue launched a debate with new ideas being discussed.[172] General Som Dutt, in his Adelphi Papers, echoed a British proposal that India should enter into a security arrangement with Japan and Australia.[173] A different dimension was added to the nuclear debate when the UN and other bodies, particularly the non-proliferation lobby, began to discuss the cost of the nuclear programme. There seemed to be a new urgency to have a community of scholars to respond to many such issues and, as India simply did not have any such manpower available, the Institute for Defence Studies and Analyses (IDSA) was started with government initiative. K. Subrahmanyam, the second director of IDSA, was a dynamic and sharp thinker on nuclear doctrine. In his writings he responded to many propositions of the non-proliferation lobby active in India and abroad.[174]

There were two salient sides to the gamut of ideas regarding the nuclear programme in light of India's foreign policy and the international arrangement of powers. On the security side was K. Subrahmanyam who insisted that India needed a clear nuclear agenda for generic security reasons. In his article on the 'Role of Nuclear Weapons in International Relations' published in July 1970, he had predicted the nuclear explosion. The other side, the foreign affairs side, was brought up by scholars like Sisir Gupta, one of the most clear-headed analysts of Indian foreign policy, with his understanding of India's neighbours and the thinking of the political establishment owing to his long stint in the Congress party's foreign affairs cell. He had been talking about the nuclear programme in a series of articles, i.e., *Break with the Past*,[175] *Problem of Indian Defence*,[176] *Role of Foreign Policy*,[177] etc.

Such was the milieu within which the nuclear policy was being formulated, and the establishment of the Centre for Disarmament Studies in JNU provided a big push to conduct detailed research on the subject. The 1970s were a bad decade for India as the anti-Indian posture of the policymakers in Washington had become apparent. Gupta critiqued the typical state department models of its geo-strategy—stable peace. Secretary of State Dean Rusk, speaking at the Manufacturers Association at Connecticut, was succinct when he said: 'We as a nation have decided that our own security requires us to take an active part in collective security arrangements in those areas which we have determined to be vital to our own security.'[178] This was arguing a case for the 'redetermination of the role and status of the regional powers in the international political system'.[179] He was predicting a very significant dimension of the world: ... the power at the disposal of the superpowers continues to grow but this does not enable them to enforce a particular order of things in the world as a whole.'[180] The problem he saw was to create a structure resting on 'many pillars rather than a few' for ensuring peace in the world.[181]

The new world order and the confidence displayed by the social scientists of India was obvious in Sisir Gupta's mapping of global politics with its centre in India. In making a case for a new world map, he made a reference to the two older models in which the regional states were jumbled up. The policies and attitudes of the superpowers towards South Asia, recast in this light, made it possible for India to contribute to the erection of a structure enabling stability and peace in Asia. Gupta was wary of the fact that the superpowers would decide to bring in the two earlier models: 'the model of absorbing the local conflicts in the overall scheme of great power rivalries' and 'the model focused on controlling and regulating great power rivalries so as to deprive the regional powers of their manoeuvrability'.[182]

Gupta also identified the challenge for the Indian foreign policy in this mapping: 'Should the great powers pursue the healthy course in a more widely based international political structure, India will have to live up to the expectations from it. On the other hand should the great powers try and apply any of the two outdated models of managing local conflicts, India will have to be prepared to prove that those models are unworkable.'[183]

In the process of enjoying the space and interaction, the IR (international relations) fraternity also began to understand the new global realities post-Vietnam and, between 1971 and 1980, the IR discipline developed with vigour. Area studies were simultaneously sustaining the discourse with IR and mutually benefiting. The NPT (Non-Proliferation Treaty), the discourse on disarmament (Strategic Arms Limitation Talks—SALT) and the explosion of India's nuclear devise caused the pro-nuclear community among the scholars to join the mainstream debate.

In the uncomfortable, sometimes violent, domestic situation, the added worry of encirclement by hostile nations brought forward the question of 'national security'. The most significant development was the evolution of a strong international relations community which had slowly and steadily emerged from the staid Commonwealth studies discipline and was now combative enough to understand the world on an equal footing. Although there were almost no Marxist scholars in the School of International Studies, except some who perfunctorily added some Marxism to curry favour with the leftist establishment.

Colonialism was viewed in terms of national sovereignty and, by the mid-1970s, one could see that the idea of non-alignment had become very robust. The Colombo summit of the non-aligned countries was held in 1976, but it was the Belgrade summit that brought the scholars together. However, the core of the community's personality could have been shaped by a new-found confidence in the country amidst very strong superpower rivalry. There were students trying to devise 'Asian alternatives to superpower models', while some tried to explain the superpower rivalry on the basis of history.[184]

The superpower rivalry in the 1970s was actually hidden under ideologically worded cold-war language. The JNU students excelled in deciphering the nuances of the intricate arms trade and their geopolitical implications better than any other institutional set up in the Third World. A mid-1970s thesis by Harpreet Mahajan on the arms trade and aid to Third World countries exposed the huge duplicity of Western countries in the whole aid business. It is in the business of aid and arms trade that the world actually had a definite pattern of division between the three worlds and their consequences to the Third World, namely, violence, instability, regime change, disproportionate spending, finances meant for human development shifted to deal with real and perceived threats to the regimes and nations, and the intricate links of the arms business groups with political groups.[185]

Superpower rivalry reached its crucial phase with the Afghanistan crisis. On 28 April 1979, the Saur Revolution took place in Afghanistan with the formation of a joint front by Nur Mohammad Taraki and Hafizullah Amin's People's Democratic Party of Afghanistan, and Barbak Karmal's Parcham. But the issues got complicated when, on 27 December 1979, the Soviet army reached the presidential palace.

With the death of Hafizullah Amin and succession by Barbak Karmal, the situation moved towards a new direction. The general tenor of the international studies scholars in JNU tended to be critical with their dispassionate analysis of the Soviet invasion and they could also see the American presence looming large.

M.S. Agwani, the leading West Asian expert, commented that the 'communist take-over in Afghanistan could offer no advantage to the Soviet Union in terms of either security or to influence relationships, which it did not already possess'.[186] He argued that the events in Afghanistan had made it handy for the United States to increase its military presence in and around the Gulf region substantially without 'evoking any serious protest from the littoral states'.[187] For Gargi Dutt and Bimal Prasad, Afghanistan was the precursor to many long-standing changes in the region.[188]

The security scenario was entering the bitterest winter of the cold war. In 1979, there was a second review of the Nuclear Non-Proliferation Treaty that India had steadfastly refused to sign as a mark of its opposition to any unequal international treaty regime. It was very clear that the presidential campaign in the USA was showing that there were vested interests which did not want détente to remain and a new arms race was being promoted. Indira Gandhi returned to power during this changing global scenario when India's immediate neighbour, Zia-ul-Huq hanged Bhutto and played the old Pakistani card of being allied to American policy. She was not at all enthused with the Soviet Union's incursion into Afghanistan and refused to endorse it when the Soviet delegation visited India with their announcement.

The increasingly intense US–Soviet rivalry in the international scenario was keenly watched and a kind of non-aligned perspective could be discerned while dealing with the history and the patterns of superpower relationships and the way they behaved with other states.[189] By the beginning of the 1980s the superpowers' approach to the Kashmir issue too was monitored closely.[190]

The 'encirclement of India' was articulated by those who understood that world affairs was more than mere national interest studies. Two young scholars, P.S. Jayaramu and C. Raja Mohan, scrutinized national security. Jayaramu wanted to historically locate and discuss how the security issues stood at the end of the Janata Party regime in 1979,[191] while Raja Mohan in his thesis, 'Nuclear Energy and The Developing Nations: A Study of Technological and Political Implications,' studied the technological and political implications in the development of nuclear energy, and he analysed the security issues in the backdrop of technological prowess.[192] The issue was hotting up particularly after the Pokhran explosion which almost crippled the Indian nuclear science programme. Matters came to a head with the US denial of nuclear fuel to Tarapur, causing a diplomatic and national uproar in 1979.

Sisir Gupta's prognosis in the 1970s that the region would see new policy harmonization was proved right. This harmonization in terms of the American and the other developed countries' perspective was greater engagement, militarily most often. The Afghanistan engagement of Soviet Russia was a great irritant to both the policy analyst and the Indian leadership as it affected the international scenario.[193] Urmila Phadnis excellently encapsulated the security dilemmas of both India and Sri Lanka in her study of their domestic politics. On the West Asian front, M.S. Agwani, K.R. Singh, and Mohammad Sadiq continued factoring in India's continued role in the changing politics of Palestine, Iran and Turkey respectively. Agwani was the leading voice of the Indian support in West Asia—particularly to the Palestinian secular cause.

Theorizing Colonialism

The discussion on imperialism and colonialism, and the writings and debates of the Marxist economists relinked the intellect to the larger world. The theories helped one understand the global economy, the colonial or feudal mode of production and the possibilities for action in the world. However, there was a felt need and a desire for new tools to freshen up the praxis; theoretical and ideological debate pivoted around this praxis and as a consequence, the structural features of knowledge production in India resurfaced. Alongside developing and making available appropriate and theoretically informed sources, the freedom in the university allowed people to connect their local understanding with universal theories, parochial concerns with national spaces, and particular identities with universal categories.

Had Indian economy undergone any transition during the colonial period? Was India to be treated as a capitalist country in the lower developmental order, like the take-off stage as suggested by W.W. Rostow, or was it something entirely different? Indians were thinking for themselves and debating among themselves and it was important for historians and economists to cogitate on the issue.

Significantly, neither Marx nor the later-day Marxists had bothered too much about the theoretical foundations vis-à-vis colonial operations in the colonies. Even before Marx wrote his voluminous *Das Kapital*, Dadabhai Naoroji had provided a graphic economic description of poverty resulting from the economic exploitation upon which British rule was based. The celebrated Marxist historians, who had travelled to and glorified India, seemed to have racial blinkers. The Indian Marxists were aware of the British tunnel vision, which was reflected in the writings of a confident generation. The debate over the characterization of agrarian economy and its class differentiation, and the argument that the bourgeoisie was more like the national bourgeoisie opened a door for discussing a distinct social formation in India. Since 1970, Bipan Chandra, for example, had been speaking of a colonial mode of production within the strictly Marxian paradigm. He suggested an improvement, which was considered an audacity, because a non-white, even if he was a Marxist, especially at a level less than a general secretary within the communist hierarchy, was not deemed worthy of making corrections or improvements.[194] Scholars in the Centre for Historical Studies like Jairus Banaji led the writing on this theme which culminated in a fierce debate in 1972.[195]

How was colonialism to be theorized? One theorizing argument was available from the Indian nationalist intelligentsia and, as early as 1965, Bipan Chandra had brought this to life in his monumental work, *Rise and Growth of Economic Nationalism in India*. However, the passion and factual details of the Naorojis, the Gokhales and the Ranades was no match for the contemporary theoretical enchantment with Lenin, Hobson and Rosa Luxemburg. There were theories of imperialism and its operation in India which drew from the theoretical formulations of Marx, Hobson, Lenin and Rosa Luxembourg and tried to explain why imperialism was the route taken by the European capitalism.[196] This was the debate which engaged European intellectuals like Leonard Woolf since the early decades of the twentieth century.

However, while imperialism developed many theoreticians and

historians, those theorizing on colonialism with first-hand experience of colonization were few and far between and when they did arise they were theoretically as well as physically suppressed. The best example is of Walter Rodney and his now famous work *How Europe Underdeveloped Africa* in 1974. He was ultimately assassinated when he ran for a political post in the West Indies. Similarly, there were historians in the mid-1970s, at the height of anti-colonial consciousness, who spoke of colonialism from this perspective.

JNU historians, primarily Bipan Chandra, were able to take India's colonial experience into the discourse on colonialism. This came into direct conflict with the tenets of the communist argument of the imperialism–capitalism debate as it was difficult to comfortably accommodate the new theory. However, it did fit well with the communists' understanding of the centrality of Lenin and then Stalin in the overthrow of capitalism. The completeness of the theory was seductive and very soon there were many works along this line of thought. The colonial mode of production thus became a template that was a major theoretical link to Stalinistic thought and assumptions.

But there were strands which did not sit comfortably with this template. There were those who disagreed with the Stalinist assumption of the centrality of communist thought and movement, particularly the Trotskyites for whom Stalin symbolized the antithesis of revolution. And then there were those who argued that the Indian experience did not fit in with the view that colonialism should be seen from the standpoint of global capitalism. Scholars have recorded this as a crucial area of discomfort that was felt by the rest of the undeveloped world as well. One major upshot was the rise of dependency theorists in Latin America and their reaction to positivism in Latin American philosophy and history.

From this discomfiture began another debate over the colonial mode of production leading to a debate on whether India had witnessed any capitalist development under the British. Irfan Habib had already set the broad outlines of the debate in his justly famous paper published in the popular journal *Enquiry* in 1965 entitled, 'Potentialities of Capitalist Development in the Economy of Mughal India'.[197] The concept of the colonial mode of production had a bearing on India's developmental experience and the prospective route to development. By 1980-81, there were very clear and distilled intellectual formulations visible on the horizon. There were those who tried to look for macroeconomic reasons for imperialism and there were others, primarily the Indian historians, who, by 1980-81, had more or less well-theorized positions on colonialism.

There was a clear demarcation between the modern and the oppressed. This is the most commonsensical view shared even by learned men like former prime minister Manmohan Singh who at a later date paid tribute to the British for gifting India with modern institutions. Bipan Chandra demonstrated how Marx was wrong in thinking that imperialism had a dual role in a colonial context like India where it had both a regenerative and an exploitative role. Comparing Marx's notes on Ireland and India, Bipan Chandra's paper on Karl Marx's understanding of colonialism was an exceptional piece. The primary question was the nature and effect of colonialism in the colonies, particularly in India.[198] It was a landmark achievement to produce such a paper that questioned one of the basic premises of a major ideological theory and paved the way for further work. Critiquing Marx's understanding of Indian colonization from within a materialist interpretation brought a certain vibrancy to the leftist scholarship that the university had produced.

By 1979-80, the world was entering one of the most dangerous phases with the old détente being questioned and the threat of an imminent nuclear war looming large. Reagan's term in the White House was beginning, and with the vow to finish off the Russians, Reagan's aggressive move towards 'Star Wars' had created a new world mood. Thatcherite Britain had already begun its move into a new economy and, with the aggressive stand on the Falklands, had shown the old colonial stance quite obviously, while the defence of Ian Smith of Rhodesia demonstrated open defiance. These manifestations were contemporary echoes of the colonialism of the past. It was now possible to perceive colonialism both old and new, and JNU used this space to usher in a new mental horizon.

JNU scholars examined the neo-economic order and determined whether India retained a colonial legacy. Harun Rashid Khan, produced an interesting write-up on the UN voting pattern and its institutional changes which mirrored the changing global power relations. JNU students were now writing on the new international order. Subhendu Sekhar Padhi and Tukaram Fulzele examined India's economic relations in political dimensions—an aspect which would, later in the late 1980s and early 1990s, burgeon as a specialized academic interest.[199]

Amit Bhaduri, one of the most outstanding economists JNU ever had, dealt with the contemporary operation of forces in his paper on 'Renegotiation of Third World Debt and Appropriate Adjustment in International Trade,' from an extremely radical left position.[200] His colleague in the economics department, Sunanda Sen, examined the nuances of international trade to discover the details of colonial operation and came out with her works during the mid-1970s and early 1980s.[201] Her work in analysing the role of international finance and trade relations in historical and contemporary terms gave the students of economics a solid empirical grounding. She was alive to the contemporary operation of colonialism and while writing on them she could throw fresh light on the operation of colonialism by unravelling trade and intricate financial relations, in 'Internationalisation of Capital, Neo-Colonialism, Unequal Exchange and Recent Trends in International Finance'.[202] Adding a contemporary political and international dimension, political scientist Bhambhri followed this up through his examination of the World Bank which more or less tried to validate the perception, with detailed explanation that the World Bank is more often than not a tool in the hands of global finance.[203]

Simultaneously, a resurgent colonial assertion was taking place. Study of Indian nationalism by the Cambridge scholars who repackaged the earlier administrative assertion that India was no nation came up with the notion of pluralist politics.[204] Anil Seal not only defended colonialism but also caricatured nationalism by arguing that the national movement was all about groups with vested interests fighting for their self-interest of 'loaves and fishes'. Once they did not get it from the colonizers, they turned against them.[205] While in the earlier ethos within which universities operated, Seal's attack might not have met with much resistance, now JNU was in fact ready with its own understanding, and the proposition by the Cambridge school, as it was christened, was perceived as ridiculous except by some sympathetic communists with a zest for attacking the Indian state and the national movement as bourgeoisie-driven.[206] This became very evident when the conservative and neo-nationalist Britain invented the subaltern studies. The latter reinforced the Cambridge school assertion of Indian nationalism as an elite upper-caste manipulation. The subalternist thought pretended at some sophistication by asserting that the elites were not only fighting a mock battle with the colonials, as they were themselves steeped in the colonial ethos, but they were actually fighting a proxy battle against the subalterns whose history and politics they wanted to appropriate.[207] However, it did not cut any ice with those that were attempting to work within the larger frame of an exciting and dynamic understanding of the nation within the campus.

Semiotics of the Material World

The 1960s were a very significant turning point for the Indian economy. It had defined the boundaries of the whole developmental discourse and the evolution of development theory. Development economics was drawing its foundational inspiration from the Indian experience where economic development was taking place alongside a democratic experience. However, the 1960s were ominous as there was unease with the direction that developmental economics was taking. It was a period of shortages and the enthusiasm for developmental planning seemed to be slacking, and by the time JNU took shape, India had undergone tremendous hardships and crises. Many economists who had cut their teeth with the planning experience, more so with a Mahalanobis, were now reviewing their premises of economic development.

From the mid-1950s there was a shortage of funding. This peaked by the 1960s when India did not have the required finances and international commitment was also not forthcoming. The financial pinch resulted in the economists elaborating their critique. Some began to critique the fundamental planning hypothesis, the Mahalanobis model, which had divided Indian economy into two sectors, and decided to concentrate on the industrial sector for investment as this was the sector to give jobs and future development.[208] One major line of criticism, however, had less to do with the planning process itself but with the effects of some of the assumptions made by the model, which the new authors found were leading to a deceleration in the economy, particularly the industrial economy. For example, one of the major critiques came from economists like Jagadish Bhagwati who echoed the very familiar Chicago University critique of Indian planning, that it was not catering to the supply side and hence supply side constraints would deter growth.[209] The economic shortages in the 1960s validated this proposition and also invited intervention at the level of the political economy. This resembled the critique of Indian planning that was put forward by Bombay University economists led by C.N. Vakil, which was extremely concerned with the inflationary aspect due to shortage of consumer goods.

The new critique that emanated from the mid-1960s onwards was on a far more intricate issue. Industrial stagnation led to serious problems as it had led to deceleration and a slackening of the economy. T.N. Srinivasan and N.S.S. Narayana blamed the crisis on the slackening of real investment, particularly in the public sector from the mid-1960s. Many economists tried to pinpoint the sectors which were affected due to the stagnation.[210] Isher Judge Ahluwalia, for example, demonstrated that it affected investment in infrastructure like electricity and the railways.[211] By 1970, the impact of the Green Revolution was visible and there were many issues that demanded the immediate attention of the economists.[212] The use of technology to improve the efficiencies in the economy moved to the forefront. The most important facet was linking of the sectoral issues to the larger global economy. By 1972, it was also apparent that without economic understanding, it was going to be difficult to study the social sciences. Therefore it was a logical conclusion to soon start up a centre dedicated to economics. Social science would then be historically and economically grounded.

Bombay University laid the groundwork for making historical connections by studying the evolution of the Indian economic history in relation to the larger processes of the global economy. Dansukhlal Tulsidas Lakdawala, the pioneer of fiscal research in India wrote his thesis on 'Justice in Taxation in India with Special Reference to Gujarat'. Similarly, Dinanath Raghunath Khatkhate, another of the respected economists, wrote his thesis on 'Monetary Policy and Economic Development of Underdeveloped Areas'. With the planning process in action, the issue of growth became a central issue under the intense scrutiny of the university scholars. R.K. Hazari, who would later go down in history for his recommendations regarding the Monopoly and Restrictive Trade Practices (MRTP), wrote a serious treatise for his thesis entitled 'An enquiry into the nature of underdevelopment: An essay on economic growth during 1953-57'. There were others in Bombay University who were working on issues closely connected with the underdeveloped country:

- Anthony D'Costa and Gennaro Zezza studied, 'Exchange Rates with Special Reference to Developing Countries';
- P.V. George worked on 'Inflation in Underdeveloped Countries'; while
- Pherozshaw Medhora examined the 'Investment Pattern in Developing Economies'.

Many key technical issues related to the larger economy, including the question of distribution, were studied by scholars in Bombay. Shantaram Wagle examined the technique of planning with special reference to underdeveloped countries, while Hannan Ezekiel pursued the old and pet interest of Bombay University, i.e., national income calculation, but this time with a larger frame of reference, the underdeveloped countries. Similarly, a scholar, Raman Pillay Priyadarshini, academically engaged with the issue of redistribution of wealth in his thesis. In the mid-1960s, P.R. Panchamukhi wrote his thesis on an issue which would in the decades to come become the most important issue before society—expenditure in the social sector. His thesis entitled, 'The Measurement of the Effects of Public Expenditure with Special Reference to Education and Health Expenditure' in many ways was pioneering work.

Bombay was, therefore, engaged with macroeconomic considerations. C.N. Vakil, B.R. Shenoy and P.R. Brahmanand would present the sharpest and detailed critique of the planning and, later, on the other economic programme as they had already developed the critique of the large colonial economy as central to their tradition. Macroeconomic consideration in Indian intellectual history developed while paying attention to issues of justice and distribution. This formed the core of the early nationalist intelligentsia's critique of the colonial regime. The early Indian economists were also responding to the same reflex of the mood nurtured by the engagement with time and society.

National income and poverty, for example, were the two principal considerations of Indian economists.[213] In 1970, V.M. Dandekar and Neelkanth Rath of Gokhale Institute in Poona brought out the famous poverty index.[214]

As we saw earlier, two important issues had emerged in the late 1960s to move the economic thinking: (a) the post–Green Revolution phase and the attendant technological changes which had an impact on agrarian relations, and (b) the issues of sectoral balance with an eye to the global economy. The economists were not part of indigenous traditions and while Krishna Bharadwaj was talking of Piero Sraffa, others were talking of Marx to generalize Indian realities. The variable of class was introduced into the study of Indian economics. There were attempts to argue in terms of 'people', but Marxist economists like Prabhat Patnaik considered the term 'class' as appropriate.

There was, however, another dimension to the way the discipline was being practised. While Krishna Bharadwaj was trying to bring a large theoretically rigorous explanatory framework of political economy where classical economics and later-day Marxist and neo-classical economy were to fuse, the Marxists were seen to be taking the discourse away towards Marxist political economy as the sole explanatory model. The indicator was the insistence on land and land reform which was voiced in the language of class as sanctioned by the Communist Party of India (increasingly associated with the CPI[M] now). The CPI(M) had begun publishing the journal *Social Scientist*, which mainly followed the party line although it also allowed space to like-minded intellectuals. But the journal effected a close and intimate relationship between intellectuals and their affiliation to the left parties.

By the 1980s, although Krishna Bharadwaj had created an aura around the Centre for Economics and Social Planning, it was rapidly being identified as the Marxist centre due to (a) popular visibility (the *Social Scientist* too began to play a role) and (b) the assumption of the critical posture of class in the analysis, which fitted well with radical politics and which had moved into the spotlight in the late 1970s.

The earlier nationalist analyses by Dandekar and others was brought forward with the help of class analyses by the historical 'political analysis school' developed by Bipan Chandra and his students. Bipan Chandra had evolved a fresh line of inquiry to delve deeper into the historical roots of class formation in modern India, an analysis pioneered by A.R. Desai in his work *Social Background of Indian Nationalism*, which was reviewed in 1948 by Chandra himself. Significantly, the Centre for Historical Studies also began its journal *Studies in History* in which one could see the seeds of the historical rooting of the politico-economic analysis.

The two leading economists in Bombay, B.R. Shenoy and P.R. Brahmananda, were men who were deeply concerned about the health of the Indian economy. Their concern was, however, at the core monetary level; in layman's language, they were concerned with the inflationary effect of the investment being planned. Until the mid-1960s, Bombay University was producing works in economics which was, in comparison to works done in other universities, mostly related to the economy of the country. They were, therefore, at the forefront of analysing macroeconomic and policy changes emanating from the Government of India's Planning Commission and economic ministries. Significantly, the Delhi School of Economics and the Planning Commission were the two centres with the largest concentration of economists. This patronage and invocation of economists by the Planning Commission for the state's planning process gave economics a commanding position in the academia by virtue of their being part of the state apparatus, although this would also prove quite debilitating for the discipline in the longer run. JNU picked up the mantle of economic thinking from Bombay University. It was quite a fortuitous coincidence that the economics department was set up by one of the alumni of Bombay University, Krishna Bharadwaj, with the added bonus of V.M. Dandekar, who was closely associated with JNU's formation.

JNU made a good entry point for larger issues of economics to be taken up as historians, political scientists, sociologists and education experts were all trying to engage with both the macro as well as micro issues. The international trade division in the School of International Studies had a different trajectory and was aligned only with international trade and not interested in entering into any debate over the larger issues affecting the domestic economy. It was purely by chance that Krishna Bharadwaj (1935–92) was in the Delhi School of Economics at the time that Vice Chancellor Parthasarathi was advised to invite her to teach in the Centre of Political Studies which she accepted.

Krishna Bahradwaj started teaching in the Centre for Political Studies where Gramsci's thoughts were hovering in the horizon with one of the first M.Phil. dissertations examining Gramsci for his unsaid and undelivered message of political praxis for the Indian communists.[215] The new economics centre in JNU had got its inspiration from the three leading figures of modern economics, Robinson, Kałecki and Sraffa. Bharadwaj had worked along Sraffa's neo-classical lines while Bhaduri was writing on capital theory and also closely following Joan Robinson.[216] Kałecki's ideas arrived in a different way and produced a different response in the mid-1970s. By 1974, along with Krishna Bharadwaj and Amit Bhaduri, the university brought in Anjan Mukherjee, a very good mathematical economist, and a Rochester University Ph.D, who had worked on Walrasian economics. From Jadavpur University arrived another Cambridge alumnus, Sunanda Sen, who had worked on international trade, and the Oxford Ph.Ds, Prabhat Patnaik and Utsa Patnaik. All the members of the faculty in the centre, barring Krishna Bharadwaj, had Oxford or Cambridge degrees. In the long-term intellectual history of this university, this had an important bearing in the way the intellectual traditions that shaped disciplines evolved in a country with a long colonial past.

Krishna Bharadwaj, the enduring academic figure of the campus in its post-1973 period, was a brilliant mathematical mind combined with a deep sense of social empathy. A graduate of Bombay University, she had moved on to work on the mathematically engaging production function analysis that the Italian-born economists and friends of the communists, Gramsci and Togliatti, were fashioning. Piero Sraffa (1898–1983) was an Italian who left Mussolini's Italy for London, when the communist party general secretary, Togliatti, smuggled Gramsci's papers through him. When Piero Sraffa's book *Production of Commodities by Means of Commodities* came out, it was given to a young student of Bombay University, Krishna Bharadwaj for review, and the review immediately brought her in touch with Sraffa. Sraffa's works on commodity production was connected and almost central to two key theoretical researches in modern economics: the critique of modern value and distribution theory, and the resurrection of the different approaches to the British classical economists, mainly Ricardo, whose work formed the foundation for Marx.

Sraffa, in his classic, *Production of Commodities by Means of Commodities*, had demonstrated that the labour theory of value is unnecessary for analysis. In his model, the relation between prices and physical magnitudes was entirely independent of values. While production function analysis could show the ways in which production behaviour influenced distribution linkages, the Marxian analysis insisted on the labour theory of value as the cornerstone of the theory of surplus value. Thus, central to the Marxian world view was the idea of exploitation.

Bharadwaj used the production function analysis in her exploration of the key sectors of the Indian economy and one could see her attempt to link the sectors to make a broad statement. Her 'Structural Linkages in Indian Industry' was keenly read.[217] The follow-up paper 'A Note on Structural Interdependence and the Concept of Key Sector' was a testimony to her strong technical mind working on the larger movement of intellectual inquiry.[218] In her input/output driven measurement of the production function analysis she strove to link the two major sectors of economy to fathom the fundamental features. In 1969, she worked on a larger empirical base when she used farm surveys to map the production conditions in Indian agriculture.[219] By 1972, she had put together her sectoral understanding into a larger framework of political economy in 'Note on Political Economics of Development'.[220] In a way, she was unconsciously laying the foundation of the political economy school in the centre she had helped set up. No wonder the first student whom she guided in the centre documented this transformation. By the mid-1980s, she had a complete repertoire of a very intricately argued trajectory of the growth of capitalism in the Indian agrarian sector, and her paper, 'A View on the Commercialisation in Indian Agriculture and the Development of Capitalism' is considered the best paper written on the subject.[221]

Amit Bhaduri was writing on the economic history of the emergence of class relations. He brought his Oxford colleague Joan Robinson into the frame who was also, at this juncture, writing in the same radical vein. While Bharadwaj had naturalized the production function analysis of Sraffa, Amit Bhaduri inducted political economy in a historically informed manner. His writings, though in no way politically motivated, would substantiate the radical left perspective of looking into the production relations. A new school was in the offing. The senior scholars of the university were now debating the course of the economy and its relationship with the state, the classes and with the global system. The debate of the evolution of Indian agrarian relations into semi-feudalism in the writings of brilliant and radical minds such as Amit Bhaduri became the centrepiece of the intellectual engagement of the whole school. He argued that there were four features of Indian semi-feudalism:

a) share cropping,
b) perpetual indebtedness of the small tenants,
c) concentration of two modes of exploitation
    (i) usury and
    (ii) landownership in the hands of the same landowner class,
d) and finally, the lack of access for small farmers to the market.

These were serious observations and required a string of theoretical and empirical foundations to critique.[222]

His colleague, Utsa Patnaik, connected the development in the rural economy to the larger theory of imperialism by presenting a critique of those who thought that imperialism was a consequence of the development of a capitalist world and that the capitalist world was made of 'production for the market', a position that the Marxist economist, Paul Sweezy, took in his critique of another Marxist economist, Maurice Dobb.[223] The debate on semi-feudalism brought the contemporary nature of capitalism to the fore. This was a tricky domain and a deep historical insight was required because historical knowledge had to be brought to bear on (a) the evaluation of feudalism and capitalism, and (b) the discourse on contemporary development. Combined with a strong historical school of political economy led by Bipan Chandra and a large school of sociology, which was engaged in bringing significant insights, it was historical opportunity for the economists to develop a formidable school to authenticate knowledge production.

While Bharadwaj used the production function analysis to determine the structure of agricultural productivity and the transport sector, some of her younger colleagues were diligently developing, along Marxian lines, a line of analysis which was centred on the demand side logic in the Indian economy. 'The failure to lift up the agrarian economy', argued Prabhat Patnaik, 'imposes limits on the growth of industry as food prices rise, real wages and hence the workers' consumption fall', which consequently affected the larger economy.[224] The economists in JNU broke new ground by going back to the original sensitivity of the early nationalist economists towards the peasants and the rural economy. This attempt to reconnect with rural economy was now to critique the Indian state's policies. The economic critique, however, resembled the position taken by the communist parties like the CPI(M).

The harmonizing of theoretical discourse to the conclusion reached by political parties outside made the economists quite often ruthlessly and arrogantly dismissive of the historical and sociological work done in the same university. This has proved to be their undoing as the visibility gained by economists was quite often at the cost of wider academic acceptance and historical opportunity to evolve.

Regional Planning and Development

This was also the time for thinking about the larger input and output analysis particularly in the field of agricultural production.[225] This found an impetus with the publication of Yogendra K. Alagh in western India. The Planning Commission saw a coming together of economists of different hues and brought a national and all-sector perspective. Sukhamoy Chakravarty pioneered multi-sectoral output modelling in order to make quantitative decisions.[226] A bias towards industrial components became increasingly visible which led to a squeezing of this initial broad perspective. The acceptance and success of the planning model as a way forward required sophisticated methodologies far beyond those that existed at the time.

Economics as a profession was on the verge of expansion at a time when there was a shortage in the economy. However, shortage of manpower did not allow large-scale exercises of modelling on a regional basis nor did it allow the idea of regional development as an auxiliary to balanced development inherent in the planning process of India to be taken forward. The idea of regional development in the discipline began to emerge in the mid-1960s in the writings of scholars like C.R. Pathak and A.R. Hashim, and therefore the idea of establishing a centre for regional planning was an excellent notion. It, however, was soon killed to suit the intellectual and personal ambition of Moonis Raza who then mooted the idea of a Centre for the Study of Regional Development (CSRD). The advent of economists from the Green Revolution belt helped the regional development centre to carry forward the old input-output exercise which now demanded more effort.

Economists like G.S. Bhalla contributed to large-scale resource and output mapping in the Punjab–Haryana belt. This kind of work also required lot of resources and various institutional sources were tapped. The ICSSR came in handy and in the successive years it forwarded research grants for works done by the centre, e.g., the centre brought the project for the 'preparation of a tribal atlas' (1974-75) which kick-started the department. The most significant feature in this was the big projects in Punjab and Haryana, the quintessential Green Revolution belt which the small group of economists brought to the centre. From 1974-75 to 1979-80, the centre applied for and received grants for studying the entire gamut of structural changes taking place in Punjab and Haryana in the wake of the Green Revolution.[227] Under the leadership of Prof. Bhalla and his colleagues G.K. Chaddha and R.K. Sharma, a veritable storehouse of information was compiled on Punjab, Haryana and the Green Revolution. The centre was humorously referred to as the Centre for Development of Punjab and Haryana.

The centre increasingly developed a pool of students who brought an all-India pattern through their comparative studies on agricultural and other regional developmental issues. The scholars and students of the department of geography were also helped by the excellent exposure to the connection and interdependencies between a diverse human population, geo-climatic variations and the actual operations of the forces of nature and human beings as economic creatures, of which the economists were quite often abundantly ignorant. Interestingly, an economist working for the American agencies realized almost four decades later that his actions to bring growth in Indian villages crippled their lives, and he titled his book, *How Thinking like an Economist Undermines Community*.[228]

CSRD had good geographers many of whom had come from the country's best training ground for geography, Aligarh Muslim University. They began to move beyond the conventional domains of geography and took up issues of development in the new intellectual climate. One of their major contributions to Indian geography was the force they brought to the idea that diversity was neither the cause of economic backwardness nor its explanation. On the strength of this argument, the centre developed its core competency on the diversity indicator and represented it in an atlas that they brought out in the 1980s. This also provided scholars with a strong inclination towards understanding the regional dimension of development.[229] The presence of some of the best Indian demographers like M.K. Premi and initially Ashok Mitra and Ashish Bose also had lent the centre a deep insight into the movements in Indian population. The centre soon developed a pattern where the same data set and the same questions were probed for different regions and provinces making an all-India comparison possible. One complete batch of students, for example, were seen mining the census data of 1961 for 'Spatial and Socio-Demographic Relationships of Large Villages and Urban Centres' under the guidance of all the demography teachers at the centre, particularly Ashok Mitra, who had been the registrar general of census and Professor Mahendra Kumar Premi.

An interesting pattern of research began to emerge when A.R. Satyanarayana studied the spatial and socio-demographic relationships of large villages and urban centres in the Mysore state. Bimla Sharma was doing it for Arunchal, Gurdarshan Singh for Jammu and Kashmir, G.S. Somawat for Gujarat, Jashomayee Devi for Maharastra, Prasanna Kumar Sahoo for Bihar, Raj Kumar Tomar for Uttar Pradesh; and S.K. Gogia for Andhra Pradesh.[230] Many research projects of a similar nature were undertaken by the centre which had the wherewithal to conduct a large comparative analysis.

However, the design of these projects was dangerously close to what the student leaders were apprehensive of in the early years when they attacked teachers for taking up sponsored researches. These data-mining exercises which the private and public agencies (like the Planning Commission or the Population Council) were looking to the university to conduct, as subcontractors, were perilously close in nature to the erstwhile sponsored researches. It was therefore no wonder that very soon the department was fulfilling the Planning Commission's requirements quite often at the cost of bringing fresh perspective on the disciplines which were changing rapidly. Similarly, the large project-oriented work had a stifling impact on the students and researchers in universities across the world as the bulk of primary work generally got transferred to the research scholars at the cost of their own individual academic growth. The paradoxical consequence that follows such a development in a multidisciplinary department is the domination by the projects.

Geography, which was brought under the umbrella of economics and demography, had a difficult terrain to tread. In the new space and with a new confidence, it did undertake some ground-breaking work on the habitation and human geography of, for example, Ladakh or the high Himalayas by Harjit Singh.[231] It was the first to switch over to a Geographical Information System (GIS); it prepared a tribal atlas demonstrating the fact that the insights gained from association with demographers and economists could be utilized to infuse some excitement into the geographer's core discipline.[232] However, the discipline as practised here was increasingly moving along the path shown to it by others. In this case, it was its cash-rich cousins like economics and demography which were stifling the growth of geography. Disciplines were gaining new insights, but at the cost of an independent growth trajectory. It had to follow a cautious path, however painful, in order to not become the spitting image of the dominant disciplines with resources infused from outside.

Decoding the Movements

The time was ripe for getting closer to the various movements of the day, and sociologists therefore began analysing them from afar. P.N. Mukherjee's study of the Naxalbari movement in the 1960s was one such initiative.[233] There was also the attempt to look into the alternative non-Marxist movements like the one led by Jayaprakash Narayan (JP), and scholars like T.K. Oommen tried to explain the movements and their leadership through non-Marxist categories.[234] The campus was also ready to understand the smaller movements with the communist movement forming their fulcrum. While there were debates on the location of classes in the politico-economic structure of the society, there were also arguments by historians like E.P. Thompson that class was a dynamic phenomenon and was in the process of being made and was not a pre-existing given as Marx indicated.[235] Also, the class formations in contemporary India required thinking about mobilization and movement slightly differently.

The deep intellectual contest between those who argued along the lines of the communist parties and those who criticized those reference frames, brought a dynamic academic repositioning of classes and movements. The historically minded saw the re-emergence—in the work of non-Marxists and other social scientists—of the old colonial administrative categorization of Indians as essentially belonging to caste and other primordial groups. There was very little place in these arguments for such modern-day formations like class, nation or world. This was the intellectual template and historiographical presuppositions that the so-called Cambridge school advocated.

The communist movement, and, in the latest phase, the Maoists, had also laid claim to the peasant movements' legacy. While one knew that the national movement had organized peasants and the whole of the post-1920s witnessed peasant movements, there was almost no detailed work, leave alone any larger theoretical treatise, to connect the movement with mobilization. The Communist Party of India at this juncture had been trying to mobilize in places like Bengal and Kerala and had been in the forefront of presenting itself as the legatee of the organized peasant movement during the pre-Independence period. The Maoists were also part of the mobilization effort and, taking Mao's line, they presented their argument that a peasant revolt was the only possible way to overthrow the present regime. Peasants were to adapt themselves to the frame of the Marxists or the Maoists depending on the denomination of the dominant communists in their area. Very few tried to argue that the peasants were the main body of the national movement which itself was one of the biggest mass movements in human history. Bipan Chandra came close to doing so when he maintained that the peasants did have a movement but it operated under a bourgeois leadership and programme. Similar was the case with labour and their connection with the larger text of Indian political and social history.[236]

Characterization of the movement began to be seriously studied by historians. One could see a sneaking appreciation of the mobilization of the peasantry by Gandhi. In September 1974, speaking to the *National*

Herald, Bipan Chandra said that Gandhi's contribution was to take the national movement to the petty bourgeoisie and the peasants, thereby giving it a broader base. The main ideology of the movement remained within the control of the bourgeoisie. He further elaborated that 'after Independence, power shifted into the hands of the bourgeoisie and therefore the character of the entire movement came to be confirmed as a mass movement under the hegemony of the bourgeoisie'.[237] While sticking to the strict Marxist class lines, the JNU historian was trying to link the class mobilization to the larger ideological core of the national movement. Two young historians, Majid Siddiqi and Mridula Mukherjee, trained at the Centre for historical Studies (CHS) by its founders, studied the peasant movements in eastern Uttar Pradesh and Punjab respectively.[238] The first issue of the journal, *Studies in History*, that the CHS brought out had an article on the labour and peasant parties during the 1920s. An examination of India's recent past was on the anvil with some confidence.

Approaching the past through the present drew many into discussing labour and its role. This immediately meant analysing political mobilization of labour from the contemporary political and intellectual perspectives. Labour not only occupied a pivotal historical role, it had a central role reserved for the future in the whole Marxist understanding. In the Leninist formulation this was the class which seemed to possess the most advanced class consciousness to bring about any revolution. For those concerned with the revolutionary praxis, an in-depth study of the labour was of utmost significance. The 1970s had not seen much labour unrest but the economic scarcity was telling. West Bengal was entering a phase characterized by intense labour unrest. The radical left intellectuals were involved with the labour at this moment in history. The communist parties, both Marxists and Maoists, thought otherwise and for them Mao's valorization of Chinese peasantry was more significant than those that placed industrial labour at the vanguard by Lenin's ideas of revolution. Both these left perspectives were to provide the template for a critique on the nature of Indian mass mobilization during the last hundred years or so and its contemporary situation. Lajpat Jagga, for example, explored the potentialities and limitations of the labour movement at a time when the freedom movement was at its peak.[239] From both these perspectives, nationalist mobilization was found to be wanting as, significantly, the character of labour's participation differed in the Indian case from those in China and Russia.

Historical perspective notwithstanding, many scholars took to studying the mobilization of labour in contemporary and ongoing locations. G. Venkatraman was examining the role of Dravida Munnetra Kazhagam in the trade union movement. The works done by the students demonstrated the dynamics of the time and the clash of these ideas. It was around 1981-82 when the Indian labour movement was entering its worst phase with the rise of Datta Samant, who was, from all possible indications, working at the behest of the Bombay capitalist classes, that the studies of labour were reaching their pinnacle.[240] The scholars in JNU were fortunate in having a rich intellectual and academic treasure trove to connect their studies and therefore did not collapse the way Bombay's labour movement crashed. Deep understanding of Marxist theories came to the rescue of many as there were enough cautions against adventurism. This caution helped them avoid the pitfalls of many fascinatingly seductive theories of revolution, like 'everyday resistance as "weapons of weak"' copied from a completely different experience and location.

Theoretical debates on Marxism and Marxist writings created an atmosphere where researching and critically looking into the inequities of the Indian social structures were seen to be of utmost importance. The study of contemporary class formation and emerging stratifications in many parts of India was now undertaken. While Jagannath Pathy examined the political elites in Orissa, K.A. Mathew was dissecting the process of class formation among plantation workers in south India. R. Vimala was trying to see whether there was an element of 'class' in the Dravidian movement. The analysis of the changing agrarian relations and the resultant stratification in Assam and Karnataka were examined by Ranjit Bhadra and G.K. Karanth respectively.[241] Suvira Jaiswal, while teaching the history of religion brought original insights into the origins of untouchability in her presidential address to the Indian History Congress in 1978.[242] All these contributions made the community sharper in its discourse on class.

The researchers were working on all segments of the movement from Maoism to Shiv Sena. The first full-scale work on the Maoists was done by a researcher, Shanta Sinha, in JNU. The limitations and the class character of movements like the one which Shiv Sena initiated, was compiled by her contemporary Dipankar Gupta.[243] It is in this context that one saw some of the most pioneering work on women also being researched. The consciousness of politics and viewing women from within a larger context influenced some of the first works on women. The work by one of the first-batch students, Rekha Chowdhry, entitled 'Women and Politics in India', and by Shipra Sen, 'The Political Women in India, Her Role and Her Status', were the beginnings of a trend of research on women.[244] In a searching work which critiqued the post-Independence failure of the Indian state to take the issue of women towards a liberatory discourse, Maitrayee Choudhury later on argued that the first draft on women did not fit into her modular understanding of contemporary India wherein the state was elitist and therefore patriarchal, and was in no way interested in really solving women's questions.[245] However, there were efforts at posing the question on a larger sociological canvas. By 1979, one saw that some of the most sensitive and powerful works on women and women's movement were written in JNU. In this sense, JNU provided the first group of works which later on provided pointers in the feminist debate on Indian women. Incidentally, the first women's journal, *Manushi*, was brought out by Madhu Kishwar, a student of history in JNU in the late 1970s and early 1980s. In the rapidly changing Indian society, early 1979 saw increasing numbers of cases of rape and bride burning, and one also saw that the rise of intellectual exercises in exploring women were rapidly changing their ideas and conception regarding 'maleness'.[246]

All these theoretical studies and discussion had produced the ability to link the local realities with the global ones. This quality is the mark of greatness of any institution. Connecting the human lives from one corner of the world to another and to reflect upon them becomes possible through such institutional spaces. The Black Movement in the United States in the 1960s was studied in JNU in the 1980s not only because R.P. Kaushik, the professor of American Studies, had incidentally worked on this earlier but also due to the desire to link some inherent commonalities regarding movement across borders. It is also significant that such work to connect human destinies and the powers constraining them achieved institutional endorsement around 1980-81.[247]

The horizon of the knowledge universe at JNU also embraced the School of Languages, which was the only place where undergraduate teaching was conducted. The pioneers there made a very conscious effort to naturalize the teaching of foreign languages while maintaining contact with their own society. A unique mosaic of variegated sensibilities and aesthetic tastes soon began to define the school where centres evolved differently from each other.

Indian languages, namely, Hindi and Urdu, located in the same centre, began a search for ideas which defined their common ancestry and the reason for the modern-day internecine clashes. There were efforts to try and look for modernity in the twentieth century Urdu literary universe.[248] Hindi, on the other hand, tried to look for the tradition of syncretism and alternative cultural paradigms. Namvar Singh's classic treatise, *In search of an Alternative Tradition*, in fact, articulated the efforts of the whole generation of language teachers here.[249] Kabir, the medieval Bhakti saint who had defied boundaries of community and religion became a kind of totem for much of this search for tradition.[250] Locating traditions to their material context became a very powerful methodological intervention by many scholars of the centre during the early phase of its evolution.

The teaching and discussion in German was informed by a sense of history for two very interesting reasons. First, a large number of faculty and students came from Poona and Bombay where German was well entrenched into Indological scholarship and the students carried that sensibility to JNU too. The other reason was the peculiar predicament related to scholarship in Germany as well as in JNU. The reality of the Nazi past and the Holocaust was a constant presence. German historians could openly debate many of these issues only in and after 1981. The serious students in JNU, however, needed to negotiate this past and the silence in the present with the strong democratic currents in India. This inspired many students of the centre to historicize literary problems and personalities in order to try and retrieve the humanistic elements from the past of modern Germany. French, on the other hand, was more tuned to the issues of state and culture. It was significant, therefore, that they began to take up issues of intercultural transactions.

Most of the centres, however, brought to JNU the radical icons of the respective linguistic contexts and contributed to enlarging the intellectual horizon of the JNU community. Spanish, in this sense remained the leader in providing the largest number of creative icons and through JNU they also entered many other universities and literary communities in the country. It is no wonder that the regular slogan of all the student marches remained the famous 1973 Chilean song, *El pueblo unidojamásseráveneido* (The people united will never be defeated) composed by Sergio Ortega in the days of resistance against the Pinochet regime in Chile. The Centre for Spanish Studies and some of its culturally active students not only hosted many of the radicals of Latin America but also gifted the song as well as the poetry of Neruda to the campus.

The inspiration of the revolutionary poets like Lu Xun and the communist revolution of China, however, provided a very peculiar context to the students of Chinese studies. They saw the romance with the Chinese revolution in the campus, but for a student who visited China, the totalitarian regime and regimented society must have been quite dampening. The result was a sense of resignation for some while others tried locating their academic quest in new pedagogic methods. In a sense, this space for innovating new pedagogies is what JNU provided its community. It is this continuous renewal of its pedagogical quest that the community of teachers and students committed themselves to in the new university.

9

Striving for a National Commons

While the intelligentsia strove to define the new space, the long struggle of the Indian scientist to create a large indigenous scientific community since the early twentieth century was coming of age.[1] The 1960s were a watershed period for the Indian scientific community for two paradoxical reasons. In 1957, the Soviet Union launched its spacecraft into orbit, and shattered the myth of American superiority in science. A feverish investment in scientific research began in the non-communist West.[2] The cold war antagonism and scientific competition had a negative impact on Indian efforts at self-reliant scientific development. India began to experience the stringent technological denial regime set up by the West. This added a renewed vigour to India's quest for self-reliance.[3]

Most of the institutions had already been set up by the mid-1960s. Electronics, defence, and even outer space had enough state support to go ahead with some kind of research. A friendly post-1956 Russian attitude was facilitating collaboration with Russia which included the establishment of an IIT in Bombay and steel plants in Bhilai and Bokaro. On the other hand, by this time the United States definitely replaced Britain and Germany as the destination for migrating Indian scientists. This was also the time when very stiff competition in the world of scientific research began to unfold with countries like Germany increasing research funding in many fields.[4] This could have resulted in widening the horizon of opportunities, but the prevailing cold war sentiments blocked any such expansion. The needs of the mid-1960s engendered a community seriously debating and considering technology transfer.[5]

Notwithstanding the expanding horizons of scientific research, the 1960s witnessed a growing sense of distrust of science, especially because science and technology began to be increasingly viewed as government projects. In the United States, for example, science was considered a big enterprise and there were question marks over its innocence and value-free status. By the late 1960s, some of those privy to policymaking realized that science's age of innocence was over and it was going to be an uphill struggle globally to make people accept science at face value. In the US, for example, the publication of *Silent Spring*[6] underscored the connection between social and environmental movements. The innocence of science was challenged. Using current research at the time, Rachel Carson reported that the harmful residuum of dichlorodiphenyltrichloroethane (DDT) in the environment was taking its toll on all creatures on planet earth. There were very high death rates especially in birds. An effective strategy used by Carson was the visualization of a spring without birds, a silent spring. Carson reported that when DDT is ingested by birds, it leads to their eggshells getting thin and brittle. If birds cannot lay eggs successfully, many young birds die. For the first time, large sections of the population rejected science and technology and demanded regulation of scientific applications. The book ultimately resulted in the ban on the pesticide DDT and the creation of the Environmental Protection Agency in 1970 in the United States.

Critiques of unalloyed valorization of natural science also began to receive academic validation, significantly from philosophical works, including works of the leading logician, W.V.O. Quine. In 1951, his paper entitled 'Two Dogmas of Empiricism' provided a foundational criticism of the division between natural science and humanities as a disciplinary divide and an analytical device.[7] In this classic paper, he pointed to the artificial division between natural science and humanities that had been created within the eighteenth-century knowledge project. It showed that the supposed dichotomy of knowledge between humanities and physical sciences were based more on dogmas than on actual categories outside the entities.[8] Thomas Kuhn, one of the historians of science at MIT, was inspired by Quine's work and took up the project of historically contextualizing science. He linked science and scientific discoveries to the social and power structures of the time.

Kuhn's *The Structure of Scientific Revolutions*, published in 1962, argued that scientific changes became 'normalized' through culture, and suppressed oppositional ideas. His work impacted scientists and non-scientists alike, suggesting that science did not proceed incrementally, but instead through irregular changes in the ways we perceive the world.[9] The way, therefore, was to prepare an intellectual critique of the complicity of the big universities, supposed to be engaged with production of knowledge, but actually engaged in the business of waging wars by the United States government the world over. From this emerged, in a subtle way, the larger critique of the university system itself as a 'corporate university', a tag made immortal by the publications of Clark Kerr's book of the same name which became a sort of the mantra for the mutinous youth of the late 1960s.[10]

Science and Its Soil

The discourse on the history of science in India was spawned by early intellectuals like Brojendranath Seal, and by Marxist scholarship in later years. The Marxist intellectuals and historians, through their work, provided a very strong academic basis for appreciating the material foundations and historical processes involved in the technological changes that take place over time. The Indian nationalist intelligentsia and later on the Marxist historians were profoundly influenced by the works of J.D. Bernal, a world-famous biologist who had pioneered works of history.[11] Joseph Needham's *History of Science* was also published at the same time, indicating the deeper structure of scientific evolution.[12] It was very important for the historians, particularly of Marxist persuasion, to understand the level of technology so that they could link it up with the level of social and political organization. It comes as no surprise, therefore, that one of the foremost historians of the agrarian system of medieval India also wrote a pioneering work on the technologies in medieval India.[13]

One of the original debates in Indian history has been regarding the nature of the Aryan settlement in the Iron Age. The rise of a republic in the sixth century based on iron tools galvanized a study of the science and technology of the time, which has since become the sine qua non for Indian historians.[14] Those who were trying to provide newer insights and linking social and cultural history were definitely trying to develop a clear picture of the relevant science and technology.[15] Interestingly, therefore, those who were making anti-science intellectual arguments also showed their antipathy to perspectives that were historical.[16]

A serious question in this regard was the possible role that the quest for progress had in a nation's development and whether the lack of such a quest was responsible for the great gulf between the advanced West and colonial India. This question had prompted the earlier generation of intellectuals to start uncovering the scientific traditions within Indian society.[17] The 1960s saw a re-examination of the same question.[18] This was the time when the historical route of evolution of the Indian society came to be debated with an added dimension, i.e., the close relationship between material life, its concomitant social processes and forms of intellectual articulation. D.D. Kosambi, an erudite mathematician working at the Tata Institute of Fundamental Research, began to develop this relationship into a complete paradigm of historical scholarship. Historians like R.S. Sharma would later try and give an excellent exposition of such a paradigm.

From S.A. Dange's tract on the Vedas to Gangadhar Adhikari's work on the other texts, the efforts undertaken by the Marxists as amateur philosophers reflected in the excellent exposition in the works of the philosopher Debi Prasad Chattopadhyaya. Chattopadhyaya, in his brilliant work on the history of materialist philosophy in India, *Lokayata*, opened up new vistas.[19] There have been two D.P. Chattopadhyayas who worked on Indian philosophy. The other D.P. Chattopadhyaya was an interesting institution builder. Apart from actively promoting Jadavpur University's philosophy department, he also helped build the Indian Council for Philosophical Research (ICPR) in the late 1970s and the early 1980s. However, his innumerable writings showed up more of the inanities in Indian philosophical discourse than any of the serious debates on moot philosophical points that had begun to emerge in the 1950s and '60s. One of the reasons behind this was the active promotion by an establishment that tried to project a notion of Indian philosophy as a project with disparate, unconnected parts. This notion of separateness, it seems, has led to very dreary and self-defeating projects.[20]

It was to the credit of the nationalist intelligentsia from the late nineteenth century that the hypothesis that science could not progress in a society enmeshed in a completely traditional outlook was emphasized. Nehru gave the best expression to this mood with his exhortation to evolve a scientific temper. Conscious of the lack of strong scientific social conditions, the intelligentsia indicated this as its first battle to usher in a scientific tradition.[21] Here both the rational as well as the empirical routes were taken and it is of signal importance that a philosopher, a very rare and original philosopher that India produced, K.C. Bhattacharya, who thought along the Kantian lines of combining the two ways.

The intelligentsia in the nineteenth century had begun to evolve a very strong rationalist route to usher in a social revolution. This enterprise was boosted by modern Western education. However, the empirical deficiency remained and, significantly, this would continue to remain the weakness impeding both the scientific and social science fields in India. The nationalist intelligentsia tried to bring in the empirical tradition and, if one examined this attempt closely, notwithstanding his projection as one against 'modern science', Gandhi became the greatest propagator of the empirical tradition in India by showing how caste taboos and the reluctance to do manual labour stymied the empirical route to a scientific tradition.

The Marxist intelligentsia inherited the nationalist intelligentsia's quest for a progressive world view by which the scientific explanations of the world around could be seen in the light of an incremental knowledge base. Colonialism and, significantly, the upsurge of new attacks on the colonies by the erstwhile colonial powers in Africa, commonly described as neo-colonialism, renewed their efforts at dominance and counter-dominance; these efforts were well understood in the 1970s and exposed the workings of the imperialist world order. The role of science and technology to counter the hegemony was also well understood. It was in this intellectual and political climate that many JNU students, not necessarily from the left, began to explore the nuances of science and technology in the global political situation.[22] The Marxist insistence on uncovering its materialist foundations provided a very robust reason for pursuing science. It is, therefore, not a coincidence that the scientific community was overwhelmingly nationalistic and progressive, and many of them were Marxists or believed in socialism to some degree.

Their commitment to a large vision inspired them to enter politics to bring change.[23]

However, an intellectual formation, informed by the distrust of science and technology of the 1960s, began to articulate an anti-Marxist discourse extremely critical of 'progressive or developmental' agenda of the nationalist intelligentsia. Inspired by the works of Kuhn and, later, Bruno Latour of Edinburgh, a strong programme in sociology was beginning to emerge in the early 1970s and '80s. By the late 1970s, following the works in the West, 'science studies' began to invite other students to unravel the issues and impediments of the evolution of sciences in India. Led by serious scholars of psychoanalysis like Ashis Nandy located at CSDS, one began to see their writings frontally attack nation, secularism, democracy and modern science—all in the name of rejecting Western modernity.[24] The arguments began to be anchored on what came to be defined in the 1980s as the 'critique of modernity' and the erstwhile nationalist intelligentsia as well as the Marxists being described as 'modernist' and 'western-oriented'. These emerging anti-Marxist and avowedly anti-left scholars tried to use the East–West dichotomy to anchor their valorizing of tradition and traditional science.

The arguments against positive science in India were taken to ludicrous extents by some psychologists in India like Ashis Nandy who confused science and technology and made a virtue of the defence of tradition by attacking scientific modes of inquiry as something Western.[25] Shiv Visvanathan provided a slightly nuanced position and, in his more sombre writings, basically argued against the technologies' empire-building efforts in India.[26] The monolithic Council for Scientific and Industrial Research (CSIR) structure, its bureaucratic organizational structure, its public persona, its heads, and the bosses of other institutions like the Indian Council for Agricultural Research (ICAR), actually gave credence to such arguments. The scientists themselves were acutely aware of this and, in a penetrative analysis, Vikram Sarabhai said: '...institution for innovation requires organization built around men. No organization chart should stand in the way of recognizing and rewarding talent.'[27]

India, at this point of time, was engaged in the work of nation building, and the sciences were seen as the main building block. The nationalist intelligentsia and leadership saw science as a panacea to the problems of lower-level education, illiteracy, poverty, malnutrition and disease. Science also meant creation of technical manpower required for the new temples of modern India. The Council for Scientific and Industrial Research (CSIR) thus came to occupy an important role. It is quite ironic that when CSIR, as a model for development of science, was getting its biggest push in the 1950s, there was a change all the world over from this model, particularly in England and later in the United States and Germany: science began moving back to the universities. There was a great opportunity in India in the mid-1960s when the 'institute model' (e.g., CSIR) exhibited deep cracks. In 1962-63, the CSIR came in for major criticism even by its biggest promoter, Jawaharlal Nehru. Bureaucratization of science had come at a time when a larger bureaucratization of the state structure was taking place. This would mean that science and technological efforts were in danger of a possible capture by a double bureaucracy. This bureaucratization was overlaid by the colonial mindset. The bureaucratization of science was beginning to suffocate science.

The urgent need of the political class for a self-reliant economy particularly in the mid-1960s produced a unique situation. A dozen scientists with deep connections with the political and bureaucratic establishment began to dominate the science and technology decision-making processes and thereby further entrenched the scientific oligarchic structure. Institutions like the Indian Council for Agricultural Research were prime examples of such a development. The need for a Green Revolution brought the council, which already had an extensive area under its operation, under the sole control of scientists-turned-science bureaucrats. Many like Sarabhai were afraid that this would strangulate innovation.

The manpower trained within the country was not sufficiently deployed but there were provisions made to directly bring foreign-trained manpower at a higher rung on the ladder with less rigorous responsibility, creating a situation which discouraged local talent—a situation that continues to prevail in many areas. Panchanan Maheshwari, the legendary botanist, who set up the department of botany in Delhi University in 1949, pointed this out in his presidential address to the Indian National Science Academy. The Indian bureaucracy and the upper classes, many of whose progenies had gone into some scientific and professional streams, now decided to milk the state in the name of science by raising the bogey of brain drain and established a scientific pool.[28]

The CSIR model, i.e., research-institution-based research systems, therefore, came under scrutiny. This was the time that universities could have taken charge of scientific research. New universities were coming up and universities like Lucknow, Osmania, Rajasthan, Saugar, Agra, and a couple of others were trying to innovate while Madras, Calcutta, Banaras, Delhi and Allahabad were also spawning good research students. New centres were about to emerge in Rajasthan which would have one of the first radiation biology labs while Banaras had a molecular biology section. Delhi University was soon to change hands to a new generation: Panchanan Maheshwari and M.M. Johri. Osmania University was trying to emerge in many areas under the dynamic leadership of Dr D.S. Reddy.

This was the time when there was a definite push in the United States to promote science in universities in a big way so as to catch up with and overtake the Soviet victory of sending the Soyuz into space. The post-Soyuz desperation of the capitalist West was overcome in 1969 with Neil Armstrong landing on the moon. However, by 1967-68, Third World countries like India had to fight hard to hold their own and develop their scientific abilities in critical areas including the controversial nuclear science programme. This and the other complicated issues of science and technology made Indian scientists realize that policymaking now required a lot more detailed and combined work. The need, it was felt, was more acute at the international level, on issues like disarmament and security where India was a regular and vocal participant. Attacks on science and technology had demolished the pre-war innocence of science.[29] At this very time in the history of science in India, when the universities were under attack for not having been able to wrest the initiative from the institutions, JNU came into being, and the vice chancellor, G. Parthasarathi, turned to M.G.K. Menon, who was on the advisory committee, for realizing his vision for science departments. In the true JNU spirit, science and technology institutes were to be brought under the university's unbiased umbrella to let the whole university body also think of science and technology related questions in an independent manner. Two such areas which evolved from this thinking were the centres for community medicine and biomedical engineering and that of science policy in developing countries.

Health Science and Engineering: Efforts at Harmony

In the original vision document compiled by V. Ramalingaswami, the department of community medicine and biomedical engineering was, eponymously, to have two components: (a) Community Medicine and (b) Biomedical Engineering. The idea was to create a centre of excellence for biomedical research and align it with the biomedical engineering department. This would have made the centre capable of understanding and designing the diagnostic equipment required by society. It would make the centre capable of pedagogic as well as policy-level intervention in health, medicine and diagnostics. The centre was envisaged in tandem with the new centre for biological sciences.

The late 1960s and early 1970s was the time when biological sciences underwent radical changes with the full implications of James Watson and Francis Crick's discovery of the double helix structure of the gene opening up new vistas in the area.[30] There was talk of aligning biology with engineering sciences to match the new requirements of the medical as well as biological sciences. These discussions were in line with M.C. Chagla's vision of integrating the All India Institute of Medical Sciences and IIT into JNU. The new university was again fortunate in having the most competent and internationally respected persons as the planners for the centre, V. Ramalingaswami and G. Parthasarathi, who aligned AIIMS and JNU along the same academic axis.

Born in Srikakulam in Andhra on 8 August 1921, Ramalingaswami was a product of Andhra University, one of the finest universities in the 1960s, from where he earned his MBBS and MD in 1944 and 1946 respectively. He went on to earn a D.Phil. and a D.Sc. in 1951 and 1967 respectively from Oxford. Ramalingaswami began his research at the Nutrition Research Laboratory, Coonoor, in the Nilgiris (now the National Institute of Nutrition, Hyderabad) in 1947. With a deep, abiding commitment, quite common in the days when people were imbued with a sense of mission to improve society by making India's poor healthy, he researched the causes of disease and searched for cures.

His pioneering research on 'protein-energy malnutrition, iodine deficiency disorders, nutritional anaemia, and liver diseases in the tropics' led many large-scale interventions in these areas. Ramalingaswami continues to be a great source of inspiration even to this day; at a time of natural and man-made calamities during the Bihar famine in 1967 and during the Bangladesh war, his leadership helped the government provide nutritional protection to millions of victims and refugees.[31] His research in the hills into the cause for widespread prevalence of goitre (swelling of the neck due to thyroid problems) led him to conduct a classic experiment in public health. It involved a population of over 100,000 people in Kangra, Himachal Pradesh. Intake of iodized salt helped reduce the disease. This work laid the foundation for the national iodine deficiency control programme and provided protection to nearly 300 million people! Ramalingaswami successfully introduced iron supplements into the diet of pregnant mothers. This measure alone led to a significant improvement in the health of women and children worldwide. His other major contribution was the discovery of a new liver disease syndrome known as Indian Childhood Cirrhosis (ICC). He joined the All India Institute of Medical Sciences (AIIMS) when it was established, and began setting up one of the best pathology departments in the world of the time.[32]

Now, he viewed the proposed department like a true scientist, i.e., field research, laboratory experiments and clinical and community-based approaches to solve problems.[33] This approach was closest to Chagla's original vision of the JNU. It would harness technology and direct it towards the questions that social scientists would ask. Technology and training would be available across disciplines, and physics, biology and medicine would all be on the same page, raising and debating the issue. Technology would, therefore, no longer be the exclusive to a privileged few. Ramalingaswami's vision was to also improve the teaching and practice of medicine in the country not only by scholastic criticism but by training the professionals, providing course material and using other methods of direct intervention.

Ramalingaswami suggested that the proposed centre should study 'the biological gradient of disease in communities' and the factors that 'determine this gradient'.[34] The studies would be designed to provide insights into: (a) medical care and medical planning with a view to improve health services and (b) developing teaching material that would be fed back to the medical colleges for an improvement in the teaching of behavioural sciences and community medicine at undergraduate and postgraduate levels in the various universities.[35]

The report merits to be quoted at length in order to discern the penetrating eye of the leading medical scientist who tried to fulfil JNU's dream project. Assuming that JNU would develop strong links with AIIMS, Ramalingaswami conceptualized that the university would, 'provide a unique opportunity for the establishment of a research and development centre that would concern itself with the study of environmental and social aspects that influence major health problems affecting the rural and urban communities in India'.[36] He explained that the 'studies require a multi-disciplinary approach including epidemiology, bio-statistics, medical care and specialized knowledge of medical science itself'.[37] It was therefore thought that the 'economics of health, the extent of capital investment in strengthening health services, the use of resources to increase medical productivity and a broadening of the horizons of health institutions and health administration through social sciences, are the broad areas of concern for the proposed centre'.[38] The results of such studies could provide a proper scientific base for restructuring the health services of the country to be better adapted to community needs. They would also make it possible to improve and enrich the teaching of community medicine.[39] Assuming the same premise of collaboration, the biomedical engineering and technological expertise of IIT, the medical expertise of AIIMS and the social science, mathematical and statistical expertise of JNU would have combined effectively to serve the Indian society.[40]

'Biomedical engineering encompasses' the proposal said, 'the fields of physical science, life science and social science, and is a true interface between technology and health care.'[41] He visualized the objective of the programme in these terms: 'Application of engineering/life science principles and techniques to study medical and health problems. And secondly, the application of bio-engineering science techniques to study the special properties of living systems.'[42]

For him, the present '"cottage industry" approach involving individually equipped doctors in medical care and community health programmes' was passé. One required to go beyond, he reasoned, and 'create systemic understanding' about the needs, and innovate practices and studies for a whole range of issues like 'patient monitoring; study of biological transport processes; the dynamics of the functioning of cardiovascular, respiratory and other systems; physiological control mechanisms and the use of artificial organs'.[43]

He also tried to knit the units together and proposed that the 'existing facilities at the All India Institute of Medical Sciences and the Indian Institute of Technology would be utilized and augmented, if necessary. The unit at the Jawaharlal Nehru University would construct programmes of research and training fully utilizing these facilities.' In one of the most futuristic notes ever seen in the field of higher education, his proposal was both practical and idealistic. He felt that there was a need to develop 'this interface territory', which could be achieved through 'several avenues leading eventually to degrees in bio-engineering or bio-technology from a variety of backgrounds'.[44] The chief problem in developing this field were the difficulties of interdisciplinary training, covering medical science, material science, chemistry, physics and mathematics. The Jawaharlal Nehru University would play a key role in bridging these areas and providing a base for advanced training and research.

The working group that was set up for going through the proposals included V. Ramalingaswami, K.S. Sanjivi, M.N. Srinivas and D. Anand. Later on, Debabar Banerjee, Udai Pareek and J.R. Bhatia were co-opted. On 29 October 1969, Ramalingaswami presented the working proposal for the unit of social medicine and community health.[45] He proposed that the university should conduct intensive research using a data set with an average of 2,000 families (10,000 persons) and 'should collect materials regarding fertility control, pre-natal and post-natal problems'.[46] 'Only such field work' he felt, 'could elicit intimate information regarding the health of families which are generally known as "hard information".'[47] This could be done by one or two groups of the body that the university would set up. The advisory committee entrusted to him the task of finding the experts and people for this.

The planning for biomedical engineering required very high-calibre thinkers who were well-versed in biophysics and its technological components. The group had some of the best people in the country in the biophysics and medical professions. A.R. Verma was one of the pioneers of crystallography along with Dr S. Ramaseshan. Dr Verma, an eminent physicist, whose paper in 1953 was cited by international contemporaries, was the director of the National Physical Laboratory. His book on crystallography published around the same time was one of the early works on the subject.[48] By the late 1990s, India had developed quite an advanced area of research in this field. Verma's work on dislocations, published in 1953, was later developed in the field of bio-sensors and became extremely useful in biomedical diagnostics and biomedical engineering. In 1964, Dorothy Hodgkin received the Nobel Prize for determining the structure of protein through X-ray crystallography. It was therefore a frontier science and the university had the advantage of having one of the front-ranking scientists as advisor. Two other members of the working group, K. Sundaram, the eminent biophysicist, and Satish Dhawan, the director of the Indian Institute of Science and also a leading space scientist, made the collegium one of the finest in the history of the Indian scientific community.[49]

Parthasarathi, however, postponed the establishment of the department because of financial constraints and his feeling that this issue could be handled by his successors. This was unfortunate. JNU and the Indian scientific community lost an opportune moment to intervene in the field of Indian medical education through this institutional and interdisciplinary collaboration. Biotechnology and biomedical engineering might have moved quite a few notches above where it has reached now, which is itself the result of the admirable strenuous efforts by the Department of Biotechnology (DBT). On the other hand, the 1970s were a period when medical education was entering a phase when it needed to forge a path of growth on its own. The rapidly intruding capital-intensive model dehumanized medical education and one realizes that had JNU created such a department, it would have intervened effectively in this situation of crisis.[50]

A Centre for Studying Science Policy

The most important project of the university and at the heart of Chagla's dream was his vision that the new university should integrate humanities with sciences. Technology transfer was the key to this.[51] In the second meeting of the Academic Advisory Committee held at

6.00 p.m. on 29 August 1969, a working group was constituted with M.G.K. Menon, B.S. Minhas, Sukhamoy Chakravarty, Anand Sarup (of the Planning Commission) and K. N. Raj for thinking of a centre for science policy. Much did not happen on this front for a while and only on 25 March 1970 was its report discussed in the seventh Academic Advisory Committee meeting. The group's paramount concern was to recruit the right scholars for this discipline and engage people who could collaborate with the natural science departments.

There were no university-based programmes in the country in 1969-70 to provide either the model or manpower for the centre. It was in the domain of economics where the issue of technological input in policymaking had been given significant thought. The historians were keen on technology and considered it an indispensable variable in the developmental paradigm. For Marxist historians, technology quite often determined entire trajectories of historical development. The possibility that JNU would associate with IIT and AIIMS in a working alliance was another idea that hovered in the horizon for those who envisioned such a programme. The fundamental interdisciplinarity was in keeping with the original concept of the centre.

The search for people to start the department and then staffing it was of utmost importance to Parthasarathi and his team of advisors. K.K. Subramanian, a leading figure in the area, was invited but he declined. B.V. Rangarao, who was with the CSIR, and an authority on the subject, was appointed. The centre was to offer courses to all undergraduate and postgraduate students of the JNU, irrespective of their discipline, and this meant they needed more manpower which needed to be trained rather than appointed. The working group decided that a graduate programme leading to the MA, M.Phil. and Ph.D degrees in this area would be ideal, and training in the primary social science disciplines such as economics, sociology and political science would be imparted to students enrolled in the programme, but the course orientation and the combination in which they were taken would be determined by faculty through mutual consultation.

The number of persons with the necessary competencies was extremely limited, even if one considered Indians working abroad. The group realized that as far as economists and sociologists were concerned, there were very few specialists in the disciplines who devoted time and energy to problems such as the economics of research and development and the sociology of scientists and scientific organizations. The centre unfortunately failed to obtain the much needed caring leadership and supportive staff. It began haltingly, and the frequent setbacks proved fatal, and it was shut down in the 1980s. The students who came to the centre from different backgrounds went on to prove themselves in various other organizations.

Emergence of Computer Science

Computer science as a discipline first appeared in the United States university scenario in the 1950s as part of either the mathematics division or electrical engineering department, and the pioneers were Stanford and Purdue Universities. Based on inexpensive drum-based computers, including the Librascope LGP-30 and IBM-650, summer school programmes in several top universities legitimized the discipline. With the almost steady evolution and innovation developing parallelly in computers and programming languages, the discipline had not yet been able to carve a niche for itself as an academic discipline either within departments like electrical engineering and mathematics or from the point of view of advanced usage in accounting, record keeping, and administrative work. It was to the credit of George Forsythe of Stanford's mathematics department whose 'prodding', according to Paul Ceruzzi, historian of computing, led to the creation of a separate division in Stanford's mathematics department in 1961, and in 1965, Stanford established the first computer science department in the USA.[52]

In the fall of 1967, Herbert Simon, Alan Perlis and Allen Newell, from Carnegie Institute of Technology at Pittsburgh wrote an eloquent and influential letter to the editor of *Science* in which they defined computer science as 'the study of computers', and it was implicit in the letter that the computer was not a static artefact but a system that carried out dynamic processes according to programmed sets of rules. They defended the study of computer sciences as a science subject—against the objections including the obvious one that computers are man-made phenomena and their study could not be one of the natural sciences. Simon, who won a Nobel Prize later, asserted that many of the natural sciences studied phenomena that were not totally divorced from human creation, and anyway, there was nothing wrong in making a science of the study of the artificial.[53]

They objected to the definition of computer science as being a study of algorithms (or programs) and not computers. For them the use of the word 'computers' here restricted the whole phenomenon. In fact, they provided evidence that the professional society is called Association for Computing Machinery (ACM). However, as Paul Cerruzi pointed out, subsequent developments ran counter to their objections and computer science evolved exactly along the algorithmic lines and the more limited algorithmic line programming.[54]

However, their letter produced one significant result and now created an urgency to defend computers intellectually, and within six months ACM came out with Curriculum 68—a set of courses that the association felt should be an 'intellectually defendable grounding in computer science for undergraduates'.[55] The curriculum emphasized the theoretical and mathematical basis for computer science. The computer hardware course was missing. Contrary to the argument of Simon and his colleagues, the curriculum saw the dropping of courses in electronics and analog computers which were part of an early course by the ACM in 1965. Now the ACM emphasized algorithmic procedures, programming languages and data structures.

In 1964, when there were merely twelve universities offering undergraduate courses, computers were introduced into the Indian academic system. Kanpur's first machine was an IBM 1620, a small computer introduced in 1959. The maturing transistor technology allowed companies to make compact solid state computers at low costs and thereby required less space than the earlier drum-based computers.[56]

The story of computers at Kanpur took the electrical engineering route as the new director, P.K. Kelkar, was trained in control systems.[57] Significantly, the arrival of computers also coincided with the recruitment of faculty and Kelkar 'hired individuals capable of running the computer centre and teaching computing, as well as others in other disciplines who would use the computer in their own research'.[58] This was a fairly significant appointment and indicated the future direction of the discipline. H.K. Kesavan arrived in January 1964 to head the electrical engineering department, and, in May, he became the first head of the computer centre. Kesavan obtained a master's degree in electrical engineering from the University of Illinois and his doctorate from Michigan State University before serving as a professor at the University of Waterloo in Ontario. Waterloo had the most powerful computers and the department, in 1967, would develop a FORTRAN compiler for another computer, i.e., WATFOR, allowing the university to run 6,000 jobs an hour—a tremendous achievement in cutting time and cost. V. Rajaraman arrived at IIT Kanpur in 1963, after earning his master's in electrical engineering at MIT and his doctorate at the University of Wisconsin, and worked in the field of analog computation. Interestingly again, Wisconsin had developed a compiler similar to Waterloo in the early 1960s.[59] Kelkar and Kesavan recruited other faculty members with training in North America, including Kesavan's former colleagues at Waterloo, H.N. Mahabala and T.R. Viswanathan, who both held doctorates in electrical engineering from the University of Saskatchewan. Now there was a complete team at the hub of the computer department.

The Content of Computer Science

While this is one part of the story where the computer and its professionals arrived, there had been a long tradition, already strong in the country, which had its origin in the Indian Statistical Institute and there were people involved in control systems in many places. Mahalanobis, a key figure in the Planning Commission since the late 1950s, was involved in developing computational methods and hence was way ahead of any other institution in the world in thinking about numbers except perhaps the Gosplan ministry of the Soviet Union. Here too there was a mingling of minds and, in the 1960s, the Society of System Sciences was formed by control systems people like Tribhuwan Prasad (of Bihar Institute of Technology [BIT] Sindri) and S. Dattagupta.[60] Parthasarathi had already entrusted M.G.K. Menon with the responsibility, and it was wise of Menon to suggest that the university ought to have a computer and system sciences stream. He also got the paper written by R. Narasimhan, the mathematician, who was also the president of the Society of System Sciences and had close links with Tribhuwan Prasad and Dattagupta.[61] Menon, as Yashpal pointed out, had involved many other scientists at TIFR in thinking about the new university. The vision document therefore must have had input from this large consultation.

When Menon, who would have probably had consultations with many others, presented the vision document for computer and system sciences, computer science was in its infancy and there were only small computers in many institutions. Almost all these computers were used as data processing machines. There were two large computer systems at TIFR and IIT Kanpur which were thought to work on large systemic applications. He was visualizing computers to provide system-and-theory building facilities in many areas of human knowledge. For example, he thought that the school of environmental and theoretical science would use the system for its 'mathematical and quantitative' needs. Similarly, social scientists, by using the computer system, would help reduce the distance that existed between the social and natural sciences. A large computer system was therefore thought of much more than just a facility for carrying out a lot of high-speed computations.

Menon provided a working plan too. He proposed the creation of two sets of groups, system and operational. The system sciences group of approximately eight to ten persons, each with a few years of post-doctoral research experience, and an equal number of immediate post-doctoral or pre-doctoral levels, a system group of about ten engineers, and about ten technical support staff, was considered ideal to start with. Half of a dozen system programmers would be useful. The details above are based on a note prepared by R. Narasimhan, professor at TIFR.

The whole vision was based on the applications of the computer facility and Menon was trying to work out ways by which the scientists and system scientists would develop the new school. TIFR had a large system that they and IIT Bombay were using. However, the vision document seemed weighed down heavily on the theoretical side including possibilities for innovating cognitive science and other new frontiers, and the vision of the environmental and life science schools which Menon had a hand in developing, provided the practical aspects. A conceptual problem in this scheme of things proved to be a major drawback for JNU.

Menon also seemed to be working with the hope, and perhaps the assumption with which Chagla thought about the university, of having the IIT as a federating body. He, therefore, did not give any role to the control system people, nor did he reserve a space for system engineering within the science school. Control engineering, the branch of engineering dealing with the regulation of systems, was a central field in the development of computing. In the late 1950s, Kelkar, along with F.C. Kohli—an MIT-trained control engineer working at Tata Electric who would later build the TATA Consultancy Services and would become its director—had established a master's degree programme in control engineering at the Victoria Jubilee Technical Institute, Bombay.

Had the computer science stream been conceived by the control system people, a more collaborative approach would have been possible with the IIT. This absence would haunt the school as well as the university forever. The computer department began to come up when the other schools had already developed their own individual identities. The faculty appointed were mainly for mathematical and algorithmic purposes as was visualized by the Association for Computing Machinery (ACM), and also by the vision document. When B.D. Nag Choudhuri began by appointing two mathematics scholars, the centre went off on a completely different track. V. Rajaraman of IIT Kanpur was approached but declined as did a few others.[62] Rajaraman's student R. Sadanand joined. However, more serious scholars felt the new university did not have a computer science culture. While IIT Kanpur, for example, quickly integrated computers into its syllabi, JNU could not do so. It was not easy for them to go out and create conditions for easy integration. A few mathematics and operation research people came in but the take-off never happened.

Menon's blueprint which suited the Tata Institute of Fundamental Research (TIFR), did not quite suit the new university. The school of environmental sciences, which came into being later in the mid-1970s, developed independently and tangentially and did not use the computer facility, thereby dashing any future hopes of a larger collaborative character of the school. Parthasarathi was fast losing interest when he could not get the men he wanted to start the school. To sum up, in the 1960s, when the computer revolution was taking off, the School of Computer and System Sciences was a great opportunity. The IIT

Kanpur experience was already there to provide a number of basic inputs. IBM, which was coming into IIT Madras, could also have been brought to JNU, but the American politics of cold war denied India any advanced technology.

Life Sciences: Baby of Circumstances

While the computer science department became a victim of historical circumstances, biological sciences accidentally became the baby of the circumstances. Massive changes were taking place in and around 1971-72, and biology began to be studied on the molecular level. In 1973, the journal *Enzymologia* changed its name to *Molecular and Cellular Biochemistry*.[63] There were interesting debates about the true character of molecular biology. C.H. Waddington saw molecular biology as an ultrastructural biology, while S.E. Luria felt that it was 'not a body of knowledge' but a programme 'of interpreting the specific structures and functions of organisms in terms of molecular structure'.[64] It was this aspect of the programme at the molecular level of biological studies that increasingly came to define the new school and the occupants of one of the largest reverse pyramidal building in the new university. It was precisely this chain of events which culminated in a crisis for the whole 'programme' itself.

In the fourth meeting of the Academic Advisory Committee held on 29 October 1969, it was decided to constitute a working group for this school of biology. M.S. Swaminathan was made its convenor. Parthasarathi was moving diplomatically as he wanted the director of the ICAR to commit his institute to a closer alliance with the university. Leading microbiologist, Obaid Siddiqi, biologist T.S. Sadasivan, and the immunologists G.P. Talwar and A.R. Gopal Ayengar were the other members of the group. They met on 10 December 1969, and discussed the proposed programmes with George Beadle, Nobel laureate and a leading authority in this field, who was visiting Delhi.[65]

In their vision document they were absolutely clear that '(i) cell biology (animal cells and virus-cell relationships) and (ii) developmental biology (differentiation, embryonic growth, etc.), will be the areas which will see maximum growth along with (iii) the evolution of neurobiology (which connects aspects of the computer and information sciences, artificial intelligence, etc., with behavioural biology)'.[66] One of the catalysts was genetics. Genetic structures were fast being decoded and it was becoming common knowledge that there was going to be a 'convergence of fields'. Thus the working group recommended a school with a sound base in modern biology, with the powerful techniques of physics, chemistry and mathematics. 'This base of modern biology, and associated techniques', they declared, could 'be considered under the broad umbrella of molecular biology' which covered 'aspects of the structures and chemistry of the very large molecular entities encountered in biology, microbial genetics and organo-chemical techniques'.[67] The breadth of the base needed and the techniques used could be seen from the following list: X-ray and neutron techniques for structural analysis; electron microscopy, radiation effects and isotopic tracer studies, chromatography, organo-chemical and biochemical techniques for analysis, synthesis and study of various interaction processes, methods in cell biology such as tissue culture and cell genetics, electro-physiology and so on.[68]

This was the beginning of the institutional basis of research on molecular biology. Tata Institute of Fundamental Research (TIFR) set up its molecular programme in 1962, and there were talks of setting up a Hyderabad centre for molecular biology. M.S. Kanungo was trying to establish a molecular biology department at BHU. The areas of research included (a) genetic transfer mechanisms in *E.coli*, (b) theoretical and experimental work on ribosome biogenesis and protein structure, (c) neurobiology, (d) molecular aspects of olfaction in drosophila, (e) yeast genetics and (f) pattern formation and molecular biology of tumour viruses. In Hyderabad, work was being done on molecular mechanisms of the action of seminal plasma and reverse transcriptases. The initial work in JNU on molecular groups began to work extensively on the protozoa parasite, *Entamoeba histolytica*, particularly on its genome structure, and also on the molecular genetics of nitrogen fixation which have also shown the presence of multiple chromosomes in *Azotobacter vinelandii*.

A sizeable initial investment was required for equipment and facilities for research in this area in contrast to what is generally provided for research in biological areas such as zoology, botany, etc., in Indian universities. However, these investments were small compared to those needed in areas such as the space sciences: astronomy and astrophysics, nuclear physics and high-energy elementary particle physics. There was sustained research activity in plant biochemistry in several places during this period, which included the study of pathways of aromatic amino acid metabolism, plant hormones, enzymes from plant sources, mechanism of drought tolerance, mechanism of host–parasite interactions, photosynthetic processes in C3 and C4 plants and the role of nitrate and nitrite reductases in nitrogen fixations. The presence of Sivatosh Mookerjee here was a great advantage as he had both name and fame, and brought in projects to kick-start the department. Gradually, radiation biology groups also began to regroup along with the plant biotechnologists, and projects began to trickle in.

In the earliest days of plant molecular biology, what was required of experimental biologists was a knowledge of a plant physiology and biochemistry. An ability to handle biological materials and ask questions about data emanating from the field was also required. These areas were fast developing as the major work on classification and chemical analysis had already been done, and skills were rapidly being developed. Availability of the restriction enzymes and other enzymes for DNA manipulation, cloning vectors, and bacterial host strains along with kits for specific operation was resulting in the discipline undergoing a complete metamorphosis.

In the meantime molecular biology was revolutionized with the discovery of the structure of DNA in 1953. There were also developments in the technique for the study of proteins. This included SDS-PAGE (sodium dodecyl sulphate polyacrylamide gel electrophoresis) for separating proteins according to size and thus also for estimating a protein's size. There were also improvements in methods to determine the three-dimensional structures of proteins.

One of the most dynamic result of all these new techniques were seen in the field of plant molecular biology. The ability to produce transgenic plants made it possible to study, in vivo, the results of introducing new or modified nuclear, and much later plastid, genes and thus bring the study of physical genes back into the study of an organism's physiology, biochemistry and development.[69] It was in this area that the Indian scientists carried out tremendous innovations, and the Haploid technique, which was contributed mainly by the plant biologists of the Delhi University, became the mainstay of the scientific take-off to advanced biological science.

There were three major schools of experimental botany around 1950.[70] At Allahabad, Sri Ranjan, founded a group that worked on various aspects of plant physiology. Govindjee, Ravinder Kaur (later Sawhney) and M.M. Laloraya were members of this group. Govindjee became a distinguished authority on photosynthesis. Laloraya did pioneering work on the mechanisms of action of plant hormones 1, 2. He later on helped establish the school of life sciences at Indore.

At Calcutta, S.M. Sircar, promoted plant physiology and biochemistry. He established a group at the botany department of the university to study seed physiology and plant hormones. In the mid-1950s, students like S.P. Sen, B.B. Biswas and others became interested in physiology and biochemistry (plant molecular biology was not born then, but it is these studies that later transformed into this new field).

Another person who significantly influenced research was R.N. Singh of Banaras. Although the botany department of the Banaras Hindu University was at the time known more for studies in algae and ecology, he did some of the first experiments on cell-free nitrogen fixation with blue-green algae. On the other hand the plant physiology traditions that developed around the nucleus of Panchanan Maheshwari, B.M. Johri, C.S. Sanwal and others in Delhi University, were experimental by nature and the department developed Haploid techniques with Sipra Guha-Mukherjee as a very dynamic central figure in the new generation.[71] P. Maheshwari, father of S. C. Maheshwari had been the soul of experimental botany at Delhi University. His magnum opus *Embryology of Angiosperms*, published by McGraw Hill in 1950, made him an inspiration for students and teachers of his generation. His interaction with some of the best in the discipline at American universities during his stay at Harvard in the late 1940s had a far-reaching influence as it helped link Indian plant and botanical research to the American experimental tradition and firmed up intellectual links with good institutions at a time when they too were transitioning to institutional advancement. He was a great teacher who kept in constant touch with many eminent authorities around the world for exchange of information—and even today his enlivening lectures on photosynthesis, nitrogen fixation and plant hormones are recalled by many.

The advent of Sudhir Sopory, one of S.C. Maheshwari's students, to the school as one of the young recruits, firmed up the plant biology component which was further strengthened when Sipra Guha-Mukherjee joined the department a couple of years later. It was a formidable plant biology community by all standards. JNU soon became an interesting meeting point of different scientific traditions. Govindjee was invited to join the school as one of the first appointments but declined. Later on Prasanna Mohanty, who had worked with him, came to the centre, and also Gaurishankar Singhal, who had worked with Joshua Rabinowicz, joined JNU.[72] S.C. Maheshwari was also appointed to the faculty, but for some reason did not join.

P.N. Srivastava had worked with the legendary Prof. D.R. Bhattacharya of Allahabad, who was in the zoology department. He worked on catfish and was soon working on finding the source of uric acid in the gut of an insect at Lucknow University.[73] He gradually moved into radiation biology and, by the mid-1960s, his explorations led to the West, after which he returned to India and joined Rajasthan University. With the help of the Ford Foundation he set up the first radiation biology lab. In the heyday of cooperation between American and Indian scientists of the pre-1967 period, Srivastava began the first radiation biology department at Rajasthan University, and from here, he and his colleague, A.R. Rao, began working on aspects of cancer.[74] They migrated to JNU in the early 1970s and made JNU their home. Thus cancer research had its small beginning with the radiation biology department.[75] JNU soon hosted the mature tradition of biochemistry from Calcutta when Asis Datta and later H.K. Das arrived at JNU. Asis Datta had also worked with Severo Ochawa, another noted scholar from Japan. The small beginning at the molecular level by Madhu Sudan Kanungo who, following his stint at Illinois, settled in Banaras Hindu University, also found expression in the late 1980s with a couple of his students who had come to work at the JNU.

In the early 1970s, JNU was host to a strong plant biology world. Plant biology at the molecular level was now creating the template for a wide range of specialities. The space for experimentation that the new environment provided enabled many scientists to venture into completely new areas of research. A trained biochemist, Asis Datta, who had been working on the pathogenesis of the rotavirus began to move towards plant culture via the studies of protein and virus. Sudhir Sopory had joined the centre in its initial phase and engaged in the Haploid technique and succeeded in contributing to plant biotechnological research to bring not only the technique to a mature phase, but also give JNU, along with Sipra Guha-Mukherjee, one of the earliest starts to fathom the technique, and develop it on a sound and original footing.

As the plant biologists were also experimenting with the 'regulation of enzymes, for example, of nitrate metabolism' there were perceptible movements towards deeper levels of 'molecular basis of cell differentiation'. This would get them closer to a new domain of 'protein, and cloning'. Sopory and Guha-Mukherjee cloned the aspartate kinase gene with a view to desensitizing the enzyme for feedback initiation and then transferring the 'desensitized' gene into crop plants for increasing their levels of essential amino acids. The move to genetic expression and exporting such expression in vitro brought the Haploid technique to its maturity.

In the meantime, those who moved to plant biology from fields like biochemistry were bringing their rich knowledge of the field into the rapidly evolving field of cell differentiation. Asis Datta was very innovative in this field. The pathogenesis of the rotavirus was now beginning to define a completely new area of development.[76] The pathogenesis experimentation was soon to bring the rich immunological experimentation close to JNU's threshold. One of the members of the advisory group, G.P. Talwar, threw in his lot with the new biology as he himself was working on a most sensitive, significant and crucial project. Vaccine development in the Third World had to face the wrath of global pharmaceutical conglomerates, with the governments supporting them in the capital cities of Paris, Washington, London and Verne. Their efforts were also frowned upon by the UN and those who were embroiled with the international diplomacy on health. It was in these circumstances that the National Immunological Institute was created by the efforts of the scientists and also by the resolve of the governments of Indira Gandhi and her successor Rajiv Gandhi.

Right from the beginning, there has always existed a bias towards population control in the Third World which geared all medical science interventions in the Third World countries towards the area of population control. Immunological intervention was incorporated into the field of reproductive health. Committed Indian scientists, however, began exploring the other concerns—cancer, food and protein fixation for increased food production.

Around the same time in the 1980s, with the combined efforts of Wall Street, and, more often than not, spectacular advertising of the possibilities of science, a lot of speculative money flooded in, thereby hailing 'biotechnology as the new thing'.[77] Many molecular biologists were working towards understanding the genetic structures and trying to figure out their technological possibilities. But the big push came from the huge money and funding politics of the US government. With the mimicking push-button tendency in science establishments, India was quick to get into the business of biotechnology. This was, to an extent, both fortunate and unfortunate. The biochemists in the institutions, and those working on technique-based areas, could easily switch over to new areas in the field. The seed had been planted to start the biotechnology department and by 1986, there were moves to start centres, and biotechnology courses were being evolved in many universities. The JNU set up a biomedical engineering unit with H.K. Das operating it as a project. A team of scientists under the leadership of Das formed the core of the new school of biotechnology. By 1989-90, the Government of India funded the project on plant molecular biology (Centre for Plant Molecular Biology [CPMB]), which later on gave direction to the two different offshoots: (a) National Institute of Plant Genome Research and (b) Centre for Molecular Medicine, with the new-generation scientists produced by the university taking leading roles in these institutions.

During this time international politics of vaccine and, as someone pointed out, aspirin, was also hotting up.[78] India, being part of the global institutional set-up, also became party to it and the cumulative result was immunological research with the inauguration of the National Institute of Immunology on 6 October 1986. At the time of its inauguration, the institute counted three major areas, namely, (a) health care, (b) population control and (c) veterinary science, as the main concerns but the prime minister felt the national immunological institute ought to also focus on research and productivity.[79] JNU generously gave 25 acres of land to the institute which ensured that the physical proximity of the institute would invite intellectual and commitment proximity.

At the structural level, however, there were deeper issues. Biological sciences had developed in the university primarily on the basis of original works being pursued in the classical biology departments in Madras, Calcutta, Delhi or Allahabad, by people who did it on account of their zeal towards it and to develop new techniques. The Haploid technique, for example, was mastered by students of Panchanan Maheshwari in Delhi University. It was a novel technique and paved the way for advanced research. Similarly, radiation biology which P.N. Srivastava and his colleagues introduced was a logical maturation from classical biology to newer areas. Students in the School of Life Sciences in JNU from the first batch onwards found interdisciplinarity on their platter. It was new and tough both for the teachers and the taught, and required the cultivation of a new cooperative spirit. The physical symbol of the new-found cooperative spirit was the setting up of what came to be known as the Central Instrumentation Facility, CIF in its abbreviated and popular nomenclature, where all the more costly and sophisticated instruments were kept for the use of the faculty and students of the whole school.

The other dimension was significant because students also received training in the necessary techniques and very soon this became a major component of the identity of the practice of postgraduate training here, something which was not imparted in many departments. It is not coincidence that one of the first doctoral theses was from a chemistry student, Alok Bhattacharya, who would use such interdisciplinary techniques.[80] The technological propensity of the new dimension in science was causing a fundamental change. One soon realized that the school was becoming another of those IITs in the campus where the students were being trained to be exported. The logic of it soon became obvious as life sciences began to acquire its own subculture in a universe where tiers of philosophical and socio-economic sections existed.

The schools of social sciences, languages and international studies were moving towards humanizing the disciplines while using the autonomous spaces provided by the political leadership in trying to carve a distinctly Indian institution; this same space was now seen as being used in the School of Life Sciences to provide a safe route to emigrate. The problem would aggravate when other institutions came up in the vicinity of the university providing more polished facilities to practise new techniques and equip the students better. This competitive need for newer facilities would further isolate the students from the larger scientific questions which would actually move science beyond mechanics and technical expertise. This tendency of the technological solution was also demonstrated when the new technically qualified students now needed separate institutions to continue working with the new confidence gained while at JNU.

The quest for technological solutions with biotechnology and molecular medicine was fast replacing the older horizon. Earlier, the sectarian attitude of the communist parties impeded the natural expansion of the university in many ways; now, the technological and financial expansion of the technology-oriented science programmes seemed like choking the philosophical and liberal bases of the university but were also trying to define science within a managerial and technocratic boundary.

The university successfully became the meeting ground of very powerful scientific and academic traditions in the early 1970s. The centres of some of the most powerful scientific traditions in India were either passing through a bad phase due to political short-sightedness or institutional collapse, or they had become moribund with the inability to inspire or excite scientific creativity in the imagination of the younger generations. One possible reason, though it needs to be researched empirically, is that 1967-68 was a significant conjuncture. The new social classes had come to higher education to find that they themselves, as well as the institutions, were not quite ready to equip them to adjust to the new situations. These new classes invoked political leadership to come to its rescue, and the clamour for reservations, and change in the medium of instruction were the two salient demands that the political mobilizers brought in to rally these sections. Institutions across the country, particularly in northern India from the 1960s onwards, witnessed this mobilization. Apart from all other issues of either empowerment or otherwise, these stratagems only brought a horizontal movement to the university's lives. There were curbs on the movement of the students and teachers.

Researchers in science began to find it increasingly difficult to move from institute to institute or state to state, as there were so many political and other artificial barriers. By the 1990s, localization began to pinch scientific research. The big cities like Calcutta or Delhi or even Madras were not hit by this quite as badly as cities like Lucknow, Jaipur, Hyderabad or Aurangabad. The faculty who wanted a dynamic situation tried to move out. JNU came in to provide a national commons for the scientists. Generally, the recruitment pattern favoured them if their competence matched the locally produced scientists—these were a good number by now. The school somehow maintained the all-India character in its appointments as it had done when it began, and people like Sivatosh Mookerjee came from Calcutta to nurture the department and the university, and so did Srivastava from Jaipur, and so on.

On another level, while there were movements of people from all walks, some of the most exciting centres like Bangalore did not have too many opportunities for postgraduate learning, and admissions were restricted; Calcutta ceased to excite young Indians after the 1950s due to the increasing urban decay and a closeness that only a non-Bengali could articulate beyond the usual euphoria of the first couple of days. It is here that Delhi's expansive openness of JNU became inviting. Thus the arid Aravalis became the unbiased green pasture for the less privileged from all communities, and unlike the caste or community clusters of IISc, Bangalore, or the institutions in Calcutta, JNU accepted everyone and so did everyone who adopted JNU as their home.

To the younger scientists, JNU was a place to hone their skills and carry on what they began. A science department cannot be run in isolation and has to be part of the larger institutional set-up. In cities like Calcutta or Poona or Delhi one could easily get the environment for the scientist to interact with a larger academic world through social and intellectual networking of the pre-Internet milieu. In relatively smaller cities and urban centres, the university has to provide the intellectual sustenance to scholars. The relative stagnation or the skewed urbanization had denuded our institutions of their inner strength and confidence. Sixty years ago, a P.N. Srivastava or a Govindjee could rise from the small villages in eastern Uttar Pradesh, but it was becoming increasingly difficult in the 1990s. The parochialization of the science departments which had already begun was being accelerated by political, linguistic and other impediments.[81] Into this hostile climate, JNU came into being and evolved as an oasis; a village which could connect people to science, to an intellectual world where scientific questions could be posed in conformity with the needs of the society, and a vision could be crafted on the scientific inquiry through a dialogue with politics, which trained to see, even without a microscope, dreams for the society. A 'national commons' in many sense had come about.

Creating a Centre for the Future

One of the difficulties that the founders faced was to create a department of Environmental and Theoretical Sciences. The menu set for it by M.G.K. Menon's introductory proposal needed very able scientists. However, G. Parthasarathi failed to get the most competent candidates for the job as they were reluctant to move to Delhi or their terms were difficult. The natural scientists, who had spent years developing their labs and establishing their own small empires, would naturally be loath to relocate to an entirely new environment. Also, by the 1970s, Calcutta had settled down a little after the Naxalite violence, and Madras had ceased to inspire as the leading scientists had either retired or had moved to Bangalore. Therefore, a beginning had to be made from scratch with new people.

Establishing departments of theoretical science seemed an uphill project as the right people were unavailable, and setting up the environmental science department seemed to be just as difficult. A via media was found by the new vice chancellor, B.D. Nag Choudhuri, when he decided to start environmental sciences and set up a department for physical sciences in lieu of theoretical sciences. However, the problem persisted as no senior physicist or chemistry or biology professor would come to an interdisciplinary department whose contours and credentials were not established. Nag Choudhuri was very fortunate to find a fine mathematical modelling professor, S.N. Biswas, to come and start the school. Prof. Biswas, as the dean summoned some of his outstanding students from abroad. L.K. Pande, J. Subba Rao and G.P. Malik joined the school. He also got Anjali Mookerjee, C.K. Varshrey, K.C. Gupta and D.K. Banerjee in the school. The school was further enriched by providing it with two existing geologists, V. Asthana and S.K. Chandra, both working at the Centre for the Study of Regional Development. While both got involved with the new school, Asthana was finally transferred to the school permanently. By 1975, the school brought two other geologists, V. Subramaniam and V. Rajamani, who came from Canada. In the meantime, located as it was in the School of Life Sciences, many colleagues from life sciences also found their way into the school. The school also got Dr J.M. Dave who was the deputy chief of the National Environmental Engineering Research Institute, Nagpur, onto its rolls.

By 1976, the vice chancellor had therefore set up a relatively good department. His own vast repertoire of scientific knowledge came in handy to achieve this. However, it was at this point that the overarching intolerance of the Emergency regime hit the centre unexpectedly. In a meeting of the school, five of the faculty members passed a no-confidence motion against the dean. Riled by the revolt of his erstwhile students, the dean, Prof. Biswas, terminated the services of the new teachers. This was a disaster for a new school. The issue was fairly serious and invited intervention from the top. Finally, after a lot of effort, the terminations were revoked but the damage to the school was permanent. It could never recover from this initial setback, known locally as the 'June massacre'.

In an age when environmental studies and interdisciplinary studies were new, and could not assure anybody a job, students came at their own risk due to their faith in the teachers. The school began to take shape with students from various backgrounds enrolling, albeit with some trepidation, into a brand new discipline of which they had no understanding. These students were very precious and needed to be handled with kid gloves as many of them thought they were lost in a black hole (as was described by a colleague in 1989).[82]

A visionary department needed good faculty and project money which was difficult to come by with the increasing UGC diktats. The physicists were there but the costly physical experiments were shelved. Biological science had become increasingly dominant in the campus and began to impinge on the school. No longer perceived as a centre for theoretical sciences, the school, housed in the School of Life Sciences, also had to endure the entry of the biological scientists in a major way. The geologists, for example, did not take very kindly this process of de-centring the physical sciences by the biological scientist. This, however, seemed a global phenomenon—the interdisciplinary departments very rarely produced good second-generation faculty from within as there remained a clash within the faculty to develop their own core areas. This could have been overcome had there been a good and strong leadership. Ever since Prof. Biswas lost his control over things in the mid-1970s things went awry.

The School of Theoretical Sciences later on came in the form of the School of Physical Sciences in 1986. In the process, the School of Environmental Sciences somehow could not generate an overall vision. The school, however, demonstrated its strength in producing one of the largest pools of environmental scientists in India. The products of the school taught, campaigned, and provided lead in research to many institutions, both governmental and non-governmental.

10

Student Marches in Aravali

> The character and the functioning of the university depend upon the trust that you place in the teaching staff of the university; they depend upon the arrangements that you make for dealing with the students of the university.[1]

The beginning of the university coincided with both the politics in the country and the general mood of the youth. The first two batches of students played quite a significant role in setting the tone of the university. The M.Phil. and Ph.D students of international studies and undergraduates of Russian studies were the first set of students to enter the new university. They, however, were not particularly known for their political proclivities except that the general tenor of international studies was apolitical, while that of Russian studies was pro–Soviet Union as they had many experts from the Soviet Union teaching and interacting with the students.

In the School of International Studies, there were eight professors and none of them could be identified with communism, Marxism or even socialism of any hue. A couple of them had strong American orientation and outlook, which was in some sense at variance with the flavour of the day. The ISIS professors had a close and regular interaction with the American think tanks and universities and therefore were not too sectarian in their attitude. Only one professor had socialistic sensibilities because of his personal proximity with Jayaprakash Narayan.

The SIS Union Merges into a New Union

SIS had a students' union that was active with Prakash Karat and a couple of active students leading it. Prakash Karat had returned from the United Kingdom where, during his studies, he had come into contact with Victor Kiernan, a Marxist and a great scholar who had taught in Lahore in the pre-Partition days. With a sharp political eye, Karat got into close contact with CPI(M) leaders like P. Sundarayya and E.M.S. Namboodiripad. This was the time for the CPI(M) to start its students' wing and Karat was an ideal choice. He was articulate and was someone acquainted with the British Marxists who were held in high esteem by even these anti-colonial communists whose minds were not totally decolonized. His being from God's own country, Kerala, also helped in befriending many gods in the party.

As soon as the Students Federation of India was set up, north India seemed to be within communist grasp. From the standpoint of CPI(M), JNU was like a clean slate where it did not have to fight it out with the likes of the Chhatra Parishad in Bengal or the National Students Union of India (NSUI) in Kerala or the socialists and the RSS in UP and Rajasthan. Karat's popularity among the mostly apolitical students of the ISIS was an excellent opportunity to establish the credentials of the fledgling party and its new students' wing.

With Karat's initiative, the SIS union was amalgamated with the SFI-led union, which had come into being following much discussion and efforts. His SIS colleagues were upset and demanded that he resign because he had not taken them into confidence.[2] A significant section of the School of International Studies was in favour of a federal structure in student politics because this would emphasize their own distinctiveness. However, some members of the SFI, who were both activists and had the idea of a liberal university union, played an instrumental role in convincing the majority of the students of the school of the rationale behind this move and the need for an integrated students' union.[3] As a result, in a general body meeting the school passed a resolution in favour of an integrated union. However, there were twenty-seven votes against as against forty-five for the proposed constitution of the union.[4]

The constitution of the union in those heady days reflected the main currents of political thought among the left and socialist movements in the country, which included the major socialist demand for representation of students in decision-making bodies and the communist demand for making academic courses relevant to the masses. The aims of the union were summed up in the constitution as:

1. The union shall strive to live up to the important role students have to play in the development and progress of our people.
2. The union shall endeavour to make our academic courses relevant to the needs of our society and meet the expectations our people have from us.
3. The union shall endeavour to democratize the structure of the decision-making in the university in order to be able to effectively strive for the relevance in our education.
4. The union shall promote and safeguard the genuine interests of the student community and link it up with the democratic movement in the country.[5]

The best feature about the union was that the entire election process was to be conducted by the students themselves without the direct involvement of university administration at any level. The first election to the JNUSU was held on 30 November 1971. An SIS researcher, O. N. Shukla, won this first election as an independent candidate for president-ship. There were no organized parties as such, and the task of this union was to organize itself structurally and financially which took almost six months. In April 1972, the union managed to establish a systematic process for the transfer of money collected for extracurricular activities from the university to the union's account. As one of the earliest students recalled, 'a draft constitution of the students' union was circulated and approved through broad consensus among the students'.[6]

The second elections to the union took place on 11 October 1972. Although the candidates did not declare their party affiliations, it was clear that V.C. Koshy was the candidate for the SFI, the student wing of the CPI(M), while J.S. Ram represented the National Students Union of India, the Congress outfit. A third candidate, Prashad, however, was an independent but came out with the best posters.[7]

The JNUSU Constitution, by making the presidential election a direct one, gave it a bit more focus than required in a university-like situation. And, although the president required consent from council members, he/she began to exude a collective personality, and this would, in the long run, turn out to be the undoing of student politics as such. It concentrated politics in a single personality, and invested a lot of time in building an artificial persona around certain people or the parties, particularly the left. All of this clashed with the avowed principles upon which the union was based.

Social Scientists Enter the University

One of the first acts of the JNU students' union was to demonstrate against the visit of British prime minister, Edward Heath, when he came to speak at the Sapru House auditorium. It was, as a contemporary recalled, 'a class act' and the 'professionalism of the organizers even took the Delhi police by surprise'. With the success of the demonstration and new-found enthusiasm, the students' union now demanded democratization of the decision-making bodies.[8] The mood was nicely captured by a contemporary who saw this as an opportunity that the political parties tried to use to penetrate JNU. He also saw how a sizeable number of the students of the School of Social Sciences tried to counter the coordinated efforts of the left parties to control the students by declaring a formation of 'Free Thinkers'.[9]

The character of the university took a dramatic turn when the School of Social Sciences (SSS) became operational. Suddenly, the university was full of scholars who were widely known for their disciplinary excellence and many for their political radicalism. Unlike the SIS students, the SSS teachers and their first batches of students came to a brand new institution and were in a mood to start fresh experiments and express the mood of the times. The teachers were, naturally, looking forward to a long phase of engagement. This was also the beginning of two completely different traditions; one (SIS) had already set up an insular institute with wide diplomatic connections and the other (SSS) was trying to start a new institutional tradition.

JNU was inhabited by many scholars who had come to represent that new-found consensus at the national level. Many from the regions and provinces were included in this panorama, e.g., the people from the literati and upper classes from Andhra Pradesh, Maharashtra,

West Bengal, Tamil Nadu, etc., who came to the university both as faculty as well as students and gave the university a profile quite different from that of any other university in modern India. When the violent linguistic agitations and the Naxalite violence took its toll on the institutions in those areas in the late 1960s, JNU provided a safe haven to scholars from centres of excellence located in the different regions.

Rasheeduddin Khan, and later, K. Seshadri, came from Hyderabad; a large contingent came from Jaipur; K.J. Mahale from Karnataka, Pramod Talgeri from Maharashtra; and Sivatosh Mookerjee and Tapas Mazumdar from Calcutta. JNU was providing space to an intellectual class who would envision academia not as an extension of the state or government department (unlike many other universities in India), but as a habitus of both mind and body. Pierre Bourdieu, the astute French sociologist, defined habitus, some years later, as a 'set of attitudes which structure the perception and practice of research: the logic of the practice of scientific labour is related to the way in which the problems are set out, explanations developed and tools forged and used'.[10]

JNU's foundational principles had envisaged a very close relationship between the students and teachers. The new faculty, particularly the social scientists, contributed much to the close rapport between teachers and students. The education minister in 1964 had envisioned a joint council for teachers and students. This was the ideal way to respond to the whole milieu of distrust that had been brewing in the campuses during the early phase of the 1960s that had led to student violence. To some diehard Marxists, e.g., Bipan Chandra, it seemed utterly impractical to have a common council or common union. Such a union could do no justice to different, and sometimes conflicting, sets of interests of the students, teachers and non-teaching staff. He, therefore, argued for separate unions for teachers, staff and students. The first president of the common council for teachers and staff, Prof. Yogendra Singh, one of the most perceptive and astute readers of Indian society, realized the impracticality of such a common council and agreed with Chandra. Soon several others joined this train of thought, and the student leaders, under the aegis of the communist parties' sympathizers, chalked out plans for a separate union.

The membership of the Communist Party of India increased with the prospects of a job in the new university, especially among the faculty of the newly established School of Languages who were either long-standing communists or new converts. This faction also had a preponderance of teachers in the social sciences stream. Thus, the political formations in JNU found their respective constituencies. The All India Students Federation (AISF), the students wing of the CPI, was like a baby born to milk and honey. The Communist Party of India (Marxist) had recently established its students wing, and, as a new organization, it was infinitely more energetic and militant. After the split in the original communist party in 1964, those who moved to the more radicalized wing of the party were mostly from Bengal, Andhra and Kerala. Extremely provincial in their outlook, they were now represented by the leaders like E.M.S. Namboodiripad, Jyoti Basu, etc., who could have otherwise lived in the CPI itself except they thought it politically pragmatic to be with the new party. The other tall leaders of the party were hard-core organizers like Pramod Dasgupta from Bengal and P. Sundarayya from Andhra. All these stalwarts raised their profiles to represent the party at the national level. Most of the leaders in CPI(M) were great mobilizers of the peasantry and they gave the new party strong orientation. As they had a strong base in their respective regions, it made their outlook more provincial rather than all-India. This was often masked by their Marxist rhetoric against capitalism, bourgeoisie, etc.

On the other hand, the CPI leaders, many of whom were the finest intellectuals and parliamentarians, e.g., S.A. Dange, Bhupesh Gupta, Hiren Mukerjee, Mohit Sen and many others, did not have the same mass base in the provinces and were located, politically, more at the all-India level—both in their parliamentary as well as intellectual lives. JNU had an advantage in this respect because the people responsible for setting it up were either very active party members or had strong leanings towards the CPI. The education minister, Nurul Hasan, had been a leading figure of the intellectual wing of the CPI and so was Moonis Raza. For the two communist parties the wound of the split was still very raw and the talk of an alliance was not highly appealing. In JNU, however, the parties attempted to converge. An alliance formed during the second student union election in 1972-73 was called the Progressive Democratic Front (PDF), and, V.C. Koshy, a political science research scholar, became the president of the union under this combine.

JNU's first MA batches, particularly in the social sciences, were articulate and some of the most talented graduates were from the best colleges in the country. For many of them the new atmosphere invited them to a discourse on freedom and decolonization, and radical alternatives. Such a student population would not be slavish followers of the communist parties; they provided the communist parties a readymade target and were accused of elitism. The new students who were the targets of the communist attack, insisted that their programme and not their class background be analysed. Many of the SFI leaders, including Karat and his comrade-in-arms, Sunit Chopra, had returned from Britain, and were therefore more elite and colonial in their academic attitude than those who were attacked as elitists.

The intellectual critique of the passionate and brilliant youth was not going to make much of a difference for these parties as their vested interests and theoretical positions were too strong to accept such critiques. The complete capture of the university was possible only through elections. The first battle lines were drawn in 1973 when mostly the social science students decided to take on the increasing dominance of the AISF and SFI leadership who were hand-in-glove with their professoriate led by Moonis Raza. The core of this was in the School of Social Sciences, primarily in the centres for history, sociology and political sciences, and they named the group 'The Free Thinkers'.

The communist parties that sought to capture some political space, particularly in the northern Indian belt, viewed the student body elections in JNU as a way to do so. Therefore, the JNU elections as well as the CPI(M)'s party-building exercise in north India were synchronous. The Free Thinkers, however, saw the elections as a means to save the university from the manipulation and control of the Stalinistic parties. The radical fringe, which claimed to be more communist than the communist parties were, also attacked the organized communist parties in order to break their ideological dominance. They themselves were just as dictatorial in their own organizational matters. The Trotskyites, for example, were perceived as a bunch of pompous intellectuals. The battle, therefore, was also for influencing the minds and controlling ideas.

Though the 1972 elections saw a political science research scholar becoming the president of the union, it was the 1973 elections which signalled a high-voltage political contest. With the arrival of the new batch of students, the Free Thinkers of JNU got a mature, political, Hindi-speaking student who was well suited to counter the SFI–AISF elitist charge. The popular slogan devised by SFI–AISF for this ongoing struggle was to take JNU to the level of Gorakhpur and BHU. Anand Kumar had become the president of the BHU during the worst phase of its history when the elected president was ousted by the manipulation of the university administration in collusion with the local RSS and local university mafia. His presence was very significant as he too came with a deep socialist ethos. Anand Kumar, an excellent reader of situation, while no match for the political acumen of Karat, had a mature and well-developed political sense. As a staunch follower of Ram Manohar Lohia, he imbibed the visceral hatred of both the Congress and the Left.[11] This made him an excellent candidate in such a volatile situation. For the social science students who wanted to counter the SFI's allegation of elitism against the university, Anand Kumar's background was a godsend: it refuted the SFI's claim that they monopolized the subaltern groups. The stage was set where left was fighting left and there was no centre and right in the picture. From the beginning, the Stalinist left practices of the Indian communist parties in particular and the Indian left in general had their first major critique in JNU.

A contemporary write up on the JNU quite graphically presents this mosaic of politics and culture of the time:

> Interest at the moment is centred on the forthcoming elections to the union of students. But the fight is not between the rightist and the leftist as was in the case of Delhi University, but among the groups of radicals of various shades of red. Everyone in JNU likes to be called progressive.
>
> This university is free from the canker of communalism. The ABVP has no base at all in the campus. Explaining this, Prof. Bipan Chandra, head of CHS, said JNU students were not easily attracted by the Jana Sangh type of ideology. Since the university only provides post-graduate courses, the students who join it are by and large mature and serious in their intellectual pursuits.[12]

The election debate was about the practices of the left and that of the communist parties. The issues of gender, race, empire and labour were discussed at great length and the syllabuses which were framed during this time were quite often reflections and insights of the struggles happening outside the campus. Topics like the character of the Indian state and the autonomy of the intellect were keenly discussed, and so was the career of socialism in India and the world.

That very year, the students and karamcharis (non-teaching staff) of JNU in a joint general body meeting decided to close the university for one day in support of a strike called by the trade unions. This joint action of the karamcharis was the result of SFI's attempt to politicize the karamcharis. In the election, the PDF had brought the karamcharis into its fold. Their election manifesto in 1972-73 clearly stated that, to make democratization meaningful it is essential that students, teachers and karamcharis are given proportional representation in all decision-making bodies. The three components must be represented in the executive council, the court and the finance committee.

The Angry Young India

The landscape of the political mind in the country showed unrest in 1974. Amitabh Bachchan was famously emerging as the angry young man while the youth in many parts of India followed the angry housewives of the Mumbai in their protest against price rise and corruption in governments. Young Turks like Chandra Shekhar, Mohan Dharia, Krishan Kant and others who until recently were supporting Indira Gandhi's nationalization of banks and coal mines as well as other policies, and were some of her ardent supporters, were now moving away and closing ranks behind a new opposition to Indira Gandhi.

This was also the time that the political differences between the CPI and the CPI(M) came to the fore. The radical, sectarian and provincial outlook of the CPI(M) was anti-Indira and anti-Congress and they would cohabit the space with the RSS if Indira could be defeated. Within the university, the Progressive Democratic Front (PDF) was under strain. Neither the SFI nor the AISF had any idea of their independent support and the AISF imagined it could sail through independently. The SFI, like the CPI(M), was becoming restive and assertive as they could sense that their politics were developing separately. This was also the time when the Trotskyites in their theoretical Marxist analyses attacked the communist parties following the Stalinist line. They isolated and attacked the SFI which was at a critical juncture. But the actual break occurred when the Chhatra Sangharsh Samiti was formed in both the Delhi University and the JNU on the issue of starting a Bihar-type agitation in the capital. AISF, in conformity with its parent party, the CPI's line, rejected the stand of the SFI to support the movement. AISF argued that it would spoil the academic life of JNU and Delhi University. In 1974, elections took place at this critical juncture.

The Free Thinkers put up their previous candidate Anand Kumar, who, because of his association with Jayaprakash Narayan's movement, had become popular in the campus by this time. In one of the meetings, almost 1,000 people gathered to listen to the leaders. The AISF put up its own candidate, Gyan Prakash, who was the erstwhile secretary in the Progressive Democratic Front. The SFI also decided to repeat Prakash Karat as its presidential candidate. For the first time, the Marxist Forum put up two candidates for student councillors from the School of Social Sciences.

This was a hard-fought election. It showed the parties their respective strengths. Although the JP movement was on the horizon, the SFI was not going to get any extra advantage as Anand Kumar, the anti-SFI candidate, belonged to the groups which were the core of the Janata movement. The opposition also exposed the duplicity of the party, e.g., its past president had clandestinely secured a scholarship from the vice chancellor, which was completely unethical for someone espousing the cause of the students. The agitation against the history centre was supported en masse by the party, which alienated the perceptive students and hardened those who had integrity in their opposition to the SFI. The serious social science students were the biggest opponents of SFI's politics because they could eloquently counter the SFI's appropriation of the progressive role. The intellectuals of the communist parties found their best critique in their first few years in JNU, which actually enriched the left and the progressive forces.

Among the 1,006 votes polled out of a total electorate of about 1200 in the 1974 election, Anand Kumar got 484 votes, Prakash Karat got 441 and the AISF candidate got only fifty-eight votes. Notwithstanding their presidential defeat, the SFI won a majority, nine, of the seats in the students council. This was the first defeat of the SFI in four elections. It also signalled the emergence of the social sciences students in the political realm with their Free Thinkers (FT). Their victory was short-lived as Anand Kumar left for the United States on a scholarship which necessitated a mid-term election. This time the Free Thinkers could not maintain the same tempo and Debi Prasad Tripathy, the SFI nominee, won the election with a margin of ninety-six votes over the FT nominee, Yogesh Sharma. AISF's crushing defeat in the poll lowered its political stature in the campus. This started a new phenomenon among the CPI-affiliated teachers who were generally responsible for the intellectual work of the party: they sympathized with the SFI inside the campus while displaying their AISF or CPI affiliation outside.

By this time, JNU had come to stay in the popular imagination with an image of political radicalism and social permissiveness. Both were true to an extent as the Left had captured the political imagination of the community but this radicalism, as a perceptive journalist reported, was not exclusively of Marxist variety. 'A group called Free Thinkers' he wrote, 'has as large a following as the SFI and includes Samajwadi Yuvajan Sabha (SYS) militants and Mr Jayaprakash Narayan's supporters. Last year its candidate Mr Anand Kumar defeated Mr Prakash Karat by 484 votes to 441 in the student union presidentship.'[13] He found the SYS supporters among the Free Thinkers no less militant than the SFI members as a number of them demonstrated in Delhi demanding the release of all prisoners and commutation of the death sentences of two Andhra Naxalites.

The Politics of the Political

The electoral plank of the parties indicated that student politics revolved around the arguments that were in vogue since the 1960s and famously agitated for by the socialists and other student groups across the country in the name of representation. In the JNU the communists also adopted the same plank and repeated the same demand, i.e., democratization in the functioning of the university, more facilities to students, etc. However, while democratization was the larger political context, politics were played at different levels. This included issues like that of admissions.

The issue regarding admissions remained a perennial bone of contention in the university's politics and reflected the communist attitude towards educational institutions. Although generally seen as part of the larger democratization demand, the admission issue in JNU was raised and advanced by the CPI(M), and the way the fringe radicals plunged into this was nothing but the communist technique of changing the class and character of an institution. The communists could be seen advocating dominance through brute numbers rather than intellectual hegemony. This technique unfortunately paid off for the communists, on most issues. However, many Marxists and many others, who had a deep affinity with the radical cause since the 1950s and were part of the larger democratic movement in the country, opposed caste-based reservations. They argued for economic and class-based positive discrimination, and insisted that even peasants, labourers, etc., be included in the reservation.[14] Their demand was based on very sound arguments:

1. The caste-based reservations would divide the students on caste lines and hamper any progressive movement to democratize the society and the polity.
2. They realized that the caste certificate would probably be falsified, as would the income certificate.

However, their arguments were attacked by the students led by the communist parties and backed by the CPI(M)- and CPI-affiliated teachers. They made a tactical line by attacking the proponents of the class line as supporters of elite students and that they were opposed to reservation of any kind. They categorized those students as elites who 'came from urban centres, good culture and spoke English'. This division was soon used to attack JNU as an elite university and became the organizing slogan of students allied to the communist parties. Prakash Karat even misrepresented the debate by writing that Bipan Chandra had opposed reservation for the Scheduled Castes and Scheduled Tribes.[15]

However, the very fact that the issue of non-elite was brought in to attack the idea of quality was quite significant, and their argument for doing away with quality was founded on their very dubious distinction between what was elite and what was non-elite. Academic quality was defined as 'an abstract concept' by the union president Koshy, whose own poor academic record was condoned by his sympathetic patrons in the new university. He saw the all-India character of the university being eroded from the beginning, and, instead of defying the declared objective, the university was admitting students normally belonging to the affluent sections and depriving the underprivileged the chance to come to this university. The party line attacked academic quality as an abstract concept meant to perpetuate the age-old reactionary policy that argues that 'academic quality' should be the sole test for a student's eligibility for higher education.[16] Significantly, the larger body of the social science faculty and students had no problem with a different admission policy: except for them it was not an issue for mobilization.

Now, this supposed elitism of JNU found many takers and more so with students coming from remote regions who, along with their political ideology, felt that the easy institutional delivery in JNU was a sign of opulence compared with the facilities available in the institutions back home—it was rather easy to paint JNU as elitist if deprivation was used as a yardstick. To buttress their point, the party attacked JNU as a model elitist institution. We have seen how Hiren Mukherjee, the CPI member in the parliament attacked the JNU Bill.[17] The attacks seemed to be real to the outsiders as they came from none other than JNU's own student leaders. This provided a veneer of authenticity to the radical image of the JNUSU presidents as they were seen to be having a 'conscience' and criticizing their own institution. Thus, union president Koshy's diatribe was read with relish by opponents of the university as well as those who wanted to be there because of its ambience of an elite university.

Calling the attempt to make JNU a centre for excellence as 'farcical' because 'given the realities of the present educational and social framework in which JNU functions', Koshy brought his conscience and dialectics into play. 'When the poverty stricken millions in India are unable to get even the basic amenities for school and undergraduate education,' Koshy's article, which many thought was written by Prakash Karat himself, argued, 'imposition of such centres from the top will only degenerate into creating elitist sanctuaries for the upper classes.'[18] 'When the overwhelming majority of college students in India are trained in a rotten educational system,' it further said, 'the concept of post graduate centres of higher learning like JNU reduces itself to a mockery. Operating within such a framework the JNU is well on the road to becoming a luxury which only a privileged few can afford under the garb of academic quality.'[19] The article went on:

> Hierarchical structure by which this university is being built, beginning from the university administration downwards, makes it all the more clear that the students come last in the priority. First come the carpets and air conditioners, then the landscape and architecture to satisfy the aesthetic sense, then the accommodation for upper echelons, accompanied by artificial lakes and swimming pools, and finally perhaps some students are needed to justify the existence of this whole set up![20]

This attack on the university as catering only to the rich and the elite and the argument that to circumvent such elitism admissions be made easier to the deprived, made a very interesting distortion in the long-term life of the university. This led to a distortion whereby the section of students who demanded affirmative action would soon be a large enough number to validate any such demands in future as well, thus constituting a permanent vested interest group within the system and enabling the left groups to cater to their constituencies, taking up these demands whenever their individual constituency levels dipped. The original attack by Prakash Karat and the communist parties of anyone opposing this criterion of affirmative action as essentially supporting elitism and therefore politically reactionary would increasingly hold sway as there was now a permanent vested group in the shape of students and their supporters in the campus. This in the long run sapped even the democratic structure required for decent debate in knowledge production.

Thus, within the first five years, there were schisms and confusion about the admission process. The SFI even managed to publish the confidential mark sheet of the history centre in a newspaper and it contained the name of a candidate who had scored brilliantly in the viva as compared to the very low grades in the academic examinations.[21] The SFI launched a campaign against CHS which was countered by the students of the centre themselves who refuted the allegations and opposed the intimidating tactics of Karat and his SFI cadres. After prolonged debate and organized attacks on those who did not agree with the elite–non-elite divide, a detailed deprivation point system was developed, mainly with the help of the geographers and applied economists, and agreed by the community. Even those who initially did not agree with many of the sharp attacks, finally gave in and assisted in the process. The admission process therefore had a large consensus.

The reports of the first couple of years make an interesting reading of the way various centres recruited people. The Centre for Historical Studies was the focus of attack by the left groups for what they perceived as elitist ways reflected in its admission. In reality, the centre admitted almost an equal number of people with deprivation points and non-deprivation points. In the Centre for the Study of Regional Development and in many of the centres the scale was higher on the side of the deprivation points. It often depended on the way the centres worked and reflected the autonomy of the centres and their weaknesses—the weaker centres could be manipulated. The Student–Faculty Committee members were there to oversee the admission proceedings. In the weaker centres they and their party higher-ups definitely intervened. Thus the academically weak centres became an easy entry point for many through different political and social networks: they could be coerced to fall in line.

On the plus side, deprivation points enabled students from a wider range of backgrounds gain admission into JNU for higher studies. Arguably, the deprivation points helped establish a national character in the university with an equitable number of students from the different states. The number of students from Maharashtra remained secularly fixed with most of them enrolling into the School of Languages, and that too particularly in the centre for German language. The number of students from Bihar kept increasing probably because of the rapidly deteriorating conditions of Bihar's institutions, and the deprivation point system and open admission of JNU provided a conducive atmosphere to join. Orissa was one of the greatest beneficiaries of the deprivation point system.

The SFI and AISF adopted the tactical line of attacking the teachers who could intellectually and administratively stand their ground. They had a strong supporter in Moonis Raza, who was not only heading the administration but was also close to the education minister who was supervising the JNU project. Many CPI cadres, who had landed jobs in the JNU, sought to bring their friends and relatives into the campus, and therefore had a stake in dominating the processes. Therefore, this communist group mainly attacked those sections in the social sciences who would probably oppose these coordinated moves.

The SFI was beginning to characterize the university as elitist. The higher teacher to student ratio seemed to be the root cause of these allegations. Koshy, and through him the CPI(M), argued that JNU showed the teacher to student ratio to be at 1:5 and in some centres 1:3, which was far below the existing national average of 1:20, seemed to them to be sheer waste. Koshy's article was in a way a veiled endorsement of the students union demand of raising the ratio to 1:10. The party was willing to allow this concession since the university was a research-oriented one.[22]

A year and a half later, Karat himself argued on the same lines in a signed article which said, the 'staff to student ratio was on an average of 1:5 in 1973, but, thanks to the union's fight for increased admission, it now averages around 1:10'.[23] The radical segment in the provincial universities in the meanwhile, were insisting that the ratio of students to teachers be increased.[24] This hiatus could be deduced as the original fault line of the Indian communists who failed to sympathize with the aspirations for an excellent institution. However, the rhetoric helped them preserve their leadership and dominance.

Attacking the university as elitist seemed to be in line with the communist critique of the institution. Changing the programmatic content would enhance both the class character and the excellence of the university—and JNU did make its voice heard. The CPI(M) believed in dominance by student cadre numbers to affect that change. Hence, the implied demand to open the university to all who could be taken in. The socialists and others chorused this demand. After the anti-Hindi agitation, the students considered anybody who spoke English elitist. Thankfully, this linguistic line of defining elitism did not take root as people soon found out that English was the lingua franca in a place of mixed communities. Language did not matter as long as the ideas were great. The JNU teachers who were intellectually and academically bright and articulate, and took stands independent of the communist parties, were personally attacked. Posters, pamphlets and open accusations in meetings saw to it that the recalcitrant fell in line or were stigmatized as reactionary, conservative, anti-student, or worse, pro-administration.

Teachers: the Class Enemy

While serious scholars who posed an intellectual threat to the party were attacked, the SFI leadership also adopted a vicious, and quite foolish, strategy, perhaps for the very first time in the annals of Indian history, of declaring teachers as the class enemy. This hurt the very foundation of the new university where the motto of trusting the teachers was adopted by the parliament itself. By this time, there were many left sympathizers in the faculty. Amongst the first critical matters taken up to demonstrate the class angle, the party attacked the administration for building two bathrooms in the faculty homes while three students were made to share one bathroom. The party claimed that this was both discrimination and elitism, and needed to be stopped. This smacked of not only foolishness of the highest order but also arrogance, which breeds such folly. A couple of years later, the same leader brought up the issue of bathroom distribution in Aligarh. Thus, bathroom socialism had its day in the sun in those early days of the JNU.

JNU was the first university in the country, which, after a lot of discussion in the first two years of its existence, adopted internal assessment as a means to test students. The course teachers themselves evaluated their students in the final semester examination. Although it was hailed as an innovation, many educationalists stood by waiting for it to fail dismally in a country like India. There was always the lurking fear of victimization in an unequal society where primordial loyalties supersede requirements of excellence or the idea of justice. The JNU community hardened its resolve to succeed on this front and not give in to the pessimism of the outside critics. Also, dismantling their innovation would have given JNU the dubious credit of pioneering self-destruction in institutions.

The SFI which considered it vital to streamline the examination system and end all intellectual autonomy in order to establish its Gleichschaltung, took the lead to bring down the JNU's innovation.

Karat wrote a stinging critique of the internal assessment system in the CPI(M) journal *Social Scientist*: this internal assessment-based semester system was 'transplanted uncritically from American or British universities like Sussex'.[25] He went on to elaborate: 'Once a teacher of an academic course marks the student's paper, there is no appeal against the grade given. There is nothing in the statutes, ordinances or rules governing academic procedures which gives the student the elementary safeguard of appealing against his grades to an authority outside the purview of the centre in which he is studying.'

In his formulation on behalf of the union was the demand that a body be created at the university level by amending the university statutes. 'If the body felt,' he wrote further, 'there is a prima facie case to enquire into the matter, it would be empowered to constitute an expert body of academics (no students) to revaluate the paper. The University Grants Commission has also recommended the setting up of a similar committee to look into the student complaints. Similarly, in the case of academic disputes for research students (on choice of topics, disagreement with supervisors, and so on), the same right of appeal would apply.'[26]

The overarching idea of JNU was attacked as futile; the rest of the criticism carried the same negativism and attack on the institution without any positive recognition of anything. However, it was the efforts of Karat and his supporter Moonis Raza that saw certain pro-student items being accepted by Parthasarathi without any hesitation. This included merit-cum-means scholarship, etc.[27]

Next year, the students' union submitted a charter of five demands. Most of the demands were accepted except three for which there were issues from both sides: (a) student representation in the executive council, (b) the setting up of a statutory body to look into the grievances of students about victimization and (c) a fixed rate of 100 rupees for quality food in the university messes.

The new vice chancellor, contended that the two subjects, namely, the appointment and service conditions of teachers and the internal evaluation system, were out of the jurisdiction of students by definition; and the very act of returning marked answer books with comments of the teacher concerned was an inbuilt check against victimization. The third demand about food subsidy, though shown as a more equitable distribution of resources, had no takers, and in fact showed the students in really poor light at a time when the general populace was fighting price rise. It was this demand which actually put off the outside population. The intellectuals and politically sympathetic sections were also not happy with this demand.

The SFI, which had the largest presence in the Students Council called a general body meeting. A resolution was passed in the meeting asking the union leadership to enter into a dialogue with the Jawaharlal Nehru University Teacher Association (JNUTA) members. As many of the JNUTA were either CPI(M) members or back-room sympathizers, the SFI assumed that the resolution would be carried through. However, this proved wrong. Many of the JNU teachers were strongly opposed to such a move because it involved curtailing autonomy, a major intellectual experiment in JNU. The students and their supporters countered by accusing the faculty of trying to camouflage their ineptitude. The issue had now snowballed into a direct attack on the teaching community by the SFI.

The students' union went on an unusual political strategy:

- First, it approached the vice chancellor who obviously rejected such a demand.
- On 31 March 1975, the union went to the students' general body with an innocuous resolution that the union leadership would enter into a dialogue with the JNUTA on the question of a statutory body against academic victimization. The original plan was to browbeat the teachers and for the left to submit an explanatory note on the 'statutory body', and when they 'clinch this issue the details of the mechanism, working, etc., can be jointly worked out by the students, teachers and the university authorities'. However this plan was scuttled by the teachers.
- As a consequence, when the CPI(M) affiliated teachers vehemently debated the issue, the SFI and its cadres considered it tantamount to a complete violation of the earlier understanding which required the discussion of the issue pertaining to the mechanism of the 'statutory body' with the teachers. The teachers, many of whom had come from active teachers' politics from various other universities, immediately perceived the

> portending danger for the long term. The supporters of the move argued that the JNU teachers were scared of being exposed and were therefore using the bogey of the right wing to stall the move to place a statutory body over and above the centre to settle academic disputes of the students and teachers.

On 1 April 1975, the JNUTA passed a resolution, saying:

> The G.B. (General Body) of the JNUTA feels that it (the situation) should be prevented from escalating into a confrontation between teachers and students. We resolve that ways and means should be found through a collective discussion between the teachers and the students before a decision on evaluating (i.e., statutory body) is taken. Meanwhile, the normal functioning of the university should not be disturbed.[28]

The Academic Council (AC) met on 4 April 1975, and passed one of the major demands of the students, viz., student representation on the executive council. The moment this was passed the JNUSU pressed for adjournment of the AC meeting before the issue of the 'statutory body' could be discussed.[29] This was serious politics as any discussion for passing a resolution would have deprived the SFI any momentum to heighten the militant consciousness of the student. The other left formations except the fringe radicals attacked the SFI on this. The union president justified himself by saying that he knew the council was not in favour of it. To many, this reeked of obstructionism rather than democratic behaviour. However, the militant mood was being created by manoeuvring a decision to go into action over its earlier decision to meet the JNUTA.

It was clear to many that the SFI leadership was hell bent on paralysing the university administration even when 'the doors of negotiation were open'. Any opposition to explore possibilities democratically began to be denounced as 'playing into the hands of the administration', a cliché which became the most enduring political tag in the university politics—strange in an institution where all administrators from the top to the bottom were teachers in the university.

It seemed like the SFI was intent on using this opportunity to radicalize the situation and force the teachers into submission for its long-term strategy. Although the Free Thinkers and AISF wanted to resolve the issue through negotiation, the SFI did not. More than 300 students squatted at the administrative block on 7 April 1975 and did not allow officials and non-teaching employees to enter the administrative building. The students must have been assured by people like Moonis Raza, who closely coordinated the SFI's political strategies, that they could keep the heat on. However, the vice chancellor, not a great friend of Moonis Raza, suddenly ordered the closure of the university indefinitely. The circular issued by the registrar said that the university was being 'closed sine die because of the abnormal situation created by the leadership of the students' union'. Later when the administrative building was closed, the students moved en masse into the library and squatted inside to prevent the authorities from closing the library. Simultaneously, the vice chancellor ordered a ban on meetings and demonstrations in the campus and sent telegrams to the parents, particularly of the girl students, to withdraw their wards from the hostel immediately. Meanwhile, a statement signed by Dr Nag Chaudhuri (vice chancellor), Professor Moonis Raza, Dr M.S. Agwani, Professor K.J. Mahale and Mr B. Roy was released, stating that the decision to close down the university was taken reluctantly.

According to the stand of the vice chancellor, the closure order of the university was taken to: (i) curb the rising tendency of the student leaders to encroach upon the rights of the authorities, and (ii) 'prevent recurrence of such incidents' in future.[30]

The general body meeting of the students decided not to vacate the hostels. There were sufficient rations in the messes for a week and the students smoothly managed the mess. They themselves cooked the food and did the dishes. The library was kept open round the clock and the students personally supervised the functioning of the laboratory complex which they commandeered following the closure order of the vice chancellor. Meetings were held frequently in the campus and a struggle fund was raised. A day after the closure, students demonstrated in unison against the authoritarian attitude of the authorities and burnt an effigy of the vice chancellor. Faculty members who had earlier supported the decision of the authorities in the JNUTA meeting became divided among themselves. Some faculty members who had left leanings started criticizing the authorities for the decision of closure without consulting any of the constituent elements of the university. But the teachers' association, in a statement passed in the meeting, condemned the effigy-burning activity of the students and urged the students' union to lift the gherao.

The AISF also called for an immediate negotiation between students and authorities and stressed that the students should take the initiative in opening a dialogue with the authorities. It alleged that the students' union (SFI-led students' union) was keeping the general body in the dark about the decisions taken to conduct the agitation and supplying them with incomplete and inaccurate information.

This precipitation of the matter by the SFI was made possible by their consistent attempts to keep the mass of students in the dark. Between 31 March 1975 and 10 April 1975 there was not one general body meeting of the students despite the AISF and SFI student councillors, in an open pamphlet on 3 April 1975, calling for 'more general body meetings'. In the meanwhile, a large group of students entered the administrative building and decided to disrupt work. The vice chancellor found it easy therefore to close the university in such a situation when student violence countrywide was a rising tide.[31] This sudden act quite perplexed the AISF and other non-SFI students, and they tried to force the president to hold a general body meeting at Godavari Hostel on 9 April 1975 at night. The president, together with the SFI student councillors, tried to disperse it without allowing anyone else to speak. When that failed, the SFI sought to disrupt the meeting—a tactic they repeated on 10 April 1975 during the general body meeting (GBM), which was abruptly adjourned before resolutions critical of the students' union leadership could be discussed. The students remained in the dark about what had actually happened on the campus and were under the false impression, created by the president that negotiations with the authorities had finally broken down.[32]

The students' union, however, tried to salvage the situation by getting leaders from the parliament to intervene. They met some of the members of the parliament and sought the immediate intervention of the Central government to resolve the crisis. The authorities, seeing the desperate action of the student leaders and the crack in student unity, threatened to stop water supply and electricity to hostels. The students, seeing the reaction of the administration, also acted with alacrity. Kumari Saraswati Menon, a resident of Jhelum Hostel, on behalf of the students union filed a writ petition in Delhi High Court imploring that 'the authorities be prohibited from evicting her from the hostel and be directed not to discontinue essential supplies like electricity and water and mess facilities'.[33]

The CPI(M) members in the parliament raised the issue and argued that the university was closed down under the instruction of the government, an allegation which Nurul Hasan, the education minister rejected outright. He in return cautioned the CPI(M) members to keep off the university as he felt that 'the unthinking action of the student leaders would jeopardize the experiment of student participation in the affairs of the university. No university can function normally when intimidation replaces dialogue and arguments are given up in favour of pressure tactics.'[34]

The tactical group within the CPI(M) tried to work out a compromise formula. It came up with the suggestions that: (i) the faculty board should be empowered to look into academic grievances of the students, (ii) an expert committee should be set up for their redressal, and (iii) student representatives should be present in the proposed committee at the screening stage.[35] The union agreed to withdraw the blockade on the condition it received a 'positive response' to the proposed suggestion from the faculty members. Knowing the generally volatile nature of the union at this point, the vice chancellor decided not to negotiate with the students' union or consider its demand 'unless the students give a definite and convincing guarantee that they will not repeat this type of disruptive activity'. This decision was taken in a meeting of the VC and the deans of the schools. Subsequently, JNUTA in its resolution requested the VC to reopen the university. On 13 April 1975, the GBM of students decided to lift the week-long blockade after getting the assurance from the JNUTA. But the VC remained indifferent to the request of the JNUTA and remained firm about his idea of the 'norms of mutual relationship', sidelining the demands of the students.

The VC insisted that the university would not reopen unless and until the students gave an assurance that they would not resort to such actions in future and laid down some conditions to be signed by the students. These conditions were:

(i) There will be no coercion, blockade or intimidation,
(ii) The decision-making processes of the university in which the students are represented shall be respected,
(iii) Students will have to accept the hostel rules,
(iv) The students in future will not interfere in the appointment and conditions of service of teachers and processes of student performance evaluation, and
(v) The students will be accountable for any loss or damage the university suffered during the week-long blockade.[36]

However, at this point the VC left for Nairobi, and Moonis Raza, the rector, took charge. Unfortunately, being a supporter of the students' union, Raza lacked the authority to confront the issue appropriately. He, therefore, insisted on the same code of conduct laid down by the VC. The JNUTA, with Moonis Raza and the CPI(M)'s persuasion and mobilizing techniques, passed a resolution: 'VC should reopen the university unconditionally'. Professor Moonis Raza seized this opportunity to reopen the university.

This agitation was one of the biggest at the JNU and had continued for several days. It also indicated how the vice chancellor would deal with a crisis. In his absence, the debate with the senior teachers and many younger teachers, a large number of whom were affiliated to the two communist parties, ended. The university was closed for a few days when the administration of the library and even the mess had been commandeered by the students. The agitation was a time when the outsiders caught their first glimpse of the workings in the students' union, and it caused a sense of resigned annoyance. However, for the JNU students, and more significantly, for those who joined later, the strike marked a glorious phase of the students' movement.

A close perusal with historical hindsight however looks at the events with slightly more cynical eyes. The agitation, which in many ways was run with dignity, catapulted the SFI as the biggest party in the campus as it not only ran the organized show, it also mobilized the younger faculty, many of whom, in the next couple of years, became the party's intellectual mainstay.[37] The agitation also saw that the students, irrespective of their party affiliation, were loyal to the union and hence, despite many of the (what came to be known as) 'diabolical moves of the SFI', they did not break student solidarity. In addition, the efforts to interact with teachers to win them over to their cause broke new ground in the interaction with and respect for them and hence, while the demand, engineered by the communist parties, was to have outside evaluators, the agitation in fact enhanced the students respect for the teachers further.

By June 1975, when Emergency was imposed, JNU was effectively a few years old. The oldest component was the SIS which was four years old. The vice chancellor was a dominant figure in the scientific circuit and had come from a defence science organization. Interestingly, he had been part of the Indo-US team and had been instrumental in de-freezing PL-480 and hence considered pro-US. These factors did not bode well for the university where the science departments had yet to be streamlined.

The Emergency was a landmark event for the JNU. The suspension of democratic rights in a campus where every talk was of scrapping democracy must have been gruelling. The teaching community baulked in fear when the JNUTA's flag bearer, an avowed militant socialist-affiliated teacher, resigned from presidentship. With the resignation of its president, the JNUTA found it difficult to hold its meetings due to lack of quorum; only teachers from the history and economics departments would attend the meetings. These few teachers would later turn lackadaisical towards the forum because it became clear to them that the forum seemed to have lost its moral authority in the university. The much proclaimed socialist leaders' solidarity disintegrated when the student who was their 'leading light' migrated to the United States. The capital seemed petrified when Sanjay Gandhi and his men brought free life to a grinding halt.

The students of Jawaharlal Nehru University, however, played a vital role in fighting the Emergency. In order to fight back the suppressive attitude of the authorities, the student activists formed an underground group (Resistance) which issued bulletins against the government and the university authorities. The first blow to JNU was the arrest of sixty students on 8 July 1975 at 5 a.m. Most of the students who were arrested were former and sitting members of the Students Council. This was a tactical move by the government to suppress the anti-government propaganda and activity of the students of Jawaharlal Nehru University.[38] It was noted that the first attack on JNU culminated in an intense resistance by the students to authority. The students on the other hand had a different skyline. The uneasy alliance between the SFI and AISF was ruptured as the CPI had supported the Emergency and CPI(M) was going along with the opposition which included the RSS.

The administration too buckled badly under the Emergency's climate of fear. Students who were identified as luminaries of the opposition, like D.P. Tripathy, could not get admission into JNU's Ph.D programme ostensibly because of the vice chancellor's intervention. This created long-term problems and a further erosion of trust with the administration and teaching community in general, who, in the eyes of the students, failed to stand their ground against the authoritarian regime, and the vice chancellor was attacked. Except for one noble exception, most centres caved in and surrendered their autonomy.

A more glaring episode was the incarceration of an M.Phil. student, Prabir Purkayastha. The freshman was seated in the university lawns, beside the School of Languages, when he was bundled into the police chief P.S. Bhinder's car and thrown in jail for almost a whole year. Lieutenant Governor Kishan Chand was told about it, and a witness later told the Shah Commission that though the authorities knew that they had picked up the wrong person, and were also told so, nobody had the courage to release him as the 'instruction' had come from the PM's house.[39]

A police officer told the commission that the deputy inspector general, P.S. Bhinder, had come straight from the prime minister's house and arrested the student on the mistaken notion that he was the union president, Devi Prasad Tripathy, who was on the police radars, despite protestations from the students present that he was not Tripathy. Mr Purkayastha told the Shah Commission that he was arrested half an hour after the striking students had prevented Mrs Maneka Gandhi, wife of Sanjay Gandhi, from entering the classrooms where she had been studying. He was held in detention under MISA (Maintenance of Internal Security Act), and Kishan Chand, the lieutenant governor, was unwilling to release him even after a year.[40] Shakti Kak, who had been with Prabir on the fateful day, gave testimony as to how Purkayastha had been grabbed by the waist with his arms and legs still sticking out of the open car door as it sped away.[41]

Emergency and the protests against the misrule it entailed not only gave the students and many teachers a cause—both academic and political—to engage with, it also effected a change in the character of the university in many ways. This was the time when educational institutions across northern India demonstrated their complete helplessness in the face of administrative interventions and student agitations, both of which adversely affected the long-term interests of the institutions. The universities of Bihar, Rajasthan, Uttar Pradesh, Madhya Pradesh and many other places in fact began to go moribund. Several career-oriented students began to gravitate towards Delhi, and JNU's relaxed admission policies began to give them hope. This, in the long run, would perhaps skew the character of the university; however, that is an issue to be examined in another context.

By the time the state of Emergency played out across the country, the student politics of JNU, notwithstanding the sectarian battles by different outfits to dominate, began to occupy a very respectable place among the political minds in the country. The JNU students, despite their sectarian ways, learnt to respect the debating culture. This culture would mark JNU's political life as uniquely different from the other campuses of the time. Unfortunately, it was also disparaged and deemed as 'foreign and non-indigenous' by those who had grown accustomed to using the students for non-academic purposes.

11

Cracks in the Structure

The Indian general elections in March 1977 had brought a government to power in which many of the socialists and the icons of the younger radical leaders enjoyed a prominent place. It also had brought the communists to power in West Bengal. The post-Emergency era of the university was a very interesting time to be in. The excitement of an imminent change from the Emergency situation, when the city's chatterati and political, bureaucratic and social elite ruled over the republic, to a more democratic society was palpable.[1]

As soon as it was apparent that there would be elections, forty-odd members of the JNU faculty took the initiative to issue an appeal to the electorate 'to vote only for those candidates who subscribed to revocation of the Emergency and other repressive measures'.[2] On the other hand there were people who, with the understanding that it was important to impose an Emergency as fascist forces and similar groups needed to be curbed, particularly the lawlessness impressed on the country by RSS, appealed to the voters to vote for Indira Gandhi's Congress for 'democracy and progress'. The group included senior professor M.S. Agwani who had taken a stand against Muslim fundamentalism and Prof. B.D. Nag Choudhuri, the vice chancellor.[3] The latter's invocations to political and other sensitivities, however, rang hollow to many as he had been seen as using the Emergency to curb the right of teachers and students to carry on with perfectly acceptable activities.

In the meantime, aspersions were cast by senior Jana Sangh leaders that JNU was spared by Indira Gandhi. On 1 March 1977, Atal Bihari Vajpayee gave a statement that Delhi University was the real target during the Emergency, referring to the 'extra wrong done to DU' as compared to the other Delhi-based university, JNU. According to Jana

Sangh, JNU's vice chancellor had a meeting with the prime minister and specifically requested that no teacher of his university should be arrested. On the other hand, 275 DU teachers were arrested.[4] It was plain to see that the left were hand-in-glove with the Congress during the Emergency.

There was another dialectic operating within the campus. The exhilaration of the post-Emergency air and the taste of new-found freedom also meant that the non-SFI students were in no mood to tolerate the SFI's overbearing attitude and demanded immediate elections. As the elections were the recruiting ground for the organization and to its ideology, the SFI wanted these to be held after the beginning of the new semester, i.e., July; however, their major opposition, the Free Thinkers, would have none of this. It led to a couple of fracases.[5] The election mood was building up. D.P. Tripathy, from UP, who had learnt the art of realpolitik from his earthy background, was emerging as the leading presidential candidate for the SFI. He was a thorough politician and understood that the CPI(M) and its student wing held the same views as the Janata Party and its socialist-minded students, and that the students' affairs within the campus were in sync with the politics outside the campus. He demanded (a) an inquiry into the excesses committed against the people in general and students in particular, (b) disbanding of the Research and Analysis Wing (RAW), and (c) revocation of the forty-second amendment to the Constitution.[6] Tripathy also held a personal grudge against the administration as he was denied admission to the M.Phil course.

In the meantime, the JNU Teachers Association elections were also due and the campus witnessed an all-round political climate. On 15 April 1977, during the JNUTA elections, the karamcharis gherao-ed the vice chancellor. They charged him with nepotism and favouritism in appointments made during the Emergency. The karamcharis were supported by the students, and the vice chancellor acceded to many of their demands. The teachers' union election was a contest between the CPI-led coalition and a radical coalition which included Harbans Mukhia with the support of the CPI(M) for the post of president, and Jaisekhar, for general secretary. The election outcome showed K.J. Mahale (144) ahead of Harbans Mukhia (104), but, for the post of general secretary, Jaisekhar (134) won over R.R. Sharma of the CPI (108).[7]

In the students union elections, the SFI adopted its old strategy of targeting the teachers and attacked the vice chancellor.[8] The basis this time, as Sitaram Yechury pointed out, was that 'during the Emergency, eleven students were denied admission on political considerations', and there was 'nothing to prevent a teacher from victimizing a student during evaluation on political grounds'.[9] Yechury did have a valid reason for reiterating the old SFI demand for 'revaluation'. The revaluation was an excellent idea as it shone a spotlight on the way the highest office of the university was involved in striking off the names of selected candidates from the list. Notwithstanding their public posture of defending human rights or fighting for Kashmir and so many other issues, the faculty of most of the centres crumbled under pressure from the administration and the students were witness to this. Schools like the School of Social Sciences had Rasheeduddin Khan, an MP, with a standing among the academia and political classes, and therefore there was no reason for his centre to buckle under. Moonis Raza, who also had close ties with the education minister and the establishment, ought to have been a source of support for the students. Some teachers in the School of International Studies were avowed socialists and had connections with the powers-that-be but they had also failed to stand their ground and students were denied admission on purely political grounds.

Following the attack on the vice chancellor, the SFI demanded that an inquiry committee be established.[10] The SFI's idea of fighting on local issues was also intended as a strategy to isolate the AISF which was facing charges for having colluded with the Emergency regime. The AISF seemed somewhat rattled by the precision of the accusations and it came out with statements almost apologizing for supporting the Emergency. Ali Javed (AISF) felt that 'the students have forgiven' the AISF because they had conceded their 'faults'.[11] He acknowledged that the AISF 'was wrong in supporting the Emergency'.[12] In order to regain lost ground, the AISF returned to their proverbial rhetoric of India's democratic politics—going to the people; in JNU parlance it meant revisiting the accusation against the university of elitism and the need to bring 'real' people in. True to tradition, Javed expressed his determination to put 'an end to the elitist character of the university'.

The University under Attack

A four-hour sit-in dharna outside the Academic Council Meeting demanded the immediate election to Student–Faculty Committees and the reintroduction of compulsory membership to the students' union.[13] While this was happening inside the campus, the media reported: 'JNU got away with quite a lot'. In addition to there being no arrests of teachers in JNU, two new schools were bestowed upon the university.

Within the campus, the election brought a complete victory for the SFI panel, which heralded an angry union as many students belonging to the party had had to face the ire of the police and at times the wrath of the administration. In the new education minister they now found a willing ear and, when some of them met him on 26 May 1977 with the demand that 'Mrs Indira Gandhi be removed from chancellorship of the university', he responded that this was not possible as 'it would involve changing the ordinance itself'. However, he added, 'it was the moral duty of Mrs Gandhi to resign because her anti-people and anti-student policies had been rejected. Strong public opinion would have to be generated to persuade her to resign the chancellorship of both JNU and Visva-Bharati'. In the same meeting he apparently assured the delegation that he would look into the charges 'against the JNU administration led by B.D. Nag Choudhuri, the registrar, A.B. Chandiramani, P.N. Sharma and Darshan Singh, the security officers'.[14] Mr P.C. Chunder, the new education minister, averred that the terms of these officers would not be extended.[15] The prime minister, Morarji Desai, did not evince any keenness in punishing those who had supported Mrs Gandhi.

The union intensified its attack against the vice chancellor for being Mrs Gandhi's accomplice in the Emergency excesses within the campus, and insisted on her resignation as chancellor.[16] The vice chancellor had terminated the contract of the architect, Kukreja Associates, and had hired a replacement, Bose and Company, which was cited as proof of his nepotism.[17] The allegations of nepotism also spilled onto the appointments made by the vice chancellor.[18] And in an act of high-handedness, Prof. S.N. Biswas, the dean of environmental sciences, had dismissed four of the faculty, K.C. Gupta, L.K. Pande,

J. Subbarao and J.C. Vaish, as they had called for a faculty meeting.[19] It was a bizarre occurrence as Prof. Biswas had himself recruited these faculty members from various other institutions to start the new school. It created confusion and bad blood. These acts, along with the suspension of a student, Ashok Lata Jain, were repeatedly mentioned by the SFI as proof of high-handedness by the authorities.

The students joined forces with the teachers within the campus and began campaigns demanding 'a commission of enquiry'. In their letters to newspapers, some students openly accused Prof. Nurul Hasan, the former education minister, of being sectarian and showing favouritism during the premiership of Mrs Indira Gandhi. He had made forty appointments by inviting people to take up posts, rather than going through the normal selection process.[20]

The anti-communist members in the parliament, mainly the RSS members and sympathizers, took this criticism further, and while speaking about the UGC report on education, Subramanian Swamy attacked JNU for being too expensive as an institution.[21] He also attacked it for being the refuge of discredited academicians who took their 'cue from Moscow'.[22] The faculty dismissed this charge on the basis of Swamy's nebulous heritage. JNU received another jolt when the UGC rejected its plan to start up honours courses.[23] The university was besieged by the communists and socialists who were attacking it from within, and Hindu communal groups and mavericks with vested interests, from outside.

Inquisition

The demand for an inquiry was on the rise and many younger teachers of the CPI(M) and socialist groupings had joined the chorus. They had a meeting with the education minister and the prime minister. There was a genuine demand to investigate the irregularities committed during the Emergency. However, many teachers were aware that these inquiries generally ended up opening a can of worms. The larger forces which were ranged against the university aggravated the situation by turning it into a witch-hunt and further damaged the institution. Notwithstanding the CPI(M) (through SFI) and the socialists spearheading the agitation for such an inquiry, on 17 February 1977, the JNUTA executive committee met and passed two resolutions, one of which said that while the teachers recognized the right of a competent authority to inquire into the functioning of the university, it reaffirmed its faith in the principle that no one should be questioned for holding any political opinion or view.[24]

It was also clear to most of the faculty that the students' organizations and many communist and socialist teachers, blinded by their ideological opposition to the Congress and the actions of Nag Choudhuri during the Emergency, were in no mood to forego a thorough inquiry into the whole university. The senior teachers, particularly from the social sciences, knew that this would have disastrous consequences for the university. JNU, being a very young university, had never undergone the dreaded and gruelling visitorial enquiry. The universities that had been subjected to this nightmare, never quite completely recovered their equilibrium after such an inquiry. It set people against people. With the Jana Sangh calling the shots within the government, the inquiry would also mean its entry through the back door and persecution of the communist elements. The SFI, however, had argued that by raising the bogey of right-wing entry, the teachers opposing outside evaluation were basically trying to hide their incompetence and preventing the democratic right of the movement to enter into the business of evaluation.

Very soon, the proceedings of the Shah Commission rivetted the attention of the country as well as the students in the campus. Students fondly reminisced about the demonstrations at the Boat Club when the prime minister's office invited their representatives inside and, on one occasion, Morarji Desai himself came out to speak to them. The stifling atmosphere of the Emergency was not there. In one such meeting, Morarji Desai had apparently asked Sitaram Yechury to dress properly and button his shirt.[25] It was in this informal atmosphere that the court meeting took place in the campus when Prime Minister Morarji Desai visited the campus. It was left to Sivatosh Mookerjee to take the lead in opposing the visitorial inquiry.[26] One beneficial aspect of the prime minister's visit was the overnight construction of the road which linked Aruna Asaf Ali Marg to Nelson Mandela Marg, which was later named Baba Gang Nath Marg. The Central Public Works Department (CPWD) also planted quite a few tall trees; an exercise that did not escape the piercing eyes of the prime minister who called the CPWD's bluff and rebuked the officers.

The international situation was worsening at this time and there was a sense of being adrift with the realization that India's foreign policy had shifted from its conventional positions, particularly in west Asia. The disclosure of the secret visit of Israel's top defence strategist, Moshe Dayan, and his meeting with Prime Minister Morarji Desai, indicated the level of penetration reached by the Israel and United States lobbies in the foreign policy administration.

It is in this atmosphere that one of the finest moments in the students' movement in the city came about. The Shah of Iran was due to visit India in February. This was the time when anti-Shah demonstrations were beginning to take the shape of a mass movement in Iran and other parts of the world as well. In such a situation, the Indian visit of the Shah was bound to generate protests. One of the leaders of the protests, Qamar Agha, who later became a leading commentator on West Asia, narrated how the demonstration was planned meticulously. He and his friend, Amarjeet Kaur, and two others, planned the whole affair in the Delhi zoo, and interacted with the anti-Shah activists in Germany who masterminded the movement.

They kept the plan of the demonstration close to their chests, and, although the media was informed, the exact location of the protest was kept secret until the last minute. The Government of India had asked the Iranian students studying in India not to go out and join any demonstration. However, the students were generally in a mood to agitate. The plan was to demonstrate before the Shah's cavalcade after it crossed the Marina Hotel and neared Connaught Place. The organizers had instructed the Iranian students the various ways by which to get into the emporium and other shops on Baba Kharak Singh Marg which opened on to the crossing of the outer circle. The JNU and Delhi University students, and other activists, climbed on to the tops of the buildings beside the Regal Building. As the cavalcade of the Shah slowed down, the students created a melee by throwing pamphlets, black flags, etc. The police managed to rescue the Shah but the demonstration was rated a success.[27] When the students reached the Iranian embassy on Barakhamba Road, the police cornered the students and around 500 students were arrested which also included seventeen Iranian students.[28]

In the meantime, notwithstanding the huge sound and fury that the students' union elections had generated, only 200 people attended the presidential debate and a journalist reported it as 'a tame affair'.[29] The main topic of discussion was whether there should be a 'limited or unlimited probe' into JNU affairs, or what Sitaram Yechury, the presidential nominee of the SFI, called 'Emergency crimes and corruption in the university administration'.[30] The SFI did not have a smooth sail. Rajan G. James, who accused SFI of being a collaborationist, polled as much as 573 votes, only seventy-five votes less than Yechury of the total 1491 votes polled. The other candidate, Sudhindra, got 263 votes.[31]

On the visitorial inquiry front, it had been decided by the prime minister's office to place complaint boxes in both JNU and Delhi University. In JNU, the complaint box was placed outside the office of the university registrar so that all those who had grievances against the university could send their written complaints to the prime minister by depositing them in the box. It came to light that the complaint box inquiring into the alleged Emergency excesses in Delhi University was retrieved by the secretariat, full to the brim. The whereabouts of the JNU box, however, remains a mystery to this day.

The strain of the aimlessness of the national polity and increase in the level of violence and aggression were reflected in the student body. The increasing aggression had something to do with the unrestrained attack on Indira Gandhi and the Congress, and, while one realized the hollowness of the Janata Party formation, one was impelled to support it. This was aggravated by increasing signs that the new formation was not only communal but also had an authoritarian streak as reflected in the Kanpur firing where many students from JNU were either involved in organizing the labour or writing their Ph.D on the labour history of the city.[32]

The Left Front under the leadership of CPI(M) came to power in the West Bengal election. With this success, the dominant left party in the campus (SFI) grew insolent and arrogant. This matched the self-righteousness of the fringe radicals with Trotskyite or Maoist sympathies. This was not a welcome sign and the popularity of the Free Thinkers and speakers like David Thomas, who had defeated the SFI candidate in the presidential election, began to reflect this uneasiness amongst the student population. The arrogance of SFI, though it was defeated in the previous union elections, was unabated. The final straw was the attack on two Free Thinkers by SFI cadre: the Bedi–Durrani affair.

When the Delhi Transport Corporation hiked bus fares in February 1979, the students launched an agitation, a common sight in West Bengal and other left-dominated parts of the country where buses were set on fire if there was even a five-paisa inflation. The students promptly hijacked a couple of buses into the JNU campus and some students were arrested but released later.[33] There followed a strike against the DTC.[34] There was a demonstration in the capital where the students clashed with the police.[35] The police, as they often did, were merely doing their routine crisis management, without being too harsh on the JNU students. However, as it happened, following the skirmishes, a male student back in the campus tea stall advised a SFI member, Mumtaj Bano, that provoking the police would yield, not laddoos, but a lathi charge, and therefore one needed to stay within one's limits. The lady either misunderstood or her report was misinterpreted, and owing to the highly charged times, Durrani and his friend Bedi were beaten up by four SFI members, Amarjit Singh Sirohi, P. Sainath, Dilip Upadhyay and Arun Sinha. [36]

A general body meeting of about 500 students demanded expulsion of the people involved. Under pressure, an inquiry committee chaired by Prof. Ravi Bakaya, a respected senior teacher with impeccable communist credentials, was constituted.[37] But the efforts were to get them absolved.[38] Their suspension was revoked.[39] The students could do the math; the teachers did not want to antagonize the SFI. The whole episode, known as the Bedi–Durrani Affair, left a lot to be desired on the justice delivery system of the institution. While the general understanding and ethos was the collegial conflict resolution, it was the preservation of the demand of the organized left parties that settled these events. It worked like this: if the person against whom there were any charges, serious or trivial, was not a member of or had no backing of any organized left parties, there would be an organized demand for the highest punishment possible. A maximalist stand was the natural stand. There was no moderation or waiting to give the person a fair trial. However, when the member was from the parties of the left, moderation, natural justice, democratic rights, etc., were the key words in vogue and anybody talking in terms of punishment was rubbished as pro-authority, pro-establishment, right-wingers and so on.

The Bedi-Durrani affair was a prime example of the kind when the serious and evidently correct charges were botched and the case was settled out of court. The collective might of the party and its own well-being took precedence over institutional well-being. In this instance, the case was mismanaged despite the fact that the Free Thinkers' demand was bolstered by a vote in the general body meeting which supported the demand for their expulsion by 412 to 292 votes.[40] The whole issue seemed to harmonize with the overarching principle on which the university was founded, that students were not criminals. Incidentally, these principles had been advocated in the 1960s by many senior nationalist members of the parliament. The leaders also sought to establish trust for the teacher as the fundamental guiding principle for the new university. Significantly, once the student movement got going, one realized the left union actually attacked the most crucial part—the issue of trust.

Amidst all these pressures, the campus was enlivened by the fair concern for animals, some wild, and some not so wild. Fluffy, Prof. Mahale's dog, had a proclivity to bite people with Marxist sympathies that warmed the hearts of the opposition. News of any such biting was relished more than the articles in the aesthetically distasteful *Panchjanya* or *Organizer* or even the Delhi tabloids. Fluffy in fact tried to silence the most vocal Marxist by nipping him not once but twice.[41] The Marxists obviously could not condone Mahale for this and his stint as acting vice chancellor was dogged by agitation and turmoil.

Maladministration Exposes Itself

Life in JNU was disturbed by acute problems in the mess and a general unrest. There were issues of inflated mess bills leading to altercations between caretakers and the mess committee in Sutlej Hostel that finally resulted in one of the biggest strikes by the mess staff on 30 January 1980.[42] The bill, which usually amounted to about Rs 110 a month, rose to Rs 150 for the previous month. Vigilant students made it a point to investigate the matter as the mess bill hike was without any particular change in the menu or quality of the food, and this was in spite of the fact that the university had scrapped fish, meat and butter from the menu due to the huge mess bill arrears. The union president met the vice chancellor about this and was told that the arrears had reached a high figure of Rs 1,80,000. This made the centralized suppliers, namely, Super Bazaar, Delhi Milk Scheme and National Agricultural Federation to stop supplies.[43] The students' union and the parties blamed the university administration for such a situation.

The Registration Mess

The winter session of 1980 began with a series of strikes, the most serious being the token strike at the School of Languages where students from the Centre for Russian Studies who were denied registration began agitating. The centre had refused thirty-two students registration for the semester. The chairperson of the department said that these students had shown no interest in their studies and that 'twenty-four of them had already left the university'. The eight who remained were using the other twenty-four to create a stir.[44] The students raised the institutional issue by pointing out that the decision not to give them registration was taken by the faculty without consulting the board of studies. They demanded that they be given provisional registration until their cases were finalized by the board.[45]

No sooner had this trouble begun than another emerged from the Centre for Persian Studies where two Ph.D candidates were not selected after the interviews. The trouble had been brewing for several months after two candidates were refused admission on the grounds that they had not done well in the interview. After a prolonged student agitation, the faculty had finally agreed to admit them after fresh interviews. However, the students insisted that the two students be admitted on the basis of their earlier interview.

The vice chancellor agreed to call a special meeting of the academic council to discuss the demand of the students. In the meantime, a meeting of the committee of advanced studies and Research (CASR) was anyway scheduled for the following Monday to discuss the issue. The students' union called for a night-long gherao. At about 3 p.m. the members of the committee, who had come to know about the decision of the students' union, sought an urgent appointment with the vice chancellor who was then in a meeting with the deans. As soon as the members of the committee walked into the vice chancellor's room, they were gherao-ed by the students. They told the vice chancellor that they were gehrao-ing the members of the committee, and the others could leave. However, Vice Chancellor K.R. Narayanan and the deans chose to stay. Thus, the VC, a number of deans and members of the committee of advanced studies spent that Monday night under gherao organized by the students' union. The gherao began at 3 p.m. and ended at 3 a.m. on Tuesday.[46] It did not result in any concrete resolution. This created further resentment among the section which was always seeking ways to intensify any struggle.[47] While the union was attacked for letting the gherao off without any tangible outcome; fifty students apparently quit the SFI on the grounds that the SFI backed out of a confrontation with the authorities.[48]

The faculty protested in full media glare over the issue of registration, particularly when the vice chancellor convened a meeting and summarily allowed eight students to register into the Centre for Russian Studies. The vice chancellor seemed to have gone soft and was 'appeasing the students out of turn'.[49] The ministry was also understandably unhappy with the wayward ways of the JNU students 'who spend years doing nothing and doing it at the expense of the taxpayer'.[50] The situation was likened to an academic war 'with a soft vice chancellor on the one side, militant students on the other, and the teachers somewhere in between'.[51] The press and the parliament were very hard on the students now, and nasty reports appeared. For example, '...seventy odd students either get fellowship or hostel; 20 to 25 take both but do not go the classes'.[52] The students in the schools of international studies and the languages were particularly targeted for such criticism.[53] The students were also accused of being careless with the library's precious collection and allegedly tore the pages and mutilated the books.[54]

In 1977, the issue of chancellorship had captured the imagination of the students when they demanded Mrs Gandhi's resignation from this post. While Mrs Gandhi's supporters in the ministry were setting the wheels in motion for her to replace Morarji Desai, the prime minister, as the chancellor, the student body and a large teaching bloc were simultaneously readying to oppose this nomination bitterly. The indignation against Emergency excesses had not diminished by the time Mrs Gandhi came back to govern in 1980. But the increased intellectual chasm, further widened by the renewed communist attack on the Congress and on Indira Gandhi personally, could have been the reason for the sustained anger of the students and a large body of teachers towards her. The senior professors were contacted sub rosa, who helped orchestrate the chain of events, and by April 1980 the prime minister had declined the offer of chancellorship. Subsequently, the executive council, which met on 26 April 1980, proposed three names for the chancellorship, namely, Satyajit Ray, D.T. Lakdawala and D.S. Kothari.[55] In due course, Dr Kothari was appointed chancellor.

The Closure of a Centre

In these turbulent times, the debate surrounding the suspension of the Centre for Science Policy flashed into the media. This centre, which was key to JNU's academic vision, continued to have teething problems right from its inception. Prof. B.V. Rangarao, notwithstanding his expertise, was not a success at leading the centre in the university setting, and, by 1979-80, the centre began to fall apart. Being an innovative programme, the students and researchers had taken quite a high risk in light of the orthodox nature of the Indian academia. The worst affected were the students when the centre buckled under. A committee was constituted under Yogendra Singh, P.N. Srivastava and Amit Bhaduri to look into the issue. The committee recommended the suspension of admissions into the centre for two to three years. Later on, yet another committee consisting of outside members V.S. Jha, B.S. Samundri and Manzoor Alam went into the working of the centre and reported that the centre had come to a standstill because Rangarao, they discovered, upset at having been deprived of headship, refused to let the others run the place. A number of other teachers, Deepak Banerjee, Matin Juberi, John Pulparampil and P.K. Mitra had abandoned ship for one reason or other. At one time Rangarao was supervising seventeen out of twenty students.[56] On the recommendations of the committee, the centre was suspended and the students were allocated to different teachers within the school of social sciences.[57]

In June, a newspaper article indicating the centre's possible revival appeared.[58] The report had cited Prof. Rangarao as saying that the closure of the centre was due to the anti-science policies of the Janata government. Four former students of the centre, Dinesh Abrol, J. Manohar Rao, R. Divakaran and Ashok Raj, wrote a strong rejoinder to the press refuting Prof. Rangarao's claim. The reality, they said, was that the suspension of the centre and the removal of Rangarao had 'nothing to do with the happenings of the last two or three years of the Janata regime'.[59] They accused the professor of several shortcomings as a teacher, ranging 'from not taking classes, to obstructing interaction with various agencies and experts inside and outside the country, infringing professional norms, manipulating the admissions and appointments, harassment of students, several of whom left the centre in frustration'.[60] The decision to suspend the centre was the only alternative left at the time because any attempt towards rehabilitation of the discredited would have only led to chaos. The entire student body of the university supported the stand of the students, and resisted the retrograde steps to revive the centre.[61] Prof. Rangarao however attributed the students' response 'to their frustration at not getting jobs at such a late age as forty'.[62]

The Centre for Science Policy was a poor illustration of institution building in the Third World, but it was picked up by the critic of JNU as 'another example of what it had begun to be associated as the *JNU malaise*'.[63] The *Hindustan Times* came out with two editorials within a couple of months highlighting the negative image of the university in the political circles of Delhi. No one bothered to appreciate the fact that this was perhaps the first time in the history of free India that a centre was closed by the university to retain its standards and the interests of the students. The internal happenings did not help the matters much to improve its image. The media soon picked on another story. S.C. Saxena working in the African studies department was treated shabbily by its head and dismissed dishonourably. The JNU teaching community took exception to this exposé.[64]

The parliament was growing weary of these altercations in JNU via the media, and a member of parliament, K.A. Rajan, asked President Sanjeeva Reddy to institute a visitorial inquiry into the affairs of the university and put an end to the irresponsible behaviour of its officials.[65]

The known basher of communists and the JNU, Subramanian Swamy, was joined by a former professor of English at Patna University, the inimitable K.K. Tiwary, known as the leader of the shouting brigade of Rajiv Gandhi, demanding an inquiry as a 'large number of CPI(M) cardholders were getting admissions and scholarships'.[66] The media got into a frenzy with a string of sensational headlines: JNU research centres do not research—centres like Centre for the Study of Science Policy (CSSP), School of Computer and System Sciences (SC&SS) and Zakir Hussain Centre for Educational Studies (ZHCES) are white elephants; JNU misadministration in admissions and scholarships given on the basis of fake income certificates.[67] The media also pointed fingers at the faculty of SIS, one of whom was supposed to have submitted articles from the Hindi weekly, *Dinman*, as his research papers—nine of them.[68] In the meantime, rumours were rife that K.R. Narayanan had resigned and that Mrs Gandhi was worried about the decline in the administrative and academic standards of the university.[69] The rumours were not baseless as K.R. Narayanan had actually resigned. The search for a new vice chancellor began in September 1980.[70]

The university was now without a head or direction and this began to be reflected in student politics too. The semblance of unity built during the Emergency years was splintering. There was no ideological or sociological unity between the communist and Janata factions. The unity which had come about during the period of struggle during the last five or six years had only been a fellowship of co-suffering. In the campus that unity had always had an ephemeral side to it as the ruling left would not allow a single inch of space to the other ideological formations. Some of the old socialists were now in a state of complete disillusionment. Generally, as succinctly put by the famous Punjabi poet, Avtar Singh Pash, the politics which emerged from the destruction of illusions have been disastrous: 'the most dangerous is when the dreams die'. The local student politics was exhibiting symptoms of disillusionment. A new students' formation known as Democratic Students Front—a combination of the Progressive Students' Organization, Progressive Students' Front and the rebel section of the SFI that lost the last JNUSU election—was trying to steal the political limelght by calling for an intensification of the struggle, including a general strike.[71]

They soon found a context—a cause—the expulsion of a student, Mathialagan, by the vice chancellor on the recommendations of the provost of Dakshinapuram. It soon became a cause célèbre. The student had not registered himself for the monsoon semester and also not cleared his mess dues. There were some confusion on all these fronts. Although double-locked, he, as the charges went, 'illegally occupied the room by unlawfully breaking open the lock in spite of warnings from the provost'.[72] In the meantime, Mathialagan was granted conditional admission. The agitation over the issue began with the boycott of classes.[73] Soon the issue became a fight between the SFI and the students supporting Rajan G. James who wanted the issue of his expulsion to be taken seriously. They declared that they had no faith in the way SFI ran the JNUSU.[74] Political rivalry spilled out into the open when the fringe radicals, the Delhi Students' Forum (DSF), noticed that the SFI was actively collaborating with the administration under the garb of 'relay fast'.[75] The karamcharis who were also mobilized did a gherao of the finance officer for their own demands, which further aggravated the situation.[76] JNU was declared closed.[77]

To make matters worse, allegations of corruption raised its ugly head. Corruption in the university administration was a regular issue, which successive student bodies had flagged, most often against the vice chancellor and other high officials whenever there was an agitation of some sort. While they got their data from the karamcharis, and kept the officials under check, it also boomeranged because the charges of corruption as a political agenda was detrimental to JNU's institutional image. However, the union's attack on the vice chancellor and others as corrupt elements came home to roost when the outside world began to question the student community's own integrity. *The Indian Express*, generally a conservative right-wing newspaper, went so far as to demand drastic action, through its editorial, 'Purge the JNU'.[78] It said JNU was 'a white elephant in every sense of the term'.[79] It was scathing in its attack saying that there were 'centres of studies where the staff outnumbered the students, and others where the petty feuds between the staff union politics and the students leave little time for serious academic work'.[80] Referring to the closure of the science policy centre, the newspaper was at its damning best: 'the so-called centre for the study in science policy had to be closed down in March for lack of even a token justification for eight years of its existence'.[81] It referred to the School of Computers and System Sciences as yet 'another bad joke that had gone on too long', where 'about a crore of rupees has been spent on it but the computers hardly ever work'.[82] The editorial then became even more mordacious:

> All these extravagancies could have been suffered but for the scandals often reported from the campus—the corruption in the administration and staff and even among the students. What is most shocking is that the parasites include those who affect a devotion to highfalutin radicalism. Some of them get admission to various courses, scholarships or fellowships through devious means or fake certificates. They do not bother to pay hostel dues. Significantly, the expulsion of a student for non-payment of arrears was the original cause of the current agitation. The tragedy of JNU is that the silent majority of genuine students are made to suffer for the misbehaviour of a few. It is time they asserted themselves. The government on its part need not wait for the present enquiry committee's report to begin a purge in JNU.[83]

The issue of the eviction of Mathialagan was now joined by that of Rajan. Rajan and others were spearheading anti-SFI politics and their argument was that the SFI was in cahoots with the administration. The political battle was now waged against the teachers but the ultimate target of the agitation was the vice chancellor. The SFI and the AISF had joined hands in the dharna outside the home of the acting vice chancellor, K.J. Mahale. The opposition councillor, Sunil Kumar Gupta, joined the indefinite hunger strike, and despite the president of JNUSU calling it off, the strike continued.[84] The SFI's decision to end the dharna was not motivated by any concern for the personal discomfort of Mahale, whose elevation to acting vice chancellorship was resented by the communist patrons and senior professors from the schools like that of international studies.[85]

While resolving to withdraw the hunger strike, the council of the students' union (it was not known how many members attended the meeting) said that it reiterated its outright opposition to the order suspending James. The resolution also noted that the students had the democratic right to all forms of peaceful protest including protests in the residential areas of people in authority.[86] Internal competition within the students union was heading for a showdown. The SFI was not comfortable with large unorganized groups carrying on the agitation completely disregarding the union. It condemned the continued hunger strike by the three pro-James students 'even after the students' council had decided to end the fast the previous day'. Meanwhile, the pro-James councillors, whose fast entered the fifth day, stated in a press release that 'they could not go with the students' council decision because it only reflected the collaborationist and anti-student policy of the SFI leadership'.[87] They said they would not break their fast until the expulsion order was revoked.[88] However, the next day, the 'police was called in to break their fast'.[89]

Commenting on 'the whole episode' the media blamed the absence of a visionary head as the real cause for what it termed the 'JNU Malaise'. One lead write-up argued that the 'university's malaise lies especially in its failure to evolve an *espirit de corps*—which is a precondition for a residential institution designed for a high degree of inter-disciplinary exchange and student teacher interaction'.[90] Its absence was, it argued and quite correctly, due to several reasons and the absence of a visionary vice chancellor was the most easily identifiable of them. The result was that 'JNU has been like an orchestra without a conductor. It is not surprising then if instead of harmony, it is producing discordant notes'.[91] It asked the government to 'nominate a suitable person committed to the institution to head the university'.[92]

Groups of students were however unrelenting and tried to push forward with their agitation. K.J. Mahale, the acting VC, was almost under siege as demonstrations and gheraos were organized outside his residence. He appealed to the students to give up their coercive and agitational approach for the redressal of their grievances. Mahale and P.N. Srivastava were gherao-ed by students for four hours in the beginning of the year.[93] The anti-SFI students of the Janata formation, also with no specific political orientation, were now moving to the fore for some kind of a showdown with the administration. The politics had gone awry. In a press release, the vice chancellor mentioned the issue of legitimate methods in exercising the right to dissent and protest. 'All manners of coercive action such as lock out, blockade, gherao, dharna, in the residential area by an individual or group had no place in the university,' he argued, and many teachers did support him. JNUTA itself met and appealed to the JNUSU to negotiate for a mutually acceptable code of civic behaviour. It also urged the university authorities not to call the police on to the campus as far as possible. While Rajan was asked to leave the hostel, there were scuffles during his eviction.[94] He accused the university officials of summoning the police and demanded the suspension of two security personnel who had allegedly beaten up students. At this juncture, the acting vice chancellor, Prof. Mahale, resigned.

With the police forcibly ending the fast of the students, the non-SFI students began their agitation. Some students associated with the democratic front gherao-ed the registrar for over two hours demanding action against the university's security staff. The general body of the teachers discussed the situation arising out of frequent confrontations between the authorities and some student groups. It condemned the behaviour of Mr James with teachers in general and the hostel authorities in particular. The teachers demanded that the university authorities take immediate action to safeguard the honour and persons of the teachers and called upon the student union to isolate those trying to foul the teacher–student relationship. The teachers also urged university authorities not to encourage police entry into the campus.[95]

Now the left-wing teachers tried to take a lead in the situation. The teachers union met and decided that they would not teach on 6 January 1981 as a protest against the gherao of the registrar. However, very few criticized the persistent coercive tactics of the students for fear of being branded as reactionary or anti-student. The residential life of the professors was not merely interspersed with coercion by the students but also by gangs outside the university—particularly the specific gangs of thieves which belonged to the now glamorized criminal tribes.[96] It was amidst this din that the local criminal gangs robbed Prof. Seshadri's house and left his poor wife badly beaten.

However, there were other areas where the students felt marginalized and resorted to agitations, e.g., when they saw an entire department, international law, going for a sojourn abroad, leaving the department without any teaching staff. Many teachers from other centres would also take a couple of months' leave before summer vacation which would amount to a six-month long vacation without actually applying for long-leave. The senior professors in the social sciences objected to this blatant misuse of the leave rules.[97] They took the initiative, and, via intervention by the academic council, tried to change the long leave incidences, which indicated a self-correcting action by the teachers—a rare event. The passion for teaching and research was the bond which made them effect this self-correction.

There were talks that distinguished academics and administrators were reluctant to don the mantle of vice chancellorship of JNU at such a critical time.[98] Three names began doing the rounds: Rais Ahmed, Ram Joshi, and Y. Nayudumma.[99] The government finally announced Dr Nayudumma's name for the vice chancellorship on 28 March 1981.[100] Dr Nayudumma was one of the foremost leather scientists in India and had contributed immensely in building the Central Leather Research Institute in Madras into a formidable institution. His association with the Council for Scientific and Industrial Research (CSIR) as its director general added to his prestige among the scientific community.[101] The decision was perhaps taken with a view to taking the science departments forward, particularly the environmental sciences, and taking steps in starting the physics department. Choosing a senior person like the DG, CSIR, to head the university was a proclamation to the entire scientific community of the political establishment's desire to push the institution forward.

Student–Teacher Divide Widens

There were, however, sharpening divisions within the university community. The student–teacher divide was widening and so were the gulf between the student formations. This indicated that the divisions were not on intellectual ground as the earlier common intellectual normative structure seemed to have been lost in the commotion of the Emergency and post-Emergency politics. In one sense, the post-1977 university was a new university. Students by this time were anyway inured to their institutions being attacked on political grounds. Respect for institutions, as such, was no longer the same as during previous years. The politics within the campus soon reflected the new political realities outside: a large number of students from Bihar, for example, had seen the collapse of the university system in their state. Many of them were party to the students' movement for Total Revolution. How did it get translated into the politics of JNU?

Use of force was a new signifier for politics in the campus. While the anti-communist mobilization was premised on the notion of countering the coercive dominance of the leftist parties, they were themselves seeming to justify the violence. The SFI, the leading communist formation, was helping such discursive legitimization with its members regularly indulging in violence. However, while one could use the levers of party hierarchy to check their violence, other groups had no such hierarchical location to check the violent behaviour of the cadres. This was one of the reasons for the increasing chasm between the sections in the university. There were, for the first time, physical assaults on teachers by the students. On 19 May 1981, for example, Prof. Rameswar Singh and Rajan James, hit each other after an altercation and, in a rare event, the case went to the local police station.[102] K.K. Trivedy, a young lecturer of history and the warden of the Ganga Hostel, was assaulted by a student, Arun K. Choudhray, who was later suspended.[103] A chowkidar was beaten up by the SFI students, which led to the arrest of the SFI office-bearer, A.S. Sirohi.[104] The presence of a large number of illegal residents in the hostels of JNU further complicated the matter and, as some girl students complained, eve-teasing was rampant in the campus: a phenomenon never heard of earlier. On 30 July 1981, twenty-eight people were evicted from various hostels.[105] To add to the mess, came the hike in the mess bill which resulted in further agitation, which was compounded by acute water shortage. The water crisis in fact almost led to the closure of the campus.[106] The situation, therefore, was unenviable for any administrator.

The events now made the two left parties come together again into an alliance for electoral purposes. The SFI panel for the central committee included A.S. Sirohi, who had been in the forefront of beating Durrani and Bedi, Sonya Gupta and Jagdiswar Gupta. The AISF proposed Ajay Patnaik's candidature. It was very clear that the panel did not reflect the intellectual life of the campus but mirrored the changed realities of politics, where JNU was synchronizing with violence, caste and community. The SFI and AISF monopolized the schools of social sciences and languages. James, who had been expelled earlier, ran for president in the student elections and brought an injunction against the result.[107]

Reaching the Heights of Oppositional Politics

The 1981 campus, with a new vice chancellor, was gradually morphing into a new political campus. Earlier, the students' politics showed signs of intellectual sparks; however, now the politics was a full-time business for many, particularly in the leftist groups. Politics was oppositional: everyone opposed everyone else. There was another stream—a visceral and almost pathological hatred for Indira Gandhi, particularly among the communists and the socialists. Followers of Namboodiripad and Lohia were united on this count. This hatred would come to the fore in October 1981 when Indira Gandhi was invited by the university to inaugurate the silver jubilee function of the School of International Studies. The students' union decided to boycott her and observe a black day.[108]

The prime minister's office must have known the wrath she invited in the JNU circle particularly for the Emergency excesses on the students and the radical mood of anti-Congress politics of the communist parties. There was, therefore, extra security arrangements at the place where she was to address the community. The appearance of the campus on that fateful day was described by a local report in such terms:

> The campus was bristling with police, security men and senior officers … Rows of riot police, helmeted and carrying guns, barricaded the shamiana. While constables strung lines of cyclone cordons around the entire area, policemen stood atop the roofs of surrounding building with searchlights mounted at vantage points … the entire area looked like some war manoeuvre and undoubtedly the staggering police presence angered the student community which viewed it as invasion.[109]

The *People's Democracy*, the organ of the CPI(M), also presented its partisan but interesting version of the event:

> At 4 p.m., when the students collected at the gates of the university, they were confronted by Congress supporters

> from Delhi University who had collected there to welcome Mrs Gandhi. This crowd comprising of anti-social elements started throwing stones at JNU students. Simultaneously the police began the lathi charge which continued non-stop until well after 6 p.m. Immediately, the word spread and all the students on the campus collected at the lawns, and those who remained in the hostels rushed down to join the protest. Virtually the whole university was there. The karamcharis also joined the protest en masse.[110]

Coming close to the election of the students' union, the Gandhi visit was a recipe for disaster from the outset. The vice chancellor, Nayudumma, had apparently told the SIS dean and other senior professors that he would prefer to hold the function at the Vigyan Bhawan as it was going to be a big event. However, the professors of the School of International Studies insisted that since the institutions had taken root here the university ought to be the place for the function.

The student politics of JNU, by all indications was moving in the same direction as the politics of the country: oppositional. And, for all practical purposes, the dominant trend in the student leadership was showing a complete identification with the oppositional politics which was markedly against Indira Gandhi. It involved an extreme and personalized attack on Mrs Gandhi.

While it was supposed to be a theoretically arrived position of the CPI(M) which saw the Indira Gandhi–led Congress as surrendering to the landlords and bureaucratic forces, there must have also been a personal factor. Indira Gandhi was instrumental in getting the first communist ministry of E.M.S. Namboodiripad dismissed in 1959. This was a unique situation in Indian history when the same Namboodiripad was the chief of the CPI(M) and there were a couple of CPI(M)-led ministries in the country, and Indira Gandhi, with the history of imposing Emergency, was at the helm of the Central government. There was therefore every reason for the CPI(M) to keep attacking the Congress for its anti-democratic stand lest the latter repeat the events of 1959 or even 1975.

It was a peculiar situation. The Congress governments in many states were visibly the most corrupt governments that India had ever had, and yet the country needed political cooperation at a time when communalism was threatening to divide it. The CPI(M), however, was convinced that the time was ripe for a militant people's movement as B.T. Ranadive's invocation to the trade unions and the central committee's resolution indicated.

Congress, on the other hand, demonstrated the complete absence of any structural innovation. The party and the government had increasingly become dependent on Indira Gandhi's personality, which also legitimized the oppositional attacks. However, she too was trying to counter it with a strong hand but there were unmistakable signs that the weakening of institutions during Emergency was recoiling now leading to cracks in the governance structures. Her own party also bore the brunt of this with disarray in its ranks and organization.[111] The campus politics was responding to the social crisis by blaming it on her and therefore designing itself as oppositional politics.

The 1980s was also the period when communal riots tore apart the country's social mosaic. In most cases, the non-communal opposition blamed Indira Gandhi and the Congress of being responsible for these upheavals. The communist parties, as the major bulwark against the communal forces also began to adopt the same stance. This had a serious ramification because the intellectual consensus that had emerged by 1969-70 with most of the forces ranged against the communal forces and their political representative, Jana Sangh and Jamat-i-Islami, was now about to be broken. When the communist parties adopted the line that questioned the anti-communal credentials of the Congress, the intellectual consensus came under tremendous strain. Thus, a large chunk of dedicated communist intellectuals, under the party lines, began to dissociate themselves from the Congress or Indira Gandhi on anti-communal fronts. The Emergency had also removed the sheen from her genuinely radical ideas in the eyes of the Indian intellectuals. Therefore, for the young radical leftist students and activists in the campus, it had increasingly become almost a non-fashionable statement to support her policies or programmes. 'Oppositional' was fast becoming the campus orthodoxy.

When the JNU students' organizations tried to move into this opposition mode, there were indications that this may mean moving out of the national consensus of the 1960s that had provided the foundational premises of the university: national integration along secular lines. The opposition to Indira Gandhi's visit also visually concretized the opposition as the metaphor for the university's intellectual template. This new metaphor now coloured the boundaries of the institution. It also began to constitute self-identification which would have long-term implications. This constituted a huge intellectual and emotional drain on the institutional well-being.

The portents of the tyranny of this opposition mode was soon evident when the JNUTA acquiesced in the students' boycott of Indira Gandhi. When 106 teachers came out criticizing the students and demanded action against them, the president of the JNUTA, C.P. Bhambhri, an avowed Marxist, who tried to align his theoretical works to the working of the political economy, immediately aligned himself with the oppositional politics. A large number of teachers, however, openly criticized the mode of protest in a democratic society. They argued that although the right to dissent is the essence of democracy, 'when expressed through undemocratic methods' it becomes the negation of democracy.[112] They invited 'all members of the university community to work together to ensure respect for democratic norms'.[113] There were however many teachers for whom the police brutality was the leading issue, which needed to be condemned. Dipankar Gupta, the treasurer of the JNUTA, for example, resigned citing police brutality as the major cause to be condemned.[114] This was followed by the JNUTA president's statement repeating the similar reasons:

> It is unfortunate that a number of teachers of JNU have considered it appropriate to go to the press to condemn students' protest against Mrs Gandhi's visit to the campus without saying a single word about the unprovoked police brutality on hundreds of students, which, to many teachers of the JNU, is a matter of prime concern. I would be failing in my duty if I did not bring this strong sentiment of a large number of teachers against the police action to the public notice.[115]

The JNUTA president's stand was soon attacked by many who rightly argued that he had no business to go to the press without consulting the JNUTA. They contended that since he spoke about the larger issues, he could have also brought them to bear on this discussion. He was therefore criticized for having given vent to his personal opinion as the

JNUTA president.[116] The president later went on to write a long piece on the different political ideologies that existed on the campus.[117]

The student politics had begun showing increasing aggression which was now to be matched by confrontation by staff who went on a long strike in September 1981. This finally led to the closure of the university on 12 August 1982.[118] The initial zeal of Nayudumma, as seen by the staff close to him, was waning. He was getting nowhere and the students, teachers and the staff were pulling in different directions.[119] He decided to resign at a time when JNU seemed to have very few friends both outside and inside. In losing Nayudumma the university, in hindsight, lost its hope to leapfrog and become a major global university. Nayudumma resigned from his post as VC in the third week of October 1982.[120]

The disorientation and anger of the students over the institutional and political disarticulation at this time was faced by the local cinema hall, Priya. The Vasant Vihar hall used to screen good and bad cinema and was a students' paradise with tickets costing Rs 3 for the front benches, affordable to both the JNU and the IIT students. When the students did not get tickets for one of the night shows of the movie *Swami Dada* they rioted, and there was a major attack on the cinema hall on 4 December 1982, the night of the last day of the monsoon semester.[121] The acting vice chancellor, P.N. Srivastava, however, saved the students from the police and other elements, and was reported to have told some police personnel that these were his own children.

JNU Faces the Flak

The activity inside the campus and the way the university was going were very keenly observed and one had a gnawing sense of ennui among the intellectual circles outside the university. The student politics was increasingly being shown to be moving to the oppositional axis, particularly to the CPI(M). The largely undefined socialist groups were quite often pushed towards militancy by the radicals who generally carried neither commitment nor responsibility to the institution as such except to avowedly make it more democratic—a term which almost became a catchphrase which could mean anything.

The intellectuals and media outside the university had a soft corner for the university in the 1970s and they were trying to interpret the university to the world outside. In addition to the ennui, the intellectuals were also experiencing a suppressed anger with the way the students were conducting themselves. Harish Khare, an old student who stayed in the university for a while before leaving for a United States degree, wrote a long piece on 'How Relevant is JNU?'.[122] A young faculty from inside, Arun Kumar, responded by asking him to do a proper audit, saying that since they at JNU were 'unable to conduct an honest enquiry, outsiders can show us what we should be attempting in any case'.[123] In the meantime, there were voices in parliament demanding 'legal action to recover the mess bill which rose up to 2,64,803 from 622 students as against a mess security of mere 62,200'.[124]

One immediately noticed an emerging pattern in these attacks. The moment the students and teachers presented a united front, a virulent attack came from the Hindu communal forces which always waited for such an occasion. *Organiser*, on 24 October 1981, a week before the university demonstrated its oppositional mettle, demanded that the 'South Delhi colleges' be affiliated 'to JNU to cure the communist menace'.[125] This was precisely the Jana Sangh strategy in Aligarh in the early 1960s. Now a Jana Sangh member in parliament, JNU teacher M.L. Sondhi, wrote a letter demanding a change in the selection committees. The founders, particularly S. Gopal and G. Parthasarathi, had structured the selection committee in such a way that the smaller centres did not become victims of the whims of the outside experts. They ensured that a couple of outside experts did not thrust their ephemeral choices on the relatively small centres. They therefore included the seniormost professor into the selection committee along with the chairperson, thereby giving the vision and aspirations of the centre a bigger say in the selection committee meetings. Now, this was the most effective tool to sustain the departmental character, notwithstanding its frequent misuse to recruit former students of the centre concerned or to keep undesirable elements out.[126]

Sondhi had been one of the critics of both Mrs Gandhi's foreign policy and the centrist orientation of the School of International Studies since the outset.[127] With the attack on Mrs Gandhi, the attack on the university began to take a strident form. On 3 December 1981, JNU's recruitment policy was attacked in the Lok Sabha.[128] The attacks came thick and fast. The discussion regarding the statistics of students not completing their Ph.D and M.Phil was in the public domain much to the chagrin of the mentors of the university. One news item said that 265 M.Phil and Ph.D degrees had remained incomplete during 1970–77.[129]

Under these circumstances, when an altogether negative image was being portrayed in the press, one heard that they had decided to change the university's admission policy. Immediately, there was an outcry against the move inside the university.[130] Outside, the members of the Janata Party raised their objections in the parliament.[131]

There were also strong protests from within the university about the way the students' leadership had emerged by painting the teachers in a completely wrong colour. A sociologist from within wrote an interesting write-up on the way the 'the friendlier leader' and 'anti-students establishment' syndrome had been developed. He wrote about how the issue of the number of students to be admitted needed to be decided carefully as they would be needing hostels. 'In the mid-seventies,' he wrote, 'under the pressure from the students' union, which attacked JNU's elitism, the numbers to be admitted were increased for schools not needing lab facilities. Additional students were accommodated by putting two students in some hostel rooms which were meant for one. In later years, additional hostel space had to be improvised on an ad hoc basis. More recently as the margin for improvisation ran out, fresh hostel capacity was not built, and new students have been largely left to their own devices.'[132] To make matters worse, older student leaders by now have started informally arranging for the newcomers to live together in groups of four or more in rooms designed for one. Over time, these leaders would convince them that the university's administration and teachers were anti-student and that the leaders were their true friends and leaders.' He also went on to write: 'In JNU, democratic rights come to include peaceful agitation which now permits virtually psychological pressure against anyone believed to be in "authority". Furthermore if a group is defined as being an adversary—say the university teachers—it has become established usage to raise slogans, calling that group shameless, VC's dog, corrupt, fascist, and so forth.'[133] To anyone who has stayed in JNU, either as a student or as a teacher, this seemed all too familiar, albeit quite bereft of the overall idea of the democracy that they claimed existed.

12

1983: The Revolution That Was Not

> A serious danger lies in the growing discord on the campus. The situation has not yet become alarming, but the future seems grim. Their own political convictions and the spotlight that is constantly turned on the campus prompt many students and teachers to see themselves as actors on the stage of history. They tend therefore to interpret events according to the role they have assumed for themselves. This may plunge the campus into tension and violence.[1]

In the summer of 1983, the political temperature at the Aravali ridges was beginning to soar as well. There was a deep conviction among a large section of students that the teachers were anti-student. This tallied with the left argument that unless the teachers conformed to the political ideas of the left—of various hues—they were definitely anti-student, or worse, agents of the state. Indian society in the meanwhile was rapidly evolving and the political situation was no longer what it was in the 1970s. Admissions to JNU had a brand new angle. There was evidence that the liberal admission policy was being used to bring in kindred spirits and kinsfolk. With the institutions of learning collapsing in eastern India, a seat in JNU was a grand prize. The lustre of a seat in JNU was enhanced by the advent of the celebrated MCA (master of computer applications) course which was almost equivalent to the American MS and therefore guaranteed a job in the newly created computer industry. Significantly, this was the department where corrupt practices in admissions were reported the most. In most cases the staff, both teaching and non-teaching, and students were involved.

Plans to amend the admission policy were mooted at this juncture. Vested groups in almost all segments of the university were, as was to be expected, not comfortable with the idea. For most of the non-teaching staff this meant fewer chances for the free entry of their wards into JNU, while for many left parties, loss of easy entry for party cadres. There were moves to counter the adoption of a new watertight admissions policy.[2] The policy was naturally deemed 'anti-students'. Relay hunger strikes were planned to demand a reversion to the old admissions policy.[3]

A Headless Institution

The year 1983 was another year of uncertainty. With the resignation of Y. Nayudumma as VC and his return to the scientific world, JNU was without a head. In fact, there was no dedicated head of the university since the days of Nag Choudhuri. His term too had been marred by the Emergency and widening chasms amongst the teachers, and between the students and teachers. In the meantime, the winds of change continued to blow irrevocably. One school was closed down while two science schools were being set up. Unfortunately, there was no Parthasarathi to give guidance, and Nag Choudhuri had neither the personality nor the time to dedicate to these enterprises.

This was also the end of an era of sequential crises in the Indian universities that began in the 1960s. Aligarh Muslim University was finally settling down with the AMU Bill and, despite strong protests from its own senior faculty, vested interests including the government of the day tried to invest it with a 'minority status'. BHU was relatively peaceful but in an academic morass, while Osmania was virtually lost in provincial oblivion. In the east, Calcutta University was beginning a new communist regimentation while Visva-Bharati continued living its peaceful localized life with local politics increasingly taking over. The institutions in UP were busy deciding whether to allow students to copy or not, thereby making a mockery of the idea of excellence. Institutions in Bihar had already collapsed into the provincial and caste quicksand. Not long afterwards, Bombay University, which already had no national standing on many fronts, was in the news when the chief minister's offspring was helped by raising her marks.[4]

The Tamil Nadu universities were a class apart, on the road to becoming the largest entrepreneurial business network whose one important product would be the software people, and any criticism would be perceived as smacking of casteism or northern Brahminical bias. But many students inclined to social sciences would drift to Delhi via a couple of attempts at the civil services exams. In this sense Delhi's emergence as the centre for the preparation for various examinations related to administration helped the universities, particularly JNU, gain a relatively better selection of students for social science research. From the south and Maharashtra, many would come to JNU to enrol themselves into courses in German or political science or sociology, or those who were taken in by the glamour of the civil services or foreign affairs would gravitate towards the School of International Studies.

The 1980s was also the time when student protest, the mainstay of the JP movement, was losing its steam as the socialists themselves were divided into many factions and, for the students, they no longer had leaders with any special charm. The communist parties, particularly the CPI(M), emerged as the most organized party following the nationwide strike of the teachers in 1986—one of the longest and biggest in independent India.[5]

1983: The Ominous Signs

The year 1983 opened with a clash between the teachers and the students. It was on the issue of a teacher, P.C. Saxena, abusing a student on caste lines. This was the time when JNU did not have any mobilization along caste lines and there were efforts to raise the issue on alternative lines. Larger democratic methods also prevented such issues being raised in a sectarian manner. Once the complaint was made, the students demanded suspension of the teacher. Students of computer science boycotted classes in protest.[6] The agitation continued for quite a while. The organization called the JNU SC/ST Welfare Association in the campus decided to file a case against the teacher. There were simultaneous demands followed by agitation by the student union for the suspension of the teacher. The students were on strike for three days to press their demand when the JNUTA offered to discuss the issue and negotiate with the JNUSU provided they retracted their demand for the suspension of Saxena and withdrew the police case against him. This created a sharp divide between the students and teachers and, on 16 February 1983, JNU teachers observed a token strike and staged a protest dharna. As the student agitation proceeded, the division grew more defined. Incidentally, there was no contest in the JNUTA election that year.[7]

The acting vice chancellor, P.N. Srivastava, chaired an emergency meeting of the executive committee on 17 February 1983, which took place in the boardroom of the neighbouring Indian Institute of Technology. They reached a consensus to seek legal opinion whether the university could appoint an inquiry committee after a criminal case had been filed against the teacher.[8] Srivastava thereafter stood firm and, despite enormous pressure from different quarters including continued strikes and dharnas, he did not agree to suspend Saxena. He said that there was a possibility that the issue would be resolved in a day or two but if the students precipitated a strike-like situation, he threatened that he would not hesitate to close down the university.[9] JNUTA in a conciliatory mood, suggested a joint inquiry into the alleged misbehaviour of Saxena, with students, teachers and members of the SC and ST Commission. The JNUTA firmly refused to accept the students' demand for suspension of Saxena, and reportedly said that they would oppose it even if Saxena was arrested, as that was not enough to prove his guilt. Only a court could possibly pronounce him guilty, and only if it was a criminal offence as such. The teachers, it is said, told the students that it was not proper to register a police complaint when a political battle was being fought.

The students' union made it clear that a case has been filed by the JNU SC/ST Welfare Association; when asked to persuade the association to withdraw its case, the students' union replied that the legal position, according to its understanding, was that once registered, a case could not be withdrawn.[10] The JNUTA made a plea to call off the strike and argued that it was undemocratic to ask for suspension without a proper enquiry.[11] Discussions dragged on as the students went on an indefinite blockade of the administrative building even as the vice chancellor requested all segments to create a congenial atmosphere.[12]

These events indicated another dimension into which the student movement was drifting: it was succumbing to the pressures of competitive politics. Competitive politics in the context of maximalist stands, as we have seen, is a dangerous and heady cocktail. The caste issue was apparently taken up by the JNU SC/ST Welfare Association whose political target was the Marxist students. This was no surprise as this was exactly what happened in Maharashtra where the Dalit leadership mobilized opinion and replaced the communist leadership, the movement happening along class lines. The students' union and parties raised the demand for punishment—a maximalist demand in order to displace the Dalit position. Earlier in August, the JNU SC/ST Welfare Association had made a similar case against another teacher.[13] The JNU students' complete failure to take the moral high ground in politics was patently obvious. Instead, in the name of democracy, they had succumbed to populism.

The goings on within the campus was not ignored by the outside world.[14] The influential Delhi newspaper, *Hindustan Times*, covered the ongoing events with a scathing attack on the university's affairs, and a screaming headline: 'Anarchy at JNU'. It wrote, 'Long ago the initiative in the university was wrested by a handful of teachers and students belonging to the two communist parties.'[15] As for the teachers, it went on to say: 'While a majority of the teachers had resigned themselves to a blatant pursuit of careerism, the committed minority bred an ethos of sectarianism.'[16] The harangue continued:

> Corrupt administrators and dishonest professors competed with each other to turn the university into an academic wasteland; to all those who questioned or cautioned about the direction JNU was taking, their refrain was to parrot the excellence and uniqueness of the university. The only distinction that the university can now claim is that it produces better pamphleteers than scholars. Today the same professional agitators among the students have turned against their initiators.
>
> As the affairs of the university became murkier, its original godfathers washed their hands of it. Those in high places like the ministry of education and the University Grants Commission, whose job it was to keep an eye on the university's development, found their misdemeanours so overwhelming that they would rather leave the can of worms unopened. By and large, the members of parliament, the press and the public suffered from JNU fatigue. The chasm between the dream and the reality of JNU was so wide that perhaps no one would lose any sleep over it if the university was simply dismantled.[17]

The general body meeting of the students took place on 24 February 1983 and it decided to boycott P.C. Saxena. Out of 770 students, 403 voted for this course of action.[18] JNU was closed for the next two days. Armed with the executive committee's approval to take necessary and appropriate action, the vice chancellor declared closure of university (sine die) on 26 February 1983, which seemed a bit of an overkill.[19] A contemporary report depicted the events in detail:

> Since Friday evening, the students have been picketing at the acting vice chancellor, P.N. Srivastava's residence as a measure of gherao. On Saturday, even visitors to the V.C.'s residence were denied admission as a part of the students' intensification programme. Authorities, finding things going from bad to worse, announced the indefinite closure of the varsity which had a student strength of over 3,000, most of them at the post-graduate level.[20]

Although the authorities asked the students to vacate the hostels at the earliest, the students, with the organizational and institutional memory, knew that they could run the hostels as they did on the previous occasion in the 1970s. Therefore the students 'broke open the locks of the messes and ran them on their own, as they had vowed they would not vacate the hostels'.[21] Srivastava, speaking to a reporter at his residence said that 'he was avoiding calling in the police despite the grave provocations from a section of students to avoid confrontation, adding that, 'after all they are our students'. At the same time, he was firm in not giving in to the threats of the students.[22]

In the meantime, the agitation continued and now members of the JNUSU continued their gherao of the acting VC for the fourth day in succession. The JNUSU members pitched tents outside Srivastava's residence to press their demand for the suspension.[23] The gherao was lifted only on 1 March 1983 after a GBM decided to lift the gherao, by a margin of 163 out of 800 students.[24] The university reopened on 2 March 1983, and teaching resumed.[25] However, all this was merely the dress rehearsal for a longer and much more painful affair in the ensuing summer.

Summer of 1983

Jalees Ahmed was a doctoral student in environmental sciences who was in the university for quite some time trying to finish his thesis. It was probably a sense of frustration which led to his surly and rude attitude towards one of the hostel wardens, M. Alam. As per the available reports, Alam was merely ensuring that the hostel rules were being followed, imposing some minor disciplinary action on Ahmed when the situation took an unfortunate turn. Alam's wife was alone at home, when Ahmed arrived and proceeded to make a scene and abused both Alam and his wife. A complaint was lodged on 4 March 1983. The next day, the provost found Ahmed's explanation unsatisfactory and he was asked to leave the hostel. As was the norm, the students intervened on Ahmed's behalf, and explained the pressure he was under with the deadline for his Ph.D thesis fast approaching. Relenting, the university, on 24 March 1983, asked him to shift to a neighbouring hostel. The order was 'defied', and, as journalist C.N. Chittaranjan wrote, 'Ahmed's friends, who should have persuaded him to comply with such a mild order, did nothing of the kind.'[26] A fresh order was issued again on 14 April 1983, asking him to shift to Ganga from Jhelum Hostel within forty-eight hours, submit an apology and pay a fine of Rs 50. When Ahmed neither complied with the order nor responded, on 27 April 1983, the provost, along with the Jhelum Hostel wardens and a couple of administrative staff went to his room and personally requested him to shift. After some initial reluctance, Ahmed agreed to move.

On the same day, the Jhelum Hostel president along with some other students came to the house of the provost of Uttarakhand at 10.30 at night to give him a charter of demands. This was when the gherao of the provost and the wardens began. M.S. Agwani, the rector, who was also the acting vice chancellor while Srivastava was away, came to negotiate. He too was gherao-ed along with two other officials, and the siege continued until late into the evening of 28 April 1983.[27] The situation seemed to have breached the codes of normal self-governing behaviour because this was turning into hooliganism of the worst kind. The students demanded reinstatement of Ahmed in the Jhelum Hostel. As the Jhelum hostel warden's room did not have a telephone connection,

Agwani was unable to communicate the necessary instructions, or call for help. Although eventually the students released Agwani, the gherao continued for the second day at the residence of another warden, Harjit Singh, where Alam had gone to. Neither Alam, nor any of his colleagues thought of summoning the police to break up the gherao.[28] M.S. Agwani made it clear to the students that 'the officials were united and would not be pressurized by such tactics'.[29]

The teachers too seemed to be gearing up for a showdown. The JNU Teachers Association passed a resolution on 29 April 1983 'unequivocally condemning' the gherao of 'any teachers', and demanded that the hostel residents lift their present siege immediately. They also spoke to the acting vice chancellor and insisted 'they wanted the university officials not to take any decision under duress'.[30]

In hindsight, one noticed a very peculiar pattern emerging. While Ahmed was simply given orders to shift to a neighbouring hostel as a disciplinary measure, the students' union had blown it all out of proportion. Henceforth the logic of the students' politics began to take control of the situation. The union was led by a combination of socialist-minded and non-communist student activists. The election of 1983 had returned a combination of anti-SFI-AISF consolidation to the central panel with a socialist-minded political science student, Nalini Ranjan Mohanty, as its president. While the organized communist groups were still smarting from the defeat, the profile of social and political behaviour in the campus had also undergone a change, and in many ways violence had crept in. For the fringe radicals, the situation was tailor-made for them, as they were used to such confrontations. Although they did not have great support in a representative situation, they were self-righteous and arrogant, and considered themselves the custodians of the revolutionary zeal of the masses and representing them in the campus. The radical fringe consisted of students and some faculty who kept their political positions aligned with the future revolution while their academic positions were adjusted to the changes in Western academia.

In the meantime, the gherao continued through the heat of the summer and, as a newspaper journalist found, it was getting 'curiouser'.[31] The gherao, for the first time, collided headlong with the teachers' association as the teachers refused to put up with it any longer and announced that they would boycott classes.[32] As this was the end semester, boycott of classes meant that the teachers would boycott the examination. This sounded an alarm bell and the students' union woke up. The president sent a letter to the JNUTA president, R.R. Sharma, and urged him, 'to call off the JNUTA's confrontational attitude against the students and support their peaceful and democratic agitation'.[33] The letter stated that the agitation had been misconstrued as one against a teacher whereas it was against Alam 'not in his capacity as a teacher but as a warden'.[34]

Alam, however, was as much a teacher as a warden. As we saw, the university planners had made a conscious choice of having the residences of the teachers and students close to each other to foster a sense of collective effort at knowledge production. Thus, the foundational ethos was not that the teachers were to be alienated—although they stayed with their families, they shared the same environment as the students. The JNUSU president's letter sounded hollow. On 2 May 1983, the eerie calm of the campus was broken suddenly by a 'silent protest march by the JNU teachers' wives, demanding immediate release of Alam who was working from the house of his co-warden Harjit Singh'.[35] The residences of the wardens of all these hostels were within their respective hostels, which abutted each other, therefore one could imagine the fear of the wardens' families as they would be at the mercy of the students.

Changing their strategy, the students decided to try an old JNU students' tactic, and the president of the Jhelum Hostel, R.P. Yadav, came forward with an allegation of corruption against the warden. Things were moving fast and the adventurists were moving to the fore to blunt the effectiveness of the union president's personal and union's collective wisdom. There were always radicals in small numbers who saw revolutionary opportunity in every action against its class enemy. Way back in the 1970s, the teachers were defined by the middle-level left as the class enemy, and that had stuck. The students' union now took 'law into their own hands'.[36] 'The students' protest in the form of a gherao had no impact on the "university authorities" who did not accede to the students' demand of setting up an inquiry committee to look into allegations of indiscipline and misbehaviour against Ahmed before transferring him.' The union had changed tack and started accusing the teachers of a confrontational attitude.

As far as the students were concerned, the prerogative for a democratic protest rested with them, which demonstrated the democratic traditions in India. They seemed to have forgotten, however, that all parties which constitute the democratic space must have the same opportunity to enter into a dialogic position no matter what their number or social position. This is how the minorities and other groups lacking numerical strength are favoured in order to have their voice heard properly and get their space in a democracy.

While the communist parties in India used the democratic space to operate in a democracy, they have not displayed much commitment to allow any other formation within that space on many occasions. The more radicalized the left, the more the space it occupied, the less space anyone else got. This explains the intellectual arrogance as well as the violent sectarianism of the more radical left in the country. Democracy, therefore, became a strategic value, not a commitment, and student politics in JNU was letting itself be guided into that route, notwithstanding the assertions of enlarging the democratic space.

According to an eyewitness account, on the night of 2 May 1983, 'a hundred students led by Mohanty and the general secretary broke open the sealed room, earlier allotted to Ahmed and restored the possession of it to him'.[37] The officiating vice chancellor convened a meeting of all deans on 3 May 1983 and reviewed the situation on the campus. It was reported that they 'had decided to take stern action against the JNU students' union president, Mohanty, who had led the students last night'.[38] An influential daily in Delhi revealed that Agwani also met the Lieutenant governor of Delhi and had briefed him about the situation.[39] In the meantime, the vice chancellor, P.N. Srivastava, returned to the city and, on 5 May 1983, the teachers' association openly issued an 'ultimatum' to the vice chancellor to the effect that he must take action against those who had broken open the Jhelum Hostel room and reinstated Ahmed. Otherwise, they said, they would boycott the examination.[40] Srivastava gave the students' leader two days to respond to the show cause in an attempt to bring some semblance of sanity to the situation. He, perhaps knowing the JNU ways of functioning, was trying to give the union a way out in the face of the strong pressure by the teachers.

Now mind games began with the students' union trying to pre-empt both the JNUTA as well as any action against the students' union members. In an early morning meeting on 7 May 1983, the students decided to boycott their exams and, as its vice-president, Sanjeev Chopra announced to the press, 'no force would be applied by the students'.[41] The battle lines had been drawn. The vice chancellor in the meantime had 'served notices to the two other students to show cause within 48 hours as to why they should not be expelled'. Their deadline was 7 May 1983. The students' union now took its second pre-emptive step as a rearguard action. It generated a statement signed by hundreds of students collectively owning up to the decision to break the lock. No one person could now be held responsible. This also pre-empted any action against the president and secretary as it could now be shown that they did not act in their individual capacities when they broke open the hostel room but had been authorized to do so by the students' union council.[42]

The university, in the meantime, witnessed a curious mix of events, in which, with the advantage of hindsight, one can see the way the university was used by various factions. While the president was leading the students in breaking the lock of Ahmed's room, another student, Asrar Ahmed, took the opportunity to break open the lock of room number 20 of the married students' hostel which had been locked by the university authorities after they had evicted its resident, Rama Shankar Yadav, who had ceased to be a registered student of the university. Rama Shankar Yadav had been on a fast-unto-death dharna outside the vice chancellor's office, which apparently entered the tenth day on 5 May 1983. Asrar Ahmed was duly served a show cause notice, the episode reflecting the situation in the university.

There were concerns from sympathetic sections. *Patriot*, an organ of the Communist Party of India, and generally sympathetic towards the students, could sense that things had got out of hand. It called the announcement of boycott as something forced and not political.[43] It was not political, as it further argued, because it found the 'students' cause "patently artificial"'. Significantly, it also found the hero of the piece an 'anti-hero' and the whole situation was not inspirational. As for the warden, the daily said he too was 'no hero', but was a decent man, who 'possessed at least a modicum of good sense to postpone the enforcement of the transfer order for a whole month when the hostel resident pleaded for a respite'.[44] However, *Patriot's* worst criticism was reserved for the union leadership which 'for no valid reason raised a local dispute to the level of an all university issue'.[45] In an almost prophetic vein the paper continued:

> The authorities and faculty of teachers have shown commendable restraint combined with dignified firmness. They have half won the battle, while the students are moving towards a resounding fall. But at what cost to the future of their alma mater—presumably a concept alien to their way of thinking.[46]

On 9 May 1983, with no response from the student leaders, Srivastava issued a letter asking the student leaders to submit their representation as their grave misconduct would invite appropriate punishment in the form of expulsion. All segments of the students' political formations seemed to have been gearing for just such a moment:

- the communist outfits were ready with their organized party cadres;
- the agitated students who had somehow wrested the union presidentship from the communists, were sensitive to any attack on their president; and
- the socialists, with not much constructive student politics behind them, included a future Central minister, Digvijay Singh, a research scholar from Bihar.

'A rumour began to go around that the vice chancellor had expelled the student,' narrated Shyam Narain Singh, who was a new but very active student. He had just sat down for lunch at his Periyar Hostel mess when the news came that Mohanty had been expelled. Immediately, he, like many others rushed to the house of the vice chancellor, i.e., house Number 104, which was about 200 metres from the hostel, in the Uttarakhand Hall of Residence. The vice chancellor was with the rector, Agwani. The house soon filled up with the students and a gherao began. The registrar, R.S. Batra was also brought in from his office, so no officials were left out. C.N. Chittaranjan, a senior journalist and champion of civil rights, seems to have reported the developments most accurately. His report also more or less captures the situation narrated to me by many who were present there:

> Students packed the VC's drawing room and filled the lawn and other space around the house. Prof. Agwani, the rector, was with the VC at the time. The registrar R.S. Batra was dragged from his office and brought to the same place. The three were made to sit in three corners, while noisy students, shouting obnoxious slogans, filled all the remaining space. Contrary to the claims later made by the students, it is learnt that whenever food was brought for the victims, such insulting slogans were raised as to make it impossible for the hostages to eat or drink. Electricity and the telephone lines were cut off. In the night, however, power was restored, because of the discomfort of the students, who were themselves from well-to-do families, rather than out of consideration for the three victims of the siege. Prof. Srivastava said that the abusive language used by the students was of a kind 'hitherto unknown in JNU, at least for the last eight years since I have been in this university'.
>
> The gherao began at about noon on May 9 1983, and only at 3 p.m. was Prof. Agwani's wife able to go in to have a look at her husband (who was a heart patient), while Prof. Srivastava's daughter, who had been sent to a colleague's house, was allowed in to see her father for a couple of minutes at 5.30 p.m. The three gherao-ed men were not allowed to talk to one another, and the vice chancellor and his colleagues were held incommunicado for a full fifty hours, during which they could hardly eat or have a wink of sleep. It appears that when any of them leaned back and closed his eyes he was pulled up with deafening noises or nudged awake and made to sit up. And outside, rumours were being spread that they were eating normal food, and that they were fine.
>
> Unable to stand the suspense and cruelty, when fifty faculty wives, with a handful of professors who had followed them to make sure they were not harmed, marched in a silent procession to the VC's besieged house to protest and plead, the rowdy group present was so vulgar as to shout offensive slogans at them.[47]

There were poignant moments to this story: Balasubramanian, a young clerk in the vice chancellor's office was admired by both students and teachers alike, and eventually went on to become the deputy registrar in the evaluation section. When he went to the vice chancellor's house on the first day of siege, presumably the students assumed he was one of them and allowed him in, and Srivastava managed to communicate to Balasubramanian to postpone the engagement of his (Srivastava's) daughter which was to take place the next day.[48] Suddenly one student recognized Balasubramanian and raised the alarm. However, he managed to quickly exit, and successfully relayed the message to defer the engagement date.

In this chaotic situation, Srivastava courageously gave three options to the union:

(a) The union must express regret for whatever they did between 27 April and 2 May 1983;
(b) It must restore status quo ante as on 27 April 1983, and the administration would simultaneously withdraw all actions contemplated against the students; and
(c) The students must accept an enquiry by a Supreme Court or high court judge into the events from 27 April to 10 May 1983.[49]

To the commentators, these were 'in the circumstances, eminently reasonable proposals'.[50] Of the few teachers who had access to the premises during the gherao, the two teachers closest to the students found these suggestions rational. However, they were obviously not heeded by the extremists present who shouted down every alternative.

The situation was rapidly deteriorating when the university doctor was finally allowed to enter and pronounced that dehydration had set in, and all three victims were in bad shape, particularly Batra. Chittaranjan reports that it was at this stage that representations were made to the lieutenant governor by the wives of some of the teachers. On 10 May, it was decided at that level that intervention could not be delayed without actually endangering the lives of those under gherao, and the police arrived, rescued the three men and arrested the thirty-seven students who resisted them.[51] Some accounts say that the police lathi-charged the students, seriously injuring some students, one of whom had his kneecap smashed.[52]

There are several different accounts of the sequence of events from this point onwards. The two clear points that began to emerge were: (a) the students went berserk and (b) they targeted their attack on people who were perceived as anti-student. The mob, which had no discernible composition, vented their frustration by indiscriminately stoning teachers' houses and cars. Specially singled out were Alam, Srivastava and the other Jhelum warden, Harjit Singh. Their houses were ransacked, and articles were damaged or stolen, books were burnt and arson attempted.[53] The attacks on the homes of both the wardens of Jhelum Hostel, Harjit Singh and Alam, were vicious. Had Harjit Singh not stood at the door stopping the crowd with a crowbar, the fates of his wife and children can only be guessed. Similarly, Alam's wife had stepped forward and shouted to the crowd to kill her before touching her husband.

Interestingly, there were instances where the students themselves surged forward to prevent the mob from further mayhem. Alam thanked a student, Jogendra, who came forward and challenged the mobbing crowd to kill him first before touching Dr Alam's wife. A similar incident was narrated by Amrik Singh, who had come to visit Bipan Chandra.

There were selective attacks on the teachers' homes. The *Mainstream* author found that the houses of teachers known to be progressive or liberal, Professor Bipan Chandra and Professor Bhambhri, were chosen for the blitzes. While the proctor, Rameswar Singh, was badly beaten up, the previous proctor, K.P. Mishra's house was attacked. There were attempts at arson as well.[54]

> ... By 7 p.m. the violence had by and large abated except for sporadic instances which continued to erupt until 9 p.m. It was only by about 7.30 p.m., around the time the police returned, that a large number of students—many of whom were not present on campus earlier—assembled on Jhelum lawns. They broke the section 144, which had been imposed and courted arrest against the police action on campus.[55]

Amrik Singh, an eminent educationist and one with a keen eye on the matters of universities, had come to JNU that afternoon to meet Bipan Chandra. Bipan Chandra's house was attacked by a group of students shouting accusations that it was he who had called in the police. Amrik Singh had parked his car near the entrance of the university. Mistaking it for another history professor's, (Satish Chandra), the mob smashed the car. A week later, he published a rare eyewitness account of the incident. To him the sequence of events was like this: 'In a commando-like move, the police rescued the VC and the two other officials from the vice chancellor's house where they had been kept under gherao for more than fifty hours. This was a little before 5 p.m. Those students who resisted the police entry into the house were taken into custody, and the police left the campus within 20 or 30 minutes. The thinking behind this quick operation seemed to be that if the police were not around there would be no possibility of a clash between the students and the police.'[56]

According to him, the students in JNU over the years 'have been steadily losing respect for their teachers. To say that the attitude of some of these students borders on contempt, would be no exaggeration.'[57] It was with this attitude that the students 'openly flouted the authority of the teachers as well as that of the administration'.[58] Amrik Singh found that the strong stand of the teachers' association by declaring that they would not conduct 'the examination till such time when suitable action against those guilty of defiance of rules had been taken' created further 'estrangement between the students and teachers'.[59]

Amrik Singh's description of the events immediately following the departure of the police is of rare value. The students, stupefied by the speedy rescue operation by the police, did not quite know how to vent their frustration. They decided to unleash their anger against the teachers. Within half an hour they were on a rampage. Amrik Singh was inside the house of Bipan Chandra, who he realized was their special target. According to his account:

> In a tidal wave, nearly fifty students started stoning a particular house. There was a brief pause and I assumed they were probably busy stoning houses other than the one in which I happened to be. The next wave came when students converged into the quadrangle and started breaking windowpanes in a systematic and ruthless manner.

> No fewer than two dozen fairly large missiles were hurled at one particular house. The stoning continued for about 15 minutes. Hardly any glass panes were left intact. We had been alerted even before the students arrived that there was going to be an attack and that some of the houses could even be burnt. Luckily arson did not take place, but the stoning was heavy.
>
> If it were not for the protective iron grills surrounding many of the homes, which impeded the entry of the marauders, I am certain that there would have been many more casualties.[60]

Prof. Amrik Singh went on to say that soon after another group of about thirty students tried to break into the house he was in. He mentioned that the crowd eventually dispersed because one student told them that he was willing to lay down his life before he allowed them to break into the house.

According to Prof Singh there were three rounds of attacks within a span of fifty minutes. All around the quadrangle there was complete chaos and remorseless stoning. A number of vehicles including his own were vandalized. Prof Singh also reported that in a number of places some students restrained the rest from breaking into houses.

The police arrived more than half an hour after the stonings were over even though they were contacted soon after the first wave of stoning.[61]

The violence at Bipan Chandra's house that Amrik Singh so graphically described was intriguing. Immediately after the police left taking with them the three gherao-ed officials, another stoning mob appeared on the scene. And a short while later, Amrik Singh observed, yet another, and this time a more organized, horde arriving and joining in with their attack of the house. The professor was saved by the strong resistance offered by a student. Chandra observed that the attacking group included some of the students whom he had served tea and for whom he had written recommendations. He felt that he had been attacked on this occasion for no reason because he had neither summoned the police nor was he in any way anti-student. Bipan Chandra was considered one of the strongest pillars of support for students. However, he admitted, this episode had strengthened his resolve to stand firm and defend the faculty, and to insist that the deans and other officials call for police assistance at the least sign of trouble, especially as two of the gherao-ed officials had heart conditions.[62]

On an earlier occasion, in 1981-82, when Mahale's house was picketed for long hours, Bipan Chandra had spoken about how gherao-ing of the teachers' houses violated the teachers' rights. While there were a large number of prevaricative statements by many teachers, Bipan Chandra had chosen to articulate clearly on the issue. Perhaps the student activists were acting on this historical memory. Perhaps this was why his house was chosen for special attack.

Soon after the violence erupted, the university authorities declared the closure of the university sine die and asked all students, including M.Phil. and Ph.D scholars to vacate their rooms in the hostels.

Many students who were not in the campus at the time of these happenings also courted arrest protesting against police action in particular and against police intervention in the university affairs in general.

Life in Jail

The students, who were arrested on the campus, were first taken to Dhaula Kuan, a major transport terminal a couple of kilometres away in the north-easterly direction on Ring Road. At this stop, the students were granted permission to go home and many promptly left for the hostel or their homes from Dhaula Kuan. Some students, however, decided not to leave as they reckoned it was getting late anyway and it would be difficult to get transport. They remained in Dhaula Kuan and were later transported to Tihar Jail. The Indian police generally give students and other minor miscreants the option to go home to save themselves the administrative and judicial red tape which accompanies throwing people in gaol. Students until recently were always treated with kid gloves unless they were radically very violent. Many students, therefore, landed in Tihar involuntarily. In Tihar they had to register their names and with a sudden surge of courage they concocted pseudonyms for themselves. One student became Romila Thapar, while another called himself Namwar Singh (an eminent professor of Hindi), son of Janwar (animal) Singh. One student became Vikas Chandra, son of Bipan Chandra, whose house, unbeknownst to them, was at that very moment under attack.

In the next couple of days, sixty-seven students, mostly girls, managed to get themselves released by exploiting the Indian jails' leniency towards the students of the prestigious university. Eight kind-hearted warders were suspended by the jail authorities. However, the jail life, which would remain an unforgettable experience for many, provided the student lessons in sociology, which was not taught in their theory-oriented campus. They had been told by their comrades-in-arms and their surplus theory theoreticians that students were, as a class, an organic intellectual, and the party was the vanguard of the revolution. Those of higher economic and social standing were immediately taken out on bail by their party comrades or family members. But the rest had to fend for themselves. Notwithstanding the general body meeting organized within the jail, life was not very pleasant for some who realized that if he had passed the main examination for the civil services and if this jail experience went on his record, the chances of fulfilling the dream of his family and himself would come to nothing. Characters like these were seen crying like children.

On the other hand there were the JP movement veterans who had been to jail previously and JNU was some sort of refuge in their post-JP-movement phase. They were there to smoothen the life of the first-timers in jail. Mohanji, for example, took Vagish Jha under his wing as an assistant in the kitchen. People like Dilip Upadhyay would soon be popular as he was seen as a friendly person by the senior inmates of the jail who were serving long sentences. Lal Chand, a science researcher, would lob his imaginary ball every other minute. However, it soon came to light that he was completely disoriented and discussion with him revealed how the authoritative and dictatorial nature of many science professors of the university was responsible for his mental state. JNU's science departments were moving towards, it seemed, the other science departments in the country.

Digvijay Singh from Bihar was a born leader in a feudal set-up and naturally the jail staff realized this and 'dada' was given a full piece of chicken one day. They had, however, never seen a students' group nurtured in a democratic environ who would soon create a big hue and cry objecting to this unequal treatment in a democratic public space like the prison, maintained by the state. Tihar witnessed a general body meeting—perhaps for the first and last time. There was no cross-party or cross-class solidarity demonstrated in getting the students released—the university itself had come forward to get them released irrespective of their affiliations.

The jail, however, was an unsure proposition for those whose party had not organized their bail, or who had nowhere to call. The journey of a lifetime had begun for many. However, they were all released gradually when the university requested withdrawal of the cases. The jail experience generally unites people with a shared common experience. However, this was not the case here as discrimination by the party, by colleagues, and even by leadership was to make the experience bitter for those who had hitherto been taught class solidarity. It also brought a cynicism instead of a new resolve. Interestingly, to a radical section, which saw revolution in every emerging opportunity, this added to their self-righteousness. It is this section, which would in future try and position itself as the intellectual vanguard of the consciousness-raising intellectual class, it was a dark beginning indeed.

Taking Responsibility

The university started its disciplinary process and initially forty students got show cause notices.[63] By June 1983, three JNU students, Mohanty, Sajal Mitra and Ahmed were rusticated for three years.[64] A retired judge of Delhi High Court, Justice Prithvi Raj, was invited to conduct the inquiry.[65] In the meantime, fourteen more students were rusticated on 19 July 1983.[66] Later on, in December, many other students, found to be involved in misdemeanours, were expelled.[67]

The process began by issuing show cause notices to these students. One of the issues was the petition which the union presented with the signatures of several students owning up to the breaking of the door lock of Ahmed's room. Most of the students disowned their signatures and some protested that their signature was taken without the true reason being explained to them. Many others said that such signatures were a routine affair and, as conscientious students, they always signed.[68]

As to the show cause notices issued to the students for participating in violent activities, most denied they were there at all. Some claimed they were not in the university, some professed to have been in the library and yet others swore they were away doing field study.[69] Those who insisted that their names were wrongly implicated also said that they did not favour the violence to which the agitating students had taken recourse. The SFI–AISF's approach to the notice was legalistic. The office-bearers like Bishnupriya Gupta, Anwar Alam and others accused the administration of conducting a wrong disciplinary process as the process mentioned no responsibility, or lack of it, of the administration for the mindless violence. This was exactly what Amrik Singh had talked about—no respect for the teachers—although the university, at the end of the day, was a community of students, teachers and the staff.[70]

There were two distinct shades to the reactions of intellectuals to the issue. The more mature left reflected their pain on seeing the events unfold and at the same time wanted to see things fall into place soon. What was interesting was the muted reaction to the students' violence and behaviour from a politically vocal group of teachers and students. There was absolutely no public censure to the ferocity of the students and the left student bodies. On the contrary, the students holding responsible positions in the union seemed to be justifying the violence. One lady office-bearer of the union and a member of the SFI commented that the vice chancellor's house was ransacked by the commandoes in civilian clothes and that the vice chancellor did not intervene when the police assaulted the students in his presence. This cynical justification bordered on sanctimonious arrogance and even several students realized this and tried to negotiate with the agitating students in an attempt to reason with them. The first public gesture condemning the act of violence came from individual initiatives in a letter signed by about 100 students from across the university issued on 31 May 1983.

The moral act of courting arrest on the evening too, as we shall see, soon gave way to the immorality of giving false names and then escaping from the jail using the leniency of the jail staff. The impersonation created problems for many whose names appeared but who had nothing to do with the whole affair. They had to appear before the court for many years even after many of the students had successfully been established in their lives. This too does not speak highly of the level of moral commitment to a cause.

While the intelligentsia and the larger society were still debating about what had happened, events continued to unfold inexorably. The outgoing president was trying to put the pieces together and restart the agitation. The vice chancellor was also determined to see the whole process through. Although there were some students who were trying to bring peace, and sought logical explanations, nobody paid much attention to their reasoning. One student did begin articulating the logic but quickly retracted his argument lest he be perceived as a renegade to cause of the revolution.[71] This is a major handicap in correctly analysing any movement where the intelligentsia is involved, as most often these analyses are based on half-truths and self-justification.

In the meantime, there were efforts to see that the university was not tarnished for ever and for mobilization of intellectuals and opinion makers. This seemed to be important in a situation like the JNU's, which had been beset with criticism from both within and without. The charge of being elitist and leftist emanated from within while the society was giving it space to experiment with a new kind of institution building. During the post-Emergency period, a serious questioning about the university and its existence began to manifest in the media and opinion makers in the capital. The Hindu communal groups also played an important role.

On 10 June 1983, Bipan Chandra and some of his friends in the Delhi Study Group organized a panel discussion on whether JNU was a sick university. Nalini Ranjan Mohanty was also a speaker in the discussion. The other speakers included V.P. Dutt, a former pro-vice-chancellor of Delhi University and an eminent intellectual of Delhi.[72] Bipan Chandra did not speak about the attack on his house, but he talked at length about the academic excellence of its faculty and its students and hoped that the crisis was part of the growth of the university.[73] For the study group, there was more at stake than just the ego of a president of a union. What was significant was that on 8 June 1983 the JNU had expelled Mohanty, Sajal Mittra and Jalees Ahmed.[74] The panel discussed how the incident was an aberration in the otherwise democratic nature of the university life. Mohanty indicated that the university should heal the rupture as soon as possible and bring the students back into its fold.

Was it going to be that easy after what was demonstrated on the evening of 9 May 1983? While the largest number who went to jail were the socialists (the new students, mostly from Bihar, etc.), those who now began to take over the reins were the SFI members, and although there was a deep-seated cynicism, there was no remorse.

The Nihilist Soul

There were serious discussions in 1989 as to why the course of student politics went the way it did in May 1983. Allegations and counter-allegations had surfaced within the collective memory of the campus. The organized party had an institutional power to sustain its own claim; the SFI and its allies, the AISF and the fringe radicals, would call the shots because the socialists, Free Thinkers and Samata Yuvajan Samaj had all but vanished from the scene. Their departure had given the space to various other formations to which the social, political and economic changes had given rise.

Surprisingly, in 1989, one realized that administratively the university was run in a very archaic manner and there were no proper chains of command. Beneath the surface of a very friendly administrative staff and collegial and non-corrupt atmosphere, there was nothing to prevent group pressure, particularly if it was from the staff or from the students. While listening to the debate as a new student, in 1989, when the 1983 incident was brought up, one thought about the possibility of a recurrence of the same politics. It was entirely possible, especially with the changing dynamics of the politics of the 1990s. Although it would not take a violent stand, with the completely changed atmosphere across the country, it would be just as corrosive for the university. Whenever the negotiations seemed to be close to a settlement, an opposing faction would raise slogans scuttling the progress made. The ultimate purpose, though shown to be revolution, at the heart of it is to humiliate anyone in authority. Tony Judt saw this in France in 1968.[75]

The 1983 violence was seen by most students in the campus as the watershed moment because it ushered in the new admissions policy which changed the character of the student body for all time to come. However, the most significant outcome was that the students were once again involved in the admissions process.

In the years to come, the admissions policy of that era was put on a pedestal because students were part of this process. The reorganization however put paid to all of these and placed a clear-cut demarcation between the students and the teachers. The SFI was instrumental in drawing this line for its own political advantage when it declared that the student and the teacher were adversaries.

As for the moot question of responsibility, most of the time it was the SFI which was held responsible for the entire violent episode: it had been in the opposition and fearful of its own loosening its grip on the reins, it had egged on the union leadership and denied it any space for negotiation. However, the reality was far more complex than just one party being responsible. The 1983 catastrophe benefited the SFI in the sense that the different political views were now no longer quite as forceful as before. It was important now to project a responsible formation to attract the new students. Both the SFI and the AISF were in a better position to do so, especially with their close association with the party-affiliated teachers, better organization and the decent middle-class demeanour of many of its cadres who were there to make careers in a respectable organization rather than to make revolutions, notwithstanding rhetoric to the contrary.

One of the biggest losses of the students' movement of 1983 was that it destroyed the potential of a socialist intellectual formation. Notwithstanding its limited vision, the socialist movement in India had been close to the Indian reality and tried to theoretically arrive at some position to mobilize people. It so happened that in the mid-1960s it became the voice of the middle castes and middle peasants and they had a sizeable hold among the youth and students in a large part of the country. In the universities like BHU, Allahabad, Patna, Lucknow, Bombay, Gorakhpur, Osmania and many others, the student intellectuals and leaders would gravitate to the socialist parties. Socialists were the natural enemies of the communist parties and the socialists kept up an intellectual fight even if quite often it was only through their journals. By the mid-1970s, JNU was emerging as a place where many students could be in touch with the socialist leaders and had some sort of camaraderie established.

In 1983, many student leaders were of a socialist inclination and their failure to lead, and not succumb to pressure by the other more intelligent and organized communist parties, dealt a deathblow to any chance of a socialist intellectual movement in JNU. This was unfortunate as a large number of the students belonged to regions where the socialists were in a dominant position and understood the society better than the communists did. The intellectuals could have given the socialist movement a better direction or at least checked the monstrosities in the shape of the various Janata Party regimes in different parts of India, characterized by their gargantuan corruption, casteism and fissiparous tendencies..

The shining part of the whole episode was the development and growth of that of human solidarity that the political and social life of the university which often evolved into a deep-seated friendship between the lower staff, common men and women in the city and the students. Many students who had nowhere to go during those fateful days when the hostels were closed down, got shelter in the houses of the security guards, peons and other people in JNU campus. In fact, the drivers of the DTC buses also came in to help the students during the crisis. One beautiful story of the humane bonding at JNU was narrated to me by an old student who had stayed with the family of a chowkidar.

13

The Rupture

Picking up pieces from the 1983 rubble, the students, teachers and the political formations began trying to put the campus back on the rails. The presence of Ph.D and M.Phil programmes assured the continuation of most of the earlier faces and practices. The communists remained unscathed. The socialists and others formations which were in the lead during the 1983 movement could not regroup themselves that easily and increasingly became of no consequence. It left the Free Thinkers to be the only force to give competition to the combined, organized strength of the Students Federation of India (SFI) and All India Students Federation (AISF). Although the fringe radicals and those groups which espoused Maoist and other revolutionary methods of violence had been exposed, a section of them were still able to don the mantle of representing JNU's anti-establishment radicalism by glorifying the violence of the previous years and vilifying a set of teachers by describing them as pro-establishment quislings.

The SFI and the CPI(M) teachers, whose brinkmanship while showing the other groups their place was in many ways responsible for the situation, blamed the anarchists and pro-establishment teachers for the events of the summer of 1983. The presence of teachers who used this situation to make themselves popular by either siding with the students or spreading the word against those who protested against the 'gherao' constituted a core around which the post-1984 political mobilization would evolve.

Perils of Adventurism: Gains Lost

The most significant discovery for outsiders as well as for the students was that the student community was not a homogeneous group as had been propagated. Many students from well-to-do families were bailed out from prison swiftly by their families or by the party bigwigs much to the chagrin of their colleagues. Many of those in the forefront of the violence were seen abandoning the cause of the revolution by taking flight to universities abroad. This disillusioned those, generally from lower echelons, who were convinced by the parties' rhetoric that the students were a class transcending their socio-economic background and working for the cause of socialist transformation. Those who either languished in jail or were rusticated were mostly from the lower-middle-class families from small towns or from backward areas like Bihar, Orissa, Andhra or western UP. But their martyr-like attitude prevented self-introspection and any frank or objective examination of the colossal damage to the institutions.

Those who did not mythologize their suffering tried to make an honest assessment of their own class position and the politics of the parties. This had serious consequences. This section of students would gradually stop taking any active roles in the party activities, particularly in those of the SFI—the most organized party—as they could see the innate 'middle-class-ness' and careerist background of the SFI functionaries and votaries. They also realized that any political action for the revolutionary goal had to be done at one's own risk—party support was commensurate with one's class or pedigree. This assessment had a serious impact on the politics of the campus as this section, emanating as they were from the small towns, peasant or lower-middle-class backgrounds, changed their attitude to politics and consequently, academia. Their disillusionment with politics would lead them to conformism.

These changes were, however, to alter the nature of the relationship among different sections of the university forever. The pre-1975 campus had a life where the line of demarcation between students and teachers was not drawn sharply and an intellectual habitus had begun to take shape. Then, intellectual and political differences notwithstanding, mutual respect and shared social concerns made the community life enjoyable despite the discomfort of the 'lonely planet' that JNU was in its hilly terrain. By 1977, new conditions emerged, and the relationships, though strained, had shared spaces and mutually respected zones. The collective conformism of the teaching community during 1975–77 had a bearing on this. With the violence of 1983, the shared mutual trust crumbled, and a silent but sharp line of delineation appeared between the students and the teachers. Trust was the first and biggest casualty.

The weakening of the students' unity encouraged the JNU administrators to effect certain changes which they considered necessary. The hostel, the space of the students, had a new character. A committee was appointed to make suggestions for the reorganization of the hostels.[1] The committee submitted its report and, by July 1984, the hostels which had been yoked into the large centralized organization under provosts and the dean, were made units unto themselves. The lunchrooms now had ex-servicemen appointed as mess managers and assistant mess managers.[2] An inter-hostel administration was set up to generally supervise the functioning of the mess staff. Ex-serviceman Harmohinder Singh was appointed as the mess advisor to the dean and he checked purchases, supplies, prices and also the quality of food and its nutrition value, etc.[3] He also coordinated the work of the mess mangers. Hostels were given some financial assets by levying a Rs 15 fee on the students annually for the mess facilities. Six students were assigned the role of mess secretaries—they looked after the working of this department and this gave the mess an autonomous character with a dominant student component.[4]

The violence had crippled the older experiment, which had evolved since 1972, of student involvement in the admissions process. The university, after a prolonged debate, abandoned the admission policy for the MA course based on marks obtained in written examinations, academic performance and interview. It now adopted a more straightforward and universally defendable method that depended on written selection tests. It was a Herculean task, considering that no outside agencies were involved, and the same teachers who were to teach the students set the question papers for entrance tests, evaluated the scripts and also travelled to the examination centres across the country. The teachers' presence at the examination centres was made mandatory. The confidentiality of the question papers set by the centres had to be maintained. An office of director of admission was created with Bipan Chandra who was given the task of formulating the new admission policy and heading it, and a team reporting to the coordinator, P.N. Sharma, worked under the director's overall supervision. P.N. Sharma did an excellent job in translating the process into reality and very soon the admission process to JNU was considered one of the best practices in India.

A comparative study on expenditure on the admission process in 1982-83 and 1984-85 showed a quantum jump, nearly rupees one lakh, on the advertisement of the admission notices, while a lot of money, viz., Rs. 43,500, was spent to conduct the examination at various centres. The MA students who joined the university in 1984, came through this admission process. The new admission system served well for the university and JNU got accolades for running the fairest selection process.[5] Thus, while the old admission process brought kudos to the university for running the most people-friendly selection, the new procedure was considered more equitable.[6]

The new procedure removed the student groups from the process of MA and BA admissions except in an informal sense where they still lobbied, supplied information and facilitated admissions for their cadres, friends, relatives and anyone who came into even informal contact with them. In this sense the freedom of the JNU atmosphere was retained. However, removal of the students as a formal body participating in the process was rather unfortunate, as in the long run it might have emerged as one of the most fascinating innovations in the university system anywhere in the world. The viva quotient of the selection process assured the teachers really fine quality researchers who may or may not have been quite so articulate in English or Hindi. This also provided easy access to the diversity of the country. The removal of the students from the admission process, elimination of the viva itself and giving the written examination the sole weightage, badly hurt many sections of the JNU society. While the interview system assured opportunities for inherent talent, there was misappropriation of the procedure by different political formations and vested interests in their attempts to get their candidates into JNU. It had also assured almost free access to the children or wards of non-teaching staff into any programme, particularly the undergraduate foreign language programmes of the university.

It is ironic that the very same political formations which helped the 'good old system' also caused its collapse. Except for the teachers affiliated to the political parties, the rest of the teaching community was utterly disgusted with the corrupt practices; therefore, very few actively opposed the changeover. The students' union declared the new admission policy 'elitist' and 'biased towards the urban and north India'. The university administration, in the next couple of years, had to defend the new policy by indicating that the new admissions were both national in character (hence not biased in favour of north Indians) and maintained a balance between the rural and urban segments (therefore non-elitist). On 26 September 1984, the vice chancellor, P.N. Srivastava, spoke on this issue, and refuted the union's claims about the degeneration of the university. For example, in 1984, of the 1,456 offered seats, only 847 students joined. The number of Scheduled Tribe and Scheduled Caste students amongst them were 183.[7] Out of the 847 students admitted, only 210 had come from public schools and 315 from rural areas.[8]

The outside world accepted the vice chancellor's arguments and also the new admission policy. *The Statesman*, in its editorial, was quite hard-hitting when it suggested that the vacant seats did not in any manner indicate that the argument for retaining the old admission process was valid. The newspaper suggested that it would perhaps be worthwhile investigating the reasons for the students' reluctance to join JNU despite being selected, rather than harping on the new admission policy. Furthermore, 'it might not be a disaster if only a limited number joined instead of a large'. This was a major blow to the students organizations, particularly of the Left, as the filling up of seats was their prime concern.

In the meantime the union took up cudgels on behalf of the bachelor's degree holders, primarily from Bihar, who had earned their bachelor's degree in two years instead of the mandatory three which was the norm in JNU and in most other universities. The union filed a petition in the court arguing that the university was irrational in making a three-year degree course the eligibility criterion because the students were not responsible for the policies of the states. However, although the courts praised the zeal of the union, they held that JNU's policy to stick to the 10+2+3 as the basic eligibility criteria was logical, and that the onus was on the state governments to change the system to the new format or support the students by offering bridge courses.[9] This put pressure on the Bihar government to switch over to the three-year graduate course, which it did by 1987-88.

What was lost was the finest experiment in the world which provided the students a key role in the most important process in a university's decision making, i.e., admissions. This had happened at a time when the universities in the West were regrouping to correct the problems in their institutional organization; the one area where they were most emphatic was removing the senior students from the campuses to the cities to fend for themselves. On the other hand, it allowed the universities to take more undergraduate and fresh students who could live on campus. India, however, was not resorting to this model. While the administration was attacked by the students, the university was attacked in the parliament. The loss of a common vision was now in the public domain and the detractors came in sharply to attack the university. Reference, for example, was made to the Public Accounts Committee's report in reiterating the wastage of resource in JNU. It reported that in 1983-84, 3,420 of 8,826 students of JNU's School of Languages dropped out without obtaining a degree. This, after the taxpayer spends Rs 11,000 annually for every student of JNU.[10]

The Beginnings of the Neo-liberal Global Regime

By 1983, the United States had seen two years of Ronald Reagan's presidency. Called 'the shooter of Berkeley', Reagan, as the governor of California, had ordered the California Highway Patrol Police to open fire on the students who were protesting in the People's Park at Berkeley in May 1969.[11] This killed the student, James Rector, creating further discontent in America. Reagan then called in the State National Guards to occupy the city of Berkeley and crack down on the protestors.[12] The coming to the world stage of the protagonist of the 'Bloody Thursday', as the shooting was referred to, was to change the political climate.[13] Reagan's predecessor, Jimmy Carter, had come to power announcing that he would reduce defence expenditure by following détente, and thereby save humanity from an impending nuclear war. Reagan challenged all these citing American helplessness in the face of the Russian invasion of Afghanistan.[14] Carter's human rights strategy was upstaged by the threat of star wars.[15] Reagan also brought to the fore American right wing's open attack on the international system which it felt was not serving American interests. The right wingers reckoned Carter had also damaged the system by invoking the human rights regime particularly in the Third World.[16]

Reagan's appeal to the Americans included the proverbial Republican agenda of cutting taxes and limiting federal government spending. Determined to take on the Soviet Union, he however did not cut back on defence expenditure.[17] A new kind of belligerence and fury of an impending nuclear war began to be heard. Reagan enunciated the then incipient idea of a clash of civilizations when he described the soviet empire and the socialist system as *evil*. This characterization held deep psychological and political implications in the Christian world as the 'evil' could only be stopped by determined efforts. Reagan came out with what came to be known as the Star Wars Missile Defence System. US international relations was now geared towards nuclear diplomacy.[18] With competitive one-upmanship in all fields, the cold war between the two superpowers began to enter its final phase.[19]

The aggressiveness in the US foreign policy was matched by or was the result of a new-found assertiveness among the conservatives and the champions of free market.[20] Michael Hardt and Antonio Negri suggested, in their new book, that one of the foundational texts for the conservatives was by Samuel Huntington which argued that too much participation or democracy was not good, neither was too much provision of welfare measures.[21] The opposition to the rise of this neo-conservatism found expression from multiple cultural rights activists from various university campuses who demanded inclusion of different ethnic groups into a share of the curriculum along with the scrapping of Western classics as compulsory reading.[22] This was the time when the cultural attack on conservatism also came in the shape of MTV attacking prudishness and puritanical cultural codes of the American society. But MTV was also the symbol of the new free-market consumerism that the American business strata wished to promote.[23]

While Reagan was committed to the old Republican ideal of reducing the state's role in the economy, Margaret Thatcher, who preceded Reagan on the international scene, had already articulated a more dynamic philosophy. Upon being elected the prime minister of UK in 1979, Thatcher, with the firm conviction that the state ought not to squander its resources, decided that the state should withdraw from works where its resources get wasted, such as the big enterprises like railways and mining. She privatized coal, railways and many other areas. Even the great universities could not escape her policy preview and she cut their funds angering the Oxford dons who later, in 1985, as a deliberate snub, voted to refuse Thatcher an honorary degree in protest against her move to make cuts in funding for higher education.[24] She denationalized the core sectors of economy but compensated Britons with liberal doses of political nationalism by boosting their confidence as inheritors of a colonial legacy. Any sense of guilt in its colonial past was sought to be erased. Complete erasure was executed with the Falkland war with Argentina which aroused unprecedented nationalism in Britain based on colonial possession. Cambridge and Oxford, while losing finances, had their colonial pride, lost in the heydays of communism and radical politics of the 1960s, restored. Britain saw horrible race riots in which the white youth targeted hapless Asians and blacks.

Neighbourly Upheavals

Within Asia, however, there were tumultuous changes. The Iranian revolution under Ayatollah Khomeini was of a very complex nature for the Indians and particularly for the intelligentsia. Indian universities, particularly Delhi University, had been home to the progressive elements within young Iranians and more so for the communist students with hundreds fleeing the Pahlavi regime's persecution. JNU also saw streams of Iranian and Kurdish students coming to the campus and adding to the radical thinking. The American role in Iran and the Middle East in propping up the Israeli state and the unjust treatment of Palestinian refugees always had the Indian intelligentsia accusing the Americans of being partisan.

The Indian sympathy had nothing to do with the Muslim population of India as was alleged. Right from the start, JNU students exhibited their pro-Palestine sympathies and the presence of the left had, in fact, steered these sympathies to larger engagement in research and activism. There were regular interactions with the Palestine Liberation Organization activists and many like Qamar Agha got completely caught up with the cause. Qamar Agha later went on to edit the Arab League's magazine. This attitude towards the Palestine question was in line with the old Indian nationalist line which Nehru had so powerfully expressed: 'West Asia is our geographical and historical kin'.

From the early 1980s, the more the Palestinians were attacked by different forces supported directly and indirectly by Israel, the more the number of protest marches and pamphlets from the JNU students in support of Palestine. On 11 August 1982, the JNU students went on a protest March in Delhi in which 100 of them were held by the local police.[25] A couple of years later, the JNU students and the local police had a day-long battle in the by-lanes of the R.K. Puram area: the former were chased in and around the stadium of the Delhi Lawn Tennis Association in the area where they had gone to protest against the Davis Cup Match between India and Israel. Many of them had to face the hard lathis (long batons) of the Delhi police.

The monarchy of Reza Shah had brutally killed thousands of Iranian communists in the 1970s and many had come to India to live as students in the Delhi University. The Shah now found his nemesis in the popular movement under the leadership of the exiled religious leader, Ayatollah Khomeini. From the beginning of 1978, there were mass protests and demonstrations against the Shah's rule which almost paralysed the country between August and December 1978. The Shah had to leave Iran into exile in mid-January 1979, and Ayatollah Khomeini returned to Teheran from Paris to a tumultuous welcome from millions of Iranians. The collapse of the royal regime was followed by a referendum which declared Iran an Islamic Republic on 1 April 1979.

All through the Iranian revolutionary process, the JNU community had opposed the United States' intervention and hoped for the collapse of Shah's regime. However, the attitude towards the Islamic revolution was ambiguous in the way many approached the issue.[26] This ambiguity remained a characteristic of many of JNU's intellectuals who could never openly come out and critique the theocratic revolution on its own terms although they were the biggest votaries of secular polity. The School of International Studies soon showed its keenness to understand the new regime's relations with other powers like the Soviets or the Saudis. This aspect of international studies, however, provided the institution a very significant insight, i.e., a long-term institutional understanding of world politics.[27]

Soon the Iran-Contra affair, the shady deal by which the Reagan government made money available through Iran to the contra rebels fighting the Sandinistas in Nicaragua was exposed.[28] This revealed how the American presidents used covert and unconstitutional ways to fund military groups in foreign lands to fight forces which the United States was opposed to. The JNU students, comprising nearly the entire left, including the radical fringes and the teachers, had been, from the beginning, very sympathetic to the Sandinistas and there were regular discussions on the issue. JNU had also become the home of many Latin American radical students doing their research. News of such covert and powerful intervention by the United States made all of them furious at its duplicity. The feeling intensified when the United States engineered a coup in Iraq and aided Saddam Husain to occupy the presidency of both the Ba'ath Party and Iraq and subsequently pushed him to wage a war on Iran, while it was undergoing internal revolutionary turmoil. This further aided the suspension of any objective assessment of the Iranian revolution on the part of JNU community. The Iranian revolution gave an impetus to the mobilizing processes in the orthodox Sunni Arab world. To make matters worse, came another angle: the Soviet armies marched into Afghanistan apparently upon the invitation of the socialist groups in Afghanistan.[29]

The scholars, and in fact a majority of Indian intellectuals and even the prime minister herself, were opposed to the Soviet intervention in Afghanistan.[30] But the issue was how to not embarrass a trusted friend at a time of very aggressive international politics. However, the non-communist intellectuals had no such qualms and they spoke the truth when they expressed their disapproval:

> We, the undersigned, condemn the Soviet Union's occupation of Afghanistan. With the help of over 40,000 troops the Soviet Union has installed a puppet regime in Kabul. The Soviet occupation of Afghanistan is a threat to the Indian sub-continent and it is imperative that this region of South Asia be kept free of Super Power rivalries. We note that the Russian invasion of Afghanistan was carried out under the pretext of the Afghan-Soviet 'Friendship' Treaty. This shows that such 'Friendship' treaties can be instruments of Soviet interference in the internal affairs of other countries. We, too, have a Friendship Treaty with the Soviet Union; we must see that the treaty will not be used to

> snatch away from us our sovereignty and freedom. We call upon all patriotic and democratic Indians to demand the immediate withdrawal of Soviet troops from Afghanistan and to support the Afghan people's resistance to Soviet occupation. If the Soviet occupation is not vacated, then the Moscow Olympics should be boycotted.[31]

The response from inside JNU was much sought after and in many circles it was assumed that the university itself supported the petition. This assumption, however, seemed somewhat misplaced as the groups of JNU students apparently blamed the Americans for the Soviet intervention in Afghanistan. They in fact led a protest rally on 9 January 1980, which went to the US embassy to protest against 'American imperialism' and its nefarious propaganda in maligning the Soviet forces which, according to them, was there on the invitation of the Afghan government.[32]

Reactions from JNU were seen as 'support of the Soviet Union due to the communist sensibilities. However, in reality, criticism emerging from JNU looked at the larger canvas (since it had the School of International Studies with experts in the field who gave the students and scholars a nuanced and broader perspective) and significantly, one constant theme, in all positions taken, was protection of 'India's national interests' rather than mere blind support of the Soviets.[33] A denouncement was however not forthcoming as the overall atmosphere was not anti-Soviet, and the Soviets were India's closest ally on many fronts. To add to this was the presence of Soviet supporters in the departments and many CPI members who were beneficiaries of Soviet munificence. No such feelings existed with the aggressive American interventions across the world, most of which were contrary to India's national interests, and this would soon prove true with the Americans sponsoring the military regime and the mujahidin in Pakistan to fight the Russians in Afghanistan. This, as intellectuals could foresee, would soon land on the Indian borders. The Khalistan movement became almost a proxy war against India by Pakistan's military regime. Therefore, the simplistic pro-American and anti-American departmental profiles were meaningless. The context was the most important fact which the area studies scholars of the US state department would not take cognizance of.[34]

The new economic and political realities were demanding new orders—both economic and political. It was an aggressive superpower rivalry which needed careful reading and calibration of statecraft. JNU scholars were alive to the rivalry and were trying to understand the intricacies of such power games. Since the power games were also conducted under the rubric of the nuclear weapons and a new arms regime which tried to destabilize détente, there were new efforts to understand the world now beyond the earlier descriptive analysis. Research could now move on to a new and more robust analytical plane in the new and larger intellectual horizon of the university. The aggressive and militaristic games by the big powers were already making a subtle transformation.

The result of the moves by the West, and particularly by the Anglo-Americans in global affairs, including their support to the Rhodesian and South African regimes, ostracized by the international community for their apartheid policy, puzzled the scholarly world. The aggressive moves by the American Navy in the Indian Ocean with regard to bases in Diego Garcia was making India uncomfortable and analysts talked about an encirclement of India. This was forcing the university to shift its global outlook and engagement with larger theoretical moorings to more concretely political and security issues. 'National interest' was now seen slightly more sympathetically than ever before. The global peace movement paradigm seemed to be a thing of the 1970s. The Peace Council, sponsored by the Soviet Union (and its intelligence units) and managed by the CPI members (some of them became quite rich in the process), was becoming ineffectual; particularly, after the Afghanistan crisis, only money and a patronage mechanism for petty party apparatchiki remained.

Back in the saddle in 1980, Indira Gandhi too must have understood that a more proactive position in global affairs was needed at this juncture when India was beginning to feel the squeeze. It was obvious that the arms trade, the new race for nuclear armaments and the new aggressiveness in the Western policy, as many JNU scholars indicated, was pushing India and many poor countries to the wall. She openly stated during her visit to Switzerland in May 1981 that the superpower rivalry was causing an arms race.[35] There was now a new thrust to the non-aligned movement as a large number of countries began to see the logic and advantage of strengthening this platform. Putting the whole scenario into a comprehensive perspective P.V. Narasimha Rao, India's polyglot foreign minister, argued that the non-aligned countries had a 'tangible and imperative stake in the practical and peaceful resolution of the problems affecting west Asia, Iran, Afghanistan, South Africa and Namibia'. He struck an important chord when he said that the recent developments in our own part of the world pose a great threat not only to regional stability but also to world peace. As non-aligned countries, all the countries in the region have a common stake in eliminating all foreign intervention and interference, whether it be the presence of foreign troops or massive arms induction, and in promoting stable relations and peaceful cooperation.'[36]

The new world beset by armed rivalry and making the poor nations economically more unstable was observed with concern by JNU scholars, and there was an urge to innovate a new institutional mechanism to help them. A New Information Order (NIO) was seen as sine qua non for such a new world.[37] To make the non-aligned movement more focused, there were now efforts to make the movement as well as other groupings like the Group of 77 more 'economically' focused. The idea of South–South cooperation, which saw the Group of 77 meeting in Havana, New York and Algiers, was a concrete move. Any similar move from the North, for example, socialist Billy Brandt's 'New Economic Order Doctrine' was viewed with creative sympathy.[38] The new sensibilities could be gleaned in the way international policies were examined. The School of International Studies seemed to now share JNU's own evolving intellectual position. A self-reliant, decolonized world order was what was needed. In 1981, the title of a scholar's work 'Imperialism, Anthropology and the Third World Reality' may well have been the title of many such works in that period.[39]

Political Challenges and Communal Consolidation

International insecurities were discussed along with the internal conflagrations. The movement against illegal migrants in Assam was becoming a mass movement under the aegis of the All Assam Students Union (AASU). The students, litterateurs and common people from across the state began to be mobilized on the issue of Bangladeshi immigrants inundating the state and threatening the cultural identity and political life of the Assamese. The issue of ethnicity, since the early decades of the twentieth century, was directly linked with the idea of the nation (and nation making) in India. Demand for Pakistan at its final moment became a demand for a territorial nation based on a certain demographic feature, i.e., religion. The subsequent demand for linguistic provinces too anchored itself on demography. Against this historical backdrop, the changes in the population profile of Assam were inevitably too sensitive to handle.

Conversion to Islam by the villagers in Meenakshipuram district in southern Tamil Nadu added fuel to the fire. The public spectacle and intense media focus got the Hindu communal organizations competing to project the issue as a sign of Hinduism being in danger. Concerns over demography, like the Assam agitation, forced people into thinking that Muslims would soon be inundating the land mass of India and that the future of India was also in danger. The creation of Pakistan, already in the historical memory, was revived every day.[40] Religious and communal groups, both Hindu and Muslim, perceived this through their respective communally coloured lenses, i.e., as a threat to their community.

The Meenakshipuram incident proved to be a catalyst for the emergence of Vishwa Hindu Parishad as a force apparently to save the Hindu religion, and came to be seen as an agent for promoting a new and militant Hindu consolidation.[41] JNU's young scholars seemed to understand the whole gamut of issues well and reflected their understanding through their work, debates and activism.[42] Those who underlined the dangers of Hindu communalism were the intellectuals who had contested the communal forces since the 1960s, mainly the intellectuals of the CPI. It was around them that the anti-communal intellectual forces tried to rally. The activities of the Jamat-i-Islami, its holding of an international conference, and the communal frenzy in Kashmir and UP were highlighted by the CPI organ, *Link*, in August 1980, when the riots in Moradabad shattered peace all around.[43]

JNU seemed to be the most hospitable place for the members of the All Assam Student Union (AASU) as many senior intellectuals gave their support to the movement. The support came primarily for two reasons: (1) it was based on linguistic sensitivities which were very basic to the political and existential sensitivities of the people there; (2) they saw the popular and democratic portents of the movement in the wide popularity of the non-violent methods being practised. The AASU students came to the campus, and the JNU students like Alokesh Barua and others played host to them, while senior professors like Bipan Chandra, C.P. Bhambhri and many others spoke supporting the movement.[44]

A kind of creeping communal chauvinism was discernible in the movement which the JNU scholars could sense. The scholars sent warnings through intermediaries and through their writings. It was soon apparent that the RSS was also active in Assam. Not long after, the Nellie and Gohpur massacres proved their suspicions correct. In Nellie about 3,300 people, mostly Muslim villagers, were killed mercilessly and what was worse, there was no sense of remorse and the local Assamese administration as well as the political classes demonstrated their extreme bias, which robbed the movement its innocence.[45] The Nellie massacre reflected the depravity of the communal ideology that touched the people in the states. The AASU tried to dissociate itself from this, but it was too late. The movement lost its sheen among many who had seen in the democratic nature of the movement a new ray of hope. One could see the spiralling effect of the movement in neighbouring Tripura, where the Tripura Upajati Juba Samiti (TUJS) mercilessly killed people in Mandai in 1980.[46]

The needed political support for the ruling party was not forthcoming from secular quarters. Worse still, Indira Gandhi was being targeted as the villain of the piece in each situation, e.g., Assam, Punjab, UP, Bengal, etc. The Congress party itself was in a quagmire with chief ministers like A.R. Antulay, Jagannath Mishra, Ramarao Adik, S. Bangarappa, Bansi Lal, Bhajan Lal, etc., becoming bywords for corruption and venality. In Andhra, the simmering discontent with the way the Congress handled its leaders led to the rise of 'Andhra Pride' in the shape of N.T. Rama Rao, the film superstar, who entered politics to save Andhra Pride. With a substantial number of students from Andhra in the campus, this provided an edge to the anti-Congress, if not pro-NTR, sentiments.

It was also the time of a very silent but perceptible improvement in the economy. The most visible aspects of the latter were the changing urban landscape: the rise of small-scale entrepreneurs. Scholars noticed a gradual change in the landholding pattern among the lower peasant classes in western UP.[47] The improvement in their landholding pattern which began during this time brought about a definite Dalit political bloc.[48] The changes in the global economy jeopardized the competitive edge of many industrial sectors like textiles, where the companies were facing obsolescence and new managerial challenges. Shifting to other sectors seemed profitable and therefore textile cities like Ahmedabad, Kanpur and Bombay became sites of industrial unrest, and the big industries resorted to violent and extralegal means against the workers.

The prolonged communal campaigns impacted on some of the crucial areas of governance and the police. In Jamshedpur, in southern Bihar, the RSS had a field day during one of the worst communal riots and in Moradabad the police opened fire on a crowd offering namaz on 13 August 1980. The most frightening result of the communal campaign of the previous decade was the sense of insecurity generated in the cities with a substantial Muslim population.[49] One of the sharpest manifestations could be seen in the riots that broke out in Meerut, situated close to Moradabad, in August 1981. The tension in Aligarh University, also close to Meerut, again reared its head with the introduction of the Aligarh Muslim University Bill in 1981, in which Indira Gandhi, in spite of opposition from many quarters including many senior scholars from the university itself like Irfan Habib, gave in to the demands of Muslim communalists and fundamentalists and gave the university what was called 'minority status'.[50] This gave credence to the Hindu communal campaign against Indira Gandhi personally and the Congress generally as appeasers of Muslims. All of these distorted the overall social and political atmosphere. Soon, over a petty altercation in Bihar Sharif, in central Bihar, a riot began on 3 May 1981 and it soon became a nightmare; and the communal violence left fifty-two dead, of which fifty were Muslims, and resulted in 12,733 Muslim refugees.

The government of Indira Gandhi, with no organized party depending on ideological and political skills, was finding it difficult to counter the communal, ideological attack which was trying to consolidate a Hindu psyche of siege. Indira Gandhi tried to maintain a balance: she prevented a Hindu consolidation by not allowing the communal groups to keep projecting her as anti-Hindu, and at the same time would not allow the minorities to feel insecure in the face of the massive communal attacks. Her visit to the Hindu temples and meeting seers seemed to indicate this. However, they were pregnant with serious social consequences by sending out wrong signals.

The bigger left party, the CPI(M), took an equidistant position between the BJP and the Congress, attacking the Congress for being responsible for the communal situation. The communists' explanation was that the communal problem was the reflection of the skewed social and economic relations, and the Congress, being the party of the big bourgeoisie and big landlords, represented that political equation. The constant attack by the secular, progressive and communist intellectuals and parties was making the situation extremely difficult for the Congress and, particularly, Indira Gandhi. These attacks provided a space for the Hindu communal BJP, which claimed to be the true secular party while calling the Congress a pseudo-secular party which was intent on appeasing Muslim communalists. The attack was so intense that diehard secularists also began to share these criticisms of the Congress and Mrs Gandhi. The Aligarh issue seemed to them to confirm these. So much so that M.C. Chagla, who was staunchly secular and spoke at the inaugural session of the BJP, also felt that the BJP was the true blue secular party.[51]

The communalization was compounded even further by the violence in Punjab. Punjab, since Partition, had witnessed clashes between its own variants of communal interests.[52] The Akali Dal, a political party based completely on religious identity and appeal, had been demanding autonomous rule for Punjab. However, in a democratic order, it had to contend with the Congress and other formations, which commanded the electoral support of the Sikhs and other sections of the population, over whom the Akalis were trying to assert their claim. In the 1960s, the Akalis clamoured for a Punjabi Suba (a separate province), which had a Punjabi-speaking majority which would extend its own political life. After a prolonged agitation, the Central leadership, despite hesitation, finally conceded the demand. As is typical of communal demands, their scope continued to expand until, by the 1970s, there were further demands in the name of autonomy, which in reality boiled down to a demand for a monopoly of the Akali Dal in state politics. The Hindu communal parties also played their part by aligning with the Akalis.

The Akalis came to power in 1977, and afterwards there was a rapid communalization of the public rhetoric and postures which increasingly gave space to the religious gurus, Gurudwara management, and finally to the semi-literate Jarnail Singh Bhindranwale, who seemed to represent the violent manifestation of the Sikh communal ideology. Hindus were systematically harassed and all methods were used to break the syncretic lives of the Punjab society, its village and cities. Frustrated by their inability to attack the Akalis, the RSS and the BJP began attacking Indira Gandhi for the partition of the province and all their other woes.

Indira Gandhi was not personally responsible for these fallouts, and in fact, she was inclined to be sympathetic to the Punjabi cause in the 1960s and '70s. However, in order to cut down the Sikh communal party's base, the Congress leadership in the state encouraged the introduction of a more virulent element, Bhindranwale, preaching and singing the glory of the Sikh religion which gradually turned into a vociferous demand for an independent Sikh state. By 1981, it was clear that outside forces were also massively entrenched and the American, Canadian as well as British expatriates, with active help from other state quarters such as Pakistan, were actively involved in the demand for a separate nation—Khalistan.

The Assam movement had found its sympathizers among all sections in JNU but when the Punjab disturbances began, the situation was different. It was geographically nearby and the scholars could see all the portents of a deep communal divide. Many teachers and most of the staff were Punjabis (in fact the lingua franca in the administration was more or less Punjabi), who grew up in the state and knew the province, pre- and post-Partition, intimately. Most could remember the history and the trajectory of the Punjabi community when Sikhs and Hindus did not have communal separation of this kind.

The communist parties, which had many adherents and writers from the campus, however, were positioned on different sides of the crisis. The CPI was fighting tooth and nail against what it perceived, and rightly so, as the rise of communalism. Senior professors like Ravi Bakaya and other CPI members were in touch with the Punjab comrades and even the chief minister, Darbara Singh, who was fighting not only the Sikh extremists and the Akalis, but also the Central home ministry which, under Zail Singh, was working on an entirely different logic. M.S. Agwani, Bipan Chandra, C.P. Bhambhri and G.S. Bhalla were regular speakers at meetings. Bipan Chandra spoke at many places in Punjab against communalism despite the grave risks involved.

The CPI(M) was more aligned to the Akalis and their demands and perceived the situation as an opportunity to see its nationalistic thesis coming to fruition with the Akali demand concretizing in the Anandpur Sahib Resolution. The party was raising its anti-Congress pitch with B.T. Ranadive and E.M.S. Namboodiripad openly denouncing the system as being in crisis. The issues that appealed to the CPI(M), and many Delhi intellectuals and journalists, were the rabid anti-Centre arguments and the talk of autonomy by the Akalis. The anti-Indira pitch in the anti-establishment, left-wing student bodies was initially euphoric, but the threat of increasing the communalization in Punjab was worrying. The student agitation in the summer of 1983, however, was based on issues that were not related to any of these intellectual or political viewpoints. Admissions into JNU were postponed from the summer of 1983 to July 1984, and so student politics too remained somewhat subdued, and therefore the students were not involved in opposing the events in Punjab— but the teachers were.

It was apparent that, amidst the rising tide of communal ideology and concomitant violence, Indira Gandhi did not have the comfort of the same intellectual consensus against communalism that was there in 1969-70. In the 1980s, most of the progressive and left intellectuals had been alienated, while the aggressive anti-Congressism of the CPI(M) made such a consensus impossible. The demoralization of institutions during and after the Emergency proved fatal. Life in JNU could not recover from the deadly attack of the unruly young mobs belonging to the total revolutionaries of the JP movement that led to a complete collapse of administrative and academic norms thereafter.

Scientific temper was conspicuously absent and the communalists were propagating the wildest of reactionary ideas. Indira Gandhi did her best to bring together the intellectuals for a consensus. In a conference at the Nehru Centre in Bombay, leading intellectuals and scientists gathered, and after prolonged deliberation, issued a statement on scientific temper as a method to combat the unscientific and reactionary ideas of the communalists. From JNU, Amit Bhaduri, Bipan Chandra and Romila Thapar were the signatories. Many intellectuals rose up in defence when Ashis Nandi, in line with his anti-modernist, anti-Congress and anti- nation-state orthodoxy, attacked the statement.

JNU proved to be an oasis for anti-communal space and discourse. Intellectually, communalism was perceived as a divisive force, and according to one analysis, the combination of big bourgeoisie and feudal landlords made communalism the ruling ideology in order to divide people.[53] The Marxists in general and those who followed the communist parties' lines within the university, and elsewhere, had been diagnosing communalization as being engineered by the feudal lords and big bourgeoisie—a neat argument fitting well with the Indian Marxists' textual explanation of reactionary movement in a society as reflecting the shades of ruling classes' use of ideological dominance.[54] Now however, they needed to respond to the more urgent and intellectually more challenging question which Lenin had once posed in history: *What is to be done?* Was fighting the feudal system the priority when the communal forces were ravaging the minds and bodies? Similarly, was it more important to fight communalism or to fight the national bourgeoisie which was seen as comprador? Was it a communal manifestation of latent forces of the nationalities wanting to be a nation? A long time ago, during 1945–47, the CPI had argued along this line upon the demand for Pakistan which it saw as a 'nationalities demand' to the chagrin of many.[55] 'Nationalities thesis' had been revived and the general secretary, Namboodiripad himself, wrote the lead article in the party's intellectual journal *Social Scientist*.[56]

Although subscribing to a version of nationalities thesis, many Marxists tried to grapple with the issue of 'communalism' seriously. The popular Marxist political scientist, Randhir Singh, linked it directly to religion and argued that that religion itself be critiqued as Marx had done. Many, like Bipan Chandra, did not concur with this view and argued that it was not religion per se but construction of community along religious lines which was at the core of the communal ideology.[57] It was a false consciousness and needed to be confronted with the help of a true consciousness.[58] This form of communalism was a specific South Asian phenomenon in modern times.[59] The attempt to probe communalism's claims revealed that it wants to pose itself as Indian nationalism. What is Indian nationalism in then was a question which became the core issue.

Imaginings in the National Commons

In the Centre for Historical Studies there was now a substantial body of research on the basis of which Bipan Chandra was advancing the theory that the Indian national movement, which he, along with all the Marxists, had all along thought was a bourgeois phenomenon, actually had a secular and democratic core to it. Its organizational and operational theories were as advanced as any other grand movement in human history. The movement according to him had developed one of the most sophisticated understanding of colonialism much before Marx wrote his magnum opus. Similarly, according to him, in the hands of the early nationalists (a term he coined to reject the nomenclature of moderates) the national movement developed a sophisticated understanding of the colonial state and also the Indian society and the ways the movement might proceed against the colonial rule.

The national movement began to be studied in its myriad dimensions testing the validity of the theory in various ways. In her research and writings, Mridula Mukherjee found that the peasants in Punjab saw their movement as part of a larger network of relationships with the communists as well as the national movement.[60] She found it quite absurd, given the large-scale evidence, that some were claiming that the nationalist leadership tried to appropriate movements of people who did not want to be with them. Visalakshi Menon explored the movement's crucial phase during 1937–39 in Uttar Pradesh.[61] The Quit India movement was studied, so were the other facets of the Indian national movement, by students like Radhika Singha, Gyanesh Kudaisya, Ravi Vasudevan and John Javos.[62] A serious study of the nature of social change and the concomitant participation in the national movement in Andhra was done by Murali Atluri.[63] Similarly, other scholars ventured into other Andhra districts which were hotbeds of radical politics in later days. While Kama Shankar Reddy tackled the national movement in the Krishna district during 1920–31, Pilli Arun Kumar, a political science student, took a slightly narrower analytical frame, viz., caste and class politics, to study Srikakulum district for the later period between 1967 and 1972.[64] Younger students like Shyam Narayan and Lata Singh were investigating the aspects of the national movement in Bihar during its most significant phase, the 1920s and '30s.[65]

In 1980, the university's own news organ, *JNU News*, announced the publication of *Indian National Movement: The Long-term Dynamics* by Bipan Chandra, which the critical reviewer thought was heralding the dawn of a new era of discourse in the studies on nationalism.[66] Though the reviewer found the equating of Gandhi with Gramsci quite outlandish, and crediting Gandhiji with 'the only historical actualization of Gramsci's strategic vision' slightly unbelievable, he felt the book would change the perspective in which the national movement should be studied and viewed.[67] It was a great achievement in retrieving the vision of the national movement and that too in such a grand manner, and done at a time when popular magazines were reporting that, in metropolitan cities, Gandhi had almost become an unknown and uncared for entity—and unfashionable to boot. The Oxford historians were only too happy to see this fate of Gandhi who was, in their view anyway, the leader of power brokers. Later, Oxford students portrayed him as not much more than a creation of rumour and hearsay.

Antonio Gramsci was a communist who spent his last years in the prison of the fascist ruler Mussolini. He had thought about the communist movement and tried to interpret both the movement and the theory in the light of his own rich understanding of European history.[68] The Communist Party of Italy was one of the most militant and active parties in Europe. In order to match the forces of the powerful right, it had to keep on improvising its tactics and strategy. The party's general secretary, Palmiro Togliatti, friend and intellectual successor of Gramsci, kept theorizing the tactics and strategy of the party to keep it alive and relevant amidst the strong anti-communist atmosphere in Italy. Gramsci's writings meant a lot to the Italian movement and he placed the communist movement in the 1940s in their specific national and political context, occupying the space by fighting the hegemony of the ruling order. He did not isolate national class struggles from their international context but was far more sensitive to their uniqueness than a host of Marxist theorists. Although he did critique the developing Bolshevism in the Communist Party of Italy (the news about Stalin's

Russia had not made its way into the West at this point in time), he insisted that western European communist movements should adopt tactics suited to their own specific context.

In his *Prison Notebook*, one of the most cited books in academia the world over, he used military metaphors to differentiate the Russian 'war of manoeuvre' with the western European 'war of position'. The latter, he claimed, was necessitated by the much stronger role played by bourgeois civil society outside of Russia perpetuating capitalist rule.[69] He made a comparison between the two giants of the communist movement, i.e., Trotsky and Lenin. The former, he said, was evidently Western and a cosmopolitan, i.e., superficially national and superficially Western or European, while Lenin on the other hand, was profoundly national and European. This comparison launched his critique of the theory of permanent revolution. For him a national revolution was to be accepted as a step towards the larger goal of socialism, as it is based on the national characteristics.

Intellectuals of the Indian left have generally looked quite seriously at the moves of the Italian Communist Party and Togliatti. This is where historians like Bipan Chandra, who were seeking the context and nature of colonialism and anti-colonial movement, saw Gramsci providing a theoretical space for a specific treatment of the Indian national movement and also of Gandhi.[70] This would, however, create problems for the communists for whom locating the movement outside global capitalism and a framework of a communist revolution was still a theoretical taboo.

Generally sympathetic to the underdog, the JNU intellectuals had taken to Gramsci not only because he was a victim of Mussolini's fascism, he was also the chief protagonist in shaping the communist party in Italy. His idea of praxis had already influenced the political science students in the 1970s when Madhu Prasad wrote a dissertation on the theme of praxis.[71] And the everyday political praxis now came to be explored through his writings by K. Srinivasulu, a political science student, for his M.Phil. thesis.[72] With the same gusto to explore the interstices between power and praxis, the young political scientists were the first to use Gramsci for their studies.[73]

The ideas of historicity and hegemony added a new dimension to the question of how ideas work in institutions in a semi-authoritarian structure or in a system wherein the pressure on the populace to be ideologically subjugated is quite subtle. This approach resonated with the Indian historical situation, particularly the way the British colonialism ruled the country. A comparative study of colonialism showed the historians that the British colonialism had a character which was different from that of the Portuguese or the French, and the JNU scholars found Gramsci's idea of hegemony useful to demonstrate that the colonial state used the instruments of oppression by disguising them as deliverance.

The ideas of Gramsci also supported the theorization of the national movement in India as an anti-hegemonic movement in which ideas and institutions of colonial hegemony were constantly attacked. Bipan Chandra put forward the concept of hegemony to support his own theorization of the national movement. The nationalist intellectuals and the leadership, according to Chandra, had worked for almost half a century to show the British as well as the Indians that the colonial policy had been increasing the immiserization of the Indian people. This breached the idea of the benevolence of the empire. He argued quite emphaticlly that this was an anti-hegemonic movement. Similarly, Gandhi, who through his mass campaign of preaching fearlessness, breached the second cardinal pillar—fear of the colonial state. Once these two hegemonic positions were attacked, the colonial system did not have the staying power, notwithstanding 'the illusion of permanence' till the very end.[74] Chandra's students, Bhagwan Josh and Shashi Joshi, began developing the theme of hegemony that Gramsci popularized.[75] The title of the book of one of his students graphically outlines this: *Independence and Partition: Loss of Hegemony*.[76]

Similarly the idea of 'war of position' was seen in the way the national movement moved step by step recovering spaces and then took time to regroup itself to launch a new wave of attack. Bipan Chandra maintained that this was struggle-compromise-struggle, which he later amended to struggle-truce-struggle. He argued that Gandhi, more than anyone else, understood this form of struggle as the only way to go forward, because a continuous struggle would not be sustainable. Bipan Chandra further said that the contest within the movement existed where the bourgeois hegemony also faced stiff opposition from the workers and peasants. Aditya Mukherjee, another of Chandra's students contended that the Indian capitalist class had been working to further its own class interest which made them back the nationalists rather than the foreign business.[77] The programme of the Congress leadership and the availability of a socialistic programmatic agenda, however, saw to it that the bourgeois hegemony was not established.

A society prejudicially known to be without history was now debating historical formations and positing the idea that there could be a new analytical mode of production, i.e., a colonial mode of production within the Marxist understanding (mode of production is Marx's contribution to human knowledge). This is how the intellectuals in post-independence countries tried to imagine their way out of the colonialism and its vestiges.

The first two volumes of S. Gopal's masterly biography of Jawaharlal Nehru not only came as the crowning achievement by the JNU historians but also led the discussion on India's development as an independent country. The 1980s brought Nehru back to centre stage when the Indian state as well as the polity was going through a bad patch.[78] Reviewing the second volume of Nehru's biography, H.Y. Sharada Prasad wrote that 'it is good to have a historian to guide us through the forest of memories, impressions, imputations and facile conclusions'. This was high praise indeed.[79] Mohit Sen, the most brilliant of the leftist intellectuals, called the volumes 'outstanding by any standards and convey a sense of restrained critical appreciation which seem admirably to convey the truth of the person and the period'.[80] The Nehru who came out of these volumes indicated a personality with a strong anti-communal and anti-caste commitment. The Indian of the 1980s needed both these commitments and, interestingly, the nation that Bipan Chandra and Gopal were reconstructing through Nehru and other figures from the national movement were exuding those commitments.

The Political Economy

Nationalism was emerging from the critique of colonialism, and sovereignty and the issue of state were discussed. However, the national economy was not in a good shape and by the 1980s; it was quite clear that India needed help to steer its stagnant economy. The 1979 budget was to take India's economy to dizzy heights of expenditure without any commensurate revenue. India's dependence on the advanced technology of the West was to increase, and the need of the hour was to have new investment and energies at both the supply and demand sides.

The university was steadily evolving a major school of political economy which was given a strong intellectual foundation by Krishna Bharadwaj.[81] It was strengthened by her colleagues, namely, Amit Bhaduri, Prabhat Patnaik and Utsa Patnaik, whose works provided stability to the lineage. Their concerns soon moved into research on the 'political economy of underdevelopment' instead of development.[82] The crisis of the mixed economy began to loom large in their writings and by the mid-eighties it became the central concern.[83] Prabhat Patnaik and Utsa Patnaik were propounding the demand side thesis from a more strident political line, and they attributed the recession in Indian economy to the depression in the agricultural sector. The state needed to intervene, invest and tax the rich rather than opening the population to the vagaries of private competition.

By the 1980s, the gargantuan state bureaucracy and its administration seemed like dinosaurs with corruption and negativity staring people in the face, and bearing all the earmarks of a typical rentier state. It would not be that easy to infuse enthusiasm in the economy from the supply side as the class interests of the sections controlling the polity and the party were still strong enough to put pressure, and Indira Gandhi herself had brought in agencies like the Monopolies and Restrictive Trade Practices (MRTP) Commission which would stifle any new initiative. The time had come to transcend to a new economic organization for a new direction. The profligate economy was running short of funds to tide it over even its immediate needs. The demand side economists of JNU were ranging themselves on an oppositional path to any change from the demand side. This explained the strong opposition to Indira Gandhi as there were indications that the state wanted some changes. The political economists allied with the CPI(M) and the intellectuals affiliated to either the CPI or the CPI(M) began to grow more stentorian, culminating in massive opposition from the university quarters when a loan was taken from the International Monetary Fund to tide over the crisis that followed the 1979 oil shock. They believed that it compromised India's sovereignty.

The diagnosis of the Indian economy by the left economists coincided with the analysis by the CPI(M). They argued, just as the party argued, that the main features of the new economy were 'lifting of controls and regulations, stimulating private enterprise, liberalization of imports of foreign goods and technology, and a lifting of curbs on foreign capital'. By 1980s these, they declared, were resulting in 'unequal income distribution, imperialist penetration, small capitalist and petty producers—centralization of capital, consequences for employment in manufacturing'.[84] Their priority included, 'employment generation by taxing the rich', import restrictions and controlling and regulating the operation of multinational capital.[85] Significantly, the public sector was considered 'a bulwark against imperialist penetration'.[86] The left theoreticians did not accept the ideological basis of the public sector—state's sovereignty and its relative autonomy from ruling combination of classes. And this is what would become a new problem.

A more managerial understanding of the economy was perceptible in the new Indian leadership. The new paradigm was in sync with the new knowledge parameters being set by the government ushered in by Rajiv Gandhi to make radical changes in many areas of the economy and its governance. Rajiv Gandhi's famous statement that the power brokers ate up all but seventeen paise of every rupee was an attack on the populism and the clientelism that existed. The left and centrist politics were both party to such populism. The communists were some of the bitterest critics of Rajiv Gandhi's new initiatives like the introduction of computers; on the plea that it would take over the people's jobs. His targeted, mission-mode approach in managing some critical areas was also looked upon with disfavour. The computer revolution in India however was launched with the arrival of the Centre for Development of Telematics (C-DOT).

The economy's pace seemed to be passing JNU by. The push for new economic sectors needed new sets of personnel, and in large numbers. There was a realization that the education system needed an overhaul in the context of the new education policy, which had been drafted single-handedly by the education minister, P.V. Narasimha Rao. However, the policy was deemed elitist and a sell-out both by the socialists and the left-wingers. JNU seemed to be on the sidelines merely watching the whole parade of strident objections to computers, management and the new ideas that the new leadership was trying out. The university's computer facility was archaic and the desire for modern management science was yet to come.

The communists had begun to feel that 'sovereignty' was at a stake. However, the historians and the other departments from the same university argued that India could take on the world as its sovereignty, which was rooted in a popular base, was very real. In this context, the CPI(M) and the left mobilized to reassert the conceptual and political idea of imperialism which it wanted to fight. The left seemed to be unaware that they were becoming almost nationalistic. On the eve of the anniversary of Indian Independence, the university organized a lecture series. There were unmistakable signs that a common universe had evolved in the dry deserts of the Aravali in the JNU. The universe comprised two intellectual lineages. One understood India as a part of global capitalism, and in their view the operation of imperialism from the outside and feudal oppression aided by comprador ruling classes from the inside would compromise the sovereignty of India.[87] The task for these intellectuals was to fight and uproot the ruling centrist forces.

The second lineage contended that, as the Indian national economy emerged out of the colonial mode of production, it did not exhibit the same type of capitalism as explained by Marx and other communist thinkers. Its politics too had evolved out of an anti-colonial mass movement and both these factors provided India with a politics and economy very different in character from its depiction in theoretical works. Any movement for socialism in India, therefore, would also need to move on a path different from Wallerstein's strategy of either waiting for a global revolution from outside or a communist revolution from within.[88]

While the first paradigm was a reading of Indian developments within global capitalism and the Marxist understanding of it, the second was historically rooted. Although both seemed to have a similar telos, the analytics were different. History was providing the check to the amorphous, undated and irresponsible wait for the global revolution. In the new issues demanding attention, i.e., environment, the language of capitalism and globalization would proliferate intellectual production. In most cases, however, a stringent historical check was the only test available. A contextualized Indian history which provided this test would now be under attack.

Conservative Rearguard: The Return of the Colonial

When consciousness about colonialism in the past and its contemporary manifestation were being examined, and the JNU community was producing some of the finest works using the autonomous intellectual space, Jack Gallagher, who had given a new colonial interpretation to modern history in 1953 and had provided one of the most sophisticated defence of colonialism, died in 1980. He had coined the expression informal empire (as different from formal empire) to shift the agency of colonization on to the colonized themselves with his theoretical sleight of hand called 'Imperialism of the Free Trade', a paper he published in 1953, the time when the high tide of imperialism in Africa was being steered by the labour leader, Bevin, the UK foreign secretary. The argument was that events in the colonies shaped the formation of the empire, thus providing the basic tenet touted by the more recent historians from the London School of Economics under the aegis of the Economic History Network, that the colonized were the agents of their own enslavement.

There must be millions of instances where the colonized were in cahoots with the colonials—the entire British army in India was comprised of Indians. The logic of viewing such assistance as agency takes away the analysis of the overarching structure of colonialism. Gallagher and his students, R. Robinson and Anil Seal, and later, C.A. Bayly produced works on Indian nationalism and the Indian National Congress which were fascinating in their antagonism bordering on almost racial hatred for Indian nationalism and the Indian National Congress.[89] It reached a kind of culmination with the publication of Judith Brown's work on Gandhi which portrayed Gandhi as the ultimate power broker who manipulated the factional power brokers and became the superpower broker, i.e., the Gandhian movement was merely a collusion of power brokers: no allowance was made to the sentiments or ideals of nationalism or anti-colonialism. The mission was followed by another Oxford student, Shahid Amin, for whom Gandhi was a chimera—a product of rumours and rumour-mongers.[90]

Up to the early 1990s, Oxford, Cambridge and the School of Oriental and African Studies were status symbols for the older landed or bureaucratic elite, and a means of class acquisition for the 'parvenus'.

It was no different in the colonial upper classes in Africa or other colonized countries. Post-colonial Britain also meticulously maintained this strategy of circulation of tutoring the colonial elite through its universities, who went on to occupy important places in the colonies. Colleges like Presidency in Calcutta or St Stephens in Delhi, for example, were the links in the chain. Colonized intellectuals of Africa spoke the same language of academia as the colonized intellectuals of the Indian metropolises like Calcutta.

The patronage structure of empirical research on colonialism was so skewed that it routinely screened out all oppositional voices. Scholars with colonial and quite often racial presuppositions found access to Indian sources denied to Indian scholars. Indian scholars, in turn, developed their own tools of approaching the same and, thanks to this, were saved from the extreme Namierism (advocated by historian Lewis Bernstein Namier, 1888–1960, who put excessive dependence on constructing history from officers' private papers apparently revealing the official mind). By the 1980s, JNU developed the strong position that the key to the India's colonial experience lay in its economic exploitation and the nationalist response against it. Research in economic history sustained the intellectual engagement with strong colonial assertions.

There were disquieting signals from different stations including the famed Delhi School of Economics which was once a citadel of research on poverty, inequality and economic history, and which produced the journal *Indian Social and Economic History Review*. In 1984, the second volume of the *Cambridge Economic History of India* covered the period between 1750 and 1950 as its subject of study. The first volume followed the course of history from 1250 to 1750 and was edited by Tapan Raychaudhuri and Irfan Habib. The second volume, edited by Dharma Kumar, from the Delhi School of Economics, and Meghnad Desai, an economist who migrated to England, differed from the first in that it was an articulation of the standard colonial position, i.e., Indian economy, industry, commerce all improved and colonialism was in more than one sense beneficial to the Indian economy—all said in so many words. The volume was overwhelmingly criticized as pandering to the colonial elite by historians and economists and its conclusions were rejected outright by serious economic historians in India.[91]

Sabyasachi Bhattacharya, who was teaching economic history at the JNU wrote a very staid piece on the economy of Eastern India during the period. Considering that this centre was the source of many offbeat theories and philosophies, people were surprised by Bhattacharya's piece. This seemed to be significant as he went on to give his presidential address in the Indian History Congress the very same year on 'social history'.[92] The relinquishment of economic history in the centre which was developing such sophisticated arguments like colonial mode of production and nationalism anchored on an economic critique of colonialism, was seen by many as capitulation.

One can argue that the communists' frequent attacks on the national movement as a bourgeois movement preserved the colonial and, in this case, Gallagherian model of Indian history. The communist rhetoric that described India as being a neo-colonial arrangement and to deny the post-Independence Indian state the credits for social transformation ran close to the Gallagherian model of characterization of the national movement as an upper-caste ruse for hiding individual and caste/class selfish motives.[93] Therefore, quite often the colonial intellectual is passed off as radical notwithstanding the absence of any ameliorative social agenda. This is what facilitated a group of scholars, trained in Thatcherite Britain's overarching conservative colour and Reagan's America, and soaked in the emergent neo-conservatism, to claim a deep radical agenda. The discourse that these politically ambitious upper-class youth articulated was the idea of balkanization, albeit in the name of mobilizing the poor, the labour or the tribals.

These products of the metropolitan universities tried to replicate themselves as the new ruling avatar with the desire to occupy intellectual leadership positions with the metropolitan university's protectorate, i.e., brand, connection, fellowship. By the 1980s, the umbrella of the British communist party which used to enrol many such Third World students into its wing had disappeared. The new product was therefore short of any working agenda to claim superior intellectual and political position from new sections which had emerged with the rise of democracy. Nation, state, secularism and democracy—these were the precise points of attack by these post-colonial colonized minds. A full-fledged conservative agenda was in operation.

The core of the conservative attack came from what came to be known as the Subaltern Studies Collective: a motley crowd of historians, political scientists and literary critics. Notwithstanding their different disciplinary locations, the group had one common denominator—their social and political positions was camouflaged in almost unreadable English phraseology which had been the hallmark of French theories after being translated into English. The second common identity of the group was its positioning in the big universities in the United Kingdom and the United States and the network with some of the radical groups in these countries. They coordinated well with resonating ideas amongst the minority radical groups in the US campuses and French salons which were now turning against the new liberal states' efforts to homogenize certain units of social and political ideas, race, class, culture, etc.

A new radical agenda in Britain, France and the United States was trying to create an anti-state and anti homogenising discourse. As part of these efforts some began to valorize anything which could attack the unity or coherence of Indian social or political system. Germany, deeply imbued with a philosophical diagnosis sans fashionable rhetoric, did not care for such discourses, and Jurgen Habermas was endeavouring to constitute an overall unifying discourse to counter any totalitarian discourse. Because of the close intellectual interaction, a large number of students were familiar with these discourses and somehow the larger community seemed to be in sync with Habermas and the discourse of solidarity and unity. The novelty of the subaltern theory did not cut much ice with a political and well-educated JNU community. Other campuses with bands of elite academics, however, began to be converted, some almost overnight.

The Communal Challenge

In JNU, many, including the members of communist parties, recognized the challenge to the state as something crucial for them as well. The state was perceived as the agency to bring social equity and be part of the democratic expansion of an essentially feudal and unequal social and economic structure. As it was the colonial state which was seen as the agent of colonial exploitation, there had been strong arguments to change the character of the post-Independence state from that of the apparatus of the colonial state.

The left wing, both the socialists and the Marxists, had accused the post-Independence Congress leadership of continuing the colonial apparatus, and hence declared that the Independence achieved was false. The state was sine qua non for a social transformation and the post-Independence state, some argued, did its utmost to dismantle linkages to colonialism in all the segments. The conservative attack on the national movement was aimed to deprive the Indian state of its historical and political legitimacy; the state and nationalism were both linked to the European modernity, and so historical and political legitimacy was pronounced to be illegitimate and therefore to be discarded. One way to discard nationalism's pre-eminence, it was argued, was to stop it from being immune to the forces of communalism, as Indian historians had been trying very hard.[94] Communalism was postulated to be the mental and textual construction of the British bureaucracy and the Indian nationalist elite.[95] There was therefore nothing wrong in communal assertions: they were expressions of community power.[96] When the demand for a separate Khalistan was raised and the Sikh communal mobilization was disrupting the Indian state, the politics of such writings were immediately challenged by those who were arguing that national movement in fact shaped the character of Indian state and that communalism favoured colonialism. Mridula Mukherjee wrote the now famous paper 'Peasant Resistance and Peasant Consciousness in Colonial India – Subaltern and Beyond'.[97] The Punjab crisis, the perils of Sikh communalism and communal riots in different parts of the country brought home the urgency to combat communalism, and the JNU scholars and students could see the centrality of the intellectual agenda in such phenomena.

The government could have easily arrested J.S. Bhindranwale who had taken over the leadership of the Khalistan movement when the Akali leadership became mute spectators to the killing of Lt Col. A.S. Atwal in the Golden Temple premises. The indecisiveness of the Central leadership let the opportunity slip by. In the ultimate stand-off, the Central leadership pulled off Operation Blue Star which brought an end to Bhindranwale and his entourage camping inside the temple. However, as this was happening, Indira Gandhi who was painted black by the Khalistanis and the other communalists was targeted for revenge, and assassinated on 31 October 1984. In the aftermath of this disaster there were massive riots in which thousands of Sikhs were mercilessly killed. The JNU students and teachers took turns to patrol the campus and save their Sikh colleagues and friends from the rampaging crowds of neighbouring villages.

By rights, the assassination of Indira Gandhi should have alienated the Akali and Sikh communal position. However, the indiscriminate killing of the Sikhs in Delhi, Kanpur and Bokaro to which the Congress leaders were party, intensified Congress baiting. Although initially providing a fresh administration, the new prime minister, Rajiv Gandhi, working under the pall of such a huge massacre, was rapidly moving into a dangerous political trap. In the Shah Bano case of 1985, he caved in to pressure from the orthodox Muslim section and amended the Indian criminal procedure code to appease this section even though he had the full support of the liberal Muslim sections, women and progressive groups. This acquiescence synchronized with the increasingly strident Hindu communal mobilization for the construction of a temple at the site of the Babri mosque.

This coincided with the ongoing mobilization for asserting that the nation was a 'religion defined category'. Therefore, it was a battle over the definition of the nation itself. Historians were now trying to carry on the debate between the national movement and the left position so that a rapprochement could be reached as the communal mobilization was already on and, as Bipan Chandra's writing had indicated, a stand on communalism was sine qua non to a project for socialism and that communalism had to be taken headlong.[98] History came back to fight politics in 1989 when the Centre for Historical Studies brought out a pamphlet which challenged the Hindu communalists for their appropriation of history. Exactly twenty years ago, it was Romila Thapar, Bipan Chandra and Harbans Mukhia who had brought out a tract on communal interpretation of history. They argued:

> Behind the present Babri Masjid–Ram Janmabhumi controversy lie issues of faith, power and politics. Each individual has a right to his or her belief and faith. But when beliefs claim the legitimacy of history, the historian has to attempt a demarcation

> between the limits of belief and historical evidence. When communal forces make claims to 'historical evidence' for the purposes of communal politics, the historian has to intervene. Historical evidence is presented here not as a polemic or as a solution to the Ram Janmabhumi–Babri Masjid conflict, for this conflict is not a matter of historical records alone. The conflict emerges from the widespread communalization of Indian politics. Nevertheless, it is necessary to review the historical evidence to the extent it is brought into play in the communalization of society.[99]
>
> The appropriation of history is a continual process in any society. But in a multi-religious society like ours, appropriations which draw exclusively on communal identities engender endless communal conflicts. And attempts to undo the past can only have dangerous consequences. It is appropriate, therefore, that a political solution is urgently found: 'Ram Janmabhumi–Babri Masjid' area be demarcated and declared a national monument.[100]

The Seductive Romance of the Campus

This author entered the sleepy little gate of JNU in the evening on 13 July 1989. Little did he realize then that the citizens of France were celebrating 200 years of their revolution which brought to us the ideas of equality, liberty and fraternity. Neither did he know then that JNU too was entering the twentieth year of its foundation. It was a fortuitous coincidence. The idea of freedom, a sustaining force for many of the intellectual battles on the JNU campus over the last twenty years, was sweeping over Europe. That continent was also the place which sustained the principles of equality and liberty in its diverse forms including the one which the communists in India espoused. Therefore, to one who was trained by the pre-war Europeans, the wave indicated larger things. But to a young mind the romance of the campus was more seductive than thinking about those changes happening thousands of miles away.

As a young student in the 1980s, reading one of the staple middle-class daily newspapers, *The Statesman*, the first and foremost wave of change that one became familiar with was the Solidarity movement in Poland. On 18 January 1989, the Communist Party of Poland voted to legalize the Solidarity.[101] On 17 April 1989, it was a legalized Solidarity that was allowed to stand for the semi-free election. On 4 June 1989, the victory of Solidarity was established in the Polish elections as the first of many anti-communist revolutions in central and eastern Europe. On 19 August 1989, the Polish president, Wojciech Jaruzelski, the man in dark glasses etched into our memory, nominated Solidarity activist, Tadeusz Mazowiecki, to be the prime minister of Poland—the first non-communist prime minister in forty-two years.[102]

In JNU, the anti-SFI students also began to be mobilized in their attack on the communists on the issue of the Tiananmen Square massacre of students. While the Aravali summers were making it unbearable for the students in Delhi, thousands of kilometres away, in Beijing, the capital city of the biggest communist country in the world, China, events were unfolding differently for students there. On 21 April 1989, students from Beijing University gathered to protest at the Tiananmen Square in Beijing, and were soon joined by students from Shanghai, Xian and Nanjing. On 19 May 1989, Zhao Ziyang, the then general secretary of the Communist Party of China, met the students indicating the party's relationship with the students. Beijing University had always had a very powerful presence which was not only displayed but also legitimized in the Chinese society.[103] However, the day after Ziyang's meeting with the students, the party imposed martial law in Beijing. The students did not relent even after the imposition of the martial law—perhaps they were given a signal from within the party to continue their agitation. The internal mechanism of the communist party, however, was rapidly changing. The students displayed their core ideology when they erected a 10-metre statue of the Goddess of Democracy on 30 May 1989. The Chinese communist party now came back into its own to counter the ideological rebellion, and crushed the rebellion with force. Four days later, on 4 June 1989, the tanks of the People's Liberation Army rolled out into the square and massacred the student demonstrators.

In the JNU campus, Sitaram Yechury (whose election slogan in 1977 was 'Achchha Kam, Achchha Nam, Sita Ram, Sita Ram'), a leading communist leader and a product of the student movement in JNU, openly targeted the bourgeois press, both American and Indian, for spreading baseless rumours to destabilize the Chinese system. It seemed pathetic and paradoxical for anyone familiar with the world events, particularly the CPI(M)-affiliated teachers, who abided by the democratic movement purely for the sake of their students, to find their communist beliefs shaken by the massacre of students in communist China. The non-SFI and non-AISF left radical sections were delighted with this turn of events, although they were far more bellicose when it came to defending their political and intellectual positions. There were now strong opinions rampant amongst the students against the communist edifice which seemed to be based on complete lies.

The regrouping began as soon as the campus reopened. JNU was one of the few institutions that had vehemently opposed the communalizing movement of the BJP through its Rath Yatra. So the RSS was more active in the campus now. The mood of the politics in the country began to change with the Congress ousted from the government, charged with corruption. Politics now seemed to be full of possibilities and by the time the university reopened in mid-July, the falsehoods of the communist claims were attacked by the more radical communist groups and supported wholeheartedly by many groups ranging from the extreme right to fringe radicals. For the fringe radicals every official, teacher or student who do not support their cause was a physical manifestation of the establishment. From their hibernation, they came back with a bang. The air was full of sound and fury, and by August the movement against the so-called establishment was in full swing. A political formation called Solidarity came into being in October 1989 to take to the field of electoral politics.

To the untutored in the politics of the campus, the fight between the SFI and the rest seemed a simple, black-and-white political fact. The truth, however, was layered in the labyrinth of ideological life of the community. All this meant that one was now in an ideological arena with no hermetic shield.

Collapse of Communism: JNU Survives

From January 1989 onwards, one was witness to tectonic changes the world over. On 20 January 1989, a rich Texan and long-time employee of the state department, George H.W. Bush, succeeded Ronald Reagan as America's forty-first president. Two weeks later, on 2 February 1989, the last of the Russian armoured column left Kabul, thereby ending the nine-year-old Russian military presence of Afghanistan. On 15 February 1989, the Soviet Union announced that the last of its troops had left Afghanistan. There were signs that not all was at peace in the Soviet Union.

A new world had begun to unfold when Mikhail Gorbachev visited China, the first soviet leader to do so since 1960. On 9 April 1989, there were reports of Soviet troops firing on protesters and killing twenty in Tbilisi Central Square. Georgia was all set to quit the Soviet Union. Events picked up pace, and, on 2 May 1989, Hungary dismantled 150 miles of barbed wire fencing along its Austrian border. A crowd of 25,000 gathered at the Heroes' Square, Budepest, to rebury Imre Nagy, the Hungarian prime minister who was executed in 1958. On 23 August 1989, the border restrictions on the Austrian side were removed. On 10 September 1989, Hungary's western borders were opened for the refugees from the German Democratic Republic. Hungary was officially declared a republic on 23 October 1989. Nearby, the East German situation was changing fast. There was a massive protest on 9 October 1989 in Leipzig, East Germany, where they demanded the legalization of opposition groups and democratic reforms. Erich Honecker was forced to step down as leader of the country and the communist government, and he resigned on 7 November 1989, though the leader of the Socialist Unity Party (SED), Egon Krenz, remained head of state. Within the next ten days momentous changes ensued:

- GDR (German Democratic Republic) opened the checkpoints in the Berlin Wall, to allow citizens to travel freely.
- The Germans began tearing down the Berlin Wall.
- On 10 November 1989, the Bulgarian Communist Party changed its name to Bulgarian Socialist Party.
- On 17 November 1989, the peaceful student demonstration in Prague, beaten back by police, began the movement to overthrow the communist regime.
- On 29 December 1989, Václav Havel was elected the president of Czechoslovakia.
- On 17 December 1989, there was an uprising in Timişoara in Romania.

- ❖ On 21 December 1989, Nicolai Ceauşescu addressed 110,000 people.
- ❖ On 22 December 1989, the army came in, and joined forces with the protesters.
- ❖ On 25 December 1989, Ion Iliescu took over the Government of Romania, and Elena and Nicolai Ceauşescu were executed on the same day.

An American strategic thinker declared that this juncture marked the end of ideology, and that history had also come to an end as the West had achieved everything that it had set its sights on.[104] If ideology was really dead, what were the students trying to achieve by defying the authorities in Tiananmen Square and being killed? There was a bitter and fierce debate at the Sutlej Hostel in the JNU campus on Tiananmen Square events. If ideology meant a belief system, political or otherwise, it was present in both locations. Perhaps the American scholar also had an ideology of sorts but was too blinkered to notice it.

One ideology which was around the corner, and increasingly mobilizing people in India into its ambit since the 1980s, was communalism. The year 1989 also saw the high tide of communal mobilization by both Hindu and Muslim forces, and the danger of Hindu forces was no longer just a perceived threat but very real. In February 1988, Ramshilas (bricks with 'Ram' written on them) were to be brought to Ayodhya, the birthplace of Rama, where a temple was being planned to be erected. In a well-thought-out strategy, it was announced during the Kumbh Mela that the Shilanyas (laying of the foundation stone), of the proposed Ram Janmabhumi temple would take place in November 1989. The Bharatiya Janata Party had planned to mobilize Hindus on the pretext of restoring Ram Janmabhumi, and moved to the fore with its Palanpur resolution to support the cultural movement. L.K. Advani led a Ram Rath Yatra from Somnath to Ayodhya to polarize the country which had become communally charged.

The communal mobilization was taking place along vitriolic conservative attack in the garb of a radical intellectual alternative. A solid phalange of the products of the metropolitan universities and the neo-conservative intellectuals now attacked the home-grown intellectual formations. It was argued that the nation state was an artificial artefact imported from the West and was better done away with. The peasant radicalism and consciousness which were to bring legitimacy of the Gandhian movement were considered a sham and the violent mobilizations were perceived as radical and potentially liberating movements. According to the group, 'state, nation and secularism' were to be replaced by 'community, society and communitarianism' respectively. 'Non-state actors' who appeared in a new wave of non-governmental organizations (NGOs), were immediately found to be a substitute for the state.

Rajni Kothari and his colleagues saw in the NGOs (which were funded by multilateral organizations with close links to the World Bank and International Monetary Fund [IMF]) the new non-party political processes and harbingers of grass-roots initiatives in India.[105] However, the socialists saw the hidden hands behind the NGOs and was ready to pounce on such valorization. One of the most critical of the leaders, Kishen Pattnayak, declared such non-party groups as dependent on foreign capital.[106]

The intellectual dilution of politics began to take its toll. In the post-colonialism writings, the East–West dichotomy was shown to be the core argument. While it provided a new arena for literary historians to churn out hundreds of books purportedly to critique the orientalist engagement of the erstwhile masters—and quite often non-masters—it also gave the radical anti-Western rhetoric a visibility to the detriment of rigorous examination of many issues. Unfortunately, this had serious repercussions.

The post-structuralists, postmodernists and subalterns in this sense were opening up, as their writings argued, a fifth column against the of the Indian intellectual life defining itself in terms of its autonomy. Such writings entered the fields of ethnicity and identity with astounding ease and began to foreground the aura of political correctness, as opposed to political action, as the proper intellectual position. One notes that many Marxist scholars, initially relishing this phenomenon with their anti-Congressism and anti-establishment world view, completely lost perspective for a while. It is at this time that many others, whose long years of intellectual struggle and rigorous practice of various disciplines, helped them stand their ground and defend the independent and self-reliant spaces won over through the last century or so. In the 1970s, in

Africa, the scholars were unfortunately overwhelmed and outmatched by the rhetoric and polemical arguments of the extremely radical organs. JNU, in many senses, withstood the onslaught of the fragmentary and counter-political discourses.

The biggest issue that the left movement faced everywhere in the world was that while it spearheaded the democratic movements, communist parties remained anti-democratic. The same remained true in JNU. The heads of the various communist groups were not only non-democratic, they were also dictatorial. There were times when there was nothing progressive or Marxist in the way many professors and students displayed their politics: personally many were crass opportunists. However, it was the continued civic and political engagement in the campus which kept the political space, and that too a communist and liberal political space, alive instead of the increasing penetration of the politics of political correctness. Communism needed just as much commitment as was required for academics. A leading Marxist social scientist, Amiya Kumar Bagchi from Calcutta, aptly described this predicament in this statement:

> As a fellow-economist ruefully admitted some years back, there is as yet no perfect socialism on earth. But along with him, I would also plead that we have to go on striving for a better system along the socialist path. For, plainly, we cannot afford the endless waste of capitalism, and the ever-present threat of having the earth blown up in a nuclear holocaust. In order to strive for socialism, we will need staunch commitment. But at the same time, we must be able to look critically at the existing systems of 'transitional socialism'. The leaders of the socialist countries have certainly been doing so.[107]

14

Hermetic Shields to Ideological Whirlpool

> I feel sir, in the fitness of things, this university ought to have been established somewhere along the banks of the Ganges so that the cultural flow of the Ganges could have mingled with the cultural unity which Nehru preached.[1]

The identity of the intellectual has been a serious philosophical issue in the West. Karl Mannheim perceived them as free-floating (*freischwebende intelligenz*) mavericks who belonged to no group at all.[2] Theodore Adorno, who was himself an exile, tried to pinpoint the location of the intellectuals within the society and came to the conclusion that they resided in a twilight zone. The intellectual is both a member of the bourgeoisie and simultaneously trying to annihilate it. The possible intransigence of the intellectual consists in being the proverbial square peg, and one whose sole business it is to demythologize.[3]

At a personal level, many JNU students became intellectuals of Adorno's kind with one caveat—they were not part of the bourgeoisie, and occupied a whole different place. Many were in exile, and in fact those from the backward regions were twice exiled. While they were exiled from the context of their own backgrounds, they were also exiled from the changed context which they faced on their possible return. They became homeless, occupying a zone where they engaged with a world which was neither the third nor the fourth.

This has been the key factor which propelled many to seek their real location, and significantly the left politics gave them a meaning well beyond mere political ideology. It gave them a vocation and a life world.

The idea that they were (or could be) organic intellectuals, as Gramsci had defined them, provided most with a true vocation to attempt to shape the political and social vision that they would like to live and work for. Most of the students who landed in the space were first or second generation into the university world. They were also part of the larger social milieu and trying to create a sphere that was different from the context of the metropolis. Thus, JNU framed a very interesting world where progressive political and social philosophy was located in the social milieu of one's own comfort. This was one of the crucial reasons for reserving seats for students from backward regions. They knew the society, they interpreted and took active part in them. What JNU did in their lives was to give them a larger overall picture, a dream, and a way to look for utopia—a telos. This made their engagement meaningful to themselves and to others.

In his deeply perspicacious work on intellectuals in the Third World, Edward Shils argued insightfully that Third World intellectuals, particularly like those in India, are too well read in the Western ideologies. This was true in the JNU context with a difference. What Shils was indicating was the colonial universities as symbolized by those of Calcutta, Madras or Bombay. They produced mimics and the alumni represented a provincialized Europe. No wonder their alumni knew it so well and rehashed it quite often: writing autobiographical tracts to legitimize their existence.[4]

Right from the very beginning, JNU, as we saw, also engaged with the contemporary trajectories of western European Marxism. The large number of people who assembled here, however, immediately indicated the major fault lines of the discourse and tried to put the corrective into it both theoretically and praxeologically. The centres that failed to do so, in fact, failed to evolve any long-term institutional identity. For example, it was in the domain of political science that the new discourse met their first intellectual interlocutors. Calcutta, and quite often Bombay, had traditionally been the first ports of call for all new ideas as well as 'imported intellectual fashions' that mimicked the colonial system. Delhi had its reasons for developing a different intellectual contour, and JNU brought a new intellectual landscape to town where the fashion and Delhi's questioning attitude to all such foreign import met against a single backdrop. The campus itself became an interesting mosaic where there were also regional twists. For the Bengali intellectual, for whom all 'new' things were liberatory, would meet the hardcore Delhi-wallah who would test all such items or ideas in the mill of governance or administerability in real life.[5] They all met in JNU and after the initial hiccups, there was a sense of acceptance. This meeting of glamour of the new and the earthiness of the practical would lend a sui generis character to JNU.

Both for the JNU students and the Indian left, discussions on Western Marxism became a significant milestone. Indian Marxism was not theoretically vacuous and quite often has an overdose of theory—Stalinistic theory. Even the French and other communist parties, which the JNU scholars studied and sympathized with, faced the same handicap. But the exhilarating debate of a large number of non-communists did not allow the left any more space and prestige than it acquired politically. The JNU and its intellectuals provided the Left the first open, unalloyed space to theoretically discuss issues of Marxism without the party bosses guiding the thought process. This space also proved to be the biggest available for the non-Marxists and anti-Marxists to intellectually take on theoretical issues and agendas with the Marxists. It is interesting that the thinkers who would critique totalitarian philosophies in the West, like C. Wright Mills, Adorno, etc., considered to be of the left, were used here to attack the totalitarianism of the communist party structure and many of the theoretical foundations of the Left.

In this context, it would be instructive to talk about one thinker who the JNU intellectuals followed quite intensely for a while—Althusser. He had argued that the 'party in France was born into a theoretical vacuum which had come to be filled by the exigencies of politics'.[6] He popularized the word 'conjuncture' and tried to intervene at the 'conjuncture of a couple of global events which included the speech of Khrushchev and the Sino-Soviet split which attacked the internationalism of the communist movement and the philosophical vacuum of French Marxism'.[7] The complex theories of Althusser took many teachers and researchers away into the world of Marxist ideas and salvaged them from feeling bad about being helpless in the politics of communism. One significant thing about the introduction was the evolution of many into serious intellectual gurus while invocation of issues like 'epistemological debate' would bring very mundane training in sociology, political science or economics into serious issues of theory.

It also happened that for many who took to such dense theories, i.e., Gramsci or Althusser, the writing and lectures became a ruse to mask theoretical and political opportunism. Quite often they were merely being verbose without saying anything concrete about the current or future possibilities in a language which was barely comprehensible to even the scholars. In JNU again, since many read such texts and engaged with them, the opportunism was soon discovered. This indicated the structural problem of knowledge production in a colonial setting. A student here takes up a theoretical project at university level, which, given the nature of college education in India, he or she is most often clueless about. After the initial training at the masters level, the students lacking linguistic and historical context of the philosophers take up a big philosophical issue for M.Phil. or Ph.D research. The discussion is followed up for the next one-and-a-half years. The moment one proceeds on a fellowship abroad, the issue is shelved for life as the no-nonsense funding organs as well as the host university abroad force the candidate to do conventional empirical work, most often on India. And, all that remains is a broken, disjointed academic programme and goalless academic trajectories. The disciplines therefore do not grow in cumulative ways.

JNU was no exception, with disciplines like political science, sociology and international studies where methods, issues and forces opposing metropolitan discourse had been very weak. Political science was mostly imitative, and the American patronage with their serious inroads had kept the development of political science across the world on a tight leash. The Marxist intervention and the historical orientation given to it by the British political science tradition which encouraged strong historiographical cultures in the different universities, allowed it to occupy some niche autonomous spaces by the mid-1980s. Looking forever for discourse provider departments, JNU no exception, brought Althusser, Gramsci and even Marcuse to be dissected and injected into localized discourses. The students and teachers followed the theoretical discourse but when they went abroad or developed these discourses into a full-fledged understanding of Indian political development or global development, they floundered phenomenally.

The case of sociology was slightly more complicated. The theories of Althusser, Gramsci, Luhmann or Giddens needed to be tested on the ground in Indian villages. Too much theory might have prevented a proper articulation of the reality. However, theory was needed even if developed indigenously. But an overarching presence of the theoretical discourse in the community remained a temptation. Thus, sociology remained precarious, like the proverbial tightrope walker, poised between temptations of theory and the dangers of losing the reality. No wonder, many, not necessarily from JNU, declared themselves anthropologists (reality checkers) abroad and sociologists (theory builders) in India.

It is at this juncture that the idea of an *organic intellectual* helped the JNU students as well as many teachers escape the disarticulating role of the discourses. In the mainstream of political debate, the intellectuals' role had reached a point in which they were for the first time giving lead to a radical hope to the state politics. JNU created a new discursive universe, and, in fact, if a prize was to be awarded for debating Althusser or Marcuse in the most linguistically varied place, JNU can easily claim to be the winner.[8]

This universe also gave the city a physical face to an intellectual: the Jholawallah (the man toting cotton shoulder bag). By the mid-1980s, the term 'Jholawallah' became an easily identifiable term of identity for the JNU intellectuals in particular and the social critic in general. The economy had been undergoing imperceptible changes and the new segments emerged from the middle classes with a new taste in dress, films, and aesthetics. Delhi being better dressed and slightly more formal than any other city in the country, the kurta-pyjama or jeans-kurta-clad JNU student had become slightly passé, and, although JNU provided the space for this transition, he managed to stand out. The JNU's stamp was also distinct in this intellectual's involvement in discussions of political and intellectual issues.

Protecting Evolved Disciplines

By the mid-1970s, the universities across the country not only erected boundaries to movement between universities, they also resisted quality in college and university teaching thereby blocking upward mobility.

There were now clear indications that the posts of vice chancellors were increasingly compromised and appointments were made with an eye to caste, community or political patronage. Universities in Karnataka, Kerala, Tamil Nadu, Bihar, Punjab and Maharashtra were sinking into a morass of mediocrity due to caste and community considerations. Many disciplines, which had taken deep root in various universities and colleges, were now beginning to face crises. Universities and colleges in many parts of the country became suddenly outdated by the increasingly changing contours of the city where they were located and by the local politics and new entrants. The political science department of Rajasthan University or philosophy department of Allahabad University were no longer able to retain or obtain internationally acclaimed faculty.

In Orissa, Karnataka, Rajasthan and Punjab, their deep-rooted political science departments were adversely hit by the crises of the 1970s and '80s. It was not only a thematic dead end, the regeneration of new scholarship was also in crisis. Rajasthan University had developed a very powerful political science tradition and by the mid-1960s they boasted of the best department in the subject. With the imposition of Hindi following the strident demands by the rioting RSS and Samajvadis, the university not only lost many teachers from across many disciplines, but political discourses began to narrow down. Instead of the department moving up the international ladder, it came to a halt. There were similar cases in several other regions in the country. Students abandoned their caste- or community-ridden campuses oozing parochial sentiments and gravitated towards JNU, a sanctuary for the national and international community. The advent of these students from all over India provided JNU one of the finest intellectual spaces in Indian history. A new tradition was in the offing and when many of these scholars returned to their regions and states they carried the seeds of these traditions, and, by the mid-1990s, the JNU alumni made a significant academic impact across the country.

JNU nurtured many regional hubs and provided core competency to these hubs. For example, the graduates who came from Kerala had a beautiful mixture of politics and pragmatism, and in JNU they found a compatible atmosphere where Marxism could be studied without reducing it to mere rhetoric—the prevailing mode in Kerala. The arrival of postgraduate students and researchers from Kerala helped

JNU blend this brand of communism with Bengal's, which was a curious mix of academic, logical and sentimental. The rootedness of the Kerala intellectuals provided a genuine earthiness and practicality to the discourse of both Marxists and anti-Marxists and avoided the purely doctrinaire approach.

Creating a New Paradigm: the North-east

JNU provided a space for many students to discuss the oppressiveness of modern state apparatuses and its physical manifestation in places like India's north-east. The military oppression and corruption were openly criticized. The Marxists, Naxals and socialist sections seriously engaged in research, which helped the dialogue reach a higher plane than mere rhetorical attack on the Indian state.

JNU incubated the Manipur University, which remained JNU's Imphal centre until 1981. This direct linkage provided an intellectual connect with the issues and discussions of a different kind. This connect also provided the local intellectual in Manipur some space which the Indian state and the security agencies do not necessarily provide in the strife-torn states there. When North-Eastern Hill University came up, it got many JNU students as faculty into its various departments. Therefore, JNU contributed in a big way in making the intellectual world of the north-east. The north-eastern students, particularly from Nagaland, Mizoram and Manipur became the harbingers of a new discursive universe. Through active realization of the peculiarities and distinctiveness of the region—the people, its history and resistance to what was called mainstream—for the first time these students met a world in JNU that fully endorsed their world view, which had been nurtured by the missionaries over their first twenty years of education. They discovered (a) how to continue holding a distinct voice in a space which was to be won and (b) the place allowed the exploration of distinct models to link the experiential part of research. The linking of the particular life world of the community to the larger geopolitical as well as theoretical issues of an expanding economy defined the JNU tradition, and this tradition soon studded the new universities to create a vibrant second generation of scholars.

Arunachal Pradesh commenced its socio-intellectual life quite afresh in the late 1960s, which was coterminous with the establishment of JNU. College, and later on, university education, began in the late 1970s, and JNU as an institution, made an enduring impact. The three colleges in Teju, Pasighat and Itanagar where many JNU students went on to teach in, benefitted from the zeal, dedication and intellectual perspective of these fresh young minds. The Arunachal University recruited candidates from JNU into their faculty when it was established—some fresh out of JNU and others transferred from their posts in other colleges. The role of these pioneers was significant. Compared to other teachers from Orissa, Bihar, Uttar Pradesh and Bengal, the intellectual hegemony that the JNU students gradually created left an indelible mark on the character of the institution and its intellectual life. Unlike the JNU students, the other faculty had originated from a limiting horizon. Interaction with the JNU students brought a different awareness to connect academics to social life. Their general irreverence for politicians and higher-ups also helped the teaching community raise its confidence level. In the early 1990s, when foreign universities needed local collaborators for their mundane and fact-finding missions, basically as data compilers, i.e., the low-end intellectual associate, they were inundated with applicants but none of whom were from JNU. The students trained by the JNU students had already begun occupying positions of intellectual, political and administrative leadership in the state and the region.

Assam has always been home to the most fascinatingly independent and creative intellectual community. The Assam Sahitya Parishad, the literary society of Assam, has been the key mover of the political history of not only Assam but also of the region through the late nineteenth century. During the second half of the twentieth century, a powerful left movement had also occupied the intellectual imagination that actively influenced the social scientists there. The Karimganj riots in the 1960s triggered an increasing tide of nativism and anti-outsider feeling. The intellectual world witnessed a sharp split over the issue of language and later domicile. In the 1980s, the Assam movement came into sharp relief. JNU gradually became the first port of call for the Assamese students on their way to Allahabad or BHU or even Delhi. Soon there was a strong Assamese presence in many social science departments. This group of students would emerge as the new sensitive set of intellectuals who would join the Assam intellectual debate from a different angle. They were sympathetic to the students' movement and, unlike the response of the Indian state at the time, the climate of JNU was also sympathetic to the movement. The student leaders often visited JNU to discuss their issues and thereby JNU also served as a link to the rest of the nation. The movement increasingly released forces inimical to the communist and leftist intellectual practices and, the post-1970s Assamese left tradition found both a haven of refuge in JNU as well as fountains of inspiration for many good works. Interestingly, as these students were not part of the Assam Sahitya Parishad, they deviated from the old political, literary and intellectual paradigm that existed in the state.

During its initial years, JNU proved to be a haven for the Bengalis who needed to escape the Naxalite extravaganza. By default, it had also become an enabling institution for those who did not secure good marks in the Calcutta University's tough 'marks(-ist)' regime. The old intellectual of Bengal did not like JNU much as they did Calcutta University. Soon the presence of some good economics teachers and historians drew students to JNU and so did the department of political science which had always been a laggard in Calcutta. Sociology was a novelty and some were drawn to it. By the late 1970s, therefore, the Calcutta students and teachers had quite a large presence in JNU. The intrinsically colonial mind of the Calcutta intellectual universe would resent any parallel centre and therefore there was always an effort to run down the JNU as being a state-sponsored, pro-establishment or a Punjabi entrepreneurial centre. Just as in many other walks of life, JNU created confusion in the Calcutta intellectual's mind—it abhorred the democratic space available here as it was the opposite of the ethos in Calcutta, which was inherently hierarchical and based on pedigree, either of the family or a degree from Cambridge or Oxford.

By the mid-1980s, several Bengali alumni from JNU began teaching in various places in Bengal and their presence helped ease the tension in many places, except in the entrenched spaces of elitist domination like the department of history of the Calcutta University which remained cocooned in a discourse originating from the metropolis while negotiating with a sectarian political outfit which refused to give space to any discordant voices.

UPSC-wallah

A significant part of the day-to-day negotiation within the university precincts was between the academics and what has been referred to as UPSC-wallahs. One of the foremost contributions of JNU in the first few years was to send some of its very best students to the civil services. There was not much difference between the serious academics and those preparing for the civil services entrance examinations, and therefore many, after their MA or M.Phil., opted for the civil services. They were significant losses to the academia. Some would-be civil servants considered plotting subversion from within while others aspired to do good for society, and many simply chose the line for academic and family reasons—one must keep in mind that employment opportunities were scarce in the 1970s. Many have risen very high, keeping their academic propensity intact. Things changed a bit in the 1980s, as academic rigour was perceived as being opposed to clearing the UPSC exams. The main reasons were:

(a) due to the gradual decline of the standard of education at the students' pre-JNU undergraduate level, in order to prepare for civil service exams they now had to start from a completely different level.

(b) by the 1980s, there were clear-cut regional specializations on the issue. Students from the backward regions and states were now more inclined to write their civil services examination as it was the only avenue for social mobility, and many such students from Orissa, Bihar, UP and other states made JNU their base to prepare for civil services.

This had an interesting outcome. There were now academic highbrows and the UPSC-wallahs. Although the civil service aspirants were now no longer seen as serious academics, the social cohesion and politics did not allow a complete rupture. This is significant because from this section emerged many good academics, journalists and scholars. One has to see the Indian society sympathetically where engaging with academics for its own sake was something very few could afford. Subjects like history, sociology and even political science had all but disappeared from many prestigious universities due to lack of state and local patronage. Qualifications in the social sciences led to declining professional standards particularly in a region with a scarcity of employment options. Students' enrolment at least for the sake of preparing for the civil services, kept the door to social sciences open.

The annual UPSC coaching has since become an almost hundred-crore-rupee business. JNU teachers, however, have come out brilliantly on this count as one cannot find a single teacher from the hundreds who has ever earned money from such coaching. The records demonstrate that the general level of scholarship required for aspirants escalated by notches over their seniors who cleared the exams during the 1950s and '60s. The talk of decline of the services will have to be seen in some other context. The UPSC candidates on JNU were linked to current issues and it gave them a competitive edge. It also brought an influx of students from smaller towns where social sciences is a no-no, and many chose to stay on. Many have argued that the UPSC had sullied the reputation of JNU and brought the academic standards down. The fact, however, is that, even without many people writing the UPSC exams, many subjects like economics showed a high dropout rate at the doctoral level. On the other hand, civil servants educated at JNU have been some of the most conscientious and honest officers in the bureaucracy with progressive value orientation. It was the JNU students who, in many parts of the country, raised their voice against corruption, bad governance or communal violence even when they were part of the administrative system.

A Home-grown Discourse

Self-reliance was practised to create a large universe of discourse and to sustain it, publication became a vital tool. The university presses, like Oxford, were extremely elitist and colonial in their outlook and manned by products of their own institutions who lived in a colonial closet. The emergent Indian scholars, many of whom came to the new university, either ignored or were ignored by these presses. Although they felt they had something critical to say, which needed to be conveyed urgently, they were too independent to rely on the old-school orientation of the existing publishing firms. The newly established publishing houses were patronized by these scholars at the time and went on to become big Indian publishers mainly for this count. This was in addition to the People's Publishing House, which was a benchmark for the best of scholarship at the time in many areas of contemporary concern as also of historical scholarship since the 1950s.

The new publishing concerns also helped the emerging academics to publish easily. Unlike what one saw in Europe and Africa, where publication costs were very high and cartels controlled the whole of the publication business, in India only some areas like Indology and a few other fields had similar cartels. They, however, did not enter the picture as JNU did not excite lucrative business prospects because it did not have the department of Sanskrit or philosophy or a conventional ancient history department where they could dump books or could earn some business abroad. The new publishers like Vikas and Rawat, and also established ones like Orient Longman, not only got good authors, but also good readers and buyers.

Scholars like Namvar Singh launched an entirely new genre, and the journal, *Alochana*, became a signature for the new mood that he helped create in the world. Similarly, the quality and substance of the regular debate was also helped by publications in the *Economic and Political Weekly*, the *Mainstream* or even the CPI magazine, *Link*, and the Hindi magazine, *Dinman*. These periodicals were not to be scoffed at as they had an impressively wide readership, and they often reached several hundred times more than one editorially truncated piece from some highbrow university press or an indexed piece in an obscure academic journal. To bolster this and following the tradition that the *American Economic Review* followed, the Centre for Historical Studies produced its own journal, *Studies in History*. The School of International Studies already had a journal, and the School of Languages launched a journal including one in Spanish, the only one in the field. In the first decade of the twentieth century, the American economists decided to launch their own journal and committed their own papers to it and soon the *American Economic Review* became not only the flagship journal of the American economists but also the best journal in the field. In a similar vein, JNU historians published their papers in their own journal which soon made the journal the best representative of historical works from the fresh scholarship. The sociologists too founded their flagship journal, *Sociological Bulletin*. The urgency of many debates made intellectuals publish rapidly and this made pamphlet writing the best mode of publication on the campus. In fact JNU may be the most productive academic space anywhere in the world in the field of write-ups by students and scholars and their animated responsiveness to the ongoing issues, with debates and rhetoric in them. Sometimes, half a dozen pamphlets distributed in the mess would charge the intellectual and political energies more than any article or book could have done.

In 1972, the organization of social science research that began around the late 1960s evolved into the Indian Council for Historical Research (ICHR) and Indian Council for Social Science Research (ICSSR). The ICSSR brought forth its journal, *Indian Social Science Review*, while the ICHR, organized around 1972, published the *Indian Historical Review*. These were now the publishing arenas for the scholars. Around this time, the CPI(M) decided to organize its intellectuals around its own journal and the *Social Scientist* was launched. Initially, when the editorial was completely subservient to the party ideology, presence of writers like Krishna Bharadwaj, for example, maintained a semblance of neutrality. However, the hegemony of the left at this point of time made the journal soon take up a major position. Many teachers of foreign languages found their creative expression in those highly ornate coffee table magazines run by the bureaucratic, crony business cartels brought out by the officials and other organizations designed to promote Indian culture abroad, i.e., the Arabic or Hispanic world. They, however, dealt a heavy blow to the development of the literary culture among the foreign language faculties as the internal journals could not compete with these ornate and highly visible journals.

The absence of a publication programme of the university undermined the university's visibility and, in the 1990s, when the demand for publishing rose in the international arena, many had to scout outside for even second-rate journals or publishing houses where the editorials were often highly antagonistic to what they termed 'the Third World perspective'.

Arrival of the Wayward

The predominant discourse and legitimizing forms of the polity was caste and, significantly enough, the intellectual discourse was coloured by it. The dominant caste's rule in the states also affected the state universities and increasingly the universities would reflect the caste composition of the polity and administration. By the 1980s, in many places there was very little to distinguish the university from being a mere extension of the state administration. Caste (in most universities in the country), or a particular tribe and even religious community as in Kashmir, or regional share (Jammu), seemed legitimate considerations.

Right from the beginning, the intellectual core which defined and constituted JNU had tried to link the regional and local realities to the larger global and intellectual trends and, therefore, from its perspective, the discourse ran differently, and it saw the communal and caste discourse as antithetical to the actual creation of an autonomous intellectual domain. JNU as a community never demanded autonomy from the state as Osmania and some other universities did. Instead, its intellectuals actually tried to define that autonomy by identifying its core in what G. Parthasarathi called 'self-reliant intellectual space'.

The connection with the international left movement and the debate therein provided the global context to the university, minus the global infrastructure. This remained the big issue. Any move to introduce the global standard would invite the wrath of the local left. In fact, the first move by the then SFI began on the issue of infrastructure, most remarkably their stand on the issue of bathrooms. One of the leaders of the federation objected to the fact that the faculty had more bathrooms per head than the students did. The same leader in later years raised the same issue to show the dreadful conditions of Aligarh University. It seemed to boil down to a scatological communism. However, the issue was taken seriously at that point in time.

The new university began to show an awesome presence of diversity—a youth from Orissa or Bihar or Maharashtra could speak the new language of academic discourse. It was a revolution of sorts in India's higher education. For the first time in India, the discussions at

JNU bypassed the colonial universities and their self-image of being an intellectual satellite.

Oxford and Cambridge had been the status markers of the new academic elite. Now suddenly a new breakthrough had come and it had the social respectability of being different. JNU, which began to occupy a different notation in the world, was the new happening place and something one did not want to miss out on.

Notes

Chapter 1

1 Submission by Kothari, D.S., 'Verbatim Report of Evidence given before the Joint Committee on the Jawaharlal Nehru University Bill, 1964', (hereafter *Report of Evidence*) Parliament of India, p. 50.

2 Mahavir Tyagi to Jawaharlal Nehru, 23 October 1963; Chagla, M.C., *Roses in December*, Bharatiya Vidya Bhawan, Bombay, 1973, p. 499.

3 Chagla to Lal Bahadur Shastri, 15 February 1965, *M.C. Chagla Papers*, Nehru Memorial Museum and Library, New Delhi, File, 75, p. 68.

4 Ibid.

5 See Nihar Ranjan Ray's critique of Gupta's stand on the UGC Report on 22 April 1958 in Rajya Sabha, see Dr Nihar Ranjan Ray, 22 April, 1958, *Rajya Sabha Debates*, Vol. XXI, No. 2, cc.96–105 Later, Chagla in reply to L.M. Singhvi's private member's bill seven years later also quoted 'number' as a major concern in the field of education: 'Fifty million boys are there in primary schools today. It is what I call an expansion explosion. We have not sufficient teachers, trained teachers, we have not sufficient schools, we have not sufficient textbooks … In all these things, what we have to remember is that the numbers are astronomical: fifty million students in primary school, about ten million in secondary schools and a million and a quarter in colleges and universities. In any scheme which we device, we are faced with these enormous numbers.' M.C. Chagla, *Rajya Sabha Debates*, 25 March 1965. See also *The Times of India*, Delhi, 26 March 1965.

6 Nehru himself was averse to the idea of having his name for the new university and had given Chagla a dressing-down when this had been brought up in conversation. Chagla M.C., *Roses in December*, p. 373.

7 Chagla, M.C., ibid.

8 Bhabha, Homi, Presidential Address at Atoms for Peace Conference, Geneva, 22 August 1955, *The Times of India*, Delhi, 23 August 1955.

9 One could see this in the life and work of Vikram Sarabhai; see, Shah, Amrita, *Vikram Sarabhai*, Penguin Books, New Delhi, 2010.

10 E.M.S. Namboodiripad, 'Modernism', *Seminar*, 63, 1964, p. 34.

11 Ibid., p. 37.

12 Gupta, Bhupesh, *Rajya Sabha Debates*, 1 September, 1965, Vol. LIII, No. 12, cc. 2301.

13 Ibid.

14 Ibid.

15 Ibid.

16 Ibid.

17 Ibid.

18 Ibid., c. 2302.

19 Ibid.

20 Ibid. On teaching socialism in the university, he was very clear: scientific socialism must be taught here. 'Therefore, have a faculty for the study of socialism. I know, in the post-graduate courses Marxism is taught but the books are always from the United States of America, which display no knowledge of Marxism at all. Therefore, Mr. Chairman, I should like a faculty to be created to impart proper education of this kind.'

21 Nussbaum, Martha C., *For Love of Country: Debating the Limits of Patriotism*, Beacon Press, Cambridge, Massachusetts, 2002; Yael, Tamir, *Liberal Nationalism*, Princeton University Press, New Jersey, 1993.

22 Asoka Mehta to M.C. Chagla, 2 December 1964, *M.C Chagla Papers*, File no. 74.

23 Ibid.

24 Ibid.

25 Ibid.

26 Ibid.

27 Ibid.

28 Ibid.

29 Ibid.
30 Ibid.
31 Ibid.
32 The members were: Shri B. Anjanappa, Shri Frank Anthony, Choudhury Brahm Prakash, Kumari Kamala Choudhury, Raja P.C. Deo Bhanj, Shri Shiv Charan Gupta, Shri Hem Barua, Pandit Jwala Prasad Jyotishi, Shri Lahri Singh, Shri Bakar Ali Mirza, Shri F.H. Mohsin, Shri H.N. Mukerjee, Shri V.T. Patil, Shri N.G. Ranga, Shrimati Renuka Ray, Shrimati Jayaben Shah, Shri M.P. Swamy, Shri Amar Nath Vidyalankar, Shri Bhishma Prasad Yadava and Shri Bhakt Darshan. *Lok Sabha Debates*, Vol. 46, No. 25, 1965, cc. 6507–09. A small note appeared in the day's newspaper, 'Scope of Nehru University', *The Times of India*, 21 September 1965.
33 Ibid., 'Partition of the country on the eve of Independence led to a tremendous influx of displaced persons with the result that population of Delhi doubled itself in two years, i.e., from 7 lakhs in 1946-47 to 14 lakhs in 1948-49'. Ibid.
34 Ibid.
35 Ibid., c. 6508
36 Ibid., c. 6509
37 Ibid., c. 6510.
38 Ibid., c. 6511.
39 A deemed university was a category used to denote institutions that had the potential to emerge as full-fledged universities over time. Ibid., c. 6514.
40 Ibid.
41 Ibid.
42 Ibid.
43 Ibid.
44 Ibid.
45 Bhakt Darshan, ibid, c. 6514.
46 M.S. Aney, Jawaharlal Nehru University Bill, 20 September 1965, *Lok Sabha Debates*, c. 6526.
47 Ibid.
48 Ibid.
49 Ibid., c., 6525
50 Ibid.
51 Ibid., c. 6720.
52 Ibid.

53 Ibid., cc. 6722–24.
54 Ibid., cc. 6518–19.
55 Ibid., c. 6535.
56 Ibid., c. 6525.
57 Ibid.
58 Ibid., c. 6543.
59 D.C. Sharma, 21 September, 1965 *Lok Sabha Debates* Vol. XLVI, No. 21 c. 6706.
60 Ibid.
61 Ibid., cc. 6526–27.
62 L.N. Singhvi, 20 September, Ibid., cc. 6537–38.
63 Ibid.
64 D.C. Sharma, 21 September, 1965 *Lok Sabha Debates* Vol. LXVI, No. 21 cc. 6706–7.
65 Chandrabhan Singh, 21 September, *Ibid.*
66 Yashpal Singh, ibid., cc. 6727–28.
67 Khadilkar, R.K., ibid., cc. 6714–16.
68 Ibid.
69 Ibid.; (see also, 'High Standard and Many Courses', *The Times of India*, Delhi, 22 September 1965.)
70 Ibid., c. 6706.
71 D.C. Sharma, 20 September, *ibid.* cc. 6577–79.
72 Ibid., c. 6708.

Chapter 2

1 Professor Tara Chand speaking on the Jawaharlal Nehru University Bill, 2 December 1965, *Rajya Sabha Debates*, Vol. LIV, No. 21 c. 3583.
2 Pradhan, R.D., *Debacle to Revival: Y.B. Chavan as Defence Minister, 1963-65*, Orient Longman, Hyderabad, 1998, pp. 248–49.
3 Ibid., p. 253.
4 Ibid., p. 296.
5 See Batabyal, Rakesh, 'The Hindu Communal Challenge, 1964-84', in Aditya Mukherjee (ed.), *A Centenary History of Indian National Congress*, Vol. V, Academic Foundation, Delhi, 2011, pp. 347–77.
6 Rao, S.L., (ed.), *Partial Memoirs of V.K.R.V. Rao*, Oxford University Press, Delhi, 2002. See also the first attempt to write a biography of

the man and his work, Mishra, Kiran, *V.K.R.V. Rao: His Life and Times*, Vikas Publishing House (P) Ltd, New Delhi, 1966.

7 Ranjan, S. and T. Raja Rao, 'Separation of organic acids by circular paper chromatography: Diurnal variations in the organic acids content in pelargonium', *Natrurewissenshaften*, Vol. 42, no. 21, 1955, p. 581.

8 Koshy, V.C., 'Jawaharlal Nehru University: A Model University? Perspective and Ideal', *Social Scientist*, Vol. 2, September 1973, pp. 46–51.

9 V.K.R.V. Rao, in 'Verbatim Report of Evidence given before the Joint Committee on the Jawaharlal Nehru University Bill, 1964', (Hereafter *Report of Evidence*), pp. 2–27.

10 *Report of Evidence*, p. 2.

11 Ibid.

12 Ibid.

13 Ibid., p. 10.

14 Ibid, p. 11.

15 Ibid. p. 25.

16 Ibid.

17 Ibid., pp. 21–22.

18 Ibid., p. 8.

19 Ibid., p. 9.

20 Ibid., p. 28.

21 Ibid.

22 Ibid., p. 15.

23 Submission by Kothari, D.S., *Report of Evidence*, p. 4.

24 Ibid., p. 46.

25 Ibid., pp. 46–47.

26 Submission by Chagla, M.C., ibid.

27 Submission by Kothari, D.S., ibid., p. 45.

28 Ibid.

29 Ibid.

30 Ibid., p. 46.

31 Ibid.

32 Ibid.

33 M. Ruthnaswamy, *Rajya Sabha Debates*, 2 December, 1965, Vol. LIV, No. 21, c. 3586.

34 Bhagwat Narayan Bhargava, ibid, c. 3524.

35 Submission by Kothari, D.S., *Report of Evidence*, p. 60.

36 Submission by Rao, V.K.R.V., ibid., p. 25.
37 Kothari, D.S., ibid, p. 4.
38 Jawaharlal Nehru University Bill, *Lok Sabha Debates*, 16 November 1966, Vol. LXI, cc. 3453–56.
39 Ibid., c. 3465.
40 Ibid., cc. 3490–92.
41 D. Thengari, 6 December, 1965, *Rajya Sabha Debates*, Vol. LIV, No. 23, c. 3806.
42 Regarding the adjustment of the Third World scholars in the little corners of anthropology or literary quarters in the American and British universities, see Arif Dirlik, *The Postcolonial Aura: Third World Criticism in the Age of Global Capitalism*, Westview Press, Boulder, 1998. Interestingly, this academic trend of privileging the local over the larger national or even international was in tune with the earlier phase of the cold-war politics when the military–industrial complex in the United States in fact favoured research and promotion of research agenda that suited the cold-war strategy of the state department. For a detailed treatment see, Robin Ron, *The Making of the Cold War Enemy*, Princeton University Press, New Jersey 1998; Simpson, C., *Universities and Empire, Money and Politics in the Social Sciences during the Cold War*, New Press, New York, 1998.
43 *JNU Bill 1964, Report of the Joint Committee, p. 58.*
44 Dissent, *Report of Evidence.*
45 Minutes of Dissent, JNU Bill, Report of Joint Committee, Rajya Sabha Secretariat, New Delhi 1965, p. xiii.
46 Ibid.
47 Ibid.
48 *Rajya Sabha Debates*, 1 December 1965, c. 3406.

'In the original scheme of this University, there was a division of the jurisdiction between the present Delhi University and the new university which is to come into existence. Now we have changed all this. 'It was pointed out in the select committee, I think with considerable force … that if this university was to start with about 17 or 18 colleges affiliated to it, the standard would immediately go down … Therefore, we decided that this university should not be an affiliating university, that the colleges which stand affiliated with the old university should continue to remain affiliated to it … And we came to the conclusion that the proper way to do so was not to take over the existing colleges but to set up and establish colleges, to run colleges which will not be affiliated colleges, but colleges which will be university colleges and which will be maintained by the university. ibid., c. 3405.

49 M B Lal, 6 December, 1965, *Rajya Sabha Debates*, Vol. LIV, No. 23, cc. 3821–22.

50 Chagla, M.C., *Rajya Sabha Debates*, 1 December, 1965, Vol. LIV, No. 20, c. 3401.

51 Ibid.

52 Sapru, P N, 1 December 1965, *Rajya Sabha Debates*, Vol. LIV, No. 20, cc. 3417–22.

53 Ibid., c. 3420–21.

54 *Rajya Sabha Debates*, 6 December 1965, Vol. LIV, No. 23, c. 3898.

55 Ibid., cc. 3907–08.

56 Submission by V.S. Jha, *Report of Evidence*, pp. 94–95.

57 Ibid.

58 Ibid, p. 94.

59 JNU Bill 1964, Report of the Joint Committee, Rajya Sabha, 1965 p. 5.

60 Ibid.

61 Ibid.,

62 Ibid., p. 54.

63 *Rajya Sabha Debates*, c. 3864.

64 Prof. Tara Chand, *Rajya Sabha Debates*, 6 December 1965, c. 3859.

65 Ibid.

66 Ibid., c. 3860.

67 Ibid.

68 Ibid., c. 3858.

69 *Rajya Sabha Debates*, 2 December 1965, c. 3583.

70 Ibid.

71 Ibid.

72 *Rajya Sabha Debates*, 2 December 1965, c. 3583.

73 Ibid.

74 Ibid., c. 3826.

75 Ibid.

76 Ibid., c. 3874.

77 Ibid., c. 3867.

78 Ibid., c. 3872.

79 Ibid., c. 3876.

80 Lal, M.B., 6 December 1965, *Rajya Sabha Debates*, Vol. LIV, No. 23, cc.3976–77.
81 White, Hayden, *Metahistory: The Historical Imagination in Nineteenth-Century Europe*, Johns Hopkins University Press, Baltimore 1975, p. 375.
82 Chagla, M.C., 16 November, *Lok Sabha Debates*, Vol LXI, No 11, c. 3429.
83 Shri Hanumanthaiya, ibid, c. 3445.

Chapter 3

1 Dr Tara Chand's suggested words in amendment no. 77 related to the preamble to the first schedule, 6 December 1965, *Rajya Sabha Debates*, Vol. LIV No. 23, c. 3898.
2 Amendment in the first schedule, ibid., c. 3909.
3 Nandy, Ashis, *The Intimate Enemy: Loss and Recovery of Self Under Colonialism*, Oxford University Press, Delhi, 1983; Chatterjee, Partha, *Nationalist Thought and the Colonial World: A Derivative Discourse*, Zed Books, London 1986; Chakravarty, Dipesh, *Provincialising Europe: Postcolonial Thought and Historical Difference*, Princeton University Press, New Jersey 2000.
4 Pandey, Gyanendra, *Construction of Communalism in Colonial North India*, Oxford University Press, Delhi, 1990.
5 It says among other things: 'The mission to include and strengthen global economic history in national systems of higher education is shared by all participants in GEHN,' Global Economic History Network, London School of Economics, http://www.lse.ac.uk/economicHistory/Research/GEHN/network/GEHNMission.aspx accessed in 2012 and re-accessed on 9 January 2014.
6 See the latest attempt in history writing in India which manifestly exhibits this same combination of rhetoric which work for the discourse of the borderless 'locals' and global.
7 Ganachari, Aravind, *Nationalism and Social Reform in Colonial Situation*, Gyan Publishing House, Delhi, 2005; Naik, J.V., 'Maharashtra's Bhau Mahajan and his Prabhakar, Dhumketu and Dnyan Darshan', *Indian Historical Review*, July 1996 and January 1997, Vol. XIII, Nos. 1 and 2, 135–152; Upadhyaya, Poonam, *Social, Political, Economic and Educational Ideas of Raja Rammohun Roy*, Mittal Publishers, Delhi, 1990; Kopf, David, *The Brahmo Samaj*

and the Shaping of the Modern Indian Mind, Princeton University Press, New Jersey, 1978; Singh, Sita Ram, *Nationalism and Social Reform in India*, Ranjit Publishers, Delhi, 1968; Panikkar, K.N., 'Intellectual and Cultural Issues in Colonial India: Some Conceptual and Historiographical Issues', Bhattacharya, and Romila Thapar (eds), *Situating India History*, Oxford University Press, Delhi, 1986; Ganguli, B.N., *Indian Economic Thought, Nineteenth Century Perspective*, Tata McGraw Hill Publishing Company, New Delhi, 1977; Joshi, V.C., *Ram Mohun Roy and Process of Modernisation in India*, NMML; New Delhi, 1974. Interestingly Rammohun Roy is absent in the new text book on Indian history published by the National Council for Education Research and Training (NCERT).

8 See, Batabyal, Rakesh, *Penguin Book of Modern Indian Speeches*, *Penguin Books*, New Delhi, 2007.

9 Omvedt, Gail, *Cultural Conflict in a Colonial Society: Non-Brahmin Movement in Western India*, Manohar, New Delhi, 1974; Sarkar, Sumit, *Modern India, 1885-1947*, Macmillan, Delhi, 1989.

10 Wolpert, Stanley, *Tilak and Gokhale: Revolution and Reform in the Making of Modern India*, University of California Press, Berkeley and Los Angeles, 1962.

11 Chandra, Bipan, *Rise and Growth of Economic Nationalism*, People's Publishing House, New Delhi 1965, (reprinted as an abridged version, Har Anand, Delhi, 2009).

12 A very recent conservative argument (after Iraq and Afghanistan intervention) on nation building from the United States has been forwarded by Fukuyama, Francis, *Nation Building, Beyond Afghanistan and Iraq*, Johns Hopkins University Press, Baltimure 2006.

13 Chandra Bipan, *Nationalism and Colonialism in Modern India*, Orient Longman, Hyderabad, 1979; Desai, A.R., *Social Background of Indian Nationalism*, Popular Prakashan, Bombay, 1948; Dutt, Rajani Palm, *India Today*, Peoples Publishing House, Bombay, 1947; Habib, Irfan, *Nationalism*, Tulika Publishers, New Delhi 2013. For a detailed representation of different views see Batabyal, Rakesh, *Penguin Book of Modern Indian Speeches*, Penguin Books, New Delhi, 2007.

14 Tilly, Charles and Gabriel Ardant, *Formation of Nation States in Western Europe*, Princeton University Press, New Jersey, 1975;

Wagner, Peter, Bjorn Wiltrock and Richard Whitley, *Discourse on Society: The Shaping of the Social Science Discipline*, Kluwer Academic Publications, Dordrecht, The Netherlands, 1991; Haupt, Claudia, *Religion-State Relations in United States and Germany*, Cambridge University Press, Cambridge, UK, 2011; Halperin, Sandra, *War and Social Change in Modern Europe: The Great Transformation, Revisited*, Cambridge University Press, Cambridge, UK, 2004; Hroch, Miloslav, *Social Preconditions of National Revival in Europe: A Comparative Analysis of the Social Composition of Patriotic Groups Among the Smaller European Nations*, Columbia University Press, New York, 2000; Hroch, Miloslav, *In the National Interest: Demands and Goals of European National Movements of the Nineteenth Century—A Comparative Perspective*, Charles University, Prague, 2000; Brubaker, Rogers, *Nationalism Reframed*, Cambridge University Press, Cambridge, UK, 1996; Smith, Anthony D., *The Nation in History: Historiographical Debates about Ethnicity and Nationalism*, John Wiley and Sons, London, 2000.

15 Chatterjee, Partha, *Nationalist Thought and the Colonial World a Derivative Discourse*, Zed Books, London, 1986. All the writings of Chatterjee are premised on this single notion and tries to prevaricate the issue of power of the colonial state.

16 Batabyal, Rakesh, *Penguin Book of Modern Indian Speeches*, Penguin Books, New Delhi, 2007.

17 This is a summarized version from his memoirs, *Roses in December*, Bharatiya Vidya Bhawan, 1973 (1980 new edition) and his private papers, *M.C. Chagla Papers*.

18 Nehru to Chagla, *M.C. Chagla Papers, Correspondence with Nehru*, pp. 1–2.

19 Ibid, p. 6.

20 Chagla, M.C., op cit.

21 Chagla, M.C., 'Law, Liberty and Life', the *Bombay Law Reporter, Journal*, May 1950, Vol. LII, pp. 138–46.

22 Ibid., p. 49.

23 Ibid., pp. 49–50.

24 Chagla, M.C., *Roses in December*, 1980, (postscript).

25 Chagla, M.C., *Roses in December*, 1973, pp. 107–08.

26 P.M.'s Secretariat, U.O. No. PMS - 18710 of 30 August 1966 in *M.C. Chagla Papers*, File No. 77, p. 112.

27 Ibid.

28 Ibid.
29 Ibid.
30 Ibid.
31 Ibid.
32 Ibid., p. 113.
33 Prime Minister to M.C. Chagla, 8 September 1966, Ibid., p. 114.
34 'U.P. government is chiefly worried by the problem of infiltration of subversive elements into the universities. The present recruitment procedures can be improved by the appointment of panels of impartial and objective selectors by the University Grants Commission.' Extract from home ministry file, 21 January 1965, Poll-I as noted by Prem Kirpal, 19 April 1965. *M.C. Chagla Papers*, File No. 75, p. 95.
35 M.C. Chagla to Gulzarilal Nanda, *M.C. Chagla Papers*, File No. 76, p. 32.
36 Ibid.
37 Ibid.
38 Ibid.
39 An important critique of the liberals and their understanding of colonial and post-Independence Indian history was presented way back in 1970 in the presidential address of Bipan Chandra. See Chandra, Bipan, 'Colonialism and Modernisation', Presidential Address, Modern Indian History, Jubbalpore, 1970, *Proceeding of Indian History Congress*, 1970. This is reproduced in a new volume. See Mukherjee, Aditya, (ed.), *The Writings of Bipan Chandra—The Making of Modern India From Marx to Gandhi*, Orient Blackswan, Hyderabad, 2012, pp. 255–291.
40 *M.C. Chagla Papers*, File No. 104, p. 1.
41 Ibid., p. 2.
42 Ibid., pp. 16–19.
43 Broadcast by M.C. Chagla from All India Radio, Bombay, on 2 February 1948, *M.C. Chagla Papers*, Subject file No. 104, p. 69.
44 Ibid.
45 Ibid.
46 M.C. Chagla to D.P. Mishra, 26 October 1965, *M.C. Chagla Papers*, File No. 76, p. 122.
47 Gulzarilal Nanda to M.C. Chagla, 28 October 1965, ibid., p. 124.
48 D.P. Mishra to M.C. Chagla, 3 November 1965, ibid., pp. 133–34.
49 Ibid.

50 Ibid.
51 M.C. Chagla to Vice Chancellors, 30 November 1965, File No. F 14/65-EM, p. 49.
52 Nayar, Kuldip, *India: The Critical Years*, Vikas Publishing House, Delhi, 1971, p. 22.
53 Krishna Kumar, quoted in Patrick French, *India*, Penguin Books, New Delhi, 2010, p. 366.
54 Chagla, M.C., *The Individual and the State*, Asia Publishing House, Bombay, 1961.
55 *Patriot*, New Delhi, 21 November 1963.
56 *Amrita Bazar Patrika*, Calcutta, 21 November 1963, p. 5.
57 See, Rao, S.L., *Partial Memories of V.K.R.V. Rao*, Oxford University Press, Delhi, 2009; Kiran Mishra, *V.K.R.V Rao, His Life and Time*, Vikas Publishing House, Delhi, 1996, and private papers of V.K.R.V. Rao, NMML.
58 'Integrated Education', inaugural speech at the 16th session of the Bombay Civil Service (Judicial Association) Conference, 9 April 1955, in *The Individual and The State*, Asia Publishing House, Bombay 1958.
59 The Model of the Second Plan provided by P.C. Mahalanobis was called the two-sector model and he gave a model of employment generation. See Mishra, Sanjeev Kumar, *Mahalonobis Approach to Planning in India*, Deep & Deep Publications, Delhi, 1994. See also Batabyal, Rakesh, *Penguin Book of Modern Indian Speeches*, Penguin Books, New Delhi, pp. 575–582.
60 Education ministers' circular, 9 January 1966, *M.C. Chagla Papers*, File No. 78, pp. 3–5.
61 M.C. Chagla to Education Ministers, EF4-2/66-TS (NCERT), ibid., File No. 78, p. 54.
62 Subhadra Joshi to Lal Bahadur Shastri, 19 November 1965, ibid., File No. 76, p. 180.
63 M.C. Chagla to T.N. Singh, Janaury 1966, ibid., File No. 77, part IV, p. 9.
64 Ibid.
65 Ibid.
66 M.C. Chagla to Nawab Ali Yavar Jung Bahadur, 27 February 1965, *M.C. Chagla Papers*, File No. 80 p. 86.
67 M.C. Chagla to Gulzarilal Nanda, 3 May 1965, ibid., File No. 80, p. 1.

68 Ibid.
69 M.C. Chagla to Lal Bahadur Shastri, 23 September 1965, ibid., p. 75.
70 Ibid.
71 Ibid.
72 M.C. Chagla to Asad Madani, 23 May 1965, ibid, pp. 5–6.
73 K.A. Hamied to M.C. Chagla, 14 July 1965, ibid., p. 43. Hamied's career demonstrated what education could do to a determined person. Born in Shahjahanpur in UP and educated in Islamia High School, Kanpur, Hamied moved to Aligarh from where he went to the Central Leather Research Institute, Madras. From Madras he got a scholarship to study in Germany where his career took a completely new turn and he returned to set up the pharmaceutical firm named CIPLA, which by the late 1960s emerged as India's answer to many multinational pharmaceutical companies. Hamied has been India's best technical pioneer (Hamied, K.A., *A Life to Remember: An Autobiography*, Lalwani Publishing House, Bombay, 1972.)
74 M.C. Chagla to Syed Mahmud, 20 May 1965, ibid., p. 3.
75 Qureshi, Z.M., 'Electoral Strategy of a Minority Pressure Group: Muslim Mazlis-e-Mushawarat', *Asian Survey*, December 1968; Shah, A.B., 'Aligarh once again', *New Quest*, May–June, 1978, pp. 143–144; Wright, Theodore P., 'Muslim Representation in India', in Donald Smith (ed.), *South Asian Politics and Religion*, Princeton University Press, New Jersey, 1966; Bipan Chandra, 'AMU and the Communalist: Dangerous Game of Appeasement', *Mainstream*, 7 March 1981.
76 M.C. Chagla to the prime minister, 31 August 1967, Appendix XII, *Roses in December, An Autobiography*, Bharatiya Vidya Bhawan, Bombay, 1973 p. 505.
77 Vice Chancellors' Conference, *Link*, 17 September 1967, pp. 12–13.
78 M.C. Chagla to the prime minister, *Roses in December*, p. 505.
79 Ibid.
80 Ibid., p. 506.
81 Ibid.
82 Ibid.
83 Ibid.
84 Ibid.

85 Ibid.

86 Bayly, Christopher Alan, *Recovering Liberties: Indian Thought in the Age of Liberalism and Empire*, Cambridge University Press, Cambridge, UK, 2012; Mehta, Uday Singh, *Liberalism and Empire: A Study in Nineteenth-Century British Liberal Thought*, University of Chicago Press, Chicago 1999.

87 Bilgrami, Akeel, 'Secular Liberalism and Moral Psychology', *Economic and Political Weekly*, Vol. 32, No. 40, 4–10 October 1997, pp. 2527–40.

Chapter 4

1 See a good introductory account of this period in the United States and in western Europe in Anderson, Terry, *The Sixties*, Pearson, New Jersey, 2011; Farrell, James J., *The Spirit of the Sixties: The Making of Postwar Radicalism*, Routledge, New York, 1997; Marwick, Arthur, *The Sixties: Cultural Revolution in Britain, France, Italy, and the United States, 1958-78*, Bloomsbury, London, 2012; Van Gosse, Richard R. Moser, *The World the Sixties Made: Politics and Culture in Recent America*, Temple University Press, Philadelphia, 2003.

2 Judt, Tony, *Post War Europe since 1945*, Penguin Books, New York 2005, p. 391.

3 Ibid., p. 394.

4 Ibid.

5 Aron, Raymond, *Memoirs: Fifty Years of Political Reflections*, Holmes and Meier, New York and London, 1990, p. 232.

6 Ibid.

7 Ibid., p. 234.

8 Di Vittorio, Antonio, *An Economic History of Europe From Expansion to Development*, Routledge, Oxford, 2006; Kindleberger, Charles P., *The World Economy and National Finance in Historical Perspective*, University of Michigan Press, Ann Arbor, Michigan, 1995; Kindleberger, Charles, *A Financial History of Western Europe*, George Allen and Unwin, London, 1984.

9 Houben, Vincent J. H., Howard Dick and J. Thomas Lindblad, *The Emergence of a National Economy: An Economic History of Indonesia, 1800-2000*, University of Hawaii Press, Honolulu, 2002; Chandra, Bipan, 'Colonial Legacy', in Bimal Jalan (ed.), *Indian*

Economy, Penguin Books, New Delhi 1991; Ivor Agyeman-Duah, *An Economic History of Ghana*, Turnaround Publishers Services, London, 2008.

10 See, Singh, Vir Bahadur (ed.), *Economic History of India, 1857-1956*, Allied Publishers, Delhi, 1981.

11 For the famine see, Singh, K. S., *The Indian Famine 1967*, People's Publishing House, New Delhi, 1975; Brass, P. R., 'The Political Uses of Crisis: The Bihar Famine of 1966-1967', in *Journal of Asian Studies*, Vol. 45, 1986, pp. 245–267; Ramalingaswami, V., Deo M.G., Guleria, J.S., Malhotra, K.K., Sood, S.K. Prakash, and R.V.N. Sinha, 'Studies of the Bihar Famine of 1966-67', in Blix, G., Y. Hofvander, and B. Vahlquist, (eds), *Famine: Nutrition and Relief Operations*, Swedish Nutrition Foundation, Uppsala, 1971; Batabyal, Rakesh, 'Famine in 20th Century India: A Historiographical Critique', paper presented at the sixth Indo-Japanese dialogue on South Asia, 21 December 2013, New Delhi.

12 Gaddis, John Lewis, *The Long Peace Inquiries into the History of the Cold War*, Oxford University Press, New York, 1987.

13 Ibid. Some new works on the cold war include, Leffler, P. Melvyn, and Odd Arne Westad (eds.), *Cambridge History of the Cold War*, Vol. 1, *Origins*, Cambridge University Press, Cambridge, U.K. 2010; Mazower, M., 'Changing Trends in the Historiography of Post-war Europe, East and West', *International Labour and Working Class History*, 58, 2000, pp. 275–82; Hogan, Michael J., *America in the World: Historiography of the American Foreign Relations since 1941*, Cambridge University Press, Cambridge, U.K. 1995; Naimark, N.M., 'Post-Soviet Russian Historiography on the Emergence of the Soviet Bloc', *Kritika*, 5, 3, Summer 2004, pp. 561–80; Xia, Y. 'The Study of Cold War International History in China: A Review of the Last Twenty Years, *Journal of Cold War Studies*, 10, 1, Winter 2008, pp. 81–115.

14 For a perceptive analysis of India's international relations as well as its foreign policy see, Karunakaran, K.P., *Outside the Contest: A Study of Nonalignment and the Foreign Policies of Some Nonaligned Countries*, People's Publishing House, New Delhi, 1963; Dutt, V.P., *India's Foreign Policy*, Vikas Publishing House, Delhi, 1984. For an analysis of India's non-aligned position, see Khan, Rasheeduddin, *Perspectives on Non-Alignment*, Kalamkar Prakashan, Delhi, 1981;

Mishra, K.P., and K.R. Narayanan, *Non-Alignment in Contemporary International Relations*, Vikas, Publishing House Delhi, 1983.

15 Verghese, B.G., has narrated the inner history of the pressure in his memoirs, *First Draft*, Tranquebar Press, Chennai, 2010, pp. 87–93.

16 B.K. Nehru, and L.K. Jha, with enormous goodwill and influence within both the US bureaucracy and leadership, can be credited with bringing the United States closer to India at this time. See Nehru, B.K., *Nice Guys Come Second*, Penguin Books, New Delhi, 1996.

17 Franckel, Francine, R., *India's Political Economy, 1947-2004: The Gradual Revolution*, Oxford University Press, Delhi, 2005, pp. 322–323; Nayar, Deepak, *India's Exports and Export Policies in the 1960's*, Cambridge University Press, Cambridge, UK, 2007, pp. 272–73. See also Sundaram, K., 'Political Response to the 1966 Devaluation: II Politicians and Parties', *EPW*, Vol. 7, No. 37, 9 September 1972, pp. 1883–92; Pupul Jayakar, *Indira Gandhi, A Biography*, Viking Books, New Delhi 1992.

18 Jayakar, Pupul, *Indira Gandhi, A Biography*, Viking Books, New Delhi, 1992.

19 Horowitz, David, *The Radical Son*, Simon and Schuster, New York, 1998.

20 P.C. Mahalanobis in Batabyal, Rakesh, *Penguin Book of Modern Indian Speeches*, Penguin Books, New Delhi, 2007, pp. 575–8. See also Mishra, S.K., *Mahalanobis Approach to Planning in India*, Deep and Deep Publications, Delhi, 1994; Gautam,Vinayshil, *Comparative Manpower Planning Practices in India, Select Indian Experience*, National Publishing House, Delhi, 1988.

21 Bundy, William P., 'Partnership in East Asia and the Pacific', *Department of State Bulletin*, 14 August 1967, pp. 195–200; see also Rusk, Dean, *As I Saw it: A Secretary of State's Memoirs*, B. Tauris, London, 1991.

22 Schrecker, Ellen, *No Ivory Tower: McCarthyism and the University*, Oxford University Press, New York, 1986; Lowen, Rebecca, *Creating the Cold War University: Transformation of Stanford*, Berkeley, California, 1997; Robin, Ron, *Making the Cold War Enemy: Culture and Politics in the Military-Intellectual Complex*, Princeton University Press, New Jersey, 2001; Simpson, C., *Universities and Empire: Money and Politics in the Social Sciences in the Cold War*, New Press, New York, 1998.

23 For a detailed study, see Gilman, Nils, *Mandarins of the Future: Modernization Theory in Cold War America*, Johns Hopkins University Press, Baltimore, 2007. For an intellectual history of Talcott Parsons's theory and its larger intellectual connections, see 'Theorist at Work', *Journal of the History of Ideas*, 71, 2 April 2010, pp. 287–311.

24 Leslie, Stuart W., *The Cold War and the American Science: The Military Industrial Complex at MIT and Stanford*, Columbia University Press, New York, 1993. See also Nelkin, Dorothy, *The Military and the University: Moral Politics at MIT*, Cornell University Press, Ithaca, 1972.

25 Rosen, George, *Western Economists and Eastern Societies: Agents of Change in South Asia, 1950-1970*, Johns Hopkins University Press Baltimore, 1985.

26 Rostow, W.W., *The Stages of Economic Growth: A Non-Communist Manifesto*, Cambridge University Press, New York, 1960.

27 See Binoy K. Roy, *US Infiltration in Indian Education*, Perspective Publications, Delhi, 1973; Malaviya, Harsh Dev, *The Danger of Right Reaction*, a Socialist Congressman Publications, Delhi, 1965.

28 Datta-Ray, Sunanda K., *Waiting for America: India and the U.S. in the New Millennium*, Harper Collins Publishers, Delhi, 2002, p. 26.

29 See for a detailed discussion Chapter 10 of the present book.

30 Cohen, Stephen, 'Indian Military and Social Change, *IDSA Journal*, No 2, 1969–70, pp. 12–29. Recently the experience of the same project was recounted for the American projects of nation building in Afghanistan and Iraq. See Fukuyama, Francis, *Nation Building, Beyond Afghanistan and Iraq*, Johns Hopkins University Press, Baltimore, 2006.

31 Ibid.

32 Schaffer, Howard, *Chester Bowles, New Dealer In Cold War*, Harvard University Press, Cambridge, Masschusetts, 1993, pp. 101–02; Bowles, Chester, *Promises to Keep: My Years in Public Life, 1914-1969*, Harper and Row, New York, 1971; Galbraith, J.K., *Ambassador's Journal: A Personal Account of the Kennedy Years*, Houghton Miffin, Boston, 1969; for a very close look at these events and processes, see, Johnson, E.A.J., *American Imperialism in the Image of Peer Gynt: Memoirs of a Professor-Bureaucrat*, University of Minnesota Press, Minnesota,1971.

33 Marglin, Stephen A., *The Dismal Science: How Thinking Like*

an Economist Undermines Community, Harvard University Press, Cambridge, Massachusetts, 2008.

34 Report on IIPA, *H.N. Kunzru Papers*, NMML.

35 See the reports of the first administrative reforms committee and second administrative reforms committee. The second committee indicates that from the post of districts until they become joint secretaries there is no proper job profile for the bureaucrats.

36 Verghese, B.G., *First Draft*, Tranquebar Press, Chennai, 2010.

37 *C.D. Deshmukh Papers*, File No. 77.

38 There were very mature student bodies of the communist parties which were ideologically and academically organized but did not have a large presence in the area.

39 Vidyarthi, L.P., *Student Unrest in Chotanagpur, 1969-70*, ICSSR Abstract of Social Science Research, National Publishing House, Delhi, 1976; Gour, P.N., *Student Unrest in the Universities of Bihar, 1967-1972*, Library Publications, Delhi, 1984; Singhvi, L.M., *Youth Unrest: Conflict of Generations*, National Publishing House, Delhi, 1972; Srinivas, M.N. 'Students in Turmoil', *Seminar*, 88, 1966.

40 Das, Arvind N., *The Republic of Bihar*, Penguin Books, 1994; Mishra, Girish, *Casteism in Bihar*, Pragati Prakashan, New Delhi, 1997.

41 Report of the University Inquiry Commission on the working of the Bihar University, 1967, cited in Gaur, *Student Unrest* ..., p. 143.

42 Ibid., p. 145.

43 Ibid. p. 150.

44 Report, p. 5, cited in ibid., p. 154.

45 Report, p. 5, cited in ibid.

46 Ibid. For a detailed treatment of caste and its destructive role in the polity and society of Bihar, see Girish Mishra, *Castesim in Bihar*, Pragati Prakashan, Delhi, 1997.

47 Ibid.

48 M.C. Chagla to D. S. Kothari, 10 June 1965, *M.C. Chagla Papers*, File No. 76, pt III.

49 Thakur, Janardan, *University News*, January 1973, p. 32.

50 Ibid.

51 *Chatterjee Committee Report on AMU*, GOI, New Delhi, 1961.

52 Ibid.

53 *Factual Analysis of Banaras Hindu University*, Gorawala, K. C. and others (sponsors), Banaras, 1958.

54 'BHU Agitation: A Political Fraud', *Link*, 5 December 1965.
55 Ibid., p. 10.
56 Ibid. Also see *M.C. Chagla Papers*, File No. 79.
57 Report of the Banaras Hindu University Inquiry Committee, July 1969, p. 81. See *Mainstream*, 16 August 1969.
58 Lelyveld, David, *Aligarh's First Generation: Muslim Solidarity in British India*, Princeton University Press, New Jersey, 1978; Maheshwari, Anil, *Aligarh Muslim University: Perfect Past and Precarious Present*, UBS Publishers, Delhi, 2001; Shah, S.Y. *Higher Education and Politics in Colonial India: A Study of Aligarh Muslim University 1875-1920*, Renaissance, Delhi, 1996.
59 Tyabji, Badruddin, *Memoirs of an Egoist*, Oxford University Press, Delhi, 1980.
60 Ibid.
61 'Shocking Incident at Aligarh', *Link*, Delhi, 2 May 1965, p. 8.
62 Hamied, K.A., op. cit., pp. 315–16.
63 *Dinman*, (Hindi) Bombay, 22 July 1965, pp. 14–15.
64 *Link*, 6 June 1965, p. 9.
65 *The Statesman*, Delhi, 5 February 1961, p. 1.
66 Central General Council, Varanasi, 10 October 1961, *Documents of Bharatiya Jana Sangh*, IV, pp. 121-22.
67 *Lok Sabha Debates*, 20 June 1961, Vol. LIX.
68 *Lok Sabha Debates*, Second series, LVI, 11 August 1961, c. 1722.
69 Ibid., cc. 1722–23.
70 Ibid.
71 *Organizer*, 18 October 1954, pp. 5 and 12; Graham, B D, *Hindu Nationalism and Indian Polities: the Origins and Development of the Bharatiya Jana Sangh*, Cambridge University Press, Cambridge, 1990.
72 Central Working Committee, Delhi, 15 August 1965, Bharatiya Jana Sangh resolution passed by Bharatiya Pratinidhi Sabha, 17 and 18 August 1965, and Working Committee on 27 and 28 September 1965, pp. 9–12. *Bharatiya Jana Sangh Documents*, documents IV, p. 77–79, cited in Graham, B.D., op. cit., p. 88. (Graham indicated some discrepancy in the wordings of two documents and says that the statement is attributed to Central General Council of 17 August 1965).
73 There were attacks on the students who wanted to join any political event anywhere. Their political acts were always construed as

Muslim communal acts and there was deliberate communal suppression in this. For details of the attacks on them on 10–11 May 1979, see, Sengupta, Vivek, 'Aligarh: Back to Violence', *Sunday*, 20 May 1979, p. 21.

74 Elliott, Carolyn, 'The Problem of Autonomy: The Osmania University Case', in Rudolph Susanne Hoeber, and Lloyd I. Rudolph, (eds.) *Education and Politics in India: Studies in Organization, Society, and Policy*, Oxford University Press, Delhi, 1972. I am indebted to Prof. Amrik Singh for giving me a graphic account of the whole case as he provided great help to Dr Reddy and the lawyers of university teachers like Gautam Mathur when the case came up to the Supreme Court.

75 M.C. Chagla to K. Brahmananda Reddy, 12 November 1965, M.C. *Chagla Papers*, File No. 76, pp. 54–55.

76 Ibid.

77 Ibid.

78 Ibid.

79 Ibid.

80 Ibid., p. 65.

81 Ibid., p. 202.

82 Ibid.

83 Ibid.

84 Ibid. p. 38.

85 Ibid.

86 Ibid., p. 34.

87 Ibid. He ended by writing: 'It is very necessary that the high tradition which he has established in the university should be fully maintained. I might add that I have discussed this matter with the P.M. and she also attaches great importance to choosing the right type of VC for Osmania University.'

88 Mellanby, Kenneth, 'Establishing a New University in Africa', *Minerva*, Volume 1, Issue 2, Winter 1963, pp. 149–58.

89 *Link*, 24 September 1967, p. 9.

90 *Indian Express*, New Delhi, 6 September 1967.

91 Ibid.

92 Ibid.

93 *Link*, 17 December 1967, p. 10.

94 *Link*, Delhi, 17 December 1967, p. 14.

95 Ibid.

96 Thapar, Romila, Bipan Chandra and Harbans Mukhia, *Communalism in the Writing of Indian History*, People's Publishing House, Delhi, 1969.

97 Ashraf, K.M., *Life and Condition of People of Hindustan*, Munshiram Manoharlal, Delhi, 1970; Mohammad Habib, *The Political Theory of the Delhi Sultanate: Including a Translation of Ziauddin Barani's Fatawa-i Jahandari, Circa 1358-59 AD*, Kitab Mahal, Allahabad, 1961; *Some Aspects of the Foundation of the Delhi Sultanate*, Kalamkar Cooperative, Delhi, 1968; and *Politics and Society in the Early Medieval Period, Collected Works of Mohammad Habib*, Vol. 1, People's Publishing House, Delhi, 1974; Koshambi, D.D., *An Introduction to the Study of Indian History*, Popular Prakashan, Bombay, 1958; *Myth and Reality: Studies in the Formation of Indian Culture*, Popular Prakashan, Bombay, 1962; and 'The Beginning of the Iron Age in India', *Journal of the Economic and Social History of the Orient*, Vol. 6, No. 3, December 1963, pp. 309–18; Sharma, R.S., *Shudras in Ancient India*, Motilal Banarasidas, Delhi, 1958; 'The Origins of Feudalism in India (c. AD 400-650)', *Journal of the Economic and Social History of the Orient*, Vol. 1, No. 3, October 1958, pp. 297–328; and *Indian Feudalism*, Macmillan, Delhi, 1965; Nurul Hasan, 'The Position of the Zamindars in the Mughal Empire', *IESHR*, Vol. 1, No. 4, 1964, pp. 107–119; *Thoughts on Indian Relations in Mughal India*, People's Publishing House, Delhi, 1973; Sukhtankar, V.S., *On the Meaning of Mahabharata*, Asiatic Society, Bombay, 1957; Dandekar, R.N., 'God in Hindu Thought', *Annals of the Bhandarkar, Oriental Research Institute*, Vol. 48/49, Golden Jubilee Volume 1917–1967, 1968, pp. 433–65.

98 Chandra, Bipan, *Rise and Growth of Economic Nationalism in India*, People's Publishing House, Bombay, 1965.

99 Thapar, Romila, Bipan Chandra and Harbans Mukhia, *Communal Interpretation of Indian History*, People's Publishing House, New Delhi, 1969.

100 Dandekar, R.N., *Some Aspects of the History of Hinduism*, Centre of Advanced Study in Sanskrit, University of Poona, Poona, 1967; Dandekar, R.N. (ed.), *Sanskrit and Maharashtra: A Symposium*, Centre of Advanced Study in Sanskrit, University of Poona, Poona, 1969.

101 Naik, J.V., 'R.G. Bhandarkar and his contribution', in M.A. Nayeem, Anrudha Ray and K. S. Mathew (eds) *Studies in the History of*

Deccan: Medieval and Modern, Pragati Publications, New Delhi, 2002.

102 Krishna, Daya, 'Three Myths about Indian Philosophy', *Diogenes*, 1966, pp. 89–103.

103 Raja, K. Kunjunni, *Indian Theories of Meaning*, Adyar Library and Research Centre, Madras, 1969; Bhattacharyya, Sibajiban, 'Descartes', *Doubt,' Philosophy and Phenomenological Research* 24 (1), 1963, pp. 106–16; 'The Middle Term', *Notre Dame Journal of Formal Logic* 9 (3), 1968, pp. 229–32; 'Some Features of Navya-Nyāya Logic', *Philosophy East and West*, 24 (3), 1974, pp. 329–42; Dharmendra Kumar, 'Logic and Inexact Predicates', *British Journal for the Philosophy of Science*, 18 March 1967, p. 211–22. See for a review of philosophical issues that are discussed during the time, Mohanty, J.N., 'Philosophy in India: 1967-1973', *Review of Metaphysics*, 28, 1974, pp. 54–84.

104 Mohanty, J.N., *Between the Two Worlds, East and West: An Autobiography*, Oxford University Press, Delhi, 2002, See for a review, Batabyal, Rakesh, *Book Review*, New Delhi, 2002.

105 Mohanty, J.N., 'Phenomenology and Existentialism: Encounter with Indian Thought', *International Philosophy Quarterly*, 12 (4), 1972, pp. 485–511.

106 Sinari, R.K., *The Structures of Indian Thought*, American Lecture Series Publication No 778, Charles C. Thomas Publisher, Springfield, Illinois, 1970.

107 Shukla, R.K., *Nature of Induction*, in Daya Krishna (ed.), *Modern Logic: Its Relevance to Science*, Impex, New Delhi, 1969.

108 Sengupta, P.K., *The Logical Structure of Science*, Centre for Advanced Study in Philosophy, Visva-Bharati, Shantiniketan, 1970.

109 Chattopadhyaya, Debi Prasad, *Lokayata: A Study in Ancient Indian Materialism*, People's Publishing House, New Delhi, 1959.

110 Chattopadhyaya, Debi Prasad, *Indian Philosophy—A Popular Introduction*, People's Publishing House, New Delhi, 1964.

111 Chattopadhyaya, Debi Prasad, *Indian Atheism—A Marxist Analysis*, Manisha, Calcutta, 1969.

112 Khundmiri, Alam, *Secularism, Islam and Modernity: Selected Essays of Alam Khundmiri*, Oxford University Press, Delhi, 2000.

113 Habib, Irfan, 'The Political Role of Sheikh Ahmad Sirhindi and Shah Waliullah' *Proceedings of the Indian History Congress*, Aligarh Session, 1960.

114 Ali, M. Athar, 'The Religious Issue in the War of Succession, 1658-59', *Medieval India Quarterly*, Vol. V, Aligarh, 1963; *Sidelights on Ideological and Religious Attitudes in the Punjab during the 17th Century*, Medieval India: A *Miscellany*, Vol. II, Asia Publishing House, Bombay, 1972.

115 Shakir, Moin, 'Islamic Modernism', *Mainstream*, 3 June, 1967; *Azad, Islam and Nationalism*, Kalamkar Prakashan, 1969; and his major work, *Khilafat to Partition: Survey of Major Political Trends Among Indian Muslims from 1919-1947*, Kalamkar Prakashan, Bombay, 1970.

116 Bhandari, Mannu, *Aapka Banti*, Radhakrishna, Delhi, 1971.

117 *Dharamyug*, Bombay, 6 April 1969.

118 *Dinman*, Bombay,12 January 1969, pp. 23–25.

119 Bender, Thomas, (ed.) *The University and the City: From Medieval Origins to the Present*, Oxford University Press, New York, 1988.

Chapter 5

1 Verbatim Report of Evidence Given Before the Joint Committee on the Jawaharlal Nehru University Bill, 1964 (Hereafter *Report of Evidence*), 18 October 1965, p. 104.

2 'My intention is', Chagla told the members of parliament, 'as soon as this bill is placed on the statute book, to appoint a vice chancellor and give him an academic advisory body, not following the example of appointing a vice chancellor after the university is established.' Jawaharlal Nehru University Bill, 1964, 1 December 1965, *Rajya Sabha Debates*, c. 3409.

3 M.S. Aney: 'a step on which, in a democracy like ours, I cannot congratulate the Government'. Ibid.

4 *Hundred Years of the University of Calcutta: A History of the University Issued in Commemoration of the Centenary Celebrations*, Volume 1, Calcutta University, Calcutta, 1957; Dongerkery, S.R., *Memories of Two Universities*, Manakatalas, Bombay, 1966; Tikekar, Aroon, *The Cloister's Pale: A Biography of the University of Mumbai*, South Asia Books, 1986; Sundaram V.A., *Banaras Hindu University, 1916-1942*, BHU, Banaras, 1942.

5 Triguna Sen, *Report of Evidence*, p.30.

6 V.S. Jha, ibid., p. 85.

7 Ibid., p. 101.

8 Ibid., p. 105.

9 Sharda Bhargava, Jawaharlal Nehru University Bill, 1964, *Rajya Sabha Debates*, 6 December 1965, cc. 3866–67.

10 Ibid., cc. 3866–76. All of them were distinguished academicians. See, for example, B.N. Prasad, 'The Summability of a Fourier Series and its Conjugate Series', Presidential Address, Section of Mathematics and Statistics, 32nd Session of the Indian Science Congress, Nagpur, 1945; 'Mathematics in India (Part A: General) and Certain Aspects of the Researches on Dirichlet Series (Part B: Technical)', Presidential Address, 27th Conference of the Indian Mathematical Society, Ahmedabad, 1961; 'Science in India (Part A: General) and Recent Researches in the Absolute Summability of Infinite Series and their Applications (Part B: Technical)', General Presidential Address, 53rd Session of the Indian Science Congress, Chandigarh, 1966.

11 Chagla, M.C., *Roses in December*, Bharatiya Vidya Bhavan, Bombay, 1973, p. 373.

12 Ibid.

13 Ibid.

14 Sharada Prasad, H.Y. (ed.) *G.P. The Man and his Work*, New Age International (P) Limited Company, New Delhi, Hyderabad, Chennai, 1998.

15 Chagla, M.C., op. cit., 1973, p. 373–74

16 G. Parthasarathi to M.C. Chagla, 6 February 1967, in *M.C. Chagla Papers*, File No. 91, p. 68.

17 G. Parthasarathi to M.C. Chagla, 7 September 1967, ibid., File No. 93, p. 52.

18 Shanmugasundaram, Dr Vedagiri, *Life and Times of the Great Twins: Dr Sir A. Ramasamy and Dr Sir A. Lakshmanasamy*, The Modern Rationalist, Chenai, November 2004.

19 Chagla did not want to be advance in this issue. *Rajya Sabha Debates*, 6 December 1965, cc. 3912–13. The debate was centred on the aphorism 'trust the teachers'. All those who favoured more than one term argued that one should start trusting teachers and allow people to do big things. Those who opposed the move had either personal grievances against some individual vice chancellor or thought that the vice chancellor would end up pursuing his personal agenda. The pervading climate of corruption and deep-seated cynicism did not allow for any grey areas.

20 Sharada Prasad, H.Y., *G.P. The Man and his Work*, p. 361.
21 Ibid., pp. 232–35.
22 Ibid., p. 41.
23 Ibid.
24 Ibid., pp. 40–41.
25 Ibid., p. 54.
26 Ibid.
27 *Rajya Sabha Debates*, 6 December 1965, c. 3891.
28 *University News*, New Delhi, August 1969, p. 7. It was at the same time that the Madras University decided to set up its postgraduate centre at Coimbatore, eventually to evolve as a new university, see ibid.
29 Ibid.
30 Mohanty, Jitendra Nath, *Between Two Worlds East and West: An Autobiography*, Oxford University Press, Delhi, 2002.
31 Minutes of the First Meeting of the Executive Council of the Jawaharlal Nehru University held on 30 September 1969.
32 Jawaharlal Nehru University Bill, 1964, *Rajya Sabha Debates*, 6 December 1965, c. 3876.
33 Ibid.
34 See, Wittner, Lawrence, *Confronting the Bomb: A Short History of the World Nuclear Disarmament Movement*, Stanford University Press, Stanford, 2009; Katsiaficas, George, *The Imagination of the New Left: A Global Analysis of 1968*, Cynthia Press, Cambridge, Massachusetts, 1987.
35 Kriesi, Hanspeter, *New Social Movements in Western Europe: A Comparative Analysis*, University of Minnesota Press, Minneapolis, 1995.
36 Minutes of the Second Meeting of the Academic Advisory Committee of the Jawaharlal Nehru University (JNU), 29 August, 1969, p. 2.
37 Ibid.
38 Ibid.
39 Ibid.
40 Ibid.
41 Ibid.
42 Jawaharlal Nehru University Bill, 1964, *Rajya Sabha Debates*, 6 December 1965, c. 3957.

43 Minutes of the Second meeting of the Executive Council of the Jawaharlal Nehru University, 27 October 1969, Item. 4.
44 Minutes of the Sixth Meeting of the Executive Council of the Jawaharlal Nehru University held on Thursday, 28 May 1970, Point 24. p. 66.
45 Thapar, Romila, *Ashoka and the Fall of Mauryan Empire*, Penguin Books, London, 1961; *A History of India*, Volume I, Penguin Books, UK, 1966.
46 Chandra, Satish, *Parties and Politics at the Mughal Court (1707 –40)*, Oxford University Press, Delhi, 2002 Reprint.
47 Minutes of the Eighth Meeting of the Executive Council of Jawaharlal Nehru University held on Friday, 11 September 1970.
48 Personal conversation with Govindjee.
49 Minutes of the Seventh Meeting of the Executive Council of JNU held on 26 July.
50 Minutes of the Eighth Meeting of the Executive Council of Jawaharlal Nehru University held on Friday, 11 September 1970.
51 Wahba Albert J., Yung-Bog Chae, Kentaro Iwasaki, Rajarshi Mazumder, Steven Sabol and Maria A.G. Sillero, 'Initiation of Protein Synthesis in Escherichia Coli; I. Purification and properties of the initiation factors,' in *Cold Spring Harbor Symposia on Quantitative Biology*, Vol. 34, pp. 285–90, Cold Spring Harbor Laboratory Press, New York, 1969.
52 Dr Chaganti is an internationally recognized leader in cancer cytogenetics and molecular genetics, and holds several patents through the Memorial Sloan Kettering Cancer Centre as well as Cancer Genetics.
53 Minutes of the Twelfth Meeting of the Executive Council of Jawaharlal Nehru University held on 20 March 1971, Annexure XIV, See. Menon, Jayaraman and Michael Smith, 'Exonuclease (phosphodiesterase) from the testes of Chinook salmon (*Oncorhynchus tshawytscha*)', *Biochemistry*, 9 (7), 1970, pp. 1584–92.
54 Minutes of the Sixth Meeting of the Executive Council of Jawaharlal Nehru University 28 May 1979.
55 Minutes of the Ninth Meeting of Executive Council of JNU held on 3 October 1970.
56 Ibid.

57 Gupta, Sisir K., *Kashmir: A Study in Indian Pakistan Relations, Asia Publishing House*, Bombay, 1966.
58 Manmohan Singh, in Sharada Prasad, H.Y., op.cit., p. 40–41.
59 Ibid.
60 Ibid.
61 Minutes of the Fourth Meeting of the Executive Council of Jawaharlal Nehru University, 22 Decmber 1969.
62 Minute of the Ninth Meeting of the Executive Council, 3 October 1970, p. 161 and also in the Minutes of the Thirteenth Meeting held on 12 June 1971.
63 Ibid., p. 99.
64 Minutes of the Seventh Meeting of the Executive Council of Jawaharlal Nehru University held on Sunday, 26 July 1970; Minutes the Seventh Meeting of the Executive Council of JNU held on 26 July 1970.
65 Minutes the Seventh Meeting of the Executive Council of JNU held on 26 July 1970.
66 Jawaharlal University Bill, 1964, *Rajya Sabha Debates*, 6 December 1965, c. 3919.
67 Ibid., see also *Rajya Sabha Debates*, 2 December 1965, c. 3514.
68 Ibid., see also *Rajya Sabha Debates*, 6 December 1965, cc. 3920–3922.
69 Ibid., c. 3921.
70 Submission by Triguna Sen, *Report of Evidence*, pp. 30–31.
71 Jawaharlal Nehru University Bill, 1964, *Rajya Sabha Debates*, 2 December 1965, p. 3529.
72 'JNU May Change Character', *Hindustan Times*, 10 May 1977.

Chapter 6

1 Minutes of the Second Meeting of the Academic Advisory Committee of the Jawaharlal Nehru University, 29 August 1969, p. 3.
2 Note by S. Gopal, Minutes of the Second Meeting of the Academic Advisory Committee of the Jawaharlal Nehru University, 29 August 1969, p. 2.
3 Ibid.
4 Ibid., p. 4.

5 Report of the Working Group on Disarmament Studies, Annexure V.

6 Memorandum of Association, *Indian Institute of International Affairs*, Government of India Press, Simla, 1943.

7 Memorandum of Association of Indian Council of World Affairs.

8 Annual Report on the Working of the ICWA, Indian Council of World Affairs, Delhi, 1956.

9 Ibid.

10 Ibid.

11 Dutt, Vidya Prakash, *India's Foreign Policy: with Special Reference to Asia and the Pacific*, Indian Council of World Affairs, 1950; 'Indo-China Impasse', *International Quarterly*, 1, 8, January-March 1952, 14–31; *East Asia, China Korea Japan, 1945-50*, OUP, London, 1958.

12 Agwani, M.S., *The United States and the Arab World*, Institute of Islamic Studies, Aligarh, 1955.

13 The address was later reproduced in Appadorai, A., 'International and Area Studies in India', *International Studies*, Sage Publication, New Delhi, London, New York, 1987, Vol. 24, No. 2.

14 The argument that there was no central polity is still carried on with sophistication by scholars in the West. That Indian polity has a segmented, fragmented existence or 'shared sovereignty' which defined much of India's political history was powerfully refuted by Indian historians. These arguments, however, are uncritically accepted by even perceptive international theory scholars. See Mallavarapu, Siddartha, 'Development of International Relations Theories in India: Traditions, Contemporary Perspectives and Trajectories,' *International Studies*, 2009, New Delhi, London and New York, Sage Publications, Vol. 46, Nos. 1& 2, pp. 165–184.

15 Dastur, Aloo Jehanbux, 'Man and His Environment with Special Reference to Professor Gedde's Valley Section,' Ph.D Thesis, Bombay University, Bombay, 1947, (later on published as *Man and His Environment*, Popular Book Depot, Bombay, 1954); Masaldan, P.N., 'Provincial Autonomy and Its Working in the United Provinces', Ph.D Thesis, Lucknow University, 1942.

16 Sirsikar, V.M., 'Studies on Political Parties and Pressure Groups', in ICSSR, *Survey of Research in Political Science, Political System*, Delhi: Allied Publishers and ICSSR, Volume I, 1979, p. 69.

17 Appadorai, A., *Economic Conditions of Southern India* (circa 1000 to 1500), 2 Vols., Madras University Press, Madras, 1936.
18 Rana, A.P., *International Relations*, Allied Publishers, Delhi and ICSSR, 1988, p. 27.
19 Bajpai, Kanti, 'International Studies in India: Bringing theory (back) home,' in Bajpai K. and S. Mallavarapu (eds.), *International Relations in India: Bringing Theory Back Home*, Orient Longman, Hyderabad, pp. 17–38.
20 Phadnis, Urmila, *Ethnicity and Nation-Building in South Asia*, Sage, New Delhi, New York and London, 1990.
21 Biray, Kolluoglu-Kirli,: 'From Orientalism to Area Studies', *C.R.: The New Centennial Review, Vol.* 3, Fall 2003, p. 103.
22 Fisher, D., *Fundamental Development of the Social Sciences: Rockefeller Philanthropy and the United States Social Science Research Council*, University of Michigan Press, Ann Arbor, 1993.
23 Biray, Kolluoglu-Kirli, *op. cit.*, p. 105.
24 Ibid.
25 Geiger, Roger L., 'American Foundation and Academic Social Sciences, 1945-1960,' *Minerva*, Vol. 26, No. 3, 1988, pp. 315–41.
26 Biray, Kolluoglu-Kirli, op. cit., p. 105.
27 Morgan, Jamie, 'The History of Contemporary Area Studies: Philosophy, Emergent Causal Relations', and 'Non-triviality of Sociology of Knowledge', in *China Review International*, Vol. 11, No. 2, Fall 2004, p. 229.
28 Leslie, Stuart A., *The Cold War and the American Science: Military Industrial Complex at MIT and Stanford*, Columbia University Press, 1993; Lowen, Rebeca, *Creating a Cold War University: The Transformation of Stanford*, University of California Press, Berkeley and Los Angeles, 1997.
29 Report of the visiting committee to Delhi University and the Indian School of International Studies to examine the problems and needs for the development of Chinese, Japanese and African studies, (referred to as Shiva Rao Committee as it was headed by Shri B. Shiva Rao, member, UGC), *H.N.Kunzru Papers*, File No. 101, p. 40.
30 Ibid., p. 31.
31 Mishra, Girish, 'The Left Challenge', in Aditya Mukherjee (ed.), *Centenary History of the Indian National Congress*, Academic Foundation, Delhi, 2011.
32 Karunakaran, K.P., *India in World Affairs, August 1947 to January*

1950, Oxford University Press, London, 1952; *India in World Affairs, February 1950 to December 1953, A Review of India's Foreign Relations.* ICWA, New Delhi 1958; *Modern Indian Political Tradition*, Allied Publishers, Bombay, 1962; *Religion and Political Awakening in India*, Meenakshi Publications, Meerut, 1965; *Outside the Contest.* People's Publishing House, New Delhi, 1963.

33 Sondhi, M.L., *Wanted A National Foreign Policy*, Jana Sangh Publication, Navchetana, New Delhi, 1968.

34 See Kishen Pattanayak, *Lok Sabha Debates*, 2 September 1966, cc. 9153–72.

35 McGarr, Paul Michael, 'Quiet Americans in India: The CIA and the Politics of Intelligence in Cold War South Asia', *Diplomatic History*, 38,5, 2014, pp. 1046–1082.

36 Appadorai to D.S. Kothari, 24 May 1964, *H.N. Kunzru Papers*, File No. 88, p. 92.

37 Ibid., pp. 98–99.

38 Ibid., p. 100.

39 H.N. Kunzru to Triguna Sen, 31 March 1967, *H.N. Kunzru Papers*, File No. 87, p. 5.

40 Ibid., p. 5.

41 Comments on the Estimates Committee report 'General Observations', ibid., pp. 88–90.

42 Ibid., p. 88.

43 Ibid., p. 89.

44 *H.N. Kunzru Papers*, File No. 88, p. 126.

45 Ibid., p. 89.

46 Report, p. 5, *H.N. Kunzru Papers*, File No. 101.

47 Ibid.

48 Ibid.

49 Ibid.

50 Ibid.

51 Ibid.

52 Ibid.

53 Khadilkar, Masani and Mani to Indira Gandhi, ibid., File No. 88, pp. 1–2.

54 Ibid.

55 A.D. Mani to Indira Gandhi, ibid., File No. 88, p. 22.

56 Ibid., p. 6.

57

1965-1966	7,12,115.00	6 lakhs
1966-1967	8,42,683.00	6·5 lakhs
1967-1968	8,53,983.00	7 lakhs
1968-1969	15,14,000.00	12 lakhs

58 Minutes of the discussion between the delegation of the board of governors and the union minister of education at his residence on Saturday, 12 April (year not mentioned but seems to be 1967) at 11.00 a.m., *H.N. Kunzru Papers*, File No. 101, pp. 59–60.
59 Ibid., p. 60.
60 Ibid.
61 Minutes of the Executive Committee Meetings, *H.N. Kunzru Papers*, File No. 88, pp. 82–87.
62 Institute of International Studies, *Lok Sabha Debates*, 3 September 1966, Vol. LIX, No. 29, cc. 9153–72.
63 Kishen Pattanayak, ibid., cc. 9153–56.
64 *H.N. Kunzru Papers*, File No., 48, pp. 70–73.
65 Item No. 10, Minutes of the Fourth Meeting of the Executive Council of JNU held on 22 December 1969. See also, resolution no. 3/EC/24-1-1970, in Annexure I, Minutes, p. 41.
66 Ibid.
67 'Negotiations with the Indian School of International Studies,' vide resolution no. 3/EC/24-1-1970, in Minutes of the Fifth Meeting of the Executive Council of Jawaharlal Nehru University, held on the 24 January 1970, Annexure I.
68 Parthasarathi to Dr Kunzru, 12 January 1970, appendix, vide resolution no. 3/ec/24-1-1970, in Annexure I, Minutes, pp. 42–43.
69 Ibid., pp. 59–61.
70 Parthasarathi, G., Inaugural Observations, Summer Institute of International Affairs and Area Studies, 15 March 1971, p. 3, in *P.N. Haksar Papers*, Instalment III, Subject File 302, p. 27.
71 Ibid.
72 Ibid.
73 Ibid.
74 Note on School of International Studies, p. 3, ibid., p. 21.
75 Parthasarathi, G. to R.K. Chabra, Secretary, University Grants Commission, also see Parthasarathi, G. to Dr George Jacob,

Chairman, University Grants Commission, 4 August 1973, ibid., pp. 25–26.

76 *H.N. Kunzru Papers*, File No. 75, pp. 236–37.

77 Ibid., p. 238.

78 Ibid., p. 182.

79 Ibid., pp. 185–86.

80 'Summary of the Meeting with Dr Nurul Hasan, 23 May 1972, ibid., pp. 10–11.

81 Ibid.

82 Minutes of the Sixth Meeting of the Executive Council of Jawaharlal Nehru University, held on Thursday, 28 May, 1970, Annexure XI, item No. 25.1 and 25.2.

Chapter 7

1 Sharada Prasad, H.Y., (ed.), *G.P. The Man and His Work: A Volume in Memory of G. Parthasarathi*, New Age International, Delhi, 1998, p. 363.

2 Angelie Multani, in *Booklet of the Alumni Association of JNU* (*AAJ*), 2008, p. 41.

3 D. Thengari, *Rajya Sabha Debates*, 6 December 1965, cc. 3842–43.

4 Minutes of the Second Meeting of the Campus Committee of JNU held on 18 May 1970, Annexure VIII, vide resolution No. 12, Executive Council (EC), 28 May 1970.

5 Development of the Campus Site – Note- I (Vide Resolution No. 7/EC/20.1.1970), Minutes of the Fifth Meeting of the Executive Council of JNU held on 24 January 1970, Annexure III, vide Resolution No. 7/AC/24 January 1970.

6 Review of the progress made with regard to engineering works at the JNU since the first meeting held on 28.1.1970, Appendix, Minutes of the Second Meeting of the Campus Committee of JNU held on 28 May, 1970, op.cit. Appendix to ibid., p. 90.

7 Harjit Singh, in *Booklet of the Alumni Association of JNU*, 2009, p. 55.

8 Rao, Joga, '5-Crore Luxury Campus for IAS Academy', *Blitz*, 20 June 1970, p. 7.

9 Ibid.

10 Submission by V. K. R.V. Rao in Verbatim Report of Evidence given before the Joint Committee on the Jawaharlal Nehru University Bill, 1964, pp. 3–4.

11 Ibid.

12 Some points suggested by Prof. Moonis Raza, Special Officer (Planning), for the consideration of the Campus Committee, vide Resolution No. 7/EC/24.1.1970, minutes of the Fifth Meeting of the Executive Council of JNU held on 24 January 1970, Annexure IV, p. 55.

13 Ibid.

14 Ibid.

15 Ibid.

16 Ibid., p. 56.

17 Ibid.

18 Ibid. p., 58.

19 Deshdeep and Vikram Soni, two physicists, campaigned for almost a decade with documents showing the place as a land of the greatest biological diversity which had been community land and that it was a completely illegal act to build on it. An empowered committee put a stay on the ongoing construction. However, mysterious are the ways of the world. The Supreme Court invalidated the stay arguing that the builder has already built quite a bit and hence recommended he be allowed to continue. The court had in fact sealed and demolished hundreds of small, medium and big constructions that were illegal across the city exactly during this period.

20 Official letter from C.J. Venkatachary to C.P. Kukreja, 6 October 1970, in appendix to Annexure XVI, 29/EC/17, Minutes of the Fifth Meeting of the Executive Council of JNU held on 24 January 1970.

21 Study in campus designs: National competition for master plan of Jawaharlal Nehru University Campus, New Delhi, 1974, JNU, New Delhi, p. 159.

22 'Report on the progress of works related to campus development', Minutes of the Twelfth Meeting of the Executive Council of JNU held on 20 March, 1971 Annexure X.

23 *Hindustan Times*, 11 June 1977.

24 Ibid.

25 Ibid.

26 Ibid.

27 *Booklet of Alumni Association of JNU*, 2008, p. 51.

28 Ibid., pp. 37–48. See also 'Meeting with Nurul Hasan', *Hindustan Times*, 31 May 1971; Letter by Ram Rattan, *Hindustan Times*, 7 June

1971; *Statesman*, 23 March 1972; *The Times of India*, 23 March 1972; *The Indian Express*, 28 March 1972.

29 *H.N. Kunzru Papers*, F.No. 75, pp. 10–11.

30 Ibid.

31 Ibid.

32 Ibid., pp. 12–13.

33 Minutes of the meeting between chairman of ICWA's library committee and JNU's representative, 24 April 1973, *H.N. Kunzru Papers*, File No. 47, pp. 1–3.

34 Sharma, Ravindra Nath, and Shiyali R. Ranganathan, *S.R. Ranganathan and the West*, Sterling Publishers, Delhi, 1992; Ranganathan, S.R., A *Librarian Looks Back: An Autobiography of Dr S.R. Ranganathan*, ABC Publishing House, Delhi, 1992; Ranganathan, Yogeswar, *S.R. Ranganathan—Pragmatic Philosopher of Information Science: A Personal Biography*, Bharatiya Vidya Bhavan, Bombay, 2001.

35 I owe this term to Purshottam Agarwal, in Suman Keshri (ed.) *JNU Mein Namwar Singh*, Rajkamal Prakashan, Delhi, 2009.

36 Interestingly enough, this has come to me from a lecture of Irfan Habib, who, while deciphering the social context of Buddhism, had argued that it was not the philosophical context but the social ethics of the time that quite often colours the religion.

37 Venkatachalapati, A.R., in *Booklet of the Alumni Association of JNU*, 2008.

38 Greer, Germaine, *Female Eunuch*, HarperCollins, New York, 1970; Freiden, Betty, *Feminine Mystique*, Harmondsworth, Pelican, New York, 1965.

39 See for example Bhandari, Mannu, *Aapka Banti*, Radhakrishna, Delhi, 1971; Shanta Rani, 'Male Character in the Hindi Stories of the 1960s', M. Phil Dissertation, JNU, 1979.

40 'Shiksha: Sahshiksha, Kitna Sahchayra,' *Dinman*, Bombay, 23 April 1972, pp. 40–41.

41 Shils, Edward, *Intellectual between Tradition and Modernity, the Indian Situation*, Mouton and Company, The Hague, 1961.

42 Shamim, M., 'A confused admission policy: JNU suffers from a clear goal,' *The Times of India*, Delhi, 22 September, 1974.

43 Proctor, Robert, *Racial Hygiene: Medicine Under the Nazis*, Harvard University Press, Cambridge, Massachusetts, 1988; Weindling, Paul,

Health, Race and German Politics Between National Unification and Nazism, Cambridge University Press, Cambridge, 1993.

44 Eric Hobsbawm, in his memoirs, narrates how many of his university friends from South Asia returned to their countries and joined the communist movement in their respective countries. See Hobsbawm, Eric, *Interesting Times*, Abacus, London, 2003.

45 Shukla, Srilal, *Rag Darbari*, Rajakamal Prakashan, Delhi, 1969.

Chapter 8

1 Bipan Chandra, cited in K.N. Sud, 'Power Struggle at Nehru University', *Hindustan Times*, New Delhi, 2 September 1974.

2 For a short biographical description of Desai, see, Shah, Ghanshyam, *Capitalist Development: Critical Essays*, Popular Prakashan, 1989, pp. 1–6. See his writings, e.g., Desai, A.R., *Social Background of Indian Nationalism*, Popular Prakashan, Bombay, 1948, *Recent Trends in Indian Nationalism*, Popular Prakashan, Bombay, 1960.

3 Eric Habsbawm comments that it was his communist circles in academia that gave him a sense of camaraderie and a unique ability to mix with people from across cultures and nations with a sense of equality. See Habsbawm, Eric, *Interesting Times*, Abacus, London, 2003.

4 China was not very comfortable with the denunciation of Stalin.

5 It is quite significant that the leadership of the CPI was more cohesive and looked like a national party with a national outlook than the CPI(M), which seemed more like a party with a strong regional and provincial outlook that began to personify its leadership's role as well.

6 Indian Council for Social Science Research, *Annual Report, 1973-74*, ICSSR, New Delhi.

7 Chandra, Bipan, *India after Independence*, Penguin Books, New Delhi, 2000; Bhambhri, C.P., *Indian State After Independence*, Shipra Publishers, Delhi, 2000; Vanaik, Achin, *Painful Transition: Bourgeois Democracy in India*, Verso, London, 1990; Kothari, Rajni, *Politics in India*, Orient Longman, Hyderabad, 1970.

8 The feeling was not confined to India alone. Many dynamic political scientists in the West also expressed the same feelings; see Kruzel,

Joseph and James Rosenau, *Journeys Through World Politics, Autobiographical Reflections*, Lexington Press, London, 1988.

9 Rao, K.V., 'Political Change and Political Scientists in India', Presidential address at the 29th Political Science Conference, 1967, *Indian Journal of Political Science*, Vol. 29, No. 1, 1968, pp. 1–17.

10 Ibid.

11 Ibid.

12 Ibid.

13 Cohen, Stephen P., 'Approaching India's Military and Security Policy, with a Detour Through Disaster Studies', *India Review*, Vol. 7, Number 4, October–December 2008, pp. 295–319.

14 Kumar, Girija, 'Servitude of the Mind', *Seminar*, No. 112, December 1968, pp. 20–24.

15 Jennings, Ivor, *British Constitution*, Cambridge University Press, Cambridge, UK., 1941, Also see, *Cabinet Government*, Cambridge University Press, Cambridge, UK, 1936.

16 Jones, W. Morris, *Parliament of India*, Pennsylvania University Press, Philadelphia, 1957; *Government and Politics of India*, B.L. Publications, Bombay, 1971.

17 Austin, Grenville, *The Indian Constitution: Cornerstone of a Nation*, Clarendon, Oxford, 1966.

18 For Clifford Geertz's sociological equivalent to Newtonian thought, see Geertz, Clifford, *After the Fact: Two Countries, Four Decades, One Anthropologist*, Harvard University Press, Cambridge, Massachusetts, 1995, p. 100; another student, Robert N. Bellah, was driven by the ideal of an abstract, content-free, theoretical science from which one could deduce the laws of social life, see 'The World Through its Theorists—In Memory of Talcott Parsons', *American Sociologist*, 15 January 1980, p. 60. I remember with fondness the month-long association with Y.B. Damle in 1997-98 in Shimla when the maestro of Indian sociologists would train me in Parsonian sociology. The whole discussion with him in those winter days began when a high- profile sociologist giving an annual lecture at Shimla got angry with an otherwise innocent theoretical question of mine. I reported this to Prof. Damle and it was Prof. Damle's turn to get angry with that sociologist as, to him, the latter actually spoke on a theme on which he had no expertise. I benefited from this anger as he would then teach me not only sociological theories but also

the Parsonian perspective in great detail. I did not know then that one day I would be helped by his training so directly.

19 Gilman, Nils, *Mandarins of the Future, Modernization Theory in the Cold War America*, Johns Hopkins Press, Baltimore, 2003, p. 100.

20 Ibid. pp. 85–86. But like other work in the same genre which has come out presenting a critique of the theories and state, it completely ignored the historical location of the intellectual world as well as the leadership in countries like India where modernization and development has been nuanced and the nationalist intelligentsia had developed quite an elaborate understanding even before the Parsonian system theory was launched. For modernization, see Naoroji, Ranade, Gokhale and Mehta. For an economic history understanding of the theme, See Bipan Chandra, 'Colonialism and Modrnization', in *Nationalism and Colonialism in Modern India*, Orient Longman, Hyderabad, 1984, pp. 1–37; for a complex sociological narrative of the processes of modernization, etc., see Singh, Yogendra, *Modernisation of Indian Tradition: A Systemic Study of Social Change*, Thomson Press, Faridabad, 1973, 1977, Reprint.

21 Gilman, Nils, op. cit. p. 113.

22 Almond, Gabriel, 'Comparative Political System', *Journal Of Politics*, 18, 3, 1956, p. 392.

23 Committee on Comparative Politics, Report on the Activities of the Committee, SSRC, New York, 1971, p. 70 as cited in Gilman, op. cit., p. 152, fn. 119.

24 Leslie, Stuart, A., *The Cold War and the American Science: Military Industrial Complex at MIT and Stanford*, Columbia University Press, New York, 1993; Lowen, Rebeca, *Creating a Cold War University: The Transformation of Stanford*, University of California Press, Berkeley and Los Angeles, 1997.

25 George, Rosen, *Western Economists and Eastern Societies: Agents of Change in South Asia, 1950-1970*, Johns Hopkins University, Baltimore, 1985.

26 Rostow, W.W., *The Stages of Economic Growth: A Non-Communist Manifesto*, Cambridge University Press, Cambridge, UK, 1960.

27 George, Rosen, op. cit.

28 Ibid.

29 Latham, Michael. E., *The Right Kind of Revolution*, University of Cornell Press, Ithaca, 2011.

30 Dean Rusk, 'Foreign Policy Problems in the Pacific', *Department of State Bulletin*, 19 November 1951, p. 824.

31 For an interesting but partisan account of the rebellion, see Mossman, James, *Rebels in Paradise, Indonesia's Civil War*, Jonathan Cape, London, 1961.

32 Cohen, Stephen, 'Indian Military and Social Change', *IDSA Journal*, Vol. 2, No. 1, 1969, p. 21. For the complete transformation of the Indonesian military, see Ruth Mcvey, 'Post-Revolutionary Transformation of Indonesian Military, Part I and II', *Indonesia*, 11, 1971, pp. 131–176 and *Indonesia*, 13, 1972, pp. 147–181.

33 A very positive account of this collaboration can be read about one of the men who helped Sumitro execute some of the policies that he encouraged the new regime to pursue, including pruning the military and getting it trained in the US. See, Mohamad, Gunawan, *Celebrating Indonesia: Fifty Years with the Ford Foundation, 1953–2003, Jakarta Ford Foundation, 2003.*

34 There was a spate of publications, which were all deprecating Sukarno as if recommending change of guard. See Penders, C.L.M., *The Life and Times of Sukarno*, Sidgwick and Jackson, New York, 1974.

35 Bell, Daniel, *The Post-Industrial Society*, Harvard University Press, Cambridge, Massachusetts, 1968.

36 Brackman, A., *Indonesian Communism*, Friedrich Praeger, New York, 1963, p. 306.

37 Wardaya, F. X. Baskara Tulus, *Cold War Shadow: United States Policy toward Indonesia, 1953-1963*, Universitas Sanata Dharma. Pusat Sejarah dan Etika Politik, Yogyakarta, 2007; Simpson, Bradley Robert, *Economists with Guns: Authoritarian Development and U.S.—Indonesian Relations, 1960-1968*, Stanford University Press, Stanford, California, 2008.

38 Geertz, Clifford, 'The Integrative Revolution: Primordial Sentiments and Civil Politics in the New States', in *The Interpretation of Cultures*, New York, Basic Books, 1963, pp. 255–310; 'After the Revolution: The Fate of Nationalism in the New States', in *The Interpretation of Cultures*, Basic Books, New York, 1971, pp. 234–54; *The Religion of Java*, Chicago, University of Chicago Press, Chicago, 1976 (1960); *Negara: The Theatre State in Nineteenth-Century, Bali*, Princeton University Press, Princeton, New Jersey, 1980; Benedict Anderson, 'Indonesia: Unity and Progress', *Current History*, February 1965, pp. 75–81; 'Old State and New Society,

Indonesia's New Order in Comparative Historical Perspective', in Anderson, Benedict ed. *Language and Power: Exploring Political Culture in Indonesia*, Cornell University Press, Ithaca, 1990, pp. 94–120.

39 'CIA and Academic Freedom', *Mainstream*, 29 April 1967, pp. 23–25.

40 Chittaranjan, C.N., 'CIA and Academic Freedom', *Mainstream*, 6 May 1967 pp. 27–29.

41 Datta-Ray, Sunanda K., *Waiting for America: India and the U.S. in the New Millennium*, HarperCollins Publishers, New Delhi, 2002, p. 26.

42 Kothari, Rajni, 'The Congress "System" in India', *Asian Survey*, 4 December 1964, 1161–73.

43 Kothari, Rajni, 'Congress System Revisited: A Decennial Review', *Asian Survey*, Vol. 14, No. 12, December 1974, pp. 1035.

44 Selig Harrison of the Center for International Policy chose to title his 1960 book *India: The Most Dangerous Decades*.

45 *The Intimate Enemy: Loss and Recovery of Self under Colonialism*, Oxford University Press, Delhi, 1983, 1988; *Alternative Sciences: Creativity and Authenticity in Two Indian Scientists*, Oxford University Press, New Delhi, 1995.

46 Khan, Rasheeduddin, 'The Muslim Leadership and Electoral Politics in Hyderabad: A Pattern of Minority Articulation', *Economic and Political Weekly*, (Hereafter *EPW*), Vol. 6, No. 15,17 April 1971, pp. 833–840.

47 Writings of Rajni Kanth remains some of the finest in the political economy tradition. See, Kanth, Rajni Kannepalli, *Breaking with the Enlightenment: The Twilight of History and the Rediscovery of Utopia*, Humanities Press International, M.E.Sharpe, New York, 1992; *Against Economics: Rethinking Political Economy*, Ashgate, New York, 1997; *Explorations in Political Economy: Essays in Criticism*, Rowman & Littlefield, New York, 1991.

48 Bhambhri, C.P., *Bureaucracy and Politics in India*, Vikas Publishing House, Delhi, 1971; *Administrators in a Changing Society*, National Publishing House, Delhi, 1972.

49 Bhambhri, C.P., 'Indian State: Conflict and Contradiction,' in Hasan, Zoya, S.N. Jha, and Rasheeduddin Khan, (eds.), *State, Political Process and Identity: Reflections on Modern India*, Sage Publications, Delhi, New York, London, 1989, pp. 73–87.

50 Bhambhri, C.P, 'Official-Non-Official Relationship in Panchayati Raj', *Indian Journal of Political Science*, October–December 1967; 'Ideology and Political Parties in India', *EPW*, Vol. 3, No. 16, 1968, p. 643; *Bureaucracy and Politics in India*, Vikas Publishing House, 1971; 'The State in Contemporary India,' *Mainstream*, 26 January 1984, pp. 44–48.

51 Bhambhri, C.P., *Elections and Political Consciousness in India: A Study*, Meenakshi Prakashan, Meerut, 1971.

52 Kothari, Rajni, *Indian Voting Behaviour: Studies of the 1962 General Elections*, Firma K.L. Mukhopadhyay, Calcutta, 1965; Verma S.P. and C.P. Bhambhri, *1967 Elections: The Urban Voter*, National Publishing House, Delhi, 1973.

53 Khan, Rasheeduddin, *Culture of India and National Integration*, Indian Institute of Advanced Study, Shimla, 1987.

54 Khan, Rasheeduddin, 'Muslim Leadership and Electoral Politics in Hyderabad: A Pattern of Minority Articulation,' *EPW*, Vol. 6, No. 15, 10 April 1971 pp. 783–794 and 'Muslim Leadership and Electoral Politics in Hyderabad: A Pattern of Minority Articulation,' *EPW*, Vol. 6, No. 16, 17 April 1971 pp. 833–840.

55 Khan, Rasheeduddin, 'The Total State: The Concept and its Manifestation in the Indian Political System' in Hasan, Zoya, S.N. Jha and Rasheeduddin Khan, *The State, Political Processes and Identity: Reflections on Modern India*, Sage Publishers, Delhi, 1989, pp. 33–72.

56 Bala, Madhu, 'Centralising Tendencies in Indian Federalism,' M.Phil Dissertation, JNU, 1976; Narula, Chand Bahadur, 'Mechanics of Conflict Resolution in the Constitution: A Study of River Water Dispute,' M.Phil Dissertation, JNU, 1976; K. R., Chakravarthi, 'Participation of States in Planning Process in India: A Case Study of Tamil Nadu', M.Phil Dissertation, JNU, 1977, Sarangi, A.K., 'Impact of Congress Party in Evolution of Indian-Federalism, 1967–1983, M.Phil Dissertation, JNU, 1983; Ram, Hari, 'Special Status in Indian Federalism: A Case Study of Jammu and Kashmir,' M.Phil Dissertation, JNU, 1978.

57 Madhur, Murli Dhar, 'Genesis of the Gorkhaland Issue, 1835–50', M.Phil Dissertation, JNU, 1989; Wariyal, H.B., 'Uttarakhand Movement: A Sociological Analysis,' M.Phil Dissertation, JNU, 1989; Joshi, Aparna, H.B., 'Women and Ecological Problems in

Uttarakhand,' 1989, Dhar, M.M., 'Genesis of the Gorkhaland Issue, 1835–1950,' M.Phil Dissertation, JNU, 1989.

58 Rekhi, Upjit Singh, 'Jharkhand Movement and Tribal Polities in Bihar,' Ph.D Thesis, JNU, 1982.

59 Krishnan, Malathi, 'The Emergence of the Jharkhand Movement in Bihar: in Historical Perspective,' M.Phil Dissertation, JNU, 1987; Jyoti, Jane Renuka 'Jharkhand Movement in Bihar: A Sociological Analysis,' M.Phil Dissertation, JNU, 1989; Pandey, Awadh Kishore, 'Social Transformation and Jharkhand Movement among the Tribes of Bihar,' M.Phil Dissertation, 1984.

60 Khaund, Bhaskar, 'Assam Movement: A Study or Socio-Economic and Cultural Dimensions,' M.Phil Dissertation, JNU, 1983; Hasan, Monirul, 'Assam Movement: Sociological Dissertation', Ph.D Thesis, JNU, 1983; Bhokt, Humayun, 'A Sociological Study of Bodo Movement,' M.Phil Dissertation, JNU, 1989.

61 Glazer. N, and D.P. Moynihan, *Ethnicity: Theory and Practice*, Harvard University Press, Cambridge, Massachusetts, 1975; the proper implication as thought of by Moynihan is best expressed in a very good biography of his by Robert Katzman (ed.), *Daniel Patrick Moynihan: The Intellectual and Public Life*, Woodrow Wilson Centre Press, Pennsylvania, 2004.

62 Mazrui, Ali, *Towards a Pax Africana*, University of Chicago Press, Chicago, 1967; *Cultural Engineering and Nation Building in East Africa*, Northwestern University Press, Evanstone, Illinois, 1972.

63 Theroux Paul, 'Obituary', *The Independent*, 15 January 1996, accessed on 14 July 2011-http://www.independent.co.uk/news/people/obituary-rajat-neogy-1324133.html

64 Love, Joseph, 'Raúl Prebisch and the Origins of the Doctrine of Unequal Exchanges', *Latin America Research Review*, Vol. 15, No. 3, 1980, pp. 45–72. I have been better served on these issues by the readings from Indian economic historians like Bipan Chandra, Amiya Bagchi, Irfan Habib, Achin Vanaik, Utsa Patnaik and Aditya Mukherjee among others than any Western economist.

65 Sourced from en. Wikipedia.org/wiki/Raúl_Prebisch (accessed on 12 May 2010). This remains the best description for general readers.

66 Frank, Andre Gunder, *Capitalism and Underdevelopment in Latin America*, Monthly Review Press, New York, 1967.

67 Frank, Andre Gunder, 'Development of Underdevelopment', *Monthly Review*, 18, 1966, pp. 17–31. His other writings too created

a revolution of sorts in the thinking about development and colonial operation. His influence on Indian Marxist scholarship has been tremendous. See Chandra, Bipan, *Nationalism and Colonialism in Modern India*, Orient Longman, Hyderabad, 1979.

68 Amin, Samir, *Accumulation on a World Scale*, Harvester Press, Sussex, 1974; *Unequal Development: An Essay on the Social Formations of Peripheral Capitalism*, translated by Brian Pearce, Harvester Press, Sussex, 1979; Arghiri, Emmanuel, *Unequal Exchange: A Study of the Imperialism Of Trade*, New Left Books, London, 1972.

69 Dasgupta, Amit, in *Booklet of the Alumni Association of JNU*, 2008, pp. 38, p. 74–79.

70 Lovejoy Paul E., 'Nigeria: The Ibadan School and its Critics', in Bogumil Jewsiewicki and David Newbury (eds) *African Historiographies: What History, for Which Africa*; Sage Publications, Beverly Hills, California, 1986; Falola, Toyin, *'Nigeria History, Politics and Affairs: Collected Essays of Adiele Afigbo'*, Africa World Press, Trenton, New Jersey, 2005.

71 Ogot, Bethwell A., *Reintroducing Man into the African World*, Anyange Press, Kisumu, Kenya, 1999; *My Footprints in the Sands of Time: An Autobiography*, Trafford Publishers, Canada, 2003; *Building on the Indigenous: Selected Essays 1981–1998*. Anyange Press, Kisumu, Kenya, 1999

72 Kimambo, I.N., A *Political History of the Pare of Tanzania, ca. 1500-1900*, East African Publishing House, Nairobi, 1969; *Mbiru: Popular Protest in Colonial Tanzania*, East African Publishing House, Nairobi, 1971; *Penetration and Protest in Tanzania: The Impact of the World Economy on the Pare, 1860-1960*, James Curry, London, 1991; *Three Decades of Historical Research at Dar es Salaam*, University of Dar es Salaam Press, Dar es Salaam,1993; (ed.), *Humanities and Social Sciences in East and Central Africa: Theory and Practice*, University of Dar es Salaam Press, Dar es Salaam, 2003.

73 Sicherman, Carol, *Becoming an African University: Makerere, 1922–2000*, Africa World Press; Trenton, New Jersey, 2005; Mills, David, 'Life on the Hill: Students and the Social History of Makerere, Africa', *The Journal of the International African Institute*, Vol. 76, No. 2, 2006, pp. 247–66.

74 Ogot, Bethwell A. Toyin Falola and E.S. Atieno Odhiambo, *The Challenges of History and Leadership in Africa: the Essays of Bethwell Allan Ogot*, Africa World Press, Trenton, New Jersey, 2002; Falola, Toyin, Harlow, U.K., Ajayi, J.F. Ade, *African Historiography: Essays in Honour of Jacob Ade Ajayi*, Longman, Harlow, UK, 1993; Ajayi, J.F. Ade, *Africa in the Nineteenth Century until the 1880s*, UNESCO, Paris 1998; Ajayi, J.F. Ade, *Milestones in Nigerian History*, Longman, Harlow, U.K., 1980; Ogot, Bethwell A., *History of the Southern Luo*, Volume 1, East African Publishing House, Nairobi, 1967.

75 Sharma, R.S., *Aspects of Political Ideas and Institutions in Ancient India*, (third education) Motilal Banarsidass, Delhi, 1991 (first published in 1959), p. xxvi. For other critiques, Spellman, J.W., *Political Theory in Ancient India*, Oxford University Press, Delhi, 1964; J. Gonda, *Ancient Indian Kingship from the Religious Point of View*, E.J. Brill, Leiden, 1969; Heesterman, J.C., *Inner Conflict of Indian Tradition*, University of Chicago Press, Chicago, 1985.

76 Sharma, R.S., *op. cit.*

77 Ibid.

78 Ibid., p. 13.

79 See for example, Shils, Edward, 'Political Development in the New States', *Comparative Study in Society and History*, 2, 1960, pp. 265–92.

80 Ibid.

81 Paul Brass, a Chicago-trained political scientist, for example, denied individuals in Uttar Pradesh any other political universe than his caste and faction. See Brass, Paul, *Factional Politics in an Indian State, Congress Party in Uttar Pradesh*, University of California Press, Berkeley and Los Angeles, 1965.

82 Thapar, Romila, *Ashoka and the Decline of the Mauryan Empire*, Oxford University Press, London, 1961. She would develop her ideas on the state later in her *From Lineage to State*, Oxford University Press, Delhi, 1984.

83 Gopal, S., *British Policy In India, 1858-1905*, Cambridge University Press, Cambridge, U.K., 1965; Gupta, Sulekh, *Agrarian Relations and Early British Rule in India: Ceded and Conquered Provinces Uttar Pradesh (1801-1833)*, Asia Publishing House, Bombay, 1963; *Agrarian Relations and Early British Rule in India*, Asia Publishing House, Bombay, 1964; Stokes, Eric, *The Peasant and the Raj:*

Studies in Agrarian Society and Peasant Rebellion in Colonial India, Cambridge University Press, Cambridge, U.K., 1980; *The English Utilitarians and India*, Oxford University Press, Delhi and Oxford, 1990; Metcalfe, T.R, *The Aftermath of Revolt 1857-1870*, Princeton University Press, New Jersey, 1965.

84 Ghoshal, U.N., *History of Indian Political Ideas*, Oxford University Press, Bombay, 1959; Kanungo, K.R, *Sher Shah and his Times*, Orient Longman, Calcutta, 1965.

85 Thapar, Romila, *Ashoka and the Decline of the Mauryan Empire*, Oxford University Press, London, 1961.

86 Bhattacharya, Sibesh, 'Land, Soil, Rainfall, Irrigation—Some Aspects of the Backdrop of Agrarian Life in the Arthasastra of Kautilya', *Indian Economic & Social History Review*, 15, 2, 1978, pp. 211–19; 'Land-System as Reflected in Kautilya's Arthasastra', *Indian Economic & Social History Review*, 16, 1, 1979, pp. 85–95.

87 Habib, Irfan, *Agrarian System of Moghul India*, Oxford University Press, Delhi, 1963; Chandra, Satish, *Party and Politics in the Mughal Court, 1707-1740*, Aligarh Muslim University Publications, Aligarh, 1959; Ali, M. Athar, *Mughal Nobility Under Aurangzeb*, Asia Publishing House, London and Bombay, 1966.

88 Shastri, K.A. Nilakantha, *The Cholas*, Madras University Historical Series, No. 9, second revised edition, Madras, 1955; Mahalingam, T.V., *South Indian Polity*, Madras University Historical Series, 21, University of Madras, Madras, 1955; Guha Amalendu, 'The Ahom Political System: An Enquiry into the State Formation Processes in Medieval Assam (1228-1714)', *Social Scientist*, New Delhi, Vol. 11, No. 12, 1983, pp. 3–34.

89 Huntington, Samuel, *Political Order in Changing Societies*, Yale University Press, New Haven, 1968; Pye, Lucien, *Aspects of Political Development*, Little Brown, Boston, 1966.

90 Dawidowicz, Lucy, *Holocaust and the Historians*, Harvard University Press, Cambridge, Massachusetts, 1981.

91 Stein, Burton, *Peasant, State and Society in Medieval South India*, Oxford University Press, Delhi, 1980.

92 Burnet, Jean, 'Robert Park and the Chicago School of Sociology: A Centennial Tribute', *Canadian Review of Sociology*, Vol. 1, No. 3, 1964, pp. 156–64.

93 Ibid.

94 Marriott, McKim (ed.), *Village India: Studies in a Little Community*, American Anthropological Association, Chicago University Press, Chicago 1955; Singer, Milton, *Traditional India: Structure and Change*, American Folklore Society, Columbus, Ohio, 1959.

95 Thapar, Romila, *From Lineage to State: Social Formation in the Mid-First Millennium B.C. in the Ganga Valley*, Oxford University Press, Delhi 1981.

96 The leading figure of this behaviouralist group was Myron Weiner whose works have been pioneering in attacking the Indian state since the 1950s. See *Politics in India, Sons of the Soil: Migration and Ethnic Conflict in India*, Princeton University Press, New Jersey, 1978.

97 Dutt, R.P., *India Today*, Manisha, Calcutta, 1947; Desai, A.R., *The Social Background of Indian Nationalism*, Popular Prakashan, Bombay, 1948.

98 Bagchi, Amiya Kumar, *The Political Economy of Underdevelopment*, Cambridge University Press, Cambridge U.K. 1982; Namboodiripad, E.M.S., 'On "Intermediate Regimes"', *EPW*, Vol. 8, No. 38, 1 December 1973, p. 2133–2140; Alavi, Hamza, 'India and the Colonial Mode of Production,' EPW, Vol. 10, No. 33–35, 1975, pp. 1236–62; Kurien, K.M., 'Class Character of Indian State', in *India—State and Society*, Orient Longman, Hyderabad, 1975; Dasgupta, Biplab, 'Class Character of the Ruling Class in India,' in K. Mathew Kurian (ed.), op. cit, pp. 115–128.

99 Kałecki, M., *Selected Essays on the Economic Growth of the Socialist and Mixed Economy*, Cambridge University Press, Cambridge, 1972.

100 E. M. S. Namboodiripad, 'On "Intermediate Regimes"', *EPW*, Vol. 8, No. 38, 1 December 1973, pp. 2133–40.

101 Ibid.

102 Gupta, Sulekh Chandra, *Indian Agriculture Evolution*, Mainstream Publications, Rajkamal Distribution, New Delhi, 1966; his earlier work, Gupta, Sulekh Chandra, *Agrarian Relations and Early British Rule in India: A Case Study of Ceded and Conquered Provinces (Uttar Pradesh) (1801-1833)*, Asia Publishing House, London, 1963, pp. xix, 338. For a very early insight into the capitalist fringe, see Thorner, Daniel, 'Coastal Andhra: Towards an Affluent Society', *EPW*, Vol. 2, No. 3–6, 1969, pp. 241–9.

103 Thorner, Daniel, op. cit.
104 Raj, K.N., *Some Economic Aspects of Bhakhra Nangal Project, A preliminary analysis on the basis of selected investment criteria*, Asia Publishing House, Bombay, 1960; 'Some questions concerning growth, transformation and planning of agriculture in the developing countries' in Proceedings of the Conference on Economic Development in South Asia held by the International Economic Association at Kandy, Ceylon, 1970, pp. 102–26.
105 Patnaik, Utsa, 'Capitalist Production in Agriculture': A note', *EPW*, Vol. 6, No. 39, 1971, pp. A-123–A130; Ashok Rudra, 'Capital Development in Agriculture: A Reply' *EPW*, Vol. 6, No. 45, 1971, p. 2291–92;
106 Patnaik, Utsa, 'Capitalist Development in Agriculture: Further Comment', *EPW*, Vol. 6, No. 52, December 1971, p. a-192.
107 Ibid.
108 Banaji, Jairus, 'Mode of Production in Indian Agriculture: A Comment,' *EPW*, Vol. 7, No. 14, April 1973, pp. 679–683.
109 Ibid., For the debate on mode of production see Patnaik, Utsa, 'On the Mode of Production in Indian Agriculture: A Reply, *EPW*, Vol. 7, No. 40, 1972, pp. 145–51.
110 Sundarayya, P., *Telangana People's Struggle and Its Lessons*, Foundation Books, Delhi, 1972.
111 Mehta, Shirin M., 'The Bardoli Satyagraha, 1928: A Case Study of a Peasant Movement and its Interrelationship with the Freedom Struggle,' Ph.D Thesis, JNU, 1977.
112 Bhattacharya, Neeladri, 'Agrarian Change in Punjab, 1880-1940,' Ph.D Thesis, JNU, 1985; Agnihotri, Indu, 'Agrarian Change in Canal Colonies:, Punjab, 1890-1935,' Ph.D Thesis, JNU, 1987.
113 Raghvan, T.C.A., 'Agrarian Change in Narmada Valley: A Study of Jabalpur, Hoshangabad and Narsinghpur Districts, 1860-1925,' Ph.D Thesis, JNU, 1981; Bandyopadhyay, Alok, 'Agrarian Change in India: A Comparative Study of Bengal and Punjab, 1901-1940 and 1950-1974,' Ph.D Thesis, JNU, 1976.
114 Bose, Pradip Kumar, 'Agrarian Structure Peasant Society and Social Change: A Study of Selected Regions in West Bengal,' Ph.D Thesis, JNU, 1979; Ram, Subas, 'Agrarian Structure of East Uttar Pradesh: With Special Reference to Sultanpur District (1856-1981),' Ph.D Thesis, JNU, 1983; Gopinath, Ravindran, 'Agrarian Structure and Transformation in Malabar, 1871-1921,' Ph.D Thesis, JNU, 1986.

115 Gurukkal, Rajan, 'The Agrarian System and Socio-Political Organization Under the Early Pandyas AD 600-1000,' Ph.D Thesis, JNU, 1984.

116 Hangloo, Rattan Lal, 'Agrarian System of Kashmir, 1846-1900 AD,' Ph.D Thesis, JNU, 1980.

117 Kurapati, Ajoy Kumar, 'The Agrarian System of Rayalaseema during the Vijayanagara Period,' M.Phil. Dissertation, JNU, 1985; Palat, Ravi Arvind, 'The Agrarian System of Jayamkondam Cholamandalam under Vijayanagar Rule (circa AD 1350-1565),' M.Phil. Dissertation, JNU, 1981; Satapathy, Pramod Kumar, 'Agrarian System in Early Medieval Orissa,' M.Phil. Dissertation, JNU, 1984.

118 Ganesh, K.N., 'Some Aspects of the Agrarian Structure in Early Medieval Venad AD 1200-1500,' Ph.D Thesis, JNU, 1979; Nand, Brahma, 'Some Aspects of the Agrarian Structure in Western India: The District of the Central Division, 1880-1930,' Ph.D Thesis, JNU, 1983.

119 Karanth, Gopal Krishna, 'Change and Continuity in Agrarian Relations: A Case Study of a Karnataka Village,' Ph.D Thesis, JNU, 1984; Singh, Jagpal, 'Changing Agrarian Relations and Politics in Western Uttar Pradesh: A Study of Meerut District (1952-85),' Ph.D Thesis, JNU, 1988.

120 Sri Lanka has produced some excellent intellectuals including R.A.L.H. Gunawardana in the late 1970s who now could see a marked decline in engagement with the issue in historical terms like the one entered by scholars like Asoka Bandarage, *Colonialism in Sri Lanka: The Political Economy of the Kandyan Highlands, 1833–1886, Mouton, Berlin, 1983*. One of the first Sri Lankan scholars, Sudarshan Seneviratne, also became one of the earliest history scholars in the campus and produced an excellent thesis entitled, 'Social Base of Early Buddhism in South East India and Sri Lanka: 3rd Century BC–3rd Century AD,' Ph.D Thesis, JNU, 1985. There were other Sri Lankan scholars too who worked here, e.g., de Silva, Jayatilaka Shanthi Ramanie, 'Changing Agrarian Relations: A Comparative Study of an Irrigated and a Non-irrigated Village in Sri Lanka,' Ph.D Thesis, JNU, 1989.

121 Suri, K. Chinnaya, 'Agrarian Movements in Andhra: 1921-1971,' Ph.D Thesis, JNU, Kumar, K., 'A Study of the Agrarian Movement in Thanjavur District,' Ph.D Thesis, JNU, 1984; Assadi, Muzaffar

Hussein, 'Agrarian Movement in Karnataka: A Study of the Rytha Sangha, 1980-85,' Ph.D Thesis, JNU, 1987.

122 Sri Kishan, 'Communist International, the CPI, and the Agrarian Question in India during the Same Period, i.e., 1920-194,' M.Phil. Dissertation, JNU, 1983.

123 Subbiah, S., 'Environmental, 'Technological and Institutional Determinants of Agricultural Productivity in Tamil Nadu: A Spatial and Temporal Analysis, 1945-55, 1969-70', M.Phil. Dissertation, JNU, 1975; Amit Cowshish, 'Impact of Green Revolution on Politics of Haryana,' M.Phil. Dissertation JNU, 1977; Luingam Luithui, 'Political Economy of Forestry in Manipur,' M.Phil. Dissertation, JNU, 1977; Parimala, G., 'Levels of Agricultural Development in Tamil Nadu: A Taluk-wise Study,' M.Phil. Dissertation, JNU, 1979; Menon, Saraswathi, 'Peasant Movement in Thanjavur,' 1940-1952, M.Phil. Dissertation, JNU, 1978.

124 Rao, C. Veerabhadra, 'Unionization of Agricultural Workers in Andhra Pradesh,' M.Phil. Dissertation, JNU, 1981; Kastala, Venkata Vijayababu, 'Politics of Agricultural Cooperatives in Andhra Pradesh: A Study of West Godavari District' Ph.D Thesis JNU; George, Jose, 'Politicization of Agricultural Workers in Kerala: A Study of Kuttanad,' Ph.D Thesis, JNU, 1980.

125 Ramesh, K., 'Tribal Development Administration in Vishakhapatnam District, Andhra Pradesh,' M.Phil. Dissertation, JNU, 1981; Rao, G. Madhu Mohan, 'A Study of the Land Reforms Legislation in Telangana Region of Andhra Pradesh,' M.Phil. Dissertation, JNU, 1981; Sangita, Satya Narayana, 'Politics, Bureaucracy and Rural Development in Andhra Pradesh,' Ph.D Thesis, JNU, 1984; Sukajit, Ningthoujam, 'Aspects of Agricultural Development in Manipur: 1970-71 to 1984-85,' M.Phil. Dissertation, JNU, 1988; Luithui, Shimreichon, 'Land and Power Structure among the Nagas,' Ph.D Thesis, JNU, 1987.

126 Singh, Lata, 'The Congress and Bihar Kisan Sabha Movement, 1934–1939', M.Phil. Dissertation, JNU, 1987.

127 Sinha, Shanta, 'Maoists in Andhra Pradesh,' Ph.D Thesis, JNU, 1976.

128 Rao, K. Nalini, 'The Anti-Mulki Agitation in Andhra Pradesh 1972-73,' M.Phil. Dissertation, JNU, 1976; Rao, Lakshmana, Nalamati, 'Rampa Rebellion in Andhra Pradesh, 1879 and 1922-1924,' M.Phil. Dissertation, JNU, 1981; Ratnam, Tripurana Venkata, 'Leadership,

Faction and Rise of Radicalism in Srikakulam District (A.P.): A Study of Congress Politics 1952-72,' Ph.D Thesis, JNU, 1978.

129 Suri, K. Chinnaya, 'Agrarian Movements in Andhra: 1921-1971,' Ph.D Thesis, JNU, 1984.

130 Rao, Satharla Nagabhushana, 'Naxalite Movement in Andhra Pradesh (1978-85): A Case Study of Adilabad, Karim Nagar & East Godavari,' M.Phil. Dissertation, JNU, 1990; Thirumali, Inukonda, 'Lords and Peasants in Telangana, 1920-48: An Enquiry into the People's Uprising in Nalgonda and Warangal Districts,' Ph.D Thesis, JNU, 1991.

131 Ramakrishnacharyulu, V, 'Veeresalingam and his Times (1848-1919),' Ph.D Thesis, JNU, 1973.

132 Reddy, M. Narayana, 'Social Movements and State Response: A Comparative Study of Three Movements in Andhra Pradesh,' M.Phil. Dissertation JNU, 1982.

133 Ramesh, K., 'Tribal Development Administration in Vishakhapatnam District, Andhra Pradesh,' Ph.D Thesis, JNU, 1981; Rao, G. Madhu Mohan, 'A Study of the Land Reforms Legislation in Telangana Region of Andhra Pradesh, Ph.D Thesis, JNU, 1980; Devi, B.R. Shyamala, 'Tribal Integration in a Developing Economy: A Study with Reference to Two Lambada Villages in Andhra Pradesh,' Ph.D Thesis, JNU, 1989.

134 Sangita, Satya Narayana, 'Politics, Bureaucracy and Rural Development in Andhra Pradesh,' Ph.D Thesis, JNU, 1984.

135 K. Bhaskaramma, 'Political Participation of Scheduled Castes: A Case Study of Khammam District in Andhra Pradesh,' M.Phil. Dissertation, JNU, 1980; Kastala, Venkata Vijayababu, 'Politics of Agricultural Cooperatives in Andhra Pradesh: A Study of West Godavari District,' Ph.D Thesis, JNU, 1983; Vidya Sagar, Kasi, 'Politics of Reserved Constituencies: A Case Study of Ibrahimpatnam Constituency, Ranga Reddy District, Andhra Pradesh, 1978-83,' M.Phil. Dissertation, JNU, 1984; Chandrasekher, T. Ganesh, 'Backward Classes and the Reservation Policy in Andhra Pradesh,' M.Phil. Dissertation, JNU, 1988.

136 Das, Aluri Sundar Kumar, 'Scheduled Caste Political Elite: A Case Study of East Godavari District, Andhra Pradesh, 1951-1981,' M.Phil. Dissertation, JNU, 1983.

137 Sema, Piketo, 'Naga Uprising: 1946-1963,' Ph.D Thesis JNU, 1979.

138 Chasie, S. K., 'The Emergence of Naga Identity, 1878-1974,' M.Phil.

Dissertation, JNU, 1981; Sakhrie, Ahu, 'Naga Movement: A Study in the Sociology of Social Movement,' M.Phil. Dissertation, JNU, 1982.

139 Siddiqi, Majid H., *The Agrarian Unrest in North India: The United Provinces 1918-1922*, Vikas Publishing House, Delhi, 1978.

140 Mukherjee, Mridula, 'Peasant Resistance and Peasant Consciousness in Colonial India-Subalterns and Beyond,' *EPW*, Vol. 23, No. 42, 8 October 1988, pp. 2111–18.

141 Chandra, Bipan, 'Capitalist Class and Nehru 1936', *EPW*, Vol. 10, No. 33–35, 06 August 1975.

142 Chenoy, Kamal Mitra, 'Industrial Policy and Big Business in India: A Case Study of FICCI, 1947-1966,' Ph.D Thesis, JNU, 1983.

143 Mukherjee, Aditya, 'The Indian Capitalist Class and Foreign Capital', *Studies in History*, Vol.1, No. 1, 1979, pp. 105–148.

144 Pande, G.C., *Studies in the Origins of Buddhism*, Motilal Banarsidass, Delhi, 1957.

145 Thapar, Romila, A *History of India: Volume 1*, Penguin Books, London, 1966.

146 Thapar, Romila, *Asoka and the Decline of the Mauryas*, Oxford University Press, Delhi, 1973.

147 Sharma, R.S., *Indian Feudalism, c 300-1200*, University of Calcutta, Calcutta, 1965; Sharma, R.S. 'Problems of Peasant Protest in Early Medieval India,' *Social Scientist*, Vol. 16, No. 9,1984, pp. 3-16.

148 Nandi, R.N., 'Growth of Rural Economy in Early Feudal India', presidential address, Ancient India Section, 45th Session of the Indian History Congress, Annamalai, 1984, p. 3.

149 Chattopadhyaya, B.D., 'Political Processes and Structure of Polity in Early Medieval India: Problems of Perspective', *Proceedings of the Indian History Congress*, Burdwan, 1980. The arguments put forward by him were already circulated to the peer group through his earlier writings. See 'Irrigation in Early Medieval Rajasthan' *Journal of Economic and Social History of the Orient*, *JESHO*, Vol. XVI, 1973, pp. 298–316; 'Trade and Urban Centres in Early Medieval North India', *Indian Historical Review*, Vol. I, No. 2, 1974, pp. 203–19; 'Origin of Rajputs: The Political, Economic and Social Processes in Early Medieval Rajasthan', *Indian Historical Review*, Vol. 3, No. 1, 1976, pp. 59–82.

150 Significantly such a communal interpretation has entered many scholarly works. Interestingly, these works are critical of both India's 'anti-colonial sentiments' as well as what it sees as the voice of its

'Muslim minority' echoing the Hindu communal historiographical positions. For such recent works, see Kumaraswamy, P.R., *India's Israel Policy*, Columbia University Press, New York, 2010.

151 *Bombay Legislative Assembly Debates*, 1947, pp. 1668–75.

152 Chagla, M.C., *Roses in December*, Bharatiya Vidya Bhawan, Bombay, 1973.

153 See, from the supposed position of the radical left, Banerjee, Sumanta, 'Devaluation of Marxism by Leftist Academics', in *EPW*, Vol. 13–14, 8 April 1978, pp. 605–608; and from the right, Nandy, Ashis, 'Self Esteem, Autonomy and Authenticity', *Seminar*, No. 222, February 1978. These attacks were countered by many, including one of the maligned scholars, Bipan Chandra, in 'Devaluation: Of What and by Whom', *EPW*, Vol. 13, No. 18, 6 May 1978, pp. 776–778.

154 See Nandy, Ashis, Seminar, No. 222, February 1978.

155 See Lloyd, Rudolph R. and Susanne Hoeber Rudolph, 'Rethinking Secularism: Genesis and Implications of the Text Book Controversy, 1977-79', *Pacific Affairs*, Vol. 56, No. 1, Spring 1983, pp. 15–37.

156 Gopal, S., 'Fear of History', Seminar 221, January 1978, New Delhi.

157 Bhambhri, C.P., 'Political Science in India – Academic Colonialism and Lessons for the Third World', *EPW*, Vol. 10, No. 18, 1975, pp. 730–35.

158 Gupta, Dipankar, 'Sociology in Indian Universities', *Mainstream*, 24 July,1975, pp. 21–22.

159 Venugopal, C.N., 'G.S. Ghurye and Radhakamal Mukherjee: 'A Comparative Sociological Appraisal of their Selected Contributions,' Ph.D Thesis, JNU, 1980. In the mid-1980s, another sociologist was studied, Archana Singh, 'The Contribution of Prof. D.N. Majumdar to the Field of Social Anthropology from a Sociology of Knowledge Perspective,' Ph.D Thesis, JNU, 1984.

160 Nanda, Bikram, 'A New Framework to Studies on Indian Tribes,' M.Phil. Dissertation, JNU, 1977.

161 Singh, Yogendra, 'Concepts and Theories of Social Change: A Trend Report', in ICSSR, A *Survey of Research in Sociology and Social Anthropology*, Vol. 1, Bombay, Popular Prakashan, 1972–74, pp. 383–431; *Modernisation of Indian Tradition: A Systemic Study of Social Change*, Thomson Press, Faridabad, 1973; *Historicity of Modernisation: A Commemoration Volume*, Thacker, Bombay, 1975, pp. 647–62.

162 One of the best examples was the Bucharest School of Sociology which became completely right-wing.

163 Ghurye, *Caste and Race in India*, Popular Prakashan, Bombay, 1969; Karve, Iravati, *Kinship Organisation in India*, Deccan College, Poona, 1953; *Hindu Society: An Interpretation*, Deccan College Research Institute, Poona 1961.

164 Louis Dumont, *Homo Hierarchicus: The Caste System and its Implications*, Weidenfeld and Nicholson, London, 1970.

165 Mukherjee, Radhakamal, *The Philosophy of Social Science*, Macmillan, Delhi, 1960. See his other works, *The Indian Working Class*, Hind Kitab, Delhi, 1945; *Destiny of Civilization*, Asia Publishing House, Bombay, 1964; *Sickness of Civilization*, Allied Publishers, Bombay, 1964.

166 D.P. Mukherjee, *Diversities: Essays in Economics, Sociology and Other Social Problems*, People's Publishing House, New Delhi, 1958; *Modern Indian Culture*, Hind Kitab, Bombay, 1945.

167 A.K. Saran, 'For a Sociology of India', *Eastern Anthropologist*, 15, 1, 1962, 53–68; 'Sociology of Knowledge and Traditional Thought', *Sociological Bulletin*, 1964-5, 13, 1, 33-46.

168 To quote Yogendra Singh: 'Social background of the student and teacher, their class character influencing the choice of problems and paradigms of research, constitute the theme of evaluation. The professional training of sociologists, their grounding in western theory and ideology along with their narrow social experiential background delimits the reflexivity of their observations.' Singh, Yogendra, 'Development of Caste Consciousness among Children from Five to Seven' *Agra University Journal of Letters*, 1959–60, p.6.

169 Rodney, Walter, *How Europe Underdeveloped Africa*, Bogle L'Ouverture Publications, London, 1972. See also Lewis, R.C., *Walter Rodney's Intellectual and Political Thoughts*, University of West Indies Press, Kingston, Jamaica, 1998.

170 Srivastava, C.P., *Lal Bahadur Shastri: India's Prime Minister, 1964-66—a Life of Truth in Politics*, Oxford University Press, Delhi, 1995.

171 Shah, A.B. *India's Defence and Foreign Policies*, Manakatalas, Bombay, 1966.

172 The debate is covered by G.G. Mirchandani, in a volume entitled *India's Nuclear Dilemma*, Popular Book Service, Delhi, 1968.

173 Dutt, Som *India and the Bomb*, Adelphi Papers, 30, IISS, London, 1966.

174 K. Subrahmanyam, 'Defence Preparations in India and China', *Bulletin of Atomic Scientists*, May 1968, pp. 28–33; *Asian Balance of Power in the Seventies: An Indian View*, IDSA, New Delhi, 1968; *A Strategy for India for a Credible Posture Against a Nuclear Adversary*, IDSA, New Delhi, 1968.

175 *Seminar*, 65, January 1965, pp. 28–31.

176 *Seminar*, 83, July 1966, pp. 10–14.

177 *Seminar*, 146, October 1971, pp. 36–39.

178 Rusk, Dean, 'Some Myths and Misconceptions about U.S. Foreign Policy', Press Release 207, 16 September 1968, *United States Department of State Bulletin*, 7 October 1968.

179 Gupta, Sisir, 'The Great Powers and the Sub-Continent: A New Phase?', *IDSA Journal*, New Delhi, Vol. IV, 1972, p. 462.

180 Ibid.

181 Ibid.

182 Ibid.

183 Ibid., p. 463.

184 Paranjpe, Shrikant B., 'The Asian Alternative to Super Power Models for Regional Security, M.Phil Dissertation, JNU, 1977; Padmavathi, S. A., 'Super-Power Diplomacy vis-à-vis the Sub-Continent 1947-55,' M.Phil Dissertation, JNU, 1974.

185 Sastri, Ravi, 'Militarization of Space: Implications for the Third World,' M.Phil. Dissertation, JNU, 1988; Naik, Yashvant Dhananjay, 'Missile Proliferation in the Third World 1970-1988,' M.Phil. Dissertation, JNU, 1989; Rao, Ravinder, 'France's Arms Sales to the Third World with Special Reference to India and Pakistan,' M.Phil. Dissertation, JNU, 1986; Alam, Mohammad, 'Changing Attitudes and Interests of Pugwash: With Special Reference to the Third World,' (M.Phil. Dissertation JNU, 1977; Assifi, Fathima, 'Arms Trade within Third World, Its Implications,' M.Phil. Dissertation, JNU, 1986; 1988; Harpreet Mahajan, 'Arms Trade and Aid to the Third World Countries, A Study with Special Reference to Indian Subcontinent,' Ph.D Thesis, JNU, 1979; Kuksal Sunil Kumar, 'Strategic Defence Initiative, A Third World Perspective,' Ph.D Thesis, JNU, 1989.

186 Agwani, M.S., 'The Saur Revolution and After', *International Studies*, June 1980, p. 557.

187 Ibid., p. 571.

188 Ibid.

189 Wasan, Navneet Rajan, 'Super Power Negotiations during the Kennedy Years,' M.Phil. Dissertation, JNU, 1978; Lal, Yogeshwar, 'Super Power Interactions: A Study of the Transition from Detente to the New Cold War,' M.Phil. Dissertation, JNU, 1984; Kumar, Narinder, 'Super Power's Intervention in the Third World: A Case Study of Nicaragua, 1979-84,' M.Phil. Dissertation, JNU, 1988.

190 Naquatee, Zeenat, 'Super Power Attitude towards the Kashmir Question,' M.Phil. Dissertation, JNU, 1984.

191 Jayaramu, P.S., 'Problems of National Security and India's Foreign Policy, 1963-79,' Ph.D Thesis, JNU, 1983.

192 Raja Mohan, C., 'Nuclear Energy and the Developing Nations: A Study of Technological and Political Implications,' Ph.D Thesis, JNU, 1982. There were more works in the same direction. For example, Chelani, Brahma, 'Indo-US Nuclear Controversy on Tarapur: Reflection in the Press of the Two Countries,' M.Phil. Dissertation, JNU, 1983; Shukla, O.N., 'Non-Proliferation Treaty and Threshold Powers: a Study of India's Attitude,' Ph.D Thesis, JNU, 1987.

193 Poulose, T.T., 'Nuclear Proliferation and the Second NPT Conference,' IDSA *Journal*, No. 2, 1980.

194 For theorization of Bipan Chandra, see Singh, Yogendra, 'Sociology of Stratification' in *Survey of Research in Sociology and Social Anthropology*, Vol. II, Satvahan, New Delhi, 1985.

195 Alavi, Hamza, 'India and the Colonial Mode of Production' in *EPW*, Vol. 10, No. 33–35, 1975, pp. 1235–62. Other participants too soon joined the debate. See Rudra, Ashok, 'India and the Colonial Mode of Production', *EPW*, Vol. 10, No. 42, 1975, pp. 1668–70. See also Jairus Banaji's spirited response to Ashok Rudra and others, *EPW*, Vol 10, No. 49, 1975, pp. 1887–92.

196 Patnaik, Prabhat, (ed.), *Lenin and Imperialism, An Appraisal of Theories and Contemporary Reality*, Orient Longman, Hyderabad, 1986.

197 Habib, Irfan, 'Potentialities of Capitalistic Development in the Economy of Mughal India,' *Journal of Economic History*, 29, 1, 1969, pp. 32–78.

198 Chandra, Bipan, 'Karl Marx, His Theories of Asian Societies and Colonial Rule,' Mimeographed, Centre for Historical Studies, JNU, 1979–80.

199 Fulzele, Tukaram U., 'The Politics of Foreign Trade in Developing Countries,' Ph.D Thesis, JNU, *1984*.

200 Bhaduri, Amit, 'Renegotiation of Third World Debt and Appropriate Adjustments in International Trade,' in Lozoya, Jorge, and A.K. Bhattacharya, (eds.), *The Financial Issues of the New International Economic Order*, Permagon Press, New York, 1980.

201 Sen, Sunanda, *Colonies and the Empire: India, 1890-1914*, Orient Longman, Calcutta, 1992.

202 Sen, Sunanda, 'Internationalisation of Capital, Neo-Colonialism, Unequal Exchange and Recent Treads in International Finance', *EPW*, Vol. 18, No. 31, 1983, pp. PE27–PE35. See also her 'New International Economic Order and Contemporary World Economic Scene', *EPW*, Vol. 16, No. 10/12, Annual Number,1981, pp. 516–525.

203 Bhambhri, C.P., *World Bank and India*, Vikas Publishing House, Delhi, 1980.

204 For a very sympathetic review by Howard Spodek, see his 'Pluralist Politics in British India: The Cambridge Cluster of Historians of Modern India', *The American Historical Review*, Vol. 84, No. 3, 1979, pp. 688–707.

205 Seal, Anil, *Emergence of Nationalism in India: Competition and Collaboration in the Later Nineteenth Century*, Cambridge University Press, Cambridge, UK, 1968.

206 Sumit Sarkar's writings in fact demonstrate this sectarian trend at its best, and very soon this trend in his writings gets assimilated within the subaltern project. A wonderful review of literature along these fragmentary notions of modern Indian history till date is presented in Sarkar, Sumit, *Modern India: 1885-1947*, Macmillan, Delhi, 1983.

207 Pandey, Gyanendra, *Construction of Communalism in Colonial Northern India*, Oxford University Press, Delhi, 1989.

208 See P.C. Mahalanobis, 'Speech at Indian Statistical Institute, Calcutta,' Batabyal, Rakesh, *Penguin Book of Modern Indian Speeches*, Penguin Books, New Delhi, 2007.

209 Bhagwati, J.N. and Padma Desai, *India: Planning for Industrialisation*, Oxford University Press, Delhi, 1970.

210 Srinivasan, T.N., and N.S.S. Narayana, 'Economic Performance since the Third Plan and its Implications for Policy', *EPW*, Vol. 12, Nos 6–8, 1977, pp. 225–39.

211 Ahluwalia, Isher Judge, *Industrial Growth in India: Stagnation Since the Mid-1960s*, Oxford University Press, Delhi, 1985.

212 Bhalla, G.S, and Alagh, Y.K., *Performance of India Agriculture: District-wise Study*, Sterling Publishers, Delhi, 1978.

213 See, Chandra, Bipan, *Rise and Growth of Economic Nationalism in India*; People's Publishing House, New Delhi, also see Batabyal, Rakesh, *Penguin Book of Modern Indian Speeches*, Penguin Books, Delhi, 2007.

214 Dandekar, V.M. and Nilakanth Rath, 'Poverty in India-I: Dimensions and Trends', *EPW*, Vol. 6, No. 1, 1971, pp. 25–27, 29-48; 'Poverty in India-II, Policies and Programme', *EPW*, Vol. 6, No. 2, 1971, pp. 106-146.

215 Madhu Prasad, 'Antonio Gramsci: Contribution to Political Theory,' M Phil Dissertation, JNU, 1975.

216 See Bhaduri, Amit, 'On the Significance of Recent Controversy on Capital Theory: A Marxian View', *Economic Journal*, Vol. 79, No. 315, pp. 532–539.

217 Bharadwaj, Krishna, 'Structural Changes in Indian Industry,' *Economic Weekly*, 18 August 1962, 1339–42.

218 Bharadwaj, Krishna, 'A Note on Structural Interdependence and the Concept of 'Key' Sectors, *Kyklos*, 19, 1966, pp. 315–19.

219 Bharadwaj, Krishna, *Production Conditions in Indian Agriculture: A Study Based on Farm Management Surveys*, Cambridge University, Press, Cambridge, 1969, 1974.

220 Bharadwaj, Krishna, 'Notes on Political Economy of Development – The Indian Case', *EPW*, Vol. 7, No. 5–7, 1972, pp. 317–28.

221 Bharadwaj, Krishna, 'A View on the Commercialisation in Indian Agriculture and the Development of Capitalism', *Journal of Peasant Studies*, 12 July 1985, pp. 8–25.

222 Bhaduri, Amit, 'A Study in Agricultural Backwardness under Semi-Feudalism', *Economic Journal*, Vol. 83, Issue 329, 1973, pp. 120–37.

223 Patnaik, Utsa, 'Neo-Marxian Theories of Capitalism and Underdevelopment: Towards a Critique', Prabhat Patnaik (ed.) *Lenin and Imperialism: An Appraisal of Theories and Contemporary Reality*, Orient Longman, Hyderabad, 1989, pp. 313–49.

224 Patnaik, Prabhat, 'Disproportionality Crisis and Cyclical Growth: A Theoretical Note,' *EPW*, Vol. 5, Nos. 5-6, February 1972 pp. 329–336.

225 Alagh, Y.K., G.S. Bhalla and S.P. Kashyap, *Structural Analysis of Gujarat, Punjab, Haryana Economies: An Input Output Study*, Allied Publishers, Delhi, 1980.

226 Chakravarty, Sukhamoy and Louis Lefeber, 'An Optimising Planning Model', *Economic Weekly*, Annual Number, February 1965, pp. 237–25. See also Manne, Alan S. and Ashok Rudra, 'A Consistency Model of India's Fourth Plan', *Sankhya*, Series B, Vol. 27, Parts 1 and 2, 1965 pp. 57–144.

227 Structural Changes in Income Distribution: A Study of the Impact of Green Revolution in Punjab and Haryana, (1975-76); Strategy of Rural Development in Selected Districts of Punjab (1976-77); Strategy of Rural Development in Selected Districts of Haryana (1976-77); Dynamics of Rural Transformation: Study of Punjab—Dynamics of Rural Transformations (1979-1980); Annual Reports of Indian Council for Social Science Research, New Delhi, 1974-75 to 1980-81.

228 Marglin, Stephen, *The Dismal Science: How Thinking Like an Economist Undermines Community*, Harvard University Press, Cambridge, Massachusetts, 2008.

229 Raza, Moonis and Amitabh Kundu, *Indian Economy: The Regional Dimension*, CSRD, JNU, 1982.

230 Masters in Population Studies Degree, Evaluation Branch, JNU, 1977.

231 Singh, Harjit, 'Ladakh: Problems of Regional Development in the context of Growth Point Strategy,' Ph.D Thesis, JNU, 1978.

232 Raza, Moonis and Aijazuddin Ahmad, *An Atlas of Tribal India: With Computed Tables of District-Level Data and its Geographical Interpretation*, Mittal Publications, Delhi, 1990.

233 Mukherjee, P.N., 'Social Movement and Social Change: Towards a Conceptual Clarification and Theoretical Framework,' *Sociological Bulletin*, Vol. 26, No. 1, 1977 pp. 38–58.

234 Oommen, T.K., *Charisma, Stability and Change: Analysis of Gramdan Bhoodan Movement in India*, Thomson Press, Delhi, 1972.

235 Thompson, E.P., *The Making of the English Working Class*, Vintage, London, 1963.

236 Chandra, Bipan, 'Peasantry and National Integration in Contemporary India,' in *Nationalism and Colonialism in Modern India*, Orient Longman, Hyderabad, 1979, pp. 328–367.

237 *National Herald*, 9 September 1974.

238 Mukherjee, Mridula, *Agrarian Structure and Peasant Movement in Punjab, 1925-1947*, Ph.D Thesis, JNU, 1993; Siddiqi, Majid Hayat, *Agrarian Unrest in North India: The United Provinces*, 1918-1922, Ph.D Thesis, JNU, 1977.

239 Jagga, Lajpat R., 'Formation of an Industrial Labour Force and Forms of Labour Protest in India, a Study of Railways, 1919-37,' Ph.D Thesis, JNU, 1983.

240 C.S. Krishna, 'Labour Movement in Tamilnadu, 1918-1933', Ph.D Thesis, JNU, 1985; Banerjee, Dipankar, 'Labour Unrest in Assam: Some Aspects of the Labour Movement Among the Non-plantation Workers 1919-39,' M Phil Dissertation, JNU, 1983; G. James, Rajan G., 'The Origins Of Trade Union Movement in Kerala: A Study of Trade Unionism Among the Coir Factory Workers of Alleppy, Kerala – 1922-1938,' M Phil Dissertation, JNU, 1978; Patel, Sujata, 'The Capitalist Class and Labour Politics: A Case Study of the Ahmedabad Millowners' Association 1918-1939,' Ph.D Thesis, JNU, 1983; Lakshmana, M., 'Labour Movement in Madras City, 1918–1939,' Ph.D Thesis, JNU, 1991; Joshi, Chitra, 'Kanpur Textile Labour: Some Structural Characteristics of the Labour Force and Aspects of the Labour Movement (1919-1939),' Ph.D Thesis, JNU, 1981; Mangalagiri, Ranjana, 'Ideology of Labour Movement in India,' M Phil Dissertation, JNU, 1985; Mohapatra, Bishnu, 'The Working Class in Third World Countries: a Critical Review of Some Theoretical Studies,' M Phil Dissertation, JNU, 1985.

241 Pathy, Jagannath, 'Political Elites of Orissa,' Ph.D Thesis, JNU, 1977; Vimala, R., 'The Non-Brahmin Movement in Tamil Nadu: The Study of its Transformation from a Social Movement to a Political Party,' M Phil Dissertation, JNU, 1979; Bhadra, Ranjit Kumar, 'Changing Social Stratification in Rural Assam,' Ph.D Thesis, JNU, 1980; Karanth, G.K.,' Change and Continuity in Agrarian Relations: A Case Study of a Karnataka Village,' 1981.

242 Jaiswal, Suvira, 'Some Recent Theories of the Origins of Untouchability: Historiographical Assessment', *Proceedings of Indian History Congress*, Osmania, 1978. In fact it was the Marxist historians who have done the pioneering and finest works on the history of caste and that too the untouchables. Beginning with R.S. Sharma's own book on Shudras in ancient India, Vivekanand Jha's work on untouchables are truly path-breaking

243 Sinha, Shanta, 'Maoists in Andhra,' Ph.D Thesis, JNU, 1977; Gupta, Dipankar, 'The Siva Sena Movement, 1969-74: A Sociological Analysis,' Ph.D Thesis, JNU, 1977.

244 Chowdhary, Rekha, 'Women and Politics in India,' M.Phil Dissertation, JNU, 1973; Sen, Shipra, 'The Political Women in India, Her Status and Role,' M Phil Dissertation, JNU, 1977.

245 Choudhury, Maitrayee, 'Trends in India's Women's Movement: A Sociological Study,' Ph.D Thesis, JNU, 1986.

246 Rani, Shanta, 'Satven Dashak ke Upanyason mein Purush Patro ki Parikalpana,' M Phil Dissertation, JNU, 1979.

247 Banerji, Sanjukta, 'The Position and Prospects of Blacks in Contemporary America: An Analysis of Ideological Perspectives and Strategies in the Black Protest Movement,' Ph.D Thesis, JNU, 1981; Joshi, Manoj, 'Place of Blacks in American Society: A Critical Study of the Debate till the Emancipation Proclamation,' Ph.D Thesis, JNU 1981; Ganpatrao, Ranveer Kashinath, 'An Assessment of "Black Protest" in the Selected Writings of Richard Wright,' M.Phil Dessertation, JNU, 1982.

248 Alam, Syed Mohammad Anwar, 'A Critical Analysis of Urdu Novel under the Progressive Writers' Movement, 1936-1947,' Ph.D Thesis, JNU, 1985; Anwar, Khurshid, *Modernism in Urdu poetry upto 1970*, Ph.D Thesis, JNU, 1987.

249 Singh, Namvar, *Doosri Paramparaki Khoj*, Rajkamal Prakahsan, Delhi, 2009.

250 Agarwal, Purshottam, 'Kabir Ki Bhakti Ka Samajik Arth,' Ph.D Thesis, JNU, 1985.

Chapter 9

1 The plea to organize the Indian scientific community was first made by P.C. Ray in his presidential address at the Indian Science Congress, 1920. See Batabyal, Rakesh, *Penguin Book of Modern Indian Speeches*, Penguin Books, New Delhi, 2007. Later on, Meghnad Saha emphasized the point that the scientific communities must be organized along the lines of Royal Scientific Society, etc. See ibid.

2 Wolf, Audra J., *Competing with the Soviets: Science, Technology, and the State in Cold War America*, Johns Hopkins University,

Baltimore, 2012; Wang, Jessica, *American Science in an Age of Anxiety: Scientists, Anticommunism, and the Cold War*, University of North Carolina Press, Chapell Hill, 1999.

3 Mukerjee, Dilip, 'Indian Science Policy Organisation and Applications,' *Minerva*, Spring 1964, Volume 2, Issue 3, pp. 360–69.

4 Keck, O., 'West German Science Policy since the 1960s: Trends and Objectives', *Research Policy*, Volume 5, Issue 2, 1976, pp. 116–57.

5 N.B. Amin, 'Trial and Tribulations of Technology Transfer,' *Industrial Times*, 15, 2, 1973, pp. 14–15. See also the proceedings of the international seminar organized by the CSIR on technology transfer, 11-13 December 1972, CSIR, New Delhi. See also the large empirical understanding of technology transfer in the brilliant Ph.D thesis by Sengupta. Sengupta, Subrata, 'European Advanced Technology: Problems and Prospect of their Transfer to the Third World with Special Reference to India,' Ph.D Thesis, JNU, 1984. Dr S. Sengupta was one of the most erudite scholars that JNU produced but died in penury and in a state of unemployment as he failed to get a job for almost a decade. His collection of books, gifted to JNU library, remains the best collection.

6 Carson, Rachel, *Silent Spring*, Houghton Mifflin, Cambridge, Massachusetts, 1962.

7 Quine, W.V.O., 'Two Dogma's of Empiricism', *Philosophical Review*, 60, 1951, pp. 20–43.

8 Ibid.

9 Kuhn, Thomas, *The Structure of Scientific Revolutions*, University of Chicago Press, Chicago, 1962; see the preface of new edition in 1970.

10 Kerr, Clark, *The Uses of the University*, Harvard University Press, Cambridge, Massachusetts, 1963.

11 Bernal, J.D., *The Social Function of Science*, Routledge, London, 1944; *Science in History* in four volumes: Volume 1: *The Emergence of Science*, MIT, Cambridge, Massachusetts, 1971; Volume 2: *The Scientific and Industrial Revolutions*; MIT, Cambridge, Massachusetts, 1971; Volume 3: *The Natural Sciences in Our Time*, Penguin Books, New York, 1969; Volume 4: *The Social Sciences: Conclusion*, Penguin Books, New York, 1969. Recently there have been a couple of good biographies of Bernal which includes one by Brenda Swann and Francis Aprahamian, *J.D. Bernal, Life in Science and Politics*, Verso, London, 1999.

12 Needham, Joseph, *Science and Civilization in China*, Cambridge University Press, Cambridge, UK, 1954. The first volume appeared in 1954, following which, twenty-three volumes have appeared until 2008. After Volume 3, there were parts in volumes. This monumental work has brought the question of science into the ambit of the social and civilizational matrix.

13 Habib, Irfan, 'Technological Changes and Society, 13th and 14th Centuries,' Presidential address at the medieval section of Indian History Congress, Varanasi Session, 1969.

14 Sharma, R.S., *Material Culture and Social Formation in Early India*, Macmillan, Delhi, 1983.

15 Kosambi, D.D., *An Introduction to the Study of Indian History*, Popular Prakashan, Bombay, 1956.

16 Nandy, Ashis, 'History's Forgotten Double', *History and Theory*, Vol. 34, No. 2, 1995, pp. 44–66.

17 Seal, Brojendranath, *Positive Sciences of the Ancient Hindus*, Longmans, Green & Co., London, 1913.

18 Sabyasachi Bhattacharya, 'Positivism in 19th Century Bengal: Diffusion of European Intellectual. Influences in India' in R. S. Sharma (ed.), *Indian Society: Historical Probings, In Memory of D. D. Kosambi*, People's Publishing House, New Delhi, 1974.

19 Chattopadhyaya, D.P., *Lokayata*: A *Study in Ancient Indian Materialism*, People's Publishing House, Bombay, 1959.

20 For a critique of this position, see, Mukherji, Nirmalangshu, 'Academic Philosophy in India', *Economic and Political Weekly*, 37, 10, 2002, pp. 231-236.

21 Chattopadhyaya, K.C., 'Lokayata System of Thought in Ancient India', *Journal of Ganganath Jha Research Institute, (JGJRI)* Allahabad, 31, 1975, pp. 137–56.

22 Deepak Kumar, *Science and the Raj: A Study of British India*, Oxford University Press, Delhi, 2006. See also Sinha, Jagdish, N., 'Science and Culture under Colonialism: India between the World Wars, *Indian Journal of History of Science*, (*IJHS*) 39, 1, 2004, pp. 101–38.

23 Starting from P.C. Ray, Shanti Swarup Bhatnagar, Meghnad Saha, and in recent times, Obaid Siddiqi, A.R. Rahman and P.M. Bhargava have been very active in speaking out in favour of scientific temper, which has been under attack from various quarters and quite often politically motivated.

24 Nandy, Ashis, *The Intimate Enemy, Loss and Recovery of Self Under Colonialism*, Oxford University Press, Delhi, 1983; *Traditions, Tyranny, and Utopias: Essays in the Politics of Awareness*, Oxford University Press, Delhi, New York, 1987; *The Illegitimacy of Nationalism: Rabindranath Tagore and the Politics of Self*, Oxford University Press, Delhi, 1994.

25 Nandy, Ashis, *Intimate Enemy*...Oxford University Press, Delhi, 1989.

26 Visvanathan, Shiv, *Organizing Science: The Making of an Industrial Research Laboratory*, Oxford University Press, Delhi, 1985; *A Carnival for Science: Essays on Science, Technology and Development*, Oxford University Press, Delhi, 1997.

27 Sarabhai, Vikram, Science Policy and National Development, ed. by Kamala Choudhary, op. cit., Chapter 2, p. 22.

28 Chatterjee, Upamanyu, *Mammaries of A Welfare State*, Penguin Books, New Delhi, 1998.

29 Sinha, Jagdish N., 'Origin of India's National Science Policy: M.L. Sircar to M.K. Gandhi, 1875-1935,' *IJHS*, 27 February 1992, 171–82.

30 Sarkar, Sahotra, *The Philosophy and History of Molecular Biology: New Perspectives*, Springer (India), New Delhi, 2001; Morange, Michel, *History of Molecular Biology*, Harvard University Press, Massachusetts, 2000.

31 Tandon, P.N. *Collected Works of Ramalingaswami*: Indian National Science Academy, Delhi, 2010.

32 Anand Kumar, T.C. 'V. Ramalingaswami: An obituary,' *Current Science*, Vol. 80, No. 12, 25 June 2001, p. 1599; for some important issues of nutrition research in India, see, Sen, Srabani, 'The Beginning of Biochemical Researches in India—A Historical Perspective', *IJHS*, 37, 3, 2002, pp. 34–65; Sen, Srabani, 'Dawn of Nutrition Research in India,' *IJHS*, 40, 1 2005 pp. 81–106; Sen, Srabani, 'Biresh Chandra Guha (1904-1962),' *IJHS*, 41, 4 2006, pp. 415–32.

33 Ramalingaswami, V., 'A Centre for the Study of Social Medicine & Community Health,' a note appended to the Minutes of the Second Academic-Advisory Committee Meeting of JNU held on 29 August 1969, pp. 1–2.

34 Ibid.

35 Ibid.

36 Ibid.

37 Ibid.

38 Ibid.

39 Ibid.

40 Ramalingaswami, V., 'Biomedical Engineering Unit', a note appended to the Second Academic Advisory Committee Meeting of JNU held on 29 August 1969, p. 1.

41 Ibid.

42 Ibid.

43 Ibid.

44 Ibid.

45 Advisory Committee Meeting, 29 October 1969.

46 Ibid.

47 Ibid.

48 Verma, A.R., *Crystal Growth and Dislocations*, Butterworths, London, 1953.

49 Sundaram, K. and R.K. Mishra, 'Calculation of Charge Densities and Bond Orders in 4-Bromoestrone and 4-Bromoestradiol K, Biochim. Biophys', *Acta*, 94, 1965, p. 601; Sundaram K. and W.P. Purcell, 'Molecular Orbital Calculations on Some Mesoionic Compounds', *International Journal of Quantum Chemistry*, 2, 1969, p. 145; Purcell W.P., and K. Sundaram, 'Electronic Structure, Antimalarial Activity and Phototoxicity of Selected Quinolinemethanol Derivatives and Analogs,' *Journal of Medicinal Chemistry*, 12, 1969, p. 18; Sundaram, K., 'A Program for Updated File Keeping, Multiple Cataloguing and Key-Word Search,' in *Automation Problems in University Libraries and Special Libraries*, published by INSDOC, Delhi, 1969; Purcell, W.P., J.A. Singer, K. Sundaram and G.L. Parks, *Quantitative Structure Activity Relationships and Molecular Orbitals in Medicinal Chemistry*, 3rd edition, A. Burger (ed.), John Wiley, New York, 1969; Sundaram, K. 'A Review of the Investigations on the Pi-Electronic Structure of DNA Bases', in *Macromolecules in Storage and Transfer of Biological Information*, Department of Atomic Energy, Government of India, Bombay, 1970.

50 I have gained valuable insight from my long interaction with many of the leading biomedical scientists and in NII, AIIMS, ICGEB, IIT and others institutions. Long interactions with Prof. Alok Ray of IIT, Amit Dinda of AIIMS and Satyajit Rath of NII have particularly been invaluable.

51 Centre for Study of Scientific and Technological Advances in Developing Societies (with reference to their economic and social implications, including the problems connected with international transfers of technology).

52 'George Forsythe and Development of Computer Science,' *Communications of the Association for Computing Machinery (ACM)*, Vol. 15, No. 8, 1972, pp. 721–26.

53 Simon, Herbert, Alan Perlis and Allen Newell, 'Letter to the Editor', *Science*, 157, 22 September 1967, pp. 1373–74.

54 Ceruzzi, Paul E., *A History of Modern Computing*, Massachusetts Institute of Technology Press, Cambridge, Massachusetts, 1998, p. 102.

55 'Curriculum 68: Recommendation for the Undergraduate Program in Computer Science,' *Communications of the ACM*, Vol. 11, No. 3, 1968, p. 147.

56 Ceruzzi, Paul E., op. cit., p. 75.

57 Bassett, Ross, 'Aligning India in the Cold War Era: Indian Technical Elites, the Indian Institute of Technology at Kanpur, and Computing in India and the United States', *Technology and Culture*, Vol. 50, No. 4, October 2009, pp. 783–810.

58 Ibid.

59 Ibid.

60 Utpal Banerjee, *Computer Education in India: Past Present and Future*, Institution of Communication Engineers, Mittal Publishers, Delhi, 1996.

61 Ibid.

62 He apparently was not very enthused by the lack of computer science culture in the new university. P.N. Sharma who had worked with Prof. Rajaraman in IIT Kanpur had been in touch with him and been instrumental in opening up dialogue with him.

63 Sarkar, Sahotra, *The Philosophy and History of Molecular Biology, New Perspectives*, Kluwer Academic Publications, Dordrecht, 1991. In 1988, *The Annual Review of Plant Physiology* changed its name to *Annual Review of Plant Physiology and Molecular Biology*.

64 Luria, S.E., 'Molecular Biology: Past Present and Future', *Bioscience*, Vol. 20, December 1970, 1289–93.

65 Beadle, who had received the Nobel Prize in 1948, was one of the pioneers in the field of genetics and had risen up to the post of the president of Chicago University. For an exciting biography of

the phenomenal life of this scientist, see, Berg, Paul, and Maxine Singer, *George Beadle: An Uncommon Farmer. The Emergence of Genetics in the 20th Century*, Cold Spring Harbor Laboratory Press, New York, 2003.

66 Menon, MGK., 'Note on the Natural Sciences,' presented before the Academic Advisory Committee of JNU on October 9, 1969 which was discussed at the fourth meeting of the Academic Advisory Committee held on 29 October 1969. Report on the Progress of Work of the Various Working Groups, Vide Resolution No. 4, Executive Council meeting held on 24 January 1970, Annexure II.

67 Ibid.

68 Ibid.

69 I have greatly benefitted from the excellent and insightful paper by Prof. S. C. Maheshwari, and S.K. Sopory, in *Current Science*, Vol. 80, No. 2, 25 January 2001. See, ibid., pp. 153–54.

70 Ibid.

71 Guha, Sipra, S. C. Maheshwari, 'In Vitro Production of Embryos from Anthers of Datura', *Nature*, 204, p. 497 (31 October 1964); Sipra Guha, S.C. Maheshwari, 'Cell Division and Differentiation of Embryos in the Pollen Grains of Datura In Vitro', *Nature*, 212, pp. 97–98 (1 October 1966); Johri, B. M., Sipra Guha, S. C. Maheshwari, 'Auxin-induced Reversal of Geotropic Response in Onion Seedlings', *Nature* 205, pp. 1026–27 (6 March 1965).

72 Brody, S.S. and G.S. Singhal, 'Spectral Properties of Chloroplast Membranes as a Function of Physiological Temperatures', *Biochemical and Biophysical Research Communications*, Volume 89, Issue 2, 27 July 1979, p. 542–546; Sharma, P.K., G.S. Singhal, 'Influence of Photoinhibition on Photosynthesis and Lipid Peroxidation', *Journal of Photochemistry and Photobiology B: Biology*, Volume 13, Issue I, 15 April 1992, pp. 83–94.

73 Srivastava, P.N. 'Thyroidal Control of Radiophosphorous Metabolism in Salmon', *Nature*, 185, p. 621, (27 February 1960); P.N. Srivastava, 'Bacterial Effect and Radiophosphorous Assimilation in Organic and Inorganic Forms in Salmon', *Nature* 187, 2 July 1960, pp. 83–84; P.N. Srivastava, 'Influence of Thyroid on Radiophosphorous Metabolism in Fish', *Nature* 188, pp. 512–13; (5 November 1960); Srivastava, P.N. and P.D. Gupta, 'Excretion of Uric Acid in Periplaneta Americana L.,' *Journal of Insect Physiology*, Volume 6, Issue 3, July 1961, pp. 163–64, IN1–IN2, 165–67.

74 Srivastava, P.N. and A. Ramesha Rao, 'PMS Response to the Ovary of the Indian Desert Gerbil, Meriones Hurrianae Jerdon, after 32 P β Irradiation', *General and Comparative Endocrinology*, Volume 2, Supplement 2, 1969, pp. 190–96.

75 Das, Padma, A. R. Rao, and P.N. Srivastava, 'Influence of 17 β Estradiol on 3 MCA-induced Cervical Carcinogenesis', *Journal of Steroid Biochemistry*, Volume 28, Supplement 1, 1987, p. 6; 'Modulatory Influences of Exogenous Estrogen on MCA-Induced Carcinogenesis in the Uterine Cervix of Mice,' *Cancer Letters*, Volume 43, Issues 1–2, 1 December 1988, pp. 73–77; 'Influence of Ascorbic Acid on MCA-Induced Carcinogenesis in the Uterine Cervix of Mice', *Cancer Letters*, Volume 72, Issues 1–2, 16 August 1993, pp. 121–25.

76 Estes, Mary K., 'Advances in Molecular Biology: Impact on Rotavirus Vaccine Development', *Journal of Infectious Disease*, Vol. 174, Supplement 1, Fifth Rotavirus Vaccine Workshop: Current Issues and Future Development, September 1996, pp. s37–s47.

77 Teitelman, Robert, *Gene Dreams, Wall Street, Academia and the Rise of Biotechnology*, Basic Books, New York, 1991.

78 Madhavi, Yennapu, 'Vaccine Policy in India,' *PLOS Med.* May 2005, 2 (5): e127. Accessed Online on 24 July 2010. www. plasmedicine.org/article/info%3Adoi%2F10.1371%2Fjournal. pmed.0020127.

79 Mitchison, Avrion, 'Immunology in India', *Nature*, 323, 30 October 1986, p. 752.

80 Bhattacharya, Alok, 'Studies on the Mechanism of Gene Expression in Yeast Candida Albicans,' Ph.D Thesis, JNU, 1976.

81 Majumdar, R. C., 'Social and International Relations in the Development of Sciences', *BNISI*, 21, 1963, pp. 3–7.

83 Personal discussion with Raj Kumar Ghosh, Ph.D in chemical sciences. He is now a citizen of Canada.

Chapter 10

1 Prof. Tara Chand, *Rajya Sabha Debates*, 2 December 1964, p. 3583. He further said: '... the students that are coming to the university are not children, they are grown up people. After three or four years they will be settled in life and will have to take decisions and do things. Why not begin to take interest in them, not as boys and girls,

but rather as men and women? And, therefore why not develop in the university such bodies and institutions as will give a chance to these young men and young women to have their say on the matters which will, after all, affect them most intimately?' Ibid.

2 Dr V.S. Sheth, in *Booklet of the Alumni Association of JNU (AAJ)*, 2009, p. 107.

3 Pattnaik, S.K., *Student Politics and Voting Behaviour: A case Study of Jawaharlal Nehru University*, Concept Publishing Co., Delhi, 1982, p. 30.

4 Ibid.

5 Ibid. Pattnaik has put all of these in one place.

6 N.D. Jayaprakash, in *Booklet of the Alumni Association of JNU*, 2009.

7 'Politicking in J. Nehru University', *The Times of India*, Delhi, 17 December 1972.

8 Dr V.S. Sheth, *AAJ*, p. 107.

9 Ibid.

10 Lenoir, Remi, 'Scientific Habitus: Pierre Bourdieu and the Collective Intellectual', *Theory, Culture & Society*, Vol. 23, No.6, 2006, pp. 23–25.

11 See his later writing on Lohia, Anand Kumar, 'Understanding Lohia's Political Sociology', *Economic And Political Weekly*, Vol. 45, No. 40, 3 October 2008, pp. 64–70.

12 'Power Struggle at Nehru University', *Hindustan Times*, 2 September 1974.

13 *The Statesman*, Delhi, 6 June 1974.

14 Shamim, M., 'A Confused Admission Policy, JNU Suffers from Lack of Clear Goal', *The Times of India*, Delhi, 21 September 1974.

15 Karat, Prakash, 'Student Movement in Jawaharlal Nehru University', *Social Scientist*, 3,10 May 1975, pp. 47–54.

16 Koshy, V.C., 'Jawaharlal Nehru University: A Model University? Perspective and Ideal', *Social Scientist*, Vol. 2, No. 2, September 1973, p. 48.

17 However, when it came to get his protégés or party leaders' 'kin appointed in the university, he was no less enterprising'.

18 Koshy, V.C, op. cit., p. 47.

19 Ibid.

20 Ibid., p. 50.

21 *The Times of India*, Delhi, 21 September 1974.

22 Koshy, V.C., op. cit.

23 Karat, Prakash, op. cit., p. 53, fn. 6.
24 Paramanand Tripathy, *Dharmayug*, 18 May, 1969.
25 Karat, Prakash, op. cit., p. 49.
26 Ibid.
27 What emerges from the above report on JNU is that it is futile to build a 'model institution' in isolation from the existing realities of our educational and social framework. All the professed aims set out for JNU were seen to have totally failed so far, and the university was being used as a 'progressive facade', an attempt to patchwork the rotten educational system that this country is burdened with. 'As such, in reality JNU is fast on the road to becoming a parasitical leech on our scarce resources for higher education.' Koshy, V.C., op. cit., p. 51.
28 Resolution of JNUTA on 1 April 1974 quoted by AISF bulletin, 'The Story of Struggle,' August 1974, as cited in Pattnaik, S.K., op. cit., p. 72, fn. 20.
29 Ibid., p. 43.
30 Ibid.
31 *The Times of India*, New Delhi, 8 April 1975.
32 Pattnaik, S.K., op. cit., pp. 39–46.
33 'Union moves to High Court,' *Hindustan Times*, 10 April 1975.
34 'Hasan won't step in to end JNU stir', *The Times of India*, New Delhi, 10 April 1975.
35 *National Herald*, Delhi, 10 April 1975.
36 'VC's conditions of reopening JNU', *The Hindu*, 15 April 1975.
37 For the later-day glorification of the strike and the demand by a CPI(M) affiliated teacher involved in the affair, see, Patnaik, Prabhat, 'On Tapas Majumdar,' *Social Scientist*, Vol. 38, No. 9–12, September–December 2010, pp. 185–187.
38 Jayaram, N., 'Sadhus No Longer', *Journal of Higher Education*, No. 7, 1979, pp. 683–699.
39 *Patriot*, 18 February 1978.
40 Ibid.
41 Ibid.

Chapter 11

1 See Singh, Tavleen, *Durbar*, Hachett India, Delhi, 2012 on the way the city's political and social elite worked during the Emergency;

see also Gujral, I.K., *Matters of Discretion: An Autobiography*, Hay House, Delhi, 2011; Dhar, P.N., *Indira Gandi, the "Emergency", and Indian Democracy*", Oxford University Press, Delhi, 2000 and Verghese, B.G., *First Draft*, Tranquebar Press, Chennai. 2010; also to see the way people fought the violation of the civil rights, Chagla, *Roses in December*, revised edition, Bharatiya Vidya Bhawan, Bombay, 1980; for some critical aspects of the Emergency, see Tarlo Emma, *Unsettling Memories: Narrative of Emergency in Delhi*, University of California Press, Berkeley and Los Angeles, 2003. For a good historical analysis of the circumstances under which the decision to impose Emergency was taken see Chandra, Bipan, *In the Name of Democracy, JP Movement and Emergency*, Penguin Books, New Delhi, 2003.

2 *Hindustan Times*, 27 February 1977. The signatories included Prof. A.K. Dasgupta, Sivatosh Mookerjee, Ashok Guha, Anirudha Gupta, S. Bhattacharya, Girija Kumar, Dhirendra Sharma and Parimal Das.

3 *Hindustan Times*, 13 March 1977.

4 *The Statesman*, Delhi, 2 March 1977.

5 *The Times of India*, Delhi, 6 March 1977.

6 Ibid., 24 March 1977.

7 *Hindustan Times*, 16 April 1977.

8 'Student Politics in Wider Perspective', *The Indian Express*, Delhi, 19 February 1977.

9 *The Statesman*, 22 April 1977.

10 Ibid.

11 Ibid.

12 Ibid.

13 *The Times of India*, New Delhi, 28 April 1977.

14 Ibid., New Delhi, 27 May 1977. Also see Minutes of the 56th Emergent Meeting of the Executive Council of JNU held on 9 November 1977 in the Committee room of the UGC, Annexure I.

15 *Patriot*, New Delhi, 27 May 1977.

16 *Hindustan Times*, New Delhi, 10 May 1977.

17 *The Times of India*, New Delhi, 21 May 1977.

18 Ibid.

19 *The Indian Express*, New Delhi, 25 May 1977.

20 Letter by Shukla, Vandana Mishra and Ramesh Dixit, *Hindustan Times*, Delhi, 3 June 1977 followed by a letter to the editor by Mangal Prasad, Atiqur Rahman, Sindhu Baghia, R.N. Mahato,

Manju Bhatia and D.K. Sharma, ibid., 7 June 1977. This was followed by yet another letter by Anil Mishra, J.K. Panigrahi, Gyan Bardhan Pathak, N. Rajan, Sanjiv Haldar and Chain Singh Panwar which reiterated the demand for an impartial commission of inquiry, ibid., 9 June 1977. All these said appointments were made using statute 28 of the university, which entitled it to invite people of exceptional calibre without making them go through the interview and normal selection process.

21 *Hindustan Times*, New Delhi, 18 July 1977.
22 *Patriot*, New Delhi, 22 July 1977.
23 *Hindustan Times*, New Delhi, 30 July 1977.
24 *Patriot*, New Delhi, 18 February 1977.
25 *Morning Echo*, New Delhi, 23 May 1978.
26 *The Statesman*, New Delhi, 15 March 1978.
27 *Patriot*, New Delhi, 6 February 1978.
28 *The Times of India*, New Delhi, 7 February 1978.
29 *Patriot*, New Delhi, 22 February 1978.
30 *The Times of India*, New Delhi, 22 February 1978; *Patriot*, New Delhi, 26 February 1978.
31 *Patriot*, New Delhi, 26 February 1978.
32 *The Times of India*, New Delhi, 18 April 1978.
33 *The Statesman*, New Delhi, 14 February 1979.
34 Ibid., 19 February 1979.
35 *Patriot*, New Delhi, 24 February 1979.
36 *Patriot*, Delhi, 24 February 1979. I must acknowledge the love and affection that I received from late Dilip Upadhyay during 1991–2002 when he occasionally would visit JNU and we would have long chats, little knowing that I would be writing the history of JNU where he would figure. He died of kidney failure in 2004.
37 *Patriot*, New Delhi, 27 February 1979.
38 Ibid., 23 February 1979.
39 *The Indian Express*, New Delhi, 22 March 1979.
40 *The Times of India*, New Delhi, 29 March 1979.
41 'Dog Days for Dons', *The Statesman*, New Delhi, 28 October 1979.
42 *The Statesman*, 31 January 1980.
43 'Starving Day at JNU', *The Statesman*, New Delhi, 31 January 1980.
44 *The Times of India*, New Delhi, 9 February 1980.
45 Ibid.
46 *The Statesman*, New Delhi, 13 February 1980.

47 Ibid.
48 *Patriot*, New Delhi, 23 February 1980.
49 *The Times of India*, New Delhi, 25 February 1980.
50 Ibid.
51 Ibid.
52 *Nav Bharat Times*, New Delhi, 25 February 1980.
53 Ibid.
54 *The Times of India*, New Delhi, 15 March 1980.
55 *The Indian Express*, New Delhi, 26 April 1980.
56 R.G. James Kuttickattu, *Hindustan Times*, 2 July 1980.
57 R.G. James Kuttickattu, *JNU: End of Science Policy; A Study of Unique Centre for Higher Learning*, Selbstveri, New Delhi, 1985.
58 *Hindustan Times*, New Delhi, 15 June 1980.
59 *Hindustan Times*, New Delhi, 1 July 1980.
60 Ibid.
61 Ibid.
62 Letter to the Editor, *Hindustan Times*, New Delhi, 7 July 1980.
63 'JNU Malaise', Ibid., 30 July 1980.
64 *The Indian Express*, New Delhi, 28 April 1980.
65 *The Times of India*, New Delhi, 27 June 1980.
66 *The Hindu*, Madras, 8 July 1980.
67 *The Indian Express*, New Delhi, 13 September 1980.
68 Ibid.
69 *Nav Bharat Times*, New Delhi, 23 June 1980.
70 'Search for new V.C.', *The Indian Express*, New Delhi, 9 September 1980.
71 *The Times of India*, New Delhi, 12 November 1980.
72 *The Times of India*, New Delhi, 18 November 1980.
73 *The Indian Express*, New Delhi, 12 November 1980.
74 *The Statesman*, New Delhi, 13 November 1980.
75 *Patriot*, New Delhi, 13 November 1980.
76 *Hindustan Times*, New Delhi, 12 November 1980.
77 *Economic* Times, New Delhi, 17 November 1980.
78 *The Indian Express*, New Delhi, 18 November 1980.
79 Ibid.
80 Ibid.
81 Ibid.
82 Ibid.
83 *The Indian Express*, New Delhi, 18 November 1980.

84 *The Times of India*, New Delhi, 14 December 1980.
85 While the representative of the union appealed to the students to adopt a compromising attitude by shifting their dharna from the residential block to the administrative wing of the university, as urged by the teachers, the SDF group strongly resented any such proposal and said that the lifting of the dharna would only mean surrendering to the dictatorial attitude of the vice chancellor.
86 *The Indian Express*, New Delhi, 17 December 1980.
87 *Hindustan Times*, New Delhi, 18 December 1980.
88 Ibid.
89 *Patriot*, New Delhi, 20 December 1980.
90 *Hindustan Times*, New Delhi, 3 December 1980.
91 Ibid.
92 Ibid.
93 Ibid., 2 January 1981.
94 *The Indian Express, Hindustan Times, National Herald*, New Delhi, 1 January 1981.
95 *The Statesman*, New Delhi, 6 January 1981.
96 *Hindustan Times*, New Delhi, 9 January 1981.
97 'JNU students protest against leave'. It said: 'Chairman of the international law department goes on leave while two faculty were already on leave', *The Times of India*, New Delhi, 15 January 1981.
98 *The Indian Express*, New Delhi, 24 March 1981.
99 *The Indian Express*, New Delhi, 24 March 1981.
100 *Sunday Statesman*, New Delhi, 29 March 1981.
101 Ibid.
102 *Hindustan Times*, New Delhi, 21 May 1981.
103 *Patriot*, New Delhi, 1 August 1981.
104 *The Statesman*, New Delhi, 31 March 1981.
105 *The Indian Express*, New Delhi, 31 July, 1981.
106 *The Times of India*, New Delhi, 25 April 1981.
107 *Hindustan Times*, New Delhi, 15 October 1981.
108 *The Times of India*, New Delhi, 29 October 1981.
109 Ibid., 31 October 1981.
110 *People's Democracy*, 8 November 1981, p. 11.
111 See Batabyal, Rakesh, 'Hindu Communal Challenge', in Mukherjee Aditya (ed.) *Centenary History of the Indian National Congress, 1964-84*, Academic Foundation, New Delhi, 2011.
112 *Hindustan Times*, Delhi, 11 November 1981.

113 Ibid.,
114 *The Statesman*, New Delhi, 10 November 1981.
115 *The Times of India*, New Delhi, 14 November 1981.
116 *The Times of India*, New Delhi, 23 November 1981.
117 *Patriot*, New Delhi, 30 December 1981.
118 *Patriot*, Delhi, 12 August 1982.
119 *The Times of India*,, Delhi, 13 October 1982.
120 *Patriot*, Delhi, 22 October 1982.
121 *Patriot*, Delhi, 5 December 1982.
122 *Hindustan Times*, Delhi, 16 May 1981.
123 Ibid., 17 May 1981.
124 *The Times of India*, 21 August 1981.
125 *Organiser*, 24 October 1981.
126 *The Times of India*, 3 December 1981.
127 For classic right-wing foreign policy statement of the 1960s and 1970s see Sondhi, M.L., *Non-Appeasement: New Directions for Indian Foreign Policy*, Abhinav Publications, Delhi, 1972.
128 *The Times of India*, 4 December 1981.
129 *Hindustan Times*, 29 April 1982.
130 *The Times of India*, 28 April 1982.
131 *National Herald*, Delhi, 24 April 1982.
132 Saberwal, Satish, 'What Has Happened at JNU', *Mainstream*, 28 May, 1983, p.9.
133 Ibid., p. 10.

Chapter 12

1 *The Statesman*, New Delhi, 6 June 1974.
2 *Patriot*, New Delhi, 25 April 1983.
3 *The Times of India*, New Delhi, 28 April 1983.
4 'Mark Sheet Racket', Ibid., 18 August 1981.
5 'UGC Responsibility', *The Times of India*, New Delhi, 4 January 1986.
6 *The Statesman*, New Delhi, 11 February 1983.
7 Ibid., 19 January 1983, p. 4.
8 Minutes of the 94th Meeting (Emergent) of the Executive Committee of JNU held on 17 February 1983 in Board Room of IIT Delhi.
9 *The Times of India*, Delhi, 17 February 1983.

10 *The Statesman*, 18 February 1983.
11 'JNU Boys Rally Before Parliament Today', *The Times of India*, Delhi, 21 February 1983.
12 Ibid., 22 February 1983.
13 *Patriot*, 29 August 1982.
14 *Patriot*, 23 February 1983.
15 *Hindustan Times*, 28 February 1983.
16 Ibid.
17 Ibid.
18 *The Statesman*, Delhi, 25 February 1983.
19 Ibid., 27 February 1983.
20 *Patriot*, 27 February 1983.
21 Ibid.
22 Ibid.
23 *The Times of India*, New Delhi, 1 March 1983.
24 *The Indian Express*, New Delhi, 2 March 1983.
25 *Hindustan Times*, New Delhi, 3 March 1983.
26 'JNU's Hour of Crisis', C.N. Chittaranjan, *Mainstream*, 21 May 1983, p. 3.
27 'JNU's Acting VC Gherao', *Hindustan Times*, New Delhi, 29 April 1983. Details of the facts can also be gleaned from the Minutes of the 96th (Emergent) Meeting of the Executive Council held on 1 June 1983, Appendix I and Appendix II.
28 Ibid.
29 *The Times of India*, New Delhi, 30 April 1983.
30 Ibid.
31 *Hindustan Times*, New Delhi, 1 May 1983.
32 *The Times of India*, New Delhi, 2 May 1983.
33 Ibid.
34 Ibid.
35 *The Statesman*, New Delhi, 3 May 1983.
36 *The Times of India*, New Delhi, 4 May 1983.
37 'JNUSU Leaders Face Action,' *National Herald*, New Delhi, 4 May 1983.
38 Ibid.
39 *The Indian Express*, New Delhi, 5 May 1983.
40 *The Times of India*, New Delhi, 6 May 1983.
41 Ibid.
42 Ibid.

43 *Patriot*, 7 May 1983.
44 Ibid.
45 Ibid.
46 Ibid.
47 Ibid., pp. 3–4.
48 N. Balasubramaniam, incidentally was appointed as a young typist in the first batch of appointments made by Parthasarathi. Author's personal interview with him was on 20 July 2006.
49 Chittaranjan, C.N. op. cit., p. 4.
50 Ramaswamy, Jugnu, 'Experiment Gone Awry', *India Today*, 15 June 1983 pp. 117–18.
51 Chittaranjan, C.N. op. cit.,
52 Ramaswamy, Jugnu, op. cit., Udai Prakash, 'Police Riding the White Elephant' (Safed Hathi par Police Ke Mahavat), *Dinman*, 22–28 May, 1983, pp. 15–16.
53 Prakash, Udai, op. cit., p. 16.
54 Chittaranjan, C.N. op. cit., p. 4.
55 Ramaswamy Jugnu, *op. cit.*, p. 118.
56 Amrik Singh, *The Times of India*, New Delhi, 17 May 1983.
57 Ibid.
58 Ibid.
59 Ibid.
60 Ibid.
61 Ibid.
62 Agwani was a heart patient and needed medicine.
63 *The Statesman*, New Delhi, 8 June 1983.
64 *The Times of India*, New Delhi, 16 June 1983.
65 *Hindustan Times*, New Delhi, 1 July 1983.
66 This included Parmar, Malik, Deo, Ramamoorthy, Nanda Kumar, Durga Charan, Jaswant Singh, Venugopal Rao, Jaljit Singh, J.M. Rao, Rabisankar, Azhar, Gufran Wali and Ganesh. *Hindustan Times*, Delhi, 19 July 1983.
67 This included Satish Kumar, Urmilesh Singh, Sudhir Gupta, Rampilla Narayana Rao, R. Sugathan, A.S. Sirohi, Bishnupriya Gupta, B. Tilak, C.P. Jivan, Syed Mohammed Anwar Alam, Rajesh Kumar Singh, Nigthoujan Devanand Singh, C. Jeyraj, Chandrabhan Prasad, Shashi Bhusan Upadhyay, Jagpal Singh and Y.K. Rajan.
68 Disciplinary Committee Files, 1983, Proctor's Office, JNU.

69 Ibid.
70 Ibid.
71 Manglik, Mukul, *The Times of India*, Delhi, 4 July 1983.
72 *Hindustan Times*, New Delhi, 11 June 1983.
73 Ibid.
74 *Patriot*, 9 June 1983.
75 It is worth insisting upon the parochial and distinctly self-regarding issues that sparked the May Events, lest the ideologically charged language and ambitious programs of the following weeks mislead us. The student occupation of the Sorbonne and subsequent street barricades and clashes with the police, notably on the nights of May 10th–11th and 24th– 25th were led by representatives of the *Jeunesse Communiste Revolutiannaire* (Trotskyist), as well as officials from established student and junior lecturer unions. But the accompanying Marxist rhetoric, while familiar enough, masked an essentially anarchist spirit whose immediate objective was the removal and humiliation of authority. Judt, Tony, *Post War: A History of Europe Since 1945*, Penguin Books, New York, 2005, p. 409.

Chapter 13

1 'Reorganisation of Mess System', *JNU News*, Delhi, March 1985, pp. 8–9.
2 Ibid
3 Ibid., p. 9.
4 Ibid.
5 Rao, K. Sudha, *Admission Policy and Practice: For Equity Access and Quality*, NUEPA, 2001, New Delhi.
6 I owe this expression to Balasubramanian, popularly known as Balu. Balu was one of the first to join the JNU secretarial staff to rise to the level of deputy registrar handling the admission and evaluation process. My interview with him was in 2007–08.
7 *JNU News*, November 1984, p. 8.
8 Ibid.
9 *Jawaharlal Nehru University Students Union* vs *Jawaharlal Nehru University*, AIR 1985 SC 567.
10 *The Statesman*, New Delhi, 3 October 1984.
11 See Stephens, Julie, *Anti-disciplinary Protest: Sixties Radicalism and Postmodernism*, Cambridge University Press, Cambridge, UK, 1998, for a theoretical perspective on student movements of the time.

12 Cannon, Lou, *President Reagan: The Role of a Lifetime*, Simon and Schuster, New York, 1991; Koh, Harold Hongju, *The National Security Constitution: Sharing Power After the Iran-Contra Affair*, Yale University Press, New Haven, 1990; Johnson Haynes, *Sleepwalking Through History: America in the Reagan Years*, W.W.Norton, New York, 2003.

13 Stephens, Julie, op. cit.

14 Cannon, Lou, *President Reagan: The Role of a Lifetime*, Simon and Schuster, New York, 1991; Johnson, Haynes, *Sleepwalking Through History: America in the Reagan Years*, W.W.Norton, New York, 2003.

15 Brzezinski, Zbigniew, *Between Two Ages—America's Role in the Technetronic Era*, Greenwood Press, New York, 1982.

16 Behera, Susmita, 'Human Rights in International Relations: A Study of U.S. Policy During the Carter Administration,' M. Phil. Dissertation, JNU, 1997; Jena, Manmatha Nath, 'US Human Rights Policy and Strategic Geo-Political Considerations vis-à-vis India and Pakistan: from Carter Administration to Clinton Administrations,' M. Phil. Dissertation, JNU, 1977.

17 Schwab, Larry, M., *Illusion of a Conservative Reagan Revolution*, Transaction Publication, New Jersey, 1991.

18 Dallek, Robert, *Ronald Reagan, The Politics of Symbolism*, pp. 129–62; for a critique of the foreign policy, see, Chomsky, Noam, *Towards a New Cold War, US Foreign Policy from Vietnam to Reagan*, The New Press, New York, 1982.

19 Kagan, Robert, *A Twilight Struggle: American Power and Nicaragua, 1977-1990*, Free Press, New York, 1996; Andrew, Christopher, *The World Was Going Our Way: the KGB and the Battle for the Third World*, Perseus Books, New York, 2005.

20 The era has now spawned a vast literary output. Some of the significant contributions from our perspective are: Haig, Alexander, *Caveat*, Weidenfeld and Nicolson, London, 1984; Collins, Robert, *Transforming America: Politics and Culture during Reagan Years*, Columbia University Press, New York, 2006; Steinfels, Peter, *The Neoconservatives: the Men who are Changing America's Politics*, Simon and Schuster, New York, 1979; Kristol, Irving, *Neoconservatism: Autobiography of an Idea*, Free Press, New York, 1995; Coser, Lewis, and Irving Howe (eds.), *The New Conservatives: A Critique from the Left*, Meridian Books, New York, 1977; Kemp,

Jack, *An American Renaissance: A Strategy for the 1980s*, Harper and Row, New York, 1979; Niskanen, William, *Reaganomics: An Insider's Account of the Policies and People*, Oxford University Press, New York, 1988; Rayack, Elton, *Not so Free to Choose: The Political Economy of Milton Friedman and Ronald Reagan*, Praeger, 1987; Moynihan, Daniel Patrick, 'Defining Deviancy Down', *The American Scholar*, Winter 1993, 17-30; Krauthammer, Charles, 'Defining Deviancy Up', *New Republic*, 22 November 1993, 20–25.

21 Hardt, Michael and Antonio Negri, *Multitude: War and Democracy in the Age of Empire*, Penguin Books, New York, 2005.

22 Bloom, Allan, *The Closing of the American Mind: How Higher Education Has Failed Democracy and Impoverished the Soul of Today's Students*, Simon and Schuster, New York, 1987.

23 McGrath, Tom, *MTV: The Making of a Revolution*, Diane Publishing Company, Pennsylvania, 1999.

24 Holmes, Martin, *The First Thatcher Government, 1979-1983*, Harvester Press, Sussex, 1985; Bosanquet, Nick, *After the New Right*, Heinemann, London, 1983.

25 *Patriot*, Delhi, 12 August 1982.

26 Baba, Noor Ahmad, 'Iranian Revolution of 1978-79: Origins and Dimensions,' M.Phil. Dissertation, JNU, 1981.

27 Defileh, Shahla, 'The Iranian Revolution and Its Impact on Iran-Saudi Arabian Relations 1978-1982,' M.Phil. Dissertation, JNU, 1984; Bhutia, 'Pulin Bihari, Irano-Soviet Relations: A study of Iranian foreign policy during the post-revolution era,' M.Phil. Dissertation, JNU, 1986.

28 Draper, Theodore, *A Very Thin Line: The Iran-Contra Affairs*, Simon and Schuster, New York, 1992; Alterman, Eric, *When Presidents Lie: History of Official Deception and its Consequences*, Penguin Books, New York, 2004.

29 Collins, Joseph, *The Soviet Invasion of Afghanistan, A Study in the Use of Force in Soviet Foreign Policy*, Lexington Books, London, 1986.

30 A fascinating recounting by M.K. Rasgotra, who was India's ambassador to Russia when Indira Gandhi and Brezhnev met, confirms that Indira Gandhi was not at all happy and refused to endorse the Soviet position.

31 Aloo Dastur, Durga Bhagwat, Vijay Tendulkar, Dhiren Narain, Manorama Savur, S.H. Deshpande, S.P. Mohanty, Vasanthi

Raman, P.V.M. Desai, R. Srinivasan, K.P. Modi, P.M. Kamath, R.N. Billimoria, Ritu Diwan, A.N. Oza, L.K. Deshpande, P.P. Desai, K. Narayan, J.P. Dixit, S. Chabria and V.B. Godre, 'Soviet Troops in Afghanistan', Letter to the Editor, *Economic and Political Weekly*, Vol. 15, No. 1, 5 January 1980, p. 5.

32 *Patriot*, New Delhi, 10 January 1980.

33 The special issue of the journal, International Studies, carried a detailed report of the issue and its ramification. *International Studies*, Sage, New Delhi, October 1980.

34 Cohen, Stephen, P., 'Approaching India's Military and Security Policy, with a Detour through Disaster Studies', *India Review*, Volume 7, Issue 4, 2008, pp. 295–319.

35 'Call for end of confrontation in Asia', *The Times of India*, Delhi, 8 May 1981.

36 Rao, P.V. Narasimha, 'Non-Alignment: Problem and Perspective', *Mainstream*, 24 May 1980, p. 7.

37 Vijayalakshmi, K.P., 'The United States and the Non–Aligned Movement, with special reference to New World Information Order 1969-1979,' Ph.D Thesis, JNU 1987; Dhar, Choudhury Rajib, 'A Case for a New World Information and Communication Order,' Ph.D Thesis, JNU 1986.

38 Chakravarty, Sukhamoy, 'Non-Alignment and International Economic Order,' Rasheduddin Khan (ed.), *Perspective on Non-Alignment*, Vikas Publishing House, Delhi, 1981.

39 Pathy, Jagannath, 'Imperialism, Anthropology and the Third World,' *EPW*, Vol. 16, No. 14, p. 623.

40 See for a full report of the conversion, *Sunday*, 7 June 1981; a full report by Kuldip Nayar, *Sunday*, 17 November 1982; also see, Shakir, Moin and H. Ghani, 'The Conversion Phenomenon', *Secular Democracy*, October 1981, pp. 15–21.

41 See Katju, Manjari, *Vishwa Hindu Parishad and Indian Politics*, Orient Longman, Hyderabad, 2003.

42 Ali Khan, Mumtaz, 'Mass Conversion of Meenakshipuram: A Sociological Enquiry,' M.Phil. Dissertation, JNU, 1983.

43 *Link*, Delhi, 31 August 1980, p. 9.

44 My long association with Prof. Alokesh Barua, one of the early students of JNU needs to be acknowledged and his experience with the AASU leaders coming to JNU remains vivid in my memory.

45 Sharma, Diganta, *Nellie 1983, Asom Andoloner Gonohotyar Postmortem*, Eklabya Prakashan, Jurhot, 2007, Kimura, Makiko, 'Memories of the Massacre: Violence and Collective Identity in the Narratives on the Nellie Incident 1', *Asian Ethnicity*, 4, 2, 2003, pp. 225–39.

46 'Mandai Massacre', *Sunday*, 24 June 1980.

47 Singh, Jagpal, *Capitalism and Dependence: Agrarian Politics in Western Uttar Pradesh 1951-1991*, Manohar, Delhi, 1992.

48 Pai, Sudha, *Dalit Assertion and the Unfinished Democratic Revolution*, Sage Publications, New Delhi, London, New York, 2002.

49 See Batabyal, Rakesh, 'Hindu Communal Challenge', in Mukherjee, Aditya, (ed.), *Centenary History of All India Congress, 1964-84*, Vol. V, Academic Foundation, Delhi, 2011.

50 Ibid.

51 See Chagla, M.C., 'The Only Alternative', Shri M.C. Chagla's address to delegates to the first plenary session of the Bharatiya Janata Party at Samata Nagar, Bandra Reclamation, Bombay on 29 December 1980.

52 Nayar, B.R., *Minority Politics in Punjab*, University of California Press, Los Angeles, 1969.

53 Ranadive, B.T., 'Intensified Crisis of the System', *Social Scientist*, November 1980, pp. 36–54.

54 Bhambhri, C.P., 'State and Communalism in India,' *Social Scientist*, Vol. 18, No. 207–08, Aug–Sept 1990, pp. 22–26.

55 Prakash, Sri, 'CPI and the Pakistan Movement', Bipan Chandra (ed.), *The Left: A Critical Appraisal*, Vikas Publishing House, Delhi, 1985.

56 Namboodiripad, E.M.S., 'The Indian National Question: Need for Deeper Study', *Social Scientist*, Vol. 10, No. 12, 1992, pp. 61–69.

57 Singh, Randhir, *Five Lectures in Marxist Mode*, Ajanta Publishers, Delhi, 1993; Bipan Chandra, *Communalism in Modern India*, Vikas Publishing House, Delhi, 1984.

58 Chandra, Bipan, Ibid.

59 Ibid.

60 Mukherjee, Mridula, 'Some Aspects of Agrarian Structure of Punjab, 1925–47', *EPW*, 15, No. 26, June 1980, pp. A 46–A 58,' 'Communists and Peasants in Punjab, A Focus on the Muzara Movement in Patiala, 1937-53', in Bipan Chandra (ed), *The*

Indian Left: Critical Appraisals, Vikas Publishing House, Delhi, 1983, pp. 401–46; 'Commercialization and Agrarian Change in pre-Independent Punjab', in K.N. Raj (ed.), *Essays on the Commercialization of Indian Agriculture*, Oxford University Press, Delhi, 1985.

61 Menon, Visalakshi, 'The Indian National Congress and Mass Mobilization—A study of U.P., 1937-39', *Studies in History*, Vol. 2, No. 2, 1980, pp. 111–140.

62 Kudaisya, Gyanesh, 'Office Acceptance and the Congress 1937-39: Premises and Perceptions,' M.Phil. Dissertation, JNU; Sharma, Gyan Prakash, 'Congress, Peasant Movement and Tenancy Legislation in Bihar, 1937-39,' M.Phil. Dissertation, JNU, 1979; Singh, Neerja, 'The Right and the Right Wing Politics in the Congress,' *1934-39*, M.Phil. Dissertation, JNU, 1984; Singha, Radhika, 'Aspects of Quit India Movement in Eastern U.P.,' M.Phil. Dissertation, JNU, 1986.

63 Atluri, Murali, 'Social Change and Nature of Social Participation in National Movement in Andhra, 1905-1934,' Ph.D Thesis, JNU, 1987.

64 Reddy, Kama Shankar, 'The National Movement in Krishna District, 1920-1931, M.Phil. Dissertation, JNU, 1988; Pilli, Arun Kumar, 'A Study of Caste and Class Politics in Srikakulum District, 1967-72, M.Phil. Dissertation, JNU, 1988.

65 Singh, Shyam Narayan, 'National Movement in Bihar, 1919-1922' M.Phil. Dissertation, JNU,1988; Singh, Lata, 'The Congress and the Bihar Kisan Sabha Movement, 1934-39,' M.Phil. Dissertation, JNU, 1987.

66 Chandra Bipan, *Indian National Movement: The Long-term Dynamics*, Vikas Publishing House, Delhi, 1988.

67 Review of Bipan Chandra's *Indian National Movement: The Long-term Dynamics*, cited in *JNU News*, 1980, p. 3.

68 For some initial good and exciting works on Gramsci and his ideas see, Davidson, Alastair, *Antonio Gramsci: Towards an Intellectual Biography*, The Merlin Press, London, 1977; Boggs, Carl, *Gramsci's Marxism*, Pluto Press, London, 1976, Joll, James, *Antonio Gramsci*, Penguin Books, London, 1978; Adamson, Walter, A *Hegemony and Revolution: Study of Antonio Gramsci's Political and Cultural Theory*, University of California Press, Berkely, Los Angels, London, 1980; Chantal, Mouffe and Anne Sassoon, 'Gramsci in France and Italy', *Economy and Society*, 6 February 1977, pp. 31–68; Morrow,

Raymond, 'Gramsci in Germany', *Telos*, 22, Winter 1974–75; pp. 174–81, Davidson A.B., 'The Varying Seasons of Gramscian Studies', *Political Studies* 20, 4 December 1972, pp. 448–61.

69 Jay, Martin, *Marxism and Totality: The Adventure of a Concept from Lucaks to Habermas*, Polity, Press, Cambridge, 1984, p. 163.

70 Chandra, Bipan, op.cit., cited in *JNU News*, 1980.

71 Prasad, Madhu, 'Gramsci's Concept of Praxis,' M.Phil. Dissertation, JNU, 1975.

72 K. Srinivasulu, 'Gramsci's Concept of Everyday Political Practice: A Study of his Factory Council Writings,' M.Phil., Dissertation, JNU, 1985.

73 Patnaik, Arun, 'Power Structure and Rural Development Programme: A Study of Digapahandi Block Orissa,' M.Phil., Dissertation, JNU, 1985.

74 Hutchins, Christopher, Illusions of Permanence: British Imperialism in India, Princeton University Press, New Jersey, 1969.

75 Josh, Bhagwan, and Shashi Joshi, *Struggle for Hegemony in India*, 1920-47, Sage Publishing House, New York, London, Delhi, 1992.

76 Mahajan, Sucheta, *Independence and Partition: Loss of Hegemony*, Sage Publishing House, New York, London, New Delhi, 1999.

77 Mukherjee, Aditya, 'The Indian Capitalist Class: Aspect of its Economic, Political and Ideological Development in the Colonial Period, 1927-47', in S. Bhattacharya and Romila Thapar (eds), *Situating Indian History*, Oxford University Press, Delhi, 1986, pp. 123–287.

78 Gopal, S., *Nehru: A Biography*, Vol. 1 & 2, Oxford University Press, Delhi, 1976 and 1979.

79 Sharada Prasad, H.Y., 'More than a Mere Prime Minister', *Mainstream*, 12 January 1980, p. 31.

80 Sen, Mohit, 'Meaning of Recalling Nehru Today', *Mainstream*, 24 May 1980, p. 11.

81 Bharadwaj, Krishna, 'Notes on Political Economy of Development – The Indian Case', *EPW*, Vol. 7, No 5–6–7, 5 February 1972, pp. 317–28; 'On Certain Theoretical Issues in Classical Political Economy, *EPW*, Vol. 13, No. 20, 20 May 1978, pp. 839–846.

82 Patnaik, Prabhat, 'On the Political Economy of Underdevelopment,' *EPW*, Vol. 8, No. 4–5–6, 3 February 1973, pp. 197–212.

83 Sanyal, Amal, Prabhat Patnaik and S.K. Rao, 'The Inflationary Process, Some Theoretical Comments,' *EPW*, Vol. 11, No. 43,

23 October 1976, pp. 1696–1710; Patnaik, Prabhat and S.K. Rao. 'Towards an Explanation of Crisis in a Mixed Underdeveloped Economy,' *EPW*, Vol. 12, No. 6–7–8, 9 February 1977, pp. 205–218.

84 Prabhat Patnaik, 'On the Political Economy of Economic "Liberalisation"', *Social Scientist*, Vol. 13 No. 7–8, 1985, pp. 3–11.

85 Ibid.

86 Ibid.

87 Lecture by Patnaik Prabhat, *JNU City Centre*, 10 August 1987, New Delhi.

88 Lecture by Bipan Chandra, 'India's Struggle for Independence,' JNU City Centre,10 August 1987, New Delhi

89 Gallagher, John, 'Congress in Decline: Bengal 1930–1939,' in Gallaghar, John, Gordon Johnson and Anil Seal (eds.) *Locality, Province and Nation: Essays on Indian Polities, 1870 to 1940*, Cambridge University Press, Cambridge, UK, 1973, pp. 269–325; Bayly C.A., *Rulers, Townsmen and Bazaars: North Indian Society in the Age of British Expansion, 1770–1870*, Cambridge University Press, Cambridge, UK, 1988; *Local Roots of Indian Politics, Allahabad, 1880–1920*, Clarendon Press, Oxford, 1975.

90 Amin, Shahid, *Event, Metaphor, Memory: Chauri Chaura 1922-1992*, Oxford University Press, Delhi, 1996.

91 Chatterjee, Suranjan, 'Economic History or an Apologia for Colonialism', *Social Scientist*, Vol. 13, No. 1, January 1985, pp. 54–70.

92 Bhattacharya, Sabyasachi, Presidential Address, Indian History Congress, *Proceedings of Indian History Congress*, 1984.

93 Gallagher, John, Gordon Johnson and Anil Seal, (eds), *Locality, Province and Nation: Essays on Indian Politics, 1870 to 1940*, Cambridge University Press, Cambridge, UK, 1973.

94 The most articulate spokespersons of this line of critics were namely, Chatterjee, Partha, *Nationalism Thought and the Colonial World: A Derivative Discourse*, Zed Books, London, 1986; Pandey, Gyanendra, *Construction of Communalism in Colonial North India*, Oxford University Press, Delhi, 1990; Sarkar, Sumit, *Modern India, 1885-1947*, Macmillan, New Delhi, 1983.

95 Pandey, Gyanendra, Ibid.

96 Ibid.

97 Mukherjee, Mridula, 'Peasant Resistance and Peasant Consciousness

in Colonial India – Subalterns and Beyond', *EPW*, Vol. 23, No. 42, 15 October 1988.

98 Mukherjee, Aditya, Bhagwan Josh, Bipan Chandra, Lajpat Jagga, Mridula Mukherjee and Sashi Joshi, 'The Communists, the Congress and the Anti-Colonial Movement,' *EPW*, Vol. 19, No. 17, 28 April, 1984, pp. 730–36; Banerjee, Sumanta, 'The Communists, The Congress and The Anti-Colonial Movement,' *EPW*, Vol. 19, No. 29, 21 July 1984, pp. 1168–72.

99 Sarvepalli Gopal, Romila Thapar, Bipan Chandra, Sabyasachi Bhattacharya, Suvira Jaiswal, Harbans Mukhia, K.N. Panikkar, R. Champakalakshmi, Satish Saberwal, B.D. Chattopadhyaya, R.N. Verma, K. Meenakshi, Muzaffar Alam, Dilbagh Singh, Mridula Mukherjee, Madhavan Palat, Aditya Mukherjee, S.F. Ratnagar, Neeladri Bhattacharya, K.K. Trivedi, Yogesh Sharma, Kunal Chakravarti, Bhagwan Josh, Rajan Gurukkal and Himanshu Ray, (Centre for Historical Studies, Jawaharlal Nehru University, New Delhi), 'The Political Abuse of History: Babri Masjid–Rama Janmabhumi Dispute,' *Social Scientist*, Vol. 18, No. 1/2 (January – February, 1990), p. 76.

100 Ibid., p. 81.

101 Dariusz Aleksandrowicz, Stephani Sonntag and Jan Wielgohs, *The Polish Solidarity Movement in Retrospect: A Story of Failure or Success?* GSFP, Berlin, 2009.

102 Zuzowski, Robert, *Political Change in Eastern Europe since 1989: Prospects for Liberal Democracy and a Market Economy*, Praeger, London, 1998.

103 Weston, Timothy B., *Power of Being Beijing University and the Chinese Intellectual Life*, University of California Press, Berkeley, 2004. I thank my students Shugguang Lee, Hui Jinag and Cheng Song for giving me a graphic idea of the Chinese university life. I also treasure the discussion on these aspects with Prof. Shen Han of Nanjing University.

104 Fukuyama, Francis, 'End of History and the Last Man', *National Interest*, Summer, 1989, pp. 3–18. In retrospect, it seems very significant that my first publication was a review of the book in a different context, see Batabyal, Rakesh, 'Ideology is not Dead', *Mainstream*, 1991.

105 Kothari, Rajni, 'The Non-Party Political Process,' *EPW*, Vol. 19, No. 5, 4 February 1984, pp. 216–24; Seth, D.L., 'Grass-roots Initiatives in

India,' *EPW*, Vol. 19, No. 6, 11 February 1984, pp. 259–62; Sethi, Harsh, 'The Immoral "Other": Debate between Party and Non-Party Groups,' *EPW*, Vol. 20, No. 9, 2 March 1985, pp. 378–80.

106 Pattanayak, Kishen, 'Non-Party Groups and Their Dependence on Foreign Money', *EPW*, Vol 20, No. 39, 28 September, 1985, pp. 1665 – 66.

107 Bagchi, Amiya Kumar 'Historicizing the Problems of Socialism', *Social Scientist*, Vol. 16, No. 10, October 1988, pp. 63–68.

Chapter 14

1 Sharma, D.C., Debate on the Jawaharlal Nehru University Bill, 21 September 1965, *Lok Sabha Debates*, LXVI, No. 21, c. 6702.

2 John Heeren, 'Karl Mannheim and the Intellectual Elite,' *The British Journal of Sociology*, Vol. 22, No. 1, March, 1971, pp. 1-15.

3 Müller-Doohm, Stefan, 'Theodor W. Adorno and Jürgen Habermas—Two Ways of Being a Public Intellectual: Sociological Observations Concerning the Transformation of a Social Figure of Modernity', *European Journal of Social Theory*, August 2005, Vol. 8, No. 3, pp. 269–280.

4 See one such tract in Chakrabarty, Dipesh, *Provincializing Europe: Postcolonial Thought and Historical Difference*, Princeton University Press, New Jersey, 2000.

5 A couple of autobiographical accounts of Bengali intellectuals in India read as beautiful parochial accounts which interestingly show how untouched they were from the city's cultural and social milieu. See, Tapan Raychaudhuri, *Bangalanama*, Ananda Publishers, Kolkata, 2007.

6 Althusser, Louis, *For Marx*, Allen Lane, The Penguin Press, London, 1965, p. 26.

7 Ibid.

8 Sengupta, Amit, 'Culture in Advanced Capitalism: A Critique of Herbert Marcuse,' M.Phil Dissertation, JNU, 1988.

Select Bibiliography

Primary Sources

Unpublished Sources

Private Papers

Bhakt Darshan Papers
C.R. Reddy Papers
H.N. Kunzru Papers
M.C. Chagla Papers,
P.N. Haksar Papers
V.K.R.V. Rao Papers

Published Sources

Newspapers and Journals

Dharmayug
Dinman
Economic and Political Weekly
Hindustan Times, Delhi
India International Quarterly
Indian Left Review
Janata
Link
Mainstream
New Age

Newsweek
Organiser
Panchajanya
People's Democracy
Quest,
Seminar,
The Statesman, Delhi
The Times of India, Delhi
Time
University News
World Marxist Review

Published Material

Annual Reports of Indian Council for Social Science Research, 1973–85.
JNU Admission Policy Papers, 1972–1983.
JNU Annual Reports, 1980–2000.
Lok Sabha Debates, 1956–1990, Selected Volumes
Rajya Sabha Debate, 1962–1990, Selected Volumes

B. Secondary Sources

Books

Agwani, M.S., *Life in Academia*, Har-Anand Publications, New Delhi, 2014.
Agwani, M.S., *West Asia War 1967*, Meenakshi Prakashan, Meerut, 1968.
Ajayi, J.F. Ade, *Milestones in Nigerian History*, Longman, London, 1980.
Alagh, Y.K., G.S. Bhalla and S.P. Kashyap, *Structural Analysis of Gujarat, Punjab, Haryana, An Input-Output Study*, Allied Publishers, Delhi, 1980.
Althusser, Louis, and Etienne Balibar, *Reading Capital*, (trans. Ben Brewster), Verso, London, 1965 (1979).
Amin, Samir, *Accumulation on a World Scale*, Harvester Press, Sussex, 1974.

Anderson, Perry, *Lineages of the Absolutist State*, New Left Books, London, 1974.

Austin, Grenville, *The Indian Constitution: Cornerstone of a Nation*, Clarendon, Oxford, 1966.

Bagchi, Amiya Kumar, *The Political Economy of Underdevelopment*, Cambridge University Press, Cambridge, UK, 1982.

Banerjee, Utpal, *Computer Education in India: Past, Present and Future*, Institution of Communication Engineers, Mittal Publishers, Delhi, 1996.

Barik, Radhakant, *Politics of JP Movement*, Radiant Publishers, Delhi, 1977.

Bell, Daniel, *The Post-Industrial Society*, Harvard University Press, Cambridge, Massachusetts, 1968.

Berg, Paul and Maxine Singer, *George Beadle: An Uncommon Farmer. The Emergence of Genetics in the 20th Century*, Cold Spring Harbor Laboratory Press, New York, 2003.

Bernal, J.D., *The Social Function of Science*, Routledge, London, 1944.

Bettelheim, Charles, *India Independent*, Monthly Review Press, New York, 1971.

Bhagwati, J.N. and Padma Desai, *India: Planning for Industrialisation*, Oxford University Press, New York, 1970.

Bhalla, G.S., and Y.K. Alagh, *Performance of Indian Agriculture: District-wise Study*, Sterling Publishers, Delhi, 1978.

Bhambhri, C.P., *Bureaucracy and Politics in India*, Vikas Publishing House, New Delhi, 1971.

Bloc, Marc (Trans. L.A. Manyon), *Feudal Society*, 2 vols., Chicago University Press, Chicago, 1961.

Bloom, Harold, *The Closing of the American Mind: How Higher Education has Failed Democracy and Impoverished the Soul of Today's Students*, Simon Schuster, New York, 1987.

Ceruzzi, Paul, E., *A History of Modern Computing*, Massachusetts Institute of Technology Press, Cambridge, Massachusetts, 1998.

Chagla, M.C., *Roses in December*, Bharatiya Vidya Bhawan, Bombay, 1973 (Revised edition, 1980).

Chandra, Bipan, 'Karl Marx, His Theories of Asian Societies and Colonial Rule', Mimeiographed, Centre for Historical Studies, JNU, 1978.

Chandra, Bipan, *Communalism in Modern India*, Vikas Publishing House, New Delhi, 1984.

Chandra, Bipan, *Indian National Movement: Long-term Dynamics*, Vikas Publishing House, New Delhi, 1986.

Chandra, Bipan, Mridula Mukherjee, Aditya Mukherjee, Sucheta Mahajan and K.N. Panikkar, *India's Struggle for Independence*, Viking, Delhi, 1988.

Chandra, Bipan, *Nationalism and Colonialism in Modern India*, Orient Longman, Hyderabad, 1979.

Chattopadhyaya, D.P., *Lokayata*, People's Publishing House, Bombay, 1959.

Chomski, Noam, *Towards a New Cold War: US Foreign Policy from Vietnam to Reagan*, The New Press, New York, 1982.

Christopher, Andrew, *The World was Going Our Way: The KGB and the Battle for the Third World*, Perseus Books, New York, 2005.

Desai, A.R., *Social Background of Indian Nationalism*, Popular Publications, Bombay, 1948.

Dobb, Maurice, *Transition from Feudalism to Capitalism*, Communist Party of Great Britain, London, 1963.

Dongerkery, S.R., *Memories of Two Universities*, Manaktalas, Bombay, 1966.

Dumont, Louis, *Homo Hierarchicus: The Caste System and its Implications*, Weidenfeld and Nicholson, London, 1970.

Frank, Andre Gunder, *Development of Underdevelopment*, Monthly Review Press, New York, 1966.

Geertz, Clifford, *After the Fact: Two Countries, Four Decades, One Anthropologist*, Harvard University Press, Cambridge, Massachusetts, 1995.

Geertz, Clifford, *The Interpretation of Cultures*, Basic Books, New York, 1971.

Ghurye, G.S., *Caste and Race in India*, Popular Prakashan, Bombay, 1969.

Gilman, Nils, *Mandarins of the Future: Modernisation Theory in the Cold War America*, Johns Hopkins University Press, Baltimore, 2003.

Gopal, S. (ed.), *Anatomy of a Confrontation: The Babri Masjid-Ramjanmabhumi Issue*, Viking, Penguin India, New Delhi, 1991.

Gopal, S., *British Policy In India, 1858-1905*, Cambridge University Press, Cambridge, UK, 1965.

Gopal, S., *Nehru: A Biography*, Vol. 1 & 2, Oxford University Press, Delhi, 1976 and 1979.

Gupta, Sulekh Chandra, *Agrarian Relations and Early British Rule in India*, Asia Publishing House, Bombay, 1964.

Habermas, Jurgen, *The Structural Transformation of the Public Sphere: An Inquiry into a Category of Bourgeois Society*, MIT Press, Cambridge, Massachusetts, 1991.

Habib, Irfan, *Agrarian System of Moghul India*, Oxford University Press, Delhi, 1963, (Revised Edition, 2000).

Hameid, K.A., *A Life to Remember: An Autobiography*, Lalwani Publishing House, Bombay, 1972.

Hobsbawm, Eric, *Interesting Times: A Twentieth Century Life*, Abacus, London, 2003.

Holmes, Martin, *The First Thatcher Government, 1979-1983*, Harvester Press, Sussex, 1985.

Horkheimer Max and Theodore Adorno, *Dialectic of Enlightenment*, Stanford University Press, Stanford, 2002.

Hroch, Miloslav, *In the National Interest: Demands and Goals of European National Movements of the Nineteenth Century, A Comparative Perspective*, Charles University, Prague, 2000.

Huntington, Samuel P., *Political Order in Changing Societies*, Yale University Press, New Haven, Connecticut, 1968.

Jaiswal, Suvira, *The Origin and Development of Vaishnavism from 200 BC to AD 500*, Munshiram Manoharlal, Delhi,1967 (1981).

Jay, Martin, *Marxism and Totality: The Adventures of a Concept from Lucaks to Habermas*, Polity Press, Cambridge, 1984.

Judt, Tony, *Past Imperfect: French Intellectuals, 1944-1956*, New York University Press, New York, 2011

Judt, Tony, *Postwar: A History of Europe Since 1945*, Random House, New York, 2011.

Kalecki, M., *Selected Essays on the Economic Growth of the Socialist and Mixed Economy*, Cambridge University Press, Cambridge, UK, 1972.

Kerr, Clark, *The Uses of the University*, Harvard University Press, Cambridge, Masschusetts, 1963.

Kimambo, I.N., *Humanities and Social Sciences in East and Central Africa: Theory and Practice*, University of Dar es Salaam Press, Dar es Salaam, 2003.

Kothari, Rajni, *Politics in India*, Orient Longman, Hyderabad, 1970.

Kristol, Irving, *Neoconservatism: Autobiography of an Idea*, Free Press, New York, 1995.

Kuhn, Thomas, *The Structure of Scientific Revolutions*, University of Chicago Press, Chicago, 1962 1970.

Leslie, Stuart A., *The Cold War and the American Science: Military Industrial Complex at MIT and Stanford*, Columbia University Press, New York, 1993.

Lowen, Rebeca, *Creating a Cold War University: The Transformation of Stanford*, University of California Press, Berkeley and Los Angeles, 1997.

Marcuse, Herbert, *One-Dimensional Man: Studies in the Ideology of Advanced Industrial Society*, Routledge and Kegan Paul, London, 1964.

Mukherjee, Radhakamal, *Destiny of Civilization*, Asia Publishing House, Bombay, 1964.

Nandy, Ashis, *The Intimate Enemy: Loss and Recovery of Self Under Colonialism*, Oxford University Press, Delhi, 1983.

Needham, Joseph, *Science and Civilization in China*, Cambridge University Press, Cambridge, UK, 1954.

Patnaik, Prabhat (ed.), *Lenin and Imperialism: An Appraisal of Theories and Contemporary Reality*, Orient Longman, Hyderabad, 1986.

Phadnis, Urmila, *Ethnicity and Nation-Building in South Asia*, Sage Publications, New Delhi, New York and London, 1990.

Poulantzas, Nicos, *State, Power and Socialism*, (trans. Patrick Camiller), Verso, London, 1978.

Raj, K.N. (ed.), *Essays on the Commercialization of Indian Agriculture*, Oxford University Press, Delhi, 1985.

Rajan, M.S., *India's Foreign Relations during the Nehru Era: Some Studies*, Asia Publishing House, Bombay,1976.

Rajan, M.S., *Nonalignment & Nonaligned Movement Retrospect and Prospect*, Vikas Publishing House, New Delhi, 1990.

Rayack, Elton, *Not so Free to Choose: The Political Economy of Milton Freidman and Ronald Reagan*, Praeger, New York, 1987.

Raza, Moonis and Amitabh Kundu, *Indian Economy: The Regional Dimension*, Centre for the Study of Regional Development, Jawaharlal Nehru University, Delhi, 1982.

Rosen, George, *Western Economists and Eastern Societies: Agents of Change in South Asia, 1950-1970*, Johns Hopkins University Press, Baltimore, 1985.

Rostow, W.W., *The Stages of Economic Growth: A Non-Communist Manifesto*, Cambridge University Press, Cambridge, UK, 1960.

Jain, S. Mohan, S.K. Sopory and Richard Veilleux, *In Vitro Haploid Production in Higher Plants*, Volume 1: Fundamental Aspects and Methods, Springer Sciences and Business Media, Dordrecht, 1996.

Sarabhai, Vikram, *Science Policy and National Development*, ed. by Kamala Choudhary, foreword by Indira Gandhi, Vikram Sarabhai Foundation, and ICSSR, 1972, (Reprint 2004).

Sarkar, Sahotra, *History and Philosophy of Molecular Biology: New Perspectives*, Kluwer Academic Publications, Dordrecht, 1991.

Sharma, R.S., *Material Culture and Social Formation in Ancient India*, Macmillan India, Delhi, 1983.

Singh, Randhir, *Five Lectures in Marxist Mode*, Ajanta Publishers, Delhi, 1993.

Singh, Yogendra, *Modernisation of Indian Tradition: A Systemic Study of Social Change*, Thomson Press, Faridabad, 1977.

Sondhi, M.L., *Wanted A National Foreign Policy* (a Jana Sangh publication,) Navchetana, Delhi, 1968.

Steinfels, Peter, *The Neoconservatives: The Men who are Changing America's Politics*, Simon Schuster, New York, 1979.

Stephens, Julie, *Anti-disciplinary Protest: Sixties Radicalism and Postmodernism*, Cambridge University Press, Cambridge, 1998.

Sundaram V.A., *Banaras Hindu University, 1916–1942*, BHU, Banaras, 1942.

Talgery, Pramod and Satyabhusan Verma, *Literature in Translation: From Cultural Transformation to Metonymic Displacement*, Popular Prakashan, Bombay, 1988.

Thapar, Romila, *Ancient Indian Social History: Some Interpretations*, Orient Longman, Hyderabad, 1979.

Thapar, Romila, *From Lineage to State: Social Formation in the Mid-First Millennium B.C. in the Ganga Valley*, Oxford University Press, Delhi, 198l.

Thomson, E.P., *The Making of the English Working Class*, Vintage, London, 1963.

Tikekar, Aroon, *The Cloister's Pale: A Biography of the University of Bombay*, South Asia Books, Bombay, 1986.

Verma, S.P., and C.P. Bhambri, *1967 Elections: The Urban Voter*, National Publishing House, Delhi, 1973.

Wagner, Peter, Bjorn Wiltrock and Richard Whitley, *The Shaping of the Social Science Discipline*, Kluwer Academic Publications, Doredrecht, 1991.

Wang, Jessica, *American Science in an Age of Anxiety: Scientists, Anticommunism, and the Cold War*, University of North Carolina Press, North Carolina, 1999.

Wolf, Audra J., *Competing with the Soviets: Science, Technology, and the State in Cold War America*, Johns Hopkins University Press, Baltimore, 2012.

Wright, Mills, C., *Sociological Imaginations*, Oxford University Press, London, 1959.

Articles

Appadorai, A, 'International and Area Studies in India', *International Studies*, Sage Publications, New Delhi, London, New York, Vol. 24, No. 2, 1987, pp. 133–43.

Bagchi, Amiya, 'Historicizing the Problems of Socialism', *Social Scientist*, Vol. 16, No. 10, October 1988, pp. 63-68.

Banaji, Jairus, 'India and the Colonial Mode of Production', Economic and Political Weekly (*EPW*), Vol. 10, No. 49, 1975, pp. 1887–89, 1891–92.

Bassett, Ross, 'Aligning India in the Cold War Era: Indian Technical Elites, the Indian Institute of Technology at Kanpur, and Computing in India and the United States', *Technology and Culture*, Vol. 50, No. 4, October 2009, pp. 783–810.

Batabyal, Rakesh, 'Area Studies, Trajectory of a Discourse', *International Studies*, Vol. 48 No. 3–4, pp. 325–36.

Batabyal, Rakesh, 'India' in Brookings Institution Working paper 'Does Fairness matter', 2010.

Bellah, Robert N., 'The World Is the World through Its Theorists: In

Memory of Talcott Parsons', *American Sociologist*, Vol. 15, No. 2, May 1980, pp. 60–62.)

Bhaduri, Amit, 'A Study in Agricultural Backwardness under Semi-Feudalism', *Economic Journal*, Vol. 83, No. 329, 1973, pp. 120–37.

Bhambhri, C.P., 'Indian State: Conflict and Contradiction', in Hasan, Zoya, S.N. Jha and Rasheeduddin Khan (eds), *State, Political Process and Identity: Reflections on Modern India*, Sage Publications, Delhi, New York, London, 1989, pp. 73–87.

Bhambhri, C.P., 'Political Science in India: Acadeic Colonialism and Lessons for the Third World', *EPW*, Vol. 10, No. 18, 1975, pp. 730–35.

Bharadwaj, Krishna, 'A View on the Commercialisation in Indian Agriculture and the Development of Capitalism', *Journal of Peasant Studies*, 12 July 1985, pp. 7–25.

Bharadwaj, Krishna, 'Note on Political Economic of Development', *EPW*, Vol. VII, No. 5–7, 1972, pp. 317–28.

Biray, Kolluoglu-Kirli,: 'From Orientalism to Area Studies', *The New Centennial Review*, Vol. 3, No. 3, Fall 2003, p. 103.

Brody, S.S., and G.S. Singhal, 'Spectral Properties of Chloroplast Membranes as a Function of Physiological Temperatures', *Biochemical and Biophysical Research Communications*, Vol. 89, No. 2, 27 July 1979, pp. 542–46.

Burnet, Jean, 'Robert Park and the Chicago School of Sociology: A Centennial Tribute', *Canadian Review of Sociology*, Vol. 1, No. 3, 1964, pp. 156–64.

Chandra, Bipan, 'AMU, and the Communalist: Dangerous Game of Appeasement', *Mainstream*, 7 March 1981, p. 6.

Chattopadhyaya, B.D., 'Origin of Rajputs: The Political, Economic and Social Processes in Early Medieval Rajasthan', *Indian Historical Review*, 1976, pp. 59–82.

Chattopadhyaya, K.C., 'Lokayata System of Thought in Ancient India', *Journal of Ganganath Jha Research Institute, (JGRI)*. Allahabad, Vol. 1, No. 31, 1975, pp. 137–56.

Cohen, Stephen, 'Indian Military and Social Change', *IDSA Journal*, Vol. 2, No. 1, 1969, p. 12–29.

Dandekar, V.M., and Nilakantha Rath, 'Poverty in India- I: Dimensions and Trends', *EPW*, Vol. 6, No. 1, 1971, pp. 25–27 and 29–48.

Dandekar, V.M., and Nilakantha Rath, 'Poverty in India-II, Policies and Programme', *EPW*, Vol. 6, No. 2, 1971, pp. 106–46.

Das, Padma, A.R. Rao and P.N. Srivastava, 'Influence of 17 β estradiol on 3 MCA-induced cervical carcinogenesis', *Journal of Steroid Biochemistry*, Vol. 28, Supplement 1, 1987, p. 6.

Das, R., and S.K. Sopory, 'Biochemistry, Biophysics', *Research Communication*, 128, 1985, pp. 1455–60.

Dastur, Aloo, et al., 'Soviet Troops in Afghanistan', Letter to the Editor, *EPW*, Vol. 15, No. 1, 5 January 1980, p. 5.

Dutt, Vidya Prakash, 'Indo-China Impasse', *International Quarterly*, Vol. 1, No. 8, January–March 1952, pp. 14–31.

Geiger, Roger L., 'American Foundation and Academic Social Sciences, 1945–1960', *Minerva*, Vol. 26, No. 3, 1988, pp. 315–41.

Gopal, S., 'Fear of History', *Seminar 221*, January 1978, pp. 71–73 and *Mainstream*, 14 January 1978, pp. 23–27.

Guha, Ramchandra, 'The Absent Liberal', *EPW*, Vol. 36, No. 50, December 2001, pp. 4663–70.

Guha, Sipra and S.C. Maheshwari, 'Cell Division and Differentiation of Embryos in the Pollen Grains of Datura in vitro,' *Nature*, Vol. 212, Issue 5057, 1966, pp. 97–98.

Guha, Sipra and S. C. Maheshwari, 'In Vitro Production of Embryos from Anthers of Datura', *Nature*, Issue 4957, 204, 1964, p. 497.

Gupta, Dipankar, 'Sociology in Indian Universities', *Mainstream*, 24 July 1975, pp. 21–22.

Gupta, Sisir, 'The Great Powers and The Sub-Continent: A New Phase?', *International Studies*, Vol. 8, No. 1–2, July 1966, pp. 447–63.

Herbert, Simon, Alan Perlis and Allen Newell, Letter to the Editor, *Science*, 22 September 1967, pp. 1373–74,

Johri, B. M., Sipra Guha, and S. C. Maheshwari, 'Auxin-induced Reversal of Geotropic Response in Onion Seedlings', *Nature*, 205, 1965, pp. 1026–27.

Kech, O., 'West German Science Policy since the 1960s: Trends and Objectives', *Research Policy*, Vol. 5 No. 2, 1976, pp. 116–57.

Khan, Rasheeduddin, 'Muslim Leadership and Electoral Politics in Hyderabad: A Pattern of Minority Articulation', *EPW*, Vol. 6, No. 16, 17 April 1971, pp. 833–40.

Khan, Rasheeduddin, 'The Total State: The Concept and Its Manifestation in the Indian Political System'; in Zoya, Hasan, S.N. Jha and Rasheeduddin Khan (eds), *The State, Political Processes and Identity: Reflections on Modern India*, Sage Publications, New Delhi, London, New York, 1989, pp. 33–72.

Knuth, Donald E., 'George Forsythe and Development of Computer Science', *Communications of the ACM*, Vol.15, No. 8, August 1972, pp. 721–26.

Kothari, Rajni, 'The Congress "System" in India', *Asian Survey*, Vol. 4, No. 12, December 1964, pp. 1161–73.

Kothari, Rajni, 'Congress System Revisited: A Decennial Review', *Asian Survey*, Vol. 14, No. 12, December 1974, pp. 1035–54.

Luria, S.E., 'Molecular Biology: Past, Present and Future,' *Bioscience*, Vol. 20, December 1970, pp. 1289–93.

Maheshwari, P., 'Indian Scientific Policy: Science and Government', Presidential Address, 33rd Annual Meeting, National Academy of Sciences, Allahabad, 1964.

Maheswari, S.C., and S.K. Sopory, 'Plant Molecular Biology in India: the Beginnings', *Current Science*, Vol. 80, No. 2, 25 January 2001, pp. 153–54.

McGarr, Paul Michael, 'Quiet Americans in India: The CIA and the Politics of Intelligence in Cold War South Asia', *Diplomatic History*, Vol. 38, No. 5, 2014, pp. 1046–82.

Mitchell, Timothy, 'The Limits of the State', *American Political Science Review*, Vol. 85, No. 1, March 1991, pp. 77–96.

Mitchison, Avrion, 'Immunology in India', *Nature*, Vol. 323, Issue 6091, 30 October 1986, p. 752.

Morgan, Jamie, 'The History of Contemporary Area Studies: Philosophy, Emergent Causal Relations, and Non-triviality of Sociology of Knowledge in China', *Review International*, Vol. 11, No. 2, Fall 2004, pp. 229–50.

Mukherjee, Aditya, 'The Indian Capitalist Class: Aspects of its Economic, Political and Ideological Development in the Colonial Period, 1927-47', in S. Bhattacharya, and Romila Thapar (ed.) *Situating Indian History*, Oxford University Press, Delhi, 1986, pp.

Mukherjee, Dileep, 'Indian Science Policy Organisation and Applications', *Minerva*. Vol. 2, No. 3, Spring 1964, pp. 360–69.

Mukerjee, Hiren, 'Reflections on Stalin Centenary', *Mainstream*, 22 December 1979, pp. 15 and 22.

Mukherjee, Mridula, 'Peasant Resistance and Peasant Consciousness in Colonial India – Subalterns and Beyond,' *EPW*, Vol. 23 No. 42, 15 October 1988, pp. 2109–20.

Mukherjee, P.N., 'Social Movement and Social Change: Towards a Conceptual Clarification and Theoretical Framework', *Sociological Bulletin*, Vol. 26, No. 1, 1977, pp. 38–59.

Namboodiripad, E.M.S., 'On Intermediate Regimes', *EPW*, Vol. 8, No. 48, 1 December 1973, pp. 2133–40.

Panikkar, K.N., 'Intellectual and Cultural Issues in Colonial India: Some Conceptual and Historiographical Issues', in Sabyasachi Bhattacharya and Romila Thapar (eds), *Situating Indian History*, Oxford University Press, Delhi, 1986.

Patnaik, Utsa, 'Neo-Marxian Theories of Capitalism and Underdevelopment: Towards a Critique', in Prabhat Patnaik (ed.), *Lenin and Imperialism: An Appraisal of Theories and Contemporary Reality*, Orient Longman, Hyderabad, 1989, pp. 313–49.

Poulose, T.T., 'Nuclear Proliferation and the Second NPT Review Conference', *IDSA Journal*, Vol. 3, No. 1, July 1980, pp. 1–5.

Quine, W.V.O., 'Two Dogmas of Empiricism', *Philosophical Review*, Vol. 60, 1951, pp. 20–43.

Raghavan, C., 'Janata and Science', *Mainstream*, Annual, 1977, pp. 113–16.

Rai, Haridwar and Roop Narain Jha, 'The Governor as the Chancellor: The Bihar Experience', *The Indian Journal of Political Science*, Vol. XXXII, No. 2, April–June 1971, pp. 125–44.

Raj, K.N., 'Some questions concerning growth, transformation and planning of agriculture in the developing countries', in *Proceedings of the Conference on Economic Development in South Asia*, held by the International Economic Association at Kandy, Ceylon, 1970, pp. 102–26.

Ramasubban, Radhika, 'What Ails CSIR?', *Mainstream*, 22 October 1977, pp. 15–18.

Rau, M. Chalapathi, 'What is Communalism?', *Link*, 31 August 1980, p.8.

Rudolph, Lloyd and Susanne Hoeber Rudolph, 'Writing India: A Career

Overview', *Indian Review*, Vol.7, No. 4, October–December 2008, pp.266–94.

Saran, A.K., 'For a Sociology of India', *Eastern Anthropologist*, Vol. 15, No. 1, 1962, pp. 53–68.

Sen, Amartya, 'On Some Debates in Capital Theory', *Economica*, New Series, Vol. 41, No. 163, August 1974, pp. 328–35.

Sen, Mohit, 'Creative Revolutionary', *Mainstream*, 19 April 1980, pp. 27–29.

Sen, Mohit, 'Distorted Study', *Mainstream*, 23 August 1980, pp. 23–25.

Sen, Sunil, 'Cambridge and the Raj', *Mainstream*, 12 January 1980, pp. 20–22.

Sengupta, Arjun, 'Aid and Development Policy in the 1990s', *EPW*, Vol. 28, No. 11, 1993, pp. 453–64.

Shah, A.B., 'Reflections on Higher Education in India in the Light of the Robbins Report', *Minerva*, Vol. II, No. 2, pp. 160–68.

Shakir, Moin and H. Ghani, 'The Conversion Phenomenon', *Secular Democracy*, October 1981, pp. 15–21.

Shils, Edward, 'Political Development in the New States', *Comparative Study in Society and History*, Vol. 2, Issue 3, 1960, pp. 265–92.

Shivaiah, 'The Behavioural Approach in Political Science: An Essay on the Meaning and Orientation of a Movement', *Indian Journal of Political Science*, Vol. 2, No. 4, October–December 1968, pp. 50–67.

Singh, Yogendra, 'Concepts and Theories of Social Change: A Trend Report', in ICSSR, *A Survey of Research in Sociology and Social Anthropology*, Vol. 1, Popular Prakashan, Bombay, 1972–74, pp. 383–431.

Sinha, Jagdish, N., 'Science and Culture under Colonialism: India between the World Wars', *Indian Journal of History of Science*, Vol. 39, No. 1, 2004, pp. 101–38.

Srivastava, P.N., and A. Ramesha Rao, 'PMS Response to the Ovary of the Indian Desert Gerbil, Meriones hurrianae jerdon, after 32 P β Irradiation', *General and Comparative Endocrinology*, Vol. 2, Supplement 2, 1969, pp. 190–96.

Theroux, Paul, 'Obituary', *The Independent*, 15 January 1996, accessed on 14 July 2011- http://www.independent.co.uk/news/people/obituary-rajat-neogy-1324133.html

Thorner, Daniel, 'Andhra: Towards an Affluent Society,' *EPW*, Vol. 2, Nos. 3–6, 1969, pp. 241–49.

JNU Theses and Dissertations

Agarwal, Purshottam, 'Kabir Ki Bhakti Ka Samajik Arth', Ph.D. Thesis, 1985.

Agnihotri, Indu, 'Agrarian Change in Canal Colonies, Punjab, 1890-1935', Ph.D Thesis, 1987.

Anwar, Khurshid, 'Modernism in Urdu Poetry up to 1970', Ph.D Thesis, 1987.

Alam, Syed Mohammad Anwar, 'A Critical Analysis of Urdu Novel under the Progressive Writers' Movement, 1936-1947', Ph.D Thesis, 1985.

Arun Kumar, P., 'A Study on Caste and Class Politics in Srikakulam District, 1967-72', M.Phil. Dissertation, 1983.

Assadi, Muzaffar Hussein, 'Agrarian Movement in Karnataka: A Study of the Rytha Sangha, 1980-85', Ph.D Thesis, 1987.

Assifi, Fahima, 'Arms Trade within Third World, Its Implications', M.Phil. Dissertation, 1986.

Atlury, Murli, 'Social Change and Nature of Social Participation in National Movement in Andhra, 1905-1934', Ph.D Thesis, 1987.

Baba, Noor Ahmad, 'Iranian Revolution of 1978-79: Origins and Dimensions', Ph.D Thesis, 1981.

Banerji, Sanjukta, 'The Position and Perspectives of Blacks in Contemporary America: An Analysis of Ideological Perspectives and Strategies in the Black Protest Movement', Ph.D Thesis, 1981.

Bhadra, Ranjit Kumar, 'Changing Social Stratification in rural Assam', Ph.D Thesis, 1980.

Bhalla, Neera, 'Studies in Isolation and Fusion of Protoplast', Ph.D Thesis, 1977.

Bhaskaramma, K., 'Political Participation of Scheduled Castes: A Case Study of Khammam District in Andhra Pradesh', M.Phil. Dissertation, 1980.

Bhattacharya, Alok, 'Studies on the Mechanism of Gene Expression in Yeast *Candida albicans*, Ph.D Thesis, 1976.

Chakrabarti, Kunal, 'Sanskritisation in Medieval Bengal, A Regional Analysis', Ph.D Thesis, 1997.

Chelani, Brahma, 'Indo-US Nuclear Controversy on Tarapur: Reflection in the Press of the Two Countries', M.Phil. Dissertation, 1983.

Choudhury, Maitrayee, 'Trends in India's Women's Movement: A Sociological Study', Ph.D Thesis, 1986.

Chowdhry, Rekha, 'Women and Politics in India', M.Phil. Dissertation, 1973.

Cowshish, Amit, 'Impact of Green Revolution on Politics of Haryana', M.Phil. Dissertation, 1977.

De Silva, Jayatilaka Shanthi Ramanie, 'Changing Agrarian Relations: A Comparative Study of an Irrigated and a Non-irrigated Village in Sri Lanka', Ph.D Thesis, 1989.

Defileh, Shahla, 'The Iranian Revolution and Its Impact on Iran-Saudi Arabian Relations, 1978-1982', M.Phil. Dissertation, 1984.

Devi, B.R. Shyamala, 'Tribal Integration in a Developing Economy: A Study with Reference to Two Lambada Villages in Andhra Pradesh', Ph.D Thesis, 1989.

Dhar Choudhury, Rajib, 'A Case for a New World Information and Communication Order', Ph.D Thesis, 1986.

Ganesh, K.N., 'Some Aspects of the Agrarian Structure in Early Medieval Venad, AD 1200-1500', Ph.D Thesis, 1979.

Ganpatrao, Ranveer Kashinath, 'An Assessment of Black Protest in the Selected Writings of Richard Wright', Ph.D Thesis, 1982.

Gopinath, Ravindran, 'Agrarian Structure and Transformation in Malabar, 1871-1921' Ph.D Thesis, 1986.

Gupta, Dipankar, 'The Siva Sena Movement, 1969-74: A Sociological Analysis', Ph.D Thesis, 1977.

Gurukkal, Rajan, 'The Agrarian System and Socio-Political Organization Under the Early Pandyas, AD 600-1000', Ph.D Thesis, 1984.

Hasan, Monirul, 'Assam Movement: Sociological Dimension', Ph.D Thesis, 1983.

Jagga, Lajpat R., 'Formation of an Industrial Labour Force and Forms of Labour Protest in India, a Study of Railways, 1919-37', Ph.D Thesis, 1983.

Jayaramu, P.S., 'Problems of National Security and India's Foreign Policy, 1963-79', Ph.D Thesis, 1983.

Joshi, Chitra, 'Kanpur Textile Labour: Some structural characteristics of the labour force and aspects of the labour movement (1919-1939)', Ph.D Thesis, 1981.

Joshi, Manoj, 'Place of Black in American Society: A Critical Study of the Debate till the Emancipation Proclamation,' Ph.D, Thesis, 1981.

Karanth, Gopal Krishna, 'Change and Continuity in Agrarian Relations: A Case Study of a Karnataka Village', Ph.D Thesis, 1984.

Khan, Mumtaj, 'Mass Conversion of Meenakshipuram: A Sociological Enquiry', M.Phil. Dissertation, 1983.

Krishna, C.S., 'Labour Movement in the Madras Presidency, 1929-33', Ph.D Thesis, 1978.

Luithui, Shimreichon, 'Land and Power Structure among the Nagas', Ph.D Thesis, 1987.

Mahajan, Harpeet, 'Arms Trade and Aid to the Third World Countries, A Study with Special Reference to Indian Subcontinent', Ph.D Thesis, 1979.

Menon, Saraswathi, 'Peasant Movement in Thanjavur, 1940-1952', M.Phil. Dissertation, 1978.

Mukherjee, Mridula, 'Agrarian Structure and Peasant Movement in Punjab, 1925-1947', Ph.D Thesis, 1993.

Nand, Brahma, 'Some Aspects of the Agrarian Structure in Western India: The District of the Central Division, 1880-1930', Ph.D Thesis, 1983.

Nanda, Bikram, 'A New Framework to Studies on Indian Tribes', M.Phil. Dissertation, 1977.

Patnaik, Arun, 'Power Structure and Rural Development Programme: A Study of Digpahandi Block, Orissa', Ph.D Thesis, 1984.

Prasad, Madhu, 'Antonio Gramsci: A Critical Analysis of His Writings', M.Phil. Dissertation, 1975.

Raghvan, T.C.A., 'Agrarian Change in Narmada Valley: A Study of Jabalpur, Hoshangabad and Narsinghpur Districts, 1860-1925', Ph.D Thesis, 1981.

Raja Mohan, C., 'Nuclear Energy and the Developing Nations: A Study of Technological and Political Implications', Ph.D Thesis, 1981.

Rani, Shanta, 'Satven Dashak Ke Upanyaso men Purush Patro ki Parikalpana', Ph.D Thesis, 1979.

Rao, G. Madhu Mohan, 'A Study of the Land Reforms Legislation in Telangana Region of Andhra Pradesh', Ph.D Thesis, 1981.

Rekhi, Upjit Singh, 'Jharkhand Movement and the Tribal Polity', Ph.D Thesis, 1982.

Sakhrie, Ahu, 'Naga Movement: A Study in the Sociology of Social Movement', Ph.D Thesis, 1982.

Sangita, Satya Narayana, 'Politics, Bureaucracy and Rural Development in Andhra Pradesh', Ph.D Thesis, 1984.

Sema, Piketo, 'Naga Uprising: 1946-1963', Ph.D Thesis, 1979.

Senaviratne, Sudarshan, 'Social Base of Early Buddhism in South-east India and Sri Lanka: 3rd century BC–3rd century AD', Ph.D Thesis, 1985.

Siddiqi, Majid Hayat, 'Peasant Movement in United Provinces, 1918-1922', Ph.D Thesis, 1977.

Singh, Jagpal, 'Changing Agrarian Relations and Politics in Western Uttar Pradesh: A Study of Meerut District (1952-85)', Ph.D Thesis, 1988.

Sinha, Shanta, 'Maoists in Andhra Pradesh', Ph.D Thesis, 1976.

Subbiah, S., 'Technological and Institutional Determinants of Agricultural Productivity in Tamil Nadu: A Spatial and Temporal Analysis, 1945-55, 1969-70' M.Phil. Dissertation, 1975.

Sukajit, Ningthoujam, 'Aspects of Agricultural Development in Manipur: 1970-71 to 1984-85', Ph.D Thesis, 1988.

Suri, K. Chinnaya, 'Agrarian Movements in Andhra: 1921-1971', Ph.D, Thesis, 1984.

Thirumali, Inukonda, 'Lords and Peasants in Telangana, 1920-48: An Enquiry into the People's Uprising in Nalgonda and Warangal Districts', Ph.D Thesis, 1991.

Venkateswarelu, K., 'Gramsci's Concept of Everyday Political Practice: A Study of His Factory Council Writings', M.Phil. Dissertation, 1985.

Acknowledgements

I do not know at what point of time I began writing this book. It was most probably the words of a dear colleague, Richa Malhotra, which motivated me to seriously look deeper into the university whose air I breathed every day. History of an institution, I began to understand as the research and writing progressed, requires a special historiographical treatment. There are innumerable people associated with an institution and they all wish to see the reflection of their own lives in the institution. A historian's account, I realized, needed to be approximate to that larger canvas of the institution (something like Plato's real entities), while at the same time not allowing the little histories to be treated merely as pale reflections of the real (big) entities. Connecting these two streams has been the underlying historiographical effort in this work. This has been an extremely difficult exercise as both the time, i.e., contemporary, and the institution, i.e., JNU, have been very dynamic; and capturing their momentum, as one can easily imagine, was quite a hard task. The story told here ends in 1989 when I joined as a student, and became both a participant in the institutional process as well as an inheritor of the traditions already evolved.

Working for the book was both exacting and exciting, almost like a lonely mind furrowing its own field. However, reading almost four to five hundred theses and dissertations of JNU scholars, in a deserted segment of the JNU library, helped me connect with the struggling minds. And that encouraged me. However, my belief that an honest and truly independent work can rarely be done with grants from foundations was an impediment in accessing financial support for the work.

All this made writing the book ultimately a labour of love. I owe a sense of gratitude to my teachers, fellow students and staff of St Xavier's

College, Ranchi, and Jawaharlal Nehru University, New Delhi, who helped shape my intellectual persona such that I was able to write the book with a sense of equanimity. I am indebted to my teachers (Late) Bipan Chandra, C.P. Bhambhri, Randhir Singh, Yogendra Singh, T.K. Oommen, (Late) Amrik Singh, (Late) G.S. Bhalla, (Late) V.P. Dutt and many others for their affection. I shall miss Visalakshi Menon who heard me read out a chapter of the book and encouraged me to keep at it.

The Academic Staff College (ASC) of JNU, where I worked for most part of the time when the book was being written, allowed me a unique window to understand the frustrations, hopes and aspirations of hundreds of scholars and lecturers from across the country. I am thankful to them for connecting me to the strong intellectual traditions pulsating silently in different parts of the land. They crave for a bit of nurturing, and at ASC we created a small nurturing incubator to keep alive those diverse struggling but stimulating traditions. I thank my colleagues Ravindranathan, Rakesh Dedha, Ramprasad, Sona Arora and others at ASC for being partners in this effort.

It was in Shimla during 1996–99 that I needed to defend the JNU model almost everyday in the discussions with the sharp and experienced minds at the Indian Institute of Advanced Study. I am grateful to (Late) Chidananda Dasgupta, Mrinal Miri, Nirmalangshu Mukherjee, Sameer Banerjee and Sanjeev Ghotge for helping me evolve beyond sectarian confines. Late Uma Banerjee too, in her silent way, was an inspiration.

My long engagement with the contemporary history and intellectual trends in eastern and central Europe allowed me insights into the working of institutions of higher learning during the socialist phase (1945 to the 1990s). I thank Prof. Janos Kornai, that genial but towering economist, for encouraging me to explore the way the changing economies were shaping institutions in the post-socialist era. Judith helped me get glimpses of the Karl Marx University, now renamed Corvenus University, in Budapest. The rich discussions with David Webermann, on those lovely summer mornings at his Budapest house, about his Harvard, Columbia, Georgia State and Central European University experiences too went a long way in seeing the career of the mind and of universities in perspective. Allaine Cerwonka shared many of her insights about the working of American and European academia. I am thankful to them.

I am indebted to Prof. Keith Hitchins, the foremost historian of modern Romanian history, for being my guide into the modern history of the region for almost three decades now. Dr Lucia and Prof. Ioana V. Chlaru Mùrarus of Bucharest University saw to it that I learnt Romanian language in the best possible way. Irina Culic at Cluj has been a good sounding board for many new ideas, and her constant efforts to push the boundaries of knowledge has been an inspiration for me. Kristoph Babinsky and Marta Warat, two close friends, helped me understand the contemporary phase of two very ancient universities, Warsaw and Jagellenion (Krakow). Premysl Rosulek was not only my guide into the central European politics but was also a good companion on the long walks in Sinaia, where only the fear of bears kept us indoors after sunset. His experience of academic life in post-socialist and the extremely bureaucratic European Union brought home to me the possible directions in which institutions may go in the future. Maja Muhic in Skopje (Macedonia), Paula in Montenegro, Maria Serketzi in Athens, Christina in Thassalaniki, and Cepil Usur and Ihsan Seddar of Ankara kept me connected to the world of the southern European universities. I thank all of them.

Olutayo Adesina, Tayo for all of us in the family, has been the founder editor of the *Nigerian Journal of Economic History* and one of the best historians of his generation heading the history department of Ibadan University in Nigeria. Our desire to transcend the colonial was generally matched by our desire to laugh aloud. I thank him and his colleague Rashid Olunayi for helping me understand the issues that have affected many good African universities including Ibadan and Ahmadu Bello since the 1970s.

I never ever dreamt that Prof. Simon Digby's long but interesting stories about the University of Oxford, where he was a fellow, would help me a decade and a half later in contextualizing my understanding of British academia. Similarly, the insights shared by some of the most eminent philosophers, Prof. Milton Fisk of Indiana University, Prof. Ned Block of New York University and Prof. Mary Hawkesworth of Rutgers University during our long conversations at different points in time helped me compare intellectual trajectories and possibilities at a global level.

The student radicalism of 1970 in Sri Lanka was crushed violently. I used this as an entry point to understand Sri Lankan universities. I must thank Prof. Sunanda Madumma Bandara, vice chancellor of Kelaniya University, and professors V.G. Kulasena, Chandana Abayarathna, Ranasinghe Piyadasa, Upali Hettiarachchi, Osantha Thalpavilla, Nisan Sakalasooriya, W.M. Semasinghe, Chaminda Abeysinghe and so many others for being intellectual partners. I must thank uncle Ananda (late Ananda Fenandopulle), Aunty Bernadine and Virginia for being part of an extended family and providing me the most serene surrounding in their beautiful home.

My stay in Japan to set up the Indian chair of contemporary history provided an opportunity to see the working of Japanese universities from close quarters. I must thank particularly Prof. Akihiko Tanaka, then the vice-president of Tokyo University and now the president of the Japan International Cooperation Agency (JICA), for sharing his involvement in positioning the Japanese universities globally. Harada Shiro, Akio Yoshida, Cheng Song, Shuguang Li, Hui Jiang (Kouki) and all my graduate students with their significant questions also made me alert to some issues that I have handled in this book.

Building JNU was a collective effort of an entire generation that wanted to have an institution of repute, and although critical of many of its future developments, they were very proud of its achievements. Prof. Amrik Singh was one of those stalwarts. It was he who helped me understand the Indian educational system and its nuances which I do not think anybody else in this country could have done better. I know for sure that he would have liked reading this book, gently commenting and critically discussing issues over a cup of tea. There are innumerable others who shared their memories, offered valuable suggestions and information. I acknowledge them with a sense of gratitude.

I must thank the librarians and the staff of Nehru Memorial Museum and Library, Jawaharlal Nehru University Library, India International Centre Library, Tokyo University Library, Central European University Library and the Library of the University of Kelaniya.

I owe a sense of gratitude to Dr Susmita Dasgupta, Dr Mohinder Singh, Arun Bali, Dr Amit Dinda, Rachana and Avjit Ghosh,

Dr Swapna Liddle and Gaurab Banerjee for being there in times of need. Exchanging notes with Bikas and Arbind, two storehouses of native knowledge about JNU, was a great experience. Doctoral students Deepak Yadav and Sangeeta Kumari extended their helping hands whenever there was a need. I express my thanks to all of them.

My special thanks to Karthika for accepting to publish the book, and to Shantanu Ray Chaudhuri for seeing it through the process. Usha Srirampudi, who had to go through a manuscript with too many disciplinary nuances, was an ideal and patient editor. Antony Thomas, editor at the last but critical stages of the book, was extremely helpful. I am indebted to all of them.

Ramakrishna and Vishnuvardhan, my sons, have been growing up along with the book and at times were the only research assistants that I could afford. I hope reading the book will give them an idea as to why their father spends so much time and energy on the university and its mundane matters.

Finally, I must acknowledge Mahalakshmi Ramakrishnan, my wife, for being such a wonderful and critical intellectual companion.